computing ESSENTIALS

Making IT work for you

COMPLETE 2011

·The O'Leary Series

Computing Concepts

- *Computing Essentials 2006* Introductory & Complete Editions
- *Computing Essentials 2007* Introductory & Complete Editions
- *Computing Essentials 2008* Introductory & Complete Editions
- *Computing Essentials 2010* Introductory & Complete Editions

Microsoft Office Applications

- *Microsoft Office 2007*
- *Microsoft Office Word 2007* Introductory & Brief Editions
- *Microsoft Office Excel 2007* Introductory & Brief Editions
- *Microsoft Office Access 2007* Introductory & Brief Editions
- *Microsoft Office PowerPoint 2007* Brief Edition

computing ESSENTIALS

Making IT work for you

COMPLETE 2011

Timothy J. O'Leary
Professor Emeritus
Arizona State University

Linda I. O'Leary

Connect
Learn
Succeed™

COMPUTING ESSENTIALS 2011 COMPLETE: MAKING IT WORK FOR YOU
Published by McGraw-Hill, a business unit of The McGraw-Hill Companies, Inc., 1221 Avenue of the Americas, New York, NY, 10020. Copyright © 2011 by The McGraw-Hill Companies, Inc. All rights reserved. No part of this publication may be reproduced or distributed in any form or by any means, or stored in a database or retrieval system, without the prior written consent of The McGraw-Hill Companies, Inc., including, but not limited to, in any network or other electronic storage or transmission, or broadcast for distance learning.

Some ancillaries, including electronic and print components, may not be available to customers outside the United States.

This book is printed on acid-free paper.

1 2 3 4 5 6 7 8 9 0 DOW/DOW 1 0 9 8 7 6 5 4 3 2 1 0

ISBN   978-0-07-351678-3
MHID   0-07-351678-3

Vice president/Editor in chief: *Elizabeth Haefele*
Vice president/Director of marketing: *John E. Biernat*
Executive editor: *Scott Davidson*
Freelance developmental editor: *Craig Leonard*
Editorial coordinator: *Alan Palmer*
Marketing manager: *Tiffany Wendt*
Lead digital product manager: *Damian Moshak*
Digital developmental editor: *Kevin White*
Director, Editing/Design/Production: *Jess Ann Kosic*
Project manager: *Marlena Pechan*
Senior production supervisor: *Janean A. Utley*
Senior designer: *Srdjan Savanovic*
Senior photo research coordinator: *Jeremy Cheshareck*
Photo researcher: *Keri Johnson*
Digital production coordinator: *Brent dela Cruz*
Cover design: *Daniel Drueger*
Interior design: *Laurie Entringer*
Typeface: *10/12 New Aster*
Compositor: *Laserwords Private Limited*
Printer: *R. R. Donnelley*
Cover credit: © *Louie Psihoyos/CORBIS*
Credits: The credits section for this book begins on page 497 and is considered an extension of the copyright page.

Library of Congress Cataloging-in-Publication Data

O'Leary, Timothy J., 1947-
    Computing essentials 2011 : making IT work for you/Timothy J. O'Leary, Linda I. O'Leary. — Complete ed.
        p. cm. — (The O'Leary series)
    Includes index.
    ISBN-13: 978-0-07-351678-3 (alk. paper)
    ISBN-10: 0-07-351678-3 (alk. paper)
    1. Computers. 2. Electronic data processing. I. O'Leary, Linda I. II. Title.
QA76.5.O4286 2011
004—dc22   2009049581

The Internet addresses listed in the text were accurate at the time of publication. The inclusion of a Web site does not indicate an endorsement by the authors or McGraw-Hill, and McGraw-Hill does not guarantee the accuracy of the information presented at these sites.

www.mhhe.com

Dedication

We dedicate this edition to our parents Irene Perley Coats, Jean L. O'Leary, and Charles D. O'Leary for all that they have sacrificed for us.

Brief Contents

Contents

Preface

The 20th century brought us the dawn of the digital information age and unprecedented changes in information technology. There is no indication that this rapid rate of change will be slowing—it may even be increasing. As we begin the 21st century, computer literacy is undoubtedly becoming a prerequisite in whatever career you choose.

The goal of *Computing Essentials* is to provide you with the basis for understanding the concepts necessary for success. *Computing Essentials* also endeavors to instill an appreciation for the effect of information technology on people and our environment and to give you a basis for building the necessary skill set to succeed in this the 21st century.

Times are changing, technology is changing, and this text is changing too. As students of today, you are different from those of yesterday. You put much effort toward the things that interest you and the things that are relevant to you. Your efforts directed at learning application programs and exploring the Web seem, at times, limitless. On the other hand, it is sometimes difficult to engage in other equally important topics such as personal privacy and technological advances.

In this text, we present practical tips related to key concepts through the demonstration of interesting applications that are relevant to your lives and by focusing on outputs rather than processes. Then, we discuss the concepts and processes.

Motivation and relevance are the keys. This text has several features specifically designed to engage and demonstrate the relevance of technology in your lives. These elements are combined with a thorough coverage of the concepts and sound pedagogical devices.

We have specifically designed the end-of-chapter materials to this text to meet the different needs of students and instructors. In addition to the traditional end-of-chapter review materials, you will find three unique categories: (1) Applying Technology is designed to help students gain a better understanding of how the technology covered in a particular chapter is used today, (2) Expanding Your Knowledge offers a deeper understanding to topics covered in that particular chapter, and (3) Writing About Technology provides the opportunity to hone essential writing skills while learning about technology issues relating to privacy, security, and ethics.

This table offers a glimpse of the unique coverage you can find at the end of each chapter.

END-OF-CHAPTER COVERAGE

Chapter	Applying Technology	Expanding Your Knowledge	Writing About Technology
1	TV Tuner Cards and Video Clips (p. 24) Digital Video Editing (p. 24) Home Networking (p. 24) Job Online (p. 451)	How Virus Protection Programs Work (p. 25) How Digital Cameras Work (p. 25) How Internet Telephones Work (p. 25) How Wireless Home Networks Work (p. 25)	Digital Photo Manipulation (p. 26) Antitrust (p. 26) Electronic Monitoring (p. 26)
2	Sharing Large Files (p. 60) Online Shopping (p. 60) Web Auctions (p. 60)	How Spam Filters Work (p. 61) How Instant Messaging Works (p. 61) Domain Registration (p. 61)	Free Speech Online (p. 62) Digital Divide (p. 62)
3	Speech Recognition (p. 96) Presentation Graphics (p. 96) Office Suites (p. 96)	How Speech Recognition Works (p. 97) Sharing Data between Applications (p. 97) Shareware (p. 97)	Acquiring Software (p. 98) Software Standards (p. 98)
4	Digital Video Editing (p. 122) Adobe Flash (p. 122) Streaming Multimedia Players (p. 122)	How Digital Video Editing Works (p. 123) Personal Web Site (p. 123) Streaming Multimedia (p. 123)	Digital Photo Manipulation (p. 124) Online Expert Systems (p. 124)
5	Virus Protection (p. 150) Windows Update (p. 150) Disk Defragmentation (p. 150)	How Virus Protection Programs Work (p. 151) Booting and POST (p. 151) Customized Desktop (p. 151)	Open Source (p. 152) Online Backup (p. 152)
6	TV Tuner Cards and Video Clips (p. 181) Desktop and Notebook Computers (p. 181) Custom System Units (p. 181)	How TV Tuner Cards Work (p. 182) How Virtual Memory Works (p. 182) Binary Numbers (p. 182)	RFIDs (p. 183) Smart Cards (p. 183)
7	WebCams and Instant Messaging (p. 215) Internet Telephones (p. 215) Voice Recognition (p. 215)	How Digital Cameras Work (p. 216) How Internet Telephones Work (p. 216) Handwriting Recognition (p. 216)	WebCams (p. 217) Voice over IP (p. 217)
8	iPods and Music from the Internet (p. 242) iPod (p. 242) USB Storage Devices (p. 242)	How Music Is Downloaded from the Internet (p. 243) File Compression (p. 243) Online Storage Services (p. 243)	CD-R and Music Files (p. 244) Archiving Electronic Records (p. 244)
9	Home Networking (p. 277) Distributed Computing (p. 277) Wireless Mobile Devices (p. 277)	How Wireless Home Networks Work (p. 278) Bittorent (p. 278) Hotspots (p. 278)	Electronic Monitoring (p. 279) Digital Rights Management (p. 279)
10	Spyware (p. 309) Personal Firewalls (p. 309) Personal Backups (p. 309)	How Web Bugs Work (p. 310) Mistaken Identity (p. 310) Air Travel Database (p. 310)	Facial Recognition (p. 311) Plagiarism (p. 311)
11	CAD (p. 335) Knowledge Work Systems (p. 335) Online Personal Information Managers (p. 335)	DVD Direct Information Systems (p. 336) Executive Support Systems (p. 336)	Consumer Information Systems (p. 337) Identity Theft (p. 337)
12	Free Database Software (p. 364) Internet Movie Database (p. 364) Online Databases (p. 364)	DVD Direct Databases (p. 365) SQL (p. 365)	Personal Information (p. 366) Database Security (p. 366)
13	Systems Design Software (p. 395) Systems Analysis Software (p. 395) Preliminary Investigation (p. 395)	DVD Direct Systems Analysis and Design (p. 396) Conversion (p. 396) UML (p. 396)	Legacy Systems (p. 397) Managing Choices (p. 397)
14	Vision Control Systems (p. 429) .NET Framework (p. 429) Integrated Development Environments (p. 429)	DVD Direct Program Development (p. 430) Source Code Generators (p. 430) Capability Maturity Model (p. 430)	Bugs (p. 431) Security and Privacy (p. 431)
15	Jobs Online (p. 451) Maintain Computer Competence (p. 451)	Your Career (p. 452) Resume Advice (p. 452)	Writing About Privacy and Ethics (p. 453) Writing About Security (p. 453)

Visual Learning

VISUAL CHAPTER OPENERS

Each chapter begins with a list of chapter competencies or objectives and provides a brief introduction to what will be covered in the chapter.

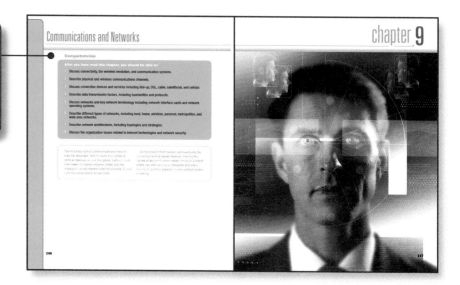

VISUAL SUMMARIES

Visual summaries appear at the end of every chapter and summarize major concepts covered throughout the chapter. Like the chapter openers, these summaries use graphics to reinforce key concepts in an engaging and meaningful way.

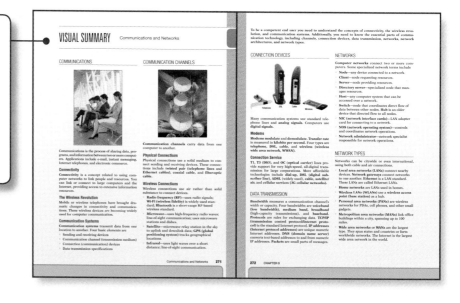

Hands-On

ENVIRONMENTAL FACTS

New "Environmental Facts" boxes appear in each chapter and focus on technology and how it can be used to reduce environmental impact.

TIPS

Tips appear within nearly every chapter and provide advice on chapter-related issues, such as how to efficiently locate information on the Web, how to speed up computer operations, and how to protect against computer viruses. Tips assist you with common technology-related problems or issues and motivate you by showing the relevance of concepts presented in the chapter to everyday life. Additional tips can be found on the O'Leary Web site at www.computing 2011.com by entering the keyword **tips**.

ON THE WEB EXPLORATIONS

At least two On the Web Explorations appear within the margins of nearly every chapter. These explorations ask you to search specific Web sites for additional information on key topics, encouraging you to expand your knowledge through Web resources.

Learning Tools

MAKING IT WORK FOR YOU

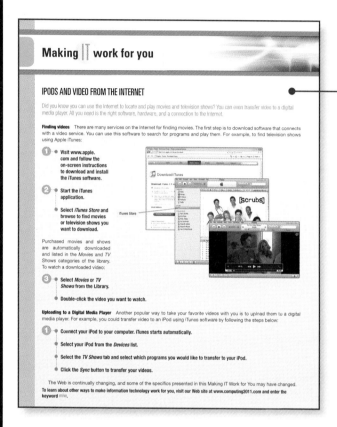

Special-interest topics are presented in the Making IT Work for You section found within nearly every chapter. These topics include protecting against computer viruses, downloading music from the Internet, and using the Internet to place free long-distance telephone calls.

Reinforcing Key Concepts

CONCEPT CHECKS

Located at points throughout each chapter, the Concept Check cues you to note which topics have been covered and to self-test your understanding of the material already discussed.

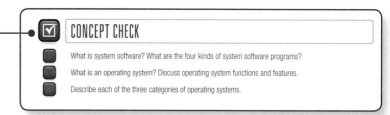

CONCEPT CHECK

What is system software? What are the four kinds of system software programs?

What is an operating system? Discuss operating system functions and features.

Describe each of the three categories of operating systems.

KEY TERMS

KEY TERMS

access speed (221)
Blu-ray Disc (BD) (230)
capacity (220)
CD (compact disc) (227)
CD-R (CD-recordable) (227)
CD-ROM (compact disc–read-only memory) (227)
CD-RW (compact disc rewriteable) (227)
cylinder (221)
density (221)
direct access (232)
disk caching (223)
DVD (digital versatile disc or digital video disc) (227)
DVD player (227)
DVD–R (DVD recordable) (230)
DVD+R (DVD recordable) (230)
DVD-RAM (DVD random-access memory) (230)
DVD-ROM (DVD–read-only memory) (227)
DVD–RW (DVD rewriteable) (230)
DVD+RW (DVD rewriteable) (230)
enterprise storage system (233)
erasable optical disc (227)
external hard drive (223)
file compression (223)
file decompression (223)
file server (233)
flash drive (225)
flash memory card (224)
floppy disk (231)
floppy disk drive (FDD) (231)
hard disk (221)
head crash (221)

hi def (high definition) (230)
high-capacity floppy disk (232)
internal hard disk (222)
land (227)
magnetic tape (232)
magnetic tape reel (232)
magnetic tape streamer (232)
mass storage (232)
mass storage devices (233)
media (220)
network attached storage (NAS) (234)
online storage service (231)
optical disc (225)
optical disc drive (227)
organizational online storage (233)
pit (227)
platter (221)
primary storage (220)
RAID system (233)
redundant array of inexpensive disks (RAID) (223)
secondary storage (220)
secondary storage device (220)
sector (221)
sequential access (232)
software engineer (234)
solid-state drive (SSD) (224)
solid-state storage (224)
storage area network (SAN) (234)
storage device (220)
tape cartridge (232)
tape library (233)
track (221)
traditional floppy disk (231)
USB drive (225)

To test your knowledge of these key terms with animated flash cards, visit our Web site at www.computing2011.com and enter the keyword terms8.

Throughout the text, the most important terms are presented in bold and are defined within the text. You will also find a list of key terms at the end of each chapter and in the glossary at the end of the book.

CHAPTER REVIEW

Following the Visual Summary, the chapter review includes material designed to review and reinforce chapter content. It includes a Key Terms list that reiterates the terms presented in the chapter, Multiple Choice questions to help test your understanding of information presented in the chapter, Matching exercises to test your recall of terminology presented in the chapter, and Open-Ended questions or statements to help review your understanding of the key concepts presented in the chapter.

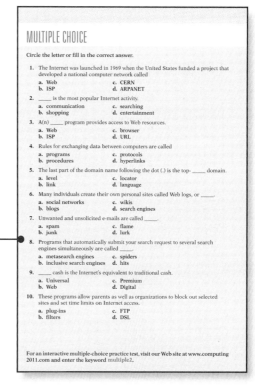

MULTIPLE CHOICE

Circle the letter or fill in the correct answer.

1. The Internet was launched in 1969 when the United States funded a project that developed a national computer network called
   a. Web   c. CERN
   b. ISP   d. ARPANET

2. _____ is the most popular Internet activity.
   a. communication   c. searching
   b. shopping   d. entertainment

3. A(n) _____ program provides access to Web resources.
   a. Web   c. browser
   b. ISP   d. URL

4. Rules for exchanging data between computers are called
   a. programs   c. protocols
   b. procedures   d. hyperlinks

5. The last part of the domain name following the dot (.) is the top-_____ domain.
   a. level   c. locator
   b. link   d. language

6. Many individuals create their own personal sites called Web logs, or _____.
   a. social networks   c. wikis
   b. blogs   d. search engines

7. Unwanted and unsolicited e-mails are called _____.
   a. spam   c. flame
   b. junk   d. lurk

8. Programs that automatically submit your search request to several search engines simultaneously are called _____.
   a. metasearch engines   c. spiders
   b. inclusive search engines   d. hits

9. _____ cash is the Internet's equivalent to traditional cash.
   a. Universal   c. Premium
   b. Web   d. Digital

10. These programs allow parents as well as organizations to block out selected sites and set time limits on Internet access.
    a. plug-ins   c. FTP
    b. filters   d. DSL

For an interactive multiple-choice practice test, visit our Web site at www.computing2011.com and enter the keyword multiple2.

The Future of Information Technology

CAREERS IN IT

Some of the fastest-growing career opportunities are in information technology. Each chapter highlights one of the most promising careers in IT by presenting job titles, responsibilities, educational requirements, and salary ranges. Among the careers covered are Webmaster, software engineer, and database administrator. You will learn how the material you are studying relates directly to a potential career path.

A LOOK TO THE FUTURE

Each chapter concludes with a brief discussion of a recent technological advancement related to the chapter material, reinforcing the importance of staying informed.

USING IT AT DVD DIRECT—A CASE STUDY

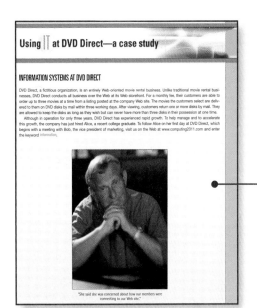

Beginning in Chapter 11 and continuing through Chapter 14, Using IT at DVD Direct—A Case Study of a fictitious organization provides an up-close look at what you might expect to find on the job in the real world. You will follow Alice, a recent college graduate hired as a marketing analyst, as she navigates her way through accounting, marketing, production, human resources, and research, gathering and processing data to help manage and accelerate the growth of the three-year-old company.

Unique End-of-Chapter Materials

APPLYING TECHNOLOGY

In each chapter, Applying Technology presents questions designed to help you gain a better understanding of how technology is being used today. One question typically relates to the chapter's Making IT Work for You topic. Other questions focus on interesting applications of technology that relate directly to you. Topics include online auctions, online Personal Information Managers, and desktop and notebook computers.

EXPANDING YOUR KNOWLEDGE

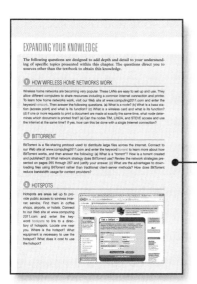

In each chapter, Expanding Your Knowledge presents questions that help you gain a deeper understanding of select topics. Typically, one question relates to a topic presented at the book's Web site, www.computing 2011.com, such as How Instant Messaging Works, How Streaming Media Works, and How Virus Protection Works. Other questions in Expanding Your Knowledge typically require Web research into carefully selected topics including robotics, multimedia, HDTV, and Internet hard drives.

WRITING ABOUT TECHNOLOGY

In each chapter, Writing About Technology presents questions relating to security, privacy, and ethical issues. The issues presented include HTML source code, antitrust legislation, RFIDs, CD-R and music files, and electronic monitoring. One objective of the Writing About Technology feature is to help you develop critical thinking and writing skills. Another objective is to help you recognize, understand, and analyze key privacy, security, and ethical issues relating to technology.

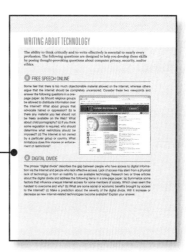

Support Materials

The Instructor's Manual offers lecture outlines with teaching notes and page references. It provides definitions of key terms and solutions to the end-of-chapter material, including multiple-choice, matching, and open-ended questions. It also offers summaries of the concept checks in each chapter. A selection of G4techTV video clips accompany this text, as do summaries for each clip.

The PowerPoint slides are designed to provide instructors with a comprehensive resource for lecture use. The slides include a review of key terms and definitions, artwork taken from the text, as well as new illustrations to further explain concepts covered in each chapter. Comprehensive teaching notes are provided for each slide.

The testbank contains over 2,200 questions categorized by level of learning (definition, concept, and application). This is the same learning scheme that is introduced in the text to provide a valuable testing and reinforcement tool. Text page references have been provided for all questions, including a level-of-difficulty rating. The testbank is offered in Word files, as well as in EZ Test format.

The instructor support materials can be downloaded at www.mhhe.com/ce2011.

G4TECHTV VIDEOS

G4techTV videos offer instructors and students video content directly related to computing that enhances the classroom or lab experience with technology programming from business and society. Video selections include "The Screen Savers" and "Pulse," which provide edgy and informative discussion. Use of these videos will help students understand how computing interacts with and contributes to business and society and will also offer an advance look at emerging technology and devices.

THE O'LEARY WEB SITE

The O'Leary Web site can be found at www.computing2011.com. Students can find a host of additional resources on the Web site, including animations of key concepts, videos relating to select Making IT Work for You applications, and in-depth coverage of select topics. Look for the Web icon throughout the text to indicate where additional related materials can be found on the Web site.

O'LEARY SERIES

The O'Leary Application Series for Microsoft® Office is available separately or packaged with *Computing Essentials*. The O'Leary Application Series offers a step-by-step approach to learning computer applications and is available in both brief and introductory versions. The introductory books are MCAS Certified and prepare students for the Microsoft Office User Certification Exam.

SIMNET® ASSESSMENT FOR OFFICE APPLICATIONS

SimNet Assessment for Office Applications provides a way for you to test students' software skills in a simulated environment. SimNet is available for Microsoft Office 2007 and provides flexibility for you in your applications course by offering:

Pre-testing options

Post-testing options

Course placement testing

Diagnostic capabilities to reinforce skills

Web delivery of test

MCAS preparation exams

Learning verification reports

For more information on skills assessment software, please contact your local sales representative, or visit us at www.mhhe.com.

Acknowledgments

We would like to extend our thanks to the professors who took time out of their busy schedules to provide us with the feedback necessary to develop the 2011 edition of this text. The following professors offered valuable suggestions on revising the text:

Ping Chen,
University of Houston

Ric Calhoun,
Gordon College

Rhonda Simms,
Dallas County Community College

Kin Lam,
Medgar Evers College

Rick Kendrick,
Antonelli College

Bill Barge,
Trine University

Shane Stevens,
Bridgewater College

Wolfgang Pelz,
The University of Akron

Kevin Halvorson,
Ridgewater College

John Jemison,
Dallas Baptist University

Rose LaMuraglia,
San Diego Community College

Dave Fitzgerald,
Jackson Community College

Terry Rigsby,
Hill College

Jackie Armstrong,
Hill College, Hillsboro Campus

Bobby Thrash,
Pearl River Community College

Mary Lou Malone,
Ohio University

Sue Vanboven,
Maricopa Community College

Wayne Machuca,
Mt. Hood Community College

Diana Hill,
Chesapeake College

Michelle Parker,
Indiana University–Purdue University Indianapolis

Diane Stark,
Maricopa Community College

Cheryl Jordan,
San Juan College

Bill Holmes,
Maricopa Community College

Cindi Nadelman,
Granite State College

Louis Berzai,
University of Notre Dame

Our thanks also go to Linda Mehlinger for all her work on revising the PowerPoint presentations and Instructor's Manual to accompany the text. We are grateful to Triad Interactive for their work in revising the testbank.

Finally, we would like to thank Robyn Ness and John Ray, who helped out with this edition. They made significant contributions to several chapters. Also thanks to Carol and Steve Willis for their indispensible contributions to this and previous editions.

About the Authors

Tim and Linda O'Leary live in the American Southwest and spend much of their time engaging instructors and students in conversation about learning. In fact, they have been talking about learning for over 25 years. Something in those early conversations convinced them to write a book, to bring their interest in the learning process to the printed page. Today, they are as concerned as ever about learning, about technology, and about the challenges of presenting material in new ways, in terms of both content and method of delivery.

A powerful and creative team, Tim combines his 25 years of classroom teaching experience with Linda's background as a consultant and corporate trainer. Tim has taught courses at Stark Technical College in Canton, Ohio, and at Rochester Institute of Technology in upstate New York, and is currently a professor emeritus at Arizona State University in Tempe, Arizona. Linda offered her expertise at ASU for several years as an academic advisor. She also presented and developed materials for major corporations such as Motorola, Intel, Honeywell, and AT&T, as well as various community colleges in the Phoenix area.

Tim and Linda have talked to and taught numerous students, all of them with a desire to learn something about computers and applications that make their lives easier, more interesting, and more productive.

Each new edition of an O'Leary text, supplement, or learning aid has benefited from these students and their instructors who daily stand in front of them (or over their shoulders). *Computing Essentials* is no exception.

computing ESSENTIALS

Making IT work for you

COMPLETE 2011

Information Technology, the Internet, and You

Competencies

After you have read this chapter, you should be able to:

1 Explain the five parts of an information system: people, procedures, software, hardware, and data.

2 Distinguish between system software and application software.

3 Discuss the three kinds of system software programs.

4 Distinguish between basic and specialized application software.

5 Identify the four types of computers and the six types of microcomputers.

6 Describe the different types of computer hardware including the system unit, input, output, storage, and communication devices.

7 Define data and describe document, worksheet, database, and presentation files.

8 Explain computer connectivity, the wireless revolution, and the Internet.

Just a few years ago, the computer was a device you might have used seated at a desk for work or school. Today computers go with us, connecting us to a world of information, our friends, and even our work. The speed of technological developments makes it easy to imagine a world where we are always connected to the Internet.

Some experts predict the Web will become seamlessly integrated into our lives. Connectivity will mean connections to our documents and data, our friends and family, and facts and figures gathered the world over. Imagine a world where the mobile device in your hand is like an expert personal assistant with access to all of these resources. Your calendar might remind you of a friend's birthday, provide suggestions for a gift, and provide a map to the store where you might want to shop on your way home from work.

chapter 1

Introduction

The purpose of this book is to help you become competent with computer technology. **Computer competency** refers to acquiring computer-related skills—indispensable tools for today. They include how to effectively use popular application packages and the Internet.

In this chapter, we present an overview of an information system: people, procedures, software, hardware, and data. It is essential to understand these basic parts and how connectivity through the Internet and the Web expands the role of information technology in our lives. Later, we will describe these parts of an information system in detail.

Fifteen years ago, most people had little to do with computers, at least directly. Of course, they filled out computerized forms, took computerized tests, and paid computerized bills. But the real work was handled by specialists. Then microcomputers came along and changed everything. Today it is easy for nearly everybody to use a computer.

- Microcomputers are common tools in all areas of life. Writers write, artists draw, engineers and scientists calculate—all on microcomputers. Students and businesspeople do all this, and more.
- New forms of learning have developed. People who are homebound, who work odd hours, or who travel frequently may take Web courses. A college course need not fit within a quarter or a semester.
- New ways to communicate, to find people with similar interests, and to buy goods are available. People use electronic mail, electronic commerce, and the Internet to meet and to share ideas and products.

People
are end users who use computers to make themselves more productive

Software
provides step-by-step instructions for computer hardware

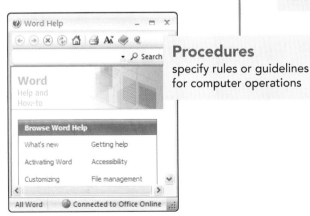

Procedures
specify rules or guidelines for computer operations

Figure 1-1 **The five parts of an information system**

To be competent with computer technology, you need to know the five parts of an information system: people, procedures, software, hardware, and data. You also need to understand connectivity, the wireless revolution, the Internet, and the Web and to recognize the role of information technology in your personal and professional life.

Information Systems

When you think of a microcomputer, perhaps you think of just the equipment itself. That is, you think of the monitor or the keyboard. Yet, there is more to it than that. The way to think about a microcomputer is as part of an information system. An **information system** has five parts: *people, procedures, software, hardware,* and *data.* (See Figure 1-1.)

- **People:** It is easy to overlook people as one of the five parts of an information system. Yet this is what microcomputers are all about—making **people, end users** like you, more productive.
- **Procedures:** The rules or guidelines for people to follow when using software, hardware, and data are **procedures.** These procedures are typically documented in manuals written by computer specialists. Software and hardware manufacturers provide manuals with their products. These manuals are provided in either printed or electronic form.

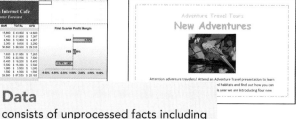

Data
consists of unprocessed facts including text, numbers, images, and sounds

Hardware
includes keyboard, mouse, monitor, system unit, and other devices

Connectivity
allows computers to share information and to connect to the Internet

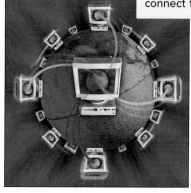

- **Software:** A **program** consists of the step-by-step instructions that tell the computer how to do its work. **Software** is another name for a program or programs. The purpose of software is to convert **data** (unprocessed facts) into **information** (processed facts). For example, a payroll program would instruct the computer to take the number of hours you worked in a week (data) and multiply it by your pay rate (data) to determine how much you are paid for the week (information).
- **Hardware:** The equipment that processes the data to create information is called **hardware.** It includes the keyboard, mouse, monitor, system unit, and other devices. Hardware is controlled by software.
- **Data:** The raw, unprocessed facts, including text, numbers, images, and sounds, are called data. Processed data yields information. Using the previous example of a payroll program, the data (number of hours worked and pay rate) is processed (multiplied) to yield information (weekly pay).

Almost all of today's computer systems add an additional part to the information system. This part, called **connectivity,** typically uses the Internet and allows users to greatly expand the capability and usefulness of their information systems.

In large computer systems, there are specialists who write procedures, develop software, and capture data. In microcomputer systems, however, end users often perform these operations. To be a competent end user, you must understand the essentials of **information technology (IT),** including software, hardware, and data.

 CONCEPT CHECK

 What are the five parts of an information system?

 What is the difference between data and information?

What is connectivity?

People

People are surely the most important part of any information system. Our lives are touched every day by computers and information systems. Many times the contact is direct and obvious, such as when we create documents using a word processing program or when we connect to the Internet. Other times, the contact is not as obvious. Consider just the four examples in Figure 1-2.

Throughout this book you will find a variety of features designed to help you become computer competent and knowledgeable. These features include Making IT Work for You, Environmental Facts, Tips, Careers in IT, On the Web Exploration, and the Computing Essentials Web site.

- **Making IT Work for You.** In the chapters that follow, you will find Making IT Work for You features that present interesting and practical IT applications. Using a step-by-step procedure, you are provided with specific instructions on how to use each application. Figure 1-3 presents a list of these applications.
- **Environmental Facts.** Today it is more important than ever that we be aware of our impact on the environment. In this chapter and the following ones, you will find Environmental Facts boxes in the margin that present important relevant environmental information.

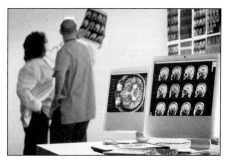

Figure 1-2 Computers in entertainment, business, education, and medicine

Application	Description
Sharing Large Files	Have you found it inconvenient or impossible to share large files with others. Perhaps you have found some video and other types of files are just too large to send as an e-mail attachment. An easy solution is to use free file-sharing services. See page 36.
Speech Recognition	Tired of using your keyboard to type term papers? Have you ever thought about using your voice to control application software? Perhaps speech recognition is just what you are looking for. See page 68.
Digital Video Editing	Do you want to make your own movie? Would you like to edit some home movies and distribute them to family and friends on DVDs? It's easy with the right equipment and software. See page 106.
Virus Protection and Internet Security	Worried about computer viruses? Did you know that others could be intercepting your private e-mail? It is even possible for them to gain access and control of your computer system. Fortunately, Internet security suites are available to help ensure your safety while you are on the Internet. See page 140.
TV Tuner Cards and Video Clips	Want to watch your favorite television program while you work? Perhaps you would like to include a video clip from a television program or from a DVD in a class presentation. It's easy using a TV tuner card. See page 168.
Web Cams and Instant Messaging	Do you enjoy chatting with your friends? Are you working on a project and need to collaborate with others in your group? What if you could see and hear your group online? Perhaps instant messaging is just what you're looking for. See page 196.
iPods and Video from the Internet	Want to use the Internet to find and play movies and television shows? Would you prefer to play the movies or shows on a digital media player? All you need is the right software, hardware, and a connection to the Internet. See page 226.
Home Networking	Computer networks are not just for corporations and schools anymore. If you have more than one computer, you can use a wireless home network to share files and printers, to allow multiple users access to the Internet at the same time, and to play interactive computer games. See page 262.
Spyware Removal	Are you concerned about maintaining your privacy while you are surfing the Web? Did you know that programs known as spyware could be monitoring your every move? Fortunately, these programs are relatively easy to detect and remove. See page 290.
Locating Job Opportunities Online	Did you know that you can use the Internet to find a job? You can browse through job openings, post your resume, and even use special programs that will search for the job that's just right for you. See page 440.

Figure 1-3 Making IT Work for You applications

tips Are you getting the most out of your computer? Here are just a few of the tips that you'll find in this book designed to make your computer faster and safer to use.

1 **Controlling spam.** Do you get a lot of unwanted e-mail advertisements? Americans receive over 200 billion spam e-mails every year. There are some basic steps that you can take to keep your inbox spam-free. See page 35.

2 **Online shopping.** Have you ever bought anything online? If not, it's likely that in the future you will join the millions who have. Consider a few guidelines to make your shopping easier and safer. See page 46.

3 **Creating and updating Web sites.** Are you thinking about creating your own Web site? Perhaps you already have one and would like to spruce it up a bit. Here are a few suggestions that might help. See page 111.

4 **Improving slow computer operations.** Does your computer seem to be getting slower and slower? Consider a few suggestions that might add a little zip to your current system. See page 164.

5 **Improving hard disk performance.** Does your internal hard-disk drive run a lot and seem slow? Are you having problems with lost or corrupted files? To clean up the disk and speed up access, consider defragging. See page 222.

6 **Protecting your privacy.** Are you concerned about your privacy while on the Web? Consider some suggestions for protecting your identity online. See page 289.

To see additional tips, visit our Web site at www.computing2011.com and enter the keyword **tips.**

Figure 1-4 **Selected tips**

- **Tips.** We all can benefit from a few tips or suggestions. Throughout this book you will find numerous Tips ranging from the basics of keeping your computer system running smoothly to how to protect your privacy while surfing the Web. For a partial list of the Tips presented in the following chapters, see Figure 1-4.

- **Careers in IT.** One of the most important decisions of your life is to decide upon your life's work or career. Perhaps you are planning to be a writer, an artist, or an engineer. Or you might become a professional in information technology. Each of the following chapters highlights a specific career in information technology. This feature provides job descriptions, projected employment demands, educational requirements, current salary ranges, and advancement opportunities.

- **On the Web Exploration.** The informational content of the Web is limitless; the challenge is to locate the information you are looking for. In this chapter and the ones that follow, you will find On the Web Exploration boxes in the margin that direct you to relevant Web information locations.

- **Computing Essentials Web site.** Throughout the text you will find numerous text references to the Computing Essentials Web site at www.computing2011.com. This site is carefully integrated with the textbook. At the site, you'll find animations, career information, tips, test review materials, and much more.

☑ **CONCEPT CHECK**

 Which part of an information system is the most important?

 Describe the Making IT Work for You, Environmental Facts, and the Tips features.

 Describe the Careers in IT, On the Web Exploration, and the Computing Essentials Web site features.

Software

Software, as we mentioned, is another name for programs. Programs are the instructions that tell the computer how to process data into the form you want. In most cases, the words *software* and *programs* are interchangeable. There are two major kinds of software: *system software* and *application software*. You can think of application software as the kind you use. Think of system software as the kind the computer uses.

System Software

The user interacts primarily with application software. **System software** enables the application software to interact with the computer hardware. System

Figure 1-5 Windows 7 and Mac OS X operating systems

software is "background" software that helps the computer manage its own internal resources.

System software is not a single program. Rather it is a collection of programs, including the following:

- **Operating systems** are programs that coordinate computer resources, provide an interface between users and the computer, and run applications. Windows 7 and the Mac OS X are two of the best-known operating systems for today's microcomputer users. (See Figure 1-5.)
- **Utilities** perform specific tasks related to managing computer resources. For example, the Windows utility called Disk Defragmenter locates and eliminates unnecessary file fragments and rearranges files and unused disk space to optimize computer operations.
- **Device drivers** are specialized programs designed to allow particular input or output devices to communicate with the rest of the computer system.

Application Software

Application software might be described as end user software. These programs can be categorized as either *basic* or *specialized applications*.

Basic applications are widely used in nearly all career areas. They are the kinds of programs you have to know to be considered computer competent. One of these basic applications is a browser to navigate, explore, and find information on the Internet. (See Figure 1-6.) The two most widely used browsers are Microsoft's Internet Explorer and Netscape's Navigator. For a summary of the basic applications, see Figure 1-7.

Specialized applications include thousands of other programs that are more narrowly focused on specific disciplines and occupations. Some of the best known are graphics, audio, video, multimedia, Web authoring, and artificial intelligence programs.

CONCEPT CHECK

Describe the two major kinds of software.

Describe three types of system software programs.

Define and compare basic and specialized applications.

Figure 1-6 Internet Explorer browser

Type	Description
Browser	Connect to Web sites and display Web pages
Word processor	Prepare written documents
Spreadsheet	Analyze and summarize numerical data
Database management system	Organize and manage data and information
Presentation graphics	Communicate a message or persuade other people

Figure 1-7 Basic applications

Hardware

Computers are electronic devices that can follow instructions to accept input, process that input, and produce information. This book focuses principally on microcomputers. However, it is almost certain that you will come in contact, at least indirectly, with other types of computers.

Types of Computers

There are four types of computers: supercomputers, mainframe computers, minicomputers, and microcomputers.

- **Supercomputers** are the most powerful type of computer. These machines are special high-capacity computers used by very large organizations. IBM's Blue Gene is one of the fastest computers in the world. (See Figure 1-8.)

- **Mainframe computers** occupy specially wired, air-conditioned rooms. Although not nearly as powerful as supercomputers, mainframe computers are capable of great processing speeds and data storage. For example, insurance companies use mainframes to process information about millions of policyholders.

- **Minicomputers,** also known as **midrange computers,** are refrigerator-sized machines. Medium-sized companies or departments of large companies typically use them for specific purposes. For example, production departments use minicomputers to monitor certain manufacturing processes and assembly-line operations.

* **Microcomputers** are the least powerful, yet the most widely used and fastest-growing type of computer. There are six types of micro-computers: *desktop, media center, notebook, netbook, tablet PC,* and *handheld computers.* (See Figure 1-9.) **Desktop computers** are small enough to fit on top of or alongside a desk yet are too big to carry around. **Media centers** blur the line between desktop computers and dedicated entertainment devices. **Notebook computers,** also known as *laptop computers,* are portable, lightweight, and fit into most briefcases. **Netbooks** are smaller, lighter, and less expensive than notebook computers. A **tablet PC** is a type of notebook computer that accepts your handwriting. This input is digitized and converted to standard text that can be further processed by programs such as a word processor. **Handheld computers** are the smallest and are designed to fit into the palm of one hand. These systems contain an entire computer system, including the electronic components, secondary storage, and input and output devices. **Personal digital assistants (PDAs)** and **smartphones** are the most widely used handheld computers.

Figure 1-8 IBM's Blue Gene supercomputer

Figure 1-9 Microcomputers

Microcomputer Hardware

Hardware for a microcomputer system consists of a variety of different devices. See Figure 1-10 for a typical desktop system. This physical equipment falls into four basic categories: system unit, input/output, secondary storage, and communication. Because we discuss hardware in detail later in this book, here we will present just a quick overview of the four basic categories.

- **System unit:** The **system unit** is a container that houses most of the electronic components that make up a computer system. Two important components of the system unit are the *microprocessor* and *memory*. (See Figure 1-11.) The **microprocessor** controls and manipulates data to produce information. **Memory** is a holding area for data, instructions, and information. One type, **random-access memory (RAM)** holds the program and data that is currently being processed. This type of memory is sometimes referred to as *temporary storage* because its contents will typically be lost if the electrical power to the computer is disrupted.

- **Input/output: Input devices** translate data and programs that humans can understand into a form that the computer can process. The most common input devices are the **keyboard** and the **mouse. Output devices** translate the processed information from the computer into a form that humans can understand. The most common output devices are **monitors** (see Figure 1-12) and **printers.**

- **Secondary storage:** Unlike memory, **secondary storage** holds data and programs even after electrical power to the computer system has been turned off. The most important kinds of secondary media are *hard disks, solid-state storage,* and *optical disks.* **Hard disks** are typically used to

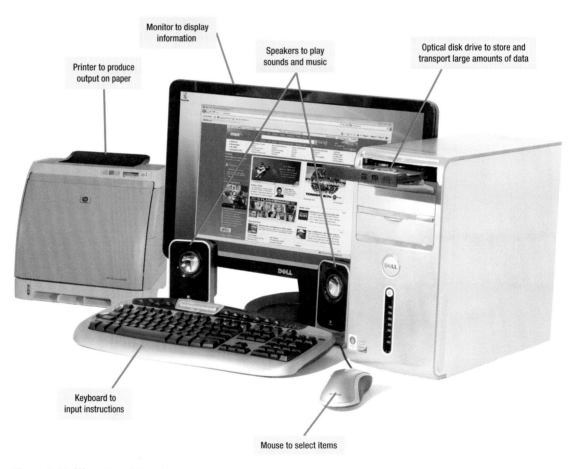

Printer to produce output on paper

Monitor to display information

Speakers to play sounds and music

Optical disk drive to store and transport large amounts of data

Keyboard to input instructions

Mouse to select items

Figure 1-10 **Microcomputer system**

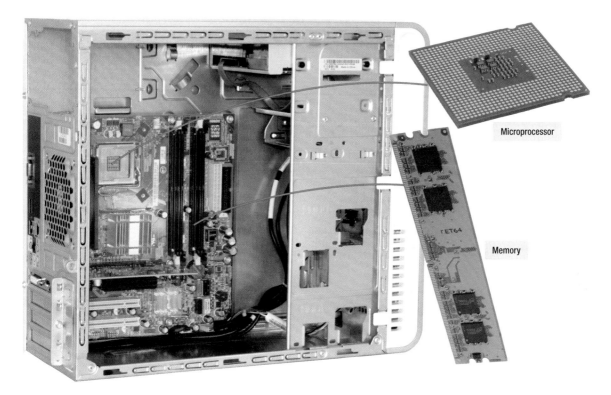

Microprocessor

Memory

Figure 1-11 **System unit**

Figure 1-12 **Monitor**

Figure 1-13 **Optical disc**

store programs and very large data files. Using rigid metallic platters and read/write heads that move across the platters, data and information are stored using magnetic charges of the disk's surface. In contrast, **solid-state storage** does not have any moving parts, is more reliable, and requires less power. It saves data and information electronically similar to RAM except that it is not volatile. Three types are **solid-state drives (SSDs)** that are used much the same way as an internal hard disk, **flash memory cards** that are widely used in portable devices, and **USB drives** that are a widely used compact storage medium for transporting data and information between computers and a variety of specialty devices. **Optical discs** use laser technology and have the greatest capacity. (See Figure 1-13.)

On the Web Explorations

To learn more about one of the leaders in the development of DVD technology, visit our Web site at

www.computing2011.com and enter the keyword dvd.

Three types of optical discs are **compact discs (CDs), digital versatile (or video) discs (DVDs),** and **high-definition (hi def) discs.**

- **Communication:** At one time, it was uncommon for a microcomputer system to communicate with other computer systems. Now, using **communication devices,** a microcomputer can communicate with other computer systems located as near as the next office or as far away as halfway around the world using the Internet. The most widely used communication device is a **modem,** which modifies telephone communications into a form that can be processed by a computer. Modems also modify computer output into a form that can be transmitted across standard telephone lines.

☑ CONCEPT CHECK

What are the four types of computers?

Describe the six types of microcomputers.

Describe the four basic categories of microcomputer hardware.

Data

Data is raw, unprocessed facts, including text, numbers, images, and sounds. As we have mentioned earlier, processed data becomes information. When stored electronically in files, data can be used directly as input for the system unit.

Four common types of files (see Figure 1-14) are

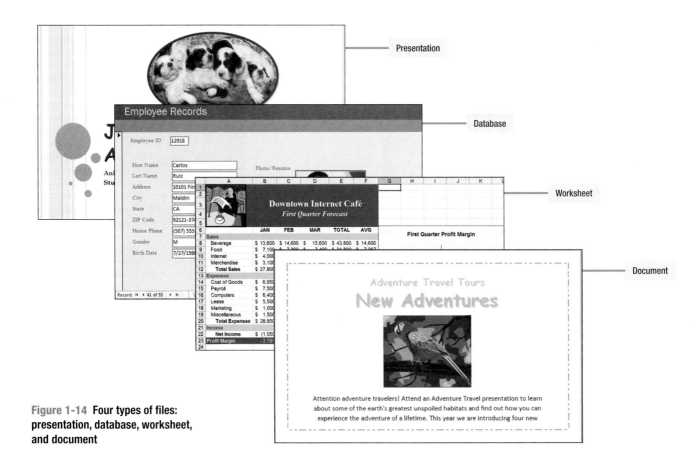

Figure 1-14 Four types of files: presentation, database, worksheet, and document

- **Document files,** created by word processors to save documents such as memos, term papers, and letters.
- **Worksheet files,** created by electronic spreadsheets to analyze things like budgets and to predict sales.
- **Database files,** typically created by database management programs to contain highly structured and organized data. For example, an employee database file might contain all the workers' names, social security numbers, job titles, and other related pieces of information.
- **Presentation files,** created by presentation graphics programs to save presentation materials. For example, a file might contain audience handouts, speaker notes, and electronic slides.

Connectivity, the Wireless Revolution, and the Internet

Connectivity is the capability of your microcomputer to share information with other computers. The single most dramatic change in connectivity in the past five years has been the widespread use of mobile or wireless communication devices. For just a few of these devices, see Figure 1-15. Many experts

Figure 1-15 **Wireless communication devices**

predict that these wireless applications are just the beginning of the **wireless revolution,** a revolution that will dramatically affect the way we communicate and use computer technology.

Central to the concept of connectivity is the **network.** A network is a communications system connecting two or more computers. The largest network in the world is the **Internet.** It is like a giant highway that connects you to millions of other people and organizations located throughout the world. The **Web** provides a multimedia interface to the numerous resources available on the Internet.

CONCEPT CHECK

- Define data. List four common types of files.

- Define connectivity and the wireless revolution.

- What is a network? Describe the Internet. What is the Web?

Careers in IT

As mentioned previously, each of the following chapters highlights a specific career in information technology. (See Figure 1-16.) Each provides specific job descriptions, salary ranges, advancement opportunities, and more. For a partial list of these careers, see Figure 1-17. For a complete list, visit our Web site at www.computing2011.com and enter the keyword **careers.**

Figure 1-16 **Software engineer**

Career	Description
Webmaster	Develops and maintains Web sites and Web resources. See page 52.
Computer support specialist	Provides technical support to customers and other users. See page 143.
Technical writer	Prepares instruction manuals, technical reports, and other scientific or technical documents. See page 207.
Software engineer	Analyzes users' needs and creates application software. See page 234.
Network administrator	Creates and maintains computer networks. See page 269.
Database administrator	Uses database management software to determine the most efficient ways to organize and access data. See page 354.
Systems analyst	Plans, designs, and maintains information systems. See page 385.
Programmer	Creates, tests, and troubleshoots computer programs. See page 419.

Figure 1-17 **Careers in information technology**

A LOOK TO THE FUTURE

Using and Understanding Information Technology Means Being Computer Competent

The purpose of this book is to help you use and understand information technology. We want to help you become computer competent in today's world and to provide you with a foundation of knowledge so that you can understand how technology is being used today and anticipate how technology will be used in the future. This will enable you to benefit from six important information technology developments.

The Internet and the Web

The Internet and the Web are considered by most to be the two most important technologies for the 21st century. Understanding how to efficiently and effectively use the Internet to browse the Web, communicate with others, and locate information are indispensable computer competencies. These issues are presented in Chapter 2, The Internet, the Web, and Electronic Commerce.

Powerful Software

The software now available can do an extraordinary number of tasks and help you in an endless number of ways. You can create professional-looking documents, analyze massive amounts of data, create dynamic multimedia Web pages, and much more. Today's employers are expecting the people they hire to be able to effectively and efficiently use a variety of different types of software. Basic and specialized applications are presented in Chapters 3 and 4. System software is presented in Chapter 5.

Powerful Hardware

Microcomputers are now much more powerful than they used to be. New communication technologies such as wireless networks are dramatically changing the ways to connect to other computers, networks, and the Internet. However, despite the rapid change of specific equipment, their essential features remain unchanged. Thus, the competent end user should focus on these features. Chapters 6 through 9 explain what you need to know about hardware. A Buyer's Guide and an Upgrader's Guide are presented at the end of this book for those considering the purchase or upgrade of a microcomputer system.

Security and Privacy

What about people? Experts agree that we as a society must be careful about the potential of technology to negatively impact our personal privacy and security. Additionally, we need to be aware of potential physical and mental health risks associated with using technology. Finally, we need to be aware of negative effects on our environment caused by the manufacture of computer-related products. Thus, Chapter 10 explores each of these critical issues in detail.

Organizations

Almost all organizations rely on the quality and flexibility of their information systems to stay competitive. As a member or employee of an organization, you will undoubtedly be involved in these information systems. Therefore, you need to be knowledgeable about the different types of organizational information systems and how they are used. Accordingly, we devote Chapters 11 through 14 to detail what you need to know about information systems and how to develop, modify, and maintain these systems.

Changing Times

Are the times changing any faster now than they ever have? Most people think so. Whatever the answer, it is clear we live in a fast-paced age. The Evolution of the Computer Age section presented at the end of this book tracks the major developments since computers were first introduced.

After reading this book, you will be in a very favorable position compared with many other people in industry today. You not only will learn the basics of hardware, software, connectivity, the Internet, and the Web, but you also will learn the most current technology. You will be able to use these tools to your advantage.

INFORMATION SYSTEMS

The way to think about a microcomputer is to realize that it is one part of an **information system.** There are five parts of an information system:

1. **People** are an essential part of the system. The purpose of information systems is to make people, or **end users** like you, more productive.
2. **Procedures** are rules or guidelines to follow when using software, hardware, and data. They are typically documented in manuals written by computer professionals.
3. **Software (programs)** provides step-by-step instructions to control the computer to convert **data** into **information.**
4. **Hardware** consists of the physical equipment. It is controlled by software and processes data to create information.
5. **Data** consists of unprocessed facts including text, numbers, images, and sound. **Information** is data that has been processed by the computer.

Connectivity is an additional part to today's information systems. It allows computers to connect and share information. To be **computer competent,** end users need to understand **information technology (IT).**

PEOPLE

People are the most important part of an information system. This book contains several features to demonstrate how people just like you use computers. These features include the following:

- **Making IT Work for You** presents several interesting and practical applications. Topics include using digital video editing and locating job opportunities.
- **Environmental Facts** discuss important and relevant environmental issues. The impact of computers and other technologies is more critical today than ever before.
- **Tips** offer a variety of suggestions on such practical matters as how to improve slow computer performance and how to protect your privacy while on the Web.
- **Careers in IT** presents job descriptions, employment demands, educational requirements, salary ranges, and advancement opportunities.
- **On the Web Explorations** direct you to important information and Web sites that relate to computers and technology.
- **Computing Essentials Web site** integrates the textbook with information on the Web including animations, career information, tips, test review materials, and much more.

To prepare for your future as a competent end user, you need to understand the basic parts of an information system: people, procedures, software, hardware, and data. Also you need to understand connectivity through the Internet and the Web and to recognize the role of technology in your professional and personal life.

SOFTWARE

Software, or **programs**, consists of system and application software.

System Software

System software enables application software to interact with computer hardware. It consists of a variety of programs:

- **Operating systems** coordinate resources, provide an interface for users and computer hardware, and run applications. Windows 7 and Mac OS X are the best-known microcomputer operating systems.
- **Utilities** perform specific tasks to manage computer resources.
- **Device drivers** are specialized programs to allow input and output devices to communicate with the rest of the computer system.

Application Software

Application software includes basic and specialized applications.

- **Basic applications** are widely used in nearly all career areas. Programs include browsers, word processors, spreadsheets, database management systems, and presentation graphics.
- **Specialized applications** focus on specific disciplines and occupations. These programs include graphics, audio, video, multimedia, Web authoring, and artificial intelligence programs.

HARDWARE

Hardware consists of electronic devices that can follow instructions, accept input, process, and produce information.

Types of Computers

Supercomputer, mainframe, minicomputer (midrange), and **microcomputer** are four types of computers. Microcomputers can be **desktop, media center, notebook, netbook, tablet PC,** or **handheld** (**PDAs** and **smartphones** are most widely used handheld microcomputers).

Microcomputer Hardware

There are four basic categories of hardware devices.

- **System unit** contains electronic circuitry, including the **microprocessor** and **memory. Random-access memory (RAM),** holds the program and data currently being processed.
- **Input/output devices** are translators between humans and computers. **Input devices** include the **keyboard** and **mouse. Output devices** include **monitors** and **printers.**
- **Secondary storage** holds data and programs. Typical media include **hard disks, solid-state storage (solid-state drives, flash memory cards,** and **USB drives),** and **optical discs (CD, DVD,** and **hi def).**
- **Communication devices** connect system units computers and the Internet. **Modems** modify output for transmission.

DATA

Data is the raw facts unprocessed about something. Common file types include

- **Document files** created by word processors.

- **Worksheet files** created by spreadsheet programs.

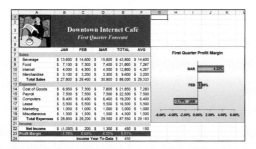

- **Database files** created by database management programs.

- **Presentation files** created by presentation graphics programs.

CONNECTIVITY AND THE INTERNET

Connectivity

Connectivity is a concept describing the ability of end users to tap into resources well beyond their desktops. **Networks** are connected computers that share data and resources.

The Wireless Revolution

The **wireless revolution** is the widespread and increasing use of mobile (wireless) communication devices.

Internet

The **Internet** is the world's largest computer network. The **Web** provides a multimedia interface to resources available on the Internet.

CAREERS IN IT

Career	Description
Webmaster	Develops and maintains Web sites and Web resources. See page 52.
Computer support specialist	Provides technical support to customers and other users. See page 143.
Technical writer	Prepares instruction manuals, technical reports, and other scientific or technical documents. See page 207.
Software engineer	Analyzes users' needs and creates application software. See page 234.
Network administrator	Creates and maintains computer networks. See page 269.
Database administrator	Uses database management software to determine the most efficient ways to organize and access data. See page 354.
Systems analyst	Plans, designs, and maintains information systems. See page 385.
Programmer	Creates, tests, and troubleshoots computer programs. See page 419.

KEY TERMS

application software (9)
basic application (9)
communication device (14)
compact disc (CD) (14)
computer competency (4)
connectivity (6,15)
data (6)
database file (15)
desktop computer (11)
device driver (9)
digital versatile disc (DVD) (14)
digital video disc (DVD) (14)
document file (15)
end user (5)
flash memory card (13)
handheld computer (11)
hard disk (12)
hardware (6)
high definition (hi def) disc (14)
information (6)
information system (5)
information technology (IT) (6)
input device (12)
Internet (16)
keyboard (12)
mainframe computer (10)
media centers (11)
memory (12)
microcomputer (11)
microprocessor (12)
midrange computer (10)
minicomputer (10)

modem (14)
monitor (12)
mouse (12)
netbook (11)
network (16)
notebook computer (11)
operating system (9)
optical disc (13)
output device (12)
people (5)
personal digital assistant (PDA) (11)
presentation file (15)
printer (12)
procedures (5)
program (6)
random access memory (RAM) (12)
secondary storage (12)
smartphone (11)
software (6)
solid-state drive (SSD) (13)
solid-state storage (13)
specialized application (9)
supercomputer (10)
system software (8)
system unit (12)
tablet PC (11)
USB drive (13)
utility (9)
Web (16)
wireless revolution (16)
worksheet file (15)

To test your knowledge of these key terms with animated flash cards, visit our Web site at www.computing2011.com and enter the keyword terms1.

MULTIPLE CHOICE

Circle the letter or fill in the correct answer.

1. People, procedures, software, hardware, and data are the five parts of a(n)
   a. competency system
   b. computer system
   c. information technology
   d. software system

2. Procedures are typically documented in manuals written by
   a. computer specialists
   b. end users
   c. Microsoft
   d. service providers

3. Which of the following is an example of connectivity?
   a. data
   b. hard disk
   c. Internet
   d. power cord

4. Windows 7 is an example of a(n)
   a. application software
   b. browser
   c. operating system
   d. shareware

5. The most powerful type of computer.
   a. mainframe computers
   b. microcomputers
   c. minicomputers
   d. supercomputers

6. The system component that controls and manipulates data in order to produce information is called the
   a. keyboard
   b. microprocessor
   c. monitor
   d. mouse

7. These devices translate data and programs that humans can understand into a form that the computer can process.
   a. display
   b. input
   c. output
   d. pointer

8. A DVD is an example of a(n)
   a. hard disk
   b. optical disc
   c. output device
   d. solid-state storage device

9. This type of file is created by word processors.
   a. worksheet
   b. document
   c. database
   d. presentation

10. Many experts are predicting that this revolution is expected to dramatically affect the way we communicate and use computer technology.
    a. graphics
    b. input
    c. memory
    d. wireless

For an interactive multiple-choice practice test, visit our Web site at www.computing2011.com and enter the keyword multiple1.

MATCHING

Match each numbered item with the most closely related lettered item. Write your answers in the spaces provided.

a. microcomputer
b. optical discs
c. output device
d. PDA
e. procedures
f. program
g. secondary storage
h. supercomputer
i. system software
j. the Internet

1. Guidelines people follow when using software. _____
2. Consists of the step-by-step instructions that tell the computer how to do its work. _____
3. Software that enables the application software to interact with the computer hardware. _____
4. The most powerful type of computer. _____
5. The least powerful and most widely used type of computer. _____
6. Translates the processed information from the computer into a form that humans can understand. _____
7. Holds data and programs even after electrical power to the system has been turned off. _____
8. Uses laser technology. _____
9. A type of handheld computer. _____
10. The largest network in the world. _____

For an interactive matching practice test, visit our Web site at www.computing2011.com and enter the keyword matching1.

OPEN-ENDED

On a separate sheet of paper, respond to each question or statement.

1. Explain the five parts of an information system. What part do people play in this system?
2. What is system software? What kinds of programs are included in system software?
3. Define and compare basic and specialized application software. Describe some different types of basic applications. Describe some types of specialized applications.
4. Describe the different types of computers. What is the most common type? What are the types of microcomputers?
5. What is connectivity? How are the wireless revolution and connectivity related? What is a computer network? What is the Internet? What is the Web?

APPLYING TECHNOLOGY

Applying Technology questions are designed to demonstrate ways that you can effectively use technology today.

Making a habit of keeping current with technology trends is a key to your success with information technology. In each of this book's chapters, the Applying Technology feature will present questions designed to help you gain a better understanding of how technology is being used today.

The first question typically relates to one of the Making IT Work for You topics. Some of these topics are listed below. Select the two that you find the most interesting and then describe why they are of interest to you and how you might use (or are using) those applications.

① TV TUNER CARDS AND VIDEO CLIPS

Want to watch your favorite television program while you work? Perhaps you would like to include a video clip from a television program or from a DVD in a class presentation. It's easy using a TV tuner card. See page 181.

② DIGITAL VIDEO EDITING

Want to make your own movie? Would you like to edit some home movies and distribute them to family and friends on DVDs? It's easy with the right equipment and software. See page 122.

③ HOME NETWORKING

Computer networks are not just for corporations and schools anymore. If you have more than one computer, you can use a wireless home network to share files and printers, to allow multiple users access to the Internet at the same time, and to play interactive computer games. See page 277.

④ LOCATING JOB OPPORTUNITIES ONLINE

Did you know that you can use the Internet to find a job? You can browse through job openings, post your resume, and even use special programs that will search for the job that's just right for you. See page 451.

EXPANDING YOUR KNOWLEDGE

Expanding Your Knowledge questions are designed to add depth and detail to your understanding of specific topics presented within this chapter. The questions direct you to sources other than the textbook to obtain this knowledge.

A deeper knowledge of select topics can greatly enhance your understanding of information technology. In each of the following chapters, the Expanding Your Knowledge feature presents questions designed to help you gain a deeper understanding of select topics.

The first question typically relates to a topic presented at our Web site at www.computing2011 .com. Some of those topics are listed below. Select the two that you find the most interesting and then describe why they are of interest to you and why they are important.

1 HOW COMPUTER VIRUS PROTECTION PROGRAMS WORK

Computer viruses are destructive and dangerous programs that can migrate through networks and operating systems. They often attach themselves to other programs, e-mail messages, and databases. It is essential to protect your computer systems from computer viruses. See page 151.

2 HOW DIGITAL CAMERAS WORK

While traditional cameras capture images on film, digital cameras capture images and convert them into a digital form. These images can be viewed immediately and saved to a disk or into the camera's memory. See page 216.

3 HOW INTERNET TELEPHONES WORK

Internet telephones offer a low-cost alternative to making long-distance calls. Using the Internet telephone (or other appropriate audio input and output devices), the Internet, a special service provider, a sound card, and special software, you can place long-distance calls to almost anywhere in the world. See page 216.

4 HOW WIRELESS HOME NETWORKS WORK

Wireless home networks are becoming very popular. They are easy to set up and use. They allow different computers to share resources including a common Internet connection and printer. See page 278.

WRITING ABOUT TECHNOLOGY

The ability to think critically and to write effectively is essential to nearly every profession. Writing about Technology questions are designed to help you develop these skills by posing thought-provoking questions about computer privacy, security, and/or ethics.

Regardless of your career path, critical thinking, analysis, and writing are essential skills. In each of the following chapters, the Writing about Technology feature presents questions about privacy, security, and ethics. These questions are designed to help you develop critical thinking, analysis, and writing skills. Some of the topics are listed below. Select two that you find the most interesting and then describe why they are of interest to you.

DIGITAL PHOTO MANIPULATION

Image editing software has made it easy to alter photographs, which in the past were accepted as visual records of real events. In some cases, the purpose of digital editing is humor and exaggeration, while other times subtle changes are used to alter a photo's deeper meaning. Some caution "seeing is believing" needs to be reconsidered for the digital age and argue that ethical standards need to be clearly established for photo manipulation. See page 124.

WEBCAMS

WebCams are almost everywhere, from dorm rooms to parking lots. They are used to communicate face-to-face with friends and family, to catch car thieves, and for any number of other applications. While acknowledging the many very positive applications of WebCams, some argue that their widespread and uncontrolled use has too many cases involving the loss of personal privacy. See page 217.

ELECTRONIC MONITORING

Surveillance of individuals occurs more frequently today than ever before. For example, the FBI has proposed the widespread use of a technology known as Carnivore to help them track terrorists. This technology supports widespread monitoring of individual Internet activity and e-mail. Privacy advocates claim that this would be an unnecessary and unneeded invasion of personal privacy. Others believe electronic surveillance is essential to protect national security. See page 279.

NOTES

The Internet, the Web, and Electronic Commerce

Competencies

After you have read this chapter, you should be able to:

1 Discuss the origins of the Internet and the Web.

2 Describe how to access the Web using providers and browsers.

3 Discuss Internet communications, including e-mail, instant messaging, social networking, blogs, microblogs, and wikis.

4 Describe search tools, including search engines, metasearch engines, and specialized search engines.

5 Evaluate the accuracy of information presented on the Web.

6 Discuss electronic commerce, including B2C, C2C, B2B, and security issues.

7 Describe these Web utilities: Web-based applications, plug-ins, filters, file transfer utilities, and Internet security suites.

Many of the earliest Web sites were digital versions of traditional resources like the dictionary, encyclopedia, or phone book. These sites made it possible to access information more easily, but they did not customize information for the user. Today it is possible to filter through this information more easily, and some Web sites are tailoring their content for each user.

Some experts predict that in the future your browser will act more like your personal assistant. Your computer will not only be capable of retrieving information from the Web, it will be able to understand and process it on your behalf. Imagine a world where your computer is like your trusted friend, able to make suggestions because it truly knows you. It may scan the Web for you and predict which of the latest films and new restaurants you might like and suggest openings on your calendar for a night out.

chapter 2

Introduction

Want to communicate with a friend across town, in another state, or even in another country? Looking for a long-lost friend? Looking for travel or entertainment information? Perhaps you're researching a term paper or exploring different career paths. Where do you start? For these and other information-related activities, most people use the Internet and the Web.

The Internet is often referred to as the Information Superhighway. In a sense, it is like a highway that connects you to millions of other people and organizations. Unlike typical highways that move people and things from one location to another, the Internet moves your ideas and information. The Web provides an easy-to-use, intuitive, multimedia interface to resources available on the Internet. It has become an everyday tool for all of us to use.

Competent end users need to be aware of the resources available on the Internet and the Web. Additionally, they need to know how to access these resources, to effectively communicate electronically, to efficiently locate information, to understand electronic commerce, and to use Web utilities.

The Internet and the Web

The **Internet** was launched in 1969 when the United States funded a project that developed a national computer network called **Advanced Research Project Agency Network (ARPANET).** The Internet is a large network that connects together smaller networks all over the globe. The **Web** was introduced in 1991 at the **Center for European Nuclear Research (CERN)** in Switzerland. Prior to the Web, the Internet was all text—no graphics, animations, sound, or video. The Web made it possible to include these elements. It provided a multimedia interface to resources available on the Internet. From these early research beginnings, the Internet and the Web have evolved into one of the most powerful tools of the 21st century.

It is easy to get the Internet and the Web confused, but they are not the same thing. The Internet is the actual network. It is made up of wires, cables, satellites, and rules for exchanging information between computers connected to the network. Being connected to this network is often described as being **online.** The Internet connects millions of computers and resources throughout the world. The Web is a multimedia interface to the resources available on the Internet. Every day over a billion users from nearly every country in the world use the Internet and the Web. What are they doing? The most common uses are the following:

- **Communicating** is by far the most popular Internet activity. You can exchange e-mail with your family and friends almost anywhere in the world. You can join and listen to discussions and debates on a wide variety of special-interest topics.

- **Shopping** is one of the fastest-growing Internet applications. You can window shop, look for the latest fashions, search for bargains, and make purchases.

- **Searching** for information has never been more convenient. You can access some of the world's largest libraries directly from your home computer. You can find the latest local, national, and international news.

- **Entertainment** options are nearly endless. You can find music, movies, magazines, and computer games. You will find live concerts, movie previews, book clubs, and interactive live games. (See Figure 2-1.)

- **Education** or **e-learning** is another rapidly emerging Web application. You can take classes on almost any subject. There are courses just for fun

On the Web Explorations

Many individuals and institutions played a part in the development of the Internet and the Web.

To learn more about the history of the Internet and Web, visit our site at www. computing2011.com and enter the keyword history.

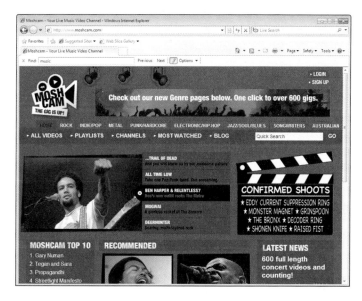

Figure 2-1 **Entertainment site**

and there are courses for high school, college, and graduate school credit. Some cost nothing to take and others cost a lot.

The first step to using the Internet and the Web is to get connected, or to gain access to the Internet.

 CONCEPT CHECK

 Describe how the Internet and the Web started.

 What is the difference between the Internet and the Web?

 List and describe five of the most common uses of the Internet and the Web.

Access

The Internet and the telephone system are similar—you can connect a computer to the Internet much like you connect a phone to the telephone system. Once you are on the Internet, your computer becomes an extension of what seems like a giant computer—a computer that branches all over the world. When provided with a connection to the Internet, you can use a browser program to search the Web.

Providers

The most common way to access the Internet is through an **Internet service provider (ISP).** The providers are already connected to the Internet and provide a path or connection for individuals to access the Internet. Your college or university most likely provides you with free access to the Internet either through its local area networks or through a **dial-up** or telephone connection. There are also some companies that offer free Internet access.

The most widely used commercial Internet service providers are national and wireless providers.

- **National service providers** like America Online (AOL) are the most widely used. They provide access through standard telephone or cable connections. Users can access the Internet from almost anywhere within the country for a standard fee without incurring long-distance telephone charges.

Figure 2-2 Browser

- **Wireless service providers** offer Internet connections for computers with wireless modems and a wide array of wireless devices.

As we will discuss in Chapter 9, users connect to ISPs using one of a variety of connection technologies including **DSL, cable,** and **wireless modems.**

Browsers

Browsers are programs that provide access to Web resources. This software connects you to remote computers, opens and transfers files, displays text and images, and provides in one tool an uncomplicated interface to the Internet and Web documents. Browsers allow you to explore, or to **surf,** the Web by easily moving from one Web site to another. Four well-known browsers are Mozilla Firefox, Apple Safari, Microsoft Internet Explorer, and Google Chrome. (See Figure 2-2.)

For browsers to connect to resources, the **location** or **address** of the resources must be specified. These addresses are called **uniform resource locators (URLs).** All URLs have at least two basic parts. (See Figure 2-3.) The first part presents the protocol used to connect to the resource. As we will discuss in Chapter 9, **protocols** are rules for exchanging data between computers. The protocol *http* is used for Web traffic and is the most widely used Internet protocol. The second part presents the **domain name.** It indicates the specific address where the resource is located. In Figure 2-3 the domain is identified as mtv.com. (Many URLs have additional parts specifying directory paths, file names, and pointers.) The last part of the domain name following the dot (.) is the **top-level domain (TLD).** It identifies the type of organization. For example, *.com* indicates a commercial site. The URL *http://www.mtv.com* connects your computer to a computer that provides information about MTV.

Once the browser has connected to the Web site, a document file is sent back to your computer. This document typically contains **Hypertext Markup Language (HTML).** The browser interprets the HTML formatting instructions and displays the document as a **Web page.** For example, when your browser first connects to the Internet, it opens up to a Web page specified in the browser settings. This page presents information about the site along with references and **hyperlinks** or **links** that connect to other documents containing related information—text files, graphic images, audio, and video clips. (See Figure 2-4.)

These documents may be located on a nearby computer system or on one halfway around the world. The links typically appear on the Web page as underlined and colored text and/or images. To access the referenced material, all you do is click on the highlighted text or image. A connection is automatically made to the computer containing the material, and the referenced material appears on your display screen.

Figure 2-3 Basic parts of a URL

Web pages also can contain special programming to add interest and activity. A language called **JavaScript** is often used to trigger simple interactive features, such as opening new browser windows and checking information entered in online forms. An advanced use of JavaScript called **AJAX** can be found on many interactive sites. This technology is used to create interactive Web sites that respond quickly, like traditional desktop application software. (Application software will be presented in Chapters 3 and 4.) **Applets** are written in the **Java** programming language. (Java and other programming languages will be presented in Chapter 14.) These programs can be downloaded quickly and run by most browsers. Java applets are used to present animation, display graphics, provide interactive games, and much more.

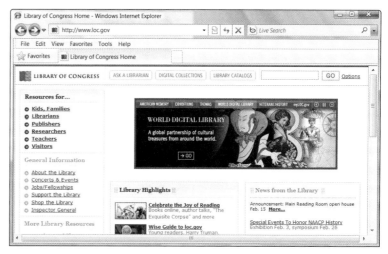

Figure 2-4 **Web page**

Today it is common to access the Internet from a variety of mobile devices like cell phones. Special browsers called **mobile browsers** are designed to run on these portable devices. (See Figure 2-5.) Unlike a traditional Web browser that is typically displayed on a large screen, a mobile browser is displayed on a very small screen and special navigational tools are required to conveniently view Web content. The Apple iPhone, for example, enables you to "pinch" or "stretch" the screen with two fingers to zoom Web content in and out.

To learn more about browsers, visit our Web site at www.computing2011 .com and enter the keyword **browsers**.

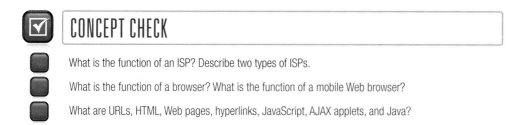

CONCEPT CHECK

What is the function of an ISP? Describe two types of ISPs.

What is the function of a browser? What is the function of a mobile Web browser?

What are URLs, HTML, Web pages, hyperlinks, JavaScript, AJAX applets, and Java?

Figure 2-5 **Mobile browser**

The Internet, the Web, and Electronic Commerce   **33**

Communication

As previously mentioned, communication is the most popular Internet activity, and its impact cannot be overestimated. At a personal level, friends and family can stay in contact with one another even when separated by thousands of miles. At a business level, electronic communication has become a standard, and many times preferred, way to stay in touch with suppliers, employees, and customers. Some popular types of Internet communication are e-mail, instant messaging, social networking, blogs, and wikis.

E-mail

E-mail or **electronic mail** is the transmission of electronic messages over the Internet. At one time, e-mail consisted only of basic text messages. Now e-mail routinely includes graphics, photos, and many different types of file attachments. People all over the world send e-mail to each other. You can e-mail your family, your co-workers, and even your senator. All you need to send and receive e-mail is an e-mail account, access to the Internet, and an e-mail program. Two of the most widely used e-mail programs are Microsoft's Outlook Express and Mozilla Thunderbird.

A typical e-mail message has three basic elements: header, message, and signature. (See Figure 2-6.) The **header** appears first and typically includes the following information:

- **Addresses:** Addresses of the persons sending, receiving, and, optionally, anyone else who is to receive copies. E-mail addresses have two basic parts. (See Figure 2-7.) The first part is the user's name and the second part is the domain name, which includes the top-level domain. In our example e-mail, *dcoats* is Dan's user name. The server providing e-mail service for Dan is *usc.edu*. The top-level domain indicates that the provider is an educational institution.

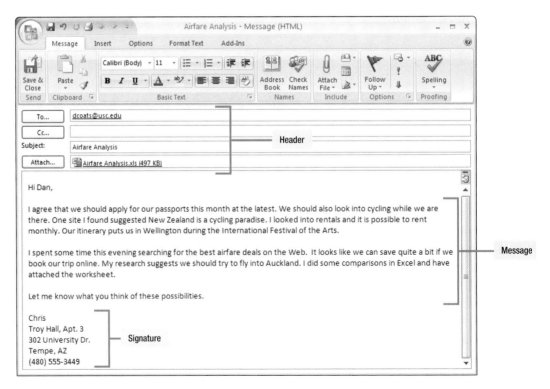

Figure 2-6 Basic elements of an e-mail message

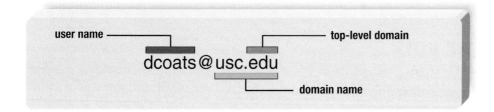

Figure 2-7 Two parts of an e-mail address

- **Subject:** A one-line description, used to present the topic of the message. Subject lines typically are displayed when a person checks his or her mailbox.
- **Attachments:** Many e-mail programs allow you to attach files such as documents and image files. If a message has an attachment, the file name appears on the attachment line. If you are sending a large file, however, there are more efficient ways to send the file. To learn more about how you can send large files, see Making IT Work for You: Sharing Large Files on pages 36 and 37.

The letter or **message** comes next. Finally, the **signature** provides additional information about the sender. Typically, this information includes the sender's name, address, and telephone number.

E-mail can be a valuable asset in your personal and professional life. However, like many other valuable technologies, there are drawbacks too. Americans receive billions of unwanted and unsolicited e-mails every year. This unwelcome mail is called **spam.** While spam is indeed a distraction and nuisance, it also can be dangerous. For example, **computer viruses** or destructive programs are often attached to unsolicited e-mail. Computer viruses and ways to protect against them will be discussed in Chapter 5.

In an attempt to control spam, anti-spam laws have been added to our legal system. For example, the CAN-SPAM Act of 2003 requires that every marketing-related e-mail provide an opt-out option. When the option is selected, the recipient's e-mail address is to be removed from future mailing lists. Failure to do so results in heavy fines. This approach, however, has had minimal impact since over 50 percent of all spam originates from servers outside the United States. A more effective approach has been the development and use of **spam blockers.** (See Figure 2-8.) These programs use a variety of different approaches to identify and eliminate spam. To learn about these approaches, visit our Web site at www.computing2011.com and enter the keyword spam.

On the Web Explorations

Almost all ISPs and online service providers offer e-mail service to their customers. But you can get this service for free from several sources.

To learn more about one of these free services, visit our site at www.computing2011.com and enter the keyword freemail.

tips

Are you tired of sorting through an inbox full of spam? Americans receive over 200 billion spam e-mails every year. Here are a few simple tips to help ensure that your inbox is spam-free:

1 **Choose a complex address.** sally_smith@hotmail.com is much more likely to get spam than 4it3scoq2@hotmail.com. Consider using a more complicated, and less personal, user name.

2 **Keep a low profile.** Many spammers collect e-mail addresses from personal Web sites, chat rooms, and message boards. Use caution when handing out your address and be sure to read the privacy policy of a site before you hand over your address.

3 **Don't ever respond to spam.** Once you respond to spam, either in interest or to opt out of a list, you have confirmed the address is valid. Valid addresses are worth more to spammers, who then sell the addresses to others.

4 **Use e-mail filter options.** Most e-mail programs have a filter option that screens incoming e-mail based on a set of preferences you choose. You can set up your inbox to accept only mail from certain addresses or to block mail from others.

5 **Use spam blockers.** There are plenty of programs available to help protect your inbox. For example, MailWasher provides an effective and free program available at www.mailwasher.com.

To see other tips, visit our Web site at www.computing2011.com and enter the keyword tips.

Instant Messaging

Instant messaging (IM) allows two or more people to contact each other via direct, live communication. To use instant messaging, you register with an instant messaging server and then specify

Spam Blocker	Site
OnlyMyEmailPersonal	www.onlymymail.com
CA Anti-Spam Plus	www.qurb.com
Vanquish vqME	www.vanquish.com

Figure 2-8 Spam blockers

Making IT work for you

SHARING LARGE FILES

Do you ever need to share large files with others? Perhaps you have found many video and other types of files can be too large to effectively send as an e-mail attachment. You could distribute large files on a CD or DVD, or by using an FTP site. A simpler alternative is to use an online file-sharing service. Using a file-sharing service makes it easy to upload and share files with anyone quickly.

Create a Custom Address   The first step is to choose a custom URL where your files will be located and upload your files to that address. To do this using the drop.io file-sharing service:

- ● **Visit http://drop.io**

- ● **Create a custom address by typing a word in the blank. For example, typing the _word_ computing will create the address http://drop.io/computing for your files.**

- ● **Click the _Add Files_ button to select files to share.**

- ● **Optionally, choose a password to protect access to your files.**

- ● **Click the _Drop it_ button to upload your selected files.**

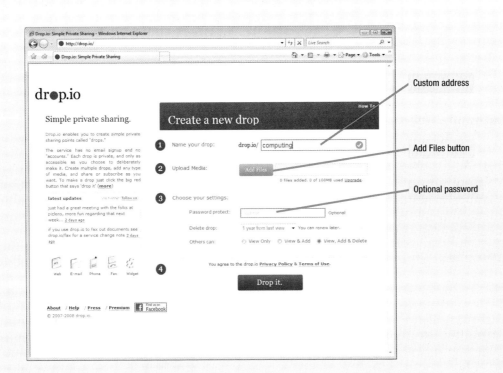

Sharing Your Address Once your files are uploaded, you can share your custom address with anyone you want to have access to your files, just as you would share any other link. For example, you might choose to send your address to others using e-mail.

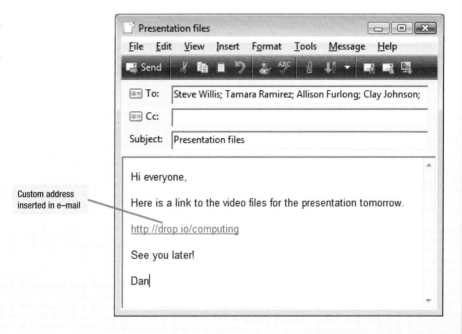

Custom address inserted in e–mail

Updating Your Files You can visit your custom address at any time from a Web browser to add, delete, or update files. For example, to add additional files to your custom address:

1 • **Visit your custom address in any Web browser (http://drop. io/*your-address*)**

• **Click the *Files* link.**

• **Click the *Add Files* button to select additional files to share.**

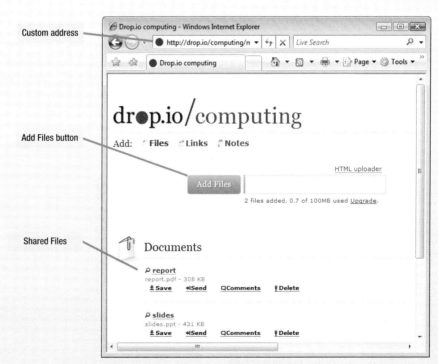

Custom address

Add Files button

Shared Files

File sharing services are continually changing and some of the specifics presented in this Making IT Work for You may have changed.

To learn about other ways to make information technology work for you, visit our Web site at www.computing2011.com and enter the keyword MIW.

a list of **friends.** Whenever you connect to the Internet, special software informs your messaging server that you are online. In response, the server will notify you if any of your friends are online. At the same time, it notifies your friends that you are online. You can then send messages directly back and forth to one another. Most instant messaging programs also include video conferencing features, file sharing, and remote assistance. Many businesses routinely use these instant messaging features. To see how instant messaging works, visit our Web site at www.computing2011.com and enter the keyword **im**.

The most widely used instant messaging services are AOL's Instant Messenger, Microsoft's MSN Messenger, and Yahoo Messenger. One limitation, however, is that many instant messaging services do not support communication with other services. For example, at the time of this writing, a user registered with AOL cannot use AOL's Instant Messenger software to communicate with a user registered with Yahoo Messenger. Recently, however, some software companies have started providing **universal instant messenger** programs that overcome this limitation. For example, Gain, Odigo, and Trillian provide instant messaging services that do support communication with other services.

Social Networking

One of the fastest-growing uses of the Internet is **social networking,** or connecting individuals to one another. Three basic categories of social networking sites are reuniting, friend-of-a-friend, and common interest.

- **Reuniting sites** are designed to connect people who have known one another but have lost touch; for example, an old high school friend that you have not seen for several years. You join a social network by connecting to a reuniting site and providing profile information such as your age, gender, name of high school, and so forth. This information is added to the reuniting site's member database. Members are able to search the database to locate individuals. Many of the sites will even notify you whenever a new individual joins that matches some parts of your profile (such as high school class). Two of the best-know reuniting sites are Classmates Online and Facebook.

- **Friend-of-a-friend sites** are designed to bring together two people who do not know one another but share a common friend. The theory is that, if you share a common friend, then it is likely that you would become friends. For example, a network could be started by one of your acquaintances by providing profile information on him- or herself and a list of friends. You could visit your acquaintance's site to connect to a friend(s) of your acquaintance. You could even join the list of friends provided at the site. Two well-known friend-of-a-friend sites are Friendster and MySpace. (See Figure 2-9.)

- **Common interest sites** bring together individuals that share common interests or hobbies. You select a networking site based on a particular interest. For

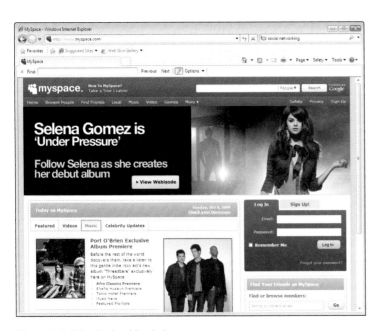

Figure 2-9 Friend-of-a-friend site

example, if you wanted to share images, you might join Flickr. If you are looking for business contacts, you might join LinkedIn. If you wanted to locate or create a special interest group, you might join Meetup.

Before providing any information to a social networking site or to any individual, consider carefully what you are disclosing. Do not provide inappropriate or overly personal information. For a list of some popular social networking sites, see Figure 2-10. To learn more about Twitter, one of the most widely used social networking sites, see Making IT Work for You: Twitter on pages 40 and 41.

Site	Description
Classmates.com	Reuniting, primarily for school, work, military
Facebook.com	Reuniting, primarily for college and high school students
Flickr.com	Common interest, image sharing
Friendster.com	Friend-of-a-friend, general
MySpace.com	Friend-of-a-friend, general
Twitter.com	Friend-of-a-friend, general
LinkedIn.com	Common interest, business
Meetup.com	Common interest, interest group meeting

Figure 2-10 **Social networking sites**

Blogs, Microblogs, and Wikis

In addition to social networking sites, there are other types of sites that help ordinary people communicate across the Web.

- Many individuals create personal Web sites, called **Web logs** or **blogs,** to keep in touch with friends and family. Blog postings are timestamped and arranged with the newest item first. Often, readers of these sites are allowed to comment. Some blogs are like online diaries with personal information; others focus on information about a hobby or theme, such as knitting, electronic devices, or good books. Although most are written by individual bloggers, there are also group blogs with multiple contributors. Some businesses and newspapers also have started blogging as a quick publishing method. Several sites provide tools to create blogs. Two of the most widely used are Blogger and WordPress. (See Figure 2-11.)

- A **microblog** publishes short sentences that only take a few seconds to write, rather than long stories or posts like a traditional blog. Microblogs are designed to keep friends and other contacts up-to-date on your interests and activities. The most popular microblogging site, **Twitter,** enables

Figure 2-11 **Blog creation site**

Making IT work for you

TWITTER

Would you like your own microblog? A microblog can help you stay in touch with friends and family, or coordinate a project with other students. It's easy using the free Twitter microblogging service.

Sign Up   To create a new Twitter account:

1 ● **Visit http://www.twitter.com.**

● **Click the *Sign up now* button.**

2 ● **Follow the on-screen instructions to create an account.**

The username you select for your new account will be used to create a custom blog address where your posts can be viewed by others. For example, tweets posted by the user **comp_essentials** can be seen at **http://twitter.com/comp_essentials**.

Sign up now button

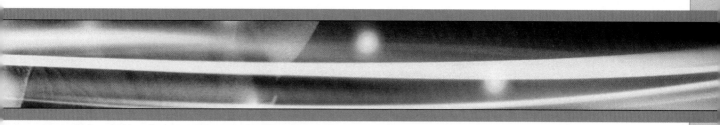

Posting and Following   Using Twitter involves posting short messages about your current status. Following others allows you to see their messages each time they post an update. To post an update to Twitter:

1

● **Enter a short message in the *What are you doing?* text box.**

● **Click the *update* button.**

Your text is immediately visible at your custom Twitter page. In addition to tweeting directly from the Twitter Web site, there are also options to tweet by sending a text message from a mobile phone, or using other software such as instant messaging applications.

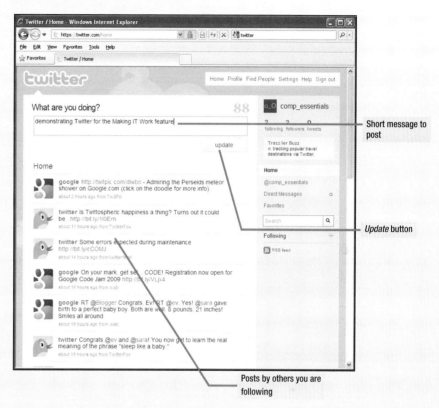

Short message to post

Update button

Posts by others you are following

To follow updates by other people, simply visit their custom blog address and click the *Follow* button.

Follow button

The Web is continually changing, and some of the specifics presented in Making IT Work for You may have changed.

To learn about other ways to make information technology work for you, visit our Web site at www.computing2011.com and enter the keyword miw.

Figure 2-12 Microblog site

you to add new content from your browser, instant messaging application, or even a mobile phone. (See Figure 2-12.)

- A **wiki** is a Web site specially designed to allow visitors to fill in missing information or correct inaccuracies. "Wiki" comes from the Hawaiian word for fast, which describes the simplicity of editing and publishing through wiki software. Wikis support collaborative writing in which there isn't a single expert author, but rather a community of interested people that builds knowledge over time. Perhaps the most famous example is Wikipedia, an online encyclopedia, written and edited by anyone who wants to contribute, that has millions of entries in over 20 languages. (See Figure 2-13.)

Creating blogs and wikis are examples of Web authoring. We will discuss Web authoring software in detail in Chapter 4. To learn more about creating your own personal Web site, visit us at www.computing2011.com and enter the keyword **blog.**

Figure 2-13 Wikipedia

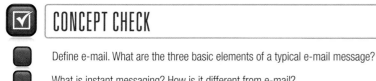
Search Tools

The Web can be an incredible resource, providing information on nearly any topic imaginable. Are you planning a trip? Writing an economics paper? Looking for a movie review? Trying to locate a long-lost friend? Information sources related to these questions, and much, much more, are available on the Web.

With over 20 billion pages and more being added daily, the Web is a massive collection of interrelated pages. With so much available information, locating the precise information you need can be difficult. Fortunately, a number of organizations called **search services** operate Web sites that can help you locate the information you need. They maintain huge databases relating to information provided on the Web and the Internet. The information stored at these databases includes addresses, content descriptions or classifications, and keywords appearing on Web pages and other Internet informational resources. Special programs called **spiders** continually look for new information and update the search services' databases. Additionally, search services provide special programs called *search engines* that you can use to locate specific information on the Web.

Are you going to use a search tool to locate some information? Here are a few tips that might help.

1. **Start with the right approach.** For general information, use a direct search. For specific information, use a keyword search.

2. **Be as precise as possible.** Use specific keywords that relate directly to the topic.

3. **Use multiple words.** Use quotation marks to identify key phrases.

4. **Use Boolean operators.** Typically, these include words such as "and," "not," and "or."

5. **Check your spelling.** Misspelling is one of the most common problems.

6. **Keep moving.** Look only at the first page of search results. If necessary, try another search using different keywords.

To see other tips, visit our Web site at www.computing2011.com and enter the keyword tips.

Search Engines

Search engines are specialized programs that assist you in locating information on the Web and the Internet. To find information, you go to a search service's Web site and use its search engine. For example, see Figure 2-14 for Yahoo's search engine. This search engine, like most others, provides two different search approaches.

- **Keyword search:** In a **keyword search,** you enter a keyword or phrase reflecting the information you want. The search engine compares your entry against its database and returns a list of **hits,** or sites that contain the keywords. Each hit includes a hyperlink to the referenced Web page (or other resource) along with a brief discussion of the information contained at that location. Many searches result in a large number of hits. For

Keyword search

Directory search

Figure 2-14 Yahoo's search engine provides keyword and directory search

example, if you were to enter the keyword *travel,* you would get thousands of hits. Search engines order the hits according to those sites that most likely contain the information requested and present the list to you in that order, usually in groups of 10.

- **Directory search:** Most search engines also provide a directory or list of categories or topics such as Autos, Finance, and Games. In a **directory search,** you select a category or topic that fits the information that you want. Another list of subtopics related to the topic you selected appears. You select the subtopic that best relates to your topic and another subtopic list appears. You continue to narrow your search in this manner until a list of Web sites appears. This list corresponds to the hit list previously discussed.

As a rule, if you are searching for general information, use the directory search approach. For example, to find general information about rock music, use a directory search beginning with the category Music and then select the subtopic Rock. If you are searching for specific information, use the keyword approach. For example, if you were looking for a specific music file, you would use a keyword search that includes the album title and/or the artist's name.

A recent study by the NEC Research Institute found that any one search engine includes only a fraction of the informational sources on the Web. Therefore, it is highly recommended that you use more than one search engine when researching important topics. See Figure 2-15 for a list of some of the most widely used search engines. Or you could use a special type of search engine called a metasearch engine.

Metasearch Engines

One way to research a topic is to visit the Web sites for several individual search engines. At each site, you would enter the search instructions, wait for the hits to appear, review the list, and visit selected sites. This process can be quite time-consuming and duplicate responses from different search engines are inevitable. Metasearch engines offer an alternative.

Search Service	Site
AOL Search	search.aol.com
Ask	www.ask.com
Google	www.google.com
MSN Search	search.msn.com
Yahoo!	www.yahoo.com

Figure 2-15 Search engines

Metasearch engines are programs that automatically submit your search request to several search engines simultaneously. The metasearch engine receives the results, eliminates duplicates, orders the hits, and then provides the edited list to you. See Figure 2-16 for a list of several metasearch engines available on the Web. One of the best known is Dogpile; see Figure 2-17.

Specialized Search Engines

Specialized search engines focus on subject-specific Web sites. Specialized sites can potentially save you time by narrowing your search. For a list of just a few selected specialized search engines, see Figure 2-18. For example, let's say you are researching a paper about the fashion industry. You could begin with a general search engine like Yahoo! Or you could go to a search engine that specializes specifically in fashion, such as infomat.com.

Metasearch Service	Site
Dogpile	www.dogpile.com
Ixquick	www.ixquick.com
MetaCrawler	www.metacrawler.com
Search	www.search.com
Clusty	www.clusty.com

Figure 2-16 Metasearch sites

Content Evaluation

Search engines are excellent tools to locate information on the Web. Be careful, however, how you use the information you find. Unlike most published material found in newspapers, journals, and textbooks, not all the information you find on the Web has been subjected to strict guidelines to ensure accuracy. In fact, anyone can publish content on the Web. Many sites, such as Wikipedia.com, allow anyone to post new material, sometimes anonymously and without critical evaluation. To learn how you can publish on the Web, visit our Web site at www.computing2011.com and enter the keyword **blog**.

To evaluate the accuracy of information you find on the Web, consider the following:

- **Authority.** Is the author an expert in the subject area? Is the site an official site for the information presented, or is the site an individual's personal Web site?

- **Accuracy.** Has the information been critically reviewed for correctness prior to posting on the Web? Does the Web site provide a method to report inaccurate information to the author?

Figure 2-17 Dogpile metasearch site

Topic	Site
Environment	www.eco-web.com
Fashion	www.infomat.com
History	www.historynet.com
Law	www.lawcrawler.com
Medicine	www.medscape.com

Figure 2-18 **Select specialized search engines**

- **Objectivity.** Is the information factually reported or does the author have a bias? Does the author appear to have a personal agenda aimed at convincing or changing the reader's opinion?
- **Currency.** Is the information up to date? Does the site specify the date when the site was updated?

CONCEPT CHECK

What are search services, search engines, and spiders?

What is the difference between a keyword and a directory search?

Compare search, metasearch, and specialized search engines.

What are the four considerations for evaluating Web site content?

Electronic Commerce

Electronic commerce, also known as **e-commerce,** is the buying and selling of goods over the Internet. Have you ever bought anything over the Internet? If you have not, there is a very good chance that you will within the next year or two. Shopping on the Internet is growing rapidly and there seems to be no end in sight.

The underlying reason for the rapid growth in e-commerce is that it provides incentives for both buyers and sellers. From the buyer's perspective, goods and services can be purchased at any time of day or night. Traditional commerce is typically limited to standard business hours when the seller is open. Additionally, buyers no longer have to physically travel to the seller's location. For example, busy parents with small children do not need to coordinate their separate schedules or to arrange for a baby sitter whenever they want to visit the mall. From the seller's perspective, the costs associated with owning and operating a retail outlet can be eliminated. For example, a music store can operate entirely on the Web without an actual physical store and without a large sales staff.

Another advantage is reduced inventory. Traditional stores maintain an inventory of goods in their stores and periodically replenish this inventory from warehouses. With e-commerce, there is no in-store inventory and products are shipped directly from warehouses.

While there are numerous advantages to e-commerce, there are disadvantages as well. Some of these disadvantages include the inability to provide immediate delivery of goods, the inability to "try on" prospective purchases, and questions relating to the security of online payments. Although these issues are being addressed, very few observers suggest that e-commerce will replace bricks-and-mortar businesses entirely. It is clear that both will coexist and that e-commerce will continue to grow.

Just like any other type of commerce, electronic commerce involves two parties: businesses and consumers. There are three basic types of electronic commerce:

- **Business-to-consumer (B2C)** involves the sale of a product or service to the general public or end

tips

Have you ever bought anything online? If not, it's likely that in the future you will join the millions that have. Here are a few suggestions on how to shop online:

1 Consult product review sites. To get evaluations or opinions on products, visit one of the many review sites on the Web such as www.consumersearch.com and www.epinions.com.

2 Use a shopping bot. Once you have selected a specific product, enlist a shopping bot or automated shopping assistants to compare prices. Two well-known shopping bots are located at www.mysimon.com and www.pricegrabber.com.

3 Consult vendor review sites. Of course, price is not everything. Before placing an order with a vendor, check their reputation by visiting vendor review sites such as www.resellerratings.com and www.bizrate.com.

To see other tips, visit our Web site at www.computing2011.com and enter the keyword tips.

users. Oftentimes this arrangement eliminates the wholesaler by allowing manufacturers to sell directly to customers. Other times, existing retail stores use B2C e-commerce to create a presence on the Web as another way to reach customers.

- **Consumer-to-consumer (C2C)** involves individuals selling to individuals. This often takes the form of an electronic version of the classified ads or an auction.
- **Business-to-business (B2B)** involves the sale of a product or service from one business to another. This is typically a manufacturer–supplier relationship. For example, a furniture manufacturer requires raw materials such as wood, paint, and varnish.

Business-to-Consumer E-Commerce

The fastest-growing type of e-commerce is business-to-consumer. It is used by large corporations, small corporations, and start-up businesses. Whether large or small, nearly every existing corporation in the United States provides some type of B2C support as another means to connect to customers. Because extensive investments are not required to create traditional retail outlets and to maintain large marketing and sales staffs, e-commerce allows start-up companies to compete with larger established firms.

The three most widely used B2C applications are for online banking, financial trading, and shopping.

- **Online banking** is becoming a standard feature of banking institutions. Customers are able to go online with a standard browser to perform many banking operations. These online operations include accessing account information, balancing check books, transferring funds, paying bills, and applying for loans.
- **Online stock trading** allows investors to research, buy, and sell stocks and bonds over the Internet. While e-trading is more convenient than using a traditional full-service broker, the greatest advantage is cost.
- **Online shopping** includes the buying and selling of a wide range of consumer goods over the Internet. (See Figure 2-19.) There are thousands of e-commerce applications in this area. Fortunately, there are numerous

environmental facts

Did you know that CDs and DVDs can take over one million years to degrade in a landfill? The migration of many applications to the Web has had a measurable impact on the environment, as fewer obsolete compact discs end up in landfills. For example, most software developers provide their programs directly over the Web as well as on CDs or DVDs. Until the time that all software is delivered this way, what can you do to limit your environmental footprint? Some companies now offer free recycling for used discs. A quick search on the Web will identify many disc recycling companies. You can also be conscientious about purchasing music and other entertainment discs. If you know you will be playing the discs on your computer or other devices that can access the Web, skip a step and buy directly online over the Web.

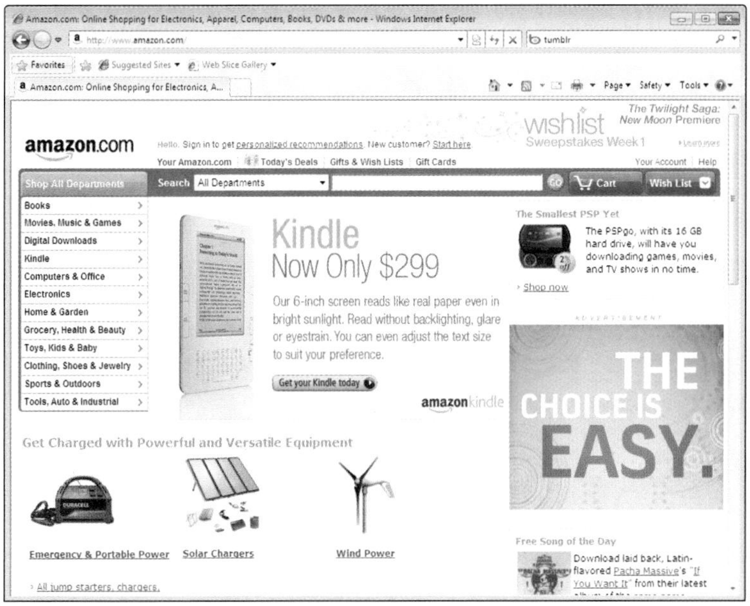

Figure 2-19 Online shopping site

Support	Site
Product comparisons	www.shopping.com
Locating closeouts	www.overstock.com
Finding coupons	www.ebates.com

Figure 2-20 Consumer support sites

Web sites that provide support for consumers looking to compare products and to locate bargains. (See Figure 2-20.)

Consumer-to-Consumer E-Commerce

A recent trend in C2C e-commerce is the growing popularity of Web auctions. **Web auctions** are similar to traditional auctions except that buyers and sellers seldom, if ever, meet face-to-face. Sellers post descriptions of products at a Web site and buyers submit bids electronically. Like traditional auctions, sometimes the bidding becomes highly competitive and enthusiastic. There are two basic types of Web auction sites:

- **Auction house sites** sell a wide range of merchandise directly to bidders. The auction house owner presents merchandise that is typically from a company's surplus stock. These sites operate like a traditional auction, and bargain prices are not uncommon. Auction house sites are generally considered safe places to shop.

- **Person-to-person auction sites** operate more like flea markets. The owner of the site provides a forum for numerous buyers and sellers to gather. While the owners of these sites typically facilitate the bidding process, they are not involved in completing transactions or in verifying the authenticity of the goods sold. (See Figure 2-21.) As with purchases at a flea market, buyers and sellers need to be cautious.

For a list of the most popular Web auction sites, see Figure 2-22.

Security

The single greatest challenge for e-commerce is the development of fast, secure, and reliable payment methods for purchased goods. The three basic payment options are check, credit card, and digital cash.

- Checks are the most traditional. Unfortunately, check purchases require the longest time to complete. After selecting an item, the buyer sends a check through the mail. Upon receipt of the check, the seller verifies that the check is good. If it is good, then the purchased item is sent out.

- Credit card purchases are faster and more convenient than check purchases. Credit card fraud, however, is a major concern for both buyers and sellers. Criminals known as **carders** specialize in stealing, trading, and using stolen credit cards over the Internet. We will discuss this and other privacy and security issues related to the Internet in Chapter 10.

Figure 2-21 Person-to-person Web auction site

Organization	Site
Amazon	www.auctions.amazon.com
WeBidz	www.webidz.com
eBay	www.ebay.com
Overstock	auctions.overstock.com

Figure 2-22 Auction sites

- **Digital cash** is the Internet's equivalent to traditional cash. Buyers purchase digital cash from a third party (a bank that specializes in electronic currency) and use it (see Figure 2-23) to purchase goods. Sellers convert the digital cash to traditional currency through the third party.

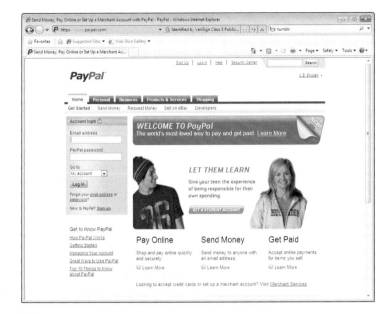

Figure 2-23 **PayPal offers digital cash**

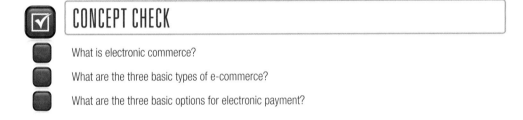

Figure 2-24 **Digital cash providers**

Organization	Site
ECash	www.ecash.com
Google	checkout.google.com
Internet Cash	www.internetcash.com
PayPal	www.paypal.com

Although not as convenient as credit card purchases, digital cash is more secure. For a list of digital cash providers, see Figure 2-24.

CONCEPT CHECK

What is electronic commerce?

What are the three basic types of e-commerce?

What are the three basic options for electronic payment?

Web Utilities

Utilities are programs that make computing easier. **Web utilities** are specialized utility programs that make using the Internet and the Web easier and safer. Some of these utilities are Internet services for connecting and sharing resources over the Internet. Others are browser-related programs that either become part of your browser or are executed from your browser. File transfer utilities allow you to copy files to and from your computer across the Internet.

Web-Based Applications

Typically, application programs are owned by individuals or organizations and stored on their computer system's hard disks. An emerging trend, however, is to free users from owning and storing applications. The most widely used **Web-based applications** are free using **Web-based services** that provide access to programs that run within your browser window. For example, Google Apps provides free access to programs with capabilities similar to Microsoft's Word, Excel, and PowerPoint. (See Figure 2-25.)

Another type of Web-based application typically runs on your desktop like a traditional application program. To use one of these, you connect to the Web site of an **application service provider (asp),** copy the application program to your computer system's memory, and then run the application. Unlike Web-based

Figure 2-25 Web-based service (Google Apps)

services, access is typically not free and the applications are more specialized. To see how application service providers work, visit our Web site at www.computing2011.com and enter the keyword **asp.**

Plug-ins

Plug-ins are programs that are automatically started and operate as a part of your browser. Many Web sites require you to have one or more plug-ins to fully experience their content. Some widely used plug-ins include

- Acrobat Reader from Adobe—for viewing and printing a variety of standard forms and other documents saved in a special format called PDF.
- Windows Media Player from Microsoft—for playing audio files, video files, and much more.
- QuickTime from Apple—for playing audio and video files. (See Figure 2-26.)
- RealPlayer from RealNetworks—for playing audio and video files.
- Shockwave from Adobe—for playing Web-based games and viewing concerts and dynamic animations.

Some of these utilities are included in many of today's browsers and operating systems. Others must be installed before they can be used by your browser. To learn more about plug-ins and how to download them, visit some of the sites listed in Figure 2-27.

Filters

Filters block access to selected sites. The Internet is an interesting and multifaceted arena. But one of those facets is a dark and seamy one. Parents, in particular, are concerned about children roaming unrestricted across the Internet. (See Figure 2-28.) Filter programs allow parents as well as

Figure 2-26 QuickTime movie at Apple.com

Plug-in	Source
Acrobat Reader	www.adobe.com
Media Player	www.microsoft.com
QuickTime	www.apple.com
RealPlayer	www.service.real.com
Shockwave	www.adobe.com

Figure 2-27 Plug-in sites

Figure 2-28 Parents play an important role in Internet supervision

Figure 2-29 Net Nanny is a Web filter

organizations to block out selected sites and set time limits. (See Figure 2-29.) Additionally, these programs can monitor use and generate reports detailing the total time spent on the Internet and the time spent at individual Web sites, chat groups, and newsgroups. For a list of some of the best-known filters, see Figure 2-30.

File Transfer Utilities

Using file transfer utility software, you can copy files to your computer from specially configured servers. This is called **downloading.** You also can use file transfer utility software to copy files from your computer to another computer on the Internet. This is called **uploading.** Three popular types of file transfer are FTP, Web-based, and BitTorrent.

- **File transfer protocol (FTP)** and **secure file transfer protocol (SFTP)** allow you to efficiently copy files to and from your computer across the Internet, and are frequently used for uploading changes to a Web site hosted by an Internet service provider. FTP has been used for decades and still remains one of the most popular methods of file transfer.
- **Web-based file transfer services** make use of a Web browser to upload and download files. This eliminates the need for any custom software to be installed. A popular Web-based file transfer service is drop.io. (See Making IT Work for You: Sharing Large Files on pages 36 and 37 to learn more about how this service works.)
- **BitTorrent** distributes file transfers across many different computers for more efficient downloads, unlike other transfer technologies where a file is copied from one computer on the Internet to another. A single file might be located on dozens of individual computers. When you download the file, each computer sends you a tiny piece of the larger file, making BitTorrent well-suited for transferring very large files. Unfortunately, BitTorrent technology often has been used for

On the Web Explorations

Some privacy groups object to the use of Web filtering programs on the grounds that they accidentally censor valuable Web content.

To learn more about this issue, visit our Web site at www.computing2011.com and enter the keyword filter.

Filter	Site
CyberPatrol	www.cyberpatrol.com
Cybersitter	www.cybersitter.com
iProtectYou Pro Web Filter	www.softforyou.com
Net Nanny	www.netnanny.com
Safe Eyes Platinum	www.safeeyes.com

Figure 2-30 Filters

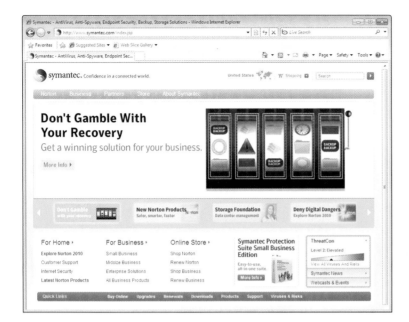

distributing unauthorized copies of copy-righted music and video.

Internet Security Suites

An **Internet security suite** is a collection of utility programs designed to maintain your security and privacy while you are on the Web. These programs control spam, protect against computer viruses, provide filters, and much more. You could buy each program separately; however, the cost of the suite is typically much less. Two of the best-known Internet security suites are McAfee's Internet Security and Symantec's Norton Internet Security. (See Figure 2-31.)

Figure 2-31 Symantec's Norton Internet Security

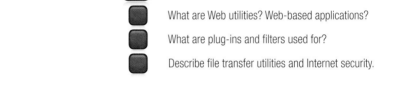

CONCEPT CHECK

What are Web utilities? Web-based applications?

What are plug-ins and filters used for?

Describe file transfer utilities and Internet security.

Careers in IT

Webmasters develop and maintain Web sites and resources. (See Figure 2-32.) The job may include backup of the company Web site, updating resources, or development of new resources. Webmasters are often involved in the design and development of the Web site. Some Webmasters monitor traffic on the site and take steps to encourage users to visit the site. Webmasters also may work with marketing personnel to increase site traffic and may be involved in development of Web promotions.

Employers look for candidates with a bachelor's degree in computer science or information systems and knowledge of common programming languages and Web development software. Knowledge of HTML is considered essential. Those with experience using Web authoring software and programs like Adobe Illustrator and Adobe Flash are often preferred. Good communication and organizational skills are vital in this position.

Webmasters can expect to earn an annual salary of $49,500 to $82,500. This position is relatively new in many corporations and tends to have fluid responsibilities. With technological advances and increasing corporate emphasis on a Web presence, experience in this field could lead to managerial opportunities. To learn about other careers in IT, visit us at www.computing2011.com and enter the keyword **careers.**

Figure 2-32 Webmaster

A LOOK TO THE FUTURE

Web-Accessible Refrigerators Will Automatically Restock Themselves

What if you could virtually tour your home from anywhere using the Web? What if your refrigerator knew what it contained and could create a grocery list to restock itself? What if you could remotely check to see if you left your wallet on the bedside table or make sure you remembered to turn the oven off? In the future, this will almost certainly be the case, as every aspect of the modern home becomes Web accessible.

Web-accessible home appliances are not a new idea. Several companies offer kitchen appliances that connect to the Internet. At present these appliances are passive, meaning that they do not have any knowledge of what food items they contain and are therefore not able to actively act to restock. In the future, however, appliances will be much more active. Refrigerators could know what food they contain and what food is needed to be fully stocked and automatically will place orders over the Internet to restock missing items.

Also, every appliance in your home might have its own Web page. Through such a Web page, you will be able to actively interact and control these appliances.

The home of the future will include more than just smart appliances. Internet cameras, high-speed Internet, and wireless technologies are converging to offer an inexpensive way to virtually visit your home from anywhere with Internet access. You will be able to follow pets to make sure they stay off the couch or search for a missing wallet you may have left on the nightstand. Coupled with Internet appliances, you could review your pantry using Internet cameras and your refrigerator's Web site to create a grocery list. You could have this list e-mailed to your grocery store and then pick up the groceries on the way home.

Could there be a downside to all this? Currently, many people's computers are infested with Internet viruses and spyware. What could happen if these malicious programs infested your home's appliances? Would it be possible that your every move in your own home could be broadcast to others over the Internet?

INTERNET AND WEB

Internet

Launched in 1969 with **ARPANET,** the **Internet** consists of the actual physical network made up of wires, cables, and satellites. Being connected to this network is often described as being **online.**

Web

Introduced in 1991 at **CERN,** the **Web** provides a multimedia interface to Internet resources.

Common Uses

The most common uses of the Internet and the Web include

- Communication—the most popular Internet activity.
- Shopping—one of the fastest-growing Internet activities.
- Searching—access libraries and local, national, and international news.
- Entertainment—music, movies, magazines, and computer games.
- Education—**e-learning** or taking online courses.

ACCESS

Once connected to the Internet, your computer seemingly becomes an extension of a giant computer that branches all over the world.

Providers

Internet service providers are connected to the Internet. The most widely used **ISPs** are **national** and **wireless.** Connection technologies include **DSL, cable,** and **wireless modems.**

Browsers

Browsers access the Web allowing you to **surf** or explore. Some related terms are

- **URLs—locations** or **addresses** to Web resources; two parts are **protocol** and **domain name; top-level domain (TLD)** identifies type of organization.
- **HTML**—commands to display **Web pages; hyperlinks (links)** are connections.
- **JavaScript**—a scripting language that adds basic interactivity and form checking to Web pages. **AJAX** allows rapid response time.
- **Applets**—special programs linked to Web pages; typically written in **Java.**
- **Mobile browsers**—run on portable devices; display on very small screens; provide special navigational tools.

To be a competent end user, you need to be aware of resources available on the Internet and Web, to be able to access these resources, to effectively communicate electronically, to efficiently locate information, to understand electronic commerce, and to use Web utilities.

COMMUNICATION

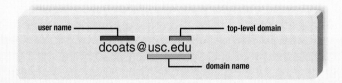

E-mail

E-mail (electronic mail) is the transmission of electronic messages. Basic elements: **header** (including **addresses, subject,** and **attachments**), **message,** and **signature. Spam** is unwanted and unsolicited e-mail that may include a **computer virus. Spam blockers** are programs that identify and eliminate spam.

Instant Messaging

Instant messaging (IM) supports live communication with **friends. Universal instant messengers** support communication with other services.

Social Networking

Social networks connect individuals to one another. Three types are

- **Reuniting sites** connect people who have lost touch with one another.
- **Friend-of-a-friend sites** bring together two people who share a common friend.
- **Common interest sites** connect individuals who share common interests or hobbies.

Blogs, Microblogs, and Wikis

A **Web log** or **blog** is an online journal with chronological postings. A **microblog** publishes short sentences; **Twitter** is the most popular microblogging site. A **wiki** is a Web site that allows people to edit or contribute to it by directly editing the pages.

SEARCH TOOLS

Search Service	Site
AOL Search	search.aol.com
Ask	www.ask.com
Google	www.google.com
MSN Search	search.msn.com
Yahoo!	www.yahoo.com

Search services maintain huge databases relating to Web site content. **Spiders** are programs that update these databases.

Search Engines

Search engines locate information on the Web. Two approaches are **keyword search** (enter keyword, and it returns a list of **hits;** good for locating specific information) and **directory search** (select from a list of topics; good for locating general information).

Metasearch Engines

Metasearch engines submit to several search engines simultaneously. Duplicate sites are eliminated, hits are ordered, and composite hits are presented.

Specialized Search Engines

Specialized search engines focus on subject-specific Web sites.

Content Evaluation

Consider the following criteria to evaluate the accuracy of information on the Web: authority, accuracy, objectivity, and currency.

ELECTRONIC COMMERCE

Organization	Site
Amazon	www.auctions.amazon.com
WeBidz	www.webidz.com
eBay	www.ebay.com
Overstock	auctions.overstock.com

Electronic commerce, or **e-commerce,** is the buying and selling of goods over the Internet. Three basic types of e-commerce are **business-to-consumer, business-to-business,** and **consumer-to-consumer.**

Business-to-Consumer E-Commerce

Most widely used **business-to-consumer (B2C)** applications are online banking, online stock trading, and online shopping.

Consumer-to-Consumer E-Commerce

Web auctions are a growing **consumer-to-consumer (C2C)** application. Two basic types are **auction house sites** and **person-to-person auction sites.**

Security

Security is the greatest challenge for online banking, online stock trading, and online shopping. Three basic payment options are check, credit card, and **digital cash.** Buyers purchase digital cash from a third party and use it to purchase goods. Sellers accept digital cash and convert to traditional currency through the third party.

WEB UTILITIES

Web utilities are specialized utility programs that make using the Internet and the Web easier and safer.

Web-Based Applications

Web-based applications free users from owning and storing applications. The programs are accessed from a Web site. **Web-based services** typically provide free access. **Application service providers (asp)** typically are not free and provide access to more specialized programs.

Plug-ins

Plug-ins are automatically loaded and operate as part of a browser. Many Web sites require specific plug-ins to fully experience their content. Some plug-ins are included in many of today's browsers; others must be installed.

Filters

Filters are used by parents and organizations to block certain sites and to monitor use of the Internet and the Web.

File Transfer Utilities

File transfer utilities copy files to (**downloading**) and from (**uploading**) your computer. Three types are

* **File transfer protocol (FTP)** and **secure file transfer protocol (SFTP)** allow you to efficiently copy files across the Internet.
* **Web-based file transfer services** make use of a Web browser to upload and download files.
* **BitTorrent** distributes file transfers across many different computers.

Internet Security Suite

An **Internet security suite** is a collection of utility programs designed to protect your privacy and security on the Internet.

CAREERS IN IT

Webmasters develop and maintain Web sites and Web resources. Bachelor's degree in computer science or information systems and knowledge of common programming languages and Web development software required. Salary range $49,500 to $82,500.

KEY TERMS

address (32, 34)
Advanced Research Project Agency
  Network (ARPANET) (30)
AJAX (33)
applets (33)
application service provider (asp) (49)
attachment (35)
auction house site (48)
BitTorrent (51)
blog (39)
browser (32)
business-to-business (B2B) (47)
business-to-consumer (B2C) (46)
cable (32)
carder (48)
Center for European Nuclear
  Research (CERN) (30)
common interest site (38)
computer virus (35)
consumer-to-consumer (C2C) (47)
dial-up (31)
digital cash (48)
directory search (44)
domain name (32)
downloading (51)
DSL (32)
e-commerce (46)
e-learning (30)
electronic commerce (46)
electronic mail (34)
e-mail (34)
file transfer protocol (FTP) (51)
filter (50)
friend (38)
friend-of-a-friend site (38)
header (34)
hit (43)
hyperlink (32)
Hypertext Markup Language
  (HTML) (32)
instant messaging (IM) (35)
Internet (30)
Internet security suite (52)
Internet service provider (ISP) (31)
Java (33)
JavaScript (33)

keyword search (43)
link (32)
location (32)
message (35)
metasearch engine (45)
microblog (39)
mobile browser (33)
national service provider (31)
online (30)
online banking (47)
online shopping (47)
online stock trading (47)
person-to-person auction site (48)
plug-in (50)
protocol (32)
reuniting site (38)
search engine (43)
search service (43)
secure file transfer protocol
  (SFTP) (51)
signature (35)
social networking (38)
spam (35)
spam blocker (35)
specialized search engine (45)
spider (43)
subject (35)
surf (32)
top-level domain (TLD) (32)
Twitter (39)
uniform resource locator (URL) (32)
universal instant messenger (38)
uploading (51)
Web (30)
Web auction (48)
Web-based application (49)
Web-based file transfer services (51)
Web-based services (49)
Web log (39)
Webmaster (52)
Web page (32)
Web utility (49)
wiki (42)
wireless modem (32)
wireless service provider (32)

To test your knowledge of these key terms with animated flash cards, visit our Web site at www.computing2011.com and enter the keyword terms2.

MULTIPLE CHOICE

Circle the letter or fill in the correct answer.

1. The Internet was launched in 1969 when the United States funded a project that developed a national computer network called
   - a. Web
   - b. ISP
   - c. CERN
   - d. ARPANET

2. _____ is the most popular Internet activity.
   - a. Communication
   - b. Shopping
   - c. Searching
   - d. Entertainment

3. A(n) _____ program provides access to Web resources.
   - a. Web
   - b. ISP
   - c. browser
   - d. URL

4. Rules for exchanging data between computers are called
   - a. programs
   - b. procedures
   - c. protocols
   - d. hyperlinks

5. The last part of the domain name following the dot (.) is the top- _____ domain.
   - a. level
   - b. link
   - c. locator
   - d. language

6. Many individuals create their own personal sites called Web logs, or _____.
   - a. social networks
   - b. blogs
   - c. wikis
   - d. search engines

7. Unwanted and unsolicited e-mails are called _____.
   - a. spam
   - b. junk
   - c. flame
   - d. lurk

8. Programs that automatically submit your search request to several search engines simultaneously are called _____.
   - a. metasearch engines
   - b. inclusive search engines
   - c. spiders
   - d. hits

9. _____ cash is the Internet's equivalent to traditional cash.
   - a. Universal
   - b. Web
   - c. Premium
   - d. Digital

10. These programs allow parents as well as organizations to block out selected sites and set time limits on Internet access.
    - a. plug-ins
    - b. filters
    - c. FTP
    - d. DSL

For an interactive multiple-choice practice test, visit our Web site at www.computing 2011.com and enter the keyword multiple2.

MATCHING

Match each numbered item with the most closely related lettered item. Write your answers in the spaces provided.

a. carders
b. wikis
c. e-commerce
d. header
e. hits
f. metasearch engine
g. plug-in
h. reuniting
i. URLs
j. Web auction

1. Addresses of Web resources. _____
2. Part of an e-mail message that includes the subject, address, and attachments. _____
3. Program that starts and operates as part of a browser. _____
4. The list of sites that contain the keywords of a keyword search. _____
5. Program that automatically submits a search request to several search engines simultaneously. _____
6. Buying and selling goods over the Internet. _____
7. Type of social networking site that reconnects people who have lost touch with one another. _____
8. Similar to a traditional auction, but buyers and sellers typically interact only on the Web. _____
9. Criminals that specialize in stealing, trading, and using stolen credit cards over the Internet. _____
10. Sites that allow visitors to easily contribute or correct content. _____

For an interactive matching practice test, visit our Web site at www.computing2011.com and enter the keyword matching2.

OPEN-ENDED

On a separate sheet of paper, respond to each question or statement.

1. Discuss the uses of the Internet. Which activities have you participated in? Which one do you think is the most popular?
2. Explain the differences between the two most common types of providers.
3. What are the basic elements of an e-mail message?
4. What is social networking? Describe the three basic categories of social networking sites.
5. Describe the different types of search engines. Give an example of the type of search each engine is best for.

APPLYING TECHNOLOGY

The following questions are designed to demonstrate ways that you can effectively use technology today. The first question relates directly to this chapter's Making IT Work for You feature.

1 SHARING LARGE FILES

Do you ever need to share large files with others? Perhaps you have found that many video and other types of files can be too large to effectively send as an e-mail attachment. To learn how to share large files, review Making IT Work for You: Sharing Large Files on pages 36 and 37. Then complete the following: (a) Describe how the drop.io file-sharing service works. (b) What is a custom address and how is it used? (c) Describe how and why you might use a file-sharing service.

2 ONLINE SHOPPING

Connect to our Web site at www.computing2011.com and enter the keyword shopping to link to a popular shopping site. Once there, try shopping for one or two products, and answer the following questions: (a) What product(s) did you shop for? Could you find the product(s) at the site? If not, then search for another product that you can locate at the site. (b) Describe your experience. Was the site easy to use? Did you find it easy to locate the product(s)? What are the pros and cons of shopping online versus at a traditional store?

3 WEB AUCTIONS

Connect to our Web site at www.computing2011.com and enter the keyword auction to link to a popular online auction. Once there, read about how the auction works and check out a few of the items up for bid. Answer the following questions: (a) What are the advantages of using a Web auction to purchase items? What are the disadvantages? (b) What are the advantages and disadvantages to selling an item on an online auction, as opposed to a traditional method (such as a classified ad in the newspaper)? (c) Have you ever bought or sold an item at an online auction? If you have, describe what you bought and how you bought it. If you have not, do you think that you will in the near future? Why or why not?

EXPANDING YOUR KNOWLEDGE

The following questions are designed to add depth and detail to your understanding of specific topics presented within this chapter. The questions direct you to sources other than the textbook to obtain this knowledge.

① HOW SPAM FILTERS WORK

Spam is an ongoing problem for e-mail users everywhere. Spam is cheap, easy to send, and difficult to track, so the problem is unlikely to disappear soon. Fortunately, spam-blocking software is available. To learn "How Spam Filters Work," visit our Web site at www.computing2011.com and enter the keyword spam. Then answer the following questions: (a) Briefly describe an advantage and a disadvantage to using each of the three types of filters to stop spam. (b) Choose one of the filters and draw a diagram depicting a spam e-mail going through this filter. Be sure to label each step. (c) Modify the diagram to show an e-mail from a friend.

② HOW INSTANT MESSAGING WORKS

One of the fastest-growing applications on the Internet is instant messaging. This extension to e-mail provides a way for friends and colleagues to communicate and share information from almost anywhere in the world. To learn "How Instant Messaging Works," visit our Web site at www.computing2011.com and enter the keyword im. Then answer the following:

As described in Step 4: Communicate, Linda, Steve, and Chris agree to meet for a movie. Then Chris tells them that he has to leave for school and disconnects. Linda and Steve continue talking, with Linda asking Steve, "Have you seen any good movies lately?" On a single page of paper, create a drawing based on the animation that describes these events beginning with Step 5 when Chris says, "Bye for now—I have to leave for school."

③ DOMAIN REGISTRATION

Individuals and businesses do not *own* domain names. Instead, names such as "yahoo.com" are *registered* with a domain name registrar for an annual fee. Conduct a Web search to locate a domain name registrar site. Review the process for registering a domain name and address the following questions: (a) List the steps involved in registering a domain name. (b) What is the cost for registering a domain name? (c) How long can a domain name be registered for?

WRITING ABOUT TECHNOLOGY

The ability to think critically and to write effectively is essential to nearly every profession. The following questions are designed to help you develop these skills by posing thought-provoking questions about computer privacy, security, and/or ethics.

1 FREE SPEECH ONLINE

Some feel that there is too much objectionable material allowed on the Internet, whereas others argue that the Internet should be completely uncensored. Consider these two viewpoints and answer the following questions in a one-page paper: (a) Should religious groups be allowed to distribute information over the Internet? What about groups that advocate hatred or oppression? (b) Is there any material you feel should not be freely available on the Web? What about child pornography? (c) If you think some regulation is required, who should determine what restrictions should be imposed? (d) The Internet is not owned by a particular group or country. What limitations does this impose on enforcement of restrictions?

2 DIGITAL DIVIDE

The phrase "digital divide" describes the gap between people who have access to digital information via the Internet and people who lack effective access. Lack of access may stem from a physical lack of technology or from an inability to use available technology. Research two or three articles about the digital divide and address the following items in a one-page paper: (a) Summarize some factors that influence unequal Internet access for some members of society. Which ones seem the hardest to overcome and why? (b) What are some social or economic benefits brought by access to the Internet? (c) Make a prediction about the severity of the digital divide. Will it increase or decrease as new Internet-related technologies become available? Explain your answer.

NOTES

Basic Application Software

Competencies

After you have read this chapter, you should be able to:

1 Discuss common features of most software applications.

2 Discuss word processors and word processing features.

3 Describe spreadsheets and spreadsheet features.

4 Discuss database management systems and database management features.

5 Describe presentation graphics and presentation graphics features.

6 Discuss integrated packages.

7 Describe software suites and the categories of software suites.

Word processing software was one of the first applications available for personal computers. Even though users were required to memorize hundreds of key combinations to format text and organize documents, these early programs made it possible to replace bulky typewriters and messy correction tape in offices and homes worldwide. Today's word processing software does not require the kind of expertise of those early versions, as they include a variety of user-friendly features that make the creation of high-quality documents easy for beginners.

As more software moves to the Web, many experts are predicting that basic application software will no longer need to be installed on your computer. The program, and your documents, will be available from any computer connected to the Internet. This kind of access makes it possible to get feedback from others or share the creation of documents easily. And you'll never have to worry about installing updates again; new features might appear overnight with instructions on their use only a click away.

On the Web Explorations

Microsoft is one of the leaders in creating software applications.

To learn more about the company, visit our Web site at www.computing2011 .com and enter the keyword microsoft.

Introduction

Not long ago, trained specialists were required to perform many of the operations you can now do with a microcomputer. Secretaries used typewriters to create business correspondence. Market analysts used calculators to project sales. Graphic artists created designs by hand. Data processing clerks created electronic files to be stored on large computers. Now you can do all these tasks—and many others—with a microcomputer and the appropriate application software.

Think of the microcomputer as an electronic tool. You may not consider yourself very good at typing, calculating, organizing, presenting, or managing information. However, a microcomputer can help you do all these things and much more. All it takes is the right kinds of software.

Competent end users need to understand the capabilities of basic application software, which includes word processors, spreadsheets, database management systems, and presentation programs. They need to know about integrated packages and software suites.

Application Software

As we discussed in Chapter 1, there are two kinds of software. **System software** works with end users, application software, and computer hardware to handle the majority of technical details. **Application software** can be described as end-user software and is used to accomplish a variety of tasks.

Application software, in turn, can be divided into two categories. One category, **basic applications,** is the focus of this chapter. These programs are widely used in nearly every discipline and occupation. They include word processors, spreadsheets, database management systems, and presentation graphics. The other category, **specialized applications,** includes thousands of other programs that are more narrowly focused on specific disciplines and occupations. Specialized applications are presented in Chapter 4.

Common Features

A **user interface** is the portion of the application that allows you to control and to interact with the program. Most applications use a **graphical user interface (GUI)** that displays graphical elements called **icons** to represent familiar objects and a mouse. The mouse controls a **pointer** on the screen that is used to select items such as icons. Another feature is the use of windows to display information. A **window** is simply a rectangular area that can contain a document, program, or message. (Do not confuse the term *window* with the various versions of Microsoft's Windows operating systems, which are programs.) More than one window can be opened and displayed on the computer screen at one time.

Traditionally, most software programs, including those in Microsoft Office 2003, use a system of menus, toolbars, dialog boxes, and buttons. (See Figure 3-1.) **Menus** present commands that are typically displayed in a **menu bar** at the top of the screen. When one of the menu items is selected, an additional list of menu options or a **dialog box** that provides additional information and requests user input may appear. **Toolbars** typically appear below the menu bar. They contain small graphic elements called **buttons** that provide shortcuts for quick access to commonly used commands.

Microsoft Office 2010 uses an interface introduced in Office 2007 that makes it easier for users to find and use all the features of an application. This new design introduces ribbons, tabs, galleries, and more. (See Figure 3-2.)

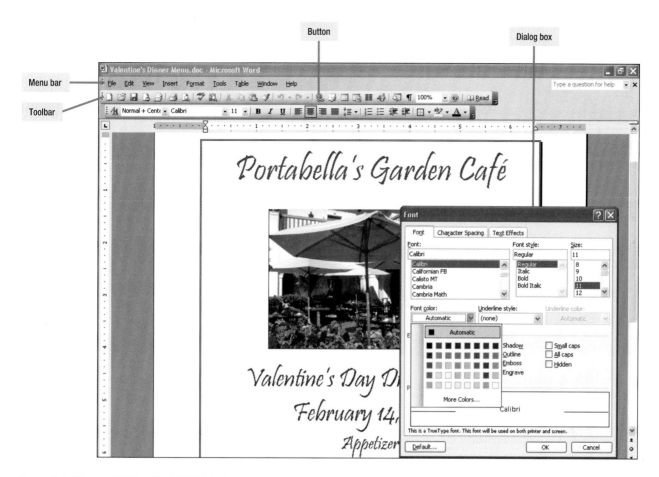

Figure 3-1 Microsoft Office Word 2003 interface

- **Ribbons** replace menus and toolbars by organizing commonly used commands into a set of tabs. These tabs display command buttons that are the most relevant to the tasks being performed by the user.
- **Tabs** are used to divide the ribbon into major activity areas. Each tab is then organized into **groups** that contain related items. Some tabs, called **contextual tabs,** only appear when they are needed and anticipate the next operations to be preformed by the user.
- **Galleries** simplify the process of making a selection from a list of alternatives. This is accomplished by displaying small graphic representations of the alternatives.

This new interface is the first major change in over a decade and promises to greatly improve user functionality and efficiency.

Some applications support **speech recognition,** the ability to accept voice input to select menu options and dictate text. See Making IT Work for You: Speech Recognition on pages 68 and 69. To learn more about how speech recognition works, visit our Web site at www.computing2011.com and enter the keyword **speech.**

CONCEPT CHECK

What is the difference between basic and specialized applications?

List some common features of most programs including Microsoft Office 2003.

Describe some of the features introduced in Microsoft Office 2007 and 2010.

Making IT work for you

SPEECH RECOGNITION

Tired of using your keyboard to type term papers? Have you ever thought about using your voice to control application software? Perhaps speech recognition is just what you are looking for.

Training the Software   The first step is to set up your microphone and train your software to recognize your voice. Using the Microsoft Windows Vista operating system:

1. ● Click *Start/Control Panel/Ease of Access/Speech Recognition Options.*

   ● Click *Start Speech Recognition.*

2. ● Complete the Microphone Setup Wizard to adjust your microphone for Speech Recognition.

3. ● Click *Start/Control Panel/Ease of Access/Speech Recognition.*

   ● Click *Train your computer to better understand you.*

   ● Read the text presented to teach the software your unique speech patterns.

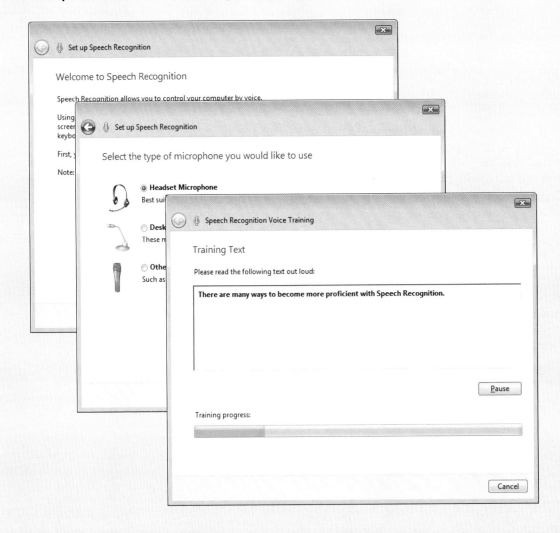

68

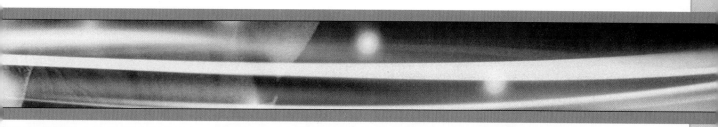

Controlling a Program   Once the software is trained, you can control many computer operations with just your voice. The Speech Reference Card is a handy guide to the commands your computer will understand. To open the Speech Reference Card:

1 • Click *Start/Control Panel/ Ease of Access/ Speech Recognition.*

• Click *Open the Speech Reference Card.*

• Click *Show All* to display a complete list of speech shortcuts, or click the print icon to print the list.

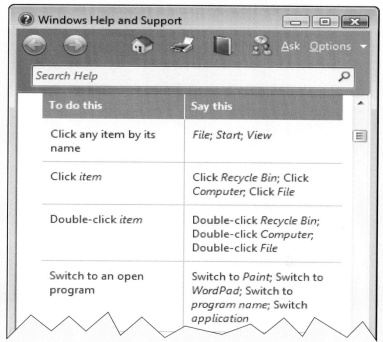

To do this	Say this
Click any item by its name	*File; Start; View*
Click *item*	Click *Recycle Bin*; Click *Computer*; Click *File*
Double-click *item*	Double-click *Recycle Bin*; Double-click *Computer*; Double-click *File*
Switch to an open program	Switch to *Paint*; Switch to *WordPad*; Switch to *program name*; Switch *application*

Dictating a Document   You can also dictate text using the Language bar. For example, to insert text into a Microsoft Word document:

1 • Say, "Open Word," to open a new Microsoft Word document.

• Dictate the text you want to appear in the document.

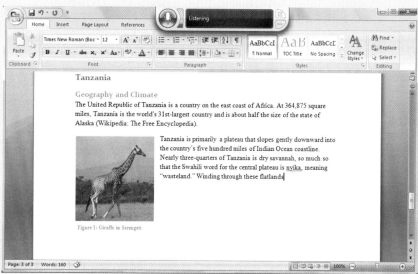

"Winding through these flatlands ..."

Although speech recognition technology continues to improve, speech recognition is not yet ready for completely hands-free operation. You will get the best results if you use a combination of your voice and the mouse or keyboard.

The Web is continually changing, and some of the specifics presented in the Making IT Work for You section may have changed.

To learn about other ways to make information technology work for you, visit our Web site at www.computing2011.com and enter the keyword miw.

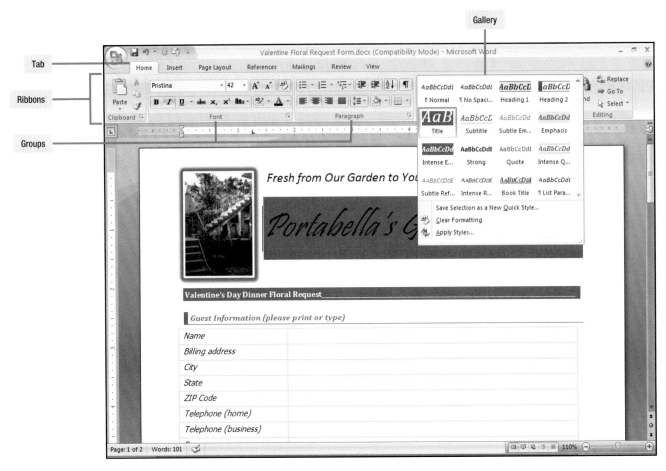

Figure 3-2 Microsoft Office Word 2007 interface

Word Processors

Word processors create text-based **documents** and are one of the most flexible and widely used software tools. All types of people and organizations use word processors to create memos, letters, and faxes. Organizations create newsletters, manuals, and brochures to provide information to their customers. Students and researchers use word processors to create reports. Word processors can even be used to create personalized Web pages.

Microsoft Word is the most widely used word processor. Other popular word processors include Corel WordPerfect and Apple Pages.

Features

Word processors provide a variety of features to make entering, editing, and formatting documents easy. One of the most basic features for entering text is **word wrap.** This feature automatically moves the insertion point to the next line once the current line is full. As you type, the words wrap around to the next line.

There are numerous features designed to support **editing** or modifying a document. One of these is a **thesaurus** that provides synonyms, antonyms, and related words for a selected word or phrase. You can quickly locate and replace selected words using the **find and replace** feature. **Spelling** and **grammar checkers** look for misspelled words and problems with capitalization, punctuation, and sentence structure. Other features are designed to improve the **format** or appearance of a document. One of the most basic is the **font** or design of the characters. (See Figure 3-3.) The height of a character is its **font size.** The appearance of characters can be enhanced using such **character effects** as **bold,** *italic,* and **colors.** Rather than individually selecting specific fonts, sizes, and formats, the **styles** feature, found in most word processors, enables users to quickly apply a predefined set of formatting characteristics to text in one easy step. **Bulleted** and **numbered lists** can make a sequence of topics easy to read.

Font	Sample
Calabri	A B C a b c
Impact	**ABCabc**
Cambria	A B C a b c
Broadway	A B C a b c

Figure 3-3 **Sample fonts**

Case

Assume that you have accepted a job as an advertising coordinator for Adventure Travel Tours, a travel agency specializing in active adventure vacations. Your primary responsibilities are to create and coordinate the company's promotional materials, including flyers and travel reports. To see how you could use Microsoft Word as the advertising coordinator for the Adventure Travel Tours, see Figures 3-4 and 3-5.

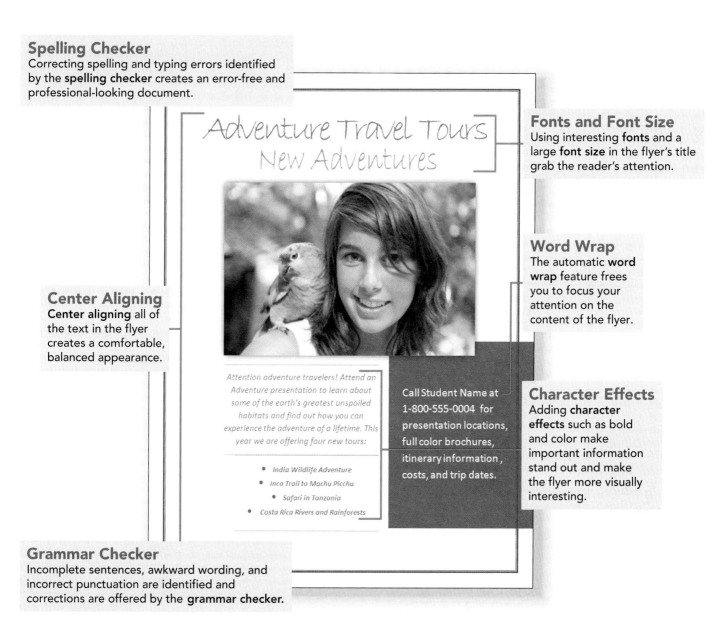

Spelling Checker
Correcting spelling and typing errors identified by the **spelling checker** creates an error-free and professional-looking document.

Fonts and Font Size
Using interesting **fonts** and a large **font size** in the flyer's title grab the reader's attention.

Word Wrap
The automatic **word wrap** feature frees you to focus your attention on the content of the flyer.

Center Aligning
Center aligning all of the text in the flyer creates a comfortable, balanced appearance.

Character Effects
Adding **character effects** such as bold and color make important information stand out and make the flyer more visually interesting.

Grammar Checker
Incomplete sentences, awkward wording, and incorrect punctuation are identified and corrections are offered by the **grammar checker.**

Attention adventure travelers! Attend an Adventure presentation to learn about some of the earth's greatest unspoiled habitats and find out how you can experience the adventure of a lifetime. This year we are offering four new tours:

- *India Wildlife Adventure*
- *Inca Trail to Machu Picchu*
- *Safari in Tanzania*
- *Costa Rica Rivers and Rainforests*

Call Student Name at 1-800-555-0004 for presentation locations, full color brochures, itinerary information, costs, and trip dates.

Figure 3-4 **Flyer**

Captions and Cross References

Identifying figures with **captions** and using **cross references** in a report make the report easier to read and more professional.

AutoCorrect

As you enter text, you occasionally forget to capitalize the first word in a sentence. Fortunately, **AutoCorrect** recognizes the error and automatically capitalizes the word.

Citations

The sources of information you used in developing the report appear in citations.

Header or Footer

Page numbers and other document-related information can be included in a **header** or **footer**.

Footnote

To include a note about Mt. Kilimanjaro, you use the **footnote** feature. This feature inserts the footnote superscript number and automatically formats the bottom of the page to contain the footnote text.

Tanzania & Peru

Tanzania

Geography and Climate

"In the midst of a great wilderness, full of wild beasts...I fancied I saw a summit...covered with a dazzlingly white cloud (qtd. in Cole 56). This is how Johann Krapf, the first outsider to witness the splendor of Africa's highest mountain, described Kilimanjaro. The peak was real, though the white clouds he "fancied" he saw were the dense layer of snow that coats the mountain.[1]

Tanzania is primarily a plateau that slopes gently downward into the country's five hundred miles of Indian Ocean coastline. Nearly three-quarters of Tanzania is dry savannah, so much so that the Swahili word for the central plateau is *nyika*, meaning "wasteland." Winding through these flatlands is the Great Rift Valley, which forms narrow and shallow lakes in its long path. Several of these great lakes form a belt-like oasis of green vegetation. Contrasting with the severity of the plains are the coastal areas, which are lush with ample rainfall. In the north the plateau slopes dramatically into Mt. Kilimanjaro.

Ngorongoro Conservation Area

Some of Tanzania's most distinguishing geographical features are found in the Ngorongoro Conservation Area.[2] The park is composed of many craters and gorges, as well as lakes, forest, and plains. Among these features is the area's namesake, the Ngorongoro Crater. The Crater is a huge expanse, covering more than one hundred square miles. On the Crater's floor, grasslands blend into swamps, lakes, rivers, and woodland. Also within the Conservation Area's perimeter is the Olduvai Gorge, commonly referred to as the "Cradle of Mankind," where in 1931 the stone

FIGURE 1 GIRAFFE IN SERENGETI

---

[1] Mt. Kilimanjaro is 19,340 feet high, making it the fourth tallest mountain in the world.

[2] The Conservation Area is a national preserve spanning 3,196 square miles.

Tanzania & Peru

2

Figure 3-5 Report

You have been asked to create a promotional advertising flyer. After discussing the flyer's contents and basic structure with your supervisor, you start to enter the flyer's text. As you enter the text, *words wrap* automatically at the end of each line. Also, while entering the text, the *spelling checker* and *grammar checker* catch spelling and grammatical errors. Once the text has been entered, you focus your attention on enhancing the visual aspects of the flyer. You add an interesting graphic and experiment with different character and paragraph formats including *fonts, font sizes, colors,* and *alignments.* See Figure 3–4. ●

creating a report

Your next assignment is to create a report on Tanzania and Peru. After conducting your research, you start writing your paper. As you enter the text for the report, you notice that the *AutoCorrect* feature automatically corrects some grammar and punctuation errors. Your report includes several figures and *tables.* You use the *captions* feature to keep track of figure and table numbers, to enter the caption text, and to position the captions. When referencing figures or tables from the text, you use the *cross reference* feature. *Footnotes* are used to further explain or comment on information in the report. You then carefully document your sources using *citations.* Finally, you prepare the report for printing by adding *header* and *footer* information. See Figure 3–5. ●

☑ CONCEPT CHECK

What do word processors do? What is word wrap?

Describe the following editing features: thesaurus, find and replace, spelling and grammar checkers.

Describe the following formatting features: font, font size, character effects, styles, numbered and bulleted lists.

Spreadsheets

Spreadsheet programs organize, analyze, and graph numeric data such as budgets and financial reports. Once used exclusively by accountants, spreadsheets are widely used by nearly every profession. Marketing professionals analyze sales trends. Financial analysts evaluate and graph stock market trends. Students and teachers record grades and calculate grade point averages.

The most widely used spreadsheet program is Microsoft Excel. Other spreadsheet applications include Apple iWork's Numbers and Corel Quattro Pro.

Features

Unlike word processors, which manipulate text and create text documents, spreadsheet programs manipulate numeric data and create workbook files. **Workbook files** consist of one or more related worksheets. A **worksheet,** also known as a **spreadsheet** or **sheet,** is a rectangular grid of **rows** and **columns.** For example, in Figure 3-6, the columns are identified by letters and the rows are identified by numbers. The intersection of a row and column creates a **cell.** For example, the cell D8 is formed by the intersection of column D and row 8.

A cell can contain text or numeric entries. **Text entries** or **labels** provide structure to a worksheet by describing the contents of rows and columns. For example, in Figure 3-6, cell B8 contains the label Food. The cell D8 contains a number identified as the food expense.

A **numeric entry** can be a number or a formula. A **formula** is an instruction to calculate or process. For example, the cell F15 contains the formula = E5–E13. This formula will calculate a value and display that value in cell F15. The value is calculated by taking the value in cell E5 and subtracting the value in cell E13. **Functions** are prewritten formulas provided by the spreadsheet program that perform calculations such as adding a series of cells. For example, the cell E13 contains the function SUM(D8:D12), which adds the values in the range from D8 to D12. A **range** is a series of continuous cells. In this case, the range includes D8, D9, D10, D11, and D12. The sum of the values in this range is displayed in cell E13. Spreadsheet programs typically provide a variety of different types of functions, including financial, mathematical, statistical, and logical functions. Some of these functions are presented in Figure 3-7.

Analytical graphs or **charts** are visual representations of data in a spreadsheet. You can readily create graphs in a spreadsheet program by selecting the cells containing the data to be charted and then selecting the type of chart to display. If you change one or more numbers in your spreadsheet, all related formulas will automatically recalculate and charts will be recreated.

tips

Have you ever wanted to draw attention to a cell in a spreadsheet? Shapes make it easy to emphasize the contents of your worksheet. If you are using Excel 2007:

1. Select *Shapes* from the *Illustrations* group on the *Insert* tab.

2. Choose a shape from the menu, click on the worksheet, and drag to create the shape.

3. While the shape is selected on the worksheet, use the *Shape Styles* group on the *Format* tab to modify its appearance.

To see additional tips, visit our Web site at www.computing2011.com and enter the keyword tips.

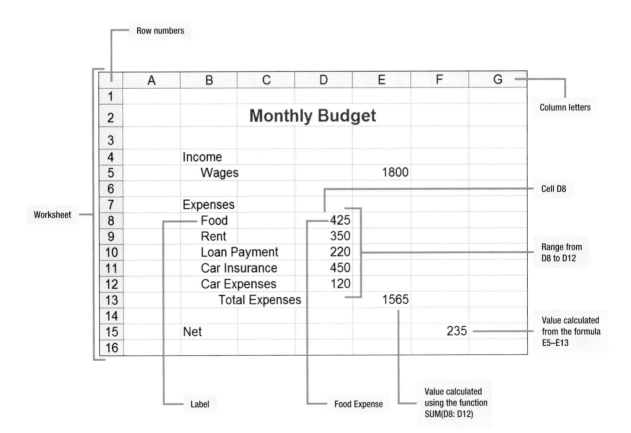

Figure 3-6 Worksheet

Type	Function	Calculates
Financial	PMT	Size of loan payments
	PV	Present value for an investment
Mathematical	SUM	Sum of the numbers in a range of cells
	ABS	Absolute value of a number
Statistical	AVERAGE	Average or mean of the numbers in a range of cells
	MAX	Largest number in a range of cells
Logical	IF	Whether a condition is true; if true, a specified value is displayed; if not true, then a different specified value is displayed
	AND	Whether two conditions are true; if both are true, then a specified value is displayed; if either one or both are not true, then a different specified value is displayed

Figure 3-7 Selected spreadsheet functions

This is called **recalculation.** The process of observing the effect of changing one or more cells is often referred to as **what-if analysis.** For example, to analyze the effect of a rent increase in the Monthly Budget worksheet in Figure 3-6, all you would need to do is replace the contents in cell D9. The entire spreadsheet, including any charts that had been created, would be recalculated automatically.

CONCEPT CHECK

What are spreadsheets used for? What is a workbook file? What is a worksheet?

Define rows, columns, cells, ranges, text, and numeric entries.

Describe the following spreadsheet features: formulas, functions, charts, recalculation, and what-if analysis.

Case

Assume that you have just accepted a job as manager of the Downtown Internet Café. This cafe provides a variety of flavored coffees as well as Internet access. One of your responsibilities is to create a financial plan for the next year. To see how you could use Microsoft Excel, the most widely used spreadsheet program, as the manager for the Downtown Internet Café, see Figures 3-8 through 3-10.

creating a sales forecast

Your first project is to develop a first-quarter sales forecast for the cafe. You begin by studying sales data and talking with several managers. After obtaining sales and expense estimates, you are ready to create the first-quarter forecast. You start structuring the *worksheet* by inserting descriptive *text entries* for the row and column headings. Next, you insert *numeric entries,* including *formulas* and *functions* to perform calculations. To test the accuracy of the worksheet, you change the values in some cells and compare the recalculated spreadsheet results with hand calculations. See Figure 3-8. ●

Worksheets

Worksheets are used for a wide range of different applications. One of the most common uses is to create, analyze, and forecast budgets.

Text Entries

Text entries provide meaning to the values in the worksheet. The rows are labeled to identify the various sales and expense items. The columns are labeled to specify the months.

	A	B	C	D	E	F
1						
2						
3			**Downtown Internet Café**			
4			*First Quarter Forecast*			
5						
6		JAN	FEB	MAR	TOTAL	AVG
7	**Sales**					
8	Beverage	$ 13,600	$ 14,600	$ 15,600	$ 43,800	$ 14,600
9	Food	$ 7,100	$ 7,300	$ 7,400	$ 21,800	$ 7,267
10	Internet	$ 4,000	$ 4,300	$ 4,500	$ 12,800	$ 4,267
11	Merchandise	$ 3,100	$ 3,200	$ 3,300	$	
12	**Total Sales**	$ 27,800	$ 29,400	$ 30,800	$ 8	
13	**Expenses**					
14	Cost of Goods	$ 6,950	$ 7,300	$ 7,600	$ 2	
15	Payroll	$ 7,500	$ 7,500	$ 7,500	$ 2	
16	Computers	$ 6,400	$ 6,400	$ 6,400	$ 1	
17	Lease	$ 5,500	$ 5,500	$ 5,500	$ 1	
18	Marketing	$ 1,000	$ 1,000	$ 1,000	$	
19	Miscellaneous	$ 1,500	$ 1,500	$ 1,500	$	
20	**Total Expenses**	$ 28,850	$ 29,200	$ 29,500	$ 87,550	$ 29,183
21	**Income**					
22	**Net Income**	$ (1,050)	$ 200	$ 1,300	$ 450	$ 150
23	**Profit Margin**	-3.78%	0.68%	4.22%	0.51%	
24			Income Year-To-Date	$ 450		

Cells

Cells can contain labels, numbers, formulas, and functions. A cell's content is indicated by the row and column labels. For example, cell D15 contains a number for the Payroll expense expected for March.

Functions

One advantage of using **functions** rather than entering formulas is that they are easier to enter. In this case, cell C20 (Total Expenses for February) contains the function SUM(C14: C19) rather than the formula = C14+C15+ C16+C17+C18+C19.

Formulas

Formulas provide a way to perform calculations in the worksheet. In this case, Cell B22 (Net Income for January) contains the formula = B12 (Total Sales for January) – B20 (Total Expenses for January).

Figure 3-8 Worksheet

creating a chart

After completing the First-Quarter Forecast for the Downtown Internet Café, you decide to *chart* the sales data to better visualize the projected growth in sales. You select the 3D column *chart type* to show each month's projected sales category. Using a variety of chart options, you enter descriptive *titles* for the chart, the x-axis, and the y-axis. Then you use *data labels* to focus attention on the growing Internet sales. Finally, you insert a *legend* to define the chart's different columns. See Figure 3-9. ●

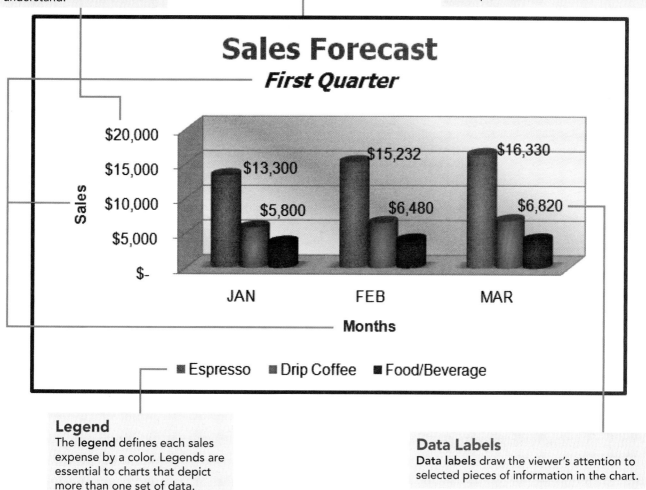

Chart Titles
Including a chart title and subtitle as well as titles along the x-axis and y-axis make the chart easier to read and understand.

Chart Types
To display the monthly expenses over the quarter, you consider several different **chart types** before selecting the 3D column chart. The 3D variation of the chart provides an interesting depth perception to the columns.

Chart
Once data is in the worksheet, it is very easy to **chart** the data. All you need to do is to select the data to chart, select the chart type, and add some descriptive text.

Legend
The **legend** defines each sales expense by a color. Legends are essential to charts that depict more than one set of data.

Data Labels
Data labels draw the viewer's attention to selected pieces of information in the chart.

Figure 3-9 Chart

analyzing your data

After presenting the First-Quarter Forecast to the owner, you revise the format and expand the *workbook* to include worksheets for each quarter and an annual forecast summary. You give each worksheet a descriptive *sheet name.* At the request of the owner, you perform a *what-if analysis* to test the effect of different estimates for payroll, and you use *Goal Seek* to determine how much Total Internet Sales would have to increase to produce a profit margin of 15 percent for the first quarter. See Figure 3-10. ●

Workbook

The first worksheet in a **workbook** is often a summary of the following worksheets. In this case, the first worksheet presents the entire year's forecast. The subsequent worksheets provide the details.

Sheet Name

Each worksheet has a unique **sheet name**. To make the workbook easy to navigate, it is a good practice to always use simple yet descriptive names for each worksheet.

What-If Analysis

What-if analysis is a very powerful and simple tool to test the effects of different assumptions in a spreadsheet.

Goal Seek

A common goal in many financial workbooks is to achieve a certain level of profit. **Goal seek** allows you to set a goal and then will analyze other parts of the workbook that would need to be adjusted to meet that goal.

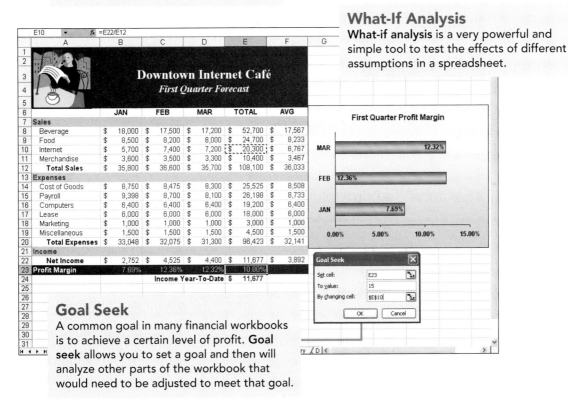

Figure 3-10 **Workbook**

Database Management Systems

A **database** is a collection of related data. It is the electronic equivalent of a file cabinet. A **database management system (DBMS)** or **database manager** is a program that sets up, or structures, a database. It also provides tools to enter, edit, and retrieve data from the database. All kinds of individuals use databases, from teachers recording grades to police officers checking criminal histories. Colleges and universities use databases to keep records on their students, instructors, and courses. Organizations of all types maintain employee databases.

Three of the most widely used database management systems designed for microcomputers are Microsoft Access, Corel Paradox, and Lotus Approach.

Features

The **relational database** is the most widely used database structure. Data is organized into related **tables.** Each table is made up of rows called **records** and columns called **fields.** Each record contains fields of data about some specific person, place, or thing.

A DBMS provides a variety of tools to create and use databases. A **sort** tool will quickly rearrange a table's records according to a selected field. A **filter** tool will quickly display only those records meeting the conditions you specify.

The greatest power of a DBMS, however, comes from its ability to quickly find and bring together information stored in separate tables using queries, forms, and reports. A **query** is a question or a request for specific data contained in a database. Database **forms** look similar to traditional printed forms. These electronic forms are displayed on the computer monitor and typically reflect the contents for one record in a table. They are primarily used to enter new records and to make changes to existing records. Data from tables and queries can be printed in a variety of different types of **reports** from a simple listing of an entire field in a table to a list of selected fields based on a query involving several tables.

Are you overwhelmed by your collection of music, videos, and books?

Would you like some help getting your life in order? Fortunately, Microsoft provides a variety of Access templates that might be just right for you. Here's how to find them:

1. Connect to office.microsoft.com.

2. Click the *Templates* tab to display the Templates Web page. Type Access in the Templates search box and click the Search button.

3. Look through the templates and select the ones that might be valuable to you.

To see more tips, visit our Web site at www.computing2011.com and enter the keyword tips.

☑ CONCEPT CHECK

What is a database? What is a DBMS? A relational database?

What are tables, records, and fields?

Describe the following DBMS features: sort, filter, query, form, and report.

Case

Assume that you have accepted a job as an employment administrator for the Lifestyle Fitness Club. One of your responsibilities is to create a database management system to replace the club's manual system for recording employee information. To see how you could use Microsoft Access, one of the most widely used relational DBMS programs, as the employment administrator for the Lifestyle Fitness Club, see Figures 3-11 and 3-12.

The first step in creating the database management system is to plan. You study the existing manual system focusing on how and what data is collected and how it is used. Next, you design the basic structure or organization of the new database system to have two related *tables*, which will make entering data and using the database more efficient. Focusing on the first table, Employees, you create the table structure by specifying the *fields*, and *primary key* field. To make the process faster and more accurate, you create a *form* and enter the data for each employee as a *record* in the table. See Figure 3-11. ●

Primary Key

The **primary key** is the unique employee identification number. You considered using the last name field as the primary key but realized that more than one employee could have the same last name. Primary keys are often used to link tables.

Fields

Fields are given field names that are displayed at the top of each table. You select the field names to describe their contents.

Table

Tables make up the basic structure of a relational database with columns containing field data and rows containing record information. This table records basic information about each employee, including name, address, and telephone number.

Record

Each **record** contains information about one employee. A record often includes a combination of numeric, text, and object data types.

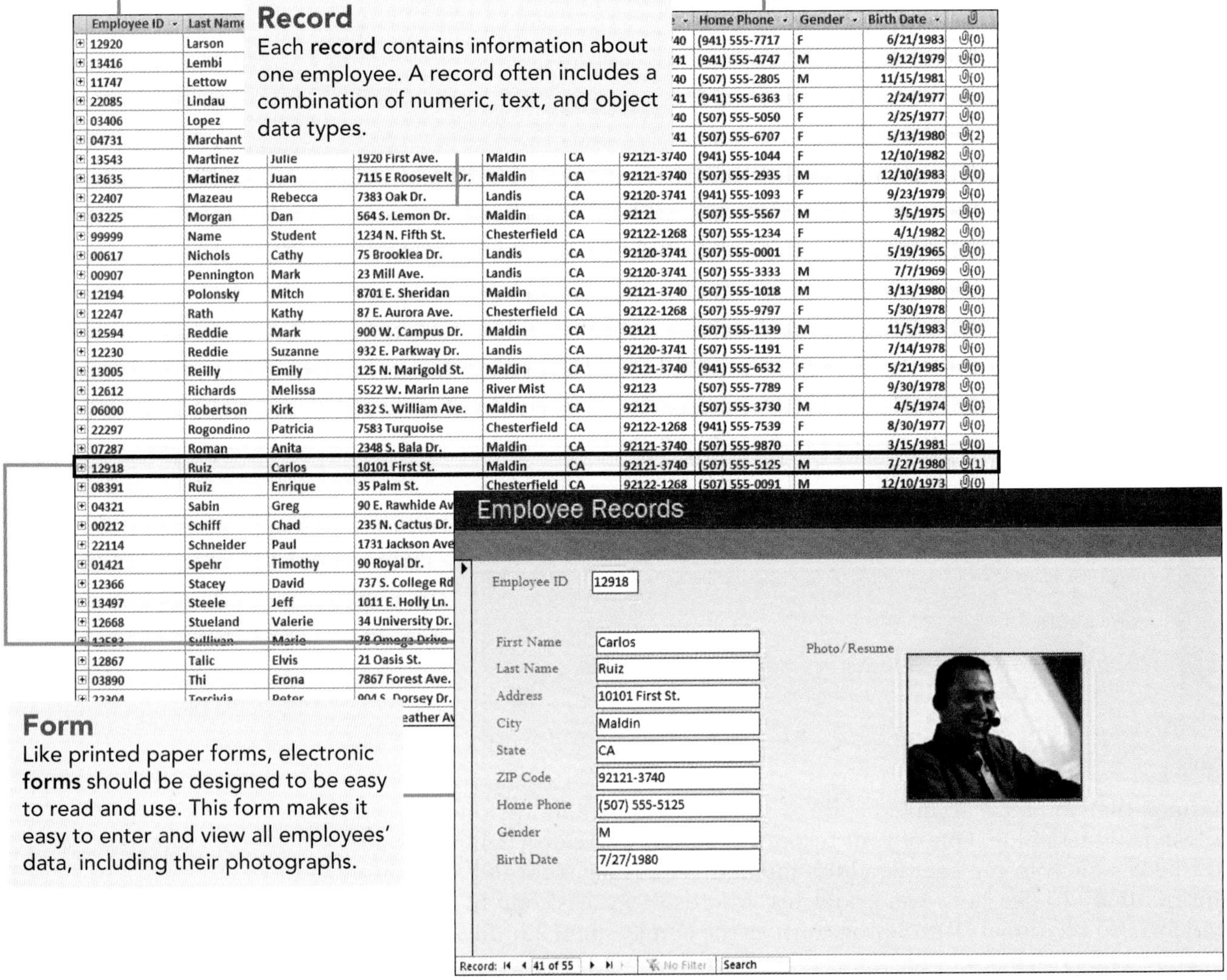

Form

Like printed paper forms, electronic **forms** should be designed to be easy to read and use. This form makes it easy to enter and view all employees' data, including their photographs.

Figure 3-11 **Table and form**

Query

Your **query** requests the names, addresses, and telephone numbers of all employees living in Maldin or Chesterfield who work in Landis.

Joined

Since the query involves two tables, they must be linked or **joined** by common fields. You chose to link the tables by the key field Employee ID.

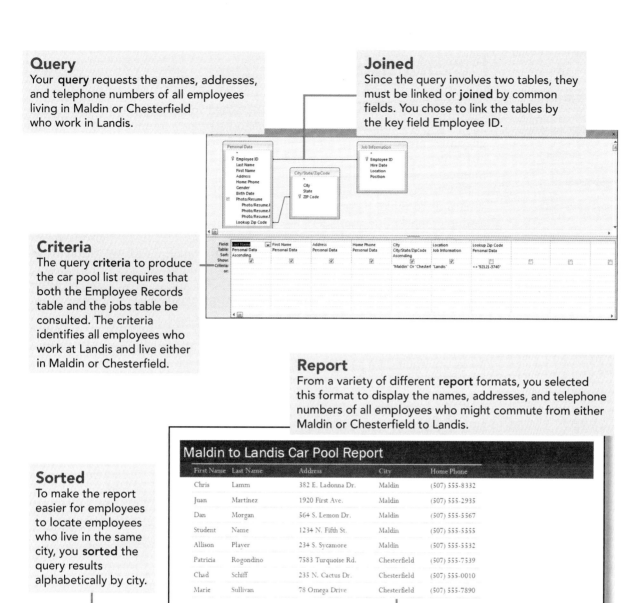

Criteria

The query **criteria** to produce the car pool list requires that both the Employee Records table and the jobs table be consulted. The criteria identifies all employees who work at Landis and live either in Maldin or Chesterfield.

Report

From a variety of different **report** formats, you selected this format to display the names, addresses, and telephone numbers of all employees who might commute from either Maldin or Chesterfield to Landis.

Maldin to Landis Car Pool Report

First Name	Last Name	Address	City	Home Phone
Chris	Lamm	382 E. Ladonna Dr.	Maldin	(507) 555-8332
Juan	Martinez	1920 First Ave.	Maldin	(507) 555-2935
Dan	Morgan	564 S. Lemon Dr.	Maldin	(507) 555-5567
Student	Name	1234 N. Fifth St.	Maldin	(507) 555-5555
Allison	Player	234 S. Sycamore	Maldin	(507) 555-5532
Patricia	Rogondino	7583 Turquoise Rd.	Chesterfield	(507) 555-7539
Chad	Schiff	235 N. Cactus Dr.	Chesterfield	(507) 555-0010
Marie	Sullivan	78 Omega Drive	Chesterfield	(507) 555-7890

Sorted

To make the report easier for employees to locate employees who live in the same city, you **sorted** the query results alphabetically by city.

Figure 3-12 Query and report

creating a query

You have continued to build the database by creating a second table named Job containing information about each employee's work location and job title. This table is linked or *joined* with the Employee Records table by the common field, Employee ID. After you completed this second table, you received a request to create car pool information for those employees who live in either Maldin or Chesterfield and work in Landis. You created a *query* using the appropriate *criteria* to create the car pool list. Then *sorting* alphabetically according to city, you created a *report* to distribute to interested employees. See Figure 3-12. ●

Presentation Graphics

On the Web Explorations

Lotus is one of the leaders in developing presentation graphics.

To learn more about the company, visit our Web site at www.computing2011 .com and enter the keyword lotus.

Research shows that people learn better when information is presented visually. A picture is indeed worth a thousand words or numbers. **Presentation graphics** are programs that combine a variety of visual objects to create attractive, visually interesting presentations. They are excellent tools to communicate a message and to persuade people.

People in a variety of settings and situations use presentation graphics programs to make their presentations more interesting and professional. For example, marketing managers use presentation graphics to present proposed marketing strategies to their superiors. Salespeople use these programs to demonstrate products and encourage customers to make purchases. Students use presentation graphics programs to create high-quality class presentations.

Three of the most widely used presentation graphics programs are Microsoft PowerPoint, Corel Presentations, and Apple Keynote.

Features

An electronic presentation consists of a series of **slides** or **pages.** Presentation programs include a variety of features to help you create effective dynamic presentations. Most include design and content templates that help you quickly create a professional-looking presentation. **Design templates** provide professionally selected combinations of color schemes, slide layouts, and special effects. **Content templates** include suggested content for each slide. Other features include tools to select alternative color schemes and slide layouts, to create animated graphics and charts, and to help you rehearse the presentation.

More advanced features include the capability to use **animations,** special effects that add action to text and graphics on a slide. Additionally, **transitions** can be used to animate how the presentation moves from one slide to the next. Other features allow you to print slides, create speaker notes, and provide handouts for your audience.

 ## CONCEPT CHECK

 What are presentation graphics programs? What are they used for?

 What are slides? What are design and content templates? What are they used for?

 What are animations and transitions? What are they used for?

Case

Assume that you have volunteered for the Animal Rescue Foundation, a local animal rescue agency. You have been asked to create a powerful and persuasive presentation to encourage other members from your community to volunteer. To see how you could use Microsoft PowerPoint, one of the most widely used presentation graphics programs, as a volunteer for the Animal Rescue Foundation, see Figures 3-13 and 3-14.

creating a presentation

You start creating the presentation using the Presentation on Product or Service *template.* The template consists of a sample presentation containing suggested content in each slide and uses a consistent design style throughout. After replacing the sample content, you are on your way to the director's office to show what you have. See Figure 3-13. ●

Customize the Template

You customize the presentation by replacing the sample text and modifying the design as needed. This includes inserting and deleting slides as needed, rearranging slide order, and inserting graphics and pictures.

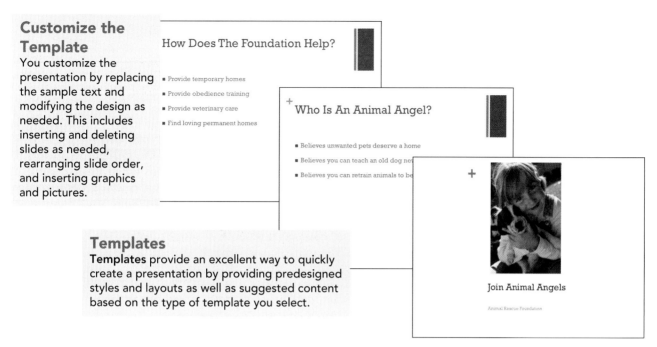

Templates

Templates provide an excellent way to quickly create a presentation by providing predesigned styles and layouts as well as suggested content based on the type of template you select.

Figure 3-13 **Presentation**

Document Theme

To make your presentation more professional and eye-catching, you select a **document theme**, built-in sets of colors, fonts, and effects that can be quickly applied to your entire presentation.

Rehearse

Now that the presentation is nearly complete, you **rehearse** it by running it electronically on the computer screen and planning what you want to say to supplement the information on the slides.

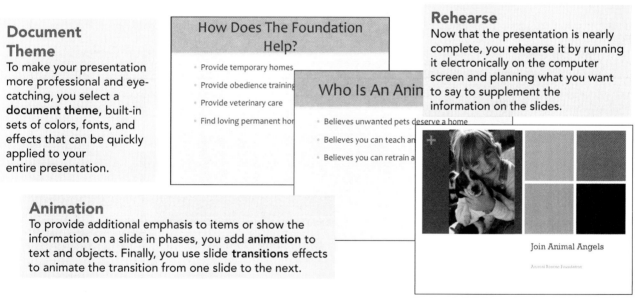

Animation

To provide additional emphasis to items or show the information on a slide in phases, you add **animation** to text and objects. Finally, you use slide **transitions** effects to animate the transition from one slide to the next.

Figure 3-14 **Revised presentation**

updating a presentation

After discussing the presentation with the director, you have some ideas to enhance the effectiveness of the message. First, you select a different document theme to change the colors, fonts, and effects used throughout the presentation. Then to add interest to the presentation as it is running, you add animation and transition effects. Then you add animations to selected objects and add slide transition effects. Finally, you practice or rehearse the presentation, create speaker notes, and print out audience handouts. You're ready to give a professionally designed, dynamic presentation. See Figure 3-14. ●

Integrated Packages

Figure 3-15 Microsoft Works

An **integrated package** is a single program that provides the *functionality* of a word processor, spreadsheet, database manager, and more. The primary disadvantage of an integrated package is that the capabilities of each function (such as word processing) are not as extensive as in the individual programs (such as Microsoft Word). The primary advantages are cost and simplicity. The cost of an integrated package is much less than the cost of the individual powerful, professional-grade application programs discussed thus far in this chapter.

Integrated packages are popular with many home users and are sometimes classified as **personal** or **home software.** The most widely used integrated package is Microsoft Works. See Figure 3-15. AppleWorks is also widely used. Both products, however, have been recently discontinued.

Case

Assume that you publish a gardening newsletter that you distribute to members of the Desert Gardening Club. Using the word processing function, you entered text, formatted titles and subtitles, and inserted several photographs. (See Figure 3-16.) Using the spreadsheet function, you analyzed daily rainfall

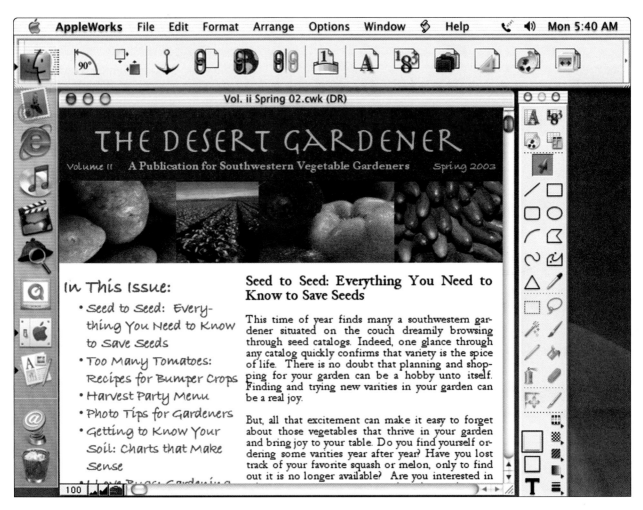

Figure 3-16 Integrated package (Microsoft Works)

for the feature article and included a chart. After completing the newsletter, you will use the database function and the membership database to print mailing labels.

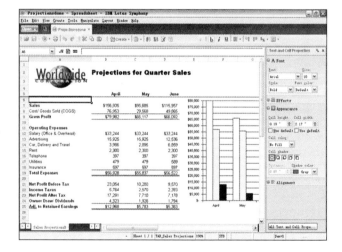
Figure 3-17 Microsoft Office

CONCEPT CHECK

What is an integrated package?

Describe the advantages and disadvantages of an integrated package.

Software Suites

A **software suite** is a collection of separate application programs bundled together and made available as a group. While the applications function exactly the same whether purchased in a suite or separately, it is significantly less expensive to buy a suite of applications than to buy each application separately. There are four basic categories of software suites:

- **Productivity suite.** Productivity suites, also known as **office software suites** or simply **office suites** contain professional-grade application programs that are typically used in a business situation. Productivity suites commonly include a word processor, spreadsheet, database manager, and a presentation application. The best known is Microsoft Office. (See Figure 3-17.) Other well-known productivity suites are Apple iWork, Sun StarOffice, Corel WordPerfect Office Suite, and Lotus SmartSuite.

- **Alternative office suites.** Traditionally, when you purchase an office suite you are licensed to use the application and a copy of the software is stored on your computer. Recently, several alternative office suites are available for free as downloadable software or as online applications. The **downloadable office suites** are stored on your desktop computer just like the traditional office suites. The **online office suites** are stored online and are available anywhere you can access the Internet. Documents created using online applications can also be stored online, making it easy to share and collaborate on documents with others. However, the downside to online applications is that you are dependent upon the server providing the application to be available whenever you need it. For this reason, when using online applications, it is important to have backup copies of your documents on your computer and to have a desktop office application available to use. Documents created using these applications are compatible with Microsoft Office. Popular downloadable office suites include StarOffice, IBM Lotus Symphony, and OpenOffice. Popular online office suites are Google Docs, Zoho, and ThinkSmart. (See Figure 3-18.) To learn more about one of the most widely used online office suites, see Making IT Work for You: Google Docs on pages 86 and 87.

Figure 3-18 IBM Lotus Symphony

Making IT work for you

GOOGLE DOCS

Do you need to collaborate with others on a document, presentation, or spreadsheet? Do you need access to a document from both home and school? Would you like to try a free alternative to traditional office software suites? If so, an online office suite might be for you. Online office suites, such as Google Docs, allow you to create and edit documents directly though a Web page with no additional software to install on your computer.

Creating a Document   To create a new online document:

1
● Visit http://docs.google.com. Follow the on-screen instructions to create a free Google account if you do not already have one.

● Click the *New* button.

● Select the type of document you want to create, such as a word processing document, presentation, or spreadsheet.

The new document is dispayed and can be edited directly through the Web page.

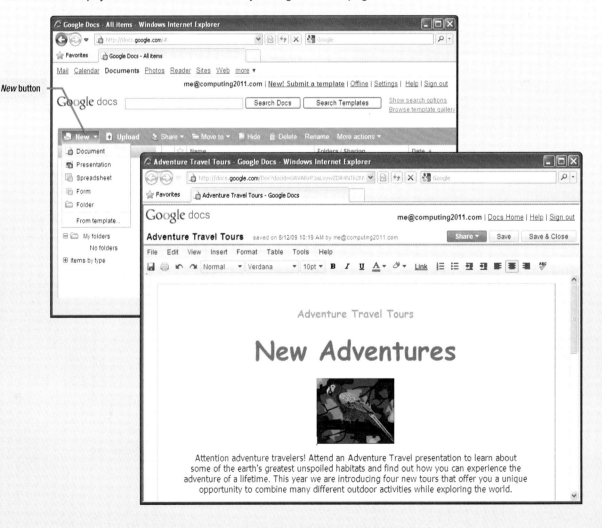

Sharing a Document To give others access to view and edit your document:

1 ● Click the *Share* button.

● Select *Invite people*...

2 ● Enter the e-mail addresses of people to invite.

● Optionally enter a brief message to the people you are inviting.

● Click the *Send* button.

The people you invited will receive an e-mail with instructions for accessing your document. You will be able to see any changes others make to the document, and they will see yours.

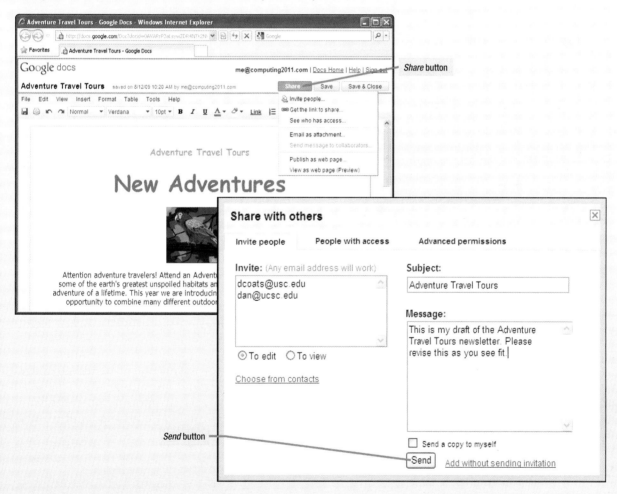

The Web is continually changing, and some of the specifics presented in Making IT Work for You may have changed.

To learn about other ways to make information technology work for you, visit our Web site at www.computing2011.com and enter the keyword miw.

- **Specialized suite.** Specialized suites focus on specific applications. These include graphics suites, financial planning suites, and many others. (Graphics suites will be discussed in Chapter 4.)
- **Utility suite.** These suites include a variety of programs designed to make computing easier and safer. Two of the best known are Norton System-Works and Norton Internet Security Suite. (Utility suites will be discussed in detail in Chapter 5.)

Many times it is convenient to share data between applications. For example, when writing a report, it may be useful to include a chart from a spreadsheet or data from a database. Data created by one application can be shared with another application in a variety of different ways, including copying and pasting, object linking, and object embedding. To learn more about sharing data between applications, visit us on the Web at www.computing2011.com and enter the keyword **sharing**.

 ## CONCEPT CHECK

 What is a software suite? What are the advantages of purchasing a suite?

 List and describe four categories of software suites?

 What is the difference between a productivity suite and a utility suite?

What is the difference between a downloadable and an online office suite?

Careers in IT

Computer trainers instruct new users on the latest software or hardware. (See Figure 3.19.) Many computer training positions are offered to those with experience with the most popular business software.

Employers look for good communication skills and teaching experience. Though a teaching degree may not be required, it may be preferred. Experience with the latest software and/or hardware is essential, but this varies depending on the position. Employers often seek detail-oriented individuals with IT experience.

Computer trainers can expect to earn an annual salary of $25,000 to $50,500. However, salary is dependent on experience and may vary drastically. Responsibilities typically include preparation of course materials, grading coursework, and continuing education in the field. Opportunities for advancement include management of other trainers and consulting work. To learn more about other careers in information technology, visit us at www.computing2011.com and enter the keyword **careers**.

Figure 3-19 Computer trainer

Agents Will Help Write Papers, Pay Bills, and Shop on the Internet

Wouldn't it be great to have your own personal assistant? Your assistant could research topics for a term paper, collect relevant information, and even suggest famous quotes that apply to your topic. Your assistant could monitor your personal budget using a spreadsheet and even evaluate the impact of a rental income. Or your assistant could punch up a classroom presentation by suggesting and locating relevant photos and videos. All this is likely with special programs called *agents*.

An agent is an intelligent program that can understand your needs and act to fulfill those needs. Today, primitive agents already exist in

many help tools to interpret user questions and to formulate appropriate responses. Computer scientists at the University of Maryland are working on the next-generation agents that may provide the most efficient way to locate information on the Web. These agents promise to understand words and the context in which they are used. They will locate Web sites that not only have the *words* you are looking for but also the *meaning.* This future is not far off, but as agent technology improves, it is only a matter of time until agents act in more autonomous ways and can help you use basic applications to do complex tasks, like prepare an essay, a budget, or a presentation.

What do you think? Should we all have our own personal agent to help us write papers, pay bills, and shop on the Internet?

APPLICATION SOFTWARE

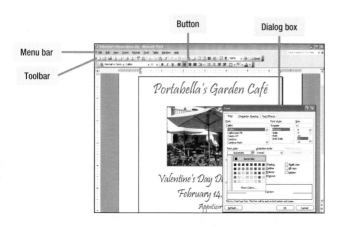

There are two basic types of software. **System software** focuses on handling technical details. **Application software** focuses on completing specific tasks or applications. Two categories are **basic applications** and **specialized applications.**

Common Features

You control and interact with a program using a **user interface. A graphical user interface (GUI)** uses **icons** selected by a mouse-controlled **pointer.** A **window** contains a document, program, or message. Most software programs, including Microsoft Office 2003, also have

- **Menus**—present commands listed on the **menu bar.**
- **Dialog box**—provides additional information or requests user input.
- **Toolbars**—contain **buttons** for quick access to commonly used commands.

Microsoft Office 2010 uses and interface introduced with Microsoft Office 2007 which includes

- **Ribbons** replace menus and toolbars.
- **Tabs** divide ribbons into major activity areas organized into **groups. Contextual tabs** automatically appear when needed.
- **Galleries** display graphic representations of alternatives.

Some applications support **speech recognition** by allowing voice input.

WORD PROCESSORS

Word processors allow you to create, edit, save, and print text-based **documents,** including flyers, reports, newsletters, and Web pages.

Features

Word wrap is a basic feature that automatically moves the insertion point to the next line. **Editing** features include

- **Thesaurus,** which provides synonyms, antonyms, and related words.
- **Find and replace,** which locates (finds), removes, and inserts (replaces) another word(s).
- **Spelling** and **grammar checkers,** which automatically locate misspelled words and grammatical problems.

Formatting features include

- **Font**—design of characters. **Font size** is the height of characters.
- **Character effects**—include **bold,** *italic,* and **colors.**
- **Styles**—feature that quickly applies predefined formats.
- **Bulleted** and **numbered lists**—used to present sequences of topics or steps.

To be a competent end user, you need to understand the capabilities of basic application software, which includes word processors, spreadsheets, database management systems, and presentation programs. You need to know how to use these applications and how data can be shared between them.

SPREADSHEETS

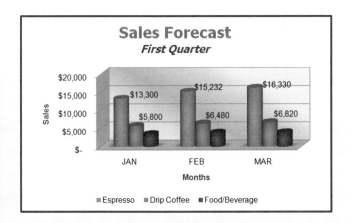

Spreadsheet programs are used to organize, analyze, and graph numeric data.

Features

Principal spreadsheet features include the following

- **Workbook files** consist of one or more related worksheets.
- **Worksheets,** also known as **spreadsheets** or **sheets,** are rectangular grids of **rows** and **columns.** Rows are identified by numbers, columns by letters.
- **Cells** are formed by the intersection of a row and column; used to hold text and numeric entries.
- **Text entries (labels)** provide structure and **numeric entries** can be numbers or formulas.
- **Formulas** are instructions for calculations. **Functions** are prewritten formulas.
- **Range** is a series of cells.
- **Analytical graphs (charts)** represent data visually.
- **Recalculation** occurs whenever a value changes in one cell that affects another cell(s).
- **What-if analysis** is the process of observing the effect of changing one or more values.

DATABASE MANAGEMENT SYSTEMS

A **database** is a collection of related data. A **database management system (DBMS),** also known as a **database manager,** structures a database and provides tools for manipulating data.

Features

Principal database management system features include the following

- **Relational database** organizes data into related tables.
- **Tables** have rows (**records**) and columns (**fields**).
- **Sort** is a tool to rearrange records.
- **Filter** is a tool to display only those records meeting specified conditions.
- **Query** is a question or request for specific data contained in a database.
- **Forms** are used to enter and edit records.
- **Reports** are printed output in a variety of forms.

PRESENTATION GRAPHICS

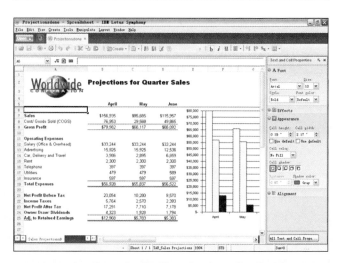

Join Animal Angels

Animal Rescue Foundation

Presentation graphics combine a variety of visual objects to create attractive, visually interesting presentations. They are excellent tools to communicate a message and to persuade people.

Features

Principal presentation graphics features include the following:

- **Slides**—individual **pages** or screens of a presentation.
- **Design templates**—professionally selected combination of color schemes, slide layouts, and special effects.
- **Content templates**—provide suggested content for each slide.
- **Animation**—adds action to text and graphics. **Transitions** animate moving from one slide to the next.

INTEGRATED PACKAGES

An **integrated package,** also known as **personal** or **home software,** is a single program that provides the functionality of several application packages. Some important characteristics include

- Functions that typically include word processing, spreadsheet, database manager, and more. Each function is not as extensive or powerful as a single-function application program.
- Less expensive than purchasing several individual application programs and simple to use.
- Popular with home users who are willing to sacrifice some advanced features for cost and simplicity.

SOFTWARE SUITES

A **software suite** is a collection of individual application packages sold together.

- **Productivity suites (office software suites or office suites)** contain professional-grade application programs.
- **Alternative office suites** include **downloadable office suites** (stored on your computer) or **online office suites** (stored online).
- **Specialized suites** focus on specific applications such as graphics.
- **Utility suites** include a variety of programs designed to make computing easier and safer.

CAREERS IN IT

Computer trainers instruct new users on the latest software or hardware. Teaching degree is preferred and experience with latest software and/or hardware is essential. Salary range $25,000 to $50,500.

KEY TERMS

analytical graph   (74)
animation   (82)
application software   (66)
basic application   (66)
bulleted list   (71)
button   (66)
cell   (73)
character effect   (71)
chart   (73)
column   (73)
computer trainer   (88)
content template   (82)
contextual tab   (67)
database   (78)
database management system
  (DBMS)   (78)
database manager   (78)
design template   (82)
dialog box   (66)
document   (70)
downloadable office suite   (85)
editing   (70)
field   (79)
find and replace   (70)
filter   (79)
font   (71)
font size   (71)
form   (79)
format   (70)
formula   (74)
function   (74)
gallery   (67)
grammar checker   (70)
graphical user interface (GUI)   (66)
group   (67)
home software   (84)
icons   (66)
integrated package   (84)
label   (74)
menu   (66)
menu bar   (66)
numbered list   (71)

numeric entry   (74)
office software suite   (85)
office suite   (85)
online office suite   (85)
page   (82)
personal software   (84)
pointer   (66)
presentation graphics   (82)
productivity suite   (85)
query   (79)
range   (74)
recalculation   (75)
record   (79)
relational database   (79)
report   (79)
ribbon   (67)
row   (73)
sheet   (73)
slide   (82)
software suite   (85)
sort   (79)
specialized application   (66)
specialized suite   (88)
speech recognition   (67)
spelling checker   (70)
spreadsheet   (73)
styles   (71)
system software   (66)
tab   (67)
table   (79)
text entry   (74)
thesaurus   (70)
toolbar   (66)
transition   (82)
user interface   (66)
utility suite   (88)
what-if analysis   (75)
window   (66)
word processor   (70)
word wrap   (70)
workbook file   (73)
worksheet   (73)

To test your knowledge of these key terms with animated flash cards, visit our Web site at www.computing2011.com and enter the keyword terms3.

MULTIPLE CHOICE

Circle the letter or fill in the correct answer.

1. This type of software works with end users, application software, and computer hardware to handle the majority of technical details.
   - **a.** application software
   - **b.** communications software
   - **c.** system software
   - **d.** Web software

2. _____ are narrowly focused on specific disciplines and occupations.
   - **a.** Basic applications
   - **b.** Business suites
   - **c.** Specialized applications
   - **d.** Utility programs

3. The primary purpose of this type of software is to create text-based documents.
   - **a.** spreadsheet
   - **b.** presentation
   - **c.** word processing
   - **d.** Web development

4. Organizations create newsletters, manuals, and brochures with this type of software.
   - **a.** graphics
   - **b.** presentation
   - **c.** spreadsheet
   - **d.** word processing

5. Letters, memos, term papers, reports, and contracts are all examples of
   - **a.** models
   - **b.** spreadsheets
   - **c.** documents
   - **d.** menus

6. Numbers and formulas entered in a cell are called
   - **a.** labels
   - **b.** numeric entries
   - **c.** intersection
   - **d.** text

7. The acronym DBMS stands for what?
   - **a.** double-blind management setup
   - **b.** document binder management system
   - **c.** data binding and marketing structure
   - **d.** database management system

8. Database _____ are primarily used to enter new records and to make changes to existing records.
   - **a.** reports
   - **b.** tables
   - **c.** forms
   - **d.** queries

9. A file that includes predefined settings that can be used to create many common types of presentations is called a
   - **a.** pattern
   - **b.** model
   - **c.** template
   - **d.** blueprint

10. A(n) _____ is a single program that provides the functionality of a word processor, spreadsheet, database manager, and more.
    - **a.** specialized application
    - **b.** integrated package
    - **c.** basic application
    - **d.** software suite

For an interactive multiple-choice practice test, visit our Web site at www.computing-2011.com and enter the keyword multiple3.

MATCHING

Match each numbered item with the most closely related lettered item. Write your answers in the spaces provided.

a. analytical
b. cell
c. integrated package
d. range
e. relational database
f. software suite
g. sort
h. spelling checker
i. what-if analysis
j. window

1. Area that contains a document, program, or message. _____
2. Type of graph or chart. _____
3. Includes the functionality of a word processor, spreadsheet, database manager, and more. _____
4. Identifies incorrectly spelled words and suggests alternatives. _____
5. The intersection of a row and column in a spreadsheet. _____
6. A collection of two or more cells in a spreadsheet. _____
7. Spreadsheet feature in which changing one or more numbers results in the automatic recalculation of all related fields. _____
8. Database structure that organizes data into related tables. _____
9. Arranging objects numerically or alphabetically. _____
10. Collection of individual applications that are bundled together. _____

For an interactive matching practice test, visit our Web site at www.computing 2011.com and enter the keyword matching3.

OPEN-ENDED

On a separate sheet of paper, respond to each question or statement.

1. Explain the difference between general-purpose and special-purpose applications.
2. Discuss the common features of most software programs. Describe the new interface introduced with Microsoft Office 2007 and used with Microsoft 2010.
3. What is the difference between a function and a formula? How is a formula related to what-if analysis?
4. What are presentation graphics programs? How are they used?
5. What is the difference between an integrated package and a software suite? What are the advantages and disadvantages of each?

APPLYING TECHNOLOGY

The following questions are designed to demonstrate ways that you can effectively use technology today. The first question relates directly to this chapter's Making IT Work for You feature.

1 SPEECH RECOGNITION

Tired of using your keyboard? Have you ever thought about speaking to your computer? Perhaps speech recognition is for you. To learn more about speech recognition, review Making IT Work for You: Speech Recognition on pages 68 and 69. Then answer the following questions: (a) What menu item is selected to begin training the software? (b) What are the verbal commands to start the Microsoft Word application? (c) Have you ever used speech recognition? If you have, describe how you used it and discuss how effective it was for you. If you have not, discuss how you might use it in the future. Be specific.

2 PRESENTATION GRAPHICS

For presentations, having the right software can help grab your audience's attention. Connect to our Web site at www.computing2011.com and enter the keyword presentation to link to a pre-sentation graphics software pack-age. Once connected, review the product's features and answer the following questions: (a) What computer hardware and software are required to use the presenta-tion graphics product? (b) List and describe three features that could help you organize or present your ideas. (c) What types of files can be embedded with a presentation using this software?

3 OFFICE SUITES

Microsoft is the leader in the office suite market, but several competing suites are also available. Visit our site at www.computing2011.com and enter the keyword office to connect to a maker of office suites. Review the site, and then answer the following questions: (a) What applications are provided in the suite? (b) What are the similarities and differences between the Microsoft and the competing office suite? (c) Which suite would you choose? Why?

EXPANDING YOUR KNOWLEDGE

The following questions are designed to add depth and detail to your understanding of specific topics presented within this chapter. The questions direct you to sources other than the textbook to obtain this knowledge.

1 HOW SPEECH RECOGNITION WORKS

Speech recognition is an emerging technology. To learn how speech recognition works, visit our Web site at www.computing2011.com and enter the keyword speech. Then answer the following: (a) Create a drawing similar to the one on our Web site that would represent dictating a mailing address for an address label. (b) What hardware is required to use voice recognition software? (c) Describe how speech recognition could enhance your use of each of the following types of applications: word processing, spreadsheet, and presentation. (d) Describe a profession that could benefit from speech recognition software. Be specific.

2 SHARING DATA BETWEEN APPLICATIONS

Sharing data between applications can be very convenient and can greatly increase your productivity. The three most common ways to share information are copy and paste, object linking, and object embedding. To learn more about sharing data between applications, visit out Web site at www.computing2011.com and enter the keyword sharing. Then respond to the following: (a) Discuss how copy and paste works. Provide a specific example. (b) What is the difference between object linking and object embedding? Provide specific examples. (c) Describe a specific situation in which you might use all three types of sharing data between applications.

3 SHAREWARE

One way to acquire new application software is by downloading shareware. Conduct a Web search for shareware programs. Connect to and explore a shareware site offering a program that might interest you. Then respond to the following: (a) What is shareware? Who creates it? (b) What does shareware cost to use? What about support if you have a problem using it? (c) What are the risks of using shareware? Be thorough. (d) Would you use shareware? Why or why not?

WRITING ABOUT TECHNOLOGY

The ability to think critically and to write effectively is essential to nearly every profession. The following questions are designed to help you develop these skills by posing thought-provoking questions about computer privacy, security, and/or ethics.

1 ACQUIRING SOFTWARE

There are three common ways to obtain new software: use public domain software, use shareware, buy commercial software. In addition to these three ways, two others are to copy programs from a friend or to purchase unauthorized copies of programs. Investigate each of these five options, and then answer the following in a one-page paper: (a) Define and discuss each option. Be sure to discuss both the advantages and disadvantages of each. (b) Which seems like the best method to you? Why? (c) Do you think there is anything wrong with obtaining and using unauthorized software? Identify and explore the key issues.

2 SOFTWARE STANDARDS

Most of the products you encounter every day, such as cars, electronics, and food, are required by law to meet certain conditions to ensure your safety and a minimum level of quality. Software, however, can be written by anyone with few of these constraints. Fortunately, some standards of certification do exist. Research a certification program for software vendors. Write a one-page paper to answer the following: (a) Describe the certification program you selected. What type of software is it intended for? (b) What requirements must software meet to receive certification? (c) Who performs the software tests to ensure compliance? (d) As a consumer of software, what additional certification requirements would you like to see? Explain your answer.

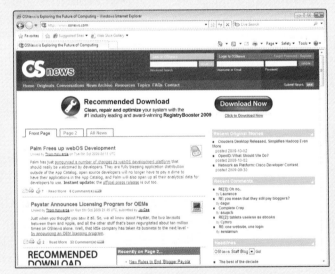

Specialized Application Software

After you have read this chapter, you should be able to:

1 Describe graphics software, including desktop publishing, image editors, illustration programs, image galleries, and graphics suites.

2 Discuss audio and video editing software.

3 Describe multimedia, including links, buttons, and multimedia authoring programs.

4 Explain Web authoring, Web site design, and Web authoring programs.

5 Describe artificial intelligence and virtual reality.

6 Discuss knowledge-based (expert) systems.

7 Describe robotics including perception systems, industrial robots, mobile robots, and household robots.

Only a few years ago, to produce an album you would need an expensive recording studio, professional musicians, and experts to run the equipment. Today's specialized application software makes it possible to record music without these expenses. Now to write, produce, record, and play an album digitally, you need a basic computer and readily available hardware and software.

Some experts suggest that someday you might even be able to create virtual digital personalities to tour and perform your music. Imagine a world where you could watch your virtual band perform your newest album from the comfort of your living room, using only your personal computer.

chapter 4

Introduction

Expect surprises—exciting and positive opportunities. The latest technological developments offer you new opportunities to extend your range of computer competency. As we show in this chapter, software that for years was available only for larger computers has become available for microcomputers. This new generation of specialized application makes it possible to perform advanced tasks at home.

For example, it is now possible, and quite common, for people to create their own Web sites. Home users also have access to software that helps manipulate and create graphic images. Many musicians and artists work from home to create complex and beautiful work using specialized applications.

Some of these same technological advances have allowed researchers and computer scientists to make advances in the field of artificial intelligence that previously were envisioned only in science fiction. Robots now provide security and assistance in homes. Virtual reality is providing opportunities in the fields of medicine and science but also commonly appears in video games.

Competent end users need to be aware of specialized applications. They need to know who uses them, what they are used for, and how they are used. These advanced applications include graphics programs, audio and video editing software, multimedia, Web authoring, and artificial intelligence, including virtual reality, knowledge-based systems, and robotics.

Specialized Applications

In the previous chapter, we discussed basic applications that are widely used in nearly every profession. This chapter focuses on specialized applications that are widely used within specific professions. (See Figure 4-1.) Specifically, we will examine

- Graphics programs for creating professional-looking published documents, for creating and editing images, and for locating and inserting graphics.
- Audio and video software to create, edit, and play music and videos.
- Multimedia programs to create dynamic interactive presentations.
- Web authoring programs to create, edit, and design Web sites.
- Artificial intelligence, including virtual reality, knowledge-based systems, and robotics.

Figure 4-1 **Specialized applications**

Graphics

In Chapter 3, we discussed analytical and presentation graphics, which are widely used to analyze data and to create professional-looking presentations. Here we focus on more specialized graphics programs used by professionals in the graphic arts profession.

Letter A

Expanded view

Figure 4-2 **Bitmap image**

Desktop Publishing

Desktop publishing programs, or **page layout programs,** allow you to mix text and graphics to create publications of professional quality. While word processors focus on creating text and have the ability to combine text and graphics, desktop publishers focus on page design and layout and provide greater flexibility. Professional graphic artists use desktop publishing programs to create documents such as brochures, newsletters, newspapers, and textbooks.

Popular desktop publishing programs include Adobe InDesign, Microsoft Publisher, and QuarkXPress. While these programs provide the capability to create text and graphics, typically graphic artists import these elements from other sources, including word processors, digital cameras, scanners, image editors, illustration programs, and image galleries.

Image Editors

One of the most common types of graphic files is bitmap. **Bitmap images,** also known as **raster images,** use thousands of dots or **pixels** to represent images. Each dot has a specific location, color, and shade. One limitation of bitmap images, however, is that when they are expanded, the images can become pixilated, or jagged on the edges. For example, when the letter A in Figure 4-2 is expanded, the borders of the letter appear jagged, as indicated by the expanded view.

Image editors, also known as **photo editors,** are specialized graphics programs for editing or modifying digital photographs. Popular image editors include Adobe Photoshop, Corel Paint Shop Pro, and Paint.NET. (See Figure 4-3.)

Paint Tools

Filter

Brush

Pen

Figure 4-3 **Adobe Photoshop**

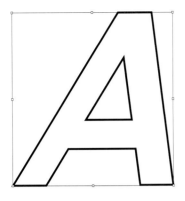

Figure 4-4 Vector image

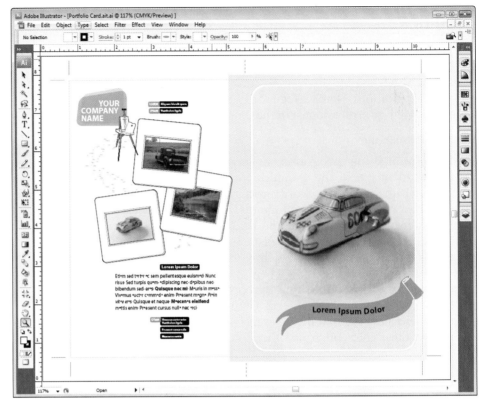

Figure 4-5 Adobe Illustrator

Illustration Programs

Vector is another common type of graphic file. While bitmap images use pixels to represent images, **vector images,** also known as **vector illustrations,** use geometric shapes or objects. (See Figure 4-4.) These objects are created by connecting lines and curves. Because these objects can be defined by mathematical equations, they can be rapidly and easily resized, colored, textured, and manipulated. An image is a combination of several objects. **Illustration programs,** also known as **drawing programs,** are used to create and edit vector images.

Popular illustration programs include Adobe Illustrator, CorelDRAW, and Inkscape. (See Figure 4-5.)

Image Galleries

Image galleries are libraries of electronic images. These images are used for a wide variety of applications from illustrating textbooks to providing visual interest to presentations. There are two basic types of electronic images in these galleries:

- **Stock photographs**—photographs on a variety of subject material from people to landscapes.
- **Clip art**—graphic illustrations representing a wide range of topics. Most applications provide access to a limited selection of free clip art. For example, in Microsoft Word, you can gain access to several pieces of clip art by issuing the command Insert>Clip Art.

There are numerous Web image galleries. (See Figure 4-6.) Some of these sites offer free images and clip art while others charge a fee.

Organization	Site
Classroom Clipart	www.classroomclipart.com
ClipArt.com	www.clipart.com
Graphics Factory	www.graphicsfactory.com
MS Office clip art	office.microsoft.com/clipart
iStockphoto	istockphoto.com
Flickr Creative Commons	www.flickr.com/creativecommons/

Figure 4-6 Selected Web image galleries

Graphics Suites

Some companies have combined or bundled their separate graphics programs in groups called **graphics suites.** The advantage of the graphics suites is that you can buy a larger variety of graphics programs at a lower cost than if purchased separately.

Two popular suites are CorelDRAW Graphics Suite and Adobe Creative Suite. CorelDRAW Graphics Suite includes five individual graphics programs plus a large library of clip art, media clips, and fonts. (See Figure 4-7.)

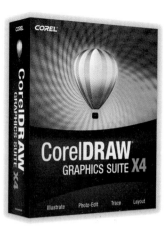

 CONCEPT CHECK

What is desktop publishing?

What is the difference between an image editor and an illustration program?

Describe image galleries. What are graphics suites?

Figure 4-7 **CorelDRAW Graphics Suite**

Audio and Video

In the past, professional-quality editing of home audio and video was a job for professional photo labs or studios. For example, if you wanted to assemble footage from all your Fourth of July picnics, you sent all the tapes to a lab and waited for a compilation tape. Now, using audio and video editing software, you can create your own compilation movies.

- **Video editing software** allows you to reorganize, add effects, and more to your digital video footage. Two commonly used video editing software programs are Apple iMovie and Windows Movie Maker. (See Figure 4-8.) These programs are designed to allow you to assemble and edit new home videos and movies from raw digital video footage. To see how digital video editors work, visit our Web site at www.computing2011.com and enter the keyword **video.** To learn how to use a digital video editor, see Making IT Work for You: Digital Video Editing on pages 106 and 107.

Figure 4-8 **Apple iMovie**

Making IT work for you

DIGITAL VIDEO EDITING

Do you want to make your own movie? Would you like to edit some home movies and distribute them to family and friends on DVDs? It's easy with the right equipment and software.

Capturing Video   You can capture video to your computer from a device such as a digital camcorder. Once captured, the video can be edited using digital video editing software. Follow the steps below to capture video from a digital camcorder using Windows Vista.

1 • **Connect the digital camcorder to your computer and turn it on.**

• **Select *Import Video*.**

• **Enter a name and select a location to save the imported video.**

2 • **Select the portion of the video to import. You can import the entire video or only a particular section.**

3 • **Preview the video as it is captured from your camera to the file you specified.**

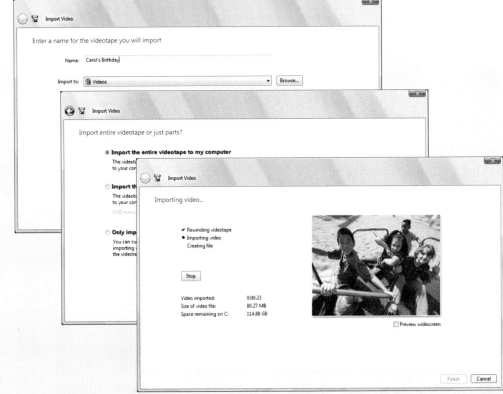

Editing a Movie Windows Movie Maker divides your captured video into clips, or scenes that make up your movie. Follow the steps below to create a movie by arranging clips and adding special effects.

1 ● Drag movie clips from the Contents Pane and arrange them in the Storyboard.

● Use the options in the Tasks Pane to add sounds, transitions, title screens, and effects to your movie.

● Use the Preview Monitor to preview your movie.

Tasks Pane

Contents Pane

Storyboard

Preview Monitor

Creating a DVD Once you have edited your movies, you can create a DVD to share with friends and family. You will need a DVD writer and a blank writable DVD. Follow the steps below to design a menu, add movies, and create your DVD.

1 ● Launch Windows DVD Maker, and click the *Choose Photos and Videos* button.

● Select the video file you created with Windows Movie Maker in the previous step.

● Click *Next* button.

2 ● Select a menu style that will be displayed when your DVD is played.

● Insert a writable DVD in your DVD drive and click the *Burn* button to create your DVD.

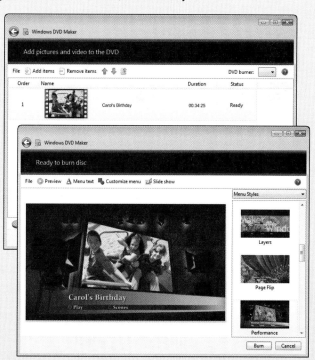

The Web is continually changing, and some of the specifics presented in this Making IT Work for You may have changed.
To learn about other ways to make information technology work for you, visit our Web site at www.computing2011.com and enter the keyword miw.

Figure 4-9 Apple GarageBand

- **Audio editing software** allows you to create and edit audio clips. Most audio editing software also has features that allow you to add audio effects, like filters, to your tracks. For example, you can use this type of software to filter out pops or scratches in an old recording. You can even use this software to create your own MP3s. Some commonly used audio editing software programs are Apple GarageBand and Sony ACID. (See Figure 4-9.)

Multimedia

Multimedia is the integration of all sorts of media into one presentation. For example, a multimedia presentation may include video, music, voice, graphics, and text. You may have seen multimedia applied in video games, Web presentations, or even a word processing document. Many of the basic application software programs you learned about in Chapter 3 include features that make the incorporation of multimedia in documents easy. Although these applications include multimedia features, they create documents that are generally accessed in a linear fashion and provide very limited user interaction.

Effective multimedia presentations incorporate user participation or interactivity. **Interactivity** allows the user to choose the information to view, to control the pace and flow of information, and to respond to items and receive feedback. When experiencing an interactive multimedia presentation, users customize the presentation to their needs. For example, Figure 4-10 presents an opening page of a multimedia presentation. Users are able to select the language to be used and decide whether to include sound.

Once used almost exclusively for computer games, interactive multimedia is now widely used in business, education, and the home. Business uses include high-quality interactive presentations, product demonstrations, and Web page design. In education, interactive multimedia is used for in-class presentations and demonstrations, distance education, and online testing. In the home, multimedia is frequently used for entertainment.

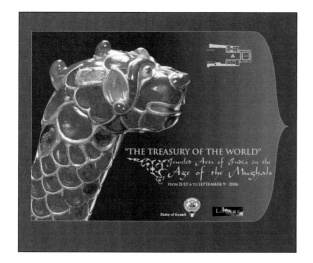

Figure 4-10 **Opening page of a multimedia presentation**

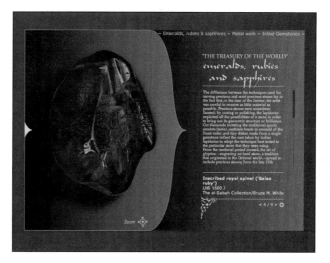

Figure 4-11 **Links and buttons are used to navigate the multimedia presentation**

Links and Buttons

An interactive multimedia presentation is typically organized as a series of related pages. Each page presents information and provides **links,** or connections, to related information. These links can be to video, sound, graphics, and text files, and to other pages and resources. By clicking special areas called **buttons** on a page, you can make appropriate links and navigate through a presentation to locate and discover information. Typically, there are several buttons on a page. You can select one, several, or none of them. You are in control. You direct the flow and content of the presentation. (See Figure 4-11.)

Multimedia Authoring Programs

Multimedia authoring programs are special programs used to create multimedia presentations. They bring together all the video, audio, graphics, and text elements into an interactive framework. Widely used authoring programs include Adobe Director and Toolbook.

On the Web Explorations

To learn more about a leading company that develops multimedia authoring programs, visit our Web site at www.computing2011.com and enter the keyword multimedia.

☑ CONCEPT CHECK

What is video editing software? What is audio editing software?

What are multimedia, interactivity, links, and buttons?

What are multimedia authoring programs?

Web Authoring

There are over a billion Web sites on the Internet, and more are being added every day. Corporations use the Web to reach new customers and to promote their products. (See Figure 4-12.) Individuals create their own personal sites, called **blogs.** Creating a site is called **Web authoring.** It begins with site design followed by creation of a document file that displays the Web site's content.

Web Site Design

A Web site is an interactive multimedia form of communication. Designing a Web site begins with determining the site's overall content. The content is then broken down into a series of related pieces of information. The overall site design is commonly represented in a **graphical map.** (See Figure 4-13.)

Notice that in the graphical map shown in Figure 4-13 each block in the map represents a Web page. Lines joining the blocks represent links to related pages of information that make up the Web site. The first page, or home page, typically serves as an introduction and supplies a table of contents. The following pages present the specific pieces or blocks of information.

Multimedia elements are added to individual pages to enhance interest and interactivity. One multimedia element found on many Web sites is moving graphics called **animations.** These animations can be simple moving text or complicated interactive features. There are many specialized programs available to aid in the creation of animation. One type of interactive animation is produced using software called Adobe Flash. **Flash** movies can be inserted as a part of the page or encompass the entire screen.

Web Authoring Programs

As we mentioned in Chapter 2, Web pages are typically HTML documents. With knowledge of HTML and a simple text editor, you can create Web pages. Even without knowledge of HTML, you can create simple Web pages using a word processing package like Microsoft Word.

More specialized and powerful programs, called **Web authoring programs,** are typically used to create sophisticated commercial sites. Also known as **Web page editors** and **HTML editors,** these programs provide support for Web site design and HTML coding. Some Web authoring programs are **WYSIWYG (what you see is what you get) editors,** which means you can build a page without interacting directly with HTML code. WYSIWYG editors preview the page described by HTML code. Widely used Web authoring programs include Adobe Dreamweaver, NetObjects Fusion, and Microsoft Expression. The Web site depicted in Figure 4-12 was created using Adobe Dreamweaver. (See Figure 4-14.)

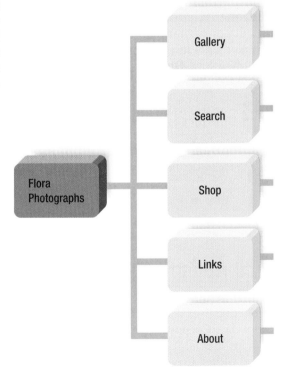

Figure 4-12 **Flora Photographs Web site**

Figure 4-13 **Partial graphical map for the Flora Photographs Web site**

WYSIWYG Editing

Dreamweaver provides tools to help you lay out pages with common elements such as text, images, and links.

HTML Coding

Using descriptions of each Web page, Adobe Dreamweaver creates HTML code for the entire site.

Web Page

Using a browser, the completed HTML document can be displayed. This is the first page of the Flora Photographs site.

Figure 4-14 Adobe Dreamweaver and the Flora Photographs Web site

Are you thinking about creating your own Web site? Perhaps you already have one and would like to spruce it up a bit? Here are a few suggestions that might help.

1 **Use a common design and theme.** Consistency in the use of colors, fonts, background designs, and navigation features gives a Web site a unified feeling and makes it easier to use.

2 **Use graphics and animations to add interest.** Graphics and animations add interest and focus the user's attention. However, they take time to download and the wait frustrates users. Be selective and limit the size of graphics. Also reuse graphics from one page to another.

3 **Make navigating your Web site easy.** Create a simple method of navigating that allows users to get to their desired information as quickly as possible. None of your content should be more than three clicks from the home page.

4 **Design your site for a standard display.** To maximize the impact of your site for the largest number of users, design it to be viewed on a monitor with a standard 1024×768 resolution.

To see additional tips, visit us at www.computing2011.com and enter the keyword tips.

Artificial Intelligence

The field of computer science known as **artificial intelligence (AI)** attempts to develop computer systems that can mimic or simulate human senses, thought processes, and actions. These include reasoning, learning from past actions, and using senses such as vision and touch. Artificial intelligence that corresponds to human intelligence is still a long way off. However, several tools that emulate human senses, problem solving, and information processing have been developed.

These modern applications of artificial intelligence are designed to help people and organizations become more productive. Many of these tools have practical applications for business, medicine, law, and so on. In the past, computers used calculating power to solve structured problems, which can be broken down into a series of well-defined steps. People—using intuition, reasoning, and memory—were better at solving unstructured problems, whether building a product or approving a loan. Organizations have long been able to computerize the tasks once performed by clerks. Now knowledge-intensive work and unstructured problems, such as activities performed by many managers, are being automated. Let us now consider three areas in which human talents and abilities have been enhanced with "computerized intelligence": virtual reality, knowledge-based systems, and robotics.

On the Web Explorations

Many people believe that the next big leap forward in computing will involve artificial intelligence.

To learn about a leading developer of artificial intelligence software, visit our Web site at www.computing2011.com and enter the keyword ai.

Virtual Reality

Suppose you could create and virtually experience any new form of reality you wished. You could see the world through the eyes of a child, a robot—or even a lobster. You could explore faraway resorts, the moon, or inside a nuclear waste dump without leaving your chair. This simulated experience is possible with virtual reality.

Figure 4-15 Virtual reality

Virtual reality is an artificial, or simulated, reality generated in 3-D by a computer. Virtual reality is also commonly known as **VR, artificial reality,** or **virtual environments.** In some cases, to navigate in a virtual space, you use virtual reality hardware including headgear and gloves. The headgear has earphones and three-dimensional stereoscopic screens (one type is called Eyephones). The gloves have sensors that collect data about your hand movements (one type is called DataGlove). Coupled with software, this interactive sensory equipment lets you immerse yourself in a computer-generated world. See Figure 4-15.

Creating virtual reality programs once required very-high-end software costing several thousands of dollars. Recently, several lower-cost yet powerful authoring programs have been introduced. One of the best known is

Second Life from Linden Labs, which allows users to create animated characters to represent themselves and to develop their own environment.

There are any number of possible applications for virtual reality. The ultimate recreational use might be something resembling a giant virtual amusement park. More serious applications can simulate important experiences or training environments such as in aviation, surgical operations, spaceship repair, or nuclear disaster cleanup. Some virtual reality strives to be an **immersive experience,** allowing a user to walk into a virtual reality room or view simulations on a **virtual reality wall.** (See Figure 4-16.)

Figure 4-16 **Virtual reality wall**

Knowledge-based (Expert) Systems

People who are expert in a particular area—certain kinds of medicine, accounting, engineering, and so on—are generally well paid for their specialized knowledge. Unfortunately for their clients and customers, these experts are expensive, not always available, and hard to replace when they move on.

What if you were to somehow capture the knowledge of a human expert and make it accessible to everyone through a computer program? This is exactly what is being done with so-called knowledge-based or expert systems. **Knowledge-based systems,** also known as **expert systems,** are a type of artificial intelligence that uses a database to provide assistance to users. These systems use a database or **knowledge base** that contains specific facts, rules to relate these facts, and user input to formulate recommendations and decisions. The sequence of processing is determined by the interaction of the user and the knowledge base. Many expert systems use so-called **fuzzy logic,** which allows users to respond to questions in a very humanlike way. For example, if an expert system asked how your classes were going, you could respond, "great," "OK," "terrible," and so on.

Over the past decade, expert systems have been developed in areas such as medicine, geology, architecture, and nature. There are expert systems with such names as Oil Spill Advisor, Bird Species Identification, and even Midwives Assistant. A system called Grain Marketing Advisor helps farmers select the best way to market their grain.

Robotics

Robotics is the field of study concerned with developing and using robots. **Robots** are computer-controlled machines that mimic the motor activities of living things. For example, Honda's Asimo robot resembles a human and is capable of walking upstairs, dancing, shaking hands, and much more. (See Figure 4-17.) Some robots can even solve unstructured problems using artificial intelligence.

Robots are used in factories, manufacturing, home security, the military, and many other fields of human endeavor. They differ from other assembly-line machines because they can be reprogrammed to do more than one task. Robots often are used to handle dangerous, repetitive tasks. There are four types of robots.

environmental facts

Did you know that robots may someday help clear our oceans of pollution? Investigators are currently exploring the use of robots and special companion ocean vessels for just that purpose. The robots would roam the ocean bottom looking for garbage, oil, and other pollutants. Once located the robots would either clean up the mess on their own or radio other robots for assistance. When full, the robots would resurface and deposit the offensive materials on the companion vessel and then go back for more. The future of robotics promises many opportunities for this kind of robotic clean up.

Figure 4-17 **Asimo**

Figure 4-18 **Industrial robot**

- **Perception systems: Perception system robots** imitate some of the human senses. For example, robots with television-camera vision systems are particularly useful. They can guide machine tools, inspect products, and secure homes.
- **Industrial robots: Industrial robots** are used to perform a variety of tasks. Examples are machines used in automobile plants to do welding, polishing, and painting. Some types of robots have claws for picking up objects and handling dangerous materials. (See Figure 4-18.)
- **Mobile robots: Mobile robots** act as transports and are widely used for a variety of different tasks. For example, the police and military use them to locate and disarm explosive devices. In the early 2000s, mobile robots entered the world of entertainment with their own television program, called *Battlebots.* You can even build your own mobile robot from a kit.
- **Household robots: Household robots** are now widely available and are designed to vacuum or scrub floors, mow lawns, patrol the house, or simply provide entertainment.

☑ CONCEPT CHECK

 Define artificial intelligence. What are virtual reality and virtual reality walls?

 Describe knowledge-based systems and fuzzy logic.

 Describe four types of robots.

Careers in IT

Desktop publishers use computers to format and create publication-ready material. (See Figure 4-19.) They may create books, magazines, newsletters, and newspapers on home computers using special application software. A large part of the job is designing page layout, importing text, and manipulating graphics. Most desktop publishers work for companies that handle commercial printing accounts. However, there are also many independent contractors.

Desktop publishing positions usually require completion of a program at a vocational school or a university. Internships and part-time work can be a valuable asset to someone pursuing this career. Employers typically look for individuals with good communication skills and artistic ability.

Desktop publishers can expect to earn an annual salary of $26,500 to $44,500. Advancement opportunities include management positions or independent contracting. To learn about other careers in information technology, visit us at www.computing2011.com and enter the keyword **careers.**

Figure 4-19 **Desktop publisher**

A LOOK TO THE FUTURE

Robots Can Look, Act, and Think Like Us

Would you like to talk with your mom through a robot that both resembles you and demonstrates your emotions on their rubber faces? What if you received a companion robot with a set of moral values? Would you trust a robot to trade the stocks in your portfolio? Researchers are currently at work on robots with the artificial intelligence needed to perform these tasks and more.

The Saya robot, with its artificial skin and muscles, is currently under development in Tokyo. Researchers hope that eventually it will be used as a communication device similar to a current Web cam. For example, you could connect to a robot that resembles you at your mother's house and communicate through it with her. You would see your mother through the robot's visual system. Your mother would hear your voice come from the robot and your emotions would be displayed on its face.

Other research is being conducted that will give robots a sense of values. It is hoped that these robots will be able to make decisions independently based on this set of values. Researchers in California are creating robots that act as surveillance instruments, capable of following a target without direction from a human. The robots can predict potential escape routes and pursue a subject through crowded areas.

The Feelix Growing project, a European research project, is developing robots that detect human emotions using simple video cameras and sensors combined with sophisticated software. These robots can then be programmed to respond with similar emotional cues. These robots recognize faces and respond to stimuli like a person would with emotions ranging from surprise to disgust. These robots might be used to help children with developmental disabilities in the near future. Someday, you might interact with a robot that can respond to how you are feeling.

All of these projects are designed to move beyond simple computing and into a decidedly human realm of emotional intelligence. Some experts have even suggested that human intelligence relies on emotional input for all important decision making. Thus, by definition, for a machine to approximate human intelligence, it would have to understand and rely on emotions. If computers could read human emotions, and had emotional intelligence of their own, it could be possible for your computer to act as a stress counselor when you stay up all night working on a project.

Computers with their own emotional intelligence could be the ultimate human companions. Computer scientists have suggested they may read your mood and play music accordingly. Or they could search through audio and video files for media you would find moving, funny, or dramatic. If computers had their own emotional sense, it is possible that they, like the humans they emulate, would require interaction for mental health.

Would you use a robot as a communication device? Do you think we should build robots with a sense of moral values? Some researchers have suggested that robots with artificial intelligence could serve as ideal supervisors and managers. What do you think? Would you like to have an "emotional" robot for a boss?

GRAPHICS

Professionals in graphic arts use specialized graphics programs.

Desktop Publishing
Desktop publishing programs (page layout programs) mix text and graphics to create professional publications.

Image Editors
Image editors (photo editors) create and modify **bitmap (raster) image** files. Images are recorded as dots or **pixels.**

Illustration Programs
Illustration programs, also known as **drawing programs,** modify **vector images (vector illustrations).** In a vector file, images are recorded as a collection of objects such as lines, rectangles, and ovals.

Image Galleries
Image galleries are libraries of electronic images, widely available from the Web. Two types are **stock photographs** and **clip art.**

Graphics Suites
A **graphics suite** is a collection of individual graphics programs sold as a unit.

AUDIO AND VIDEO

Recent advances in video and audio technology allow individuals to assemble near-professional-quality video and audio footage.

Video Software
Video editing software allows you to reorganize, add effects, and more to digital video.

Audio Software
Audio editing software allows you to create and edit audio clips. You can add audio effects, like filters, to your tracks. You can create MP3s.

To be a competent end user, you need to be aware of specialized applications. You need to know who uses them, what they are used for, and how they are used. Specialized applications include graphics programs, audio and video editing software, multimedia, Web authoring, and the field of artificial intelligence.

MULTIMEDIA

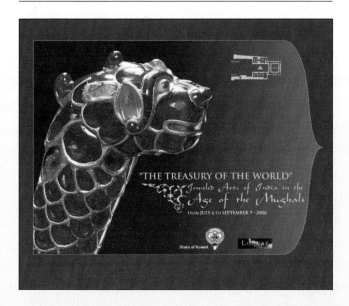

Multimedia integrates all sorts of media into one presentation. An essential feature is user participation or **interactivity.**

Links and Buttons

A multimedia presentation is organized as a series of related pages. Pages are **linked,** or connected, by clicking **buttons.**

Multimedia Authoring Programs

Multimedia authoring programs bring together video, audio, graphics, and text elements in an interactive framework.

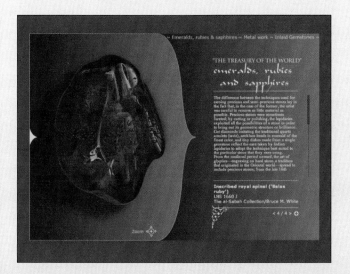

WEB AUTHORING

Blogs are personal Web sites. Creating Web sites is called **Web authoring.** It begins with Web site design, followed by creating a document file that displays the Web site content.

Web Site Design

Web sites are an interactive multimedia form of communication.

Graphical maps use linked blocks to represent a Web site's overall content. Typically, blocks represent individual Web pages and links indicate relationships between related pages.

The first Web page (home page) usually introduces the site and supplies a table of contents. Multimedia elements are added to pages. **Animations** are moving graphics. **Flash** is a widely used application for Web animation.

Web Authoring Programs

Web sites can be created using a simple text editor or word processor. **Web authoring programs,** also known as **Web page editors** or **HTML editors,** are specifically designed to create Web sites. They provide support for Web site design and HTML coding. Some offer **WYSIWYG (what you see is what you get) editors.**

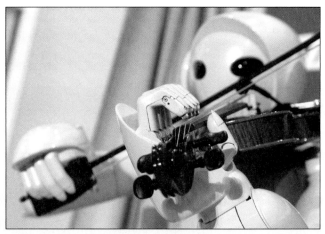

Artificial intelligence (AI) attempts to develop computer systems that mimic human senses, thought processes, and actions.

Virtual Reality

Virtual reality (VR, artificial reality, or **virtual environments)** creates computer-generated simulated environment using sensory equipment, including head gear and gloves.

Applications include recreational and other areas such as aviation, surgical operations, spaceship repair, and nuclear disaster cleanup. Some applications strive for **immersive experiences** and can be viewed on **virtual reality walls.**

Knowlege-Based (Expert) Systems

Knowledge-based (expert) systems are programs that duplicate the knowledge that humans use to perform specific tasks. **Knowledge bases** are databases containing facts and rules. **Fuzzy logic** allows users to respond to questions in a very humanlike way.

Robotics

Robotics is concerned with developing and using robots. **Robots** are computer-controlled machines that mimic the motor activities of living things. Four types of robots are

- **Perception systems** imitate human senses such as vision.
- **Industrial robots** perform a variety of tasks such as welding, polishing and painting.
- **Mobile robots** act as transports for such things as locating and disarming explosive devices.
- **Household robots** are designed to vacuum and scrub floors, mow lawns, patrol the house, or provide entertainment.

CAREERS IN IT

Desktop publishers use computers to format and create publication-ready material. Vocational or university degree is preferred plus good communication skills and artistic ability. Salary range $26,500 to $44,500.

KEY TERMS

animation (110)
artificial intelligence (AI) (112)
artificial reality (112)
audio editing software (108)
bitmap image (103)
blog (109)
button (109)
clip art (104)
desktop publisher (114)
desktop publishing program (103)
drawing program (104)
expert system (113)
Flash (110)
fuzzy logic (113)
graphical map (110)
graphics suite (105)
household robot (114)
HTML editor (110)
illustration program (104)
image editors (103)
image gallery (104)
immersive experience (113)
industrial robot (114)
interactivity (108)
knowledge base (113)

knowledge-based system (113)
link (109)
mobile robot (114)
multimedia (108)
multimedia authoring program (109)
page layout program (103)
perception system robot (114)
photo editors (103)
pixel (103)
raster image (103)
robot (113)
robotics (113)
stock photograph (104)
vector (104)
vector illustration (104)
vector image (104)
video editing software (105)
virtual environment (112)
virtual reality (112)
virtual reality wall (113)
VR (112)
Web authoring (109)
Web authoring program (110)
Web page editor (110)
WYSIWIG editors (110)

To test your knowledge of these key terms with animated flash cards, visit our Web site at www.computing2011.com and enter the keyword terms4.

MULTIPLE CHOICE

Circle the letter or fill in the correct answer.

1. Graphic programs widely used in the graphic arts profession include _____.
   a. desktop publishing programs, image editors, and illustration programs
   b. artificial intelligence, virtual reality, and illustration programs
   c. megamedia programs, image editors, and desktop publishing programs
   d. virtual reality, desktop publishing programs, and illustration programs

2. Image editors are used for creating and editing _____.
   a. bitmap images   c. text
   b. vector images   d. HTML codes

3. Programs used to create or modify vector images are called _____.
   a. illustration programs   c. graphical modifiers
   b. image editors   d. bit publishing packages

4. Pages in a multimedia presentation typically provide _____ or connections to related information.
   a. blogs   c. logs
   b. links   d. maps

5. The overall site design is commonly represented in a _____ map.
   a. visual   c. documentary
   b. HTML   d. graphical

6. _____ are Web authoring tools that present a visual representation of a page described by HTML code.
   a. Artificial intelligence   c. WYSIWYG editors
   b. Image editors   d. Virtual reality

7. A field of computer science that attempts to develop computer systems that can mimic or simulate human senses.
   a. AI   c. VR
   b. HTML   d. WYSIWIG

8. Users can interact in a fully immersed 3-D environment using _____.
   a. unstructured problems   c. HTML
   b. virtual reality   d. robotics

9. Fuzzy logic is
   a. used to respond to questions in a humanlike way
   b. a new programming language used to program animation
   c. the result of fuzzy thinking
   d. a term that indicates logical values greater than one

10. Robots used in automobile plants would be classified as
    a. perception system robots   c. mobile robots
    b. industrial robots   d. knowledge robots

For an interactive multiple-choice practice test, visit our Web site at www.computing2011.com and enter the keyword multiple4.

MATCHING

Match each numbered item with the most closely related lettered item. Write your answers in the spaces provided.

a. AI
b. bitmap
c. desktop publishing
d. fuzzy logic
e. graphical map
f. graphics suite
g. image editor
h. link
i. multimedia
j. vector image

1. Integrates all sorts of media into one presentation. _____
2. Graphics program for creating and editing bitmap images. _____
3. Programs used to create multimedia presentations. _____
4. Diagram of a Web site's overall design. _____
5. Program that allows you to mix text and graphics to create publications of professional quality. _____
6. Group of graphics programs offered at lower cost than if purchased separately. _____
7. Connection on a multimedia page to related information. _____
8. Graphics file made up of thousands of pixels. _____
9. Graphics file made up of a collection of objects, such as rectangles, lines, and ovals. _____
10. Attempts to develop computer systems that mimic or simulate human thought processes and actions. _____

For an interactive matching practice test, visit our Web site at www.computing2011.com and enter the keyword matching4.

OPEN-ENDED

On a separate sheet of paper, respond to each question or statement.

1. Describe graphics, including desktop publishers, image editors, illustration programs, image galleries, and graphics suites.
2. Discuss audio and video editing software.
3. What is multimedia? Discuss interactivity, links, and buttons.
4. Describe Web authoring, including Web site design and Web authoring programs.
5. Discuss three areas of artificial intelligence.

APPLYING TECHNOLOGY

The following questions are designed to demonstrate ways that you can effectively use technology today. The first question relates directly to this chapter's Making IT Work for You feature.

1 DIGITAL VIDEO EDITING

Have you ever thought of making your own movie? Would you like to edit some home videos and distribute them to family and friends on DVDs? It's easy with the right equipment and software. To learn more about digital video editing, review Making IT Work for You: Digital Video Editing, on pages 106 and 107. Then answer the following questions: (a) Briefly describe the steps necessary to begin transferring video from a camcorder to your computer. (b) Where can you preview your movie in Windows Movie Maker? (c) What is Windows DVD Maker and what is it used for?

2 ADOBE FLASH

Web sites aren't all just text and pictures anymore. Many are taking advantage of browser plug-ins that add new functionality and display abilities to Web browsers, as we discussed in Chapter 2. One of the most popular plug-ins is Adobe Flash. Visit our Web site at www.computing2011.com and enter the keyword flash for a link to the Adobe site. Once connected, read about Flash and answer the following questions: (a) What is Flash? What types of content can it display? (b) How is the Flash plug-in obtained? (c) What types of companies are using Flash in their Web page designs? (d) Do you think Flash is a valuable Web page addition or just a flashy distraction? Explain your answer.

3 STREAMING MULTIMEDIA PLAYERS

Streaming multimedia files come in many varieties. There are several formats for streaming audio and video files available, each with is own advantage. To play these files, a user needs software known as a *player,* which must support the type of file the user wishes to play. Visit our Web site at www.computing2011.com and enter the keyword streaming for a link to a popular streaming multimedia player. Read about the player and then answer the following questions: (a) What types of streaming multimedia files can be played with this player? (b) How does the user receive and install the player? (c) As streaming multimedia becomes more widely available on the Internet, how might the role of player software change? Be specific.

EXPANDING YOUR KNOWLEDGE

The following questions are designed to add depth and detail to your understanding of specific topics presented within this chapter. The questions direct you to sources other than the textbook to obtain this knowledge.

1 HOW DIGITAL VIDEO EDITING WORKS

The falling prices of digital camcorders and improvements in computer technology have made digital video editing affordable for individuals. To learn more about digital video editing, visit our Web site at www.computing2011.com and enter the keyword video. Then answer the following questions: (a) What hardware is needed to capture video from a VCR tape? Why is this hardware necessary? (b) How can video editing software be used to improve a video? (c) What are some common ways to share videos?

2 PERSONAL WEB SITE

Would you like a personal Web site but don't want to deal with learning HTML? There are many services available to get you started. To learn more about personal Web sites, visit our Web site at www.computing2011.com and enter the keyword blog. Then answer the following questions: (a) What are Web logs? What are they used for? (b) What is Blogger.com? Describe the following features provided by Blogger.com: templates, upload file, hyperlink, post, publish, and view Web page. (c) Have you ever created a Web log or other types of personal Web site? If you have, describe how you created it and what you used it for. If you have not, discuss why and how you might use one.

3 STREAMING MULTIMEDIA

Many Web sites are now enhanced with streaming multimedia. Some sites offer streaming audio or video to augment text, such as news sites with file footage. For others, the content *is* the streaming multimedia, such as Internet radio or animation sites. Locate several Web sites that offer streaming multimedia and pick one to review. Then answer the following: (a) Define "streaming multimedia." (b) What type of streaming multimedia did the site offer? Who is the intended audience? (c) In what ways was the experience limited? Be specific.

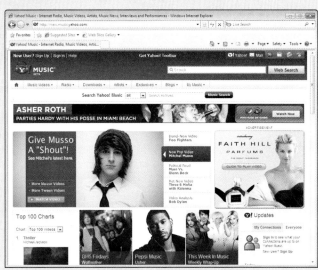

WRITING ABOUT TECHNOLOGY

The ability to think critically and to write effectively is essential to nearly every profession. The following questions are designed to help you develop these skills by posing thought-provoking questions about computer privacy, security, and/or ethics.

① DIGITAL PHOTO MANIPULATION

Image editing software has made it easy to alter photographs, which in the past were accepted as visual records of real events. In some cases, the purpose of digital editing is humor and exaggeration, while other times subtle changes are used to alter a photo's deeper meaning. Research examples of digital photo editing that resulted in controversy and then answer the following questions in a one-page paper: (a) Do you see any ethical issues related to altering photographs? (b) What do you consider the boundary between acceptable photo editing and deceptive or misleading practices? (c) Do you feel the old saying "seeing is believing" needs to be reconsidered for the digital age? Defend your answers.

② ONLINE EXPERT SYSTEMS

Expert systems have been integrated into many Web sites for consumers. For example, health-related Web sites help patients "self-diagnose" illnesses before seeing a physician. Research Web sites that make expert systems available and address the following items in a one-page paper: (a) Define "expert system." (b) What benefits do these expert systems offer the user? (c) Are there ways these systems could be harmful? What responsibilities do users of online expert systems have? (d) What responsibilities do providers of online expert systems have?

NOTES

System Software

After you have read this chapter, you should be able to:

1 Describe the differences between system software and application software.

2 Discuss the four types of system software.

3 Discuss the basic functions, features, and categories of operating systems.

4 Describe Windows, Mac OS, UNIX, Linux, and virtualization.

5 Describe the purpose of utilities and utility suites.

6 Identify the five most essential utilities.

7 Discuss Windows utility programs.

8 Describe device drivers, including Windows' Add a Device Wizard and Update.

Just a few years ago, the operating system installed on a computer determined much of its function. The application software you wanted to use may have only worked with one type of operating system. Today more applications are cross platforms, which means that the software runs on more than one operating system. And as more software becomes Web-based, the operating system becomes less central in the lives of daily users.

Some experts predict that in the future people might never really interact with the operating system on their computers at all. And because most software is moving to the Web, the user interface of the future will most likely take a form similar to a browser window. Imagine a world where your computer is like your TV. The inner workings of your TV, and the software that may be running behind the scenes, are unimportant. It's the content the TV connects to that really matters.

chapter 5

Introduction

When most people think about computers, they think about surfing the Web, creating reports, analyzing data, storing information, making presentations, and any number of other valuable applications. We typically think about applications and application software. Computers and computer applications have become a part of the fabric of our everyday lives. Most of us agree that they are great . . . as long as they are working.

We usually do not think about the more mundane and behind-the-scenes computer activities: loading and running programs, coordinating networks that share resources, organizing files, protecting our computers from viruses, performing periodic maintenance to avoid problems, and controlling hardware devices so that they can communicate with one another. Typically, these activities go on behind the scenes without our help.

That is the way it should be, and the way it is, as long as everything is working perfectly. But what if new application programs are not compatible and will not run on our current computer system? What if we get a computer virus? What if our hard disk fails? What if we buy a new digital video camera and can't store and edit the images on our computer system? What if our computer starts to run slower and slower?

These issues may seem mundane, but they are critical. This chapter covers the vital activities that go on behind the scenes. A little knowledge about these activities can go a long way to making your computing life easier. To effectively use computers, competent end users need to understand the functionality of system software, including operating systems, utility programs, and device drivers.

System Software

End users use application software to accomplish specific tasks. For example, we use word processors to create letters, documents, and reports. However, end users also use system software. **System software** works with end users, application software, and computer hardware to handle the majority of technical details. For example, system software controls where a word processing program is stored in memory, how commands are converted so that the system unit can process them, and where a completed document or file is saved. See Figure 5-1.

System software is not a single program. Rather it is a collection or a system of programs that handle hundreds of technical details with little or no user intervention. System software consists of four types of programs:

- **Operating systems** coordinate computer resources, provide an interface between users and the computer, and run applications.
- **Utilities** perform specific tasks related to managing computer resources.
- **Device drivers** are specialized programs that allow particular input or output devices to communicate with the rest of the computer system.
- **Language translators** convert the programming instructions written by programmers into a language that computers understand and process.

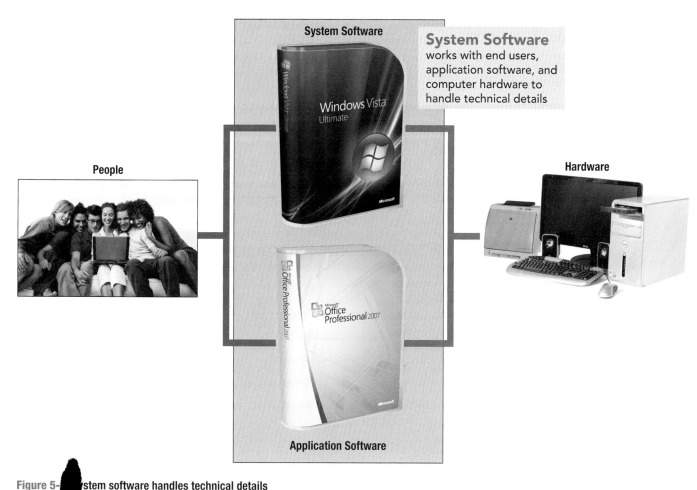

People

System Software

System Software works with end users, application software, and computer hardware to handle technical details

Hardware

Application Software

Figure 5- stem software handles technical details

Operating Systems

An **operating system** is a collection of programs that handle many of the technical details related to using a computer. In many ways, an operating system is the most important type of computer program. Without a functioning operating system, your computer would be useless.

Functions

Every computer has an operating system and every operating system performs a variety of functions. These functions can be classified into three groups:

- **Managing resources:** Operating systems coordinate all the computer's resources including memory, processing, storage, and devices such as printers and monitors. They also monitor system performance, schedule tasks, provide security, and start up the computer.
- **Providing user interface:** Operating systems allow users to interact with application programs and computer hardware through a **user interface.** Many older operating systems used a character-based interface in which users communicated with the operating system through written commands such as "Copy A: assign.doc C:". Almost all newer operating systems

use a **graphical user interface (GUI).** As we discussed in Chapter 3, a graphical user interface uses graphical elements such as icons and windows.

- **Running applications:** Operating systems load and run applications such as word processors and spreadsheets. Most operating systems support **multitasking,** or the ability to switch between different applications stored in memory. With multitasking, you could have Word and Excel running at the same time and switch easily between the two applications.

Features

Starting or restarting a computer is called **booting** the system. There are two ways to boot a computer: a warm boot and a cold boot. A **warm boot** occurs when the computer is already on and you restart it without turning off the power. A warm boot can be accomplished in several ways. For many computer systems, they can be restarted by simply pressing a sequence of keys. Starting a computer that has been turned off is called a **cold boot.** To learn more about booting your computer system and POST (power on self-test), visit our Web site at www.computing2011.com and enter the keyword boot.

You typically interact with the operating system through the graphical user interface. Most provide a place, called the **desktop,** that provides access to computer resources. (See Figure 5-2.) Operating systems have several features in common with application programs, including

- **Icons**—graphic representations for a program, type of file, or function.
- **Pointer**—controlled by a mouse, trackpad, or touchscreen, the pointer changes shape depending upon its current function. For example, when shaped like an arrow, the pointer can be used to select items such as an icon.
- **Windows**—rectangular areas for displaying information and running programs.
- **Menus**—provide a list of options or commands.
- **Dialog boxes**—provide information or request input.
- **Help**—provides online assistance for operating system function procedures.

Most operating systems store data and programs in a systems and folders. Unlike the traditional filing cabinet, computer files aners are stored on a storage device such as your hard disk. **Files** are useore data and programs. Related files are stored within a **folder,** and fornizational purposes, a folder can contain other folders. For example, youight organize

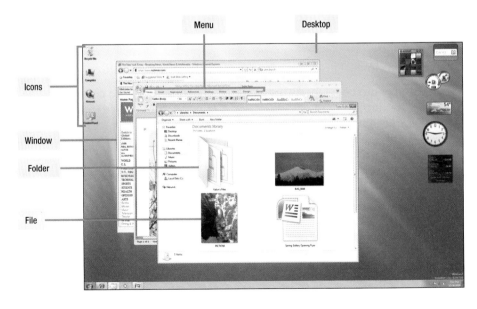

Figure 5-2 Desktop

your electronic files in the *My Documents* folder on your hard disk. This folder could contain other folders, each named to indicate its contents. One might be "Computers" and could contain all the files you have created (or will create) for this course.

Categories

While there are hundreds of different operating systems, there are only three basic categories: embedded, network, or stand-alone.

- **Embedded operating systems** are used for handheld devices such as smart phones, cable and satellite television tuner boxes, video game systems, and other small electronics. (See Figure 5-3.) The entire operating system is stored within or embedded in the device. The operating system programs are permanently stored on ROM, or read-only memory, chips. Popular embedded operating systems include Windows CE and Windows XP Embedded.

- **Network operating systems (NOS)** are used to control and coordinate computers that are networked or linked together. Many networks are small and connect only a limited number of microcomputers. Other networks, like those at colleges and universities, are very large and complex. These networks may include other smaller networks and typically connect a variety of different types of computers.

  Network operating systems are typically located on one of the connected computers' hard disks. Called the **network server,** this computer coordinates all communication between the other computers. Popular network operating systems include NetWare, Windows Server, and UNIX.

- **Stand-alone operating systems,** also called **desktop operating systems,** control a single desktop or notebook computer. (See Figure 5-4.)

Figure 5-3 Handheld devices have embedded operating systems

Figure 5-4 Stand-alone operating system

These operating systems are located on the computer's hard disk. Often desktop computers and notebooks are part of a network. In these cases, the desktop operating system works with the network's NOS to share and coordinate resources. In these situations, the desktop operating system is referred to as the *client operating system*. Popular desktop operating systems include Windows, Mac OS, and various versions of UNIX and Linux.

The operating system is often referred to as the **software environment** or **platform.** Almost all application programs are designed to run with a specific platform. For example, Apple's iMovie software is designed to run with the Mac OS environment. Many applications, however, have different versions, each designed to operate with a particular platform. For example, one version of Microsoft Office is designed to operate with Windows. Another version is designed to operate with Mac OS.

 CONCEPT CHECK

 What is system software? What are the four kinds of system software programs?

 What is an operating system? Discuss operating system functions and features.

 Describe each of the three categories of operating systems.

Windows

Microsoft's **Windows** is by far the most popular microcomputer operating system today with nearly 90 percent of the market. Because its market share is so large, more application programs are developed to run under Windows than any other operating system. Windows comes in a variety of different versions and is designed to run with Intel and Intel-compatible microprocessors such as the Core 2 Quad and Atom series. For a summary of Microsoft's desktop operating systems, see Figure 5-5.

There are many versions of Windows. The latest, **Windows 7,** was released in 2009. (See Figure 5-6.) Compared to the previous system, **Windows Vista,** Windows 7 provides several improvements including:

- Improved handwriting recognition for tablet computers.
- A taskbar that features previews, large icons, and personalization features.
- Advanced searching capabilities for finding files and content on your computer.

Name	Description
Windows 98	Stand-alone operating system
Windows 2000 Professional	Upgrade to Windows NT Workstation
Windows ME	Upgrade to Windows 98 specifically designed for home users
Windows XP	Upgrade to Windows 2000 with improved interface, stability, and reliability
Windows Vista	Upgrade to Windows XP with improved security, three-dimensional workspace, and filtering capabilities.
Windows 7	Microsoft's latest operating system with improved user experience, speed, and stability

Figure 5-5 Microsoft desktop operating systems

Figure 5-6 Windows 7

Mac OS

Apple introduced its Macintosh microcomputer and operating system in 1984. It provided one of the first GUIs, making it easy even for novice computer users to move and delete files. Designed to run with Apple computers, **Mac OS** is not nearly as widely used as the Windows operating system. As a result, fewer application programs have been written for it. Nonetheless, Mac OS is considered to be one of the most innovative operating systems. It is a powerful, easy-to-use operating system that is popular with professional graphic designers, desktop publishers, and many home users.

One of the latest versions of the Macintosh operating system is **Mac OS X.** (See Figure 5-7.) This operating system provides a wide array of powerful features including Spotlight and Dashboard Widgets. **Spotlight** is an advanced search tool that can rapidly locate files, folders, e-mail messages, addresses, and much more. **Dashboard Widgets** are a collection of specialized programs that will constantly update and display information. Some versions of Mac OS X also include **Boot Camp,** which allows Macintosh computers to run both the Mac OS and the Windows operating system.

Unix and Linux

The **UNIX** operating system was originally designed to run on minicomputers in network environments. Now, it is also used by powerful microcomputers and by servers on the Web. There are a large number of different versions of UNIX. One receiving a great deal of attention today is **Linux.**

Figure 5-7 Mac OS X

Linux was originally developed by a graduate student at the University of Helsinki, Linus Torvalds, in 1991. He allowed free distribution of the operating system code and encouraged others to modify and further develop the code. Linux is a popular and powerful alternative to the Windows operating system. (See Figure 5-8.)

Virtualization

As we have discussed, application programs are designed to run with particular operating systems. What if you wanted to run two or more applications each requiring a different operating system? One solution would be to install each of the operating systems on a different computer. There is, however, a way in which a single physical computer can support multiple operating systems that operate independently. This approach is called **virtualization.**

With **virtualization software,** the physical machine can be logically separated into separate and independent virtual computers known as **virtual machines.** Each virtual machine appears to the user as a separate independent computer with its own operating system. The operating system of the physical machine is known as the **host operating system.** The operating system for each virtual machine is known as the **guest operating system.** Users can readily switch between virtual computers and programs running on them. (See Figure 5-9.)

 CONCEPT CHECK

What is Windows? What is Windows Vista? What is Windows 7?

What is Mac OS? Spotlight? Dashboard Widgets? Boot Camp?

What is UNIX? What is Linux?

What are virtualization and virtualization software? What are host and guest operating systems?

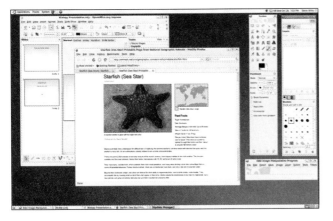

Figure 5-8 Linux

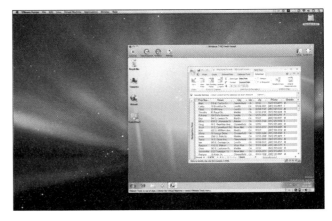

Figure 5-9 Windows 7 running within a window on the Mac OS X operating system

Utilities

Ideally, microcomputers would continuously run without problems. However, that simply is not the case. All kinds of things can happen—internal hard disks can crash, computers can freeze up, operations can slow down, and so on. These events can make computing very frustrating. That's where utilities come in. **Utilities** are specialized programs designed to make computing easier. There are hundreds of different utility programs. The most essential are

- **Troubleshooting** or **diagnostic programs** that recognize and correct problems, ideally before they become serious.
- **Antivirus programs** that guard your computer system against viruses or other damaging programs that can invade your computer system.
- **Uninstall programs** that allow you to safely and completely remove unneeded programs and related files from your hard disk.
- **Backup programs** that make copies of files to be used in case the originals are lost or damaged.
- **File compression programs** that reduce the size of files so they require less storage space and can be sent more efficiently over the Internet.

Did you know you can search the content of e-mail messages, files, notes and contacts all at once using a simple utility in Windows Vista? Here's how:

1 Click *Start* and begin typing the term you want to search for into the *Search Programs and Files* blank.

2 As you type, a list of files and other items containing your search term is displayed.

3 Continue typing to further narrow the list, or click an item in the list to view it instantly.

To see additional tips, visit our Web site at www.computing2011.com and enter the keyword tips.

Most operating systems provide some utility programs. Even more powerful utility programs can be purchased separately or in utility suites.

Windows Utilities

The Windows operating systems are accompanied by several utility programs, including Backup and Restore, Disk Cleanup, and Disk Defragmenter.

Backup and Restore is a utility program included with the many versions of Windows that makes a copy of all files or selected files that have been saved onto a disk. It helps to protect you from the effects of a disk failure. For example, you can select *Backup and Restore* from the Windows 7 Maintenance menu to create a backup for your hard disk as shown in Figure 5-10.

When you surf the Web, a variety of programs and files are saved on your hard disk. Many of these and other files are not essential. **Disk Cleanup** is a troubleshooting utility that identifies and eliminates nonessential files. This frees up valuable disk space and improves system performance.

For example, by selecting Disk Cleanup from the Windows 7 System Tools menu, you can eliminate unneeded files on your hard disk as shown in Figure 5-11.

As we will discuss in detail in Chapter 8, files are stored and organized on a disk according to tracks and sectors. A **track** is a concentric ring. Each track is divided into wedge-shaped sections called **sectors.** (See Figure 5-12.) The operating system tries to save a file on a single track across contiguous sectors. Often, however, this is not possible and the file has to be broken up, or **fragmented,** into small parts that are stored wherever space is available. Whenever a file is retrieved, it is reconstructed from the fragments. After a period of time, a hard disk becomes highly fragmented, slowing operations.

1 Click *Start*, and then select *Maintenance* from the *All Programs* menu.

● Select *Backup and Restore*, and then click *Set up backup*.

● Choose the destination for the backup.

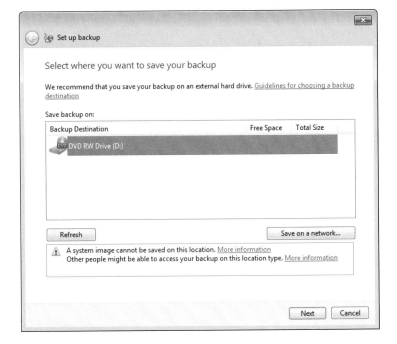

2 Choose the files you want to back up.

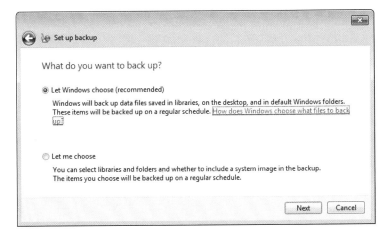

3 Set up Backup Wizard to back up the selected files.

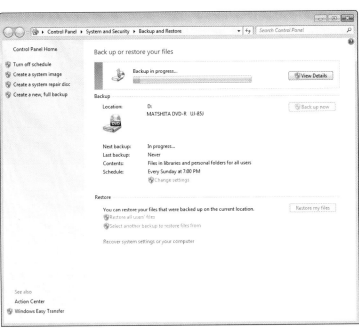

Figure 5-10 Backup and Restore utility

1 Click *Start*, and then select *Accessories* from the *All Programs* menu.

• Select *Disk Cleanup* from the *System Tools* menu.

• Review the files suggested for cleanup, and then click *OK*.

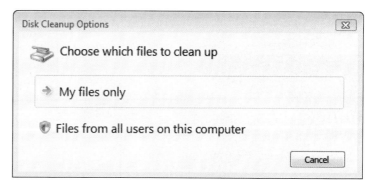

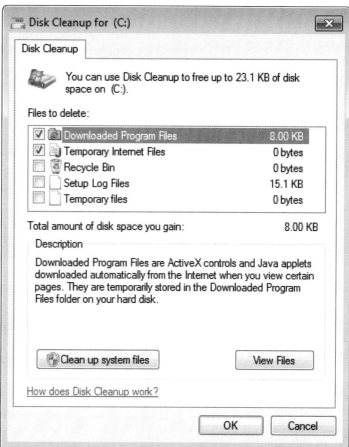

2 The utility cleans the selected files.

Figure 5-11 Disk Cleanup utility

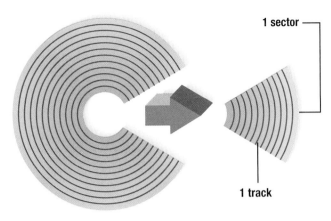

1 sector

1 track

Figure 5-12 Tracks and sectors

Disk Defragmenter is a utility program that locates and eliminates unnecessary fragments and rearranges files and unused disk space to optimize operations. For example, by selecting Disk Defragmenter from the Windows 7 System Tools menu, you can defrag your hard disk as shown in Figure 5-13.

Utility Suites

Like application software suites, **utility suites** combine several programs into one package. Buying the package is less expensive than buying the programs separately. The three best-known utility suites are McAfee Office, Norton SystemWorks, and V Communications System-Suite. (See Figure 5-14.) These suites provide a variety of utilities, including programs that will protect your system from dangerous programs called computer **viruses.** You can "catch" a computer virus many ways, including by opening attachments to e-mail messages and downloading software from the Internet. (We will discuss computer viruses in detail in Chapter 10.)

① Click *Start.*

 Select *Accessories* from the *All Programs* menu.

 Select *Disk Defragmenter* from the *System Tools* menu. If necessary, click *Continue.*

② Click the *Defragment disk* button to begin defragging.

 If necessary, choose the drive you want to defragment.

 When defragmentation is complete for the selected drive, view the report or close the window.

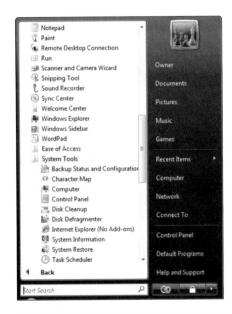

Figure 5-13 Disk Defragmenter utility

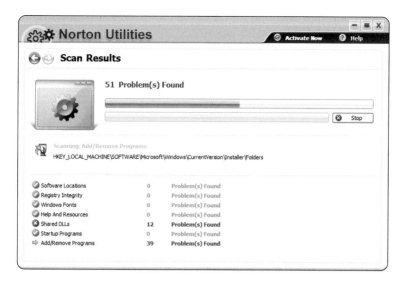

Figure 5-14 **Norton SystemWorks**

To learn more about virus protection, visit our Web site at www.computing 2011.com and enter the keyword **virus.** Also see Making IT Work for You: Virus Protection and Internet Security on pages 140 and 141.

CONCEPT CHECK

Discuss the five most essential utilities.

Describe Windows Backup and Restore, Disk Cleanup, and Disk Defragmenter.

What is the difference between a utility and a utility suite?

Device Drivers

Every device, such as a mouse or printer, that is connected to a computer system has a special program associated with it. This program, called a **device driver** or simply a **driver,** works with the operating system to allow communication between the device and the rest of the computer system. Each time the computer system is started, the operating system loads all of the device drivers into memory.

Whenever a new device is added to a computer system, a new device driver must be installed before the device can be used. Windows supplies hundreds of different device drivers with its system software. For many devices, the appropriate drivers are automatically selected and installed when the device is first connected to the computer system. For others, the device driver must be manually installed. Fortunately, Windows provides wizards to assist in this process. For example, Windows' **Add a Device Wizard** provides step-by-step guidance for selecting the appropriate hardware driver and installing that driver. If a particular device driver is not included with the Windows system software, the product's manufacturer will supply one. Many times these drivers are available directly from the manufacturer's Web site.

You probably never think about the device drivers in your computer. However, when your computer behaves unpredictably, you may find reinstalling or updating

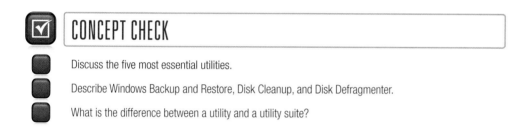

On the Web Explorations

Utility software can make your computer faster, safer, and more productive.

To learn more about a market leader of utility software, visit our Web site at www.computing2011.com and enter the keyword utility.

Making IT work for you

VIRUS PROTECTION AND INTERNET SECURITY

Are you worried that a computer virus will erase your personal files? Did you know that others could be intercepting your private e-mail? It is even possible for others to gain access to and control over your computer system. Fortunately, Internet security suites are available to help ensure your safety while you are on the Internet.

Getting Started   The first step is to install an Internet security suite. Once installed, the software will continually work to ensure security and privacy. For example, to install McAfee Security Center follow the instructions below.

1 ● **Connect to www.mcafee.com and follow the instructions to subscribe to this Internet security suite.**

2 ● **Follow the instructions at the Web site to download and install the security suite on your computer.**

SecurityCenter McAfee SecurityCenter runs a number of programs continually to monitor your computer. Some of Security Center's most powerful features include VirusScan, PersonalFirewall, and SiteAdvisor. You can modify the way these programs run with the McAfee SecurityCenter.

VirusScan is a program that controls how frequently the computer system is searched for computer viruses. When a file is checked, it is compared to the profile of known viruses. Once a virus is detected, the infected file is quarantined or deleted.

PersonalFirewall is a program that monitors all inbound and outbound traffic to a computer system. It limits access to authorized users and applications.

SiteAdvisor is a program that helps protect your privacy online. It installs in your Web browser, and warns you of potentially harmful Web sites as you surf.

The Web is continually changing, and some of the specifics presented in this Making IT Work for You may have changed.

To learn about other ways to make information technology work for you, visit our Web site at www.computing2011.com and enter the keyword miw.

your device drivers solves your problems. Windows makes it easy to update the drivers on your computer using **Windows Update,** as shown in Figure 5-15.

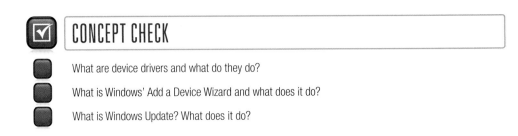

CONCEPT CHECK

What are device drivers and what do they do?

What is Windows' Add a Device Wizard and what does it do?

What is Windows Update? What does it do?

❶ Access *Windows Update* from the *All Programs* list of the *Start* menu.

Click *Check for updates.*

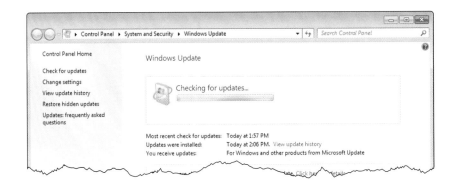

❷ Review the list of recommended updates.

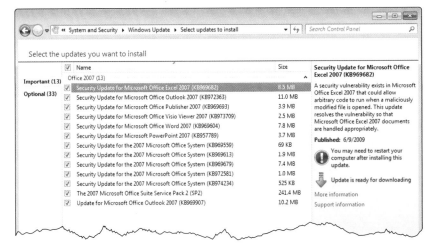

❸ Click *Install updates* to download updates to your computer.

Figure 5-15 Using Windows Update

Careers in IT

Computer support specialists provide technical support to customers and other users. (See Figure 5.16.) They also may be called technical support specialists or help-desk technicians. Computer support specialists manage the everyday technical problems faced by computer users. They resolve common networking problems and may use troubleshooting programs to diagnose problems. Most computer support specialists are hired to work within a company and provide technical support for other employees and divisions. However, it is increasingly common for companies to provide technical support as an outsourced service.

Employers generally look for individuals with a bachelor's degree to fill computer support specialist positions. Degrees in computer science or information systems may be preferred. However, because demand for qualified applicants is so high, those with practical experience and certification from a training program increasingly fill these positions. Employers seek individuals with good analytical and communication skills. Those with good people skills and customer service experience have an advantage in this field.

Computer support specialists can expect to earn an annual salary of $32,000 to $53,500. Opportunities for advancement are very good and may involve design and implementation of new systems. To learn about other careers in information systems, visit us at www.computing2011.com and enter the keyword **careers**.

Figure 5-16 Computer support specialist

A LOOK TO THE FUTURE

Self-Healing Computers Could Mean an End to Computer Crashes and Performance Problems

Wouldn't it be nice if computers could fix themselves? What if you never had to worry about installing or updating software? What if your computer could continually fine-tune its operations to maintain peak performance? What if your computer could fight off viruses and malicious attacks from outsiders? For many people, this sounds too good to be true. Maintenance and security tasks like these can be time-consuming and frustrating.

Now imagine you run a business and unless these tasks are performed, you will lose valuable time and money. It is not a pleasant daydream and it quickly becomes a nightmare without properly trained systems administrators to keep servers running smoothly. Yet many experts predict that supercomputers and business systems are not far from becoming too complex for humans to oversee. Recent news from IBM makes the dream of a self-repairing, self-updating, and self-protecting server seem ever closer.

IBM has announced plans to concentrate research efforts on developing just such a server. The project, called the Autonomic Computing Initiative (ACI), hopes to free businesses from the time-consuming maintenance and the complexity of business infrastructure. IBM hopes the new system will be self-regulating and virtually invisible. They believe ACI has the potential to revolutionize the way businesses run.

Autonomic computing is a system that allows machines to run with little human intervention. Such computers would not have self-awareness, but rather would be self-correcting. Autonomic processes in machines are modeled after autonomic processes in the human body. For example, you are not consciously breathing as you read this. Instead, your body monitors and maintains your respiration without your constant input. Scientists hope autonomic computing will behave in a similar manner and maintain self-regulating systems without intervention.

Autonomic machines would be able to sense security flaws and repair them. They would be able to sense slow computer operations and take corrective action. They would be able to sense new equipment, format it, and test it. These goals are impressive and the autonomic computer is still in development.

As technology continues to develop, many computer systems have become too complex for human maintenance. This progress makes autonomic computing more valuable now than ever. However, it is important to note that autonomic computing is not artificial intelligence because autonomic machines do not have human cognitive abilities or intelligence. Instead, these machines have knowledge of their own systems and the capability to learn from experiences to correct errors in such systems.

Given the potential for a self-maintaining server, the possibility of a similar system designed for a microcomputer seems less like a dream and more like a reality. What do you think—will microcomputers someday care for themselves?

SYSTEM SOFTWARE

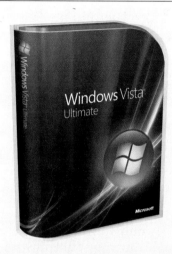

System software works with end users, application programs, and computer hardware to handle many details relating to computer operations.

Not a single program but a collection or system of programs, these programs handle hundreds of technical details with little or no user intervention.

Four kinds of systems programs are operating systems, utilities, device drivers, and language translators.

- **Operating systems** coordinate resources, provide an interface between users and the computer, and run programs.

- **Utilities** perform specific tasks related to managing computer resources.

- **Device drivers** allow particular input or output devices to communicate with the rest of the computer system.

- **Language translators** convert programming instructions written by programmers into a language that computers can understand and process.

OPERATING SYSTEMS

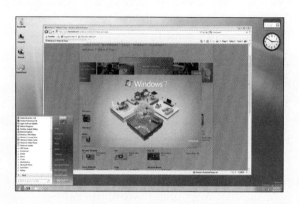

Operating systems (software environments, platforms) handle technical details.

Functions

Functions include managing resources, providing a **user interface** (most newer operating systems use a **graphical user interface,** or **GUI**), and running applications (**multitasking** allows switching between different applications stored in memory).

Features

Booting starts (**cold**) or restarts (**warm**) a computer system. The **desktop** provides access to computer resources. Common features include **icons, pointers, windows, menus, dialog boxes,** and **Help.** Data and programs are stored in a system of **files** and **folders.**

Categories

Three categories of operating systems are

- **Embedded**—used with handheld computers; operating system stored within device.

- **Network (NOS)**—controls and coordinates networked computers; located on the **network server.**

- **Stand-alone (desktop)**—controls a single computer; located on the hard disk.

Operating systems are often called **software environments** or **platforms.**

To effectively use computers, competent end users need to understand the functionality of system software, including operating systems, utility programs, and device drivers.

OPERATING SYSTEMS

Windows

Windows, the most widely used operating system, is designed to run with Intel and Intel-compatible microprocessors. There are numerous versions of Windows. **Windows 7** is the most recent version of Windows. It provides improved handwriting recognition; taskbar with previews, large icons, and personalization features; and advanced search capabilities.

Mac OS

Mac OS, an innovative, powerful, easy-to-use operating system, runs on Macintosh computers. Recent versions provide **Spotlight,** an advanced search tool, and **Dashboard Widgets,** a collection of specialized programs. Some versions of MAC OS X come with **Boot Camp,** which allows Macintosh computers to run both Mac OS and Windows operating systems.

UNIX and Linux

UNIX was originally designed to run on minicomputers in network environments. Now, it is used by powerful microcomputers and servers on the Web. There are many different versions of UNIX. One version, **Linux,** is a popular and powerful alternative to the Windows operating system.

Virtualization

Virtualization is a process that allows a single physical computer to support multiple operating systems that operate independently. **Virtualization software** creates **virtual machines. Host operating systems** run on the physical machine. **Guest operating systems** operate on virtual machines.

UTILITIES

Utilities make computing easier. The most essential are **troubleshooting (diagnostic), antivirus, uninstall, backup,** and **file compression.**

Windows Utilities

Windows operating systems are accompanied by several utility programs, including **Backup and Restore, Disk Cleanup,** and **Disk Defragmenter** (eliminates unnecessary **fragments; tracks** are concentric rings; **sectors** are wedge-shaped).

Utility Suites

Utility suites combine several programs into one package. Computer **viruses** are dangerous programs.

DEVICE DRIVERS

Device drivers (drivers) allow communication between hardware devices. **Add a Device Wizard** gives step-by-step guidance to install printer drivers. **Windows Update** automates the process of updating device drivers.

CAREERS IN IT

Computer support specialists provide technical support to customers and other users. Degrees in computer science or information systems are preferred plus good analytical and communication skills. Salary range $32,000 to $53,500.

KEY TERMS

Add a Device Wizard   (139)
antivirus program   (135)
Backup and Restore   (135)
backup program   (135)
Boot Camp   (133)
booting   (130)
cold boot   (130)
computer support specialist   (143)
Dashboard Widgets   (133)
desktop   (130)
desktop operating system   (131)
device driver (128, 139)
diagnostic program   (135)
dialog box   (130)
Disk Cleanup   (135)
Disk Defragmenter   (138)
driver   (139)
embedded operating systems   (131)
file   (130)
file compression program   (135)
folder   (130)
fragmented   (135)
graphical user interface (GUI)   (130)
guest operating system   (134)
Help   (130)
host operating system   (134)
icon   (130)
language translator   (128)
Linux   (133)
Mac OS   (133)

Mac OS X   (133)
menu   (130)
multitasking   (130)
network operating systems (NOS)   (131)
network server   (131)
operating system (128, 129)
platform   (132)
pointer   (130)
sector   (135)
software environment   (132)
Spotlight   (133)
stand-alone operating system   (131)
system software   (128)
track   (135)
troubleshooting program   (135)
uninstall program   (135)
UNIX   (133)
user interface   (129)
utility (128, 135)
utility suite   (138)
virtualization   (134)
virtualization software   (134)
virtual machine   (134)
virus   (138)
warm boot   (130)
window   (130)
Windows   (132)
Windows 7   (132)
Windows Update   (142)
Windows Vista   (132)

To test your knowledge of these key terms with animated flash cards, visit our Web site at www.computing2011.com and enter the keyword terms5.

MULTIPLE CHOICE

Circle the letter or fill in the correct answer.

1. Software that allows your computer to interact with the user, applications, and hardware is called
   a. application software
   b. word processor
   c. system software
   d. database software

2. In order for a computer to understand a program, it must be converted into machine language by a(n) _____.
   a. operating system
   b. utility
   c. device driver
   d. language translator

3. "GUI" stands for
   a. gnutella universal interface
   b. graphic uninstall/install
   c. graphical user interface
   d. general utility interface

4. A(n) _____ boot occurs when a computer is restarted without turning off the power.
   a. cold
   b. warm
   c. direct
   d. indirect

5. _____ is the most widely used operating system.
   a. Windows
   b. Mac OS
   c. UNIX
   d. Linux

6. This operating system is most popular with graphic designers and those who work in multimedia.
   a. Windows Vista
   b. Linux
   c. Mac OS
   d. UNIX

7. This operating system was originally designed to run on minicomputers used in a network environment.
   a. Linux
   b. UNIX
   c. Windows
   d. Mac OS

8. A concentric ring on a hard disk is referred to as a
   a. track
   b. sector
   c. table
   d. segment

9. These programs guard your computer against malicious programs that may invade your computer system.
   a. file compression program
   b. antivirus program
   c. backup program
   d. troubleshooting program

10. Every time the computer system is started, the operating system loads these into memory.
    a. driver updates
    b. device managers
    c. device drivers
    d. Windows updates

For an interactive multiple-choice practice test, visit our Web site at www.computing2011.com and enter the keyword multiple5.

MATCHING

Match each numbered item with the most closely related lettered item. Write your answers in the spaces provided.

a. desktop OS
b. embedded OS
c. file compression program
d. Linux
e. multitasking
f. NOS
g. platform
h. Spotlight
i. system software
j. track

1. Concentric ring on a disk. _____
2. An advanced search tool. _____
3. A computer's ability to run more than one application at a time. _____
4. Operating systems completely stored within ROM. _____
5. Operating system used to control and coordinate computers that are linked together. _____
6. Another name for software environment. _____
7. An operating system located on a single stand-alone hard disk. _____
8. One popular, and free, version of the UNIX operating system. _____
9. Collection of programs that handle technical details. _____
10. Program that reduces the size of files for efficient storage. _____

For an interactive matching practice test, visit our Web site at www.computing2011.com and enter the keyword matching5.

OPEN-ENDED

On a separate sheet of paper, respond to each question or statement.

1. Describe system software. What are the four types of system programs?
2. What are the basic functions of every operating system? What are the three basic operating system categories?
3. Explain the differences and similarities between Windows, Mac OS, and Linux. Discuss visualization.
4. Discuss utilities. What are the five most essential utilities? What is a utility suite?
5. Explain the role of device drivers. Discuss the Add a Device Wizard and Windows Update.

APPLYING TECHNOLOGY

The following questions are designed to demonstrate ways that you can effectively use technology today. The first question relates directly to this chapter's Making IT Work for You feature.

VIRUS PROTECTION

Worried about computer viruses? Did you know that others could be intercepting your private e-mail? It is even possible for them to gain access and control over your computer systems. Fortunately, Internet security suites are available to help ensure your safety while you are on the Internet. To learn more about virus protection, review Making IT Work for You: Virus Protection and Internet Security on pages 140 and 141. Then answer the following questions: (a) What are viruses? What are Internet security suites? What do they do? (b) Have you ever experienced a computer virus? If you have, describe the virus, how you got it, and what you did to get rid of it. If you have not, have you taken any special precautions? Discuss the precautions. Do you think it's possible that you may have one now and not know it, or do you think that you have just been lucky? (c) What is a personal firewall? What does it do?

WINDOWS UPDATE

Windows Update is a utility built into Windows that monitors and controls the process of keeping the computer up to date. Connect to our Web site at www.computing2011.com and enter the keyword update to link to the Windows Update Web site. Read the information about Windows Update. Then answer the following questions: (a) How does Windows Update work? (b) How does a user know when he or she requires an update? (c) What is the process for initiating an update using Windows Update? (d) In what ways can Windows Update be automated?

③ DISK DEFRAGMENTATION

In addition to the Disk Defragmenter utility built in to Windows, several products are available to perform this task and help improve your computer's performance. Visit our Web site at www.computing2011.com and enter the keyword defrag to learn more about one of these utilities. Then answer the following: (a) What is fragmentation? (b) How does this utility correct fragmentation? (b) Can this utility be automated to run on a regular schedule? (d) What is the procedure to automate this utility? Be specific.

EXPANDING YOUR KNOWLEDGE

The following questions are designed to add depth and detail to your understanding of specific topics presented within this chapter. The questions direct you to sources other than the textbook to obtain this knowledge.

1 HOW VIRUS PROTECTION PROGRAMS WORK

Computer viruses are destructive and dangerous programs that can migrate through networks and operating systems. They often attach themselves to other programs, e-mail messages, and databases. It is essential to protect your computer system from computer viruses. To learn how virus protection programs work, visit our Web site at www.computing2011.com and enter the keyword virus. Then answer the following: (a) Briefly describe the four steps taken by virus protection programs. (b) What is signature scanning? (c) What is heuristic detection and how is it different from signature scanning? (d) Do you use a virus protection program? If yes, what program(s) do you use and has it been effective? If no, do you plan to in the near future? Why or why not?

2 BOOTING AND POST

Computers do a considerable amount of work before a user even hits a key. Knowing how a computer starts up can be an invaluable tool for fixing a broken computer or getting working computers to run at peak efficiency. To learn how a computer starts up, visit our Web site at www.computing 2011.com and enter the keyword boot. Then answer the following: (a) Briefly describe the four steps of a cold boot. (b) When booting up, what does the microprocessor do first? (c) What does BIOS stand for? (d) Advanced users often customize their BIOS and POST. What benefits can users achieve by modifying their BIOS or POST?

3 CUSTOMIZED DESKTOP

There are several ways to customize your computer's desktop to make it more interesting, informative, or efficient. To learn about customizations, connect to our Web site at www.computing2011.com and enter the keyword desktop, and then address the following: (a) Summarize some of the customizations you found. (b) Briefly explain how these customizations are added to a user's computer. (c) Explain how customization could make your computing experience more enjoyable or productive.

WRITING ABOUT TECHNOLOGY

The ability to think critically and to write effectively is essential to nearly every profession. The following questions are designed to help you develop these skills by posing thought-provoking questions about computer privacy, security, and/or ethics.

1 OPEN SOURCE

The Linux operating system is one of the most famous examples of open source software. In an open source model, the underlying code for an application is freely available for other computer programmers to improve and redistribute it. This is much different from traditional models of development in which software companies hold the copyright to software and prevent others from imitating it. Research the concept of open source software and write a one-page paper responding to the following questions: (a) What is the basic licensing model for open source projects? (b) What are some examples of corporations that have supported or contributed to open source projects? (c) What might be some of the benefits of open source development? What are some of the drawbacks? Explain your answer.

2 ONLINE BACKUP

One of the best ways to safeguard important personal or corporate data is to use an online backup service. Research three or four online backup services and then answer the following questions in a one-page paper: (a) What are the general features of online backup services? (b) What types of emergencies do online backups help with that other backup methods do not? (c) How are backups scheduled? (d) Is this service a replacement for making backups locally? Why or why not?

NOTES

The System Unit

Competencies

After you have read this chapter, you should be able to:

1. Describe the six basic types of system units.

2. Discuss how a computer can represent numbers and encode characters electronically.

3. Describe each of the major system unit components.

4. Discuss microprocessors, including microprocessor chips and specialty processors.

5. Discuss memory including RAM, ROM, and flash memory.

6. Discuss expansion slots and cards.

7. Describe five principal types of expansion buses.

8. Compare standard, specialized, and legacy ports.

9. Discuss power supply for desktop and notebook computers.

The first computer ever built was too big to fit into a modern home, but today's computer chips are smaller than our fingertips. These tiny circuits are the brains inside your computer. They run the video game you are playing *and* keep track of the tiny movements of your mouse as you play.

chapter 6

Introduction

Why are some microcomputers more powerful than others? The answer lies in three words: speed, capacity, and flexibility. After reading this chapter, you will be able to judge how fast, powerful, and versatile a particular microcomputer is. As you might expect, this knowledge is valuable if you are planning to buy a new microcomputer system or to upgrade an existing system. (The Buyer's Guide and the Upgrader's Guide at the end of this book provide additional information.) It also will help you to evaluate whether or not an existing microcomputer system is powerful enough for today's new and exciting applications. For example, with the right hardware, you can use your computer to watch TV while you work and to capture video clips for class presentations.

Sometime you may get the chance to watch when a technician opens up a microcomputer. You will see that it is basically a collection of electronic circuitry. While there is no need to understand how all these components work, it is important to understand the principles. Once you do, you will be able to determine how powerful a particular microcomputer is. This will help you judge whether it can run particular kinds of programs and can meet your needs as a user.

Competent end users need to understand the functionality of the basic components in the system unit, including the system board, microprocessor, memory, expansion slots and cards, bus lines, ports, cables, and power supply units.

System Unit

The **system unit,** also known as the **system chassis,** is a container that houses most of the electronic components that make up a computer system. There are a variety of different categories or types of system units.

Categories

All computer systems have a system unit. For microcomputers, there are six basic types (see Figure 6-1):

- **Desktop system units** typically contain the system's electronic components and selected secondary storage devices. Input and output devices, such as a mouse, keyboard, and monitor, are located outside the system unit. This type of system unit is designed to be placed either horizontally or vertically.
- **Media center system units** blur the line between desktop computers and dedicated entertainment devices. Media center system units use powerful desktop system hardware with specialized graphics cards for interfacing with televisions and other home entertainment devices. A special operating system like Microsoft Windows Media Center provides on-demand TV programs, movies, music, and games.
- **Notebook system units** are portable and much smaller. These system units contain the electronic components, selected secondary storage devices, and input devices (keyboard and pointing device). Located outside the system unit, the monitor is attached by hinges. Notebook system units are often called **laptops.**
- **Netbook system units** are similar to notebook system units. They are, however, smaller, less powerful, and less expensive. **Netbooks** are designed to support on-the-go Web browsing and e-mail access. They reduce space and weight by leaving out components such as optical drives.
- **Tablet PC system units** are similar to notebook system units. **Tablet PCs** are highly portable devices that support the use of a stylus or pen to input

Desktop

Media Center

Notebook

Netbook

Tablet PC

Handheld

Figure 6-1 Basic types of system units

commands and data. There are two basic types. One type is effectively a notebook computer that accepts stylus input and has a monitor that swivels and folds onto its keyboard. The other type has a removable keyboard. With the keyboard attached, this second type can be used like a traditional notebook computer. With the keyboard detached, the unit is more portable and all input is typically with a stylus.

• **Handheld computer system units** are the smallest and are designed to fit into the palm of one hand. These systems contain an entire computer system, including the electronic components, secondary storage, and input and output devices. **Personal digital assistants (PDAs)** and **smartphones** are the most widely used handheld computers.

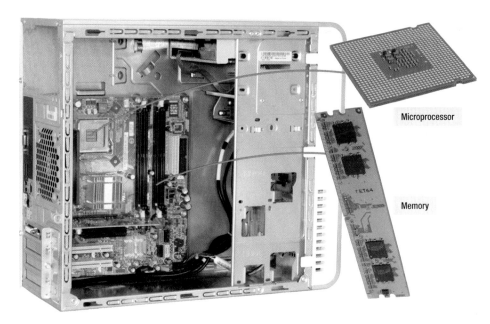

Figure 6-2 **System unit components**

Components

While the actual size may vary, each type of system unit has the same basic system components including system board, microprocessor, and memory. (See Figure 6-2.) Before considering these components, however, a more basic issue must be addressed. How do we as human beings communicate with and control all this electronic circuitry?

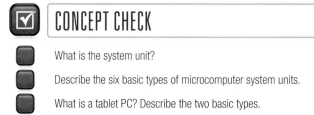

CONCEPT CHECK

What is the system unit?

Describe the six basic types of microcomputer system units.

What is a tablet PC? Describe the two basic types.

Electronic Data and Instructions

Have you ever wondered why it is said that we live in a digital world? It's because computers cannot recognize information the same way you and I can. People follow instructions and process data using letters, numbers, and special characters. For example, if we wanted someone to add the numbers 3 and 5 together and record the answer, we might say "please add 3 and 5." The system unit, however, is electronic circuitry and cannot directly process such a request.

Our voices create **analog,** or continuous, signals that vary to represent different tones, pitches, and volume. Computers, however, can recognize only **digital** electronic signals. Before any processing can occur within the system unit, a conversion must occur from what we understand to what the system unit can electronically process.

Numeric Representation

What is the most fundamental statement you can make about electricity? It is simply this: It can be either on or off. Indeed, there are many forms of technology that can make use of this two-state on/off, yes/no, present/absent arrangement. For instance, a light switch may be on or off, or an electric circuit open or closed. A specific location on a tape or disk may have a positive charge or a negative charge. This is the reason, then, that a two-state or binary system is used to represent data and instructions.

The decimal system that we are all familiar with has 10 digits (0, 1, 2, 3, 4, 5, 6, 7, 8, 9). The **binary system,** however, consists of only two digits—0 and 1. Each 0 or 1 is called a **bit**—short for binary digit. In the system unit, the 1 can be represented by a positive charge and the 0 by no electrical charge. In order to represent numbers, letters, and special characters, bits are combined into groups of eight called **bytes.** Whenever you enter a number into a computer system, that number must be converted into a binary number before it can be processed. To learn more about binary systems and binary arithmetic, visit our Web site at www.computing2011.com and enter the keyword binary.

Any number can be expressed as a binary number. Binary numbers, however, are difficult for humans to work with because they require so many digits. Instead, binary numbers are often represented in a format more readable by humans. The **hexadecimal system,** or **hex,** uses 16 digits (0, 1, 2, 3, 4, 5, 6, 7, 8, 9, A, B, C, D, E, F) to represent binary numbers. Each hex digit represents four binary digits, and two hex digits are commonly used together to represent 1 byte (8 binary digits). (See Figure 6-3.) You may have already seen hex when selecting a color in a Web site design or drawing application, or when entering the password for access to a wireless network.

Decimal	Binary	Hex
0	00000000	00
1	00000001	01
2	00000010	02
3	00000011	03
4	00000100	04
5	00000101	05
6	00000110	06
7	00000111	07
8	00001000	08
9	00001001	09
10	00001010	0A
11	00001011	0B
12	00001100	0C
13	00001101	0D
14	00001110	0E
15	00001111	0F

Figure 6-3 Numeric representations

Character Encoding

As we've seen, computers must represent all numbers with the binary system internally. What about text? How can a computer provide representations of the nonnumeric characters we use to communicate, such as the sentence you are reading now? The answer is character encoding schemes or standards.

Character encoding standards assign a unique sequence of bits to each character. Historically, microcomputers used the **ASCII (American Standard Code for Information Interchange)** to represent characters while mainframe computers used **EBCDIC (Extended Binary Coded Decimal Interchange Code).** These schemes were quite effective; however, they are limited. ASCII, for example, only uses 7 bits to represent each character, which means that only 128 total characters could be represented. This was fine for most characters in the English language but was not large enough to support other languages such as Chinese and Japanese. These languages have too many characters to be represented by the 7-bit ASCII code.

The explosion of the Internet and subsequent globalization of computing has led to a new character encoding called **Unicode.** The Unicode standard is the most widely used character encoding standard and is recognized by virtually every computer system. The first 128 characters are assigned the same sequence of bits as ASCII to maintain compatibility with older ASCII-formatted information. However, Unicode uses a variable number of bits to represent each character, which allows non-English characters and special characters to be represented.

CONCEPT CHECK

What is the difference between an analog and a digital electronic signal?

What are decimal and binary systems? How are they different?

Compare EBCDIC, ASCII, and Unicode.

System Board

On the Web Explorations

Improvements in system unit components are being made every day.

To learn more about a company on the forefront of these technologies, visit our Web site at www.computing2011.com and enter the keyword component.

The **system board** is also known as the **motherboard.** The system board controls communications for the entire computer system. Every component of the system unit connects to the system board. It acts as a data path and traffic monitor, allowing the various components to communicate efficiently with one another. External devices such as the keyboard, mouse, and monitor could not communicate with the system unit without the system board.

On a desktop computer, the system board is typically located at the bottom of the system unit or along one side. It is a large flat circuit board covered with a variety of different electronic components including sockets, slots, and bus lines. (See Figure 6-4.)

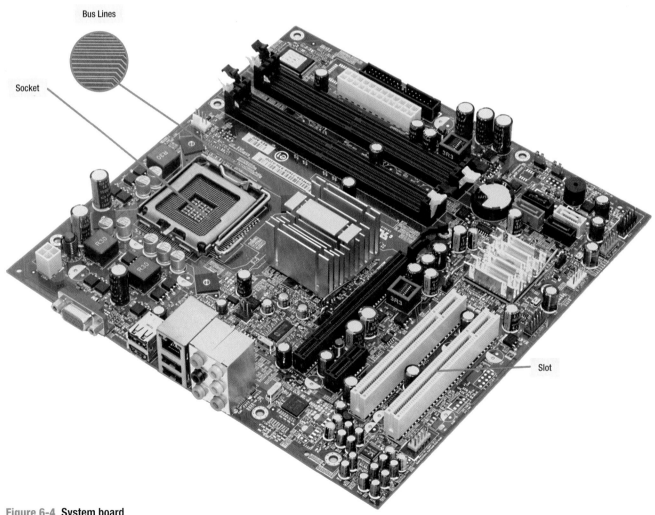

Figure 6-4 **System board**

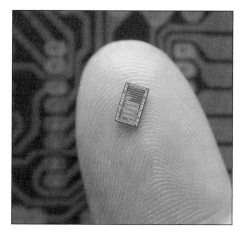

Figure 6-5 **Chip**

Figure 6-6 **Chip mounted onto a carrier package**

- **Sockets** provide a connection point for small specialized electronic parts called chips. **Chips** consist of tiny circuit boards etched onto squares of sandlike material called silicon. These circuit boards can be smaller than the tip of your finger. (See Figure 6-5.) A chip is also called a **silicon chip, semiconductor,** or **integrated circuit.** Chips are mounted on **carrier packages.** (See Figure 6-6.) These packages either plug directly into sockets on the system board or onto cards that are then plugged into slots on the system board. Sockets are used to connect the system board to a variety of different types of chips, including microprocessor and memory chips.
- **Slots** provide a connection point for specialized cards or circuit boards. These cards provide expansion capability for a computer system. For example, a modem card plugs into a slot on the system board to provide a connection to the Internet.
- Connecting lines called **bus lines** provide pathways that support communication among the various electronic components that are either located on the system board or attached to the system board. (See Figure 6-7.)

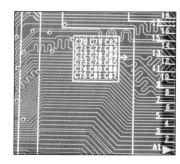

Figure 6-7 **Bus lines**

Notebook, tablet PC, and handheld system boards are smaller than desktop system boards. However, they perform the same functions as desktop system boards.

 CONCEPT CHECK

 What is the system board and what does it do?

 Define and describe sockets, slots, and bus lines.

 What are chips? How are chips attached to the system board?

Microprocessor

In a microcomputer system, the **central processing unit (CPU)** or **processor** is contained on a single chip called the **microprocessor.** The microprocessor is the "brains" of the computer system. It has two basic components: the control unit and the arithmetic-logic unit.

Unit	Speed
Microsecond	Millionth of a second
Nanosecond	Billionth of a second
Picosecond	Trillionth of a second

Figure 6-8 Processing speeds

On the Web Explorations

The most powerful microprocessors are capable of multicore and 64-bit processing.

To learn more about one of the manufacturers of these chips, visit our Web site at www.computing2011.com and enter the keyword multi.

- **Control unit:** The **control unit** tells the rest of the computer system how to carry out a program's instructions. It directs the movement of electronic signals between memory, which temporarily holds data, instructions, and processed information, and the arithmetic-logic unit. It also directs these control signals between the CPU and input and output devices.
- **Arithmetic-logic unit:** The **arithmetic-logic unit,** usually called the **ALU,** performs two types of operations: arithmetic and logical. **Arithmetic operations** are, as you might expect, the fundamental math operations: addition, subtraction, multiplication, and division. **Logical operations** consist of comparisons. That is, two pieces of data are compared to see whether one is equal to (=), less than (<), or greater than (>) the other.

Microprocessor Chips

Chip processing capacities are often expressed in word sizes. A **word** is the number of bits (such as 16, 32, or 64) that can be accessed at one time by the CPU. The more bits in a word, the more data a computer can process at one time. As mentioned previously, eight bits group together to form a byte. A 32-bit-word computer can access 4 bytes at a time. A 64-bit-word computer can access 8 bytes at a time. Therefore, the computer designed to process 64-bit words is faster. Other factors affect a computer's processing capability including how fast it can process data and instructions.

The processing speed of a microprocessor is typically represented by its **clock speed,** which is related to number of times the CPU can fetch and process data or instructions in a second. Older microcomputers typically process data and instructions in millionths of a second, or microseconds. Newer microcomputers are much faster and process data and instructions in billionths of a second, or nanoseconds. Supercomputers, by contrast, operate at speeds measured in picoseconds—1,000 times as fast as microcomputers. (See Figure 6-8.) Logically, the higher a microprocessor's clock speed, the faster the microprocessor. However, some processors can handle multiple instructions per cycle or tick of the clock; this means that clock speed comparisons can only be made between processors that work the same way.

The two most significant recent developments in microprocessors are the 64-bit processor and the multicore chip. Until recently, 64-bit processors were only used in large mainframe and supercomputers. All of that is changing as 64-bit processors have become standard for most of today's desktop and laptop computers.

The other recent development is the multicore chip. As mentioned previously, a traditional microcomputer's CPU is typically contained on a single microprocessor chip. A new type of chip, the **multicore chip,** can provide two or more separate and independent CPUs. These chips allow a single computer to run two or more operations at the same time. For example, a dual-core process could have one core computing a complex Excel spreadsheet while the other is running a multimedia presentation. More significantly, however, is the potential for microcomputers to run very large, complex programs that previously required expensive and specialized hardware.

For multicore processors to be used effectively, computers must understand how to divide tasks into parts that can be distributed across each core—an operation called **parallel processing.** Operating systems such as Windows Vista and Mac OS X support parallel processing. Software developers use this technology for a wide range of applications from scientific programs to sophisticated computer games.

See Figure 6-9 for a table of popular microprocessors.

Specialty Processors

In addition to microprocessor chips, a variety of more specialized processing chips have been developed.

- **Coprocessors** are specialty chips designed to improve specific computing operations. One of the most widely used is the **graphics coprocessor,** also called a **GPU (graphics processing unit).** These processors are designed to handle a variety of specialized tasks such as displaying 3-D images and encrypting data.

- **Smart cards** are plastic cards the size of a regular credit card that have an embedded specialty chip. Many colleges and universities provide smart cards to their students for identfication.

- Many cars have as many as 70 separate specialty processors to control nearly everything from fuel efficiency to satellite entertainment and tracking systems.

- **RFID tags** are specialty chips embedded in merchandise to track their location. The International Civil Aviation Organization has proposed inserting RFID chips in over a billion passports to track visitors as they enter or leave the United States.

Processor	Manufacturer	Description
Atom	Intel	32- and 64-bit, single- and dual-core
Core 2 Duo	Intel	64-bit, dual-core
Core 2 Quad	Intel	64-bit, quad-core
Xeon	Intel	64-bit, dual- and quad-core
Athlon 64 X2	AMD	64-bit, dual-core
Nano	Via	64-bit, low power
Cell	Sony/Toshiba/IBM	64-bit, eight-core

Figure 6-9 Popular microprocessors

CONCEPT CHECK

Name and describe the two components of a microprocessor.

Define word, clock speed, multicore chip, and parallel processing.

What are specialty processors? Describe coprocessors, smart cards, and RFID tags.

Memory

Memory is a holding area for data, instructions, and information. Like microprocessors, **memory** is contained on chips connected to the system board. There are three well-known types of memory chips: random-access memory (RAM), read-only memory (ROM), and flash memory.

RAM

Random-access memory (RAM) chips hold the program (sequence of instructions) and data that the CPU is presently processing. (See Figure 6-10.) RAM is called temporary or volatile storage because everything in most types of RAM is lost as soon as the microcomputer is turned off. It is also lost if there is a power

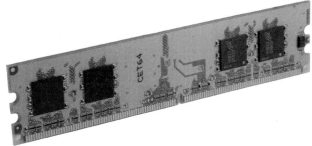

Figure 6-10 RAM chips mounted on circuit board

Unit	Capacity
Megabyte (MB)	1 million bytes
Gigabyte (GB)	1 billion bytes
Terabyte (TB)	1 trillion bytes

Figure 6-11 Memory capacity

failure or other disruption of the electric current going to the microcomputer. Secondary storage, which we shall describe in Chapter 8, does not lose its contents. It is permanent or nonvolatile storage, such as the data stored on a hard disk. For this reason, as we mentioned earlier, it is a good idea to frequently save your work in progress to a secondary storage device. That is, if you are working on a document or a spreadsheet, every few minutes you should save, or store, the material.

Cache (pronounced "cash") **memory** improves processing by acting as a temporary high-speed holding area between the memory and the CPU. The computer detects which information in RAM is most frequently used and then copies that information into the cache. When needed, the CPU can quickly access the information from the cache.

Having enough RAM is important! For example, to use Microsoft Office 2007 effectively, you need a minimum of 256 MB of RAM to hold the program and another 512 MB–1024 MB of RAM for the operating system.

Some applications, such as photo editing software, may require even more. Fortunately, additional RAM can be added to a computer system by inserting an expansion module called a **DIMM** (**dual in-line memory module**) into the system board. The capacity or amount of RAM is expressed in bytes. There are three commonly used units of measurement to describe memory capacity. (See Figure 6-11.)

Other types of RAM include DRAM, SDRAM, DDR, and Direct RDRAM. To learn more about these other types of RAM, visit our Web site at www.computing 2011.com and enter the keyword **ram.**

Even if your computer does not have enough RAM to hold a program, it might be able to run the program using **virtual memory.** Most of today's operating systems support virtual memory. With virtual memory, large programs are divided into parts and the parts are stored on a secondary device, usually a hard disk. Each part is then read into RAM only when needed. In this way, computer systems are able to run very large programs. To learn more about how virtual memory works, visit our Web site at www.computing2011.com and enter the keyword **memory.**

ROM

Read-only memory (ROM) chips have information stored in them by the manufacturer. Unlike RAM chips, ROM chips are not volatile and cannot be changed by the user. "Read only" means that the CPU can read, or retrieve, data and programs written on the ROM chip. However, the computer cannot write—encode or change—the information or instructions in ROM.

ROM chips typically contain special instructions for detailed computer operations. For example, ROM instructions are needed to start a computer, to access memory, and to handle basic keyboard input.

Flash Memory

Flash memory offers a combination of the features of RAM and ROM. Like RAM, it can be updated to store new information. Like ROM, it does not lose that information when power to the computer system is turned off.

Flash memory is used for a wide range of applications. For example, it is used to store the startup instructions for a computer. This information would include the specifics concerning the amount of RAM and the type of keyboard, mouse, and secondary storage devices connected to the system unit. If changes are made to the computer system, these changes are reflected in flash memory.

See Figure 6-12 for a summary of the three types of memory.

Type	Use
RAM	Programs and data
ROM	Fixed start-up instructions
Flash	Flexible start-up instructions

Figure 6-12 Memory

☑ CONCEPT CHECK

⬜ What is memory? Name and describe three types.

⬜ What are cache memory, DIMM, and virtual memory?

⬜ Define ROM and flash memory.

Expansion Slots and Cards

Most microcomputers allow users to expand their systems by providing **expansion slots** on the system board. Users can insert optional devices known as **expansion cards** into these slots. (See Figure 6-13.) Ports on the cards allow cables to be connected from the expansion cards to devices outside the system unit. (See Figure 6-14.) There are a wide range of different types of expansion cards. Some of the most commonly used expansion cards are

- **Advanced graphics cards** provide high-quality 3D graphics and animation for games and simulations.
- **Sound cards** accept audio input from a microphone and convert it into a form that can be processed by the computer. Also, these cards convert internal electronic signals to audio signals so they can be heard from external speakers or home theater systems.
- **Modem cards** allow distant computers to communicate with one another by converting electronic signals from within the system unit into electronic signals that can travel over telephone lines and other types of connections.
- **Network interface cards (NIC),** also known as **network adapter cards,** are used to connect a computer to a network. (See Figure 6-15.) The network allows connected computers to share data, programs, and hardware. The network adapter card typically connects the system unit to a cable that connects to the network, or it provides a wireless connection.

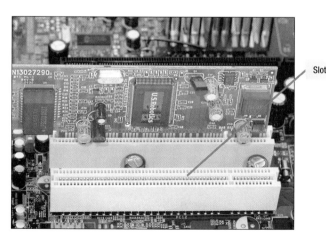

Figure 6-13 Expansion cards fit into slots on the system board

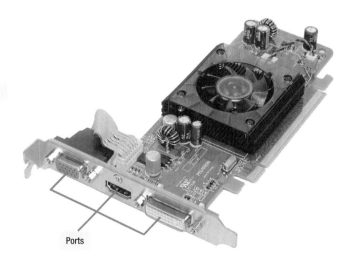

Slot

Ports

Figure 6-14 Expansion card with three ports

The System Unit **165**

- Now you can watch television, capture video, and surf the Internet at the same time. **TV tuner cards** contain a TV tuner and a video converter that changes a traditional TV signal into one that can be displayed on your monitor. To see how TV tuner cards work, visit our Web site at www.computing2011.com and enter the keyword **tv.** To learn about using TV tuner cards, see Making IT Work for You: TV Tuner Cards and Video Clips on pages 168 and 169.

Plug and Play was originally a set of specific hardware and software standards developed by Intel, Microsoft, and others. As hardware and software have evolved, however, Plug and Play has become a generic term that is associated with the ability to plug any device into a computer and have it play or work immediately. Some devices, however, are not plug and play and require that new device drivers be installed, as discussed in Chapter 5.

To meet the size constraints of notebook and handheld computers, small credit card–sized expansion cards have been developed. These cards plug into PCM-CIA (called **PC Cards**) or, most recently, **ExpressCard** slots. (See Figure 6-16.)

☑ CONCEPT CHECK

- What are expansion slots and cards? Name five expansion cards.

- Discuss Plug and Play.

- What are PC card and ExpressCard slots?

tips

Having problems or want to upgrade your system and would like professional help? Here are a few suggestions:

1 **Select a reputable computer store.** Consider local as well as national chain stores. Check them out with the Better Business Bureau.

2 **Visit the store with your computer.** Ideally, have a knowledgeable friend accompany you. Describe the problem and get a written estimate. Ask about the company's warranty.

3 **Tag your system.** If you leave the system, attach a tag with your name, address, and telephone number.

4 **Pay by credit card.** If a dispute occurs, many credit card companies will intervene on your side.

To see additional tips, visit our Web site at www.computing2011.com and enter the keyword tips.

Figure 6-15 **Network interface card**

Figure 6-16 **PC card**

Bus Lines

A **bus line**—also known simply as a **bus**—connects the parts of the CPU to each other. Buses also link the CPU to various other components on the system board. (See Figure 6-17.) A bus is a pathway for bits representing data and instructions. The number of bits that can travel simultaneously down a bus is known as the **bus width.**

A bus is similar to a multilane highway that moves bits rather than cars from one location to another. The number of traffic lanes determines the bus width. A highway (bus line) with more traffic lanes (bus width) can move traffic (data and instructions) more efficiently. For example, a 64-bit bus can move twice as much information at a time as a 32-bit bus. Why should you even care about what a bus line is? Because as microprocessor chips have changed, so have bus lines. Bus design or bus architecture is an important factor relating to the speed and power for a particular computer. Additionally, many devices, such as expansion boards, will work with only one type of bus.

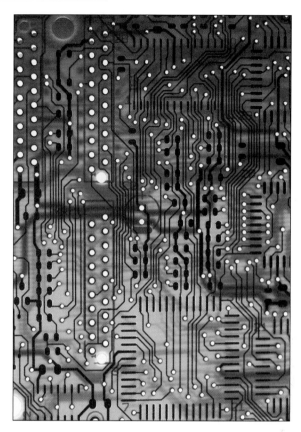

Figure 6-17 Bus is a pathway for bits

Expansion Buses

Every computer system has two basic categories of buses. One category, called **system buses,** connects the CPU to memory on the system board. The other category, called **expansion buses,** connects the CPU to other components on the system board, including expansion slots.

Computer systems typically have a combination of different types of expansion buses. The principal types are PCI, USB, Firewire, SATA, and PCIe.

- **Peripheral component interconnect (PCI)** was originally developed to meet the video demands of graphical user interfaces. When first introduced, it had a 32-bit bus width and was over 20 times faster than the older buses that it replaced. Almost all PCI buses are now 64-bit and are very common on older computers.

- **Universal serial bus (USB)** is widely used today. It combines with a PCI bus on the system board to support several external devices without using expansion cards or slots. External USB devices are connected from one to another or to a common point or hub and then onto the USB bus. The USB bus then connects to the PCI bus on the system board. The current USB standard, USB 2.0, is soon to replaced by the recently announced USB 3.0.

- **FireWire buses** are similar to USB buses. Although reports differ, FireWire buses are generally considered slightly faster than the USB 2.0 bus. Both are used to support a variety of specialized applications such as digital camcorders and video editing devices.

- **Serial Advanced Technology Attachment (SATA)** buses are one of the newest buses. It is much faster than USB 2.0 and FireWire buses and is now widely used to connect high-speed storage devices to the system board.

- **PCI Express (PCIe)** is another recently developed bus. It is widely used in many of today's most powerful computers. Unlike the PCI bus and most other buses that share a single bus line or path with several devices, the PCIe bus provides a single dedicated path for each connected device. PCIe buses are much faster and are replacing the PCI bus.

Making IT work for you

TV TUNER CARDS AND VIDEO CLIPS

Want to watch your favorite television program while you work? Perhaps you would like to include a video clip from television in a class presentation. It's easy using a TV tuner card.

Viewing Once a TV tuner card has been installed, you can view your favorite TV shows, even while running other applications such as PowerPoint. For example, you could use a Hauppauge TV tuner product and Hauppauge software as shown below.

1 ● **Launch the WinTV application.**

● **Size and move the television application window.**

● **Select a channel to view.**

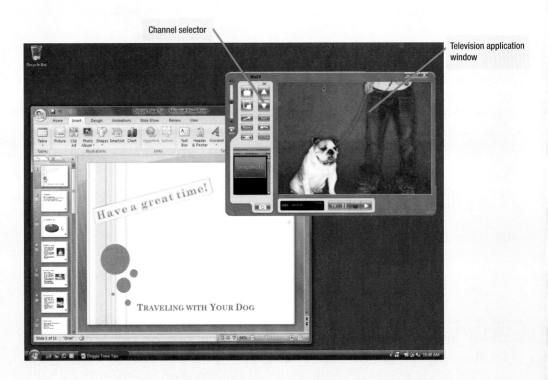

Channel selector

Television application window

Capturing You can capture the video playing in the TV window into a digital file by following the steps shown below.

1 ● Click the *Record* button to begin recording.

● Click the *Stop* button to stop recording.

● Select a location and name to save your captured video file.

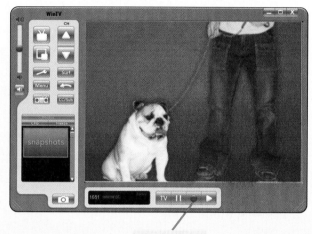

Record/Stop button

Using Once captured in a file, a video can be used in any number of ways. It can be added to a Web page, attached to an e-mail, or added to a class presentation. For example, you could include a video clip in a PowerPoint presentation by following the steps below.

1 ● Select the *Insert* tab, and then select *Movie* from the Media Clips group.

● Select the video file you saved in the previous step.

● Choose whether the video file should start automatically, or only when you click it during your presentation.

● Drag and resize the inserted movie clip as needed.

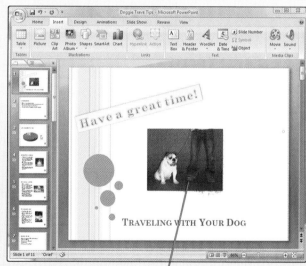

Inserted movie clip

TV tuner cards are relatively inexpensive and easy to install. Some factors limiting their performance on your computer are the speed of your processor, the amount of memory, and secondary storage capacity.

TV tuner cards are continually changing, and some of the specifics presented in this Making IT Work for You may have changed.

To learn about other ways to make information technology work for you, visit our Web site at www.computing2011.com and enter the keyword miw.

What is a bus and what is bus width?

 What is the difference between a system and an expansion bus?

 Discuss the five principal types of buses.

Ports

A **port** is a socket for external devices to connect to the system unit. (See Figure 6-18.) Some ports connect directly to the system board while others connect to cards that are inserted into slots on the system board. Some ports are standard features of most computer systems and others are more specialized.

Standard Ports

Most microcomputers come with a standard set of ports for connecting a monitor, keyboard, and other peripheral devices. The most common ports include

- **VGA (Video Graphics Adapter)** and **DVI (Digital Video Interface) ports** provide connections to analog and digital monitors, respectively.

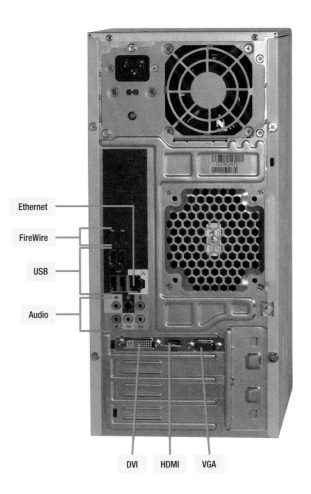

Figure 6-18 **Ports**

DVI has become the most commonly used standard, but VGA ports are still provided on almost all systems for compatibility with older/lower-cost monitors.

- **Universal serial bus (USB) ports** can be used to connect several devices to the system unit and are widely used to connect keyboards, mice, printers, and storage devices to the system unit. A single USB port can be used to connect many USB devices to the system unit.
- **FireWire ports** provide high-speed connections to specialized FireWire devices such as camcorders and storage devices.
- **Ethernet ports** are a high-speed networking port that has become a standard for many of today's computers. Ethernet allows you to connect multiple computers for sharing files, or to a DSL or cable modem for high-speed Internet access.

Specialized Ports

In addition to standard ports, there are numerous specialty ports including S/PDIF, HDMI, and MIDI.

- **Sony/Philips Digital Interconnect Format (S/PDIF)** ports are also known as **optical audio connections.** These ports are used to integrate computers into high-end audio and home theatre systems.
- **High Definition Multimedia Interface (HDMI)** ports provide high-definition video and audio, making it possible to use a computer as a video jukebox or an HD video recorder.
- **Musical instrument digital interface (MIDI)** ports are a special type of serial port for connecting musical instruments like an electronic keyboard to a sound card. The sound card converts the music into a series of digital instructions. These instructions can be processed immediately to reproduce the music or saved to a file for later processing.

Legacy Ports

In the past, additional ports were common on microcomputer systems to connect specific types of devices. These older ports, known as **legacy ports,** have largely been replaced by faster, more flexible ports such as the universal serial bus (USB).

- **Serial ports** were used for a wide variety of purposes, such as connecting a mouse, keyboard, modem, and many other devices to the system unit. Serial ports sent data one bit at a time and were good for sending information over long distances.
- **Parallel ports** were used to connect external devices that needed to send or receive a lot of data over a short distance. These ports typically sent eight bits of data simultaneously across eight parallel wires. Parallel ports were mostly used to connect printers to the system unit.
- **Keyboard** and **mouse ports** were used to connect keyboards and mice to the system unit. Different types of keyboard ports existed for different types of keyboards, making some keyboards incompatible with some system units.
- **Infrared Data Association (IrDA) ports** were used to provide a wireless mechanism for transferring data between devices. Instead of cables, the

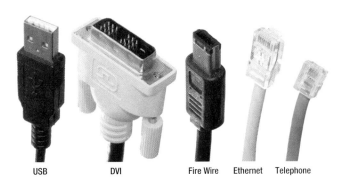

Figure 6-19 **Cables**

IrDA ports from each device were directly aligned and infrared light waves were used to transmit data. One of the most common applications was to transfer data from either a handheld or notebook computer to a desktop computer.

- **Game ports** were used to connect video game controllers and joysticks.

Cables

Cables are used to connect exterior devices to the system unit via the ports. One end of the cable is attached to the device and the other end has a connector that is attached to a matching connector on the port. (See Figure 6-19.)

Power Supply

Computers require direct current (DC) to power their electronic components and to represent data and instructions. DC power can be provided indirectly by converting alternating current (AC) from standard wall outlets or directly from batteries.

- Desktop computers have a **power supply unit** located within the system unit. (See Figure 6-20.) This unit plugs into a standard wall outlet, converts AC to DC, and provides the power to drive all of the system unit components.
- Notebook computers use **AC adapters** that are typically located outside the system unit. (See Figure 6-21.) AC adapters plug into a standard wall outlet, convert AC to DC, provide power to drive the system unit components, and can recharge the batteries. Notebook computers can be operated either using an AC adapter plugged into a wall outlet or using battery power. Notebook batteries typically provide sufficient power for four to six hours before they need to be recharged.

Figure 6-20 **Power supply unit**

Figure 6-21 **AC adapter**

- Like notebook computers, handheld computers use AC adapters located outside the system unit. Unlike notebook computers, however, handheld computers typically operate only using battery power. The AC adapter is used to recharge the batteries.

☑ CONCEPT CHECK

What are ports? What do they do?

Describe four standard, three specialized, and five legacy ports.

What is a power supply unit? What is an AC adaptor?

Careers in IT

Computer technicians repair and install computer components and systems. (See Figure 6-22.) They may work on everything from personal computers and mainframe servers to printers. Some computer technicians are responsible for setting up and maintaining computer networks. Experienced computer technicians may work with computer engineers to diagnose problems and run routine maintenance on complex systems. Job growth is expected in this field as computer equipment becomes more complicated and technology expands.

Employers look for those with certification in computer repair or associate degrees from vocational schools. Employment usually begins with training, but most employers expect applicants to have prior technical experience. Computer technicians also can expect to continue their education to keep up with technological changes. Good communication skills are important in this field.

Computer technicians can expect an hourly wage of $13.50 to $22.50. Opportunities for advancement typically come in the form of work on more advanced computer systems. Some computer technicians move into customer service positions or go into sales. To learn more about other careers in information technology, visit us at www.computing2011.com and enter the keyword **careers.**

Figure 6-22 **Computer technician**

A LOOK TO THE FUTURE

As You Walk out the Door, Don't Forget Your Computer

Wouldn't it be nice if you could conveniently access the Internet wirelessly at any time during the day? What if you could send and receive e-mail while jogging without touching a screen, or send a friend live video of what you are looking at? What If a computer on your body could help you remember the names of people at a party? Of course, many people currently use wireless phone technology when they are away from their home or office. What if these users could accomplish these tasks with an even smaller, more portable, and less intrusive system? Will people be wearing computers rather than carrying them?

Wearable computers already exist for specialized military and industrial use. Imagine using your hands to prepare a meal or work on a car with instruc-

tions and diagrams instantly available in your line of sight. Some of these systems are composed of a computer that is worn inside a jacket or in a belt and a head-mounted display. The display allows you to see the equivalent of a desktop monitor via a small screen that is worn in front of one eye or projected onto the inside of a regular pair of eyeglasses. Such devices might be used in airports by security personnel. These devices are currently being used by the U.S. Department of Defense for military applications and by the Toronto Blue Jays to end long lines at ticket windows. When coupled with face recognition technology, these products provide security personnel portable and instant communication with the command center. Police and security officers may someday use this technology to check IDs and verify your identity.

Experts say that wearable computers will be used by surgeons in operating rooms to "view" their patients. Will we be wearing computers soon? Some of us already are. And some experts predict the majority of us will employ a wearable computer before the end of the decade. Many computer manufacturers are currently working on wearable computers, and there is even a wearable computer fashion show that showcases the latest designs.

Many people are already wearing their computers, and making use of this mobile technology to read e-mail while waiting in lines or even studying their notes for the next exam. What do you think? Will people someday grab their keys and their computers before they leave the house? Will your computer one day be housed in your jacket? Do you see any potential issues that might come up if wearable computers were widespread?

VISUAL SUMMARY   The System Unit

SYSTEM UNIT

System unit (system chassis) contains electronic components.

Categories

There are six basic categories of system units: **desktop, media center, notebook (laptop), netbook, tablet PC**, and **handheld**.

Components

Each type of system unit has the same basic components including system board, microprocessor, and memory.

ELECTRONIC REPRESENTATION

Human voices create **analog** (continuous) signals; computers only recognize **digital** electronic signals.

Numeric Representation

Data and instructions can be represented electronically with a two-state or **binary system** of numbers (0 and 1). Each 0 or 1 is called a **bit**. A **byte** consists of eight bits. **Hexadecimal system (hex)** uses 16 digits to represent binary numbers.

Character Encoding

Character encoding standards assign unique sequences of bits to each character. Three standards are **ASCII (American Standard Code for Information Interchange)**, **EBCDIC (Extended Binary Coded Decimal Interchange Code)**, and **Unicode.**

SYSTEM BOARD

The **system board (motherboard)** connects all system components and allows input and output devices to communicate with the system unit. It is a flat circuit board covered with these electronic components:

- **Sockets** provide connection points for **chips (silicon chips, semiconductors, integrated circuits)**. Chips are mounted on **carrier packages.**
- **Slots** provide connection points for specialized cards or circuit boards.
- **Bus lines** provide pathways to support communication.

To be a competent end user, you need to understand how data and programs are represented electronically. Additionally, you need to understand the functionality of the basic components in the system unit: system board, microprocessor, memory, expansion slots and cards, bus lines, and ports and cables.

MICROPROCESSOR

Processor	Manufacturer	Description
Atom	Intel	32- and 64-bit, single- and dual-core
Core 2 Duo	Intel	64-bit, dual-core
Core 2 Quad	Intel	64-bit, quad-core
Xeon	Intel	64-bit, dual- and quad-core
Athlon 64 X2	AMD	64-bit, dual-core
Nano	Via	64-bit, low power
Cell	Sony/Toshiba/IBM	64-bit, eight-core

The **microprocessor** is a single chip that contains the **central processing unit (CPU)** or **microprocessor.** It has two basic components:

- **Control unit** tells the computer system how to carry out program instructions.
- **Arithmetic-logic unit (ALU)** performs **arithmetic** and **logical operations.**

Microprocessor Chips

A **word** is the number of bits that can be accessed by the microprocessor at one time. **Clock speed** represents the number of times the CPU can fetch and process data or instructions in a second. Older microprocessors process data and instructions in microseconds; newer ones process in nanoseconds. Supercomputers process in picoseconds.

The two most significant developments are 64-bit processors and **multicore chips. Parallel processing** requires programs that allow multiple processors to work together to run large complex programs.

Specialty Processors

Specialty processors include **graphics coprocessors** also known as **GPU** or **graphics processing unit** (process graphic images), **smart cards** (plastic cards containing embedded chips), processors in automobiles (monitor fuel efficiency, satellite entertainment, and tracking systems), and **RFID tags** (track merchandise).

MEMORY

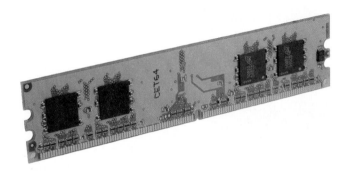

Memory holds data, instructions, and information. There are three types of memory chips: RAM, ROM, and **flash memory.**

RAM

RAM (random-access memory) chips are called temporary or volatile storage because their contents are lost if power is disrupted.

- **Cache memory** is a high-speed holding area for frequently used data and information.
- **DIMM (dual in-line memory module)** is used to expand memory.
- **Virtual memory** divides large programs into parts that are read into RAM as needed.

ROM

ROM (read-only memory) chips are nonvolatile storage and control essential system operations.

Flash Memory

Flash memory is a type of memory that does not lose its contents when power is removed. It is used to store information about a computer's configuration.

Unit	Capacity
Megabyte (MB)	1 million bytes
Gigabyte (GB)	1 billion bytes
Terabyte (TB)	1 trillion bytes

EXPANSION SLOTS AND CARDS

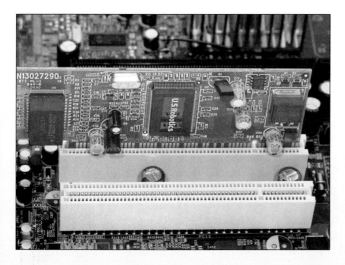

Most computers allow users to expand their systems by providing **expansion slots** on their system boards to accept **expansion cards.**

Examples of expansion cards include **advanced graphics cards, sound cards, modem cards, network interface cards (NIC; network adapter cards), and TV tuner cards.**

Plug and Play is the ability for a computer to recognize and configure a device without human interaction.

PC Card and **ExpressCard** slots accept credit card–sized expansion cards in notebook computers.

BUS LINES

Bus lines, also known as **buses,** provide data pathways that connect various system components. **Bus width** is the number of bits that can travel simultaneously.

Expansion Buses

System buses connect CPU and memory. **Expansion buses** connect CPU and slots. Five principal expansion bus types are **PCI (peripheral component interconnect), USB (universal serial bus), FireWire bus, SATA (Serial Advanced Technology Attachment), and PCIe (PCI Express).**

PORTS

Ports are connecting sockets on the outside of the system unit.

Standard Ports

Four standard ports are

- **VGA (Video Graphics Adapter)** and **DVI (Digital Video Interface)**—provide connections to monitors.
- **USB (universal serial bus)**—widely used to connect keyboards, mice, printers, and storage devices; one port can connect several devices to system unit.
- **FireWire**—almost twice as fast as USB 2.0; provide connections for specialized FireWire devices.
- **Ethernet**—high-speed networking port that has become a standard for many of today's computers.

Specialized Ports

Three specialty ports are

- **S/PDIF (Sony/Philips Digital Interface)** for high-end audio and home theatre systems, **HDMI (High Definition Multimedia Interface)** for high-definition digital audio and video, **and MIDI** for digital music.

Legacy Ports

Legacy ports have largely been replaced by faster, more flexible ports such as the universal serial bus (USB). These ports include **serial, parallel, keyboard, mouse,** and **Infrared Data Association (IrDA).**

Cables

Cables are used to connect external devices to the system unit via ports.

POWER SUPPLY

Power supply units convert AC to DC; they are located within the desktop computer's system unit. **AC adapters** power notebook computers and tablet PCs and recharge batteries.

CAREERS IN IT

Computer technicians repair and install computer components and systems. Certification in computer repair or associate degrees from vocational schools required. Hourly wage $13.50 to $22.50.

KEY TERMS

AC adapter (172)
advanced graphics
  card (165)
analog (158)
arithmetic-logic unit
  (ALU) (162)
arithmetic
  operation (162)
ASCII (159)
binary system (159)
bit (159)
bus (167)
bus line (161, 167)
bus width (167)
byte (159)
cable (172)
cache memory (164)
carrier package (161)
central processing unit
  (CPU) (161)
character encoding
  standards (159)
chip (161)
clock speed (162)
computer
  technician (173)
control unit (162)
coprocessor (163)
desktop system
  unit (156)
digital (158)
DIMM (164)
DVI (Digital Video
  Interface) port (171)
EBCDIC (159)
Ethernet ports (171)
expansion bus (167)
expansion card (165)
expansion slot (165)
ExpressCard (166)
FireWire bus (167)
FireWire port (171)
flash memory (164)
game port (172)
GPU (163)

graphics
  coprocessor (163)
handheld computer
  system unit (157)
hexadecimal system
  (hex) (159)
High Definition
  Multimedia Interface
  (HDMI) (171)
Infrared Data Association
  (IrDA) port (171)
integrated circuit (161)
keyboard port (171)
laptop computer (156)
legacy port (171)
logical operation (162)
media center system
  unit (156)
memory (163)
microprocessor (161)
modem card (165)
motherboard (159)
mouse port (171)
multicore chips (162)
musical instrument
  digital interface
  (MIDI) (171)
netbook (156)
netbook system
  unit (156)
network adapter
  card (165)
network interface card
  (NIC) (165)
notebook system
  unit (156)
optical audio
  connections (171)
parallel port (171)
parallel
  processing (162)
PC card (166)
PCI Express
  (PCIe) (167)

peripheral component
  interconnect
  (PCI) (167)
personal digital assistant
  (PDA) (157)
Plug and Play (166)
port (170)
power supply unit (172)
processor (161)
random-access memory
  (RAM) (163)
read-only memory
  (ROM) (164)
RFID tag (163)
semiconductor (161)
Serial Advanced
  Technology Attachment
  (SATA) (167)
serial port (171)
silicon chip (161)
slot (161)
smart card (163)
smartphone (157)
socket (161)
Sony/Philips Digital
  Interconnect Format
  (S/PDIF) (171)
sound card (165)
system board (160)
system bus (167)
system chassis (156)
system unit (156)
tablet PC (156)
tablet PC system
  unit (156)
TV tuner card (166)
Unicode (159)
universal serial
  bus (167)
universal serial bus
  (USB) port (171)
VGA (Video Graphics
  Adapter) port (170)
virtual memory (164)
word (162)

To test your knowledge of these key terms with animated flash cards, visit our Web site at www.computing2011.com and enter the keyword terms6.

MULTIPLE CHOICE

Circle the letter or fill in the correct answer.

1. The container that houses most of the electronic components that make up a computer system is known as the
    a. arithmetic-logic unit
    b. central processing unit
    c. RFID
    d. system unit

2. The smallest unit in a digital system is a
    a. byte
    b. bit
    c. word
    d. character

3. The _____ controls communications for the entire computer system.
    a. arithmetic-logic unit
    b. semiconductor
    c. motherboard
    d. coprocessor

4. These provide expansion capability for a computer system.
    a. sockets
    b. slots
    c. bytes
    d. bays

5. The _____ tells the rest of the computer how to carry out a program's instructions.
    a. ALU
    b. control unit
    c. system unit
    d. motherboard

6. A 32-bit word computer can access _____ bytes at a time.
    a. 4
    b. 8
    c. 16
    d. 32

7. These chips are specifically designed to handle the processing requirements related to displaying and manipulating 3-D images.
    a. graphics coprocessors
    b. arithmetic-logic unit processors
    c. control unit processors
    d. CISC chips

8. This type of memory improves processing by acting as a temporary high-speed holding area between the memory and the CPU.
    a. RAM
    b. ROM
    c. cache memory
    d. flash memory

9. _____ refers to a computer's ability to configure and use a device without human interaction.
    a. CPU
    b. Plug and Play
    c. Cache
    d. ALU

10. _____ ports connect special types of music instruments to sound cards.
    a. BUS
    b. CPU
    c. USB
    d. MIDI

For an interactive multiple-choice practice test, visit our Web site at www.computing 2011.com and enter the keyword multiple6.

MATCHING

a. bus width
b. cables
c. control unit
d. expansion card
e. ExpressCard
f. port
g. RAM
h. smart card
i. system bus
j. system unit

1. Houses most of the electronic components in a computer system. _____
2. The number of bits that can travel down a bus at the same time. _____
3. Tells the computer system how to carry out a program's instructions. _____
4. A credit card–sized piece of plastic with an embedded chip. _____
5. Volatile storage that holds the program and data the CPU is currently processing. _____
6. Connects the CPU to memory. _____
7. Plugs into slots on the system board. _____
8. A type of slot used by notebook computers. _____
9. Connecting socket on the outside of the system unit. _____
10. Connects input and output devices to the system unit via the ports. _____

For an interactive matching practice test, visit our Web site at www.computing2011.com and enter the keyword matching6.

OPEN-ENDED

On a separate sheet of paper, respond to each question or statement.

1. Describe the six basic types of system units.
2. Describe the two basic components of the CPU.
3. What are the differences and similarities between the three types of memory?
4. Identify five expansion cards and describe the function of each.
5. Identify and describe four standard ports, three specialized ports, and five legacy ports.

APPLYING TECHNOLOGY

The following questions are designed to demonstrate ways that you can effectively use technology today. The first question relates directly to this chapter's Making IT Work for You feature.

① TV TUNER CARDS AND VIDEO CLIPS

Want to watch your favorite television program while you work? Perhaps you would like to include a video clip in a class presentation. It's easy using a video TV card. To learn more about this technology, review Making IT Work for You: TV Tuner Cards and Video Clips on pages 168 and 169. Then visit our Web site at www.computing2011.com and enter the keyword tuner. Play the video and answer the following: (a) Describe the two windows that open when the TV icon is selected. (b) What are the basic functions of the control box? (c) What is the command sequence to insert a video clip into a PowerPoint presentation?

② DESKTOP AND NOTEBOOK COMPUTERS

Are you thinking about purchasing a new computer? Visit our Web site at www.computing2011.com and enter the keyword computer to link to a site that presents information about the newest desktop and notebook computers. Check out different desktop and notebook models and then answer the following questions: (a) If you were to purchase a desktop computer, which one would you select? Describe how it would fit your needs and print out its specifications. (b) If you were to purchase a notebook computer, which one would you select? Describe how it would fit your needs and print out its specifications. (c) If you had to choose between the desktop and notebook, which one would you choose? Why?

③ CUSTOM SYSTEM UNITS

When it is time for you to purchase your next computer, you might consider shopping online. A big advantage to choosing a computer online instead of in a store is that many computer manufacturers allow you to customize your new computer and build it to order. Visit our Web site at www.computing2011.com and enter the keyword custom to connect to a retailer of customized computers and use their online tools to customize and price a computer that meets your current needs. Then answer the following questions: (a) Which of the three types of system units did you configure? (b) What microprocessor did you choose? (c) How much and what type of memory option did you choose? (d) Would you purchase the computer you customized? Why or why not?

EXPANDING YOUR KNOWLEDGE

The following questions are designed to add depth and detail to your understanding of specific topics presented within this chapter. The questions direct you to sources other than the textbook to obtain this knowledge.

1 HOW TV TUNER CARDS WORK

The advent of digital TV and the success of digital video recorders have made TV tuner cards a popular addition to many computers. TV tuner cards allow you to watch and record TV shows on your computer, even while running other applications. To learn more about how TV tuner cards work, visit our Web site at www.computing2011.com and enter the keyword tv. Then answer the following questions: (a) What are some examples of inputs to a TV tuner card? (b) What is the function of a TV tuner card? (c) Where can the TV tuner card send the video signal once it is converted?

2 HOW VIRTUAL MEMORY WORKS

Typically before a program can be executed, it must be read into RAM. Many programs, however, are too large to fit into many computer systems' RAM. One option is to increase the RAM in the system. Another way is to use virtual memory. To learn more about how virtual memory works, visit our Web site at www.computing2011.com and enter the keyword memory. Then answer the following: (a) What is virtual memory? (b) Define page file, page, and paging. (c) What is thrashing?

3 BINARY NUMBERS

Binary numbers are the most basic unit that computers use to perform tasks. To learn more about how binary numbers work, visit our Web site at www.computing2011.com and enter the keyword binary. Then answer the following questions: (a) What character is represented by the binary number 01000011 in ASCII code? (b) What is the binary result of 1011 + 0010? What is the decimal equivalent to this number? (c) How many numbers can be represented with 1 bit (one binary "place")? How many by 2 bits? How many by 3 bits?

WRITING ABOUT TECHNOLOGY

The ability to think critically and to write effectively is essential to nearly every profession. The following questions are designed to help you develop these skills by posing thought-provoking questions about computer privacy, security, and/or ethics.

RFIDS

RFIDs have been touted by the media as an up-and-coming technology for several years. These tiny chips (that can be embedded in virtually everything) can be used to identify groceries, vehicles, and even people! Without knowing where RFID readers are placed and where RFID chips are embedded, it is unclear what information we might be sharing about ourselves and who we might be sharing it with. Write a one-page paper that addresses the following items: (a) What benefits do you see in using RFIDs in daily life? Explain your answers. (b) What privacy issues does an RFID raise for consumers? (c) Describe how RFIDs might be misused.

② SMART CARDS

There have been numerous proposals in recent years to use smart card technology for personal identification, such as driver's licenses or a national ID card. Advocates claim that this would reduce identity fraud because the cards would contain biometric information such as a fingerprint scan. Research smart card technology on the Web and then answer the following questions in a one-page paper: (a) What are the benefits of using smart cards for identification? List several examples. (b) What privacy concerns exist? Be specific. (c) Would you be in favor of using smart cards for personal identification? Why or why not?

Input and Output

After you have read this chapter, you should be able to:

1 Define input.

2 Describe keyboard entry including the different types of keyboards and keyboard features.

3 Discuss pointing devices including mice, touch screens, joysticks, and styluses.

4 Describe scanning devices including optical scanners and card readers.

5 Discuss image capturing devices including digital cameras and digital video cameras.

6 Define output.

7 Discuss monitor features, flat-panel, CRT, e-book readers, data projectors, and HDTVs.

8 Define printing features as well as ink-jet, laser, dot-matrix, thermal, plotter, photo, and portable printers.

9 Discuss audio-output devices.

10 Define combination input and output devices.

In the beginning the only input device was the keyboard. Every task on the computer began with a line of typed text. And most computers did not even have speakers; the only output was through a simple monitor and a dot-matrix printer. Today's input and output devices are much more diverse and sophisticated, allowing users to interact with their computers with their voice or handwriting.

Some experts predict in the future input devices will rely on gesture recognition. Computers will view human movement and interpret those gestures as commands. Output devices are expected to become more powerful as well. Imagine a world where the flick of your wrist controls the lights in your house or even starts your household appliances.

chapter 7

Introduction

How do you send instructions and information to the CPU? How do you get information out? Here we describe one of the most important places where computers interface with people. We input text, music, and even speech, but we probably never think about the relationship between what we enter and what the computer processes. People understand language, which is constructed of letters, numbers, and punctuation marks. However, at a basic level, computers can understand only the binary machine language of 0s and 1s. Input devices are essentially translators. Input devices translate numbers, letters, and actions that people understand into a form that computers can process.

Have you ever wondered how information processed by the system unit is converted into a form that you can use? That is the role of output devices. While input devices convert what we understand into what the system unit can process, output devices convert what the system unit has processed into a form that we can understand. Output devices translate machine language into letters, numbers, sounds, and images that people can understand.

Competent end users need to know about the most commonly used input devices, including keyboards, mice, scanners, digital cameras, voice recognition, and audio-input devices. Additionally, they need to know about the most commonly used output devices, including monitors, printers, and audio output devices. And end users need to be aware of combination input and output devices such as fax machines, multifunctional devices, and Internet telephones.

What Is Input?

Input is any data or instructions that are used by a computer. They can come directly from you or from other sources. You provide input whenever you use system or application programs. For example, when using a word processing program, you enter data in the form of numbers and letters and issue commands such as to save and to print documents. You also can enter data and issue commands by pointing to items, or using your voice. Other sources of input include scanned or photographed images.

Input devices are hardware used to translate words, sounds, images, and actions that people understand into a form that the system unit can process. For example, when using a word processor, you typically use a keyboard to enter text and a mouse to issue commands. In addition to keyboards and mice, there are a wide variety of other input devices. These include pointing, scanning, image capturing, and audio-input devices.

Keyboard Entry

One of the most common ways to input data is by **keyboard.** As mentioned in Chapter 6, keyboards convert numbers, letters, and special characters that people understand into electrical signals. These signals are sent to, and processed by, the system unit. Most keyboards use an arrangement of keys given

Figure 7-1 Ergonomic keyboard

the name QWERTY. This name reflects the keyboard layout by taking the letters of the first six alphabetic characters found on the top row of keys displaying letters.

Keyboards

There are a wide variety of different keyboard designs. They range from the full-sized to miniature and from rigid to flexible. There are even virtual keyboards that project an interactive key layout onto a flat surface. The most common types are

- **Traditional keyboards**—full-sized, rigid, rectangular keyboards that include function, navigational, and numeric keys.
- **Ergonomic keyboards**—similar to traditional keyboards. The keyboard arrangement, however, is not rectangular and a palm rest is provided. They are designed specifically to alleviate wrist strain associated with the repetitive movements of typing. (See Figure 7-1.)
- **Wireless keyboards**—transmit input to the system unit through the air. By eliminating connecting wires to the system unit, these keyboards provide greater flexibility and convenience.
- **PDA keyboards**—miniature keyboards for PDAs and smart phones to send e-mail, create documents, and more. (See Figure 7-2.)
- **Virtual keyboards**—display an image of a keyboard on a touch screen device. The screen functions as the actual input device, which is why the keyboard is considered virtual. Virtual keyboards are common on tablet computers and mobile devices.

Features

A computer keyboard combines a typewriter keyboard with a **numeric keypad,** used to enter numbers and arithmetic symbols. It also has many special-purpose keys. Some keys, such as the CAPS LOCK key, are **toggle keys.** These

On the Web Explorations

People are spending more time at their computers than ever before. Consequently, the need for ergonomic keyboards is increasing.

To learn more about one manufacturer of ergonomic keyboards, visit our Web site at www.computing2011.com and enter the keyword ergonomic.

Figure 7-2 PDA keyboard

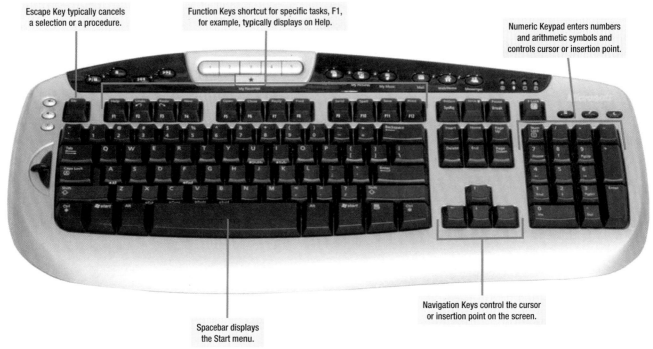

Escape Key typically cancels a selection or a procedure.

Function Keys shortcut for specific tasks, F1, for example, typically displays on Help.

Numeric Keypad enters numbers and arithmetic symbols and controls cursor or insertion point.

Navigation Keys control the cursor or insertion point on the screen.

Spacebar displays the Start menu.

Figure 7-3 Keyboard features

keys turn a feature on or off. Others, such as the CTRL key, are **combination keys,** which perform an action when held down in combination with another key. To learn more about keyboard features, see Figure 7-3.

CONCEPT CHECK

What is input? What are input devices?

Discuss the five most common types of keyboard.

Define some common keyboard features?

Pointing Devices

Pointing, of course, is one of the most natural of all human gestures. Pointing devices provide a comfortable interface with the system unit by accepting pointing gestures and converting them into machine-readable input. There are a wide variety of different pointing devices, including the mouse, joystick, touch screen, and stylus.

Mice

A **mouse** controls a pointer that is displayed on the monitor. The **mouse pointer** usually appears in the shape of an arrow. It frequently changes shape, however, depending on the application. A mouse can have one, two, or more buttons, which are used to select command options and to control the mouse pointer on the monitor. Some mice have a **wheel button** that can be rotated to scroll through information that is displayed on the monitor.

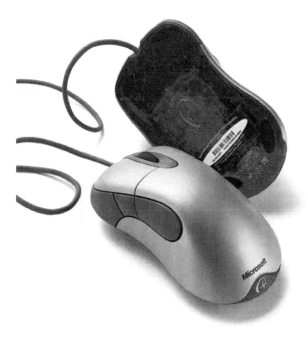

Figure 7-4 **Optical mouse**

Figure 7-5 **Trackball**

Although there are several different mouse types, there are three basic designs:

- **Optical mouse** has no moving parts and is currently the most widely used. It emits and senses light to detect mouse movement. An optical mouse can be used on almost any surface with high precision. (See Figure 7-4.)
- **Mechanical mouse** has a ball on the bottom and is attached with a cord to the system unit. As you move the mouse across a smooth surface, the roller rotates and controls the pointer on the screen.
- **Cordless** or **wireless mouse** is a battery-powered device that typically uses radio waves or infrared light waves to communicate with the system unit. These devices eliminate the mouse cord and free up desk space.

Three devices similar to a mouse are trackballs, touch pads, and pointing sticks. You can use the **trackball,** also known as the **roller ball,** to control the pointer by rotating a ball with your thumb. (See Figure 7-5.) You can use **touch pads** to control the pointer by moving and tapping your finger on the surface of a pad. (See Figure 7-6.) You can use a **pointing stick,** located in the middle of the keyboard, to control the pointer by directing the stick with one finger. (See Figure 7-7.)

Figure 7-6 **Touch pad**

Figure 7-7 **Pointing stick**

Figure 7-8 **A touch screen**

Touch Screens

A **touch screen** is a particular kind of monitor with a clear plastic outer layer. Behind this layer are crisscrossed invisible beams of infrared light. This arrangement enables someone to select actions or commands by touching the screen with a finger. Touch screens are easy to use, especially when people need information quickly. They are commonly used at restaurants, automated teller machines (ATMs), and information centers. (See Figure 7-8.)

Multi-touch screens can be touched with more than one finger, which allows for interactions such as rotating graphical objects on the screen with your hand or zooming in and out by pinching and stretching your fingers. Multi-touch screens are commonly used on mobile devices such as the Apple iPhone, as well as some notebook computers and desktop monitors. (See Figure 7-9.)

Joysticks

The **joystick** is a popular input device for computer games. You control game actions by varying the pressure, speed, and direction of the joystick. Additional controls, such as buttons and triggers, are used to specify commands or initiate specific actions. (See Figure 7-10.)

Stylus

A **stylus** is a penlike device commonly used with tablet PCs and PDAs. (See Figure 7-11.) A stylus uses pressure to draw images on a screen. Often, a stylus interacts with the computer through handwriting recognition software. **Handwriting recognition software** translates handwritten notes into a form that the system unit can process.

Figure 7-9 **Multi-touch screen**

Figure 7-10 **Joystick**

Stylus

Figure 7-11 **Stylus**

CONCEPT CHECK

What is a pointing device? Describe four pointing devices.

Describe three basic mouse designs.

Define touch screens, joysticks, and styluses.

Scanning Devices

Scanners move across text and images. Scanning devices convert scanned text and images into a form that the system unit can process. There are four types of scanning devices: optical scanners, card readers, bar code readers, and character and mark recognition devices.

Optical Scanners

An **optical scanner,** also known simply as a scanner, accepts documents consisting of text and/or images and converts them to machine-readable form. These devices do not recognize individual letters or images. Rather, they recognize light, dark, and colored areas that make up individual letters or images. Typically, scanned documents are saved in files that can be further processed, displayed, printed, or stored for later use. There are three basic types of optical scanners: flatbed, document, and portable. (See Figure 7-12.)

- **Flatbed scanner** is much like a copy machine. The image to be scanned is placed on a glass surface and the scanner records the image from below.

Flatbed scanner

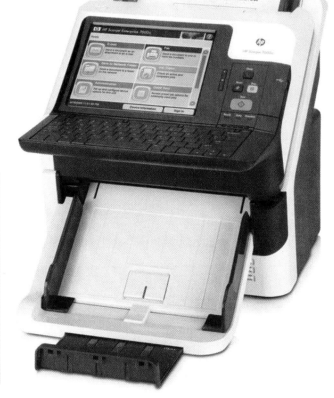

Portable scanner

Document scanner

Figure 7-12 Three types of scanners

- **Document scanner** is similar to a flatbed scanner except that it can quickly scan multipage documents. It automatically feeds one page of a document at a time through a scanning surface.
- **Portable scanner** is typically a handheld device that slides across the image, making direct contact.

Optical scanners are powerful tools for a wide variety of end users, including graphics and advertising professionals who scan images and combine them with text. Lawyers and students use portable scanners as a valuable research tool to record information.

Card Readers

Nearly everyone uses a credit card, debit card, access (parking or building) card, and/or some type of identification card. These cards typically have the user's name, some type of identification number, and signature embossed on the card. Additionally, encoded information is often stored on the card as well. Card readers interpret this encoded information. There are two basic types:

- By far the most common is the **magnetic card reader.** The encoded information is stored on a thin magnetic strip located on the back of the card.

Figure 7-13 Radio frequency card reader

Figure 7-14 Bar code reader

When the card is swiped through the magnetic card reader, the information is read.

- **Radio frequency card readers** are not as common but more convenient because they do not require the card to actually make contact with the reader. The card has a small **RFID (radio frequency identification)** microchip that contains the user's encoded information. Whenever the card is passed within a few inches of the card reader, the user's information is read. (See Figure 7-13.)

Bar Code Readers

You are probably familiar with **bar code readers** or **scanners** from grocery stores. (See Figure 7-14.) These devices are either handheld **wand readers** or **platform scanners.** They contain photoelectric cells that scan or read **bar codes,** or the vertical zebra-striped marks printed on product containers.

Almost all supermarkets use electronic cash registers and a bar code system called the **Universal Product Code (UPC).** At the checkout counter, electronic cash registers use a bar code reader to scan each product's UPC code. The codes are sent to the supermarket's computer, which has a description, the latest price, and an inventory level for each product. The computer processes this input to update the inventory level and to provide the electronic cash register with the description and price for each product. These devices are so easy to use that many supermarkets are offering customers self-checkout stations.

Character and Mark Recognition Devices

Character and mark recognition devices are scanners that are able to recognize special characters and marks. They are specialty devices that are essential tools for certain applications. Three types are

- **Magnetic-ink character recognition (MICR)**—used by banks to automatically read those unusual numbers on the bottom of checks and deposit slips. A special-purpose machine known as a reader/sorter reads these numbers and provides input that allows banks to efficiently maintain customer account balances.
- **Optical-character recognition (OCR)**—uses special preprinted characters that can be read by a light source and changed into machine-readable code. A common OCR device is the handheld wand reader. (See Figure 7-15.) These are used in department stores to read retail price tags by reflecting light on the printed characters.
- **Optical-mark recognition (OMR)**—senses the presence or absence of a mark, such as a pencil mark. OMR is often used to score standardized multiple-choice tests.

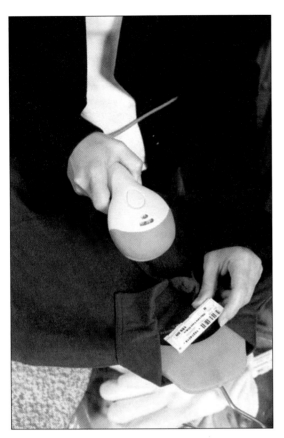

Figure 7-15 Wand reader

 CONCEPT CHECK

 How are pointing and scanning devices different?

 Describe four types of scanners.

 Describe three common character and mark recognition devices.

Image Capturing Devices

Optical scanners, like traditional copy machines, can make a copy from an original. For example, an optical scanner can make a digital copy of a photograph. Image capturing devices, on the other hand, create or capture original images. These devices include digital cameras and digital video cameras.

Digital Cameras

Digital cameras are similar to traditional cameras except that images are recorded digitally on a disk or in the camera's memory rather than on film and then downloaded, or transferred, to your computer. (See Figure 7-16.) You can take a picture, view it immediately, and even place it on your own Web page, within minutes.

To learn more about how digital photography works, visit us on the Web at www.computing2011.com and enter the keyword **photo.** Digital photographs can be shared easily with others over the Internet.

Digital Video Cameras

Unlike traditional video cameras, **digital video cameras** record motion digitally on a disk or in the camera's

Figure 7-16 Digital camera

Built-in WebCam

Attached WebCam

Figure 7-17 Two types of WebCams

memory. Most have the capability to take still images as well. **Web-Cams** are specialized digital video cameras that capture images and send them to a computer for broadcast over the Internet. Some Web-Cams are built-in while others are designed to be attached to the computer monitor. (See Figure 7-17.) To learn more about WebCams, visit our Web site at www.computing2011.com and enter the keyword **webcam**. To learn how you can videoconference, see Making IT Work for You: WebCams and Instant Messaging on pages 196 and 197.

Audio-Input Devices

Audio-input devices convert sounds into a form that can be processed by the system unit. By far the most widely used audio-input device is the microphone. Audio input can take many forms, including the human voice and music.

Voice Recognition Systems

Voice recognition systems use a microphone, a sound card, and special software. These systems allow users to operate computers and other devices as well as to create documents using voice commands. Examples include voice-controlled dialing features on mobile phones, navigation on GPS devices, and control of car audio systems such as Microsoft Sync. Specialized portable voice recognition systems are widely used by doctors, lawyers, and others to record dictation. (See Figure 7-18.) These devices are able to record for several hours before connecting to a computer system to edit, store, and print the dictated information. Some systems are even able to translate dictation from one language to another, such as from English to Japanese.

Figure 7-18 Portable voice recognition system

Making IT work for you

WEBCAMS AND INSTANT MESSAGING

Do you enjoy chatting with your friends? Are you working on a project and need to collaborate with others in your group? What if you could see and hear your group online? Perhaps instant messaging is just what you're looking for. It's easy and free with an Internet connection and the right software.

Sending Messages   In instant messaging applications, your friends are added to a list of contacts that shows you when they are online and available to chat. For example, you could use Windows Live Messenger as follows:

1 ● Add contacts by clicking the *Add a Contact* button and following the on-screen instructions.

● Double-click the name of a friend in the *Online* section.

● Enter your message in the window that appears.

● Click the *Send* button.

Your message appears on your friend's screen instantly. Your friend can then continue the conversation by following the steps above.

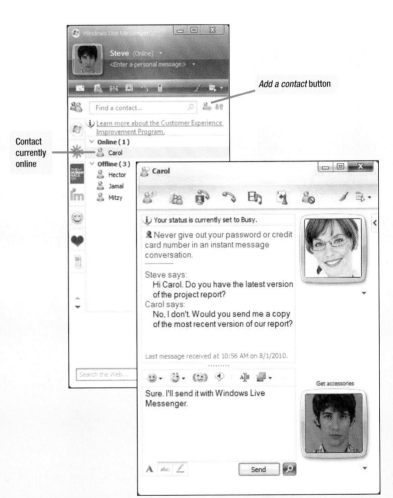

Add a contact button

Contact currently online

Transferring Files   While chatting, it is sometimes useful to share a file. For example, you might want to send a copy of a report you have been working on to a classmate to review. To send a file during an online chat:

① • Click the *Share files* button and select *Send a file or photo. . .*

  • Browse your computer for the file you want to share and click *Open*.

Your friend is given an option to accept your file. A notification appears in your conversation when your file upload is complete. An additional notification is added when your friend has completed the download of your file. You can continue to chat throughout this process.

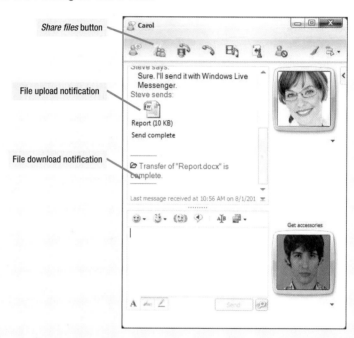

Share files button

File upload notification

File download notification

Using a WebCam   In addition to typing text messages, some instant messaging software allows you to have voice or video conversations over the Internet so you can see and hear the person you are collaborating with. To do this, both users must have a microphone and speakers, as well as Web cameras for video conferencing. You could hold a video conference using Windows Live Messenger by following these steps.

① • Start a conversation with a contact as shown on the previous page.

  • Click the *Video call* button.

Your friend is given the option to accept the video conference. Once he or she accepts, the video conference begins.

Video call button

Video image of your friend

Video image you are sending

The Web is continually changing, and some of the specifics presented in this Making IT Work for You may have changed.
To learn about other ways to make information technology work for you, visit our Web site at www.computing2011.com and enter the keyword miw.

What Is Output?

Output is processed data or information. Output typically takes the form of text, graphics, photos, audio, and/or video. For example, when you create a presentation using a presentation graphics program, you typically input text and graphics. You also could include photographs and even add voice narration. The output would be the completed presentation.

Output devices are any hardware used to provide or to create output. They translate information that has been processed by the system unit into a form that humans can understand. There are a wide range of output devices. The most widely used are monitors, printers, and audio-output devices.

Monitors

The most frequently used output device is the **monitor.** Also known as **display screens,** monitors present visual images of text and graphics. The output is often referred to as soft copy. Monitors vary in size, shape, and cost. Almost all, however, have some basic distinguishing features.

Features

The most important characteristic of a monitor is its clarity. **Clarity** refers to the quality and sharpness of the displayed images. It is a function of several monitor features, including resolution, dot pitch, refresh rate, size, and aspect ratio.

Pixel

Figure 7-19 Monitor resolution

- **Resolution** is one of the most important features. Images are formed on a monitor by a series of dots or **pixels (picture elements).** (See Figure 7-19.) Resolution is expressed as a matrix of these dots or pixels. For example, many monitors today have a resolution of 1,600 pixel columns by 1,200 pixel rows for a total of 1,920,000 pixels. The higher a monitor's resolution (the more pixels), the clearer the image produced. See Figure 7-20 for the most common monitor resolutions.

- **Dot (pixel) pitch** is the distance between each pixel. Most newer monitors have a dot pitch of .31 mm (31/100th of a millimeter) or less. The lower the dot pitch (the shorter the distance between pixels), the clearer the images produced.

- **Refresh rate** indicates how often a displayed image is updated or refreshed. Most monitors operate at a rate of 75 hertz, which means that the monitor is refreshed 75 times each second. Images displayed on monitors with refresh rates lower than 75 hertz appear to flicker and can cause eye strain. The faster the refresh rate (the more frequently images are redrawn), the better the quality of images displayed.

- Size, or active display area, is measured by the diagonal length of a monitor's viewing area. Common sizes are 15, 17, 19, 21, and 24 inches.
- **Aspect ratio** is determined by the width of a monitor divided by its height. Common aspect ratios for monitors are 4:3 (standard, similar to traditional television pictures) and 16:10 (wide screen).

Standard	Pixels
SVGA	800 × 600
XGA	1,024 × 768
SXGA	1,280 × 1,024
UXGA	1,600 × 1,200
QXGA	2,048 × 1,536
QXSGA	2,560 × 2,048

Figure 7-20 Resolution standards

Flat-Panel Monitors

Flat-panel monitors are the most widely used type of monitor today. Compared to other types, they are thinner, are more portable, and require less power to operate. (See Figure 7-21.)

Many of today's flat-panel monitors are **LCD (liquid crystal display)**. There are two basic types: passive-matrix and active-matrix. **Passive-matrix** or **dual-scan monitors** create images by scanning the entire screen. This type requires very little power, but the clarity of the images is not as sharp. **Active-matrix** or **thin film transistor (TFT) monitors** do not scan down the screen; instead, each pixel is independently activated. They can display more colors with better clarity. Active-matrix monitors are more expensive and require more power.

OLED (organic light-emitting diode) is a newer technology and is becoming widely used. Unlike LCD, OLED technology has the benefits of lower power consumption and longer battery life, as well as possibilities for much thinner displays.

Cathode-Ray Tubes

Until recently, the most common type of monitor for the office and the home was the **cathode-ray tube (CRT)**. (See Figure 7-22.) These monitors are typically placed directly on the system unit or on the desktop. CRTs are similar in size and technology to televisions. Compared to other types of monitors, their

Figure 7-21 Flat-panel monitor

Figure 7-22 CRT monitor

primary advantages are low cost and excellent resolution. Their primary disadvantages are that they are bulky, are less energy efficient, and occupy a considerable amount of space on the desktop.

Other Monitors

There are several other types of monitors. These monitors are used for more specialized applications, such as reading books, making presentations, and watching television. Three of these specialized devices are E-book readers, data projectors, and high-definition television.

Figure 7-23 **E-book reader**

- **E-book readers** are handheld, book-sized devices that display text and graphics. To learn more about one of the most widely used e-book readers, see Making IT Work for You: Amazon Kindle on page 201. Using content downloaded from the Web or from special cartridges, these devices are used to read newspapers, magazines, and entire books. (See Figure 7-23.) These devices use a special type of screen called **electronic paper** or **e-paper** that requires power only when changing pages, and not the entire time a page is displayed on the screen.

- **Data projectors** are specialized devices similar to slide projectors. These devices, however, connect to microcomputers and project computer output just as it would appear on a monitor. Data projectors are commonly used for presentations almost anywhere from the classroom to the boardroom.

- **High-definition television (HDTV)** delivers a much clearer and more detailed wide-screen picture than regular television. Because the output is digital, users can readily freeze video sequences to create high-quality still images. The video and still images can then be digitized, edited, and stored on disk for later use. This technology is very useful to graphic artists, designers, and publishers.

On the Web Explorations

HDTV is a higher-quality alternative to standard-definition television.

To learn more about HDTV, visit our Web site at www.cmputing2011.com and enter the keyword hdtv.

CONCEPT CHECK

 What is output? What are output devices?

 Define these monitor features: resolution, dot pitch, refresh rate, size, and aspect ratio.

 Describe flat-panel, CRT, and other more specialized monitors.

AMAZON KINDLE

E-book readers are a great way to enjoy reading on the go. Did you know they can also help you stay current in your profession? Many e-book readers feature subscriptions to newspapers and magazines, including publications that will keep you up-to-date on topics important to your career. Some devices, such as the Amazon Kindle, can even download subscriptions automatically wherever you are without the need for a computer connection.

Subscribing To subscribe to a magazine using the Kindle:

1 ● **Press the *Menu* button and select *Shop in Kindle Store***

Turn Wireless Off

Shop in Kindle Store

View Archived Items

Search

Settings

Experimental

Sync & Check for Items

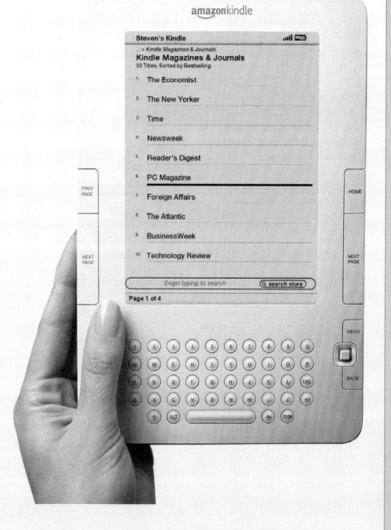

2 ● **Select *Magazines* from the *Browse* menu.**

Browse:

Books - *Over 300,000 titles available*

Newspapers

Magazines

Blogs

3 ● **Select a publication of interest and follow the on-screen instructions to complete your subscription.**

The Web in continually changing, and some of the specifics presented in Making IT Work for You may have changed.

To learn about other ways to make information technology work for you, visit our Web site at www.computing2011.com and enter the keyword miw.

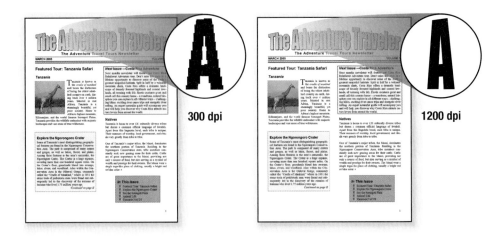

300 dpi   1200 dpi

Figure 7-24 Dpi comparison

Printers

You probably use a printer with some frequency to print homework assignments, photographs, and Web pages. **Printers** translate information that has been processed by the system unit and present the information on paper. Printer output is often called hard copy.

Features

There are many different types of printers. Almost all, however, have some basic distinguishing features, including resolution, color capability, speed, and memory.

- **Resolution** for a printer is similar to monitor resolution. It is a measure of the clarity of images produced. Printer resolution, however, is measured in **dpi (dots per inch).** (See Figure 7-24.) Most printers designed for personal use average 1,200 dpi. The higher the dpi, the better the quality of images produced.
- Color capability is provided by most printers today. Users typically have the option to print either with just black ink or with color. Because it is more expensive to print in color, most users select black ink for letters, drafts, and homework. Color is used more selectively for final reports containing graphics and for photographs.
- Speed is measured in the number of pages printed per minute. Typically, printers for personal use average 15 to 19 pages per minute for single-color (black) output and 13 to 15 pages per minute for color output.
- Memory within a printer is used to store printing instructions and documents waiting to be printed. The more memory in a printer, the faster it will be able to create large documents.

Ink-Jet Printers

Ink-jet printers spray ink at high speed onto the surface of paper. This process not only produces a letter-quality image but also permits printing to be done in a variety of colors, making them ideal for select special applications. (See Figure 7-25.) Ink-jet printers are the most widely used printers. They are reliable, quiet, and relatively inexpensive. The most costly aspect of ink-jet printers is replacing the ink cartridges. For this reason, most users specify black ink for the majority of print jobs and use the more expensive color printing for select applications. Typical ink-jet printers produce 17 to 19 pages per minute of black-only output and 13 to 15 pages of color output.

Laser Printers

The **laser printer** uses a technology similar to that used in a photocopying machine. Laser printers use a laser light beam to produce images with excellent letter and graphics quality. More expensive than ink-jet printers, laser printers are faster and are used in applications requiring high-quality output. (See Figure 7-26.)

There are two categories of laser printers. **Personal laser printers** are less expensive and are used by many single users. They typically can print 15 to 17 pages a minute. **Shared laser printers** typically support color, are more expensive, and are used (shared) by a group of users. Shared laser printers typically print over 50 pages a minute.

Figure 7-25 A special-application ink-jet printer

On the Web Explorations

For fast high-quality printouts, laser printers are the standard.

To learn more about a company that makes laser printers, visit our Web site at www.computing2011.com and enter the keyword printer.

Figure 7-26 Laser printer

environmental facts

Did you know that the ingredients in most printer cartridges contain hazardous chemicals? In fact, much of the production of new printer ink and toner has moved to third-world nations as a result of pollution concerns. One approach to minimizing the impact is to recycle printer cartridges. However, some have approached the problem from a completely different direction. What if the ink your printer used was a by-product readily available in your house? At least one manufacturer thinks this is the way of the future. Their new green printer design uses coffee grounds to print your text and images.

Figure 7-27 **Photo printer**

Other Printers

There are several other types of printers. These printers include dot-matrix printers, thermal printers, plotters, photo printers, and portable printers:

- **Dot-matrix printers** form characters and images using a series of small pins on a print head. Once a widely used microcomputer printer, they are inexpensive and reliable but quite noisy. In general, they are used for tasks where high-quality output is not required.
- **Thermal printers** use heat elements to produce images on heat-sensitive paper. These printers are widely used with ATMs and gasoline pumps to print receipts.
- **Plotters** are special-purpose printers for producing a wide range of specialized output. Using output from graphics tablets and other graphical input devices, plotters create maps, images, and architectural and engineering drawings. Plotters are typically used by graphic artists, engineers, and architects to print out designs, sketches, and drawings.
- **Photo printers** are special-purpose printers designed to print photo-quality images from digital cameras. (See Figure 7-27.) Most photo printers print 3 × 5" or 4 × 6" images on glossy, photo-quality paper.
- **Portable printers** are usually small and lightweight printers designed to work with a notebook computer. Portable printers may be ink-jet or laser printers, print in black and white or color, and connect with USB.

☑ **CONCEPT CHECK**

▢ Discuss these printer features: resolution, color capability, speed, and memory.

▢ Compare ink-jet printers and laser printers.

▢ Discuss dot-matrix, thermal, plotter, photo, and portable printers.

Figure 7-28 **Digital music player**

Audio-Output Devices

Audio-output devices translate audio information from the computer into sounds that people can understand. The most widely used audio-output devices are **speakers** and **headphones.** These devices are connected to a sound card in the system unit. The sound card is used to capture as well as play back recorded sounds. Audio-output devices are used to play music, vocalize translations from one language to another, and communicate information from the computer system to users.

Creating voice output is not anywhere near as difficult as recognizing and interpreting voice input. In fact, voice output is quite common. It is used with many soft-drink machines, telephones, and cars. It is used as a reinforcement tool for learning, such as to help students study a foreign language. It also is used in many supermarkets at the checkout counter to confirm purchases. One of its most powerful capabilities is to assist the physically challenged.

Digital music players, also known as **digital media players,** are specialized devices for storing, transferring, and playing audio files. Older players are only able to play music saved in a special compressed audio file format known as MP3. Today, most players are able to use a wide variety of audio files. Many are capable of displaying video files as well. Some of the best-known audio and video players are the Apple iPod, Creative Zen, Microsoft Zune, and iRiver. (See Figure 7-28.)

Combination Input and Output Devices

Many devices combine input and output capabilities. Sometimes this is done to save space. Other times it is done for very specialized applications. Common combination devices include fax machines, multifunctional devices, Internet telephones, and terminals.

Fax Machines

A **fax machine** is a standard tool in nearly every office. At one time, all fax machines were separate stand-alone devices for sending and receiving images over telephone lines. Now, most computer systems have that capability with the simple addition of a fax/modem board. To send a fax, these devices scan the image of a document converting the light and dark areas into a format that can be sent electronically over standard telephone lines. To receive a fax, these devices reverse the process and print the document (or display the document on your monitor) using signals received from the telephone line.

Multifunctional Devices

Multifunctional devices (MFD) typically combine the capabilities of a scanner, printer, fax, and copy machine. These multifunctional devices offer a cost and space advantage. They cost about the same as a good printer or copy machine but require much less space than the single-function devices they replace. Their disadvantage is that the quality and functionality are not quite as good as those of the separate single-purpose devices. Even so, multifunctional devices are widely used in home and small business offices.

Internet Telephones

Internet telephones are specialized input and output devices for receiving and sending voice communication. (See Figure 7-29.)

Voice over IP (VoIP) is the transmission of telephone calls over computer networks. Also known as **telephony, Internet telephony,** and **IP telephony** VoIP uses the Internet rather than traditional communication lines to support voice communication. To place telephone calls using Internet telephony requires a high-speed Internet connection and special software and/or hardware. Skype and Vonage are two examples of popular Internet telephony service providers. The three most popular approaches are

- **Computer-to-computer** communications allow individuals to place free long-distance calls. This application requires that both parties have a computer and that their computers are on and connected to the Internet when a call is placed. The required software is available from a variety of sources for free or at very low cost.
- **Computer-to-traditional telephone** communications allow a user to call almost any traditional telephone from his or her computer. Only the person making the call needs to have a computer connected to the Internet. The calling party subscribes to a special Internet phone service provider that supplies the required software and charges a small monthly and/or per-minute fee. To see how this works, visit our Web site at www.computing2011.com and enter the keyword **phone.**
- **Traditional telephone-to-traditional telephone** communications do not require a computer. The calling party subscribes to a special Internet phone service provider that supplies a special hardware adapter that connects a traditional telephone to the Internet. The cost for this service is similar to the computer-to-traditional telephone approach.

Compared to traditional telephone calls, Internet-supported calls may have a lower sound quality and may have an audio delay. However, most users report that this difference is not significant.

On the Web Explorations

Multifunctional devices save space and money, making them a favorite in home offices and small businesses.

To learn more about MFDs, visit our Web site at www.computing2011.com and enter the keyword mfd.

Figure 7-29 Internet telephone

☑ CONCEPT CHECK

What are the two most widely used audio-output devices?

Describe the following combination devices: fax machine, MFD, and Internet telephone.

Describe the three most popular Internet telephony approaches.

Careers in IT

Technical writers prepare instruction manuals, technical reports, and other scientific or technical documents. (See Figure 7-30.) Most technical writers work for computer software firms, government agencies, or research institutions. They translate technical information into easily understandable instructions or summaries. As new technology continues to develop and expand, the need for technical writers who can communicate technical expertise to others is expected to increase.

Technical writing positions typically require a college degree in communications, journalism, or English and a specialization in, or familiarity with, a technical field. However, individuals with strong writing skills sometimes transfer from jobs in the sciences to positions in technical writing.

Technical writers can expect to earn an annual salary in the range of $46,500 to $76,500. Advancement opportunities can be limited within a firm or company, but there are additional opportunities in consulting. To learn about other careers in information technology, visit us at www.computing2011.com and enter the keyword **careers.**

Figure 7-30 **Technical writer**

A LOOK TO THE FUTURE

Crashing Through the Foreign Language Barrier

Have you ever wished you could speak more than one language fluently? What if you could speak hundreds of languages instantly? Would you like to have your own personal interpreter to accompany you whenever you traveled to a foreign country? What if you could take a picture of a foreign road sign or restaurant menu and have it immediately translated for you? Technology called machine translation (MT) may soon exist to do all of these things. The military and private sector are funding a variety of research projects on electronic interpreters, and the commercial opportunities are enormous. The worldwide translation services market is an over $8 billion a year industry and is expected to grow even more.

Prototype portable handheld electronic interpreters are currently in a testing phase at the U.S. Office of Naval Research. In fact, it is expected that these devices will be widely used in the near future. The company Speech-Gear has developed software called Compadre that takes verbal statements in one language, converts the statements to text, translates that text to another language, and then vocalizes the translated text. And it does all this in two seconds! The military is particularly interested in instant electronic interpreters as they focus on peacekeeping objectives. More than ever before, U.S. soldiers find themselves needing to communicate with non-English-speaking civilians to settle disputes and maintain order.

Despite advances in translation software, several challenges remain. Current translation techniques are labor intensive; they require linguists and programmers to create large lists of words and their corresponding meanings. Unfortunately, computers have a difficult time understanding idioms, such as "It is raining cats and dogs." They may also have difficulty correctly identifying words by their context. For example, the sentences "The stove is hot" and "The latest tech gadget is hot" use the same word, *hot,* but it has a very different meaning in each sentence. Researchers have been working on a solution to these problems. One is the EliMT project. Instead of translating from word to word, EliMT compares books that have been translated in different languages, looking for sentence fragment patterns. By comparing sentence fragments, it is hoped that translation programs will be able to identify word groupings and translate them into another language's comparable word grouping, essentially translating concepts instead of individual words. Other systems are supplementing machine translation with expert human translators for verification of unusual phrases.

What are the uses for such software and devices? Will the average person want or need an electronic translator? What type of professions and professionals will use them? What industries would benefit most from electronic translators? How could you use this technology?

INPUT

Input is any data or instructions used by a computer. Input devices translate words, images, and actions into a form a computer can process.

Keyboards

Keyboards are the most common way to input data. The most common types are

- **Traditional**—full-sized, rigid, rectangular.
- **Ergonomic**—designed to minimize wrist strain.
- **Wireless**—no wire provides greater flexibility.
- **PDA**—miniature keyboards for PDAs and smart phones.
- **Virtual**—an image of a keyboard displayed on a touch screen device.

Features include **numeric keypads, toggle keys,** and **combination keys.**

Pointing Devices

Pointing devices accept pointing gestures and convert them to machine-readable input.

- **Mouse** controls a **mouse pointer. A wheel button** rotates to scroll through information. Three basic mouse designs are **optical, mechanical,** and **cordless (wireless).** Similar devices include **trackball (roller ball), touch pad,** and **pointing stick.**
- **Touch screens** operations are controlled by finger touching the screen. **Multi-touch screens** can be touched with more than one finger; commonly used on mobile devices such as the Apple iPhone.

INPUT

- **Joystick** operations are controlled by varying pressure, speed, and direction.
- **Stylus** is a penlike device used with tablet PCs and PDAs. **Handwriting recognition software** translates handwritten notes.

Scanning Devices

Scanners move across text and graphics. Scanning devices convert scanned text and images into a form that can be processed by the system unit.

- **Optical scanners** record light, dark, and colored areas of scanned text or images. There are three types: **flatbed, document,** and **portable.**
- **Card readers** interpret encoded information. Two types: **magnetic** (reads **magnetic strip**) and **radio frequency** (reads **RFID** microchip) card readers.

To be a competent end user, you need to be aware of the most commonly used input and output devices. These devices are translators for information into and out of the system unit. Input devices translate words, sounds, and actions into symbols the system unit can process. Output devices translate symbols from the system unit into words, images, and sounds that people can understand.

INPUT

- **Bar code readers** are used with electronic cash registers in supermarkets. **Wand readers** or **platform scanners** read **UPC** codes that are used to determine product descriptions and prices and to update inventory levels.
- Character and mark recognition devices recognize special characters and marks. Three types: **MICR** (read by readers/sorters), **OCR**, and **OMR.**

Image Capturing Devices

Image capturing devices create or capture original images. These devices include **digital cameras** (images downloaded to system unit for further processing and/or printing) and **digital video cameras. WebCams** capture and send images over the Internet, one design is built-in and the other is attached.

Audio-Input Devices

Audio-input devices convert sounds into a form that can be processed by the system unit. Audio input takes many forms, including the human voice and music. **Voice recognition systems** use a combination of a microphone, a sound card, and special software.

OUTPUT

Output is data or information processed by a computer. Output devices translate processed text, graphics, audio, and video into a form humans can understand.

Monitors

Monitors (display screens) present visual images of text and graphics. Monitor output is described as soft copy.

Clarity is a function of several monitor features including **resolution** (expressed as matrix of **pixels** or **picture elements**), **dot (pixel) pitch, refresh rate,** size, and **aspect ratio.**

- **Flat-panel monitors** have become the standard for computer systems. Many are **LCD (liquid crystal display).** Two basic types are **passive-matrix (dual-scan)** and **active-matrix (thin film transistor, TFT).** OLED (organic light-emitting diode) is newer technology requiring lower power consumption, longer battery life, and potential for thinner displays.

OUTPUT

- **Cathode-ray tubes (CRTs)** use technology similar to a television. Compared to flat-panels, CRTs are bulky, require more electricity to run, and occupy considerable space on the desktop.

Three specialized types of monitors are **e-book readers** (screen known as **electronic paper** or **e-paper**), **data projectors**, and **high-definition television (HDTV)**.

Printers

Printers translate information processed by the system unit and present the information on paper. Output from printers is described as hard copy. Some distinguishing features of printers include **resolution** (measured in **dpi** or **dots per inch**), color capability, speed, and memory.

- **Ink-jet printers** spray ink to produce high-quality output. These printers are inexpensive and the most widely used type of printer.
- **Laser printers** use technology similar to photo-copying machines. Two categories are **personal** and **shared.**

Other printers include **dot-matrix printers, thermal printers, plotters, photo printers,** and **portable printers.**

Audio-Output Devices

Audio-output devices translate audio information from the computer into sounds that people can understand. **Speakers** and **headphones** are the most widely used audio-output devices.

Digital music players (digital media players) store, transfer, and play audio files. Many players also display video files.

COMBINATION DEVICES

Combination devices combine input and output capabilities. Common types include

Fax Machines

Fax machines send and receive images via standard telephone lines.

Multifunctional Devices

Multifunctional devices (MFD) typically combine the capabilities of a scanner, printer, fax, and copy machine.

Internet Telephones

Internet telephones receive and send voice communication. **Voice over IP (VoIP)**, also known as **telephony, Internet telephony,** and **IP telephony,** use the Internet to transmit telephone calls. Three approaches are computer-to-computer, computer-to-traditional telephone, and traditional telephone-to-traditional telephone.

CAREERS IN IT

Technical writers prepare instruction manuals, technical reports, and other documents. Bachelor's degree in communication, journalism, or English and a specialization in, or familiarity with, a technical field required. Salary range $46,500 to $76,500.

KEY TERMS

active-matrix (199)
monitor (198)
aspect ratio (199)
bar code (193)
bar code reader (193)
bar code scanner (193)
cathode-ray tube (CRT)
  monitor (199)
clarity (198)
combination key (188)
cordless mouse (189)
data projector (200)
digital camera (194)
digital media
  player (205)
digital music
  player (205)
digital video
  camera (194)
display screen (198)
document scanner (192)
dot-matrix printer (204)
dot pitch (198)
dots-per-inch (dpi) (202)
dual-scan monitor (199)
e-book reader (200)
e-paper (200)
electronic paper (200)
ergonomic
  keyboard (187)
fax machine (205)
flat-panel monitor (199)
flatbed scanner (191)
handwriting recognition
  software (190)
headphones (205)
high-definition television
  (HDTV) (200)
ink-jet printer (202)
Internet telephone (206)

Internet telephony (206)
IP telephony (206)
joystick (190)
keyboard (186)
laser printer (203)
liquid crystal display
  (LCD) (199)
magnetic card
  reader (192)
magnetic-ink character
  recognition
  (MICR) (194)
mechanical mouse (189)
monitor (198)
mouse (188)
mouse pointer (188)
multifunctional device
  (MFD) (206)
multi-touch
  screen (190)
numeric keypad (187)
optical-character
  recognition
  (OCR) (194)
optical-mark recognition
  (OMR) (194)
optical mouse (189)
optical scanner (191)
organic light-emitting
  diode (OLED) (199)
passive-matrix
  monitor (199)
PDA keyboard (187)
personal laser
  printer (203)
photo printer (204)
picture elements (198)
pixel (198)
pixel pitch (198)
platform scanner (193)

plotter (204)
pointing stick (189)
portable printer (204)
portable scanner (192)
printer (202)
radio frequency card
  reader (193)
radio frequency
  identification
  (RFID) (193)
refresh rate (198)
resolution (198, 202)
roller ball (189)
shared laser
  printer (203)
speakers (205)
stylus (190)
technical writer (207)
telephony (206)
thermal printer (204)
thin film transistor (TFT)
  monitor (199)
toggle key (187)
touch pad (189)
touch screen (190)
trackball (189)
traditional
  keyboard (187)
Universal Product Code
  (UPC) (193)
virtual keyboard (187)
Voice over IP
  (VoIP) (206)
voice recognition
  system (195)
wand reader (193)
WebCam (195)
wheel button (188)
wireless keyboard (187)
wireless mouse (189)

To test your knowledge of these key terms with animated flash cards, visit our Web site at www.computing2011.com and enter the keyword terms7.

MULTIPLE CHOICE

Circle the letter or fill in the correct answer.

1. Hardware used to translate words, sounds, images, and actions that people understand into a form that the system unit can process is known as
   a. device drivers
   b. device readers
   c. input devices
   d. output devices

2. This type of keyboard provides the greatest amount of flexibility and convenience by eliminating cables connected to the system unit.
   a. ergonomic
   b. network
   c. traditional
   d. wireless

3. The mouse _____ usually appears in the shape of an arrow.
   a. indicator
   b. marker
   c. meter
   d. pointer

4. _____ describes the relationship between the height and width of a monitor.
   a. Aspect ratio
   b. Dot pitch
   c. Dpi
   d. Resolution

5. This type of pointing device has crisscrossed invisible beams of infrared light that are protected with a clear plastic outer layer.
   a. joystick
   b. optical mouse
   c. pointing stick
   d. touch screen

6. A Universal Product Code is read by what type of scanner?
   a. bar code
   b. flatbed
   c. MICR
   d. OCR

7. _____ input devices convert sounds into a form that can be processed by the system unit.
   a. Audio
   b. Electrolyzing
   c. Plotting
   d. WebCam

8. The most important characteristic of a monitor is its
   a. clarity
   b. dot pitch
   c. resolution
   d. viewable size

9. This type of printer uses technology similar to photocopying machines.
   a. ink-jet
   b. laser
   c. portable
   d. thermal

10. _____ is a specialized input and output device for receiving and sending voice communication.
    a. Fax machine
    b. Laser
    c. MFD
    d. Scanner

For an interactive multiple-choice practice test, visit our Web site at www.computing2011.com and enter the keyword multiple7.

MATCHING

Match each numbered item with the most closely related lettered item. Write your answers in the spaces provided.

a. clarity
b. CRT
c. dpi
d. HDTV
e. joystick
f. stylus
g. TFT
h. thermal
i. toggle
j. UPC

1. These keys turn a feature on or off. _____
2. A pointing device widely used for computer games. _____
3. Penlike device commonly used with tablet PCs and PDAs. _____
4. Type of bar code used in supermarkets. _____
5. Refers to quality and sharpness of displayed images. _____
6. Type of monitor similar to a traditional television set. _____
7. Monitors that have independently activated pixels. _____
8. Delivers a much clearer widescreen picture than regular television. _____
9. Measurement used to determine a printer's resolution. _____
10. Printer that uses heat to produce images on heat-sensitive paper. _____

For an interactive matching practice test, visit our Web site at www.computing2011. com and enter the keyword matching7.

OPEN-ENDED

On a separate sheet of paper, respond to each question or statement.

1. Define input devices.
2. Describe the different types of keyboard, pointing, scanning, image capturing, and audio-input devices.
3. Describe the three categories of output devices.
4. Define output devices.
5. What are combination input and output devices? Give examples of such devices.

APPLYING TECHNOLOGY

The following questions are designed to demonstrate ways that you can effectively use technology today. The first question relates directly to this chapter's Making IT Work for You feature.

1 WEBCAMS AND INSTANT MESSAGING

Do you enjoy chatting with friends? Are you working on a project and need to collaborate with others in your group? What if you could see and hear your group online? Perhaps instant messaging and WebCams are just what you're looking for. It's easy and free with an Internet connection and the right software. To learn more about WebCams and instant messaging, review Making IT Work for You: Web-Cams and Instant Messaging on pages 196 and 197. Then answer the following questions: (a) How do you add a new friend to Windows Live Messenger? (b) What hardware is necessary to video conference with Windows Live Messenger? (c) Describe the steps for sharing a file using Windows Live Messenger. Be sure to include both the steps you take and those your friend must take to receive the file.

2 INTERNET TELEPHONES

Do you need a cheaper way to stay in touch with friends and family? Did you know you can use your computer and the Internet to make long-distance calls to regular phones? All you need is some software and an Internet connection to get started. To learn more about this technology, visit our Web site at www.computing2011.com and enter the keyword phone. Then answer the following questions: (a) Which Internet phone service provider is featured in the examples? (b) What are the sliders used for in the Setup Wizard? (c) Which button is clicked to end a call?

3 VOICE RECOGNITION

Through voice recognition technology you can control your computer or dictate a term paper. Connect to our Web site at www.computing2011.com and enter the keyword voice to link to a leader in voice recognition software. Once there, read about the product's features and then answer the following: (a) Describe the features offered by the voice recognition software. (b) What input devices are required to use this software? (c) Do you think voice recognition software will replace keyboards and mice as primary input devices? Justify your answer.

EXPANDING YOUR KNOWLEDGE

The following questions are designed to add depth and detail to your understanding of specific topics presented within this chapter. The questions direct you to sources other than the textbook to obtain this knowledge.

 ## HOW DIGITAL CAMERAS WORK

While traditional cameras capture images on film, digital cameras capture images, then convert them into a digital form. These images can be viewed immediately and saved to a disk or into the camera's memory. To learn more about how digital cameras work, visit our Web site at www.computing2011.com and enter the keyword photo. Then answer the following questions: (a) What is a CCD and what is its function? (b) What is an ADC and what is its function? (c) How are images transported from a digital camera to a computer?

 ## HOW INTERNET TELEPHONES WORK

Internet telephones offer a low-cost alternative to making long-distance calls. Using the Internet telephone (or other appropriate audio-input and audio-output devices), the Internet, a special service provider, a sound card, and special software, you can place long-distance calls to almost anywhere in the world. To learn more about how Internet telephony works, visit our Web site at www.computing2011.com and enter the keyword phone. Then answer the following questions: (a) What input and output devices are used? (b) What advantages and disadvantages would these devices have compared to an Internet telephone? (c) If Chris were to place a call to Steve, would she incur traditional long-distance charges? Why or why not? (d) Create a drawing similar to the animation that would represent computer-to-computer telephony. Be sure to include and number the appropriate steps.

 ## HANDWRITING RECOGNITION

Handwriting recognition is a developing technology for direct input. Conduct a Web search with the keywords "handwriting recognition" to learn more about this technology. Then answer the following questions: (a) What types of devices and applications use handwriting recognition now? (b) What are some applications where handwriting recognition is the best choice for input? Why is this the case? (c) What are current limitations of handwriting recognition?

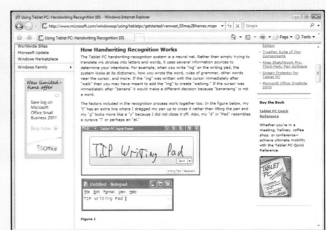

WRITING ABOUT TECHNOLOGY

The ability to think critically and to write effectively is essential to nearly every profession. The following questions are designed to help you develop these skills by posing thought-provoking questions about computer privacy, security, and/or ethics.

1 WEBCAMS

Many WebCams broadcast live views of public places, such as university campuses, football stadiums, and city centers. Anyone with a WebCam and the right software can set up a WebCam broadcast. Visit our Web site at www.computing2011.com and enter the keyword broadcast to link to a directory of public WebCams. Once connected, browse a few WebCam broadcasts and write a one-page paper that answers the following questions: (a) What WebCam broadcasts did you view? Describe the experience. (b) How does a user list his or her WebCam on the directory site? (c) Do you think WebCams can be used to enhance security? Justify your answer. (d) Do you think Web-Cams can be a violation of personal privacy? Justify your answer.

2 VOICE OVER IP

Voice over IP (VoIP) offers many benefits when compared to traditional telephone service. These include cost savings, installation convenience, and wide availability over existing high-speed Internet systems. However, there are some downsides. For example, unlike wired phone lines, VoIP is not automatically switched to generator backup during power outages. Also, 911 emergency service requires address lookup, which is easier to maintain for landlines. Consider the following questions and discuss your answers. Write a one-page summary of your analysis that answers the following questions: (a) What responsibility do VoIP providers have to their users regarding availability of emergency services? (b) What balance would you strike between service cost and issues of public safety? Explain your answer.

Secondary Storage

Competencies

After you have read this chapter, you should be able to:

1 Distinguish between primary and secondary storage.

2 Discuss the important characteristics of secondary storage including media, capacity, storage devices, and access speed.

3 Describe hard disk platters, tracts, sectors, and head crashes.

4 Compare internal and external hard drives.

5 Discuss performance enhancements including disk caching, RAIDs, file compression, and file decompression.

6 Define solid-state storage including solid-state drives, flash memory, and USB drives.

7 Define optical storage including compact, digital versatile, and high-definition discs.

8 Describe more specialized storage such as online storage services, floppy disk drives, and magnetic tape.

9 Discuss mass storage devices, enterprise storage systems, and storage area networks.

Floppy disks were once the only way to distribute software and the only way to share files between personal computers. These disks were everywhere, and they were essential, but they were also extremely fragile. Today's compact discs and USB flash drives are more reliable and hold more information than hundreds of floppy disks, but many believe there are still advances in this field ahead.

Some experts predict that the future of secondary storage is holographic. Compact discs use two dimensions to record data, but advances in optics now make it possible to record data in three dimensions. This holographic data storage could make it possible to inexpensively store hundreds of today's DVDs on one disc. Imagine buying a disk that holds hundreds of movies, for less than the cost of one of today's DVDs.

chapter **8**

Introduction

Secondary storage devices are used to save, to back up, and even to transport files consisting of data or programs from one location or computer to another. Not long ago, almost all files contained only numbers and letters. The demands for saving these files were easily met with low-capacity storage devices.

Data storage has expanded from text and numeric files to include digital music files, photographic files, video files, and much more. These new types of files require secondary storage devices that have much greater capacity.

Secondary storage devices have always been an indispensable element in any computer system. They have similarities to output and input devices. Like output devices, secondary storage devices receive information from the system unit in the form of the machine language of 0s and 1s. Rather than translating the information, however, secondary storage devices save the information in machine language for later use. Like input devices, secondary storage devices send information to the system unit for processing. However, the information, since it is already in machine form, does not need to be translated. It is sent directly to memory (RAM), where it can be accessed and processed by the CPU.

Competent end users need to be aware of the different types of secondary storage. They need to know the capabilities, limitations, and uses of hard disks, solid-state drives, optical discs, and other types of secondary storage. Additionally, they need to be aware of specialty storage devices for portable computers and to be knowledgeable about how large organizations manage their extensive data resources.

Storage

An essential feature of every computer is the ability to save, or store, information. As discussed in Chapter 6, random-access memory (RAM) holds or stores data and programs that the CPU is presently processing. Before data can be processed or a program can be run, it must be in RAM. For this reason, RAM is sometimes referred to as **primary storage.**

Unfortunately, most RAM provides only temporary or volatile storage. That is, it loses all of its contents as soon as the computer is turned off. Its contents also are lost if there is a power failure that disrupts the electric current going into the system unit. This volatility results in a need for more permanent or nonvolatile storage for data and programs. We also need external storage because users need much more storage capacity than is typically available in a computer's primary or RAM memory.

Secondary storage provides permanent or nonvolatile storage. Using **secondary storage devices** such as a hard disk drive, data and programs can be retained after the computer has been shut off. This is accomplished by *writing* files to and *reading* files from secondary storage devices. Writing is the process of saving information *to* the secondary storage device. Reading is the process of accessing information *from* secondary storage. This chapter focuses on secondary storage devices.

Some important characteristics of secondary storage include

- **Media** are the actual physical material that holds the data and programs. (See Figure 8-1.)
- **Capacity** measures how much a particular storage medium can hold.
- **Storage devices** are hardware that reads data and programs from storage media. Most also write to storage media.

Figure 8-1 Secondary storage media

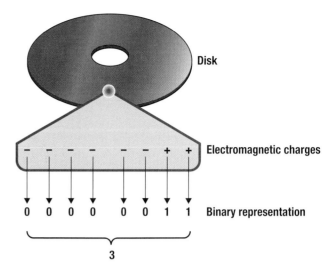

Figure 8-2 How charges on a disk surface store the number 3

- **Access speed** measures the amount of time required by the storage device to retrieve data and programs.

Most desktop microcomputer systems have hard and optical disk drives, as well as ports where additional storage devices can be connected.

Figure 8-3 Tracks and sectors

Hard Disks

Hard disks save files by altering the magnetic charges of the disk's surface to represent 1s and 0s. Hard disks retrieve data and programs by reading these charges from the magnetic disk. Characters are represented by positive (+) and negative (−) charges using the ASCII, EBCDIC, or Unicode binary codes. For example, the number 3 would require a series of 8 charges. (See Figure 8-2.) **Density** refers to how tightly these charges can be packed next to one another on the disk.

Hard disks use rigid metallic **platters** that are stacked one on top of another. Hard disks store and organize files using tracks, sectors, and cylinders. **Tracks** are rings of concentric circles without visible grooves. Each track is divided into invisible wedge-shaped sections called **sectors.** (See Figure 8-3.) A **cylinder** runs through each track of a stack of platters. Cylinders are necessary to differentiate files stored on the same track and sector of different platters. When a hard disk is formatted, tracks, sectors, and cylinders are assigned.

Hard disks are sensitive instruments. Their read/write heads ride on a cushion of air about 0.000001 inch thick. It is so thin that a smoke particle, fingerprint, dust, or human hair could cause what is known as a head crash. (See Figure 8-4.)

A **head crash** occurs when a read/write head makes contact with the hard disk's surface or with particles on its surface. A head crash is a disaster for a

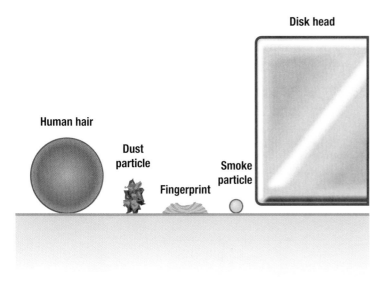

Disk head

Human hair

Dust particle

Fingerprint

Smoke particle

Figure 8-4 Materials that can cause a head crash

hard disk. The disk surface is scratched and some or all of the data is destroyed. At one time, head crashes were commonplace. Now, fortunately, they are rare.

There are two basic types of hard disks: internal and external.

Internal Hard Disk

An **internal hard disk** is located inside the system unit. These hard disks are able to store and retrieve large quantities of information quickly. They are used to store programs and data files. For example, nearly every microcomputer uses its internal hard disk to store its operating system and major applications such as Word and Excel.

To see how a hard disk works, visit our Web site at www.computing2011.com and enter the keyword **disk.**

To ensure adequate performance of your internal hard disk and the safety of your data, you should perform routine maintenance and periodically make backup copies of all important files. For hard-disk maintenance and backup procedures, refer to Chapter 5's coverage of the Windows utilities Backup and Restore, Disk Cleanup, and Disk Defragmenter.

External Hard Drives

While internal hard disks provide fast access, they have a fixed amount of storage and cannot be easily removed from the system cabinet. External hard disks typically connect to a USB or FireWire port on the system unit, are easily removed, and effectively provide an unlimited amount of storage. (See Figure 8-5.)

tips

Does your internal hard disk run a lot and seem slow? The problem could be with fragmented files—files that when saved were broken into pieces (fragments) and stored in different locations on your hard disk, which take longer for the hard disk to access. Defragging rearranges the file parts so they are stored in adjacent locations. To clean up the disk and speed up access times, consider defragmenting. If you are using Windows Vista:

1 Start Disk Defragmenter. Type *defrag* into the Start menu search box and press Enter to open the Disk Defragmenter utility. Click *Defragment* now to begin defragmenting your disk.

2 Keep working. You can continue running other applications while your disk is being defragmented. Unfortunately, your computer operates more slowly, and Disk Defragmenter takes longer to finish.

3 Automate. Windows 7 will defragment your disk for you automatically. Click *Configure schedule* in the Disk Defragmenter utility to set this to a time that is convenient for you.

To see additional tips, visit our Web site at www.computing 2011.com and enter the keyword tips.

Figure 8-5 External hard drive

External hard drives use the same basic technology as internal hard disks and are used primarily to complement an internal hard disk. Because they are easily removed, they are particularly useful to protect or secure sensitive information. Other uses for external drives include backing up the contents of the internal hard disk and providing additional hard-disk capacity.

Performance Enhancements

Three ways to improve the performance of hard disks are disk caching, redundant arrays of inexpensive disks, and file compression/decompression.

Disk caching improves hard-disk performance by anticipating data needs. It performs a function similar to cache memory discussed in Chapter 6. While cache memory improves processing by acting as a temporary high-speed holding area between memory and the CPU, disk caching improves processing by acting as a temporary high-speed holding area between a secondary storage device and the CPU. Disk caching requires a combination of hardware and software. During idle processing time, frequently used data is read from the hard disk into memory (cache). When needed, the data is then accessed directly from memory. The transfer rate from memory is much faster than from the hard disk. As a result, overall system performance is often increased by as much as 30 percent.

Figure 8-6 **RAID storage device**

Redundant arrays of inexpensive disks (RAID) improve performance by expanding external storage, improving access speed, and providing reliable storage. Several inexpensive hard-disk drives are connected to one another. These connections can be by a network or within specialized RAID devices. (See Figure 8-6.) The connected hard-disk drives are related or grouped together, and the computer system interacts with the RAID system as though it were a single large-capacity hard-disk drive. The result is expanded storage capability, fast access speed, and high reliability. For these reasons, RAID is often used by Internet servers and large organizations.

File compression and **file decompression** increase storage capacity by reducing the amount of space required to store data and programs. File compression is not limited to hard-disk systems. It is frequently used to compress files on DVDs, CDs, and flash drives as well. File compression also helps to speed up transmission of files from one computer system to another. Sending and receiving compressed files across the Internet is a common activity.

File compression programs scan files for ways to reduce the amount of required storage. One way is to search for repeating patterns. The repeating patterns are replaced with a token, leaving enough tokens so that the original can be rebuilt or decompressed. These programs often shrink files to a quarter of their original size. To learn more about file compression, visit our Web site at www.computing2011.com and enter the keyword **compression.**

You can compress and decompress files using specialized utilities such as WinZip. Or, if a specialized utility is not available, you can use utility programs in Windows. For a summary of performance enhancement techniques, see Figure 8-7.

On the Web Explorations

A computer can be a library, a jukebox, even a home entertainment system, but to do any of these tasks requires large amounts of hard-disk space.

To learn more about the leaders in high-capacity hard disks, visit our Web site at www.computing2011.com and enter the keyword capacity.

Technique	Description
Disk caching	Uses cache and anticipates data needs
RAID	Linked, inexpensive hard-disk drives
File compression	Reduces file size
File decompression	Expands compressed files

Figure 8-7 **Performance enhancement techniques**

CONCEPT CHECK

Discuss four important characteristics of secondary storage.

What are the two types of hard disks? Briefly describe each.

What is density? What are tracks, sectors, cylinders, and head crashes?

List and describe three ways to improve the performance of hard disks.

Solid-State Storage

Unlike hard disks, which rotate and have read/write heads that move in and out, **solid-state storage** devices have no moving parts. Data and information are stored and retrieved electronically directly from these devices much as they would be from conventional computer memory.

Solid-State Drives

Solid-state drives (SSDs) are designed to be connected inside a microcomputer system the same way an internal hard disk would be but contain solid-state memory instead of magnetic disks to store data. (See Figure 8-8.) SSDs are faster and more durable than hard disks. SSDs also require less power, which can lead to increased battery life for laptops and mobile devices. SSDs are more expensive and generally have a lower capacity than hard disks, but this is changing as the popularity of SSDs continues to increase.

Flash Memory

Flash memory cards are small solid-state storage devices widely used in portable devices such as mobile phones and GPS navigation systems. (See Figure 8-9.) Flash memory also is used in a variety of specialized input devices to capture and transfer data to desktop computers.

Figure 8-8 **Solid-state drive**

Figure 8-9 **Flash memory card**

For example, flash memory is used to store images captured from digital cameras and then to transfer the images to desktop and other computers. Flash memory is used in digital media players like the iPod to store and play music and video files. To learn more about digital video players, see Making IT Work for You: iPods and Video from the Internet on page 226.

USB Drives

USB drives, or **flash drives,** are so compact that they can be transported on a key ring. (See Figure 8-10.) These drives conveniently connect directly to a computer's USB port to transfer files and can have capacities ranging from 1 GB to 256 GB, with a broad price range to match. Due to their convenient size and large capacities, USB drives have become a very popular option for transporting data and information between computers, specialty devices, and the Internet. To learn more about using flash drives to transport data, see Making IT Work for You: Flash Camcorders and YouTube on pages 228 and 229.

 ## CONCEPT CHECK

 What is solid-state storage?

 Compare solid-state technology to that used in hard disks.

 What are SSDs? What is flash memory? What are USB drives?

Optical Discs

Today's **optical discs** can hold over 50 gigabytes of data. (See Figure 8-11.) That is the equivalent of millions of typewritten pages or a medium-sized library all on a single disc. Optical discs are having a great impact on storage today, but we are probably only beginning to see their effects.

In optical-disc technology, a laser beam alters the surface of a plastic or metallic disc to represent data. Unlike hard disks, which use magnetic charges to represent 1s and 0s, optical discs use reflected light. The 1s and 0s are represented

Figure 8-10 **USB drive**

Figure 8-11 **Optical disc**

Making IT work for you

IPODS AND VIDEO FROM THE INTERNET

Did you know you can use the Internet to locate and play movies and television shows? You can even transfer video to a digital media player. All you need is the right software, hardware, and a connection to the Internet.

Finding videos   There are many services on the Internet for finding movies. The first step is to download software that connects with a video service. You can use this software to search for programs and play them. For example, to find television shows using Apple iTunes:

iTunes Store

1 • Visit www.apple. com and follow the on-screen instructions to download and install the iTunes software.

2 • Start the iTunes application.

• Select *iTunes Store* and browse to find movies or television shows you want to download.

Purchased movies and shows are automatically downloaded and listed in the *Movies* and *TV Shows* categories of the library. To watch a downloaded video:

3 • Select *Movies* or *TV Shows* from the Library.

• Double-click the video you want to watch.

Uploading to a Digital Media Player   Another popular way to take your favorite videos with you is to upload them to a digital media player. For example, you could transfer video to an iPod using iTunes software by following the steps below:

1 • Connect your iPod to your computer. iTunes starts automatically.

• Select your iPod from the *Devices* list.

• Select the *TV Shows* tab and select which programs you would like to transfer to your iPod.

• Click the *Sync* button to transfer your videos.

The Web is continually changing, and some of the specifics presented in this Making IT Work for You may have changed.

To learn about other ways to make information technology work for you, visit our Web site at www.computing2011.com and enter the keyword miw.

by flat areas called **lands** and bumpy areas called **pits** on the disc surface. The disc is read by an **optical disc drive** using a laser that projects a tiny beam of light on these areas. The amount of reflected light determines whether the area represents a 1 or a 0. To see how an optical disc drive works, visit our Web site at www.computing2011.com and enter the keyword optical.

Like hard disks, optical discs use tracks and sectors to organize and store files. Unlike the concentric tracks and wedge-shaped sectors used for hard disks, however, optical discs typically use a single track that spirals toward the center of the disc. This single track is divided into equally sized sectors.

Figure 8-12 DVD disc drive

Compact Disc

Compact disc, or as it is better known, **CD,** is one of the most widely used optical formats. CD drives are standard on many microcomputer systems. Typically, CD drives can store from 650 MB (megabytes) to 1 GB (gigabyte) of data on one side of a CD.

There are three basic types of CDs: read only, write once, and rewritable:

- **Read only—CD-ROM,** which stands for **compact disc–read-only memory,** is similar to a commercial music CD. *Read only* means it cannot be written on or erased by the user. Thus, you as a user have access only to the data imprinted by the publisher. CD-ROMs are used to distribute large databases and references. They also are used to distribute large software application packages.

- **Write once—CD-R,** which stands for **CD-recordable,** can be written to once. After that they can be read many times without deterioration but cannot be written on or erased. CD-R drives often are used to archive data and to record music downloaded from the Internet.

- **Rewriteable—CD-RW** stands for **compact disc rewritable.** Also known as **erasable optical discs,** these discs are very similar to CD-Rs except that the disc surface is not permanently altered when data is recorded. Because they can be changed, CD-RWs are often used to create and edit multimedia presentations.

Digital Versatile Disc

DVD stands for **digital versatile disc** or **digital video disc.** This is a newer format that has replaced CDs as the standard optical disc. DVDs are very similar to CDs except that more data can be packed into the same amount of space. (See Figure 8-12.) DVD discs can store 4.7 GB to 17 GB on a single DVD disc—17 times the capacity of CDs. There are three basic types of DVDs, similar to CDs: read only, write once, and rewriteable.

- **Read only—DVD-ROM** stands for **digital versatile disc–read-only memory.** DVD-ROM drives are also known as **DVD players.** DVD-ROMs are having a major impact on the video market. While CD-ROMs are effective for

Are you concerned about damaging your optical discs? Actually, they are quite durable, and taking care of them boils down to just a few basic rules.

1 **Don't stack.** Don't stack or bend discs.

2 **Don't touch.** Don't touch the recording surfaces. Hold only by their edges.

3 **Don't remove.** Never attempt to remove a disc when it is rotating and in use.

4 **Avoid extreme conditions.** Keep discs from extreme heat and direct sunlight.

5 **Use storage boxes.** Store discs in plastic storage boxes.

Of course, the best protection is to make a backup or duplicate copy of your disc.

To see additional tips, visit our Web site at www.computing 2011.com and enter the keyword tips.

FLASH CAMCORDERS AND YouTube

Would you like to make short videos to share with family and friends? Traditional camcorders can be expensive, and often require a special connection to transfer video to your computer. Recently, flash memory–based camcorders have made creating digital video simpler and more affordable, and connect to your computer as easily as other flash memory secondary storage devices.

Capture   To capture video using a Pure Digital Flip camcorder:

1 • **Press the record button to record what you see on the view screen.**

• **Press the record button again to stop recording.**

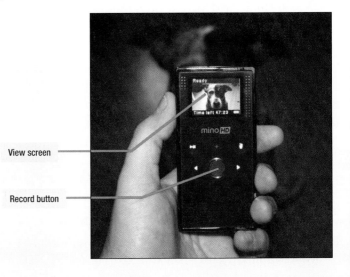

View screen

Record button

Connect   Connecting the camcorder to your computer is as simple as connecting other secondary storage devices such as USB flash drives:

1 • **Slide the switch on the side of the camcorder to extend the built-in USB connector.**

• **Plug the camcorder directly into a USB port on your computer.**

USB connector

Slide to extend USB connector

Share The FlipShare software included with the camcorder allows you to save your video to your computer, e-mail videos to friends, or upload videos directly to Internet sites such as YouTube and MySpace.

The Web is continuously changing, and some of the specifics presented in this Making IT Work for You may have changed. To learn about other ways to make information technology work for you, visit our Web site at www.computing2011.com and enter the keyword miw.

distributing music, they can only contain just over an hour of fair-quality video. DVD-ROMs can provide over two hours of high-quality video and sound comparable to that found in motion picture theaters. The motion picture industry has rapidly shifted video distribution from video cassettes to DVD-ROMs.

- **Write once—DVD+R** and **DVD−R** are two competing write-once formats. Both stand for **DVD recordable.** Each has a slightly different way in which it formats its discs. Fortunately, most new DVD players can use either format. These drives are typically used to create permanent archives for large amounts of data and to record videos. DVD recordable drives are rapidly replacing CD-R drives due to their massive capacity.

- **Rewriteable—DVD+RW, DVD−RW,** and **DVD-RAM** are the three most widely used formats. DVD+RW and DVD−RW stand for **DVD rewriteable. DVD-RAM** stands for **DVD random-access memory.** Each format has a unique way of storing data. Unfortunately, older DVD players typically can read only one type of format. Newer DVD players, however, are able to read and use any of the formats. Rewriteable DVD disc drives have rapidly replaced CD rewriteable drives. Applications range from recording video from camcorders to developing multimedia presentations that include extensive graphics and video.

High-Definition Discs

While CDs and DVDs are the most widely used optical discs today, the future belongs to discs of even greater capacity. While DVD discs have sufficient capacity to record standard-definition movies and music, they are insufficient for recording high-definition video, which requires about four times as much storage. This next generation of optical disc is called **hi def (high definition),** with a far greater capacity than DVDs. The hi def standard is **Blu-ray Disc (BD).** The name comes from the blue-colored laser that is used to read the disc.

Blu-ray Discs have a capacity of 25 to 50 gigabytes, more than 10 times the capacity of a standard single-layer DVD. Although Blu-ray media are the same size as other optical media, the discs require special drives. Most of these drives are capable of reading standard DVDs and CDs in addition to Blu-ray.

Like CDs and DVDs, Blu-ray has three basic types: read only, write once, and rewriteable. As with any optical disc, a device with recording capabilities is required for writing data.

For a summary of the different types of optical discs, see Figure 8-13.

☑ CONCEPT CHECK

- How is data represented on optical discs?
- Compare CD and DVD formats. Why did DVDs replace CDs?
- What is hi def? What is Blu-ray? Compare Blu-ray to standard DVD.

Format	Typical Capacity	Description
CD	650 MB to 1 GB	Once the standard optical disc
DVD	4.7 GB to 17 GB	Current standard
Blu-ray	25 GB to 50 GB	Hi-def format, large capacity

Figure 8-13 Types of optical discs

Other Types of Secondary Storage

For the typical microcomputer user, the three basic storage options—hard disk, optical disc, and solid-state storage—are complementary, not competing. Almost all microcomputers have one hard-disk drive and one optical drive, with USB ports that can support portable solid-state drives. For many users, these secondary storage devices are further complemented with more specialized storage such as online storage services, floppy disk drives, and magnetic tape.

Online Storage Services

Online storage services provide users with storage space that can be accessed from a Web site. (See Figure 8-14.) This type of storage has several advantages compared to other types of secondary storage including low cost and the flexibility to access information from any location using the Internet. Because all information must travel across the Internet, however, access speed is slower. Another consideration is that users are dependent on the availability and security procedures of the service site. Because of these limitations, online storage services are typically used as a specialized secondary storage device and not for storing highly personalized or sensitive information.

Typically, service sites focus on supplying their services either to businesses or to individuals. The business-oriented sites provide faster access and greater security for a fee. The individual-focused sites provide limited storage for much lower cost and some sites are free. (See Figure 8-15.)

Figure 8-14 **An online storage service**

Floppy Disks

Floppy disks are portable or removable storage media that were once commonly used to transport relatively small word processing, spreadsheet, and other types of files. (See Figure 8-16.) They use flexible flat circular pieces of Mylar plastic that have been coated with a magnetic material. Like hard disks, **floppy disk drives (FDD)** store data and programs by altering the electromagnetic charges on the disk's surface. As with hard disks, files are stored and organized according to tracks and sectors.

There are two kinds of floppy disks: traditional and high-capacity. The **traditional floppy disk**

Focus	Company	Location
Individual	iBackup	www.ibackup.com
Individual	Apple	www.me.com
Individual	xDrive	www.xdrive.com
Business	Amerivault	www.amerivault.com
Business	Mozy	www.mozy.com

Figure 8-15 **Online storage services**

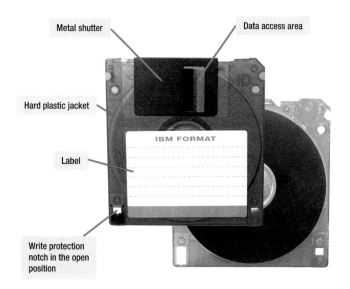

Figure 8-16 **Floppy disk**

Figure 8-17 **Magnetic tape cartridge**

is the 1.44 MB 2HD 3½-inch disk; 2HD means two-sided, high-density. These disks have a capacity of 1.44 megabytes—the equivalent of over 350 typewritten pages. Like the traditional floppy, the **high-capacity floppy disks** are 3½ inches in diameter. However, they are able to store more information, are thicker, and require special disk drives. These disks typically have a 100 MB, 250 MB, or 750 MB capacity—over 500 times as much as a standard floppy disk.

Magnetic Tape

On a traditional audiotape, you may have to fast-forward or rewind through several feet of tape to find a particular song. Finding a song on an audio compact disc, in contrast, can be much faster. You select the track, and the disc player moves directly to it. That, in brief, represents the two different approaches to external storage. The two approaches are called **sequential access** and **direct access.**

Disks provide fast direct access. Tapes provide slower sequential access. With tape, information is stored in sequence, such as alphabetically. For example, all the grades of students at your school could be recorded on tape arranged alphabetically by their last names. To find the grades for one student, say Chris Reed, the search would begin at the start of the tape and search alphabetically past all the last names beginning with A to Q before ultimately reaching Reed. This may involve searching several inches or feet, which takes time.

Like floppy and hard disks, **magnetic tape** stores data and programs by altering the electromagnetic charges on a recording surface. Although slower to access specific information, magnetic tape is an effective and commonly used tool for backing up data. At one time, mainframe computers used **magnetic tape reels** exclusively. This type of tape is typically ½ inch wide and 1½ miles long and provides massive storage capacity. Now, most mainframes as well as microcomputers use **tape cartridges** or **magnetic tape streamers** to back up data. (See Figure 8-17.)

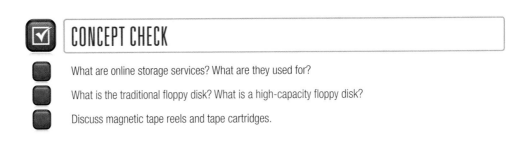

CONCEPT CHECK

What are online storage services? What are they used for?

What is the traditional floppy disk? What is a high-capacity floppy disk?

Discuss magnetic tape reels and tape cartridges.

Mass Storage Devices

It is natural to think of secondary storage media and devices as they relate to us as individuals. It may not be as obvious how important these matters are to organizations. **Mass storage** refers to the tremendous amount of secondary storage required by large organizations. **Mass storage devices** are specialized high-capacity secondary storage devices designed to meet organizational demands for data.

Enterprise Storage System

Most large organizations have established a strategy called an **enterprise storage system** to promote efficient and safe use of data across the networks within their organizations. (See Figure 8-18.) Some of the mass storage devices that support this strategy are

- **File servers**—dedicated computers with very large storage capacities that provide users access to fast storage and retrieval of data.
- **Network attached storage (NAS)**—similar to a file server except simpler and less expensive; widely used for home and small business storage needs.
- **RAID systems**—larger versions of the specialized devices discussed earlier in this chapter that enhance organizational security by constantly making backup copies of files moving across the organization's networks.
- **Tape library**—device that provides automatic access to data archived on a large collection or library of tapes.
- **Organizational online storage**—high-speed Internet connection to a dedicated remote organizational online storage site.

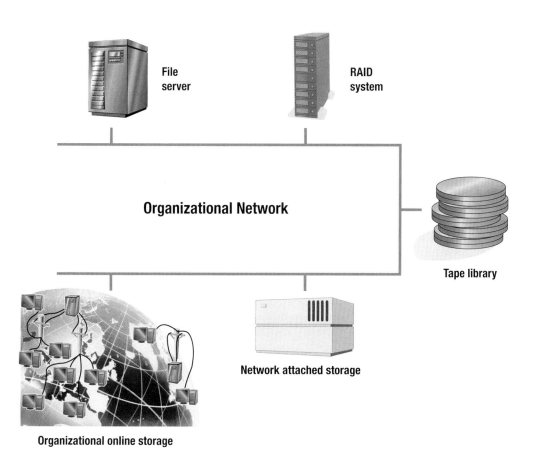

Figure 8-18 Enterprise storage system

Storage Area Network

A recent mass storage development is **storage area network (SAN)** systems. SAN is an architecture to link remote computer storage devices, such as enterprise storage systems, to computers such that the devices are as available as locally attached drives. In a SAN system, the user's computer provides the file system for storing data, but the SAN provides the disk space for data.

The key to a SAN is a high-speed network, connecting individual computers to mass storage devices. Special file systems prevent simultaneous users from interfering with each other. SANs provide the ability to house data in remote locations and still allow efficient and secure access.

CONCEPT CHECK

- Define mass storage and list five mass storage devices.
- What is an enterprise storage system?
- What is a storage area network system?

Careers in IT

Software engineers analyze users' needs and create application software. (See Figure 8-19.) Software engineers typically have experience in programming but focus on the design and development of programs using the principles of mathematics and engineering. They rarely write code themselves.

A bachelor's degree in computer science or information systems and an extensive knowledge of computers and technology are required by most employers. Internships may provide students with the kinds of experience employers look for in a software engineer. Those with specific experience with networking, the Internet, and Web applications may have an advantage over other applicants. Employers typically look for software engineers with good communication and analytical skills.

Software engineers can expect to earn an annual salary in the range of $63,000 to $98,500. Advancement opportunities are usually tied to experience. Experienced software engineers may be promoted to project manager or have opportunities in systems design. To learn about other careers in information technology, visit us at www.computing2011.com and enter the keyword **careers.**

Figure 8-19 **Software engineer**

A LOOK TO THE FUTURE

Will Cloud Computing Rain on Secondary Storage?

Recently, many applications that would have required installation on your computer to run have moved to the Web. Numerous Web sites now exist to provide application services. This is known as *cloud computing,* where the Internet acts as a "cloud" of servers that supply applications as a *service* rather than a *product.* Many examples already exist. For example, you may have created a word processing document or spreadsheet online using Google Apps, managed your financial information using Mint .com, or stored files and folders using Amazon S3.

With cloud computing, data is typically stored on the application provider's server. The processing power of the service provider's server is used to run applications, with the local computer responsible only for displaying the results. The applications and data can be accessed from any Internet-ready device. This means that even devices with little storage, memory, or processing power, such as mobile phones, can run the same powerful applications as a desktop computer.

The benefits to this arrangement are numerous. Imagine how much easier it would be to deploy or upgrade a customer relationship management software application in a large company. In the past, an IT professional would need to visit every computer the company owned to install the software from disk and manage licensing for the number of computers the software was purchased for. With software delivered as a service, the company can simply purchase the appropriate number of accounts from the service provider and direct employees to use the provider's Web site.

As wireless access to the Internet becomes available in more locations, devices used to store or transport information might use the network instead. For example, if you could instantly access music and video across the network from anywhere, would you still use CDs, DVDs, or portable music devices? Would you need a CD or USB storage to transport files from your home computer to school if they were centrally located on the Web?

Could cloud computing spell the end for secondary storage? With faster connections to the Internet and newer Internet-ready devices, will it be necessary to store data or install software on one's personal computer? What issues do you see with storing sensitive personal data on a provider's system rather than your own? What might happen, for example, if a provider were to go out of business or raise the price for using the application? Can you think of any applications that would not work well as a service?

STORAGE

RAM is **primary storage.** Most RAM is volatile, meaning that it loses its contents whenever power is disrupted. **Secondary storage** provides nonvolatile storage. Secondary storage retains data and information after the computer system is turned off.

Writing is the process of saving information to **secondary storage devices.** Reading is the process of accessing information from secondary storage devices.

Important characteristics of secondary storage include

- **Media**—actual physical material that retains data and programs.
- **Capacity**—how much a particular storage medium can hold.
- **Storage devices**—hardware that reads and writes to storage media.
- **Access speed**—time required to retrieve data from a secondary storage device.

HARD DISKS

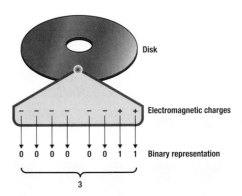

Hard disks use rigid metallic **platters** that provide a large amount of capacity. They store data and programs by altering the electromagnetic charges on the platter's surface. Files are organized according to **tracks, sectors,** and **cylinders. Density** refers to how tightly electromagnetic charges can be packed next to one another on the disk.

A **head crash** occurs when the hard disk makes contact with the drive's read/write heads.

Two types of hard disks are internal and external hard disks.

Internal Hard Disk
Internal hard disks are located within the system unit. Used to store programs and data files.

External Hard Drives
Unlike internal hard disks, **external hard drives** are removable. External drives use the same basic technology as internal disks.

To be a competent end user, you need to be aware of the different types of secondary storage. You need to know their capabilities, limitations, and uses. There are three widely used storage media: hard disk, solid-state storage, and, optical disc.

HARD DISKS

Performance Enhancements

Three ways to improve hard disk performance are disk caching, RAID, and file compression and decompression.

- **Disk caching**—provides a temporary high-speed holding area between a secondary storage device and the CPU; improves performance by anticipating data needs and reducing time to access data from secondary storage.
- **RAID (redundant array of inexpensive disks)**—several inexpensive hard-disk drives are connected together; improves performance by providing expanded storage, fast access, and high reliability.
- **File compression** and **decompression**—files compressed before storing and then decompressed before being used again; improves performance through efficient storage.

SOLID-STATE STORAGE

Solid-state storage devices have no moving parts and are more reliable and require less power than hard disks.

Solid-State Drives

Solid-state drives are similar to internal hard disk drives except they use solid-state memory; are faster, more durable, and more expensive; and generally provide less capacity.

Flash Memory

Flash memory cards are small solid state storage devices that are widely used with notebook computers. They are used with a variety of specialized input devices including digital cameras to store and transfer images and digital media players like the iPod to store and transfer music and video files.

USB Drives

USB drives (flash drives) are so small that they fit onto a key ring. These drives connect to a computer's USB port and are widely used to transfer data and information between computers, specialty devices, and the Internet.

OPTICAL DISCS

Optical discs use laser technology. 1s and 0s are represented by **pits** and **lands. Optical disc drives** project light and measure the reflected light.

Compact Disc

Compact discs (CDs) have typical capacity of 650 MB to 1 GB. Three types are **CD-ROM (compact disc–read-only memory), CD-R (CD-recordable** (CD-R drives are also known as CD burners)), and **CD-RW (compact disc rewritable, erasable optical discs).**

Digital Versatile Disc

DVDs (digital versatile discs, digital video discs) have far greater capacity than CDs (4.7 GB to 17 GB). Three types are **DVD-ROM (digital versatile disc–read-only memory; DVD players** are drives), write once **(DVD+R, DVD−R),** and rewriteable **(DVD+RW, DVD−RW, DVD−RAM).**

High-Definition Discs

Hi-def (high-definition) Blu-ray Discs are the next standard optical disc. **Blu-ray Discs (BDs)** have a capacity of 25 GB to 50 GB. Same size as other optical media, but much greater capacity and requires special drives. Three basic types: read only, write once, and rewriteable.

OTHER TYPES

The three basic storage options (hard, solid-state, and optical) are complementary and not necessarily competitive. Many users complement with more specialized devices including

- **Online storage services**—Web-based, low-cost storage. Accessible from any Internet connection, these drives are often slow and security is an issue.
- **Traditional** and **high-capacity floppy disks**—portable, removable storage media that were once widely used. Like a hard disk, they store data and programs by charging the disk surface.
- **Magnetic tape—sequential access** (disks provide **direct access**) used primarily for backing up data. **Magnetic tape reels** were widely used with mainframes. Now **tape cartridges (magnetic tape streamers)** are most widely used for mainframes and microcomputers.

MASS STORAGE

Mass storage refers to the tremendous amount of secondary storage required by large organizations. **Mass storage devices** are specialized high-capacity secondary storage devices.

Most large organizations have established a strategy called an **enterprise storage system** to promote efficient and safe use of data across the networks within their organizations.

Mass storage devices that support this strategy are **file servers, network attached storage (NAS), RAID systems, tape libraries,** and **organizational online storage.** A **storage area network (SAN)** is a method of using enterprise-level remote storage systems as if they were local to your computer.

CAREERS IN IT

Software engineers analyze users' needs and create application software. Bachelor's degree in computer science or information systems and extensive knowledge of computers and technology required. Salary range $63,000 to $98,500.

KEY TERMS

access speed   (221)
Blu-ray Disc (BD)   (230)
capacity   (220)
CD (compact disc)   (227)
CD-R (CD-recordable)   (227)
CD-ROM (compact disc–read-only
   memory)   (227)
CD-RW (compact disc
   rewriteable)   (227)
cylinder   (221)
density   (221)
direct access   (232)
disk caching   (223)
DVD (digital versatile disc or digital
   video disc)   (227)
DVD player   (227)
DVD−R (DVD recordable)   (230)
DVD+R (DVD recordable)   (230)
DVD-RAM (DVD random-access
   memory)   (230)
DVD-ROM (DVD–read-only
   memory)   (227)
DVD−RW (DVD rewriteable)   (230)
DVD+RW (DVD rewriteable)   (230)
enterprise storage system   (233)
erasable optical disc   (227)
external hard drive   (223)
file compression   (223)
file decompression   (223)
file server   (233)
flash drive   (225)
flash memory card   (224)
floppy disk   (231)
floppy disk drive (FDD)   (231)
hard disk   (221)
head crash   (221)

hi def (high definition)   (230)
high-capacity floppy disk   (232)
internal hard disk   (222)
land   (227)
magnetic tape   (232)
magnetic tape reel   (232)
magnetic tape streamer   (232)
mass storage   (232)
mass storage devices   (233)
media   (220)
network attached storage (NAS)   (233)
online storage service   (231)
optical disc   (225)
optical disc drive   (227)
organizational online storage   (233)
pit   (227)
platter   (221)
primary storage   (220)
RAID system   (233)
redundant array of inexpensive disks
   (RAID)   (223)
secondary storage   (220)
secondary storage device   (220)
sector   (221)
sequential access   (232)
software engineer   (234)
solid-state drive (SSD)   (224)
solid-state storage   (224)
storage area network (SAN)   (234)
storage device   (220)
tape cartridge   (232)
tape library   (233)
track   (221)
traditional floppy disk   (231)
USB drive   (225)

To test your knowledge of these key terms with animated flash cards, visit our Web
site at www.computing2011.com and enter the keyword terms8.

MULTIPLE CHOICE

Circle the letter or fill in the correct answer.

1. RAM is referred to as _____ storage.
   a. direct
   b. nonvolatile
   c. secondary
   d. sequential

2. The amount of time required by a storage device to retrieve data and programs is its
   a. access speed
   b. capacity
   c. memory
   d. storage

3. How tightly the bits can be packed next to one another on a disk is referred to as
   a. tracks
   b. sectors
   c. density
   d. configuration

4. Thick, rigid metal platters that are capable of storing and retrieving information at a high rate of speed are known as
   a. hard disks
   b. soft disks
   c. flash memory
   d. SAN

5. This type of storage device has no moving parts.
   a. hard disks
   b. floppy disks
   c. optical discs
   d. solid state

6. The data on an optical disc is represented by flat areas called _____ on the disc surface.
   a. surfaces
   b. flats
   c. lands
   d. pits

7. DVD stands for
   a. digital video data
   b. direct video disc
   c. digital versatile disc
   d. direct versatile disc

8. _____ is the hi-def standard.
   a. Blu-ray
   b. CD-ROM
   c. DVD+R
   d. Max RL

9. Tape is described as using this type of access.
   a. magneto-optical
   b. DVD
   c. direct
   d. sequential

10. Specialized high-capacity secondary storage device designed to meet organizational demands for data.
    a. Blue-ray Disc
    b. hi def
    c. mass storage
    d. floppy disk

For an interactive multiple-choice practice test, visit our Web site at www.computing 2011.com and enter the keyword multiple8.

MATCHING

Match each numbered item with the most closely related lettered item. Write your answers in the spaces provided.

a. access speed
b. file compression
c. flash memory card
d. hi def
e. online storage service
f. RAID
g. RAM
h. solid-state storage
i. track
j. USB drive

1. A type of storage that is volatile. _____
2. Time required to retrieve data and programs. _____
3. A solid-state storage device small enough to fit onto a key ring. _____
4. Closed concentric ring on a disk on which data is recorded. _____
5. Several connected inexpensive hard-disk drives. _____
6. Increases storage capacity by reducing the amount of space required to store data and programs. _____
7. Stores data electronically and has no moving parts. _____
8. A credit card–sized solid-state storage device used in portable computers. _____
9. Provides free or low-cost storage available at special Web sites. _____
10. The next generation of optical discs. _____

For an interactive matching practice test, visit our Web site at www.computing2011.com and enter the keyword matching8.

OPEN-ENDED

On a separate sheet of paper, respond to each question or statement.

1. What are the two types of hard disks? Describe three ways to improve hard disk performance.
2. Compare solid-state and hard disk storage.
3. What are the three most common optical disc formats? What is Blu-ray?
4. Discuss online storage services, floppy disks, and magnetic tape. What are the advantages and disadvantages of each?
5. Discuss mass storage systems including enterprise storage systems and storage area networks.

APPLYING TECHNOLOGY

The following questions are designed to demonstrate ways that you can effectively use technology today. The first question relates directly to this chapter's Making IT Work for You feature.

1 IPODS AND VIDEO FROM THE INTERNET

Did you know that you could use the Internet to locate movies and television shows, download them to your computer, and transfer them to a portable media player to watch on the go? All it takes is the right software, hardware, and a connection to the Internet. To learn more about using portable media players, review Making IT Work for You: iPods and Video from the Internet on page 226. Then answer the following questions: (a) What item is clicked in the iTunes application to locate movies and television shows? (b) Which television show was selected for purchase in the Making IT Work feature? (c) Describe the procedure to transfer video from the iTunes application to an iPod.

2 IPOD

Apple's iPod is a personal portable music player that stores a large number of digital music files. Connect to our Web site at www.computing2011.com and enter the keyword ipod to link to the iPod Web site. Once connected, read about the features and capabilities of iPod, and then answer the following questions: (a) How are music files transferred to iPod? (b) What type of secondary storage does iPod use? (c) What is iPod's storage capacity?

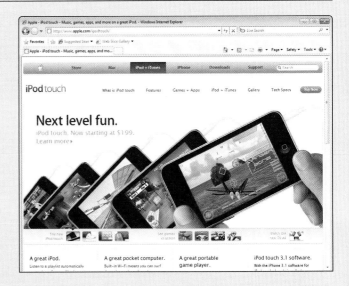

3 USB STORAGE DEVICES

Do you need to carry more data than will fit on a single floppy disk or CD? A USB storage device might be for you. These devices store large amounts of data in a package small enough to travel with your car keys. Connect to our Web site at www.computing2011.com and enter the keyword keychain to link to a site that features USB storage devices. Explore the site and then answer the following questions: (a) What type of secondary storage do USB storage devices use? (b) How is data transferred to and from computer systems? (c) What system software are the USB storage devices compatible with? (d) What are typical capacities of the USB storage devices?

EXPANDING YOUR KNOWLEDGE

The following questions are designed to add depth and detail to your understanding of specific topics presented within this chapter. The questions direct you to sources other than the textbook to obtain this knowledge.

① HOW MUSIC IS DOWNLOADED FROM THE INTERNET

One of the most popular activities on the Internet is to locate and download music files. Using a CD-R drive, the files are saved onto an optical disc. These discs can then be played in a variety of different types of devices. To learn more about how music is downloaded, visit our Web site at www.computing2011.com and enter the keyword music. Then answer the following questions: (a) Go to the Web and find a Web site where you can download music from the Internet. What Web site did you find? How much do they charge to download music? (b) When you download music from the Internet, where is it stored on your computer? (c) Name three ways you can play music from the Internet.

② FILE COMPRESSION

A common problem for computer users is that they run out of hard disk space. File compression software can open up space on a full hard drive, improve system performance, and make files easier to find and organize. To learn more about file compression, visit our Web site at www.computing2011.com and enter the keyword compression. Then answer the following questions: (a) What are the two types of file compression? How do they differ? (b) What type of file compression is used for home movies? Why? (c) What type of file compression is used for a resume? Why? (d) Research a compression/decompression utility on the Web. What types of files does your utility create? Is this a lossy or lossyless file compression?

③ ONLINE STORAGE SERVICES

Online storage services offer remote file storage or backup. Research an online storage service on the Web and then answer the following questions: (a) What online storage service did you research? (b) What is the cost for using the service, and what features do you get for that price? (c) How are files accessed from and uploaded to the service? (d) What assurances does the service provider offer concerning availability of your data? What about security?

WRITING ABOUT TECHNOLOGY

The ability to think critically and to write effectively is essential to nearly every profession. The following questions are designed to help you develop these skills by posing thought-provoking questions about computer privacy, security, and/or ethics.

1 CD-R AND MUSIC FILES

Creating a custom CD of your favorite music is a popular use of secondary storage. Many sites on the Web offer free music that you can download. However, not all music files that are available on the Internet are freely distributable. Consider the following questions and write a one-page paper addressing them: (a) Is it fair to make a copy on your computer of a CD you have purchased? (b) Would it be fair to give a burned copy of a CD to a friend? What if the friend would not have otherwise purchased that CD? (c) People have been making illegal copies of music cassette tapes for some time. Why is using the Internet to make and distribute copies of music receiving so much attention?

2 ARCHIVING ELECTRONIC RECORDS

At one time in the recent past, floppy disks were the standard for storing and exchanging files. However, they do not have the capacity to store most of today's video, image, and music files. As a result, floppy disk drives are no longer a standard feature on many computers, which instead offer optical drives for CDs and DVDs. Consider the following questions and address the following items in a one-page paper: (a) Do you currently back up or save documents that you want to keep for the future, including digital photos, e-mail messages, and school projects? If so, which media do you use? (b) Are there electronic files you feel you may want to access far into the future? (c) What does the demise of floppy disks suggest about the challenges of archiving important documents for future generations? Explain your answer.

NOTES

Communications and Networks

Competencies

After you have read this chapter, you should be able to:

1 Discuss connectivity, the wireless revolution, and communication systems.

2 Describe physical and wireless communications channels.

3 Discuss connection devices and services including dial-up, DSL, cable, satellite/air, and cellular.

4 Describe data transmission factors, including bandwidths and protocols.

5 Discuss networks and key network terminology including network interface cards and network operating systems.

6 Describe different types of networks, including local, home, wireless, personal, metropolitan, and wide area networks.

7 Describe network architectures, including topologies and strategies.

8 Discuss the organization issues related to Internet technologies and network security.

The first truly global communications network was the telegraph, which made it possible to send a message across the globe. Letters could take weeks to travel between cities, but the telegraph cut the transmission to minutes. E-mail cuts the transmission to seconds.

Some predict that humans will eventually be connected with a neural network, making the cables of any kind unnecessary. Imagine a world where you can send your thoughts and ideas directly to another person's mind, without typing or talking.

chapter 9

Introduction

We live in a truly connected society. We can communicate almost instantaneously with others worldwide; changing events from the smallest of countries and places are immediately broadcast to the world; our e-mail messages are delivered to handheld devices; cars access the Internet to provide driving instructions and solve mechanical problems. Even household appliances can connect to the Internet and be remotely controlled. The communications and information options we have at our fingertips have changed how we react and relate to the world around us.

As the power and flexibility of our communication systems have expanded, the sophistication of the networks that support these systems has become increasingly critical and complex. The network technologies that handle our cellular, business, and Internet communications come in many different forms. Satellites, broadcast towers, telephone lines, even buried cables and fiber optics carry our telephone messages, e-mail, and text messages. These different networks must be able to efficiently and effectively integrate with one another.

Competent end users need to understand the concept of connectivity, wireless networking, and the elements that make up network and communications systems. Additionally, they need to understand the basics of communications channels, connection devices, data transmission, network types, network architectures and organizational networks.

Communications

Computer communications is the process of sharing data, programs, and information between two or more computers. We have discussed numerous applications that depend on communication systems, including

- **E-mail**—provides a fast, efficient alternative to traditional mail by sending and receiving electronic documents.
- **Instant messaging**—supports direct, "live" electronic communication between two or more friends or buddies.
- **Internet telephone**—provides a very low-cost alternative to long-distance telephone calls using electronic voice and video delivery.
- **Electronic commerce**—buying and selling goods electronically.

In this chapter, we will focus on the communication systems that support these and many other applications. Connectivity, the wireless revolution, and communication systems are key concepts and technologies for the 21st century.

Connectivity

Connectivity is a concept related to using computer networks to link people and resources. For example, connectivity means that you can connect your microcomputer to other computers and information sources almost anywhere. With this connection, you are linked to the world of larger computers and the Internet. This includes hundreds of thousands of Web servers and their extensive information resources. Thus, becoming computer competent and knowledgeable becomes a matter of knowing not only about connectivity through networks to microcomputers, but also about larger computer systems and their information resources.

The Wireless Revolution

The single most dramatic change in connectivity and communications in the past few years has been the widespread use of mobile telephones with wireless Internet connectivity. Students, parents, teachers, businesspeople, and others routinely talk and communicate with these devices. It is estimated that over 3 billion mobile telephones are in use worldwide. This wireless technology allows individuals to stay connected with one another from almost anywhere at any time.

So what's the revolution? While wireless technology was originally used primarily for voice communications, many of today's cell phones support e-mail, Web access, and a variety of Internet applications. In addition, wireless technology allows a wide variety of nearby devices to communicate with one another without any physical connection. You can share a high-speed printer, share data files, and collaborate on working documents with a nearby co-worker without having your computers connected by cables or telephone—wireless communication. Highspeed Internet wireless technology allows individuals to connect to the Internet and share information from almost anywhere in the world. (See Figure 9-1.) But is it a revolution? Most experts say yes and that the revolution is just beginning.

Figure 9-1 **Wireless revolution**

Communication Systems

Communication systems are electronic systems that transmit data from one location to another. Whether wired or wireless, every communication system has four basic elements. (See Figure 9-2.)

- **Sending and receiving devices.** These are often a computer or specialized communication device. They originate (send) as well as accept (receive) messages in the form of data, information, and/or instructions.
- **Communication channel.** This is the actual connecting or transmission medium that carries the message. This medium can be a physical wire or cable, or it can be wireless.
- **Connection devices.** These devices act as an interface between the sending and receiving devices and the communication channel. They convert

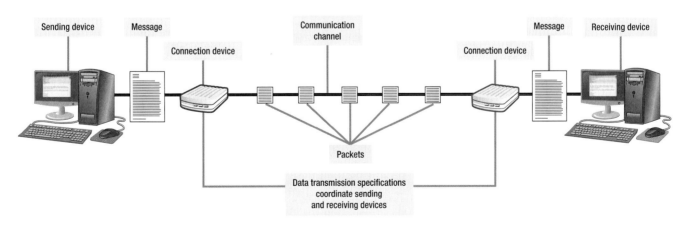

Figure 9-2 **Basic elements of a communication system**

outgoing messages into packets that can travel across the communication channel. They also reverse the process for incoming messages.

- **Data transmission specifications.** These are rules and procedures that coordinate the sending and receiving devices by precisely defining how the message will be sent across the communication channel.

For example, if you wanted to send an e-mail to a friend, you could create and send the message using your computer, the *sending device*. Your modem, a *connection device*, would modify and format the message so that it could travel efficiently across *communication channels*, such as telephone lines. The specifics describing how the message is modified, reformatted, and sent would be described in the *data transmission specifications*. After your message traveled across the channel, the receiver's modem, a connection device, would reform it so that it could be displayed on your friend's computer, the *receiving device*. (Note: This example presents the basic communication system elements involved in sending e-mail. It does not and is not intended to demonstrate all the specific steps and equipment involved in an e-mail delivery system.)

 ## CONCEPT CHECK

- Define computer communications and connectivity.
- What is the wireless revolution?
- Describe the four elements of every communication system.

Communication Channels

Communication channels are an essential element of every communication system. These channels actually carry the data from one computer to another. There are two categories of communication channels. One category connects sending and receiving devices by providing a physical connection, such as a wire or cable. The other category is wireless.

Physical Connections

Figure 9-3 **Twisted-pair cable**

Physical connections use a solid medium to connect sending and receiving devices. These connections include telephone lines (twisted pair), coaxial cable, and fiber-optic cable.

- **Twisted-pair cable** consists of pairs of copper wire that are twisted together. Both standard **telephone lines** and **Ethernet cables** use twisted-pair. (See Figure 9-3.) Ethernet cables are commonly used in networks and to connect a variety of components to the system unit.

Figure 9-4 **Coaxial cable**

- **Coaxial cable,** a high-frequency transmission cable, replaces the multiple wires of telephone lines with a single solid-copper core. (See Figure 9-4.) In terms of the number of telephone connections, a coaxial cable has over 80 times the transmission capacity of twisted pair. Coaxial cable is used to deliver television signals as well as to connect computers in a network.

- **Fiber-optic cable** transmits data as pulses of light through tiny tubes of glass. (See Figure 9-5.) In terms of the number of telephone connections, fiber-optic cable has over 26,000 times the transmission capacity of twisted-pair cable. Compared to coaxial cable, they are lighter and more

Figure 9-5 **Fiber-optic cable**

Standard	Maximum speed
802.11b	11 Mbps
802.11a	54 Mbps
802.11g	54 Mbps
802.11n	600 Mbps

Figure 9-6 **Wi-Fi standards**

reliable at transmitting data. They transmit information using beams of light at light speeds instead of pulses of electricity, making them far faster than copper cable. Fiber-optic cable is rapidly replacing twisted-pair cable telephone lines.

Wireless Connections

Wireless connections do not use a solid substance to connect sending and receiving devices. Rather, they use the air itself. Primary technologies used for wireless connections are radio frequency, microwave, satellite, and infrared.

Figure 9-7 **Microwave dish**

- **Radio frequency (RF)** uses radio signals to communicate between wireless devices. For example, cellular telephones and many Internet-enabled devices use RF to place telephone calls and/or to connect to the Internet. Some end users connect their notebook or handheld computers to a cellular telephone to access the Web from remote locations. Most home or business wireless networks are based on a technology called **Wi-Fi (wireless fidelity).** A number of standards for Wi-Fi exist, and each can send and receive data at a different speed. (See Figure 9-6.) **Bluetooth** is a short-range radio communication standard that transmits data over short distances of up to approximately 33 feet. Bluetooth is widely used for wireless headsets, printer connections, and handheld devices.

- **Microwave** communication uses high-frequency radio waves. Like infrared, microwave communication provides line-of-sight communication because microwaves travel in a straight line. Because the waves cannot bend with the curvature of the earth, they can be transmitted only over relatively short distances. Thus, microwave is a good medium for sending data between buildings in a city or on a large college campus. For longer distances, the waves must be relayed by means of microwave stations with microwave dishes or antennas. (See Figure 9-7.)

- **Satellite** communication uses satellites orbiting about 22,000 miles above the earth as microwave relay stations. Many of these are offered by Intelsat, the International Telecommunications Satellite Consortium, which is owned by 114 governments and forms a worldwide communication system. Satellites rotate at a precise point and speed above the earth. They can amplify and relay microwave signals from one transmitter on the ground to another. Satellites can be used to send and receive large volumes of data. Uplink is a term relating to sending data to a satellite. Downlink refers to receiving data from a satellite. The major drawback to satellite communication is that bad weather can sometimes interrupt the flow of data.

One of the most interesting applications of satellite communications is for global positioning. A network of 24 satellites owned and managed by the Defense Department continuously sends location information to earth. **Global positioning system (GPS)** devices (See Figure 9-8.) use that information to uniquely

Figure 9-8 **GPS navigation**

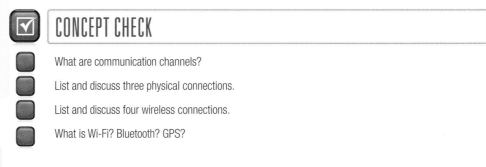

Channel	Description
Twisted pair	Twisted copper wire, used for standard telephone lines and Ethernet cables
Coaxial cable	Solid copper core, more than 80 times the capacity of twisted pair
Fiber-optic cable	Light carries data, more than 26,000 times the capacity of twisted pair
Radio frequency	Radio waves connect wireless devices including cell phones and computer components
Microwave	High-frequency radio waves, travels in straight line through the air
Satellite	Microwave relay station in the sky, used by GPS devices
Infrared	Infrared light travels in a straight line

Figure 9-9 Communication channels

determine the geographical location of the device. Available in many automobiles to provide navigational support, these systems are often mounted into the dash with a monitor to display maps and speakers to provide spoken directions. Many of today's cell phones, including the Apple iPhone, use GPS technology for handheld navigation.

* **Infrared** uses infrared light waves to communicate over short distances. It is sometimes referred to as line-of-sight communication because the light waves can only travel in a straight line. This requires that sending and receiving devices must be in clear view of one another without any obstructions blocking that view. One of the most common applications is to transfer data and information from a portable device such as a notebook computer or PDA to a desktop computer.

For a summary of communication channels, see Figure 9-9.

☑ CONCEPT CHECK

- What are communication channels?
- List and discuss three physical connections.
- List and discuss four wireless connections.
- What is Wi-Fi? Bluetooth? GPS?

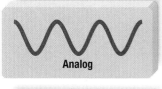

Analog

Digital

Figure 9-10 Analog and digital signals

Connection Devices

A great deal of computer communication takes place over telephone lines. However, because the telephone was originally designed for voice transmission, telephones typically send and receive **analog signals,** which are continuous electronic waves. Computers, in contrast, send and receive **digital signals.** (See Figure 9-10.) These represent the presence or absence of an electronic pulse—the on/off binary signals we mentioned in Chapter 6. To convert the digital signals to analog signals and vice versa, you need a modem.

Modems

The word **modem** is short for *modulator-demodulator*. **Modulation** is the name of the process of converting from digital to analog. **Demodulation** is the process of converting from analog to digital. The modem enables digital microcomputers to communicate across different mediums, including telephone wires, cable lines, and radio waves.

The speed with which modems transmit data varies. This speed, called **transfer rate,** is typically measured in **thousands of bits (kilobits) per second (Kbps).** (See Figure 9-11.) The higher the speed, the faster you can send and receive information. For example, transferring an image like Figure 9-10 might take 75 seconds with a 33.6 Kbps modem and only 45 seconds with a 56 Kbps modem. To learn more about transfer rates, visit our Web site at www.computing2011.com and enter the keyword **rate.**

There are four commonly used types of modems: telephone, DSL, cable, and wireless. (See Figure 9-12.)

- A **telephone modem** is used to connect a computer directly to a telephone line. These modems can be either internal or external. Internal modems are on an expansion card that plugs into a slot on the system board. An external modem is typically connected to the system unit through a serial or USB port.

- A **DSL (digital subscriber line)** modem uses standard phone lines to create a high-speed connection directly to your phone company's offices. These devices are usually external and connect to the system unit using either USB or Ethernet ports.

- A **cable modem** uses the same coaxial cable as your television. Like a DSL modem, a cable modem creates high-speed connections using the system unit's USB or Ethernet port.

Unit	Speed
Kbps	thousand bits per second
Mbps	million bits per second
Gbps	billion bits per second

Figure 9-11 Typical transfer rates

Telephone   DSL   Cable   Wireless

Figure 9-12 Basic types of modems

- A **wireless modem** is also known as a **WWAN (wireless wide area network) modem.** It is usually a small plug-in USB or ExpressCard device that provides very portable high-speed connectivity from virtually anywhere.

Connection Service

For years, large corporations have been leasing special high-speed lines from telephone companies. Originally, these were copper lines, known as **T1** lines, that could be combined to form higher-capacity options known as **T3** or **DS3** lines. These lines have largely been replaced by **optical carrier (OC)** lines, which are substantially must faster.

While the special high-speed lines are too costly for most individuals, Internet service providers (as discussed in Chapter 2) do provide affordable connections. These include dial-up, DSL, cable, satellite/air, and cellular services.

- **Dial-up service** uses existing telephones and telephone modems to connect to the Internet. For years this had been the most widely used service; however, it is very slow and is being replaced by other higher-speed connection services.
- **Digital subscriber line (DSL) service** is provided by telephone companies using existing telephone lines to provide high-speed connections. **ADSL (asymmetric digital subscriber line)** is one of the most widely used types of DSL. DSL is much faster than dial-up.
- **Cable service** is provided by cable television companies using their existing television cables. These connections are faster than DSL.
- **Satellite/air connection services** use satellites to provide wireless connections. While slower than DSL and cable modem, satellite/air connections are available almost anywhere that a satellite-receiving disk can be aimed at the southern skies.
- **Cellular services** use **3G cellular networks** to provide wireless connectivity to the Internet. Although not as fast as the other services, cellular services are rapidly growing in popularity for mobile devices such as cell phones and laptop computers.

For a comparison of typical user connection costs and speeds, see Figure 9-13.

☑ CONCEPT CHECK

What is the function of a modem?

Compare four types of modems.

What is a connection service?

Compare five affordable connection services.

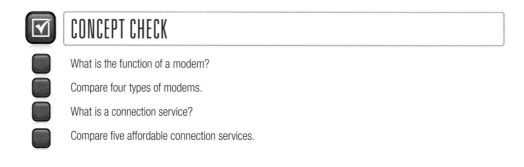

Type	Monthly Fee	Speed	Seconds to Receive Image
Dial-up	$10	56 Kbps	45.0 seconds
DSL	30	1.5 Mbps	1.5 seconds
Cable	40	8 Mbps	0.32 second
Satellite/air	75	900 Kbps	2.8 seconds
Cellular	55	768 Kbps	3.2 seconds

Figure 9-13 Typical user connection costs and speeds

Data Transmission

Several factors affect how data is transmitted. These factors include bandwidth and protocols.

Bandwidth

Bandwidth is a measurement of the width or capacity of the communication channel. Effectively, it means how much information can move across the communication channel in a given amount of time. For example, to transmit text documents, a slow bandwidth would be acceptable. However, to effectively transmit video and audio, a wider bandwidth is required. There are four categories of bandwidth.

- **Voiceband,** also known as **low bandwidth,** is used for standard telephone communication. Microcomputers with telephone modems and dial-up service use this bandwidth. While effective for transmitting text documents, it is too slow for many types of transmission, including high-quality audio and video.
- **Medium band** is used in special leased lines to connect minicomputers and mainframes as well as to transmit data over long distances. This bandwidth is capable of very high-speed data transfer.
- **Broadband** is widely used for DSL, cable, and satellite connections to the Internet. Several users can simultaneously use a single broadband connection for high-speed data transfer.
- **Baseband** is widely used to connect individual computers that are located close to one another. Like broadband, it is able to support high-speed transmission. Unlike broadband, however, baseband can only carry a single signal at one time.

Protocols

For data transmission to be successful, sending and receiving devices must follow a set of communication rules for the exchange of information. These rules for exchanging data between computers are known as **protocols.**

The standard protocol for the Internet is **TCP/IP (transmission control protocol/Internet protocol).** The essential features of this protocol involve (1) identifying sending and receiving devices and (2) breaking information into small parts for transmission across the Internet.

- **Identification:** Every computer on the Internet has a unique numeric address called an **IP address (Internet protocol address).** Similar to the way a postal service uses addresses to deliver mail, the Internet uses IP addresses to deliver e-mail and to locate Web sites. Because these numeric addresses are difficult for people to remember and use, a system was developed to automatically convert text-based addresses to numeric IP addresses. This system uses a **domain name server (DNS)** that converts text-based addresses to IP addresses. For example, whenever you enter a URL, say www.computing2011.com, a DNS converts this to an IP address before a connection can be made. (See Figure 9-14.)
- **Packetization:** Information sent or transmitted across the Internet usually travels through numerous interconnected networks. Before the message is sent, it is reformatted or broken down into small parts called **packets.** Each packet is then sent separately over the Internet, possibly traveling different routes to one common destination. At the receiving end, the packets are reassembled into the correct order.

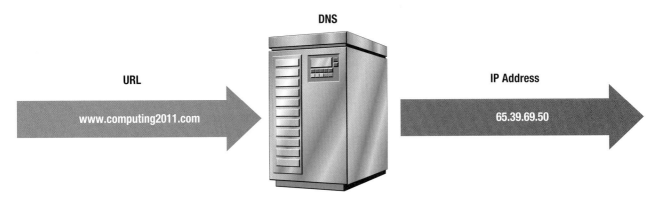

Figure 9-14 DNS converts text-based addresses to numeric IP addresses

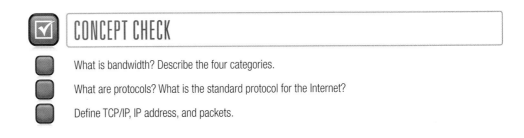

CONCEPT CHECK

What is bandwidth? Describe the four categories.

What are protocols? What is the standard protocol for the Internet?

Define TCP/IP, IP address, and packets.

Networks

A **computer network** is a communication system that connects two or more computers so that they can exchange information and share resources. Networks can be set up in different arrangements to suit users' needs. (See Figure 9-15.)

Terms

There are a number of specialized terms that describe computer networks. These terms include

- **Node**—any device that is connected to a network. It could be a computer, printer, or data storage device.
- **Client**—a node that requests and uses resources available from other nodes. Typically, a client is a user's microcomputer.
- **Server**—a node that shares resources with other nodes. Dedicated servers specialize in performing specific tasks. Depending on the specific task, they may be called an application server, communication server, database server, file server, printer server, or Web server.
- **Directory server**—a specialized server that manages resources, such as user accounts, for an entire network.
- **Host**—any computer system that can be accessed over a network.
- **Switch**—central node that coordinates the flow of data by sending messages directly between sender and receiver nodes. A **hub** previously filled this purpose by sending a received message to all connected nodes, rather than just the intended node.

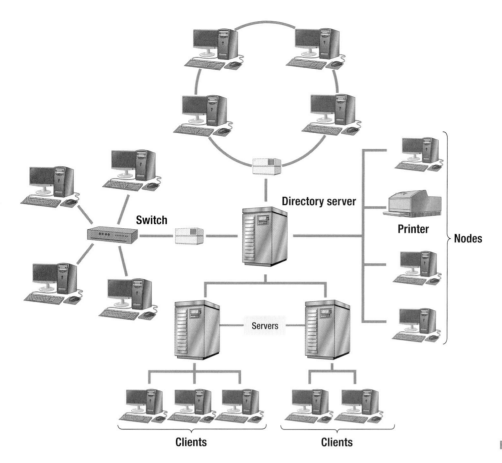

Figure 9-15 **Computer network**

- **Network interface cards (NIC)**—as discussed in Chapter 6, these are expansion cards located within the system unit that connect the computer to a network. Sometimes referred to as a LAN adapter.
- **Network operating systems (NOS)**—control and coordinate the activities of all computers and other devices on a network. These activities include electronic communication and the sharing of information and resources.
- **Network administrator**—a computer specialist responsible for efficient network operations and implementation of new networks.

A network may consist only of microcomputers, or it may integrate microcomputers or other devices with larger computers. Networks can be controlled by all nodes working together equally or by specialized nodes coordinating and supplying all resources. Networks may be simple or complex, self-contained or dispersed over a large geographical area.

CONCEPT CHECK

What is a computer network? What are nodes, clients, servers, directory servers, hosts, and switches?

What is the function of an NIC and an NOS?

What is a network administrator?

Clearly, different types of channels—cable or air—allow different kinds of networks to be formed. Telephone lines, for instance, may connect communications equipment within the same building or within a home. Networks also may be citywide and even international, using both cable and air connections. Local area, metropolitan area, and wide area networks are distinguished by the geographical area they serve.

Local Area Networks

Networks with nodes that are in close physical proximity—within the same building, for instance—are called **local area networks (LANs).** Typically, LANs span distances less than a mile and are owned and operated by individual organizations. LANs are widely used by colleges, universities, and other types of organizations to link microcomputers and to share printers and other resources. For a simple LAN, see Figure 9-16.

The LAN represented in Figure 9-16 is a typical arrangement and provides two benefits: economy and flexibility. People can share costly equipment. For instance, the four microcomputers share the laser printer and the file server, which are expensive pieces of hardware. Other equipment or nodes also may be added to the LAN—for instance, more microcomputers, a mainframe computer, or optical-disc storage devices. Additionally, the **network gateway** is a device that allows one LAN to be linked to other LANs or to larger networks. For example, the LAN of one office group may be connected to the LAN of another office group.

There are a variety of different standards or ways in which nodes can be connected to one another and ways in which their communications are controlled in a LAN. The most common standard is known as **Ethernet.** LANs using this standard are sometimes referred to as Ethernet LANs.

Home Networks

While LANs have been widely used within organizations for years, they are now being commonly used by individuals in their homes and apartments. These LANs, called **home networks,** allow different computers to share resources, including a common Internet connection. Computers can be connected in a variety of ways, including electrical wiring, telephone wiring, and special cables. One of the simplest ways, however, is without cables, or wireless.

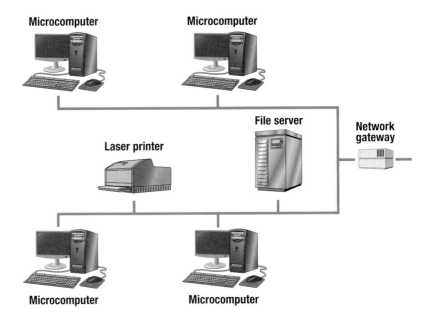

Figure 9-16 Local area network

Wireless LAN

A wireless local area network is typically referred to as a **wireless LAN (WLAN).** It uses radio frequencies to connect computers and other devices. All communications pass through the network's centrally located **wireless access point** or **base station.** This access point interprets incoming radio frequencies and routes communications to the appropriate devices. To see how home networks work, visit our Web site at www.computing2011.com and enter the keyword **network.**

To learn more about how to set up and use a wireless home network, see Making IT Work for You: Home Networking on pages 262 and 263.

Personal Area Network

A **personal area network (PAN)** is a type of wireless network that works within a very small area—your immediate surroundings. PANs connect cell phones to headsets, PDAs to other PDAs, keyboards to cell phones, and so on. These tiny, self-configuring networks make it possible for all of our gadgets to interact wirelessly with each other. The most popular PAN technology is Bluetooth, with a maximum range of around 30 feet. Virtually all wireless peripheral devices available today use Bluetooth, including the controllers on popular game systems like the PlayStation and Wii.

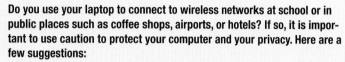

Do you use your laptop to connect to wireless networks at school or in public places such as coffee shops, airports, or hotels? If so, it is important to use caution to protect your computer and your privacy. Here are a few suggestions:

1. **Use a firewall.** A personal firewall is essential when connecting your computer directly to public networks. Some firewalls, such as the one built into Windows Vista, can be set to use more restrictive rules for public networks.

2. **Turn off file sharing.** Turning off file-sharing features in your operating system will ensure that no one can read or delete your files, or add infected files to your computer.

3. **Avoid typing sensitive information.** When possible, avoid sites that require personal information such as passwords or credit card numbers for home.

4. **Turn it off.** Turn off your laptop's wireless connection when you are not using it. This prevents automatic connections to wireless networks you do not authorize and limits your exposure to public networks.

To see additional tips, visit our Web site at www.computing2011.com and enter the keyword tips.

Metropolitan Area Networks

The next step up from the LAN is the **MAN**—the **metropolitan area network.** MANs span distances up to 100 miles. These networks are frequently used as links between office buildings that are located throughout a city.

Unlike a LAN, a MAN is typically not owned by a single organization. Rather, it is either owned by a group of organizations who jointly own and operate the network or by a single network service provider who provides network services for a fee.

Wide Area Networks

Wide area networks (WANs) are countrywide and worldwide networks. These networks provide access to regional service (MAN) providers and typically span distances greater than 100 miles. They use microwave relays and satellites to reach users over long distances—for example, from Los Angeles to Paris. Of course, the widest of all WANs is the Internet, which spans the entire globe.

The primary difference between a LAN, MAN, and WAN is the geographical range. Each may have various combinations of hardware, such as microcomputers, minicomputers, mainframes, and various peripheral devices.

For a summary of network types, see Figure 9-17.

CONCEPT CHECK

 Describe LANs, home networks, wireless LAN, and PAN.

 What is a MAN? What is a WAN?

Type	Description
LAN	Local area network; located within close proximity
Home	Local area network for home and apartment use; typically wireless
WLAN	Wireless local area network; all communication passes through access point
PAN	Personal area network; connects digital devices, such as PDAs
MAN	Metropolitan area network; typically spans cities with coverage up to 100 miles
WAN	Wide area network for countrywide or worldwide coverage; the Internet is the largest WAN

Figure 9-17 **Types of networks**

Network Architecture

Network architecture describes how a network is arranged and how resources are coordinated and shared. It encompasses a variety of different network specifics, including network topologies and strategies. Network topology describes the physical arrangement of the network. Network strategies define how information and resources are shared.

Topologies

A network can be arranged or configured in several different ways. This arrangement is called the network's **topology.** While many different topologies can be used for networks, six basic categories represent the past and present.

The past is represented by two network topologies that can still be found today but have been replaced in large part by newer, more efficient topologies. These older or legacy networks are

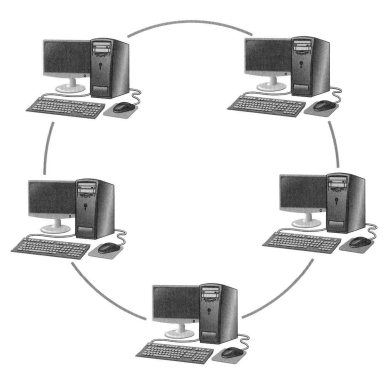

- **Bus network**—each device is connected to a common cable called a **bus** or backbone and all communications travel along this bus.

- **Ring network**—each device is connected to two other devices, forming a ring. (See Figure 9-18.) When a message is sent, it is passed around the ring until it reaches the intended destination.

Both of these legacy topologies pass messages device-to-device in sequence, which causes several disadvantages. A single incorrectly configured or malfunctioning device could cause errors or even bring the whole network down. Since all messages must pass through all nodes between the source and destination, bandwidth usage is high, making this type of topology slow and less efficient. Finally, security is a greater challenge since intermediate devices receive messages that are not intended for them.

The present is represented by four network topologies that are widely used today. These current network topologies are

Figure 9-18 **Ring network**

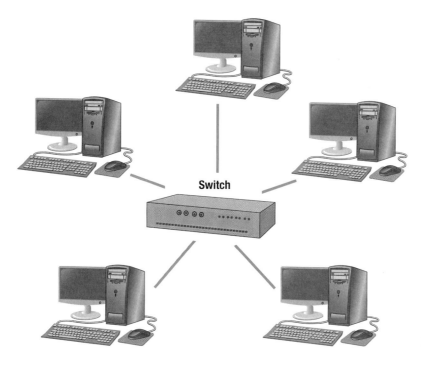

Figure 9-19 **Star network**

- **Star network**—each device is connected directly to a central network switch. (See Figure 9-19.) Whenever a node sends a message, it is routed to the switch, which then passes the message along to the intended recipient. The star network is the most widely used network topology today. It is applied to a broad range of applications from small networks in the home to very large networks in major corporations.
- **Tree network**—each device is connected to a central node, either directly or through one or more other devices. The central node is connected to two or more subordinate nodes that in turn are connected to other subordinate nodes, and so forth, forming a treelike structure. (See Figure 9-20.) This

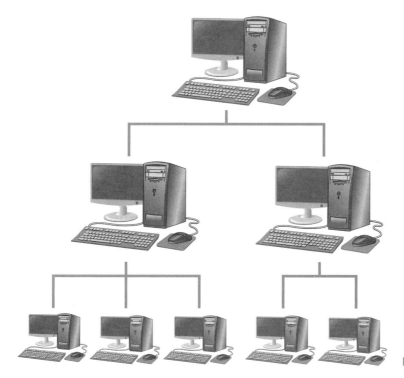

Figure 9-20 **Tree network**

Making IT work for you

HOME NETWORKING

Computer networks are not just for corporations and schools anymore. If you have more than one computer, you can use a home network to share files and printers, to allow multiple users access to the Internet at the same time, and to play multiplayer computer games.

Installing the Access Point A wireless access point is a device that broadcasts wireless signals for the network and is the gateway to the Internet for the wireless network. To set up a wireless access point using Windows Vista:

① ● Click *Start/ControlPanel/Network and Internet/ Network and Sharing Center.*

● Click *Set up a connection or network.*

● Choose *Set up a wireless router or access point.*

② ● Follow the on-screen instructions, which might include opening a special Web page to configure your access point.

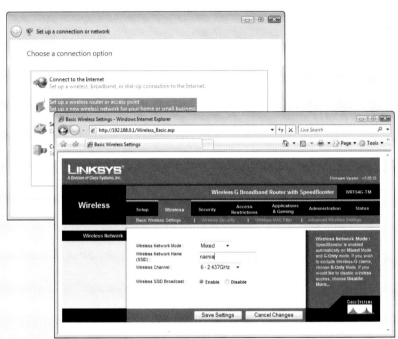

Connecting Computers Each computer on a wireless network requires a wireless network card. Many laptops and some desktops come equipped with a wireless network card built-in. Add-on cards can also be purchased. Once a computer is equipped with a wireless network card, it is simple to connect it to the wireless network. For example, to connect to a wireless network using Windows Vista:

① ● Click *Start/Connect To.*

● Select the name of the network you configured in the previous step.

● Enter the password you chose in the previous step to connect to the wireless network.

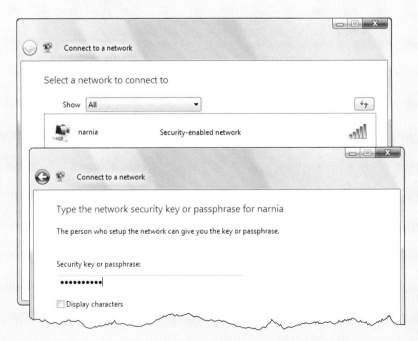

Using the Network   Now your wireless devices are ready to share their resources. Some common uses are file and printer sharing, online gaming, Internet phone, and streaming music and video.

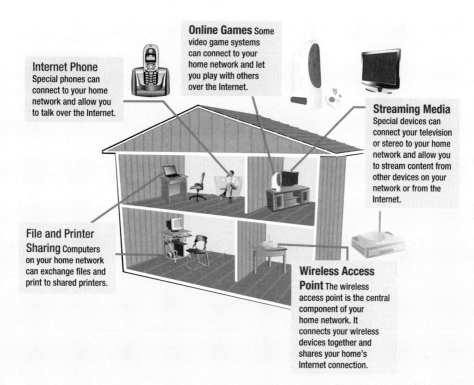

Internet Phone
Special phones can connect to your home network and allow you to talk over the Internet.

Online Games Some video game systems can connect to your home network and let you play with others over the Internet.

Streaming Media
Special devices can connect your television or stereo to your home network and allow you to stream content from other devices on your network or from the Internet.

File and Printer Sharing Computers on your home network can exchange files and print to shared printers.

Wireless Access Point The wireless access point is the central component of your home network. It connects your wireless devices together and shares your home's Internet connection.

Home networks are continually changing, and some of the specifics presented in this Making IT Work for You may have changed.

To learn about other ways to make information technology work for you, visit our Web site at www.computing2011.com and enter the keyword miw.

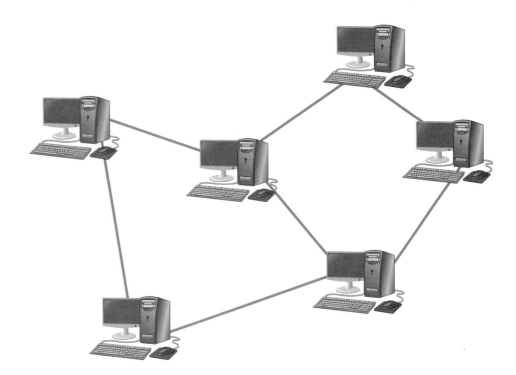

Figure 9-21 **Mesh network**

network, also known as a **hierarchical network,** is often used to share corporatewide data.

- **Hybrid network**—is a combination of different topologies. For example, large organizations today typically have a complex network of smaller networks. These smaller networks have been created over time and use a variety of different topologies. Connected together, these smaller networks form a hybrid network.

- **Mesh network**—this topology is the newest type and does not use a specific physical layout (such as a star or a tree). Rather, the mesh network requires that each node have more than one connection to the other nodes. The resulting pattern forms the appearance of a mesh. (See Figure 9-21.) If a path between two nodes is somehow disrupted, data can be automatically rerouted around the failure using another path. Wireless technologies are frequently used to build mesh networks.

For a summary of the network topologies, see Figure 9-22.

Topology	Description
Bus	Past; all devices connected to a bus
Ring	Past; each device connected to two other devices
Star	Present; each device connected to central switch
Tree	Present; each device connected directly or indirectly to central node; hierarchical topology
Hybrid	Present; combination of different topologies
Mesh	Present each device connected to more than one other device

Figure 9-22 **Network topologies**

CONCEPT CHECK

 What is a network topology?

 Describe two past topologies.

Describe four present topologies.

Strategies

Every network has a **strategy,** or way of coordinating the sharing of information and resources. The most common network strategies are terminal, client/server, peer-to-peer, and distributed.

In a **terminal server network,** processing power is centralized in one large computer, with the capacity to handle a large number of connections. The nodes connected to this host computer are either terminals with little or no processing capabilities or microcomputers running special terminal emulation software such as Windows Remote Desktop. (See Figure 9-23.)

Many airline reservation systems are terminal server networks. A large central computer maintains all the airline schedules, rates, seat availability, and so on. Travel agents use terminals to connect to the central computer and to schedule reservations. Although the tickets may be printed along with travel itineraries at the agent's desk, nearly all processing is done at the central computer.

One advantage of terminal server networks is the centralized location and control of technical personnel, software, and data. One disadvantage is the lack of control and flexibility for the end user. Another disadvantage is that terminal server networks do not use the full processing power available with microcomputers.

Client/server networks use central computers to coordinate and supply services to other nodes on the network. The server provides access to resources such as Web pages, databases, application software, and hardware. (See Figure 9-24.) This strategy is based on specialization. Server nodes coordinate and supply specialized services, and client nodes request the services.

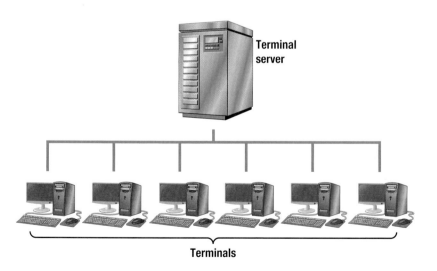

Figure 9-23 **Terminal server network**

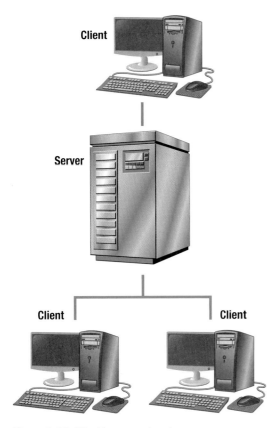

Figure 9-24 **Client/server network**

Commonly used server operating systems are Windows Server, Mac OS X Server, Linux, and Solaris.

Client/server networks are widely used on the Internet. For example, each time you open a Web browser, your computer (the client) sends out a request for a specific Web page. This request is routed over the Internet to a server. This server locates and sends the requested material back to your computer.

One advantage of the client/server network strategy is the ability to handle very large networks efficiently. Another advantage is the availability of powerful network management software to monitor and control network activities. The major disadvantages are the cost of installation and maintenance.

In a **peer-to-peer (P2P) network,** nodes have equal authority and can act as both clients and servers. (See Figure 9-25.) The most common way to share games, movies, and music over the Internet is to use a P2P network. For example, special file-sharing software such as eDonkey or BitTorrent can be used to obtain files located on another microcomputer and also can provide files to other microcomputers.

P2P networks are rapidly growing in popularity as people continue to share information with others around the world. The primary advantage is that they are easy and inexpensive (often free) to set up and use. One disadvantage of P2P networks is the lack of security controls or other common management functions. For this reason, few businesses use this type of network to communicate sensitive information.

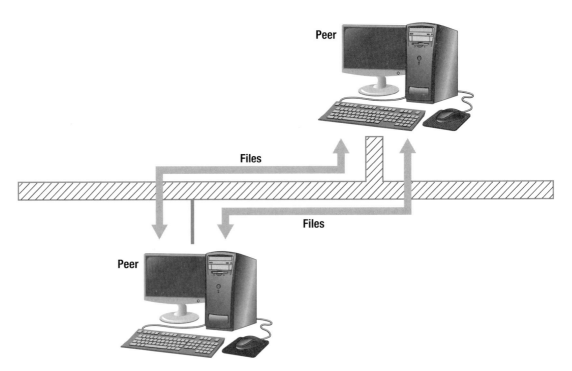

Figure 9-25 **Peer-to-peer network**

Strategy	Description
Terminal	Centralized processing power, location, and control; underutilized processing power of microcomputers
Client/server	Clients request services; servers provide services and coordination; efficient network management software; expensive
Peer-to-peer	All nodes act as clients and servers; easy and inexpensive; lacks security controls
Distributed	Nodes share resources from different locations; used in decentralized organizations

Figure 9-26 Network strategies

In a **distributed processing network,** processing capability is located and shared at different nodes or locations. This type of strategy is common for decentralized organizations where divisional offices have their own computer systems. The computer systems in the divisional offices are networked to the organizations's main or centralized computer.

For a summary of network strategies, see Figure 9-26.

CONCEPT CHECK

What is a network strategy?

Discuss the four most common network strategies.

Organizational Networks

Computer networks in organizations have evolved over time. Most large organizations have a complex and wide range of different network configurations, operating systems, and strategies. These organizations face the challenge of making these networks work together effectively and securely.

Internet Technologies

Many organizations today employ Internet technologies to support effective communication within and between organizations using intranets and extranets.

*   An **intranet** is a *private* network within an organization that resembles the Internet. Like the *public* Internet, intranets use browsers, Web sites, and Web pages. Typical applications include electronic telephone directories, e-mail addresses, employee benefit information, internal job openings, and much more. Employees find surfing their organizational intranets to be as easy and as intuitive as surfing the Internet.

*   An **extranet** is a *private* network that connects *more than one* organization. Many organizations use Internet technologies to allow suppliers and others limited access to their networks. The purpose is to increase efficiency and reduce costs. For example, an automobile manufacturer has hundreds of suppliers for the parts that go into making a car. By having access to the car production schedules, suppliers can schedule and deliver parts as they

are needed at the assembly plants. In this way, operational efficiency is maintained by both the manufacturer and the suppliers.

Network Security

Large organizations face the challenge of ensuring that only authorized users have access to network resources, sometimes from multiple geographic locations or across the Internet. Securing large computer networks requires specialized technology. Three technologies commonly used to ensure network security are firewalls, intrusion detection systems, and virtual private networks.

- A **firewall** consists of hardware and software that control access to a company's intranet and other internal networks. Most use a special computer or software called a **proxy server.** All communications between the company's internal networks and the outside world pass through this server. By evaluating the source and the content of each communication, the proxy server decides whether it is safe to let a particular message or file pass into or out of the organizations' network. (See Figure 9-27.)

- **Intrusion detection systems (NIDS)** work with firewalls to protect an organization's network. These systems use sophisticated statistical techniques to analyze all incoming and outgoing network traffic. Using advanced pattern matching and heuristics, a NIDS system can recognize signs of a network attack and disable access before an intruder can do damage.

- **Virtual private networks (VPN)** create a secure private connection between a remote user and an organization's internal network. Special VPN protocols create the equivalent of a dedicated line between a user's home or laptop computer and a company server. The connection is heavily encrypted and, from the perspective of the user, it appears that their workstation is actually located on the corporate network.

Like organizations, end users have security challenges and concerns. We need to be concerned about the privacy of our personal information. In the

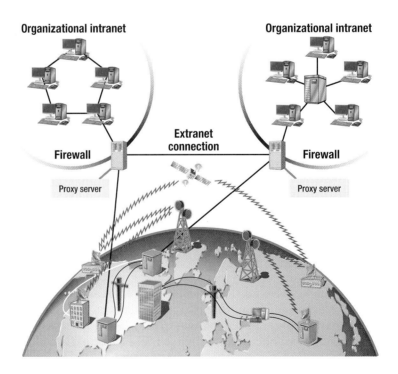

Figure 9-27 Intranets, extranets, firewalls, and proxy servers

next chapter, we will discuss personal firewalls and other ways to protect personal privacy and security.

On the Web Explorations

A popular and free NIDS system is Snort.

To learn more about Snort and try it on your own computer, visit our Web site at www.computing2011.com and enter the keyword snort.

☑ CONCEPT CHECK

- What are Internet technologies? Compare intranets and extranets.

- What is a firewall? What is a proxy server?

- What are intrusion detection systems?

- What are virtual private networks?

Careers in IT

Network administrators manage a company's LAN and WAN networks. (See Figure 9-28.) They may be responsible for design, implementation, and maintenance of networks. Responsibilities usually include maintenance of both hardware and software related to a company's intranet and Internet networks. Network administrators are typically responsible for diagnosing and repairing problems with these networks. Some network administrators are responsible for planning and implementations of network security as well.

Employers typically look for candidates with a bachelor's degree in computer science or information systems and practical networking experience. Experience with network security and maintenance is preferred. Technical certification also may be helpful in obtaining this position. Because network administrators are involved directly with people in many departments, good communication skills are essential.

Network administrators can expect to earn an annual salary of $48,500 to $79,000. Opportunities for advancement typically include upper management positions. This position is expected to be among the fastest-growing jobs in the near future. To learn about other careers in information technology, visit us at www.computing2011.com and enter the keyword **careers**.

Figure 9-28 Network administrator

Telepresence Lets You Be There without Actually Being There

How would you like to speak with distant friends or family as though they were in the same room at the touch of a button? Can you imagine receiving a physical examination from a doctor thousands of miles away? All this and more could be possible in the future thanks to the emerging technology known as *telepresence*.

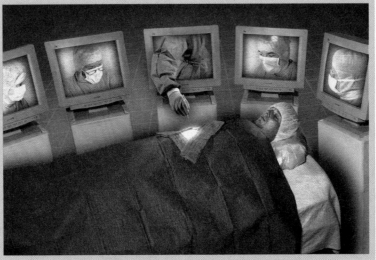

Telepresence seeks to create the illusion that you are actually at a remote location, seeing, hearing, and someday maybe even feeling as though you were really there. Today's early telepresence implementations mainly focus on an extension of video-conferencing, allowing rooms of people in different locations to conduct meetings as though they are sitting across a table from one another, an illusion created with very high definition video, acoustically tuned audio systems, and high-speed networks. However, telepresence could someday go beyond simple voice and video conferencing available today, and the applications seem endless.

Telepresense might be used to allow people to work in hazardous areas from a safe remote location. Doctors and medical specialists might be able to perform surgeries on people unable to travel. You might use telepresense as a vacation. Imagine touring remote cities or going on a deep sea diving expedition without hassle or risk.

Cisco is already marketing one video-based telepresence solution, known as Cisco Tele-Presence. At schools like MIT, developments are being made in the areas of holography, which is technology that creates 3-dimensional images called holograms, and sophisticated sensors that might pave the way to advanced telepresence. In the coming decade, you might be able to virtually interact with others with no video screen at all.

How would you use telepresence? What benefits do you see from this technology? How might telepresense impact travel in the future? Do you see any disadvantages?

COMMUNICATIONS

Communications is the process of sharing data, programs, and information between two or more computers. Applications include e-mail, instant messaging, Internet telephones, and electronic commerce.

Connectivity

Connectivity is a concept related to using computer networks to link people and resources. You can link or connect to large computers and the Internet, providing access to extensive information resources.

The Wireless Revolution

Mobile or wireless telephones have brought dramatic changes in connectivity and communications. These wireless devices are becoming widely used for computer communication.

Communication Systems

Communication systems transmit data from one location to another. Four basic elements are

- Sending and receiving devices
- Communication channel (transmission medium)
- Connection (communication) devices
- Data transmission specifications

COMMUNICATION CHANNELS

Communication channels carry data from one computer to another.

Physical Connections

Physical connections use a solid medium to connect sending and receiving devices. These connections include **twisted pair (telephone lines and Ethernet cables), coaxial cable,** and **fiber-optic cable.**

Wireless Connections

Wireless connections use air rather than solid substance to connect devices.

- **Radio frequency (RF)**—uses radio signals; **Wi-Fi (wireless fidelity)** is widely used standard; **Bluetooth** is a short-range RF-based wireless standard.
- **Microwave**—uses high-frequency radio waves; line-of-sight communication; uses microwave stations and dishes.
- **Satellite**—microwave relay station in the sky to uplink and downlink data; **GPS (global positioning system)** tracks geographical locations.
- **Infrared**—uses light waves over a short distance; line-of-sight communication.

To be a competent end user you need to understand the concepts of connectivity, the wireless revolution, and communication systems. Additionally, you need to know the essential parts of communication technology, including channels, connection devices, data transmission, networks, network architectures, and network types.

CONNECTION DEVICES

Telephone   DSL   Cable   Wireless

Many communication systems use standard telephone lines and **analog signals**. Computers use **digital signals**.

Modems

Modems modulate and **demodulate. Transfer rate** is measured in **kilobits per second.** Four types are **telephone, DSL, cable,** and **wireless (wireless wide area network, WWAN).**

Connection Service

T1, T3 (DS3), and **OC (optical carrier)** lines provide support for very high-speed, all-digital transmission for large corporations. More affordable technologies include **dial-up, DSL (digital subscriber line), ADSL** (widely used), **cable, satellite/air,** and **cellular services (3G cellular networks).**

DATA TRANSMISSION

Bandwidth measures a communication channel's width or capacity. Four bandwidths are **voiceband (low bandwidth), medium band, broadband** (high-capacity transmissions), and **baseband. Protocols** are rules for exchanging data. **TCP/IP (transmission control protocol/Internet protocol)** is the standard Internet protocol. **IP addresses (Internet protocol addresses)** are unique numeric Internet addresses. **DNS (domain name server)** converts text-based addresses to and from numeric IP addresses. **Packets** are small parts of messages.

NETWORKS

Computer networks connect two or more computers. Some specialized network terms include

- **Node**—any device connected to a network.
- **Client**—node requesting resources.
- **Server**—node providing resources.
- **Directory server**—specialized node that manages resources.
- **Host**—any computer system that can be accessed over a network.
- **Switch**—node that coordinates direct flow of data between other nodes. **Hub** is an older device that directed flow to all nodes.
- **NIC (network interface cards)**—LAN adapter card for connecting to a network.
- **NOS (network operating system)**—controls and coordinates network operations.
- **Network administrator**—network specialist responsible for network operations.

NETWORK TYPES

Networks can be citywide or even international, using both cable and air connections.

- **Local area networks (LANs)** connect nearby devices. **Network gateways** connect networks to one another. **Ethernet** is a LAN standard. These LANs are called Ethernet LANs.
- **Home networks** are LANs used in homes.
- **Wireless LANs (WLANs)** use a **wireless access point (base station)** as a hub.
- **Personal area networks (PANs)** are wireless networks for PDAs, cell phones, and other small gadgets.
- **Metropolitan area networks (MANs)** link office buildings within a city, spanning up to 100 miles.
- **Wide area networks** or **WANs** are the largest type. They span states and countries or form worldwide networks. The Internet is the largest wide area network in the world.

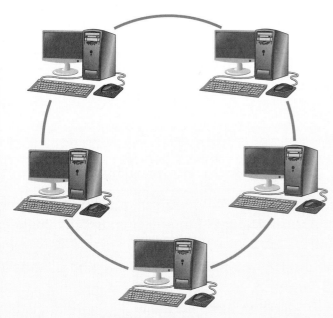

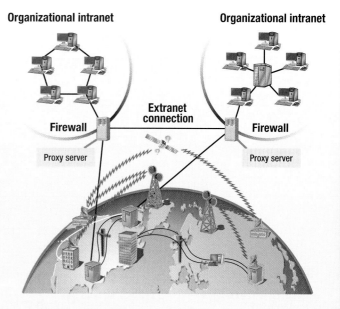

Network architecture describes how a computer network is configured and what strategies are employed.

Topologies

A network's configuration is called its **topology.**

- **Bus** and **ring networks**—older or legacy topologies; pass messages device-to-device in sequence; are less efficient.
- **Star, tree (hierarchical),** and **hybrid networks**—are widely used today; less likely to break down; more efficient, better security.
- **Mesh network**—newest; each node has two or more connecting nodes; data can be routed around disrupted paths.

Strategies

Every network has a **strategy,** or way of sharing information and resources.

Strategy	Description
Terminal	Centralized processing power, location, and control; underutilized processing power of microcomputers
Client/server	Clients request services; servers provide services and coordination; efficient network management software; expensive
Peer-to-peer	All nodes act as clients and servers; easy and inexpensive; lacks security controls
Distributed	Nodes share resources from different locations; used in decentralized organizations

Internet Technologies

Internet technologies support effective communication using intranets and extranets.

- **Intranet**—private network within an organization; uses browsers, Web sites, and Web pages. Typical applications include electronic telephone directories, e-mail addresses, employee benefit information, internal job openings, and much more.
- **Extranet**—like intranet except connects *more than one* organization; typically allows suppliers and others limited access to their networks.

Network Security

Three technologies commonly used to ensure network security are firewalls, intrusion detection systems, and virtual private networks.

- **Firewall**—controls access; all communications pass through **proxy server.**
- **Intrusion detection systems (NIDS)**—work with firewalls; use sophisticated statistical techniques to recognize and disable network attacks.
- **Virtual private network (VPN)**—creates secure private connection between remote user and organization's internal network.

CAREERS IN IT

Network administrators manage a company's LAN and WAN networks. Bachelor's degree in computer science or information systems and practical networking experience required. Salary range $48,500 to $79,000.

KEY TERMS

3G cellular network (254)
analog signal (252)
asymmetric digital
  subscriber line
  (ADSL) (254)
bandwidth (255)
baseband (255)
base station (259)
Bluetooth (251)
broadband (255)
bus (260)
bus network (260)
cable modem (253)
cable service (254)
cellular service (254)
client (256)
client/server
  network (265)
coaxial cable (250)
communication
  channel (249)
communication
  system (249)
computer network (256)
connectivity (248)
demodulation (253)
dial-up service (254)
digital signal (252)
digital subscriber line
  (DSL) (253)
digital subscriber line
  (DSL) service (254)
directory server (256)
distributed processing
  network (267)
domain name server
  (DNS) (255)
DS3 (254)
Ethernet (258)
Ethernet cable (250)
extranet (267)
fiber-optic cable (250)

firewall (268)
global positioning system
  (GPS) (251)
hierarchical
  network (264)
home network (258)
host (256)
hub (256)
hybrid network (264)
infrared (252)
intranet (267)
intrusion detection
  system (NIDS) (268)
IP address (Internet
  protocol address) (255)
kilobits per second
  (Kbps) (253)
local area network
  (LAN) (258)
low bandwidth (255)
medium band (255)
mesh network (264)
metropolitan area
  network (MAN) (259)
microwave (251)
modem (253)
modulation (253)
network
  administrator (257, 268)
network
  architecture (260)
network gateway (258)
network interface card
  (NIC) (257)
network operating system
  (NOS) (257)
node (256)
optical carrier (OC) (254)
packet (255)
peer-to-peer (P2P)
  network (266)

personal area network
  (PAN) (259)
protocol (255)
proxy server (268)
radio frequency
  (RF) (251)
ring network (260)
satellite (251)
satellite/air connection
  service (254)
server (256)
star network (261)
strategy (265)
switch (256)
T1 (254)
T3 (254)
telephone line (250)
telephone modem (253)
terminal server
  network (265)
topology (260)
transfer rate (253)
transmission control
  protocol/Internet
  protocol (TCP/IP) (255)
tree network (261)
twisted pair cable (250)
virtual private network
  (VPN) (268)
voiceband (255)
wide area network
  (WAN) (259)
Wi-Fi (wireless
  fidelity) (251)
wireless access
  point (259)
wireless LAN
  (WLAN) (259)
wireless modem (254)
wireless wide area network
  (WWAN) modem (254)

To test your knowledge of these key terms with animated flash cards, visit our Web site at www.computing2011.com and enter the keyword terms9.

MULTIPLE CHOICE

Circle the letter or fill in the correct answer.

1. Connectivity is a concept related to
   a. transmitting information, either by computer or by phone
   b. the interconnections within a computer
   c. using computer networks to link people and resources
   d. being in an active session with your computer

2. The transmission medium that carries the data is referred to as the
   a. send and receive device
   b. communication channel
   c. protocol
   d. gateways

3. Bluetooth is a type of radio wave information transmission system that is good for about
   a. 30 feet
   b. 30 yards
   c. 30 miles
   d. 300 miles

4. Special high-speed lines used by large corporations to support digital communications are known as
   a. satellite/air connection service lines
   b. cable modems
   c. ExpressCards
   d. T1 and T3 lines

5. The rules for exchanging data between computers are called
   a. interconnections
   b. synchronous packages
   c. protocols
   d. data transmission synchronization

6. Two or more computers connected so that they can communicate with each other and share information are called a
   a. satellite
   b. protocol
   c. broadcast
   d. network

7. A node that shares resources with other nodes is called a
   a. client
   b. server
   c. host
   d. NOS

8. The arrangement of the computers in a network is called the
   a. NOS
   b. topology
   c. node layout
   d. protocol

9. How a network is arranged and how it shares information and resources is called a network _____.
   a. topology
   b. strategy
   c. protocol
   d. architecture

10. A(n) _____ protects an organization's network from outside attack.
    a. fortress
    b. extranet
    c. DNS
    d. firewall

For an interactive multiple-choice practice test, visit our Web site at www.computing 2011.com and enter the keyword multiple9.

MATCHING

Match each numbered item with the most closely related lettered item. Write your answers in the spaces provided.

a. bandwidth
b. Bluetooth
c. client
d. peer-to-peer
e. DNS
f. firewall
g. infrared
h. packets
i. TCP/IP
j. topology

1. Wireless connection that uses light waves over short distances. _____
2. Uses RF to transmit data over short distances up to 33 feet. _____
3. Measurement of the capacity of a communication channel. _____
4. Standard protocol for the Internet. _____
5. Broken-down parts of a message sent over the Internet. _____
6. Converts text-based addresses to and from IP addresses. _____
7. A node that requests resources from other nodes. _____
8. The configuration of a network. _____
9. Network strategy in which each node has equal authority. _____
10. Protects network from external threats. _____

For an interactive matching practice test, visit our Web site at www.computing2011.com and enter the keyword matching9.

OPEN-ENDED

On a separate sheet of paper, respond to each question or statement.

1. Define and discuss connectivity, the wireless revolution, and communications.
2. Identify and describe the various physical and wireless communication channels.
3. Identify the standard Internet protocol and discuss its essential features.
4. Discuss past and present network topologies.
5. Define and discuss four common network strategies.

APPLYING TECHNOLOGY

The following questions are designed to demonstrate ways that you can effectively use technology today. The first question relates directly to this chapter's Making IT Work for You feature.

1 HOME NETWORKING

Computer networks are not just for corporations and schools anymore. If you have more than one computer, you can use a home network to share files and printers, to allow multiple users access to the Internet at the same time, and to play multiplayer computer games. To learn more about this technology, review Making IT Work for You: Home Networking on pages 262 and 263. Then answer the following: (a) Describe the window shown for the setup of the wireless access point. What brand of access point is demonstrated? (b) What name is used for the wireless home network? (c) What are four common uses for a wireless home network?

2 DISTRIBUTED COMPUTING

When networked computers are not in use, their processing power can be combined with other networked computers to perform a common task. In some cases, the problems that can be solved by many individual computers are far too large to be solved by any single computer. Connect to our site at www.computing2011.com and enter the keyword distributed for a link to a site that features distributed computing. Explore the site and answer the following questions: (a) What type of problem does this site solve with distributed computing? (b) How do users donate unused computer time to this project? (c) Would you donate your extra computer time to a distributed computing project? Why or why not?

3 WIRELESS MOBILE DEVICES

Recent advances in technology allow mobile devices to communicate on the go faster than ever before. Visit our Web site at www.computing2011.com and enter the keyword moblie to link to a Web site featuring connected mobile devices. Once connected, review the latest products and then answer the following questions: (a) What support for Internet connection is available? How fast is the connection? (b) Are the connection options you researched in part (a) available where you live? Is there any place they are not available? (c) What is required to connect a mobile device to the Internet? (d) What type of Internet information is accessible? Is there any type that is not accessible?

EXPANDING YOUR KNOWLEDGE

The following questions are designed to add depth and detail to your understanding of specific topics presented within this chapter. The questions direct you to sources other than the textbook to obtain this knowledge.

1 HOW WIRELESS HOME NETWORKS WORK

Wireless home networks are becoming very popular. These LANs are easy to set up and use. They allow different computers to share resources including a common Internet connection and printer. To learn how home networks work, visit our Web site at www.computing2011.com and enter the keyword network. Then answer the following questions. (a) What is a node? (b) What is a base station (access point) and what is its function? (c) What is a wireless card and what is its function? (d) If one or more requests to print a document are made at exactly the same time, what node determines which document is printed first? (e) Can the nodes TIM, LINDA, and STEVE access and use the Internet at the same time? If yes, how can this be done with a single Internet connection?

2 BITTORRENT

BitTorrent is a file-sharing protocol used to distribute large files across the Internet. Connect to our Web site at www.computing2011.com and enter the keyword torrent to learn more about how BitTorrent works, and then answer the following: (a) What is a "torrent"? How is a torrent created and published? (b) What network strategy does BitTorrent use? Review the network strategies presented on pages 265 through 267 and justify your answer. (c) What are the advantages to downloading files using BitTorrent rather than traditional client-server methods? How does BitTorrent reduce bandwidth usage for content providers?

3 HOTSPOTS

Hotspots are areas set up to provide public access to wireless Internet service. Find them in coffee shops, airports, or hotels. Connect to our Web site at www.computing 2011.com and enter the keyword hotspots to link to a directory of hotspots. Locate one near you. Where is the hotspot? What equipment is necessary to use the hotspot? What does it cost to use the hotspot?

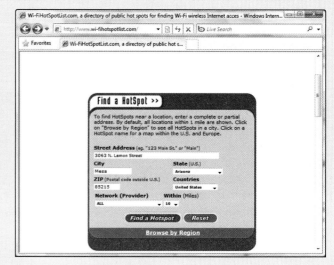

WRITING ABOUT TECHNOLOGY

The ability to think critically and to write effectively is essential to nearly every profession. The following questions are designed to help you develop these skills by posing thought-provoking questions about computer privacy, security, and/or ethics.

1 ELECTRONIC MONITORING

Programs known as "sniffers" are sometimes used to monitor communications on corporate networks. Recently, the FBI unveiled a technology known as Carnivore that can monitor an individual's Internet activity and eavesdrop on e-mail messages. Write a one-page paper that answers the following questions: (a) Is it a violation of an employee's privacy for an organization or corporation to use sniffer programs to monitor communications on their network? (b) Is it a violation of privacy for a government agency such as the FBI to use programs like Carnivore to monitor communications on the Internet? (c) Under what conditions are the types of monitoring discussed in parts (a) and (b) acceptable and ethical? (d) How can these conditions be enforced?

2 DIGITAL RIGHTS MANAGEMENT

In response to the issue of sharing copyrighted material over computer networks discussed in this chapter, many different forms of digital rights management, or DRM, have been proposed. However, DRM is controversial and hotly debated by industry groups and consumer advocates. Use the Web to research DRM, and then write a one-page paper titled "Digital Rights Management" that addresses the following topics: (a) Define "digital rights management." (b) What systems have been proposed for DRM? (c) Why are some consumers opposed to these systems? (d) Do you think DRM is a fair solution to online piracy? Justify your answer.

Privacy and Security

Competencies

After you have read this chapter, you should be able to:

1. Identify the most significant concerns for effective implementation of computer technology.

2. Discuss the primary privacy issues of accuracy, property, and access.

3. Describe the impact of large databases, private networks, the Internet, and the Web on privacy.

4. Discuss online identity and the major laws on privacy.

5. Describe the security threats posed by computer criminals including employees, hackers, crackers, organized crime, and terrorists.

6. Discuss computer crimes including creation of viruses and worms and implementation of denial of service attacks and Internet scams.

7. Detail ways to protect computer security.

8. Discuss computer ethics including copyright law and plagiarism.

9. Describe ways to protect copyrights and to identify plagiarism, including digital rights management and Turnitin.

In the past, protecting your privacy may have required a paper shredder and an unlisted phone number. Today it is possible to learn the complete life history of a stranger with a few clicks of the mouse.

Some experts believe that in the future details about your entire life may be available online and could be collected and analyzed by the businesses you frequent. Imagine a world where the grocery store where you regularly shop knows what you browse for online and suggests recipes or changes to your diet accordingly.

chapter 10

Introduction

The tools and products of the information age do not exist in a world by themselves. As we said in Chapter 1, a computer system consists not only of software, hardware, data, and procedures, but also of people. Because of people, computer systems may be used for both good and bad purposes.

There are more than 300 million microcomputers in use today. What are the consequences of the widespread presence of this technology? Does technology make it easy for others to invade our personal privacy? When we apply for a loan or for a driver's license, or when we check out at the supermarket, is that information about us being distributed and used without our permission? When we use the Web, is information about us being collected and shared with others?

Does technology make it easy for others to invade the security of business organizations like our banks or our employers? What about health risks to people who use computers? What about the environment? Do computers pose a threat to our ecology?

This technology prompts lots of questions—very important questions. Perhaps these are some of the most important questions for the 21st century. Competent end users need to be aware of the potential impact of technology on people and how to protect themselves on the Web. They need to be sensitive to and knowledgeable about personal privacy, organizational security, ergonomics, and the environmental impact of technology.

People

As we have discussed, information systems consist of people, procedures, software, hardware, and data. This chapter focuses on people. (See Figure 10-1.) While most everyone agrees that technology has had a very positive impact on people, it is important to recognize the negative, or potentially negative, impacts as well.

Effective implementation of computer technology involves maximizing its positive effects while minimizing its negative effects. The most significant concerns are

* **Privacy:** What are the threats to personal privacy and how can we protect ourselves?

Figure 10-1 People are part of an information system

- **Security:** How can access to sensitive information be controlled and how can we secure hardware and software?
- **Ethics:** How do the actions of individual users and companies affect society?

Let us begin by examining privacy.

Privacy

As you have seen, computing technology makes it possible to collect and use data of all kinds, including information about people. The Web sites you visit, the stores where you shop, and the television shows you watch are all examples of information about you. How would you feel if you learned such information was being collected or shared? Would it matter who was collecting it, or how it was being used, or whether it was even correct?

Privacy concerns the collection and use of data about individuals. There are three primary privacy issues:

- **Accuracy** relates to the responsibility of those who collect data to ensure that the data is correct.
- **Property** relates to who owns data and rights to software.
- **Access** relates to the responsibility of those who have data to control and who is able to use that data.

Large Databases

Large organizations are constantly compiling information about us. The federal government alone has over 2,000 databases. Every day, data is gathered about us and stored in large databases. For example, telephone companies compile lists of the calls we make, the numbers called, and so on. A special telephone directory (called a **reverse directory**) lists telephone numbers sequentially. (See Figure 10-2.) Using it, government authorities and others can easily get the names, addresses, and other details about the persons we call.

Credit card companies keep similar records. Supermarket scanners in grocery checkout counters record what we buy, when we buy it, how much we buy, and the price. Financial institutions, including banks and credit unions, record how much money we have, what we use it for, and how much we owe. Publishers of magazines, newspapers, and mail-order catalogues have our names, addresses, phone numbers, and what we order.

A vast industry of data gatherers known as **information resellers** or **information brokers** now exists that collects and sells such personal data. Using publicly available databases and in many cases nonpublic databases, information resellers create **electronic profiles** or highly detailed and personalized descriptions of individuals. Very likely, you have an electronic profile that includes your name, address, telephone number, Social Security number, driver's license number, bank account numbers, credit card numbers, telephone records, and shopping and purchasing patterns. Information resellers sell these electronic profiles to direct marketers, fundraisers, and others. Many provide these services on the Web for free or for a nominal cost. (See Figure 10-3.)

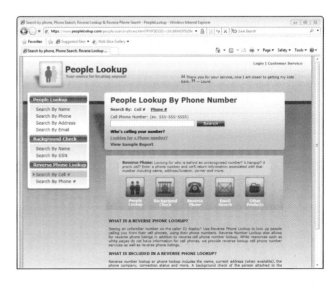

Figure 10-2 Reverse directory Web site

Figure 10-3 Information reseller's Web site

Figure 10-4 Google Street View

Your personal information, including preferences, habits, and financial data, has become a marketable commodity. This raises many issues, including

- **Collecting public, but personally identifying information:** What if people anywhere in the world could view detailed images of you, your home, or your car? Using detailed images captured with a specially equipped van, Google's Street View project allows just that. Street View makes it possible to take a virtual tour of many cities and neighborhoods from any computer with a connection to the Internet. (See Figure 10-4.) Although the images available on Street View are all taken in public locations, some have objected to the project as being an intrusion on their privacy.

- As digital cameras and Webcams become cheaper and software becomes more sophisticated, it is likely that many more issues involving personal privacy in public spaces will need to be addressed. Such a combination of computing technologies could, for example, make real-time tracking of individuals in public places possible.

- **Spreading information without personal consent:** How would you feel if an employer were using your medical records to make decisions about hiring, placement, promotion, and firing? A survey of Fortune 500 companies found that over one-third were using medical records for just these purposes.

How would you feel if someone obtained a driver's license and credit cards in your name? What if that person then assumed your identity to buy clothes, cars, and a house? It happens every day. Every year, nearly 10 million people are victimized in this way. It is called **identity theft.** Identity theft is the illegal assumption of someone's identity for the purposes of economic gain. It is one of the fastest-growing crimes in the country. To learn more about identity theft and how to minimize your risk, visit our Web site at www.computing2011.com and enter the keyword **theft.**

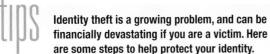

tips

Identity theft is a growing problem, and can be financially devastating if you are a victim. Here are some steps to help protect your identity.

1 Never give personal information on the Internet or in response to e-mail. One common scam known as *phishing* involves e-mail that has been forged to appear to come from your bank or school.

2 Only do business on the Internet with companies you know to be legitimate, or large companies with a solid reputation.

3 When selling a computer, be sure to completely remove all personal information from the hard drive. Many programs are available to ensure data is completely removed.

4 Check your credit reports from the three major credit bureaus for unusual activity or inaccuracy at least once a year.

To see more tips, visit our Web site at www.computing 2011.com and enter the keyword tips.

- **Spreading inaccurate information:** How would you like to be turned down for a home loan because of an error in your credit history? This is much more common than you might expect. What if you could not find a job or were fired from a job because of an error giving you a serious criminal history? This can and has happened due to simple clerical errors. In one case, an arresting officer while completing an arrest warrant incorrectly recorded the Social Security number of a criminal. From that time forward, this arrest and the subsequent conviction became part of another person's electronic profile. This is an example of **mistaken identity** in which the electronic profile of one person is switched with another.

It's important to know that you have some recourse. The law allows you to gain access to those records about you that are held by credit bureaus. Under the **Freedom of Information Act,** you are also entitled to look at your records held by government agencies. (Portions may be deleted for national security reasons.)

CONCEPT CHECK

 What are the three primary privacy issues?

 What are information resellers, electronic profiles, identity theft, and mistaken identity?

 What is the Freedom of Information Act?

Private Networks

Suppose you use your company's electronic mail system to send a co-worker an unflattering message about your supervisor or to send a highly personal message to a friend. Later you find the boss has been spying on your exchange. This is legal and a recent survey revealed that nearly 75 percent of all businesses search employees' electronic mail and computer files using so-called **snoopware.** (See Figure 10-5.) These programs record virtually everything you do on your computer. One proposed law would not prohibit this type of electronic monitoring but would require employers to provide prior written notice. Employers also would have to alert employees during the monitoring with some sort of audible or visual signal.

On the Web Explorations

Several organizations monitor the legislation on privacy issues.

To learn more about one such organization, visit our Web site at www.computing2011.com and enter the keyword privacy.

The Internet and the Web

When you send e-mail on the Internet or browse the Web, do you have any concerns about privacy? Most people do not. They think that as long as they are using their own computer and are selective about disclosing their names or other personal information, then little can be done to invade their personal privacy. Experts call this the **illusion of anonymity** that the Internet brings.

As we discussed in Chapter 9, every computer on the Internet is identified by a unique number known as an IP address. IP addresses can be used to trace Internet activities to their origin, allowing computer security experts and law enforcement officers to investigate computer crimes such as unauthorized access to networks or sharing of copyrighted files without permission.

Figure 10-5 **Snoopware**

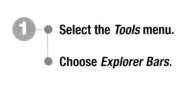

1 ● Select the *Tools* menu.

● Choose *Explorer Bars.*

2 ● Select *History.*

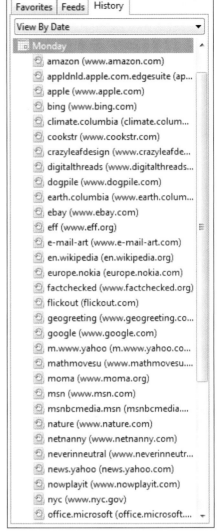

Figure 10-6 **Viewing history files**

When you browse the Web, your browser stores critical information onto your hard disk, typically without your explicit permission or knowledge. For example, your browser creates a **history file** that includes the locations of sites visited by your computer system. This history file can be displayed by your browser. To view the history file using Internet Explorer version 8.0, follow the steps in Figure 10-6.

Another way your Web activity can be monitored is with **cookies,** or small pieces of information that are deposited on your hard disk from Web sites you have visited. Typically, cookies are deposited without your explicit knowledge or consent. While cookies are harmless in and of themselves, what makes them potentially dangerous is that they can store information about you without your knowledge. Using them, a record of what sites you visit, what you do at the sites, and other information you provide can be created. To view the cookies on a hard drive using Internet Explorer version 8.0, follow the steps in Figure 10-7.

There are two basic types of cookies: traditional and ad network. Most cookies can be displayed by your browser.

● **Traditional cookies** provide information to a single site. When you first visit a site, a cookie is deposited with information that identifies you

1 Select *Tools* from the menu bar.

Choose *Internet Options*.

2 Select *Settings* in the *Browsing history* section of the *General* tab.

Click *View files*.

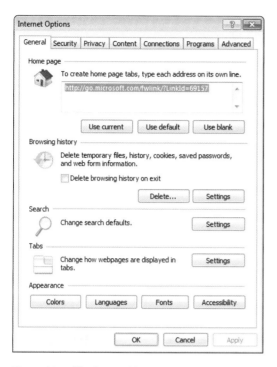

Figure 10-7 **Viewing cookies**

specifically (such as information you provided on a form). Any further pages you visit on the site will have access to the cookie and be able to read its contents. When you leave the site, the cookie is usually saved. When you revisit, the cookie is reactivated and the information accessed. Most cookies are intended to provide customized service. For example, when you revisit an electronic commerce site, you can be greeted by name, presented with customized advertising banners, and directed to Web pages promoting items you have previously purchased.

• **Ad network** or **adware cookies** record your activities across different sites. Once deposited onto your hard drive, they can be activated and accessed from many of the Web sites that you visit. These cookies are deposited on your hard disk by organizations that compile and market the information. Two such organizations are DoubleClick and Avenue A.

Most browsers are able to control many types of cookies. For example, Internet Explorer version 8.0 provides settings to selectively block cookies from being deposited onto a system's hard disk. (See Figure 10-8.)

The term **spyware** is used to describe a wide range of programs that are designed to secretly record and report an individual's activities on the Internet. Ad network cookies are just one type of spyware. Two other types are Web bugs and computer monitoring software.

• **Web bugs** are small images or HTML code hidden within an e-mail message. When a user opens an e-mail containing a Web bug, information is

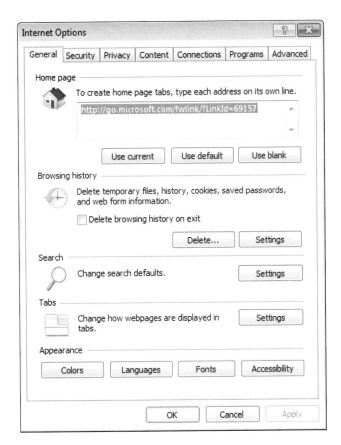

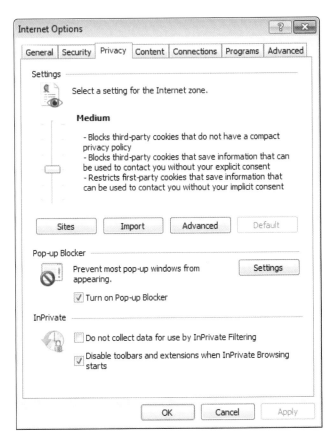

Figure 10-8 **Blocking cookies**

sent back to the source of the bug. One of the most common Web bugs is used by companies that sell active mailing lists to spammers. This bug is simply an invisible graphic embedded into an e-mail message. When the e-mail is opened, a request is sent to display the graphic without the reader's knowledge. The request is sent to a remote server that then knows that this e-mail address is active. Although this Web bug does no serious harm, others are more dangerous. To see how Web bugs can work, visit our Web site at www.computing2011.com and enter the keyword **bugs.**

- **Computer monitoring software** is the most invasive and dangerous type of spyware. These programs record every activity and keystroke made on your computer system, including credit card numbers, bank account numbers, and e-mail messages. Also known as **keystroke loggers,** computer monitoring software can be deposited onto your hard drive without your knowledge either from the Web or by someone installing the programs directly onto your computer. The previously mentioned snoopware is a type of computer monitoring software used by businesses to monitor their employees. Computer monitoring software also has been used by the FBI and the CIA to collect incriminating evidence on suspected terrorists and organized crime members. These programs are also widely used by private investigators, criminals, and spouses.

Unfortunately, it is more difficult to remove Web bugs and computer monitoring software than ad network cookies because they are more difficult to detect. There are over 90,000 active spyware programs, and chances are you have one or more of them on your computer. A recent study reported finding an average of 28 active spyware programs on microcomputers it had evaluated.

A category of programs known as **antispyware** or **spy removal programs,** which are designed to detect and remove cookies, Web bugs, and monitoring software, has evolved to battle the threat. (See Figure 10-9.) For a list of some of these programs, see Figure 10-10. To learn more about protecting yourself from spyware, see Making IT Work for You: Spyware Removal on pages 290 and 291.

Figure 10-9 **Protect your privacy**

Online Identity

Another aspect of Internet privacy comes from **online identity,** the information that people voluntarily post about themselves online. With the popularity of social networking, blogging, and photo- and video-sharing sites, many people post intimate details of their lives without considering the consequences. Although it is easy to think of online identity as something shared between friends, the archiving and search features of the Web make it available indefinitely to anyone who cares to look. How would you feel if information you posted about yourself on the Web kept you from getting a job?

Program	Web Site
Windows Defender	www.microsoft.com
Ad-Aware	www.lavasoft.com
CounterSpy	www.counterspy.com
Spy Doctor	www.spydoctor.com
Spy Sweeper	www.spysweeper.com

Figure 10-10 **Antispyware programs**

Major Laws on Privacy

Some federal laws governing privacy matters have been created. For example, the **Gramm-Leach-Bliley Act** protects personal financial information, the **Health Insurance Portability and Accountability Act (HIPAA)** protects medical records, and the **Family Educational Rights and Privacy Act (FERPA)** restricts disclosure of educational records. To learn more about existing privacy laws, visit our Web site at www.computing2011.com and enter the keyword **law.**

Most of the information collected by private organizations is not covered by existing laws. However, as more and more individuals become concerned about controlling who has the right to personal information and how that information is used, companies and law makers will respond.

tips

What can you do to protect your privacy while on the Web? Here are a few suggestions.

1 **Encrypt sensitive e-mail.** Encrypt or code sensitive e-mail using special encryption programs.

2 **Shield your identity.** Use an anonymous remailer or special Web site that forwards your e-mail without disclosing your identity.

3 **Block cookies.** Use your browser or a cookie-cutter program to block unwanted cookies.

4 **Check for Web bugs and computer monitoring software.** Use spy removal programs to check for Web bugs and computer monitoring software.

5 **Notify providers.** Instruct your service provider or whomever you use to link to the Internet not to sell your name or any other personal information.

6 **Be careful.** Never disclose your telephone number, passwords, or other private information to strangers.

To see more tips, visit our Web site at www.computing2011.com and enter the keyword tips.

Making IT work for you

SPYWARE REMOVAL

Have you installed any free software from the Internet? Did you know seemingly harmless software might actually be spying on you, even sending personal information to advertisers or worse? Fortunately, spyware removal software is available to help keep your personal information private.

Finding and Removing Spyware Once spyware removal software is installed on your system, you can scan your system for known spyware and remove it. Follow the steps below to find and remove spyware using Ad-Aware.

1 • Connect to www.lavasoft.com and follow the on-screen instructions to download and install the Ad-Aware software.

2 • Launch the Ad-Aware application.

• Click the *Scan Now* button.

• Click the *Scan* button to begin scanning for spyware.

• Review the results of the scan, and place a checkmark next to any detected items you would like to remove.

• Click the *Remove* button to remove the detected spyware from your system.

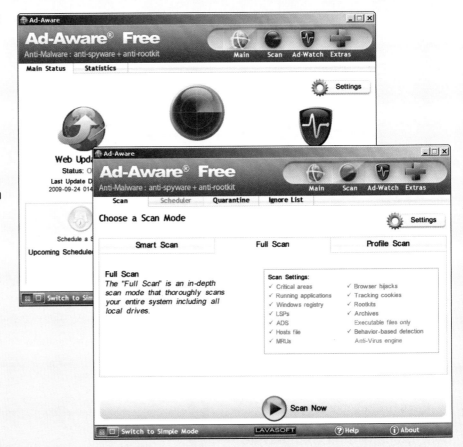

Automating Spyware Removal To protect your system from spyware, it is recommended that you run your spyware removal software automatically. If you purchase the Plus or Pro version of Ad-Aware, you can follow the steps below to set Ad-Aware to run automatically on a regular schedule.

1 • Click the *Scan* button.

• Click the *Schedule* button.

2 • Choose how frequently you would like your system scanned for spyware.

• Click the *Add* button to add your selection to the scheduler.

Ad-Aware will now run automatically on the days and times you selected.

Staying Up to Date Now that your system is protected from spyware, you'll want to keep it that way. Spyware removal programs keep a profile of known spyware, which must be updated from time to time. Follow the steps below to update the spyware profile in Ad-Aware.

1 • Click the *Web Update* button.

2 • Click the *Update* button.

Ad-Aware connects to the Internet and updates its spyware profile. The newest Ad-Aware reference file is installed automatically. You can now follow the steps in the "Finding and Removing Spyware" section to rid your system of the latest known spyware.

The Web is continually changing, and some of the specifics presented in this Making IT Work for You may have changed.

To learn about other ways to make information technology work for you, visit our Web site at www.computing2011.com and enter the keyword miw.

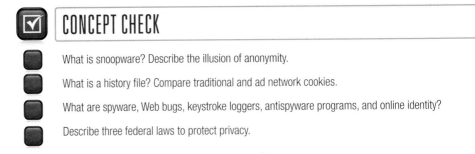

CONCEPT CHECK

What is snoopware? Describe the illusion of anonymity.

What is a history file? Compare traditional and ad network cookies.

What are spyware, Web bugs, keystroke loggers, antispyware programs, and online identity?

Describe three federal laws to protect privacy.

Security

We are all concerned with having a safe and secure environment to live in. We are careful to lock our car doors and our homes. We are careful about where we walk at night and whom we talk to. This is personal security. What about computer security? What if someone gains unauthorized access to our computer or other computers that contain information about us? What if someone steals our computer or other computers that contain information about us? What are the major threats to computer security, and how can we be protected?

Computer Criminals

A **computer crime** is an illegal action in which the perpetrator uses special knowledge of computer technology. Typically, computer criminals are either employees, outside users, hackers, crackers, organized crime members, or terrorists.

- **Employees:** The largest category of computer criminals consists of those with the easiest access to computers—namely, employees. Sometimes the employee is simply trying to steal something from the employer— equipment, software, electronic funds, proprietary information, or computer time. Sometimes the employee is acting out of resentment and is trying to get back at the company.
- **Outside users:** Not only employees but also some suppliers or clients may have access to a company's computer system. Examples are bank customers who use an automated teller machine. Like employees, these authorized users may be able to obtain confidential passwords or find other ways of committing computer crimes.
- **Hackers and crackers:** Some people think of these two groups as being the same, but they are not. **Hackers** are people who create or improve programs and share those programs with fellow hackers. Typically, they are not criminals. **Crackers,** on the other hand, create and share programs designed to gain unauthorized access to computer systems or disrupt networks. Their motives are malicious and can be very destructive and costly. Typically, they are criminals.
- **Organized crime:** Members of organized crime groups have discovered that they can use computers just as people in legitimate businesses do, but for illegal purposes. For example, computers are useful for keeping track of stolen goods or illegal gambling debts. In addition, counterfeiters and forgers use microcomputers and printers to produce sophisticated-looking documents such as checks and driver's licenses.
- **Terrorists:** Knowledgeable terrorist groups and hostile governments could potentially crash satellites and wage economic warfare by disrupting

navigation and communication systems. The Department of Defense reports that its computer systems are probed approximately 250,000 times a year by unknown sources.

Computer Crime

The FBI estimates that businesses lose trillions of dollars a year from computer crimes. The number of these crimes has tripled in the past two years. Computer crime can take various forms including the creation of malicious programs, denial of service attacks, Internet scams, theft, and data manipulation.

Malicious Programs Hackers and crackers are notorious for creating and distributing malicious programs. These programs are called **malware,** which is short for **mal**icious soft**ware.** They are specifically designed to damage or disrupt a computer system. The three most common types of malware are viruses, worms, and Trojan horses.

- **Viruses** are programs that migrate through networks and operating systems, and most attach themselves to different programs and databases. While some viruses are relatively harmless, many can be quite destructive. Once activated, these destructive viruses can alter and/or delete files. Some delete all files on the hard disk and can damage system components. Creating and knowingly spreading a virus is a very serious crime and a federal offense punishable under the **Computer Fraud and Abuse Act.**

  Unfortunately, new computer viruses are appearing all the time. The best way to stay current is through services that keep track of viruses on a daily basis. For example, the Virus Radar On-line project tracks the most serious virus threats. See Figure 10-11.

- **Worms** are a special type of virus that does not attach itself to programs and databases. Rather it fills a computer system with self-replicating information, clogging the system so that its operations are slowed or stopped. A recent worm traveled across the world within hours, stopping tens of thousands of computers along its way. Internet worms also can be carriers of more traditional viruses. Once the traditional virus has been deposited by a worm onto an unsuspecting computer system, the virus will either activate immediately or lie dormant until some future time.

Viruses and worms typically find their way into microcomputers through e-mail attachments and programs downloaded from the Internet. Because viruses can be so damaging, computer users are advised to never open an e-mail attachment from an unknown source and to exercise great care in accepting new programs and data from any source.

As we discussed in Chapter 5, antivirus programs alert users when certain kinds of viruses and worms enter their system. Some of the most widely used are Dr. Solomon's Anti-Virus, McAfee VirusScan, eSafe, and Norton AntiVirus. Unfortunately, new viruses are being developed all the time, and not all viruses can be detected. (See Making IT Work for You: Virus Protection and Internet Security on pages 140 and 141 in Chapter 5.)

- **Trojan horses** are programs that come into a computer system disguised as something else. Trojan horses are not viruses. Like worms, however,

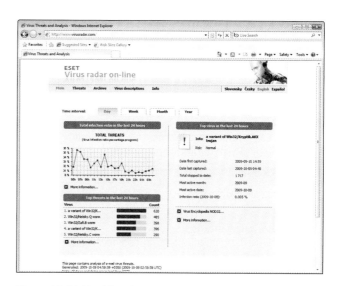

Figure 10-11 Tracking viruses

they can be carriers of viruses. The most common types of Trojan horses appear as free computer games and free screen saver programs that can be downloaded from the Internet. Once the Trojan horse is downloaded onto a computer system, the viruses are deposited and ready to activate. One of the most dangerous types of Trojan horse claims to provide free antivirus programs. They begin by locating and disabling any existing virus protection programs before depositing a virus.

Zombies are computers infected by a virus, worm, or Trojan horse that allows them to be remotely controlled for malicious purposes. A collection of zombie computers is known as a **botnet,** or **robot network.** Botnets harness the combined power of many zombies for malicious activities like password cracking or sending junk e-mail. Because they are formed by many computers distributed across the Internet, botnets are hard to shut down even after they are detected. Unfortunately for individual computer owners, it can also be difficult to detect when a personal computer has been compromised.

Denial of Service A **denial of service (DoS) attack** attempts to slow down or stop a computer system or network by flooding a computer or network with requests for information and data. The targets of these attacks are usually Internet service providers (ISP) and specific Web sites. Once under attack, the servers at the ISP or the Web site become overwhelmed with these requests for service and are unable to respond to legitimate users. As a result, the ISP or Web site is effectively shut down.

Internet Scams A **scam** is a fraudulent or deceptive act or operation designed to trick individuals into providing personal information or spending their time and money for little or no return. An **Internet scam** is simply a scam using the Internet. Internet scams are becoming a serious problem and have created financial and legal problems for thousands of people. Almost all of the scams are initiated by a mass mailing to unsuspecting individuals.

A technique often employed by scammers is **phishing** (pronounced "fishing"). Phishing attempts to trick Internet users into thinking a fake but official-looking Web site or e-mail is legitimate. Phishing has grown in sophistication, replicating entire Web sites like PayPal to try to lure users into divulging their financial information.

See Figure 10-12 for a list of common types of Internet scams.

tips

Are you concerned about catching a virus? Here are a few suggestions that might help:

1. **Use an antivirus program.** Install antivirus programs on all computer systems you use and run them frequently.

2. **Check disks.** Before using any floppy or CD, check for viruses.

3. **Check all downloads.** Check all files downloaded from the Internet.

4. **Update your antivirus program.** New viruses are being developed daily, and the virus programs are continually being revised. Update your antivirus program frequently.

To see more tips, visit our Web site at www.computing 2011.com and enter the keyword tips.

Theft Theft can take many forms—of hardware, of software, of data, of computer time. Thieves steal equipment and programs, of course, but there are also white-collar crimes. These crimes include the theft of data in the form of confidential information such as preferred-client lists. Another common crime is the use (theft) of a company's computer time by an employee to run another business.

Data Manipulation Finding entry into someone's computer network and leaving a prankster's message may seem like fun, which is why hackers do it. It is still against the law. Moreover, even if the manipulation seems harmless, it may cause a great deal of anxiety and wasted time among network users.

The **Computer Fraud and Abuse Act** makes it a crime for unauthorized persons even to view—let alone

Type	Description
Identity theft	Individual(s) pose as ISPs, bank representatives, or government agencies requesting personal information. Once obtained, criminal(s) assume a person's identity for a variety of financial transactions.
Chain letter	Classic chain letter instructing recipient to send a nominal amount of money to each of five people on a list. The recipient removes the first name on the list, adds his or her name at the bottom and mails the chain letter to five friends. This is also known as a pyramid scheme. Almost all chain letters are fraudulent and illegal.
Auction fraud	Merchandise is selected and payment is sent. Merchandise is never delivered.
Vacation prize	"Free" vacation has been awarded. Upon arrival at vacation destination, the accommodations are dreadful but can be upgraded for a fee.
Advance fee loans	Guaranteed low-rate loans available to almost anyone. After applicant provides personal loan-related information, the loan is granted subject to payment of an "insurance fee."

Figure 10-12 Common Internet scams

copy or damage—data using any computer across state lines. It also prohibits unauthorized use of any government computer or a computer used by any federally insured financial institution. Offenders can be sentenced to up to 20 years in prison and fined up to $100,000.

For a summary of computer crimes, see Figure 10-13. For a brief history of computer crimes, visit our Web site at www.computing2011.com and enter the keyword **crime.**

Other Hazards

There are plenty of other hazards to computer systems and data besides criminals. They include the following:

- **Natural hazards:** Natural forces include fires, floods, wind, hurricanes, tornadoes, and earthquakes. Even home computer users should store backup disks of programs and data in safe locations in case of fire or storm damage.
- **Civil strife and terrorism:** Wars, riots, and terrorist activities are real risks in all parts of the world. Even people in developed countries must be mindful of these acts.
- **Technological failures:** Hardware and software don't always do what they are supposed to do. For instance, too little electricity, caused by a brownout or blackout, may cause the loss of data in primary storage. Too much

Computer Crime	Description
Malicious programs	Include viruses, worms, and Trojan horses
DoS	Causes computer systems to slow down or stop
Internet scams	Are scams over the Internet usually initiated by e-mail and involving phishing
Theft	Includes hardware, software, and computer time
Data manipulation	Involves changing data or leaving prank messages

Figure 10-13 Computer crimes

Figure 10-14 Crashes can result in lost data

electricity, as when lightning or some other electrical disturbance affects a power line, may cause a **voltage surge,** or **spike.** This excess of electricity may destroy chips or other electronic components of a computer.

Microcomputer users should use a **surge protector,** a device that separates the computer from the power source of the wall outlet. When a voltage surge occurs, it activates a circuit breaker in the surge protector, protecting the computer system.

Another technological catastrophe occurs when a hard-disk drive suddenly crashes, or fails (as discussed in Chapter 8), perhaps because it has been bumped inadvertently. If the user has forgotten to make backup copies of data on the hard disk, data may be lost. (See Figure 10-14.)

- **Human errors:** Human mistakes are inevitable. Data-entry errors are probably the most commonplace and, as we have discussed, can lead to mistaken identity. Programmer errors also occur frequently. Some mistakes may result from faulty design, as when a software manufacturer makes a deletion command closely resembling another command. Some errors may be the result of sloppy procedures. One such example occurs when office workers save important documents under file names that are not descriptive and not recognizable by others.

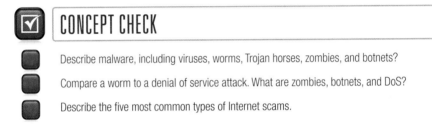

CONCEPT CHECK

Describe malware, including viruses, worms, Trojan horses, zombies, and botnets?

Compare a worm to a denial of service attack. What are zombies, botnets, and DoS?

Describe the five most common types of Internet scams.

Measures to Protect Computer Security

Security is concerned with protecting information, hardware, and software from unauthorized use as well as from damage from intrusions, sabotage, and natural disasters. Considering the numerous ways in which computer systems and data can be compromised, we can see why security is a growing field. Some of the principal measures to protect computer security are restricting access, encrypting messages, anticipating disasters, and preventing data loss.

Restricting Access Security experts are constantly devising ways to protect computer systems from access by unauthorized persons. Sometimes security is a matter of putting guards on company computer rooms and checking the identification of everyone admitted. Other times it is using **biometric scanning** devices such as fingerprint and iris (eye) scanners. (See Figure 10-15.)

Oftentimes it is a matter of being careful about assigning passwords to people and of changing the passwords when people leave a company. **Passwords** are secret words or phrases (including numbers) that must be keyed into a computer system to gain access. For many applications on the Web, users assign their own passwords.

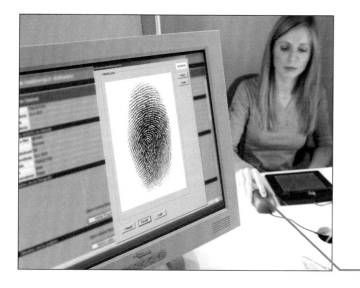

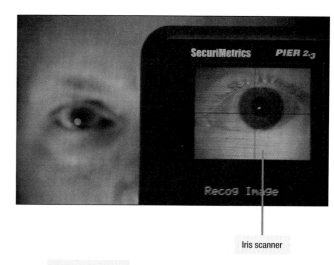

Iris scanner

Fingerprint scanner

Figure 10-15 Biometric scanning devices

The strength of a password depends on how easily it can be guessed. A **dictionary attack** uses software to try thousands of common words sequentially in an attempt to gain unauthorized access to a user's account. For this reason, words, names, and simple numeric patterns make poor passwords. It is also important not to reuse passwords for different accounts. If one account is compromised, that password might be tried for access to other systems as well. For example, if a low-security account such as an online Web forum is compromised, that password could also be tried on higher-security accounts such as banking Web sites.

As mentioned in previous chapters, most major corporations today use special hardware and software called firewalls to control access to their internal computer networks. **Firewalls** act as a security buffer between the corporation's private network and all external networks, including the Internet. All electronic communications coming into and leaving the corporation must be evaluated by the firewall. Security is maintained by denying access to unauthorized communications. To learn how to use Windows Vista's built-in firewall, visit our Web site at www.computing 2011.com and enter the keyword firewall.

Encrypting Data Whenever information is sent over a network or stored on a computer system, the possibility of unauthorized access exists. The solution is **encryption,** the process of coding information to make it unreadable except to those who have a special piece of information known as an **encryption key,** or, simply, **key.** Some common uses for encryption include

- **E-mail encryption:** Protects e-mail messages as they move across the Internet. One of the most widely used personal e-mail encryption programs is Pretty Good Privacy. (See Figure 10-16.)
- **File encryption:** Protects sensitive files by encrypting them before they are stored on a hard drive.

Figure 10-16 Encrypted e-mail

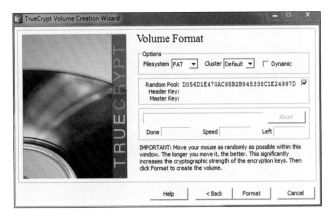

Figure 10-17 **File encryption**

Files can be encrypted individually, or specialized software can be used to encrypt all files automatically each time they are saved to a certain hard drive location. (See Figure 10-17.)

- **Web site encryption:** Secures Web transactions, especially financial transactions. Web pages that accept passwords or confidential information like a credit card number are often encrypted.
- **Virtual Private Networks: Virtual private networks (VPNs)** encrypt connections between company networks and remote users such as workers connecting from home. This connection creates a secure virtual connection to a company LAN across the Internet.
- **Wireless network encryption:** Restricts access to authorized users on wireless networks.

Anticipating Disasters Companies (and even individuals) should prepare themselves for disasters. **Physical security** is concerned with protecting hardware from possible human and natural disasters. **Data security** is concerned with protecting software and data from unauthorized tampering or damage. Most large organizations have a **disaster recovery plan** describing ways to continue operating until normal computer operations can be restored.

Preventing Data Loss Equipment can always be replaced. A company's *data*, however, may be irreplaceable. Most companies have ways of trying to keep software and data from being tampered with in the first place. They include careful screening of job applicants, guarding of passwords, and auditing of data and programs from time to time. Some systems use redundant storage to prevent loss of data even when a hard drive fails. We discussed RAID in Chapter 6, which is a commonly used type of redundant storage. Backup batteries protect against data loss due to file corruption during unexpected power outages.

Making frequent backups of data is essential to prevent data loss. Backups are often stored at an off-site location to protect data in case of theft, fires, floods, or other disasters. Incremental backups store multiple versions of data at different points in time to prevent data loss due to unwanted changes or accidental deletion.

See Figure 10-18 for a summary of the different measures to protect computer security.

On the Web Explorations

How strong is your password?

To test password strength, visit our Web site a www.computing2011.com and enter the keyword password.

CONCEPT CHECK

Discuss biometric scanning, passwords, dictionary attack, and firewalls.

What is encryption? What is Pretty Good Privacy?

Define physical security, data security, and disaster recovery plans.

Measure	Description
Restricting	Limit access to authorized persons using such measures as passwords and firewalls
Encrypting	Code all messages sent over a network
Anticipating	Prepare for disasters by ensuring physical security and data security through a disaster recovery plan
Preventing	Routinely copy data and store it at a remote location

Figure 10-18 Measures to protect computer security

tips

What can you do to protect the security of your microcomputer system? Here are a few suggestions.

1. **Avoid viruses, spyware, and spam:** Install, use, and periodically update virus protection, antispyware, and antispam programs. All incoming files should be checked for viruses before they are executed or saved.
2. **Avoid attachments:** Never run an e-mail attachment with an .exe extension unless you are sure of its source.
3. **Update software:** Occasionally programs (especially operating systems) have security weaknesses. Software manufacturers often provide corrective code to eliminate the security holes. This code is often referred to as a patch.
4. **Guard the computer:** If you are concerned that your computer may be stolen, put a cable lock on it. If you subscribe or belong to an online information service, do not leave passwords nearby in a place accessible to others. Etch your driver's license number into your equipment. That way it can be identified in the event it is recovered after theft.

To see more tips, visit our Web site at www.computing2011.com and enter the keyword tips.

Ethics

What do you suppose controls how computers can be used? You probably think first of laws. Of course, that is right, but technology is moving so fast that it is very difficult for our legal system to keep up. The essential element that controls how computers are used today is *ethics*.

Ethics, as you may know, are standards of moral conduct. **Computer ethics** are guidelines for the morally acceptable use of computers in our society. We are all entitled to ethical treatment. This includes the right to keep personal information, such as credit ratings and medical histories, from getting into unauthorized hands. These issues, largely under the control of corporations and government agencies, were covered earlier in this chapter. Now we'll examine two important issues in computer ethics where average users have a role to play.

Copyright and Digital Rights Management

Copyright is a legal concept that gives content creators the right to control use and distribution of their work. Materials that can be copyrighted include paintings, books, music, films, and even video games. Some users choose to make unauthorized copies of digital media, which violates copyright. For example, making an unauthorized copy of a digital music file for a friend might be a copyright violation.

Software piracy is the unauthorized copying and distribution of software. According to a recent study, software piracy costs the software industry over $30 billion annually. The **Digital Millennium Copyright Act** establishes the right of a program owner to make a backup copy of any program. The act also establishes that none of these copies may be legally resold or given away. This may come as a surprise to those who copy software from a friend, but that's the law. It is also illegal to download copyright-protected music and videos from the Internet.

To prevent copyright violations, corporations often use **digital rights management (DRM).** DRM encompasses various technologies that control access to electronic media and files. Typically, DRM is used to (1) control the number of devices that can access a given file as well as (2) limit the kinds of devices that can access a file. Although some companies see DRM as a necessity to protect their rights, some users feel they should have the right to use the media they buy—including movies, music, software, and video games—as they choose.

Today, there are many legal sources for digital media. Television programs can be watched online, often for free, on television-network-sponsored sites. Sites like Pandora allow listeners to enjoy music at no cost. There are several online stores for purchasing music and video content. A pioneer in this area is Apple's iTunes Music Store. (See Figure 10-19.)

Plagiarism

Another ethical issue is **plagiarism,** which means representing some other person's work and ideas as your own without giving credit to the original source. Although plagiarism has been a problem long before the invention of computers, computer technology has make plagiarism easier. For example, simply cutting and pasting content from a Web page into a report or paper may seem tempting to an overworked student or employee.

Correspondingly, computer technology has made it easier than ever to recognize and catch **plagiarists.** For example, services such as Turnitin are dedicated to preventing Internet plagiarism. This service will examine the content of a paper and compare it to a wide range of known public electronic documents including Web page content. In this way, Turnitin can identify an undocumented paper or even parts of an undocumented paper. (See Figure 10-20.)

Figure 10-19 iTunes Music Store Web Site

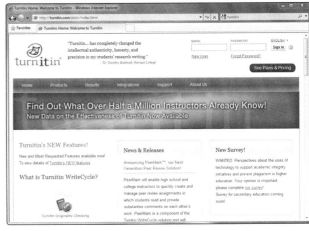

Figure 10-20 Turnitin Web Site

CONCEPT CHECK

 What is the distinction between ethics and computer ethics?

 Define copyright, software privacy, the Digital Millennium Copyright Act, and digital rights management.

 What is plagiarism? What is Turnitin and what does it do?

Careers in IT

Cryptography is the science of disguising and revealing encrypted information; in terms of information technology, cryptography usually refers to keeping any intercepted information private. For example, such information may be financial data, like banking and credit card information used in online shopping, or private e-mail and correspondence. **Cryptographers** design systems, break systems, and do research on encryption. (See Figure 10-21.) Responsibilities typically do not include building and maintaining the computer networks that use cryptography; these are the duties of security engineers and network administrators. In general, cryptographers are mathematicians who specialize in making and breaking codes.

Many cryptographers work as consultants or professors of cryptography, yet there are full-time positions available at some large corporations or for the government. A PhD in cryptography is usually an essential prerequisite for a position as a cryptographer. However, all cryptographers must have broad experience in both mathematics and computer science or information systems.

Cryptographers can expect to earn an annual salary of $60,000 to over $100,000. Opportunities for advancement typically depend on experience; the most competitive field will be research positions in the military and at universities. Those with experience in computer science and information technology should be among the most employable mathematicians and increasingly in demand. To learn more about becoming a cryptographer, visit us at www.computing2011.com and enter the keyword **careers.**

Figure 10-21 **Cryptographer**

A LOOK TO THE FUTURE

A Webcam on Every Corner

Wireless Internet connections are becoming widely available in public places. At the same time, digital video and still camera technology is becoming more sophisticated and cheaper. As a result, images of public places are more accessible than ever before. Mobile phones are now equipped with cameras and Internet connectivity, and such devices are likely to improve in quality and speed in the future.

In 2007, Google launched Google Street View, a Web site that collected digital photographs from a car that drove around the streets of major cities and associated them with physical addresses. Since that time, many more cities have been added. This allowed users to take "virtual site-seeing tours" from the comfort of their homes. A person could explore the streets of Manhattan or San Francisco, for example,

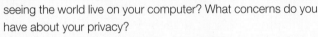

or catch a glimpse of a destination before booking a hotel. However, this service stirred controversy when some of the images captured inadvertently showed people in embarrassing situations or engaged in illegal activities. The U.S. Department of Defense even banned this service from displaying images of military bases.

In the future, you might be able to see live video of a vacation spot, or even check in on your house while you are traveling. Public webcams continue to grow in popularity, and new technology will enhance the images produced so very fine details can be observed. However, others might be able to observe your activities with a simple Web search. What do you think about public webcams? Can you think of some benefits of seeing the world live on your computer? What concerns do you have about your privacy?

PRIVACY

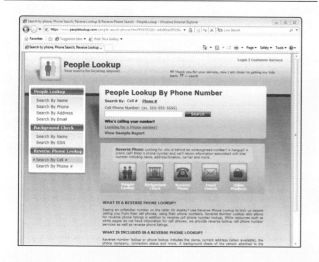

Effective implementation of computer technology involves maximizing positive effects while minimizing negative effects. The most significant concerns are **privacy, security,** and **ethics.**

Large Databases

Large organizations are constantly compiling information about us. **Reverse directories** list telephone numbers followed by subscriber names. **Information resellers (information brokers)** collect and sell personal data. **Electronic profiles** are compiled from databases to provide highly detailed and personalized descriptions of individuals.

Identity theft is the illegal assumption of someone's identity for the purposes of economic gain. **Mistaken identity** occurs when an electronic profile of one person is switched with another. The **Freedom of Information Act** entitles individuals access to governmental records relating to them.

Private Networks

Many organizations monitor employee e-mail and computer files using special software called **snoopware.**

The Internet and the Web

Many people believe that, while using the Web, little can be done to invade their privacy. This is called the **illusion of anonymity.**

PRIVACY

History files record locations of visited sites. **Cookies** store and track information. Two basic types are **traditional cookies** and **ad network cookies (adware cookies).**

Spyware are programs designed to secretly record and report Internet activities. Ad network cookies are one type of spyware. Another type—**computer monitoring (keystroke loggers)**—watches what you do, while **Web bugs** provide information back to spammers about activity on your e-mail account. **Antispyware (spy removal programs)** detects Web bugs and monitoring software.

Online Identity

With the popularity of social networking, blogging, photo- and video-sharing sites, many people post personal information and sometimes intimate details of their lives without considering the consequences. This creates an **online identity.** With the archiving and search features of the Web, this identity is indefinitely available to anyone who cares to look for it.

Major Laws on Privacy

The **Gramm-Leach-Bliley Act** protects personal financial information; the **Health Insurance Portability and Accountability Act (HIPAA)** protects medical records; and the **Family Educational Rights and Privacy Act (FERPA)** restricts disclosure of educational records.

To be a competent end user, you need to be aware of the potential impact of technology on people. You need to be sensitive to and knowledgeable about personal privacy, organizational security, and ethics.

SECURITY

Computer Criminals

Computer criminals include employees, outside users, hackers and crackers, organized crime, and terrorists.

- **Hackers**—create or improve programs and share those programs with fellow hackers. Typically are not criminals.
- **Crackers**—share programs designed to gain unauthorized access to computer systems or disrupt networks. Typically are criminals.

Computer Crime

Computer crime is an illegal action involving special knowledge of computer technology.

- Malicious programs, or **malware,** include **viruses** (the **Computer Fraud and Abuse Act** makes spreading a virus a federal offense), **worms** (self-replicate across a network), and **Trojan horses** (enter a computer system disguised as something else). Antivirus programs alert users when certain viruses and worms enter their systems.
- **Zombies** are remotely controlled infected computers used for malicious purposes. A collection of zombie computers is known as a **botnet,** or **robot network.**
- **Denial of service attack (DoS)** is an attempt to shut down or stop a computer system or network. It floods a computer or network with requests for information and data. Servers

SECURITY

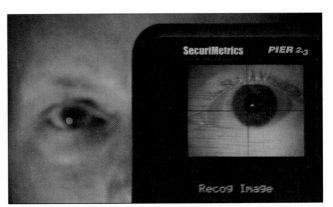

under attack are unable to respond to legitimate users.

- **Scams** are fraudulent or deceptive acts or operations designed to trick individuals into spending their time and money with little or no return. Common **Internet scams** include identity theft, chain letters, auction fraud, vacation prizes, and advance fee loans. These are frequently coupled with **phishing** Web sites or e-mails.
- Theft takes many forms including stealing hardware, software, data, and computer time.
- Data manipulation involves changing data or leaving prank messages. The **Computer Fraud and Abuse Act** helps protect against data manipulation.
- Other hazards include natural disasters, civil strife, terrorism, technological failures (**surge protectors** protect against **voltage surges** or **spikes**), and human error.

Measures to Protect Computer Security

Security is concerned with keeping hardware, software, data, and programs safe from unauthorized personnel and unforeseen events. Some measures are restricting access by using **biometric scanning** devices, **passwords,** and **firewalls;** encrypting data using **encryption keys** for e-mail, Web site, **VPN,** and wireless network **encryption;** anticipating disasters (**physical** and **data security, disaster recovery plans**); and preventing data loss.

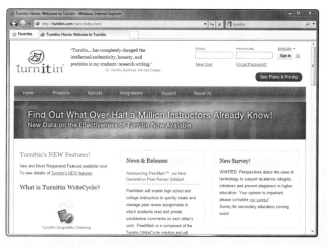

What do you suppose controls how computers can be used? You probably think first of laws. Of course, that is right, but technology is moving so fast that it is very difficult for our legal system to keep up. The essential element that controls how computers are used today is *ethics*.

Ethics are standards of moral conduct. **Computer ethics** are guidelines for the morally acceptable use of computers in our society. We are all entitled to ethical treatment. This includes the right to keep personal information, such as credit ratings and medical histories, from getting into unauthorized hands.

Copyright and Digital Rights Management

Copyright is a legal concept that gives content creators the right to control use and distribution of their work. Materials that can be copyrighted include paintings, books, music, films, and even video games.

Software piracy is the unauthorized copying and distribution of software. The software industry loses over $30 billion annually to software privacy. Two related topics are the Digital Millennium Copyright Act and digital rights management.

- **Digital Millennium Copyright Act** establishes the right of a program owner to make a backup copy of any program and disallows the creation of copies to be sold or given away. It is also illegal to download copyright-protected music and videos from the Internet.
- **Digital rights management (DRM)** is a collection of technologies designed to prevent

copyright violations. Typically, DRM is used to (1) control the number of devices that can access a given file as well as (2) limit the kinds of devices that can access a file.

Today, many legal sources for digital media exist, including

- Television programs that can be watched online, often for free, on television-network-sponsored sites.
- Sites like Pandora that allow listeners to enjoy music at no cost.
- Online stores that legally sell music and video content. A pioneer in this area is Apple's iTunes Music Store.

Plagiarism

Plagiarism is the illegal and unethical representation of some other person's work and ideas as your own without giving credit to the original source. Examples of plagiarism include cutting and pasting Web content into a report or paper.

Recognizing and catching **plagiarists** is relatively easy. For example, services such as **Turnitin** are dedicated to preventing Internet plagiarism. This service examines a paper's content and compares it to a wide range of known public electronic documents including Web page content. Exact duplication or paraphrasing is readily identified.

CAREERS IN IT

Cryptographers design encryption algorithms, break codes, and provide support to national security efforts. PhD in mathematics and broad experience in computer science are required. Salary range $60,000 to over $100,000.

KEY TERMS

access (283)
accuracy (283)
ad network cookie (287)
adware cookie (287)
antispyware (289)
biometric scanning (296)
botnet (294)
computer crime (292)
computer ethics (299)
Computer Fraud and Abuse
    Act (293, 294)
computer monitoring software (288)
cookies (286)
copyright (299)
cracker (292)
cryptographer (301)
cryptography (301)
data security (297)
denial of service (DoS) attack (294)
dictionary attack (297)
Digital Millennium Copyright
    Act (300)
digital rights management
    (DRM) (300)
disaster recovery plan (298)
electronic profile (283)
encryption (297)
encryption key (297)
ethics (299)
Family Educational Rights and Privacy
    Act (FERPA) (289)
firewall (297)
Freedom of Information Act (285)
Gramm-Leach-Bliley Act (289)
hacker (292)
Health Insurance Portability and
    Accountability Act (HIPAA) (289)

history file (286)
identity theft (284)
illusion of anonymity (285)
information broker (283)
information reseller (283)
Internet scam (294)
key (297)
keystroke logger (288)
malware (293)
mistaken identity (285)
online identity (289)
password (296)
phishing (294)
physical security (298)
plagiarism (300)
plagiarist (300)
privacy (283)
property (283)
reverse directory (283)
robot network (294)
scam (294)
security (283)
snoopware (285)
software piracy (300)
spike (296)
spy removal program (289)
spyware (287)
surge protector (296)
traditional cookies (286)
Trojan horse (293)
virtual private network (VPN) (297)
virus (293)
voltage surge (296)
Web bug (287)
worm (293)
zombie (294)

To test your knowledge of these key terms with animated flash cards, visit us at www.computing2011.com and enter the keyword terms10.

MULTIPLE CHOICE

Circle the letter or fill in the correct answer.

1. Reverse _____ list telephone numbers followed by subscriber names.
   a. directories
   b. order
   c. databases
   d. listings

2. The privacy issue that relates to the responsibility of controlling who is able to use data is
   a. access
   b. property
   c. accuracy
   d. encryption

3. Two basic types of cookies are _____.
   a. advanced and remedial
   b. traditional and natural
   c. natural and ad network
   d. ad network and traditional

4. A small image or other HTML code that is hidden within in an e-mail message is called a _____.
   a. virus
   b. worm
   c. denial-of-service attack
   d. Web bug

5. People who create or improve programs and share those programs are _____.
   a. employees
   b. hackers
   c. crackers
   d. members of organized crime

6. An attempt to slow down or stop a computer system or network by flooding the system with requests for information is called a
   a. virus
   b. worm
   c. denial-of-service attack
   d. Trojan horse

7. Secret words or phrases used to gain access to a computer system are called
   a. encryption
   b. codes
   c. crackers
   d. passwords

8. Computer _____ are guidelines for the morally acceptable use of computers in our society.
   a. business demands
   b. ethics
   c. laws
   d. security requirements

9. Copyright is a(n) _____ concept that gives content creators the right to control use and distribution of their work.
   a. economic
   b. ethical
   c. legal
   d. moral

10. _____ is a collection of technologies designed to prevent copyright violations.
    a. DBMS
    b. DoS
    c. DRM
    d. RSS

For an interactive multiple-choice practice test, visit us at www.computing 2011.com and enter the keyword multiple10.

MATCHING

Match each numbered item with the most closely related lettered item. Write your answers in the spaces provided.

a. ad network
b. computer crime
c. cracker
d. DoS
e. firewall
f. illusion of anonymity
g. property
h. snoopware
i. virus checkers
j. worm

1. Relates to who owns data and rights to software. _____
2. Programs that record virtually every activity on a computer system. _____
3. Belief that there is little threat to personal privacy via the Internet. _____
4. A type of cookie that records activities across different sites. _____
5. Illegal action involving special knowledge of computer technology. _____
6. Gains unauthorized access to a system for malicious purposes. _____
7. Replicates itself over a network—spreading to other systems automatically. _____
8. An attack that overwhelms Web sites with data, making them inaccessible. _____
9. Programs that alert users when certain viruses enter a system. _____
10. Security hardware and software that controls access to internal computer networks. _____

For an interactive matching practice test, visit our Web site at www.computing 2011.com and enter the keyword matching10.

OPEN-ENDED

On a separate sheet of paper, respond to each question or statement.

1. Discuss the impact of large databases, private networks, the Internet, and the Web on privacy.
2. Discuss the various kinds of computer criminals.
3. What are the principal measures used to protect computer security? What is encryption? How is it used by corporations and individuals?
4. What is a copyright? Discuss software piracy, the Digital Millennium Copyright Act, and digital rights management.
5. What is plagiarism? Discuss how computers make plagiarism easy and tempting to busy people and how a plagiarist can be easily identified.

APPLYING TECHNOLOGY

The following questions are designed to demonstrate ways that you can effectively use technology today. The first question relates directly to this chapter's Making IT Work for You feature.

1 SPYWARE

Have you installed any free software from the Internet? Did you know that seemingly harmless software might actually be spying on you, even sending personal information to advertisers or worse? Fortunately, spyware removal programs can help. After reviewing Making IT Work for You: Spyware Removal on pages 290 and 291, answer the following: (a) Define spyware and discuss how it works. (b) Describe the process for downloading and installing Lavasoft's Ad-Aware. (c) Describe the capabilities of Ad-Aware. (d) Do you think that spyware might be on your computer? If yes, how do you suppose the spyware was deposited onto your system? If no, why are you so confident?

2 PERSONAL FIREWALLS

At one time, firewalls were used only for large servers. Today firewalls are available for almost any device that connects to the Internet and are essential to ensure security. Connect to our Web site at www.computing2011.com and enter the keyword security to link to a personal firewall product for home users. Once connected, read about the firewall and then answer the following: (a) Is this firewall a hardware or software solution? (b) Describe the procedure for installing the firewall. (c) What types of security risks does this firewall protect against? (d) Are there any security risks the firewall does not cover? If so, how can those risks be reduced?

3 PERSONAL BACKUPS

Do you make backups of your files? If your computer crashed or was lost or stolen today, would you be able to recover all your important data? Backup systems used to be just for large companies and organizations, but today personal backup software makes it simple to keep your information safe. Visit our Web site at www.computing2011.com and enter the keyword backup to link to a site about personal backup software. Once connected, explore the site, and briefly answer the following: (a) Where does the backup software store the backups it makes? (b) Describe the steps necessary to back up a computer using the software. (c) Describe the steps necessary to restore files to a computer from a previous backup using the software.

EXPANDING YOUR KNOWLEDGE

The following questions are designed to add depth and detail to your understanding of specific topics presented within this chapter. The questions direct you to sources other than the textbook to obtain this knowledge.

1 HOW WEB BUGS WORK

The Internet is popular because it is fast, cheap, and open to everyone. These qualities also make it an ideal tool for criminals. Unscrupulous people can use programs called Web bugs to spy on you when you use the Internet. To learn more about how Web bugs work, visit our Web site at www.computing2011.com and enter the keyword bugs. Then answer the following questions: (a) How can a Web bug infect your computer? (b) When a Web bug is delivered by e-mail, it typically sends a copy of that e-mail back to the server. What is the significance or purpose of this activity? (c) Do you think Web bugs are really a privacy concern? Do you think your computer may have one? How could you find out?

2 MISTAKEN IDENTITY

A simple typo can result in mistaken identity. Such mistakes can have a tremendous impact on a person's career, family, and future. To learn more about mistaken identity, visit our Web site at www.computing2011.com and enter the keyword id. Then answer the following questions: (a) Have you been a victim of mistaken identity? If so, please discuss. (b) If your response was "yes," how would you verify that mistaken identity has occurred? (c) Perhaps you have been a victim without knowing it. List the questions that should be considered.

3 AIR TRAVEL DATABASE

To curb possible terrorist threats, the government has implemented a controversial database, known as the Computer Assisted Passenger Pre-screening System (CAPPS). This database determines a "possible threat score" for each individual to determine whether he or she can fly. Research CAPPS on the Internet and then answer the following questions: (a) How does CAPPS determine who is a security risk? (b) What personal information is gathered by CAPPS? (c) How might CAPPS infringe on personal privacy?

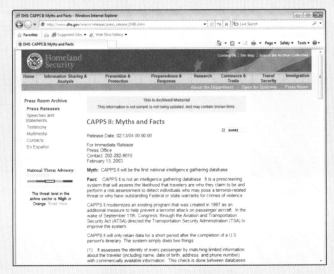

WRITING ABOUT TECHNOLOGY

The ability to think critically and to write effectively is essential to nearly every profession. The following questions are designed to help you develop these skills by posing thought-provoking questions about computer privacy, security, and/or ethics.

 ## FACIAL RECOGNITION

As new technologies emerge that promise to enhance our security, our privacy may be at stake. A recent example is the introduction of facial recognition systems in public places for use by police officers. Such systems have recently caught the attention of privacy advocates, as well as the ACLU. Research facial recognition systems on the Web and then write a one-page paper titled "Facial Recognition" that addresses the following topics: (a) Describe how facial recognition technology works. (b) How can facial recognition technology enhance security? (c) In what ways might facial recognition technology compromise privacy? (Hint: Consider security cameras in department or grocery stores.) (d) Do you approve of facial recognition technology? Explain your answer.

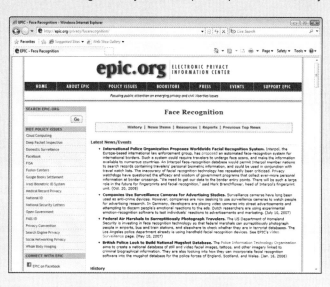

 ## PLAGIARISM

Suspicious of cheating, a professor at the University of Virginia developed a program to compare the term papers of his current and past students. Alarmingly, he found that 122 students' work suggested plagiarizing. Consider the implications of this case and then write a one-page paper titled "Plagiarism" that addresses the following questions: (a) With more and more academic submissions being stored in an electronic format and available online, how is it easier to copy another's work? (b) For the same reason, how is detecting an unoriginal work easier? (c) Have you ever copied and pasted text from a Web site or other electronic document and passed it off as your own? (d) How does "borrowing" work in this way affect other students? What about the original author? Explain.

Information Systems

Competencies

After you have read this chapter, you should be able to:

1 Explain the functional view of a organization and describe each function.

2 Describe the management levels and the informational needs for each level in an organization.

3 Discuss how information flows within an organization.

4 Discuss computer-based information systems.

5 Distinguish among a transaction processing system, a management information system, a decision support system, and an executive support system.

6 Distinguish between office automation systems and knowledge work systems.

7 Explain the difference between data workers and knowledge workers.

One of the challenges that has emerged as technology becomes more consistent and available is to filter through the data. In a large corporation there may be so much data available to management that it is unusable. Today's managers and executives need access to timely and complete information about the daily operations of their business.

Some experts predict that artificial intelligence may some day filter the facts and figures available to executives. Imagine a world where an executive can expect around-the-clock service from the computer sitting on the desk.

chapter 11

Introduction

An information system is a collection of people, procedures, software, hardware, and data (as we discussed in Chapter 1). They all work together to provide information essential to running an organization. This is information that will successfully produce a product or service and, for profit-oriented enterprises, derive a profit.

Why are computers used in organizations? No doubt you can easily state one reason: to keep records of events. However, another reason might be less obvious: to help make decisions. For example, point-of-sale terminals record sales as well as which salesperson made each sale. This information can be used for decision making. For instance, it can help the sales manager decide which salespeople will get year-end bonuses for doing exceptional work.

The Internet, communication links, and databases connect you with information resources as well as information systems far beyond the surface of your desk. The microcomputer offers you access to a greater quantity of information than was possible a few years ago. In addition, you also have access to better-quality information. As we show in this chapter, when you tap into a computer-based information system, you not only get information—you also get help in making decisions.

Competent end users need to understand how the information flows as it moves through an organization's different functional areas and management levels. They need to be aware of the different types of computer-based information systems, including transaction processing systems, management information systems, decision support systems, and executive support systems. They also need to understand the role and importance of databases to support each level or type of information system.

Organizational Information Flow

Computerized information systems do not just keep track of transactions and day-to-day business operations. They also support the vertical and horizontal flow of information within the organization. To understand this, we need to understand how an organization is structured. One way to examine an organization's structure is to view it from a functional perspective. That is, you can study the different basic functional areas in organizations and the different types of people within these functional areas.

As we describe these, consider how they apply to a hypothetical manufacturer of sporting goods, the HealthWise Group. This company manufactures equipment for sports and physical activities. Their products range from soccer balls to surfboards. (See Figure 11-1.)

Like many organizations, HealthWise Group can be viewed from a functional perspective with various management levels. Effective operations require an efficient and coordinated flow of information throughout the organization.

Functions

Depending on the services or products they provide, most organizations have departments that specialize in one of five basic functions. These are accounting, marketing, human resources, production, and research. (See Figure 11-2.)

- **Accounting** records all financial activity from billing customers to paying employees. For example, at HealthWise, the accounting department tracks all sales, payments, and transfers of funds. It also produces reports detailing the financial condition of the company.

- **Marketing** plans, prices, promotes, sells, and distributes the organization's goods and services. At HealthWise, goods include a wide range of products related to sports and other types of physical activity.

- **Human resources** focuses on people—hiring, training, promoting, and any number of other human-centered activities within the organization. This function relates to people in each of the functional areas, including accountants, sales representatives, human resource specialists, production workers, and research scientists.

- **Production** actually creates finished goods and services using raw materials and personnel. At HealthWise, this includes manufacturing a variety of sports equipment, including surfboards.

- **Research** identifies, investigates, and develops new products and services. For example, at HealthWise, scientists are investigating a light, inexpensive alloy for a new line of weight-training equipment.

Figure 11-1 Manufacturing surfboards

Although the titles may vary, nearly every large and small organization has departments that perform these basic functions. Whatever your job in an organization, it is likely to be in one of these functional areas.

Management Levels

Most people who work in an organization are not managers, of course. At the base of the organizational pyramid are the assemblers, painters, welders, drivers, and so on. These people produce goods and services. Above them are various levels of managers—people with titles such as supervisor, director, regional manager, and vice president. These are the people who do the planning, leading, organizing, and controlling necessary to see that the work gets done. At HealthWise, for example, the northwest district sales manager directs and coordinates all the salespeople in her area. Other job titles might be vice president of marketing, director of human resources, or production manager. In smaller organizations, these titles are often combined.

Management in many organizations is divided into three levels. (See Figure 11-3.)

- **Supervisors:** Supervisors manage and monitor the employees or workers. Thus, these managers have responsibility relating to *operational matters*. They monitor day-to-day events and immediately take corrective action, if necessary. (See Figure 11-4.)

- **Middle management:** Middle-level managers deal with *control, planning* (also called *tactical planning*), and *decision making*. They implement the long-term goals of the organization.

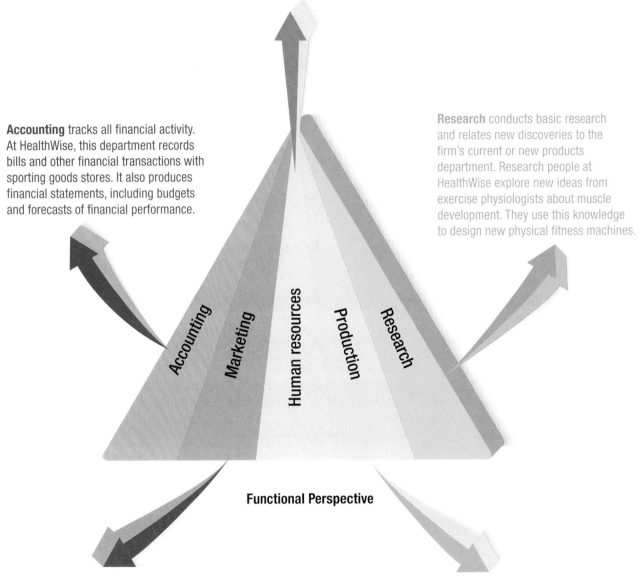

Human resources finds and hires people and handles matters such as sick leave and retirement benefits. In addition, it is concerned with evaluation, compensation, and professional development.

Accounting tracks all financial activity. At HealthWise, this department records bills and other financial transactions with sporting goods stores. It also produces financial statements, including budgets and forecasts of financial performance.

Research conducts basic research and relates new discoveries to the firm's current or new products department. Research people at HealthWise explore new ideas from exercise physiologists about muscle development. They use this knowledge to design new physical fitness machines.

Accounting

Marketing

Human resources

Production

Research

Functional Perspective

Marketing handles planning, pricing, promoting, selling, and distributing goods and services to customers. At HealthWise, they even get involved with creating a customer newsletter that is distributed via the corporate Web page.

Production takes in raw materials and people work to turn out finished goods (or services). It may be a manufacturing activity or—in the case of a retail store— an operations activity. At HealthWise, this department purchases steel and aluminum to be used in weight-lifting and exercise machines.

Figure 11-2 **The five functions of an organization**

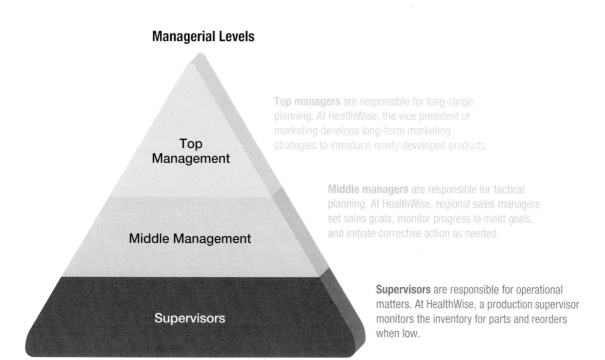

Managerial Levels

Top Management

Middle Management

Supervisors

Top managers are responsible for long-range planning. At HealthWise, the vice president of marketing develops long-term marketing strategies to introduce newly developed products.

Middle managers are responsible for tactical planning. At HealthWise, regional sales managers set sales goals, monitor progress to meet goals, and initiate corrective action as needed.

Supervisors are responsible for operational matters. At HealthWise, a production supervisor monitors the inventory for parts and reorders when low.

Figure 11-3 **Three levels of management**

- **Top management:** Top-level managers are concerned with *long-range planning* (also called *strategic planning*). They need information that will help them to plan the future growth and direction of the organization.

Information Flow

Each level of management has different information needs. Top-level managers need information that is summarized in capsule form to reveal the overall condition of the business. They also need information from outside the organization because top-level managers need to forecast and plan for long-range events. Middle-level managers need summarized information—weekly or monthly reports. They need to develop budget projections and to evaluate the performance of supervisors. Supervisors need detailed, very current, day-to-day information on their units so that they can keep operations running smoothly.

To support these different needs, information *flows* in different directions. (See Figure 11-5.) For top-level managers, the flow of information from within the organization is both vertical and horizontal. The top-level managers, such as the chief executive officer (CEO), need information from below and from all departments. (See Figure 11-6.) They also need information from outside the organization. For example, at HealthWise, they are deciding whether to introduce a line of hockey equipment in the southwestern United States. The vice president of marketing must look at relevant data. Such data might include availability of ice rinks and census data about the number

Figure 11-4 **Supervisors monitor day-to-day events**

Information Flow

Top managerial–level information flow is vertical, horizontal, and external. At HealthWise, the vice president of marketing communicates vertically (with regional sales managers), horizontally (with other vice presidents), and externally to obtain data to forecast sales.

Middle managerial–level information flow is vertical and horizontal. At HealthWise, regional sales managers communicate vertically (with district sales managers and the vice president of marketing) and horizontally with other middle-level managers.

Supervisory-level information flow is primarily vertical. At HealthWise, production supervisors monitor worker activities to ensure smooth production. They provide daily status reports to middle-level production managers.

Figure 11-5 **Information flow within an organization**

of young people. It also might include sales histories on related cold-weather sports equipment.

For middle-level managers, the information flow is both vertical and horizontal across functional lines. For example, the regional sales managers at HealthWise set their sales goals by coordinating with middle managers in the production department. They are able to tell sales managers what products will be produced, how many, and when. The regional sales managers also must coordinate with the strategic goals set by the top managers. They must set and monitor the sales goals for the supervisors beneath them.

For supervisory managers, information flow is primarily vertical. That is, supervisors communicate mainly with their middle managers and with the workers beneath them. For instance, at HealthWise, production supervisors rarely communicate with people in the accounting department. However, they are constantly communicating with production-line workers and with their own managers.

Now we know how a large organization is usually structured and how information flows within the organization. But how is a computer-based information system likely to be set up to support its needs? And what do you, as a microcomputer user, need to know to use it?

Figure 11-6 **Top-level managers handle both vertical and horizontal information flow**

CONCEPT CHECK

 What are the five basic functions within an organization?

 What are the three levels of management? Discuss each level.

 Describe the flow of information within an organization.

Computer-Based Information Systems

Almost all organizations have computer-based **information systems.** Large organizations typically have formal names for the systems designed to collect and use the data. Although different organizations may use different names, the most common names are transaction processing, management information, decision support, and executive support systems. (See Figure 11-7.)

- **Transaction processing system:** The **transaction processing system (TPS)** records day-to-day transactions, such as customer orders, bills, inventory levels, and production output. The TPS helps supervisors by generating databases that act as the foundation for the other information systems.
- **Management information system:** The **management information system (MIS)** summarizes the detailed data of the transaction processing system in standard reports for middle-level managers. Such reports might include weekly sales and production schedules.
- **Decision support system:** The **decision support system (DSS)** provides a flexible tool for analysis. The DSS helps middle-level managers and others in the organization analyze a wide range of problems, such as the effect of events and trends outside the organization. Like the MIS, the DSS draws on the detailed data of the transaction processing system.
- **Executive support system:** The **executive support system (ESS),** also known as the **executive information system (EIS),** is an easy-to-use system that presents information in a very highly summarized form. It helps top-level managers oversee the company's operations and develop strategic plans. The ESS combines the internal data from TPS and MIS with external data.

Information Systems

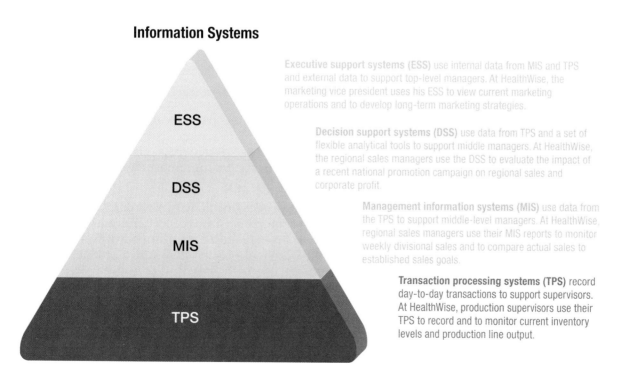

Executive support systems (ESS) use internal data from MIS and TPS and external data to support top-level managers. At HealthWise, the marketing vice president uses his ESS to view current marketing operations and to develop long-term marketing strategies.

Decision support systems (DSS) use data from TPS and a set of flexible analytical tools to support middle managers. At HealthWise, the regional sales managers use the DSS to evaluate the impact of a recent national promotion campaign on regional sales and corporate profit.

Management information systems (MIS) use data from the TPS to support middle-level managers. At HealthWise, regional sales managers use their MIS reports to monitor weekly divisional sales and to compare actual sales to established sales goals.

Transaction processing systems (TPS) record day-to-day transactions to support supervisors. At HealthWise, production supervisors use their TPS to record and to monitor current inventory levels and production line output.

Figure 11-7 **Four kinds of computer-based information systems**

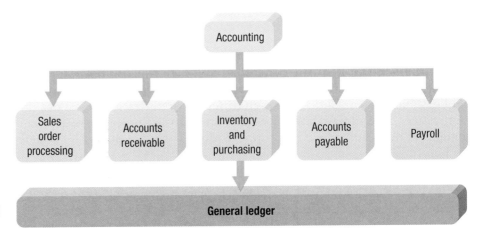

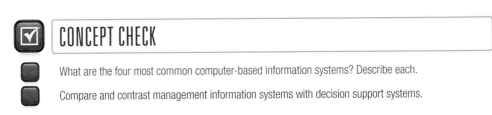

Figure 11-8 Transaction processing system for accounting

☑ **CONCEPT CHECK**

What are the four most common computer-based information systems? Describe each.

Compare and contrast management information systems with decision support systems.

Transaction Processing Systems

A *transaction processing system (TPS)* helps an organization keep track of routine operations and records these events in a database. For this reason, some firms call this the **data processing system (DPS).** The data from operations—for example, customer orders for HealthWise's products—makes up a database that records the transactions of the company. This database of transactions is used to support an MIS, DSS, and ESS.

One of the most essential transaction processing systems for any organization is in the accounting area. (See Figure 11-8.) Every accounting department handles six basic activities. Five of these are sales order processing, accounts receivable, inventory and purchasing, accounts payable, and payroll. All of these are recorded in the general ledger, the sixth activity.

Let us take a look at these six activities. They will make up the basis of the accounting system for almost any office you might work in.

- The **sales order processing** activity records the customer requests for the company's products or services. When an order comes in—a request for a set of barbells, for example—the warehouse is alerted to ship a product. (See Figure 11-9.)
- The **accounts receivable** activity records money received from or owed by customers. HealthWise keeps track of bills paid by sporting goods stores and by gyms and health clubs to which it sells directly.
- The parts and finished goods that the company has in stock are called **inventory**—all exercise machines in the warehouse,

Figure 11-9 Customer orders are sent to the warehouse via sales order processing

for example. (See Figure 11-10.) An **inventory control system** keeps records of the number of each kind of part or finished good in the warehouse. **Purchasing** is the buying of materials and services. Often a **purchase order** is used. This is a form that shows the name of the company supplying the material or service and what is being purchased.

- **Accounts payable** refers to money the company owes its suppliers for materials and services it has received—steel and aluminum, for example.

- The **payroll** activity is concerned with calculating employee paychecks. Amounts are generally determined by the kind of job, hours worked, and kinds of deductions (such as taxes, Social Security, medical insurance). Paychecks may be calculated from employee time cards or, in some cases, supervisors' time sheets.

- The **general ledger** keeps track of all summaries of all the foregoing transactions. A typical general ledger system can produce income statements and balance sheets. **Income statements** show a company's financial performance—income, expenses, and the difference between them for a specific time period. **Balance sheets** list the overall financial condition of an organization. They include assets (for example, buildings and property owned), liabilities (debts), and how much of the organization (the equity) is owned by the owners.

There are many other transaction systems that you come into contact with every day. These include automatic teller machines, which record cash withdrawals; online registration systems, which track student enrollments; and supermarket discount cards, which track customer purchases.

 CONCEPT CHECK

 What is the purpose of a transaction processing system?

 Describe the six activities of a TPS for accounting.

Management Information Systems

A *management information system (MIS)* is a computer-based information system that produces standardized reports in summarized structured form. (See Figure 11-11.) It is used to support middle managers. An MIS differs from a transaction processing system in a significant way. Whereas a transaction processing system *creates* databases, an MIS *uses* databases. Indeed, an MIS can draw from the databases of several departments. Thus, an MIS requires a *database management system* that integrates the databases of the different departments. Middle managers need summary data often drawn from across different functional areas.

An MIS produces reports that are *predetermined*. That is, they follow a predetermined format and always show the same kinds of content. Although reports may differ from one industry to another, there are three common categories of reports: periodic, exception, and demand.

The Sports Company
Regional Sales Report

Region	Actual Sales	Target	Difference
Central	$166,430	$175,000	($8,570)
Northern	137,228	130,000	7,228
Southern	137,772	135,000	2,772
Eastern	152,289	155,000	(2,711)
Western	167,017	160,000	7,017

Figure 11-11 Management information system report

- **Periodic reports** are produced at regular intervals—weekly, monthly, or quarterly, for instance. Examples are HealthWise's monthly sales and production reports. The sales reports from district sales managers are combined into a monthly report for the regional sales managers. For comparison purposes, a regional manager is also able to see the sales reports of other regional managers.

- **Exception reports** call attention to unusual events. An example is a sales report that shows that certain items are selling significantly above or below marketing department forecasts. For instance, if fewer exercise bicycles are selling than were predicted for the northwest sales region, the regional manager will receive an exception report. That report may be used to alert the district managers and salespeople to give this product more attention.

- The opposite of a periodic report, a **demand report** is produced on request. An example is a report on the numbers and types of jobs held by women and minorities. Such a report is not needed periodically, but it may be required when requested by the U.S. government. At HealthWise, many government contracts require this information. It is used to certify that HealthWise is within certain government equal-opportunity guidelines.

CONCEPT CHECK

What is the purpose of a management information system?

Describe the three common categories of MIS reports.

Decision Support Systems

Managers often must deal with unanticipated questions. For example, the HealthWise manager in charge of manufacturing might ask how a strike would affect production schedules. A *decision support system (DSS)* enables managers to get answers to such unexpected and generally nonrecurring kinds of problems. Frequently, a team is formed to address large problems. A **group decision support system (GDSS)** is then used to support this collective work.

A DSS, then, is quite different from a transaction processing system, which simply records data. It is also different from a management information system, which summarizes data in predetermined reports. A DSS is used to analyze data. Moreover, it produces reports that do not have a fixed format. This makes the DSS a flexible tool for analysis.

At one time, most DSSs were designed for large computer systems. Now, microcomputers, with their increased power and sophisticated software, such as spreadsheet and database programs, are widely used for DSS. Users of a DSS are managers, not computer programmers. Thus, a DSS must be easy to use—or most likely it will not be used at all. A HealthWise marketing manager might want to know which territories are not meeting their monthly sales quotas. To find out, the executive could query the database for all "SALES < QUOTA." (See Figure 11-12.)

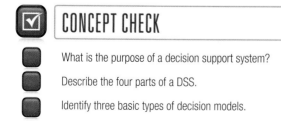

Figure 11-12 Decision support system query results for SALES < QUOTA

How does a decision support system work? Essentially, it consists of four parts: the user, system software, data, and decision models.

- The **user** could be you. In general, the user is someone who has to make decisions—a manager, often a middle-level manager.
- **System software** is essentially the operating system—programs designed to work behind the scenes to handle detailed operating procedures. In order to give the user a good, comfortable interface, the software typically is menu- or icon-driven. That is, the screen presents easily understood lists of commands or icons, giving the user several options.
- **Data** in a DSS is typically stored in a database and consists of two kinds. **Internal data**—data from within the organization—consists principally of transactions from the transaction processing system. **External data** is data gathered from outside the organization. Examples are data provided by marketing research firms, trade associations, and the U.S. government (such as customer profiles, census data, and economic forecasts).
- **Decision models** give the DSS its analytical capabilities. There are three basic types of decision models: strategic, tactical, and operational. **Strategic models** assist top-level managers in long-range planning, such as stating company objectives or planning plant locations. **Tactical models** help middle-level managers control the work of the organization, such as financial planning and sales promotion planning. **Operational models** help lower-level managers accomplish the organization's day-to-day activities, such as evaluating and maintaining quality control.

☑ CONCEPT CHECK

What is the purpose of a decision support system?

Describe the four parts of a DSS.

Identify three basic types of decision models.

Executive Support Systems

Using a DSS requires some training. Many top managers have other people in their offices running DSSs and reporting their findings. Top-level executives also want something more concise than an MIS—something that produces very focused reports.

Executive support systems (ESSs) consist of sophisticated software that, like an MIS or a DSS, can present, summarize, and analyze data from an organization's databases. However, an ESS is specifically designed to be easy to use. This is so that a top executive with little spare time, for example, can obtain essential information without extensive training. Thus, information is often displayed in very condensed form with informative graphics.

Consider an executive support system used by the president of HealthWise. It is available on his microcomputer. The first thing each morning, the president calls up the ESS on his display screen, as shown in Figure 11-13. Note that the screen gives a condensed account of activities in the five different areas of the company. (These are Accounting, Marketing, Production, Human Resources, and Research.) On this particular morning, the ESS shows business in four areas proceeding smoothly. However, in the first area, Accounting, the percentage of late-paying customers—past due accounts—has increased by 3 percent. Three percent may not seem like much, but HealthWise has had a history of problems with late payers, which has left the company at times strapped for cash. The president decides to find out the details. To do so, he selects 1. Accounting.

Within moments, the display screen displays a graph of the past due accounts. (See Figure 11-14.) The status of today's late payers is shown in red. The status of late payers at this time a year ago is shown in yellow. The differences between today and a year ago are significant and clearly presented. For example, approximately $60,000 was late 1 to 10 days last year. This year, over $80,000 was late. The president knows that he must take some action to speed up customer payments. (For example, he might call this to the attention of the vice president of accounting. The vice president might decide to implement a new policy that offers discounts to early payers or charge higher interest to late payers.)

ESSs permit a firm's top executives to gain direct access to information about the company's performance. Most provide direct electronic communication links to other executives. Some systems provide structured forms to help

Figure 11-13 **Opening screen for an executive information system**

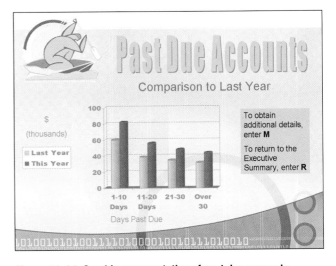

Figure 11-14 **Graphic representation of past due accounts**

Type	Description
TPS	Tracks routine operations and records events in databases, also known as data processing systems
MIS	Produces standardized reports (periodic, exception, and demand) using databases created by TPS
DSS	Analyzes unanticipated situations using data (internal and external) and decision models (strategic, tactical, and operational)
ESS	Presents summary information in a flexible, easy-to-use, graphical format designed for top executives

Figure 11-15 **Summary of information systems**

managers streamline their thoughts before sending electronic memos. In addition, an ESS may be organized to retrieve information from databases outside the company, such as business-news services. This enables a firm to watch for stories on competitors and stay current on relevant news events that could affect its business. For example, news of increased sports injuries caused by running and aerobic dancing, and the consequent decrease in people's interest in these activities, might cause HealthWise to alter its sales and production goals for its line of fitness-related shoes.

For a summary of the different types of information systems, see Figure 11-15.

CONCEPT CHECK

 What is the purpose of an executive support system?

 Describe the four types of information systems.

 How is an ESS similar to and different from an MIS or DSS?

Other Information Systems

We have discussed only four information systems: TPS to support lower-level managers, MIS and DSS to support middle-level managers, and ESS to support top-level managers. There are many other information systems to support different individuals and functions. The fastest-growing are information systems designed to support information workers.

Information workers distribute, communicate, and create information. They are the organization's secretaries, clerks, engineers, and scientists, to name a few. Some are involved with distribution and communication of information (like the secretaries and clerks; see Figure 11-16). They are called **data workers.** Others are involved with the creation of information (like the engineers and scientists). They are called **knowledge workers.**

Two systems to support information workers are

- **Office automation systems: Office automation systems (OASs)** are designed primarily to support data workers. These systems focus on managing documents, communicating, and scheduling. Documents are managed using word processing, Web authoring, desktop publishing, and other image technologies. **Project managers** are programs designed to schedule, plan, and control project resources. Microsoft

Figure 11-16 **Secretaries and clerks are data workers**

Figure 11-17 Videoconferencing: Individuals and groups can see and share information

Project is the most widely used project manager. **Videoconferencing systems** are computer systems that allow people located at various geographical locations to communicate and have in-person meetings. (See Figure 11-17.)

- **Knowledge work systems: Knowledge workers** use OAS systems. Additionally, they use specialized information systems called **knowledge work systems (KWSs)** to create information in their areas of expertise. For example, engineers involved in product design and manufacturing use **computer-aided design/computer-aided manufacturing (CAD/CAM) systems.** (See Figure 11-18.) These KWSs consist of powerful

Figure 11-18 CAD/CAM: Knowledge work systems used by design and manufacturing engineers

microcomputers running special programs that integrate the design and manufacturing activities. CAD/CAM is widely used in the manufacture of automobiles and other products.

CONCEPT CHECK

 What is an information worker?

 Who are data workers? What type of information system is designed to support them?

Who are knowledge workers? What type of information system is designed to support them?

Careers in IT

Information systems managers oversee the work of programmers, computer specialists, systems analysts, and other computer professionals. (See Figure 11-19.) They create and implement corporate computer policy and systems. These professionals consult with management, staff, and customers to achieve goals.

Most companies look for individuals with strong technical backgrounds, sometimes as consultants, with a master's degree in business. Employers seek individuals with strong leadership and excellent communication skills. Information systems managers must be able to communicate with people in technical and nontechnical terms. Information systems management positions are often filled with individuals who have been consultants or managers in previous positions. Those with experience in computer and network security will be in demand as businesses and society continue to struggle with important security issues.

Information systems managers can expect an annual salary of $79,000 to $129,500. Advancement opportunities typically include leadership in the field. To learn more about other careers in information systems, visit us at www.computing2011.com and enter the keyword **careers**.

Figure 11-19 **Information systems manager**

Oftentimes, More Information Is Too Much Information

Have you ever questioned the value of technology? Has it really helped us and made us more productive? Is it possible that the various devices intended to increase our productivity have actually had the opposite effect?

E-mail, cell phones, notebook computers, and the Web are great. They allow us to communicate, work almost anywhere, and have access to vast amounts of data. However, unless we are careful, they can create "information overload" and have a negative effect on our ability to get work done.

Several recent studies have found that e-mail is the major source of information overload. It was recently reported that a typical knowledge worker in a large corporation sends and receives over 100 e-mail messages a day. Furthermore, the study concluded that the majority of these messages are not necessary. Here are some tips to control e-mail overload:

- **Be selective.** Look first at the subject line in an e-mail—read only those of direct and immediate interest to you. Look next at the sender line—read only those from people important to you; postpone or ignore the others.

- **Remove.** After reading an e-mail, respond if necessary; then either file it in the appropriate folder or delete it.

- **Protect.** Limit your e-mail by giving your address only to those who need it.

- **Be brief.** When responding, be concise and direct.

- **Stop spam.** Spam is unwanted e-mail advertisements. Avoid mailing lists, complain to those who send spam, and ask to have your name removed from their mailing list.

- **Don't respond.** You do not have to respond to an e-mail. Be selective; respond only to those worthy of your time.

Is information overload part of your future?

Using IT at DVD Direct—a case study

INFORMATION SYSTEMS AT DVD DIRECT

DVD Direct, a fictitious organization, is an entirely Web-oriented movie rental business. Unlike traditional movie rental businesses, DVD Direct conducts all business over the Web at its Web storefront. For a monthly fee, their customers are able to order up to three movies at a time from a listing posted at the company Web site. The movies the customers select are delivered to them on DVD disks by mail within three working days. After viewing, customers return one or more disks by mail. They are allowed to keep the disks as long as they wish but can never have more than three disks in their possession at one time.

Although in operation for only three years, DVD Direct has experienced rapid growth. To help manage and to accelerate this growth, the company has just hired Alice, a recent college graduate. To follow Alice on her first day at DVD Direct, which begins with a meeting with Bob, the vice president of marketing, visit us on the Web at www.computing2011.com and enter the keyword information.

"She said she was concerned about how our members were connecting to our Web site."

INFORMATION FLOW

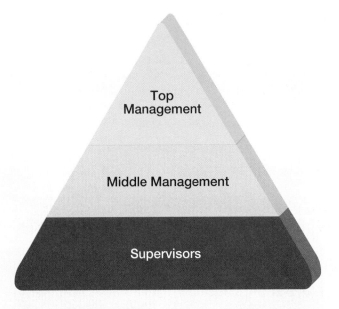

Information flows in an organization through functional areas and between management levels.

Functions

Most organizations have separate departments to perform five functions:

- **Accounting**—tracks all financial activities and generates periodic financial statements.
- **Marketing**—advertises, promotes, and sells the product (or service).
- **Production**—makes the product (or service) using raw materials and people to turn out finished goods.
- **Human resources**—finds and hires people, handles such matters as sick leave, retirement benefits, evaluation, compensation, and professional development.
- **Research**—conducts product research and development, monitors and troubleshoots new products.

Management Levels

The three basic management levels are

- **Top-level**—concerned with long-range planning and forecasting.
- **Middle-level**—deals with control, planning, decision making, and implementing long-term goals.
- **Supervisors**—control operational matters, monitor day-to-day events, and supervise workers.

Information Flow

Information flows within an organization in different directions.

- For **top-level managers,** the information flow is primarily upward from within the organization and into the organization from the outside.
- For **middle-level managers,** the information flow is horizontal and vertical within departments.
- For **supervisors,** the information flow is primarily vertical.

To be a competent end user, you need to understand how information flows through functional areas and management levels. You need to be aware of the different types of computer-based information systems, including transaction processing systems, management information systems, decision support systems, and executive support systems.

INFORMATION SYSTEMS

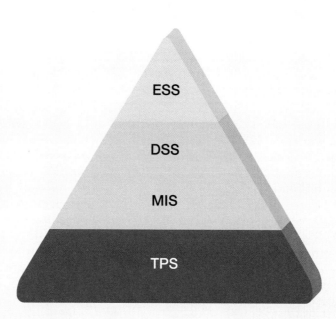

All organizations have computer-based **information systems**, including the following.

Transaction Processing Systems

Transaction processing systems (TPS), also known as **data processing systems (DPS)**, record day-to-day transactions. An example is in accounting, which handles six activities: **sales order processing, accounts receivable, inventory (inventory control systems)** and **purchasing, accounts payable, payroll,** and **general ledger.** General ledger is used to produce **income statements** and **balance sheets.**

Management Information Systems

Management information systems (MIS) produce predetermined **periodic, exception,** and **demand reports.** Management information systems use database management systems to integrate the databases of different departments.

Decision Support Systems

Decision support systems (DSS) enable managers to get answers for unanticipated questions. Teams formed to address large problems use **group decision support systems (GDSS).** A decision support system consists of the **user, system software, data—internal** and **external,** and **decision models.** Three types of decision models are **strategic, tactical,** and **operational.**

Executive Support Systems

Executive support systems (ESS) assist top-level executives. An executive support system is similar to MIS or DSS but easier to use. ESSs are designed specifically for top-level decision makers.

Other Information Systems

Many other systems are designed to support **information workers** who create, distribute, and communicate information. Two such systems are

- **Office automation systems (OAS)** support **data workers** who are involved with distribution and communication of information. **Project managers** and **videoconferencing systems** are OAS.

- **Knowledge work systems (KWS)** support **knowledge workers,** who create information. Many engineers use **computer-aided design/computer-aided manufacturing (CAD/CAM)** systems.

KEY TERMS

accounting (315)
accounts payable (321)
accounts receivable (320)
balance sheet (321)
computer-aided design/computer-
   aided manufacturing (CAD/CAM)
   system (326)
data (323)
data processing system (DPS) (320)
data worker (325)
decision model (323)
decision support system (DSS) (319)
demand report (322)
exception report (322)
executive information system
   (EIS) (319)
executive support system (ESS) (319)
external data (323)
general ledger (321)
group decision support system
   (GDSS) (323)
human resources (315)
income statement (321)
information system (319)
information systems manager (327)
information worker (325)
internal data (323)
inventory (320)

inventory control system (321)
knowledge work system (KWS) (326)
knowledge worker (325)
management information system
   (MIS) (319)
marketing (315)
middle management (315)
office automation system
   (OAS) (325)
operational model (323)
payroll (321)
periodic report (322)
production (315)
project manager (325)
purchase order (321)
purchasing (321)
research (315)
sales order processing (320)
strategic model (323)
supervisor (315)
system software (323)
tactical model (323)
top management (317)
transaction processing system
   (TPS) (319)
user (323)
videoconferencing system (326)

To test your knowledge of these key terms with animated flash cards, visit our
Web site at www.computing2011.com and enter the keyword terms11.

MULTIPLE CHOICE

Circle the letter or fill in the correct answer.

1. The department in charge of recording all financial activity is the _____ department.
   a. human resources
   b. accounting
   c. marketing
   d. production

2. This management level deals with control, planning, and decision making.
   a. supervisory
   b. middle-managerial
   c. stockholder
   d. top-managerial

3. This level of management needs summarized information such as weekly or monthly reports.
   a. top management
   b. middle management
   c. supervisors
   d. stockholders

4. Top-level managers use _____ to help oversee the company's operations and develop strategic plans.
   a. TPS
   b. MIS
   c. DSS
   d. ESS

5. The money that the company owes for goods or services is handled by
   a. accounts receivable
   b. inventory
   c. sales order processing
   d. accounts payable

6. Management information systems produce reports that are _____; they always follow the same format and show the same types of information.
   a. predetermined
   b. encrypted
   c. graphically simplified
   d. dynamic

7. These types of systems would most likely be used to assist a manager in getting answers to unexpected and generally nonrecurring kinds of problems.
   a. TPS
   b. MIS
   c. DSS
   d. ESS

8. These systems permit a firm's top executives to gain direct access to information about the company's performance.
   a. TPS
   b. MIS
   c. ESS
   d. DSS

9. _____ workers distribute, communicate, and create information.
   a. White-collar
   b. Data mine
   c. Information
   d. Organization

10. These systems are computer systems that allow people located at various locations to communicate and have live meetings.
    a. project managers
    b. videoconferencing
    c. telemarketing
    d. data conferencing

For an interactive multiple-choice practice test, visit our Web site at www.computing 2011.com and enter the keyword multiple11.

MATCHING

Match each numbered item with the most closely related lettered item. Write your answers in the spaces provided.

a. DSS

b. exception report

c. GDSS

d. general ledger

e. knowledge workers

f. MIS

g. periodic report

h. supervisor

i. tactical models

j. TPS

1. Manager responsible for administration and monitoring workers. _____
2. System that records day-to-day transactions. _____
3. Computer-based information system that produces standardized reports in summarized, structured form. _____
4. Activity that produces income statements and balance sheets based on all transactions of a company. _____
5. Report generated at regular intervals. _____
6. Report that calls attention to unusual events. _____
7. Flexible tool for analysis that helps managers make decisions about unstructured problems. _____
8. System used to support the collective work of a team addressing large problems. _____
9. Models that help middle managers control the work of the organization. _____
10. Individuals involved in the creation of information. _____

For an interactive matching practice test, visit our Web site at www.computing 2011.com and enter the keyword matching11.

OPEN-ENDED

On a separate sheet of paper, respond to each question or statement.

1. Name and discuss the five common functions of most organizations.
2. Discuss the roles of the three kinds of management in a corporation.
3. What are the four most common computer-based information systems?
4. Describe the different reports and their roles in managerial decision making.
5. What is the difference between an office automation system and a knowledge work system?

APPLYING TECHNOLOGY

The following questions are designed to demonstrate ways that you can effectively use technology today.

1 CAD

Many companies model plans or products using computer-aided design, or CAD. To learn more about one of these products, visit our Web site at www.computing2011.com and enter the keyword cad. Connect to the product's site and read about the features of the product. Then answer the following: (a) What type of modeling is the product used for? (b) What are its basic features? (c) Cite some specific applications for the product. (d) Are there any special or advanced features that set it apart from other CAD software?

2 KNOWLEDGE WORK SYSTEMS

Companies always want to tailor their Web sites to the needs of their customers to stay competitive; sites that are easier to navigate or provide the desired information quicker will be most in demand by consumers. One way to accomplish this is with Web site knowledge work software that monitors traffic on a Web server and provides reports that summarize visitors' activities. Visit our Web site at www.computing2011.com and enter the keyword knowledge to link to a company that delivers such software. Once connected, review the company's products and then answer the following questions: (a) What events can the software monitor for? Briefly describe each. (b) How are reports about Web site usage delivered? What information do they include? (c) How can a company apply this information to improve its Web site? Provide specific examples.

3 ONLINE PERSONAL INFORMATION MANAGERS

An important element for many personal information systems is a personal information manager, or PIM. PIMs can be either stored on your system's hard disk or accessed from the Web. Using the Web, locate and explore two or three online PIMs and then answer the following questions in a one-page paper: (a) Describe the common features of online PIMs. (b) What is the advantage of using an online PIM versus one that is stored on your system's hard disk? (c) What are the disadvantages? (d) Of the PIMs you reviewed, which would you choose? Why?

EXPANDING YOUR KNOWLEDGE

The following questions are designed to add depth and detail to your understanding of specific topics presented within this chapter. The questions direct you to sources other than the textbook to obtain this knowledge.

1 DVD DIRECT INFORMATION SYSTEMS

To learn about DVD Direct, visit us on the Web at www.computing2011.com and enter the keyword information. DVD Direct is similar to several real-world DVD rental companies. Connect to one of these companies' Web sites by visiting our Web site at www.computing 2011.com and enter the keyword rental. Once connected, explore the site and then answer the following questions: (a) How are DVD Direct and this company similar? (b) How are they different? (c) Does this company offer streaming video downloads? (d) If DVD Direct wanted to provide delivery via streaming video, what would you anticipate would be their greatest challenges?

2 EXECUTIVE SUPPORT SYSTEMS

Research at least three different executive support systems using a Web search. Review each and then answer the following questions: (a) Which ESSs did you review? (b) What are the common features of ESSs? (c) What specific types of decisions was each ESS designed to aid in? (d) What type of company is likely to use each? Provide some examples.

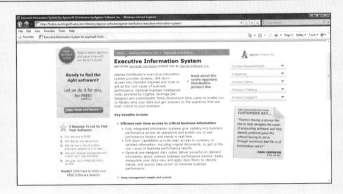

WRITING ABOUT TECHNOLOGY

The ability to think critically and to write effectively is essential to nearly every profession. The following questions are designed to help you develop these skills by posing thought-provoking questions about computer privacy, security, and/or ethics.

1 CONSUMER INFORMATION SYSTEMS

Some companies specialize in maintaining information systems that accumulate consumer information. When you apply for a job, loan, or insurance policy, the business you are dealing with might purchase access to such information to verify your credentials. However, not all requests for your personal information are so harmless. In 2005, the company ChoicePoint revealed that it had accidentally sold personal information for nearly 140,000 people to fraudulent businesses. Write a one-page paper on the topic of consumer information providers that addresses the following: (a) Which companies did you research? (b) What types of personal information do these companies collect? Be specific. (c) Can you find out what information has been collected about you? How? (d) What precautions have been taken to ensure that personal data is not distributed illegitimately?

2 IDENTITY THEFT

Identity theft occurs when someone acquires your personal information and uses it to hijack your finances. A common scenario is a thief using your Social Security number to open a credit card account in your name. When the thief does not pay, it is your credit history that is blemished. Consider this scam thoroughly and then answer the following questions in a one-page paper: (a) List three steps an individual should take to avoid identity theft. (b) List three steps a corporation that maintains your personal data in their information system should take to safeguard your data. (c) How can Internet activities contribute to the likelihood of identity theft? How can this be prevented?

Databases

Competencies

After you have read this chapter, you should be able to:

1 Distinguish between the physical and logical view of data.

2 Describe how data is organized: characters, fields, records, tables, and databases.

3 Define key fields and how they are used to integrate data in a database.

4 Define and compare batch processing and real-time processing.

5 Describe databases, including the need for databases, and database management systems (DBMS).

6 Describe the five common database models: hierarchical, network, relational, multidimensional, and object-oriented.

7 Distinguish among individual, company, distributed, and commercial databases.

8 Discuss strategic database uses and security concerns.

The earliest databases were maintained without computers, using record books and filing cabinets. The information stored in those books and filing cabinets began to move to digital format as the availability of secondary storage devices increased, and the cost of that storage dropped. Today almost all data kept by large organizations is stored in a database management system, and those books and filing cabinets are disappearing.

Some experts predict that the organization and access of databases will change radically in the near future. There are many opportunities to upload data from mobile devices, and computers are now able to compile and sort that data without human intervention. Imagine a world where your phone uploads your path through an amusement park, that data is processed, and other users in the park are given advice on their phones about the best time to ride a roller coaster or how to find the snow cone stand with the shortest line.

chapter .12

Introduction

Like a library, secondary storage is designed to store information. How is this stored information organized? What are databases and why do you need to know anything about them?

Only a few years ago, a computer was considered to be an island with only limited access to information beyond its own hard disk. Now, through communication networks and the Internet, individual computers have direct electronic access to almost unlimited sources of information.

In today's world, almost all information is stored in databases. They are an important part of nearly every organization including schools, hospitals, banks, and retail stores. To effectively compete in today's world, you need to know how to find information and understand how it is stored.

Competent end users need to understand data fields, records, tables, and databases. They need to be aware of the different ways in which a database can be structured and the different types of databases. Also, they need to know the most important database uses and issues.

Data

As we have discussed throughout this book, information systems consist of people, procedures, software, hardware, and data. This chapter focuses on the last element, **data,** which can be defined as facts or observations about people, places, things, and events. More specifically, this chapter focuses on how databases are used to store, organize, and use data.

Not long ago, data was limited to numbers, letters, and symbols recorded by keyboards. Now, data is much richer and includes

- Audio captured, interpreted, and saved using microphones and voice recognition systems.
- Music downloaded from the Internet, captured from MIDI devices, and from other sources. (See Figure 12-1.)
- Photographs captured by digital cameras, edited by image-editing software, and shared with others over the Internet.
- Video captured by digital video cameras, TV tuner cards, and WebCams.

There are two ways or perspectives to view data. These perspectives are the *physical view* and the *logical view*. The **physical view** focuses on the actual format and location of the data. As discussed in Chapter 6, data is recorded as digital bits that are typically grouped together into bytes that represent characters using a coding scheme such as Unicode. Typically, only very specialized computer professionals are concerned with the physical view. The other perspective, the **logical view,** focuses on the meaning, content, and context of the data. End users and most computer professionals are concerned with this view. They are involved with actually using the data with application programs. This chapter presents the logical view of data and how data is stored in databases.

CONCEPT CHECK

Describe some of the different types of data.

What is the physical view of data?

What is the logical view of data?

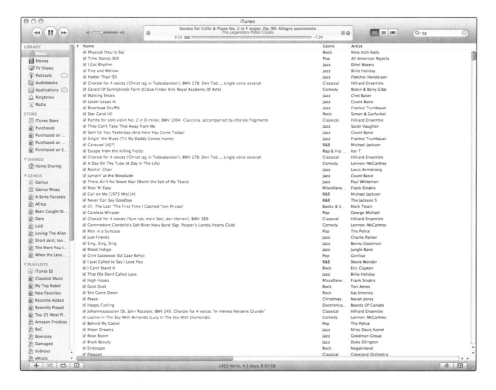

Figure 12-1 Apple's iTunes database of music files

Data Organization

The first step in understanding databases is to learn how data is organized. In the logical view, data is organized into groups or categories. Each group is more complex than the one before. (See Figure 12-2.)

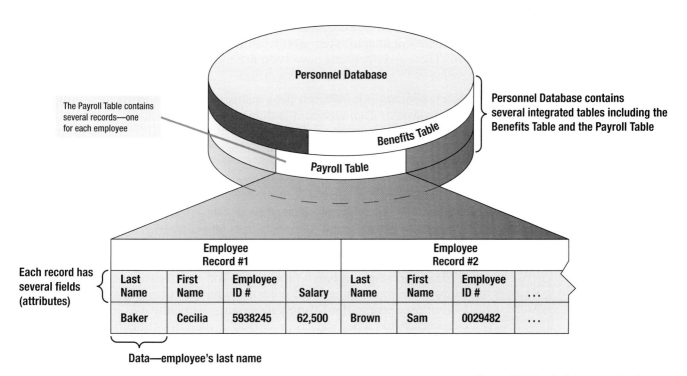

Figure 12-2 Logical data organization

- **Character:** A **character** is the most basic logical data element. It is a single letter, number, or special character, such as a punctuation mark, or a symbol, such as $. For example, in Figure 12-2 the letter *B* is the first letter of an employee's last name.
- **Field:** The next higher level is a **field** or group of related characters. In our example, Baker is in the data field for the Last Name of an employee. It consists of the individual letters (characters) that make up the last name. A data field represents an **attribute** (description or characteristic) of some **entity** (person, place, thing, or object). For example, an employee is an entity with many attributes, including his or her last name.
- **Record:** A **record** is a collection of related fields. A record represents a collection of attributes that describe an entity. In our example, the payroll record for an employee consists of the data fields describing the attributes for one employee. These attributes are First Name, Last Name, Employee ID, and Salary.
- **Table:** A **table** is a collection of related records. For example, the payroll table would include payroll information (records) for the employees (entities).
- **Database:** A **database** is an integrated collection of logically related tables. For example, the Personnel Database would include all related employee tables including the Payroll Table and the Benefits Table.

Key Field

Each record in a database has at least one distinctive field, called the **key field.** Also known as the **primary key,** this field uniquely identifies the record. As we discussed in Chapter 3, tables can be related or connected to other tables by common key fields.

For most employee databases, the key field is an employee identification number. Key fields in different tables can be used to integrate the data in a database. For example, in the Personnel Database, both the Payroll and the Benefits tables include the field Employee ID. Data from the two tables could be related by combining all records with the same key field (Employee ID).

Batch versus Real-Time Processing

Traditionally, data is processed in one of two ways. These are batch processing, or what we might call "later," and real-time processing, or what we might call "now." These two methods have been used to handle common record-keeping activities such as payroll and sales orders.

- **Batch processing:** In **batch processing,** data is collected over several hours, days, or even weeks. It is then processed all at once as a "batch." If you have a bank credit card, your bill probably reflects batch processing. That is, during the month, you buy things and charge them to your credit card. Each time you charge something, an electronic copy of the transaction is sent to the credit card company. At some point in the month, the company's data processing department puts all those transactions (and those of many other customers) together and processes them at one time. The company then sends you a single bill totaling the amount you owe. (See Figure 12-3.)
- **Real-time processing:** Totaling up the sales charged to your bank credit card is an example of batch processing. You might use another kind of card—your bank's automated teller machine (ATM) card—for the second kind of processing. **Real-time processing,** also known as **online processing,** occurs when data is processed at the same time the transaction occurs. As you use your ATM card to withdraw cash, the system automatically computes the balance remaining in your account. (See Figure 12-4.)

1. You use your credit card to make several purchases throughout the month.

2. The credit card company records your and all other card holders' purchases.

3. Once a month, the credit card company produces monthly statements for each of its card holders.

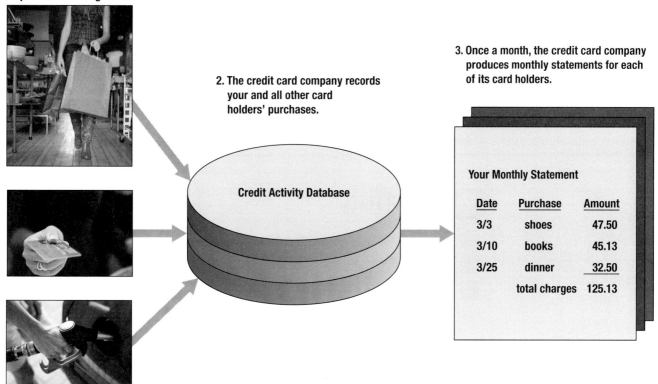

Credit Activity Database

Your Monthly Statement

Date	Purchase	Amount
3/3	shoes	47.50
3/10	books	45.13
3/25	dinner	32.50
	total charges	125.13

Figure 12-3 Batch processing: Monthly credit card statements

1. You request a $200 withdrawal at an ATM.

2. The ATM immediately sends the electronic request to your bank.

3. The bank processes the request by first verifying that you have sufficient funds to cover the request.

Request

Approval

Customer Accounts Database

Checking Acc't Table

Last Name	First Name	Acc't Bal.
Baker	Cecilia	1,200

6. The ATM dispenses $200 to you.

5. The bank sends an electronic approval and reduces your account balance by $200.

4. The bank determines your account balance is $1,200.

Figure 12-4 Real-time processing: ATM withdrawal

At one time, only magnetic tape storage, and therefore only sequential access storage (as we discussed in Chapter 8), was available. All processing then was batch processing and was done on mainframe computers. Even today, a great deal of mainframe time is dedicated to this kind of processing. Many smaller organizations, however, use microcomputers for this purpose.

Real-time processing is made possible by the availability of disk packs and direct access storage (as we described in Chapter 8). Direct access storage makes it possible to go quickly and directly to a particular record. (In sequential access storage, by contrast, the user must wait for the computer to scan several records one at a time. It continues scanning until the desired record is located.)

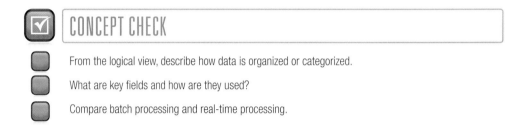

CONCEPT CHECK

From the logical view, describe how data is organized or categorized.

What are key fields and how are they used?

Compare batch processing and real-time processing.

Databases

Many organizations have multiple files on the same subject or person. For example, records for the same customer may appear in different files in the sales department, billing department, and credit department. This is called **data redundancy.** If the customer moves, then the address in each file must be updated. If one or more files are overlooked, problems will likely result. For example, a product ordered might be sent to the new address, but the bill might be sent to the old address. This situation results from a lack of **data integrity.**

Moreover, data spread around in different files is not as useful. The marketing department, for instance, might want to offer special promotions to customers who order large quantities of merchandise. However, they may be unable to do so because the information they need is in the billing department. A database can make the needed information available.

Need for Databases

For both individuals and organizations, there are many advantages to having databases:

- **Sharing:** In organizations, information from one department can be readily shared with others. Billing could let marketing know which customers ordered large quantities of merchandise.
- **Security:** Users are given passwords or access only to the kind of information they need. Thus, the payroll department may have access to employees' pay rates, but other departments would not.
- **Less data redundancy:** Without a common database, individual departments have to create and maintain their own data and data redundancy results. For example, an employee's home address would likely appear in

several files. Redundant data causes inefficient use of storage space and data maintenance problems.

- **Data integrity:** When there are multiple sources of data, each source may have variations. A customer's address may be listed as "Main Street" in one system and "Main St." in another. With discrepancies like these, it is probable that the customer would be treated as two separate people.

Database Management

In order to create, modify, and gain access to a database, special software is required. This software is called a **database management system,** which is commonly abbreviated **DBMS.**

Some DBMSs, such as Microsoft Access and FileMaker Pro, are designed specifically for microcomputers. Other DBMSs are designed for specialized database servers. DBMS software is made up of five parts or subsystems: *DBMS engine, data definition, data manipulation, application generation,* and *data administration.*

- The **DBMS engine** provides a bridge between the logical view of the data and the physical view of the data. When users request data (logical perspective), the DBMS engine handles the details of actually locating the data (physical perspective).
- The **data definition subsystem** defines the logical structure of the database by using a **data dictionary** or **schema.** This dictionary contains a description of the structure of data in the database. For a particular item of data, it defines the names used for a particular field. It defines the type of data for each field (text, numeric, time, graphic, audio, and video). An example of an Access data dictionary form is presented in Figure 12-5.
- The **data manipulation subsystem** provides tools for maintaining and analyzing data. Maintaining data is known as **data maintenance.** It

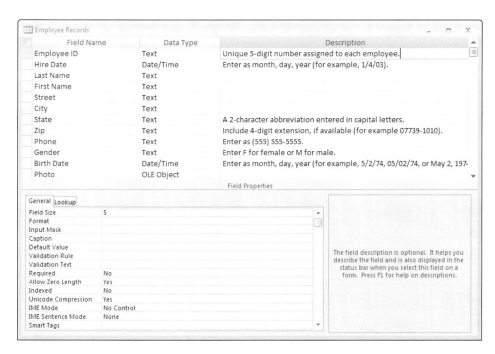

Figure 12-5 Access data dictionary form

Figure 12-6 Access data entry form

involves adding new data, deleting old data, and editing existing data. Analysis tools support viewing all or selected parts of the data, querying the database, and generating reports. Specific tools include **query-by-example** and specialized programming languages called **structured query languages (SQL).** (Structured query languages and other types of programming languages will be discussed in Chapter 14.)

- The **application generation subsystem** provides tools to create data entry forms and specialized programming languages that interface or work with common and widely used programming languages such as C or Visual Basic. See Figure 12-6 for a data entry form created by the application generation subsystem in Access.

- The **data administration subsystem** helps to manage the overall database, including maintaining security, providing disaster recovery support, and monitoring the overall performance of database operations. Larger organizations typically employ highly trained computer specialists, called **database administrators (DBAs),** to interact with the data administration subsystem. Additional duties of database administrators include determining **processing rights** or determining which people have access to what kinds of data in the database.

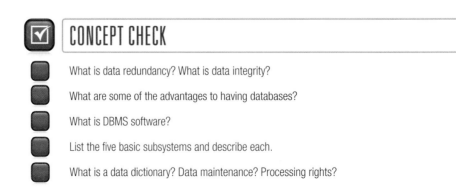

CONCEPT CHECK

- What is data redundancy? What is data integrity?

- What are some of the advantages to having databases?

- What is DBMS software?

- List the five basic subsystems and describe each.

- What is a data dictionary? Data maintenance? Processing rights?

DBMS Structure

DBMS programs are designed to work with data that is logically structured or arranged in a particular way. This arrangement is known as the **database model.** These models define rules and standards for all the data in a database. For example, Microsoft Access is designed to work with databases using the relational data model. Five common database models are *hierarchical, network, relational, multidimensional,* and *object-oriented.*

Hierarchical Database

At one time, nearly every DBMS designed for mainframes used the hierarchical data model. In a **hierarchical database,** fields or records are structured in nodes. **Nodes** are points connected like the branches of an upside-down tree. Each entry has one **parent node,** although a parent may have several **child nodes.** This is sometimes described as a **one-to-many relationship.** To find a particular field, you have to start at the top with a parent and trace down the tree to a child.

The nodes farther down the system are subordinate to the ones above, like the hierarchy of managers in a corporation. An example of a hierarchical database is a system to organize music files. (See Figure 12-7.) The parent node is the music library for a particular user. This parent has four children, labeled "artist." Coldplay, one of the children, has three children of its own. They are labeled "album." The *Greatest Hits* album has three children, labeled "song."

The problem with a hierarchical database is that if one parent node is deleted, so are all the subordinate child nodes. Moreover, a child node cannot be added unless a parent node is added first. The most significant limitation is the rigid structure: one parent only per child, and no relationships or connections between the child nodes themselves.

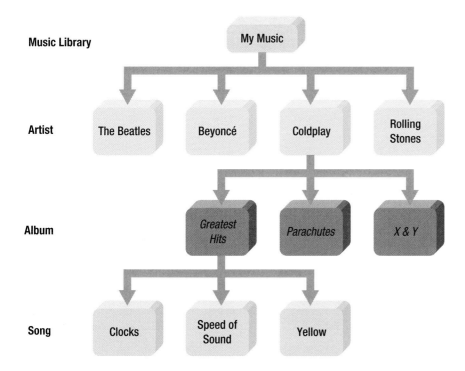

Figure 12-7 Hierarchical database

Network Database

Responding to the limitations of the hierarchical data model, network models were developed. A **network database** also has a hierarchical arrangement of nodes. However, each child node may have more than one parent node. This is sometimes described as a **many-to-many relationship.** There are additional connections—called **pointers**—between parent nodes and child nodes. Thus, a node may be reached through more than one path. It may be traced down through different branches.

For example a university could use this type of organization to record students taking classes. (See Figure 12-8.) If you trace through the logic of this organization, you can see that each student can have more than one teacher. Each teacher also can teach more than one course. Students may take more than a single course. This demonstrates how the network arrangement is more flexible and in many cases more efficient than the hierarchical arrangement.

Relational Database

A more flexible type of organization is the **relational database.** In this structure, there are no access paths down a hierarchy. Rather, the data elements are stored in different tables, each of which consists of rows and columns. A table and its data is called a **relation.**

An example of a relational database is shown in Figure 12-9. The Vehicle Owner Table contains license numbers, names, and addresses for all registered drivers. Within the table, a row is a record containing information about one driver. Each column is a field. The fields are License number, Last Name, First Name, Street, City, State, and Zip. All related tables must have a **common data item** (key field) enabling information stored in one table to be linked with information stored in another. In this case, the three tables are related by the License number field.

Police officers who stop a speeding car look up the driver's information in the Department of Motor Vehicles database (Figure 12-10) using the driver's license number. They also can check for any unpaid traffic violations in the Outstanding Citations Table. Finally, if the officers suspect that the car is stolen, they can look up what vehicles the driver owns in the Vehicle Table.

The most valuable feature of relational databases is their simplicity. Entries can be easily added, deleted, and modified. The hierarchical and network databases are more rigid. The relational organization is common for microcomputer

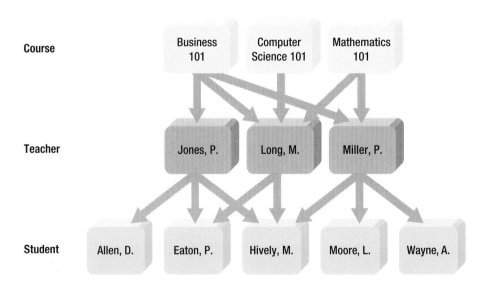

Figure 12-8 **Network database**

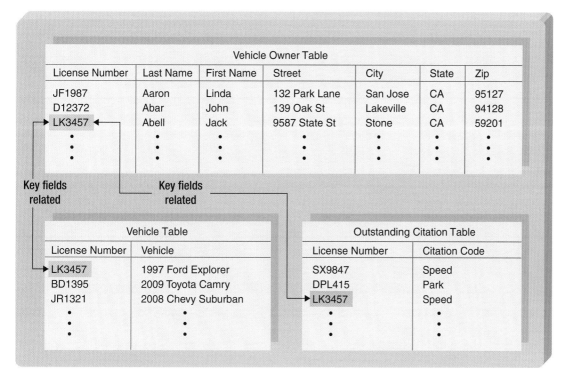

Figure 12-9 **Relational database**

Vehicle Owner Table						
License Number	Last Name	First Name	Street	City	State	Zip
JF1987	Aaron	Linda	132 Park Lane	San Jose	CA	95127
D12372	Abar	John	139 Oak St	Lakeville	CA	94128
LK3457	Abell	Jack	9587 State St	Stone	CA	59201

Key fields related · Key fields related

Vehicle Table	
License Number	Vehicle
LK3457	1997 Ford Explorer
BD1395	2009 Toyota Camry
JR1321	2008 Chevy Suburban

Outstanding Citation Table	
License Number	Citation Code
SX9847	Speed
DPL415	Park
LK3457	Speed

DBMSs such as Access, Paradox, dBASE, and R: Base. Relational databases are also widely used for mainframe and minicomputer systems.

Multidimensional Database

The multidimensional data model is a variation and an extension of the relational data model. While relational databases use tables consisting of rows and columns, **multidimensional databases** extend this two-dimensional data model to include additional or multiple dimensions, sometimes called a **data cube.** Data can be viewed as a cube having three or more sides and consisting of cells. Each side of the cube is considered a dimension of the data. In this way, complex relationships between data can be represented and efficiently analyzed.

Multidimensional databases provide several advantages over relational databases. Two of the most significant advantages are

* **Conceptualization.** Multidimensional databases and data cubes provide users with an intuitive model in which complex data and relationships can be conceptualized.
* **Processing speed.** Analyzing and querying a large multidimensional database can be much faster. For example, a query requiring just a few seconds on a multidimensional database could take minutes or hours to perform on a relational database.

Object-Oriented Database

The other data structures are primarily designed to handle structured data such as names, addresses, pay rates, and so on. **Object-oriented databases** are more flexible and store data as well as instructions to manipulate

Figure 12-10 **The Department of Motor Vehicles may use a relational database**

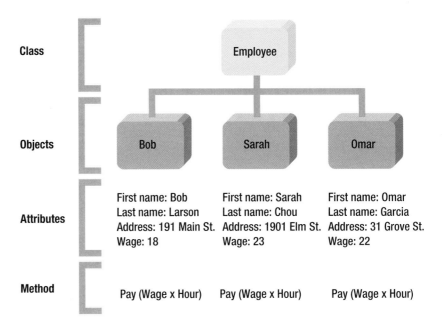

Class   Employee

Objects   Bob   Sarah   Omar

Attributes

First name: Bob
Last name: Larson
Address: 191 Main St.
Wage: 18

First name: Sarah
Last name: Chou
Address: 1901 Elm St.
Wage: 23

First name: Omar
Last name: Garcia
Address: 31 Grove St.
Wage: 22

Method   Pay (Wage x Hour)   Pay (Wage x Hour)   Pay (Wage x Hour)

Figure 12-11 **Object-oriented database**

the data. Additionally, this structure is ideally designed to provide input for object-oriented software development, which is described in Chapter 14.

Object-oriented databases organize data using classes, objects, attributes, and methods.

- **Classes** are general definitions.
- **Objects** are specific instances of a class that can contain both data and instructions to manipulate the data.
- **Attributes** are the data fields an object possesses.
- **Methods** are instructions for retrieving or manipulating attribute values.

For example, a health club might use an object-oriented employment database. (See Figure 12-11.) The database uses a class, Employee, to define employee objects that are stored in the database. This definition includes the attributes First name, Last name, Address, and Wage and the method Pay. Bob, Sarah, and Omar are objects each with specific attribute values. For example the object Bob has the stored values Bob, Larson, 191 Main St, 18. While hierarchical and network databases are still widely used, the relational, multidimensional, and object-oriented data models are more popular today.

For a summary of DBMS organization, see Figure 12-12.

Organization	Description
Hierarchical	Data structured in nodes organized like an upside-down tree; each parent node can have several children; each child node can have only one parent
Network	Like hierarchical except that each child can have several parents
Relational	Data stored in tables consisting of rows and columns
Multidimensional	Data stored in data cubes with three or more dimensions
Object-oriented	Organizes data using classes, objects, attributes, and methods

Figure 12-12 **Summary of DBMS organization**

Types of Databases

Databases may be small or large, limited in accessibility or widely accessible. Databases may be classified into four types: *individual, company, distributed, and commercial.*

Individual

The **individual database** is also called a **microcomputer database.** It is a collection of integrated files primarily used by just one person. Typically, the data and the DBMS are under the direct control of the user. They are stored either on the user's hard-disk drive or on a LAN file server.

There may be many times in your life when you will find this kind of database valuable. If you are in sales, for instance, a microcomputer database can be used to keep track of your customers. If you are a sales manager, you can keep track of your salespeople and their performance. If you are an advertising account executive, you can keep track of what work and how many hours to charge each client.

Company

Companies, of course, create databases for their own use. The **company database** may be stored on a central database server and managed by a database administrator. Users throughout the company have access to the database through their microcomputers linked to local or wide area networks.

As we discussed in Chapter 11, company databases are the foundation for management information systems. For instance, a department store can record all sales transactions in the database. A sales manager can use this information to see which salespeople are selling the most products. The manager can then determine year-end sales bonuses. Or the store's buyer can learn which products are selling well or not selling and make adjustments when reordering. A top executive might combine overall store sales trends with information from outside databases about consumer and population trends. This information could be used to change the whole merchandising strategy of the store.

Distributed

Many times the data in a company is stored not in just one location but in several locations. It is made accessible through a variety of communications networks. The database, then, is a **distributed database.** That is, not all the data in a database is physically located in one place. Typically, database servers on a client/server network provide the link between the data.

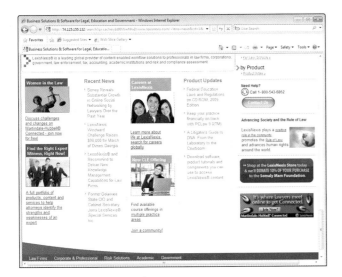

Figure 12-13 Commercial database (LexisNexis)

For instance, some database information can be at regional offices. Some can be at company headquarters, some down the hall from you, and some even overseas. Sales figures for a chain of department stores, then, could be located at the various stores. But executives at district offices or at the chain's headquarters could have access to these figures.

Commercial

A **commercial database** is generally an enormous database that an organization develops to cover particular subjects. It offers access to this database to the public or selected outside individuals for a fee. Sometimes commercial databases are also called **information utilities** or **data banks.** An example is LexisNexis, which offers a variety of information-gathering and reporting services. (See Figure 12-13.)

Some important commercial databases are the following:

- **CSi:** Offers consumer and business services, including electronic mail.
- **Dialog Information Services:** Offers business information, as well as technical and scientific information.
- **Dow Jones Interactive Publishing:** Provides world news and information on business, investments, and stocks.
- **LexisNexis:** Offers news and information on legal, public records, and business issues.

Most of the commercial databases are designed for organizational as well as individual use. Organizations typically pay a membership fee plus hourly use fees. Often, individuals are able to search the database to obtain a summary of available information without charge. They pay only for those items selected for further investigation.

See Figure 12-14 for a summary of the four types of databases.

CONCEPT CHECK

List four types of databases and describe each.

Give a brief example of each type of database.

Type	Description
Individual	Integrated files used by just one person
Company	Common operational or commonly used files shared in an organization
Distributed	Database spread geographically and accessed using database server
Commercial	Information utilities or data banks available to users on a wide range of topics

Figure 12-14 Summary of the four types of databases

Database Uses and Issues

Databases offer great opportunities for productivity. In fact, in corporate libraries, electronic databases are now considered more valuable than books and journals. However, maintaining databases means users must make constant efforts to keep them from being tampered with or misused.

Strategic Uses

Databases help users to keep up to date and to plan for the future. To support the needs of managers and other business professionals, many organizations collect data from a variety of internal and external databases. This data is then stored in a special type of database called a **data warehouse.** A technique called **data mining** is often used to search these databases to look for related information and patterns.

There are hundreds of databases available to help users with both general and specific business purposes, including

- *Business directories* providing addresses, financial and marketing information, products, and trade and brand names.
- *Demographic data,* such as county and city statistics, current estimates on population and income, employment statistics, census data, and so on.
- *Business statistical information,* such as financial information on publicly traded companies, market potential of certain retail stores, and other business data and information.
- *Text databases* providing articles from business publications, press releases, reviews on companies and products, and so on.
- *Web databases* covering a wide range of topics, including all of the above. As mentioned earlier, Web search sites like Google maintain extensive databases of available Internet content.

Security

Precisely because databases are so valuable, their security has become a critical issue. As we discussed in Chapter 10, there are several database security concerns. One concern is that personal and private information about people stored in databases may be used for the wrong purposes. For instance, a person's credit history or medical records might be used to make hiring or promotion decisions. Another concern is unauthorized users gaining access to a database. For example, there have been numerous instances in which a computer virus has been launched into a database or network.

Security may require putting guards in company computer rooms and checking the identification of everyone admitted. Some security systems electronically check fingerprints. (See Figure 12-15.) Security is particularly important to organizations using WANs. Violations can occur without actually entering secured areas. As mentioned in previous chapters, most major corporations today use special hardware and software called **firewalls** to control access to their internal networks.

Figure 12-15 **Security: Electronic fingerprint scanner**

 CONCEPT CHECK

- What is a data warehouse? What is data mining?
- What are some database security concerns?
- What is a firewall?

Careers in IT

Database administrators use database management software to determine the most efficient ways to organize and access a company's data. (See Figure 12-16.) Additionally, database administrators are typically responsible for maintaining database security and backing up the system. Database administration is a fast-growing industry and substantial job growth is expected.

Database administrator positions normally require a bachelor's degree in computer science or information systems and technical experience. Internships and prior experience with the latest technology are a considerable advantage for those seeking jobs in this industry. It is possible to transfer skills learned in one industry, such as finance, to a new career in database administration. In order to accomplish this objective, many people seek additional training in computer science.

Database administrators can expect to earn an annual salary of $48,500 to $85,000. Opportunities for advancement include positions as a chief technology officer or other managerial opportunities. To learn more about other careers in information technology, visit us at www.computing2011.com and enter the keyword **careers.**

Figure 12-16 **Database administrator**

A LOOK TO THE FUTURE

Every Book Ever Written ... at Your Fingertips

Database technology continues to evolve, and massive amounts of digital storage that seemed impossible only a few years ago are now available and affordable. In the future, you will likely be able to access every document ever produced by man just as easily as you currently search the Web. Recently, several projects are under way to digitize, analyze, and store a vast amount of information.

The Google Book Search is a massive database containing millions of books. Google, numerous libraries, and an increasing number of authors have been working together to expand this database. Books are scanned using special cameras and high-speed scanners. The digital images are recognized using optical character recognition, and the content is analyzed. The results are stored in databases, which make the text searchable. This technology allows users to cross-reference thousands of books for a given search term.

The challenges of supporting a database this large are a topic of ongoing research. By some estimates, the Google project alone is scanning more than 1 million books per year. To make sense of all this information, advanced data mining and search techniques must be developed. In the future, a database might help you find quotes and articles related to a particular topic in a way never before possible. A single search could return a wide variety of writings on a topic, all without leaving your desk.

The Google Book Search project has been the target of some opposition regarding the legality of indexing copyrighted works. The service provides users with excerpts of texts within the database, even if that work is under copyright restriction that would otherwise prevent redistribution.

What do you think? Should databases like these be allowed to store and access copyrighted materials? Who owns the scanned material? Would you use a database like this?

Using IT at DVD Direct—a case study

DATABASES AT DVD DIRECT

DVD Direct, a fictitious organization, is an entirely Web-oriented movie rental business. Its members order movies from DVD Direct's Web site and the movies are delivered on DVD disks by mail. Members can keep the movies as long as they wish before returning them by mail. However, a member can have at most three movies out at one time.

A recent internal study at DVD Direct discovered that many current and potential customers with high-bandwidth Internet connections would prefer to have movies delivered over the Internet. Further, the study indicated that current customers who recently switched to high-bandwidth connections were very likely to drop their DVD Direct membership. Top management has become concerned that if DVD Direct does not address these findings, it will continue to lose high-bandwidth members and it may no longer be able to compete in the online movie rental business. This has led Carol, DVD Direct's CEO, to consider some dramatic changes to its business model—the way it does business.

So far, this issue has been formally discussed only in high-level meetings. However, the rumor mill has been working and almost everyone in the company knows that some type of change is in the works. Alice, a recently hired market analyst, has joined the company at this critical moment for DVD Direct and is about to learn more about the proposed changes. To follow Alice as she meets with Bob, the vice president of marketing, visit us on the Web at www.computing2011.com and enter the keyword databases.

"I want you to focus on some critical database issues."

DATA

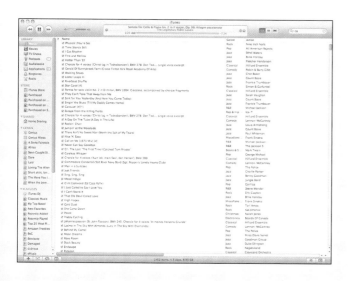

Data consists of facts or observations about people, places, things, and events.

Data Types

Not long ago, data was limited to numbers, letters, and symbols. Now data includes

- Audio—captured, interpreted, and saved using microphones and voice recognition systems.
- Music—downloaded from the Internet and captured from other sources, rearranged, and used to create customized CDs.
- Photographs—captured by digital cameras, edited by image-editing software, and shared with others over the Internet.
- Video—captured by digital video cameras and TV tuner cards, saved, and used in presentations.

Data Views

There are two ways or perspectives to view data: the *physical view* and the *logical view*.

- **Physical view** focuses on actual format and location of data; very specialized computer professionals are concerned with this view.
- **Logical view** focuses on meaning and content of data; end users and most computer professionals are concerned with this view.

DATA ORGANIZATION

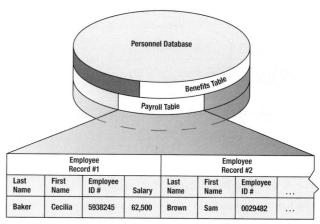

Data is organized by the following groups:

- **Character**—the most basic logical element, consisting of individual numbers, letters, and special characters.
- **Field**—next level, consisting of a set of related characters, for example, a person's last name. A data field represents an **attribute** (description or characteristic) of some **entity** (person, place, thing, or object).
- **Record**—a collection of related fields; for example, a payroll record consisting of fields of data relating to one employee.
- **Table**—a collection of related records; for example, a payroll table consisting of all the employee records.
- **Database**—an integrated collection of related tables; for example, a personnel database contains all related employee tables, including the payroll and the benefits tables.

Key Field

A **key field (primary key)** is the field in a record that uniquely identifies each record.

- Tables can be related (connected) to other tables by key fields.
- Key fields in different files can be used to integrate the data in a database.
- Common key fields are employee ID numbers and driver's license numbers.

To be a competent end user, you need to understand data fields, records, tables, and databases. You need to be aware of the different ways in which a database can be structured and the different types of databases. Also, you need to know the most important database uses and issues.

DATA ORGANIZATION

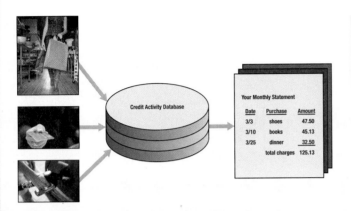

Batch versus Real-Time Processing

Traditionally, data is processed in one of two ways: batch or real-time processing.

- **Batch processing**—data is collected over time and then processed later all at one time (batched). For example, monthly credit card bills are typically created by processing credit card purchases throughout the past month.
- **Real-time processing (online processing)**—data is processed at the same time the transaction occurs; direct access storage devices make real-time processing possible. For example, a request for cash using an ATM machine initiates a verification of funds, approval or disapproval, disbursement of cash, and an update of the account balance.

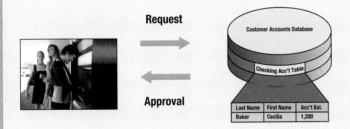

DATABASES

A **database** is a collection of integrated data— logically related files and records.

Need for Databases

Advantages of databases are sharing data, improved security, reduced **data redundancy**, and higher **data integrity**.

Database Management

A **database management system (DBMS)** is the software for creating, modifying, and gaining access to the database. A DBMS consists of five subsystems:

- **DBMS engine** provides a bridge between logical and physical data views.
- **Data definition subsystem** defines the logical structure of a database using a **data dictionary** or **schema**.
- **Data manipulation subsystem** provides tools for **data maintenance** and data analysis; tools include **query-by-example** and **structured query language (SQL)**.
- **Application generation subsystem** provides tools for creating data entry forms with specialized programming languages.
- **Data administration subsystem** manages the database; **database administrators (DBAs)** are computer professionals who help define **processing rights**.

DBMS STRUCTURE

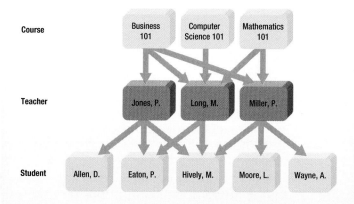

DBMS programs are designed to work with specific data structures or **database models.** These models define rules and standards for all the data in the database. Five principal database models are *hierarchical, network, relational, multidimensional,* and *object-oriented.*

Hierarchical Database

Hierarchical database uses **nodes** to link and structure fields and records; entries may have one **parent node** with several **child nodes** in a **one-to-many relationship.**

Network Database

Network database is like hierarchical except a child node may have more than one parent in a **many-to-many relationship;** additional connections are called **pointers.**

Relational Database

Relational database data is stored in tables (**relations**); related tables must have a **common data item** (key field). A table and its data is called a **relation.**

Multidimensional Database

Multidimensional databases extend two-dimensional relational tables to three or more dimensions, sometimes called a **data cube.**

Multidimensional databases offer more flexible structures than relational databases, providing a more intuitive means of modeling data.

Object-Oriented Database

Object-oriented databases store data, instructions, and unstructured data. Data is organized using *classes, objects, attributes,* and *methods.*

- **Classes** are general definitions.
- **Objects** are specific instances of a class that can contain both data and instructions to manipulate the data.
- **Attributes** are the data fields an object possesses.
- **Methods** are instructions for retrieving or manipulating attribute values.

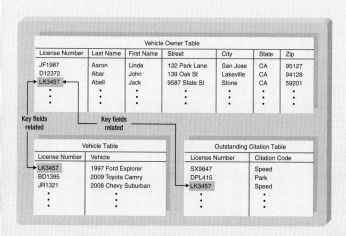

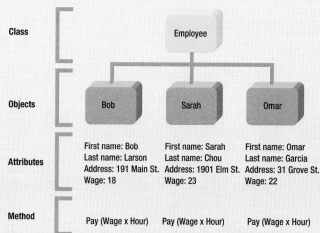

There are four types of databases:

Individual

Individual database or **microcomputer database** is used by one person.

Company or Shared

Company databases are usually stored on a central server and accessed by multiple people. These databases are typically used for company operations.

Distributed

Distributed database is spread out geographically; not all data is physically located in one place; it is accessible by communications links.

Commercial

Commercial databases are generally enormous and cover particular subjects; also known as **information utilities** and **data banks**.

Databases offer a great opportunity for increased productivity; however, security is always a concern.

Strategic Uses

Data warehouses are a new type of database that supports data mining. **Data mining** is a technique for searching and exploring databases for related information and patterns.

Databases available for general and specific business purposes include business directories, demographic data, business statistical information, text databases, and Web databases.

Security

Two important security concerns are illegal use of data and unauthorized access. Most organizations use **firewalls** to protect their internal networks.

CAREERS IN IT

Database administrators use database management software to determine the most efficient ways to organize and access a company's data. They are also responsible for database security and system backup. Bachelor's degree in computer science or information systems and technical experience required. Salary range $48,000 to $90,000.

KEY TERMS

application generation
  subsystem   (346)
attribute (342, 350)
batch processing   (342)
character   (342)
child node   (347)
class   (350)
commercial database   (352)
common data item   (348)
company database   (351)
data   (340)
data administration subsystem   (346)
data bank   (352)
data cube   (349)
data definition subsystem   (345)
data dictionary   (345)
data integrity   (344, 345)
data maintenance   (345)
data manipulation subsystem   (345)
data mining   (353)
data redundancy   (344)
data warehouse   (353)
database   (342)
database administrator
  (DBA)   (346, 353)
database management system
  (DBMS)   (345)
database model   (347)
DBMS engine   (345)
distributed database   (351)
entity   (342)

field   (342)
firewall   (353)
hierarchical database   (347)
individual database   (351)
information utility   (352)
key field   (342)
logical view   (340)
many-to-many relationship   (348)
method   (350)
microcomputer database   (351)
multidimensional database   (349)
network database   (348)
node   (347)
object   (350)
object-oriented database   (349)
one-to-many relationship   (347)
online processing   (342)
parent node   (347)
physical view   (340)
pointers   (348)
primary key   (342)
processing rights   (346)
query-by-example   (346)
real-time processing   (342)
record   (342)
relation   (348)
relational database   (348)
schema   (345)
structured query language (SQL)   (346)
table   (342)

To test your knowledge of these key terms with animated flash cards, visit our Web site at www.computing2011.com and enter the keyword terms12.

MULTIPLE CHOICE

Circle the letter or fill in the correct answer.

1. Facts or observations about people, places, things, or events are stored as
   - **a.** numbers
   - **b.** information
   - **c.** statistics
   - **d.** data

2. Which sequence is ordered from the least to the most complex?
   - **a.** character, record, field, database, table
   - **b.** character, field, record, table, database
   - **c.** character, field, record, database, table
   - **d.** character, table, record, field, database

3. A collection of related tables is called a
   - **a.** character
   - **b.** database
   - **c.** field
   - **d.** record

4. When data is processed at the same time that a transaction occurs, it is called
   - **a.** batch processing
   - **b.** group processing
   - **c.** real-time processing
   - **d.** consignment processing

5. The software used to create and modify a database is called a(n)
   - **a.** DBMS
   - **b.** DBMFA
   - **c.** MDBS
   - **d.** DMBS

6. In a network database model, each child node may have more than one parent node. This relationship is called
   - **a.** one-to-many
   - **b.** one-to-one
   - **c.** many-to-many
   - **d.** combined join

7. In the relational database model, a column represents a
   - **a.** character
   - **b.** record
   - **c.** file
   - **d.** field

8. A database whose data is not located in just one place is said to be
   - **a.** distributed
   - **b.** fragmented
   - **c.** centralized
   - **d.** split

9. Commercial databases are also known as
   - **a.** data warehouses
   - **b.** information utilities
   - **c.** DBMS engines
   - **d.** key fields

10. A technique used to search databases looking for related information and patterns is
    - **a.** data mining
    - **b.** data modeling
    - **c.** data retrieving
    - **d.** data culling

For an interactive multiple-choice practice test, visit our Web site at www.computing2011.com and enter the keyword multiple12.

MATCHING

Match each numbered item with the most closely related lettered item. Write your answers in the spaces provided.

a. data dictionary
b. DBMS
c. table
d. key field
e. logical
f. multidimensional
g. network database
h. SQL
i. real-time
j. relational database

1. End users and most computer professionals use this data view. _____
2. A collection of records. _____
3. The common field by which tables in a database are related. _____
4. Processing that occurs where data is processed when the transaction occurs. _____
5. Software required to create, modify, and gain access to a database. _____
6. Defines the logical structure of a database. _____
7. A specialized programming language typically included in the data manipulation subsystem. _____
8. Database with hierarchical arrangement of nodes in which each child node may have more than one parent node. _____
9. Database structure in which data is organized into related tables. _____
10. DBMS structure that extends the two-dimensional relational data model. _____

For an interactive matching practice test, visit our Web site at www.computing 2011.com and enter the keyword matching12.

OPEN-ENDED

On a separate sheet of paper, respond to each question or statement.

1. Describe the five logical data groups or categories.
2. What is the difference between batch processing and real-time processing?
3. Identify and define the five parts of DBMS programs.
4. Describe each of the five common database models.
5. What are some of the benefits and limitations of databases? Why is security a concern?

APPLYING TECHNOLOGY

The following questions are designed to demonstrate ways that you can effectively use technology today.

1 FREE DATABASE SOFTWARE

Did you know that advanced database management software can be obtained for free? Visit our Web site at www.computing2011.com and enter the keyword mysql to connect to a site that features free database software. Read about this software and then answer the following questions: (a) What is MySQL? What is its basic functionality? (b) How does MySQL compare to commercial software like Microsoft Access in terms of performance? (c) What support is available to users of MySQL? How is it provided? (d) Would you recommend MySQL as an IT solution? Why or why not?

2 INTERNET MOVIE DATABASE

One popular commercial database is the Internet Movie Database, or IMDB. Connect to our Web site at www.computing2011.com and enter the keyword movie to link to the IMDB site. Once connected, try making a couple of queries and then answer the following questions: (a) What types of information does the IMDB contain? (b) What queries did you try? What were the results? (c) Based on your knowledge of databases, would you expect the IMDB to be relational or hierarchical? Justify your answer.

3 ONLINE DATABASES

As an Internet user, you have access to many interesting and informative databases via the Web. Locate at least five online databases that contain information that is interesting to you by conducting a Web search using the keywords "online database." Conduct a query of each database and then answer the following: (a) Give the URL and a brief description of each online database you reviewed. (b) What features are common to online databases? (c) Which provided the most relevant or interesting information? Will you use this site again? Why or why not?

EXPANDING YOUR KNOWLEDGE

The following questions are designed to add depth and detail to your understanding of specific topics presented within this chapter. The questions direct you to sources other than the textbook to obtain this knowledge.

 DVD DIRECT DATABASES

DVD Direct customers currently use the Internet to order videos. The videos are sent and returned by mail. DVD Direct is exploring the use of streaming video to deliver videos through the Internet. This change would significantly impact the way it does business. To learn more about DVD Direct, visit us on the Web at www.computing2011.com and enter the keyword databases. (a) Describe how DVD Direct currently stores movie data. (b) Create a drawing similar to Figure 12-2 that shows how DVD Direct uses batch processing. (c) What changes would be required to support online delivery of movies? (d) Create a drawing similar to Figure 12-3 that shows how DVD Direct could use real-time processing. (e) Compare the advantages and disadvantages of batch and real-time processing.

 SQL

Structured query language (SQL) is the most widely used language for database interaction today. Connect to our Web site at www.computing2011.com and enter the keyword sql to link to a site that gives an overview of SQL. Explore the site and answer the following: (a) What type of database is SQL designed for? (b) What database tasks can SQL be used for? (c) List some popular databases that use SQL. (d) In the DVD Direct case in the chapter, Alice is considering changes to the current database system. How might SQL be used to help accomplish that task? Be specific.

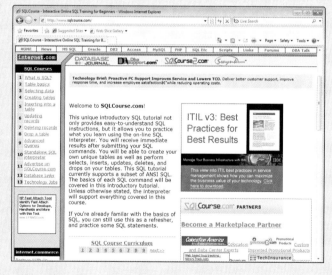

WRITING ABOUT TECHNOLOGY

The ability to think critically and to write effectively is essential to nearly every profession. The following questions are designed to help you develop these skills by posing thought-provoking questions about computer privacy, security, and/or ethics.

1 PERSONAL INFORMATION

Corporations currently collect information about the purchases you make and your personal spending habits. Sometimes corporations will share information to build a more informative profile about you. There have been proposals for legislation to regulate or halt this type of exchange. Consider how you feel about this exchange of information and then answer the following questions in a one-page paper: (a) What ethics and privacy concerns are related to corporations sharing personal data? (b) How might the consumer benefit from this? (c) Could this harm the consumer? What could happen if your grocery store shared information about your purchases with your life insurance carrier? (d) What rights do you feel consumers should have with regard to privacy of information collected about them? How should these rights be enforced? Defend your answer.

2 DATABASE SECURITY

Securing the data in a database is typically as important a concern as its design. Research database security on the Web and then write a one-page paper that addresses the following topics: (a) Describe a few security risks that databases must be protected against. (b) Describe some steps that can be taken to ensure that a database is secured. (c) In the DVD Direct case in the chapter, Harvey cited some security concerns for the new database design. Summarize those concerns and add any others you think would be important. (d) What obligations does DVD Direct have to the copyright owners of the streaming videos to keep its data secure? What obligations does it have to its customers?

Systems Analysis and Design

After you have read this chapter, you should be able to:

1 Describe the six phases of the systems life cycle.

2 Identify information needs and formulate possible solutions.

3 Analyze existing information systems and evaluate the feasibility of alternative systems.

4 Identify, acquire, and test new system software and hardware.

5 Switch from an existing information system to a new one with minimal risk.

6 Perform system audits and periodic evaluations.

7 Describe prototyping and rapid applications development.

In the past the creation of a new system sometimes took so long that it was outdated and abandoned by a company even before its premiere. The systems life cycle was initially designed to address this real concern about the time required to build a new process within a business.

Today, in addition to the formalized approach offered by the life cycle, systems analysts have powerful design and prototyping tools available to speed the creation of a new business system from start to finish. Additionally, social networking has reached the business realm, making information exchange between divisions easier than ever. The future of this process will almost certainly include the latest advances in technology, and become more collaborative as technology does.

chapter 13

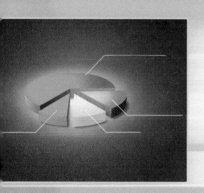

Introduction

Most people in an organization are involved with an information system of some kind. For an organization to create and effectively use a system requires considerable thought and effort. Fortunately, there is a six-step process for accomplishing this. It is known as systems analysis and design.

Big organizations can make big mistakes. For example, General Motors spent $40 billion putting in factory robots and other high technology in its automaking plants. It then removed much of this equipment and reinstalled that basic part of the assembly line, the conveyor belt. Why did the high-tech production systems fail? The probable reason was that GM did not devote enough energy to training its workforce in using the new systems.

The government also can make big mistakes. In one year, the Internal Revenue Service computer system was so overwhelmed it could not deliver tax refunds on time. How did this happen? Despite extensive testing of much of the system, not all testing was completed. Thus, when the new system was phased in, the IRS found it could not process tax returns as quickly as it had hoped.

Both of these examples show the necessity for thorough planning—especially when an organization is trying to implement a new kind of system. Systems analysis and design reduces the chances for such spectacular failures.

Competent end users need to understand the importance of systems analysis and design. They need to be aware of the relationship of an organization's chart to its managerial structure. Additionally, they need to know the six phases of the systems development life cycle: preliminary investigation, systems analysis, systems design, systems development, systems implementation, and systems maintenance.

Systems Analysis and Design

We described different types of information systems in the last chapter. Now let us consider: What, exactly, is a **system**? We can define it as a collection of activities and elements organized to accomplish a goal. As we saw in Chapter 11, an *information system* is a collection of hardware, software, people, procedures, and data. These work together to provide information essential to running an organization. This information helps to produce a product or service and, for profit-oriented businesses, derive a profit.

Information about orders received, products shipped, money owed, and so on, flows into an organization from the outside. Information about what supplies have been received, which customers have paid their bills, and so on, also flows within the organization. To avoid confusion, the flow of information must follow a route that is defined by a set of rules and procedures. However, from time to time, organizations need to change their information systems. Reasons include organizational growth, mergers and acquisitions, new marketing opportunities, revisions in governmental regulations, and availability of new technology.

Systems analysis and design is a six-phase problem-solving procedure for examining and improving an information system. The six phases make up the **systems life cycle.** (See Figure 13-1.) The phases are as follows:

1. *Preliminary investigation:* The information problems or needs are identified.
2. *Systems analysis:* The present system is studied in depth. New requirements are specified.

3. *Systems design:* A new or alternative information system is designed.
4. *Systems development:* New hardware and software are acquired, developed, and tested.
5. *Systems implementation:* The new information system is installed and adapted to the new system, and people are trained to use it.
6. *Systems maintenance:* In this ongoing phase, the system is periodically evaluated and updated as needed.

In organizations, this six-phase systems life cycle is used by computer professionals known as **systems analysts.** These people study an organization's systems to determine what actions to take and how to use computer technology to assist them. A recent survey by *Money* magazine compared salary, prestige, and security of 100 widely held jobs. The top job classification was computer engineer, followed by computer systems analyst.

As an end user, working alone or with a systems analyst, it is important that you understand how the systems life cycle works. In fact, you may *have* to use the procedure. More and more end users are developing their own information systems. This is because in many organizations there is a three-year backlog of work for systems analysts. For instance, suppose you recognize that there is a need for certain information within your organization. Obtaining this information will require the introduction of new hardware and software. You go to seek expert help from systems analysts in studying these information needs. At that point you discover that the systems analysts are so overworked it will take them three years to get to your request! You can see, then, why many managers are learning to do these activities themselves. In any case, learning the six steps described in this chapter will raise your computer competency. It also will give you skills to solve a wide range of problems. These skills can make you more valuable to an organization.

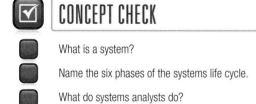

Figure 13-1 The six-phase systems life cycle

CONCEPT CHECK

- What is a system?
- Name the six phases of the systems life cycle.
- What do systems analysts do?

Phase 1: Preliminary Investigation

The first phase of the systems life cycle is a **preliminary investigation** of a proposed project to determine the need for a new information system. This usually is requested by an end user or a manager who wants something done that is not presently being done. For example, suppose you work for

Figure 13-2 **Preliminary investigation**

Advantage Advertising, a fast-growing advertising agency. Advantage Advertising produces a variety of different ads for a wide range of different clients. The agency employs both regular staff workers and on-call freelancers. One of your responsibilities is keeping track of the work performed for each client and the employees who performed the work. In addition, you are responsible for tabulating the final bill for each project. (See Figure 13-2.)

How do you figure out how to charge which clients for which work done by which employees? This kind of problem is common to many service organizations (such as lawyers' and contractors' offices). Indeed, it is a problem in any organization where people charge for their time and clients need proof of hours worked.

In Phase 1, the systems analyst—or the end user—is concerned with three tasks: (1) briefly defining the problem, (2) suggesting alternative solutions, and (3) preparing a short report. (See Figure 13-3.) This report will help management decide whether to pursue the project further. (If you are an end user employing this procedure for yourself, you may not produce a written report. Rather, you would report your findings directly to your supervisor.)

Defining the Problem

Defining the problem means examining whatever current information system is in use. Determining what information is needed, by whom, when, and why is accomplished by interviewing and making observations. If the information system is large, this survey is done by a systems analyst. If the system is small, the survey can be done by the end user.

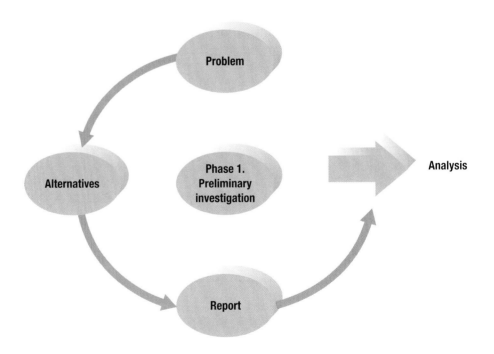

Figure 13-3 **Phase 1: Preliminary investigation**

For example, suppose Advantage Advertising account executives, copywriters, and graphic artists currently just record the time spent on different jobs on their desk calendars. (Examples might be "Client A, telephone conference, 15 minutes"; "Client B, design layout, 2 hours.") After interviewing several account executives and listening to their frustrations, it becomes clear that the approach is somewhat disorganized. (See Figure 13-4.) Written calendar entries are too unprofessional to be shown to clients. Moreover, a large job often has many people working on it. It is difficult to pull together all their notations to make up a bill for the client. Some freelancers work at home, and their time slips are not readily available. These matters constitute a statement of the problem: The company has a manual time-and-billing system that is slow and difficult to implement.

Figure 13-4 One step in defining problems with the current system is to interview executives

As an end user, you might experience difficulties with this system yourself. You're in someone else's office, and a telephone call comes in for you from a client. Your desk calendar is back in your own office. You have two choices. You can always carry your calendar with you, or you can remember to note the time you spent on various tasks when you return to your office. The secretary to the account executive is continually after you (and everyone else at Advantage) to provide photocopies of your calendar. This is so that various clients can be billed for the work done on various jobs. Surely, you think, there must be a better way to handle time and billing.

Suggesting Alternative Systems

This step is simply to suggest some possible plans as alternatives to the present arrangement. For instance, Advantage could hire more secretaries to collect the information from everyone's calendars (including telephoning those working at home). Or it could use the existing system of network-linked microcomputers that staffers and freelancers presently use. Perhaps, you think, there is already some off-the-shelf packaged software available that could be used for a time-and-billing system. At least there might be one that would make your own job easier.

Preparing a Short Report

For large projects, the systems analyst writes a report summarizing the results of the preliminary investigation and suggesting alternative systems. The report also may include schedules for further development of the project. This document is presented to higher management, along with a recommendation to continue or discontinue the project. Management then decides whether to finance the second phase, the systems analysis.

For Advantage Advertising, your report might point out that billing is frequently delayed. It could say that some tasks may even "slip through the cracks" and not get charged at all. Thus, as the analyst has noted, you suggest the project might pay for itself merely by eliminating lost or forgotten charges.

CONCEPT CHECK

What is the purpose of the preliminary investigation phase?

What are the three tasks the systems analyst is concerned with during this phase?

Phase 2: Systems Analysis

In Phase 2, **systems analysis,** data is collected about the present system. This data is then analyzed, and new requirements are determined. We are not concerned with a new design here, only with determining the *requirements* for a new system. Systems analysis is concerned with gathering and analyzing the data. This usually is completed by documenting the analysis in a report. (See Figure 13-5.)

Gathering Data

When gathering data, the systems analyst—or the end user doing systems analysis—expands on the data gathered during Phase 1. He or she adds details about how the current system works. Data is obtained from observation and

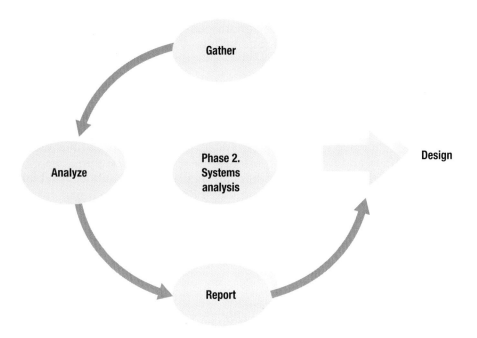

Figure 13-5 Phase 2: Systems analysis

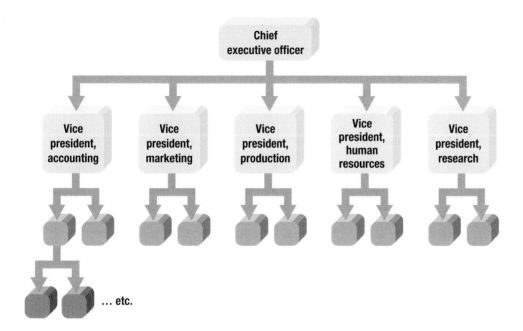

Figure 13-6 **Example of an organization chart**

interviews. In addition, data may be obtained from questionnaires given to people using the system. Data also is obtained from studying documents that describe the formal lines of authority and standard operating procedures. One document is the **organization chart,** which shows levels of management and formal lines of authority. (See Figure 13-6.) You might note that an organization chart resembles the hierarchy of three levels of management we described in Chapter 11. The levels are top managers, middle managers, and supervisors.

Note in our illustration in Figure 13-6 that we have preserved the department labeled "Production." However, the name in an advertising agency might be something like "Creative Services." Obviously, the products an advertising agency produces are ads: radio and television commercials, magazine and newspaper ads, billboard ads, and so on. In any case, if the agency is working on a major advertising campaign, people from several departments might be involved. There also might be people from different management levels within the departments. Their time charges will vary, depending on how much they are paid.

Analyzing the Data

In the data analysis step, the idea is to learn how information currently flows and to pinpoint why it isn't flowing appropriately. The whole point of this step is to apply logic to the existing arrangement to see how workable it is. Many times, the current system is not operating correctly because prescribed procedures are not being followed. That is, the system may not really need to be redesigned. Rather, the people in it may need to be shown how to follow correct procedures.

Many different tools are available to assist systems analysts and end users in the analysis phase. Some of the principal ones are as follows:

- **Checklists:** Numerous checklists are available to assist in this stage. A checklist is a list of questions. It is helpful in guiding the systems analyst and end user through key issues for the present system.

Figure 13-7 **Example of a grid chart**

Forms (input)	Reports (output)		
	Client billing	Personnel expense	Support cost
Time sheet	✓	✓	
Telephone log	✓		✓
Travel log	✓		✓

For example, one question might be "Can reports be prepared easily from the files and documents currently in use?" Another might be "How easily can the present time-and-billing system adapt to change and growth?"

- **Top-down analysis method:** The top-down analysis method is used to identify the top-level components of a complex system. Each component is then broken down into smaller and smaller components. This approach makes each component easier to analyze and deal with.

  For instance, the systems analyst might look at the present kind of bill submitted to a client for a complex advertising campaign. The analyst might note the categories of costs—employee salaries, telephone and mailing charges, travel, supplies, and so on.

- **Grid charts:** A grid chart shows the relationship between input and output documents. An example is shown in Figure 13-7 that indicates the relationship between the data input and the outputs.

  For instance, a time sheet is one of many inputs that produces a particular report, such as a client's bill. Other inputs might be forms having to do with telephone conferences and travel expenses. On a grid sheet, rows represent inputs, such as time sheet forms. Columns represent output documents, such as different clients' bills. A check mark at the intersection of a row and column means that the input document is used to create the output document.

- **Decision tables:** A decision table shows the decision rules that apply when certain conditions occur. Figure 13-8 shows a decision table to evaluate

Figure 13-8 **Example of a decision table**

Conditions	Decision rules			
	1	2	3	4
1. Project less than $10,000	Y	Y	N	N
2. Good credit history	Y	N	Y	N
Actions	1	2	3	4
1. Accept project	✓	✓	✓	
2. Require deposit		✓	✓	
3. Reject project				✓

whether to accept a client's proposed advertising project. The first decision rule applies if both conditions are met. If the project is less than $10,000 and if the client has a good credit history, the firm will accept the project without requiring a deposit.

- **System flowcharts:** System flowcharts show the flow of input data to processing and finally to output, or distribution of information. An example of a system flowchart keeping track of time for advertising "creative people" is shown in Figure 13-9. The explanation of the symbols used appears in Figure 13-10. Note that this describes the present manual, or noncomputerized, system. (A system flowchart is not the same as a program flowchart, which is very detailed. Program flowcharts are discussed in Chapter 14.)

- **Data flow diagrams:** Data flow diagrams show the data or information flow within an information system. The data is traced from its origin through processing, storage, and output. An example of a data flow diagram is shown in Figure 13-11. The explanation of the symbols used appears in Figure 13-12.

- **Automated design tools:** Automated design tools are software packages that evaluate hardware and software alternatives according to requirements given by the systems analyst. They are also called **computer-aided software engineering (CASE) tools.** These tools are not limited to systems analysis. They are used in systems design and development as well. CASE tools relieve the systems analysts of many repetitive tasks, develop clear documentation, and, for larger projects, coordinate team member activities.

For a summary of the analysis tools, see Figure 13-13.

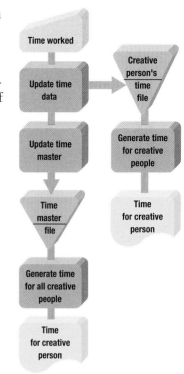

Figure 13-9 Example of a system flowchart

Documenting Systems Analysis

In larger organizations, the systems analysis stage is typically documented in a report for higher management. The **systems analysis report** describes the current information system, the requirements for a new system, and a possible development schedule. For example, at Advantage Advertising, the system flowcharts show the present flow of information in a manual time-and-billing

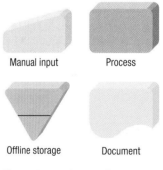

Figure 13-10 System flowchart symbols

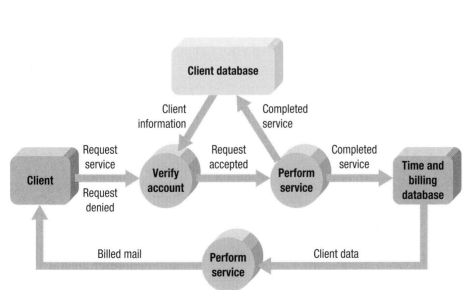

Figure 13-11 Example of a data flow diagram

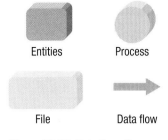

Entities   Process

File   Data flow

Figure 13-12 Data flow diagram symbols

Tool	Description
Checklist	Provides a list of questions about key issues
Top-down analysis	Divides a complex system into components, beginning at the top
Grid chart	Shows relationships between inputs and outputs
Decision table	Specifies decision rules and circumstances when specific rules are to be applied
System flowchart	Shows movement of input data, processing, and output or distribution of information
Data flow diagram	Shows data flow within an organization or application
Automated design tools	Automates the analysis, design, and development of information systems

Figure 13-13 Summary of analysis tools

system. Some boxes in the system flowchart might be replaced with symbols showing where a computerized information system could work better.

Management studies the report and decides whether to continue with the project. Let us assume your boss and higher management have decided to continue. You now move on to Phase 3, systems design.

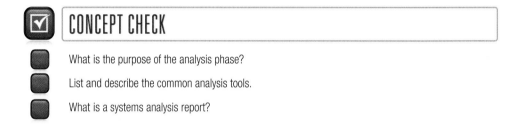

CONCEPT CHECK

What is the purpose of the analysis phase?

List and describe the common analysis tools.

What is a systems analysis report?

Phase 3: Systems Design

Phase 3 is **systems design.** It consists of three tasks: (1) designing alternative systems, (2) selecting the best system, and (3) writing a systems design report. (See Figure 13-14.)

Designing Alternative Systems

In almost all instances, more than one design can be developed to meet the information needs. Systems designers evaluate each alternative system for feasibility. By feasibility we mean three things:

* **Economic feasibility:** Will the costs of the new system be justified by the benefits it promises? How long will it take for the new system to pay for itself?
* **Technical feasibility:** Are reliable hardware, software, and training available to make the system work? If not, can they be obtained?

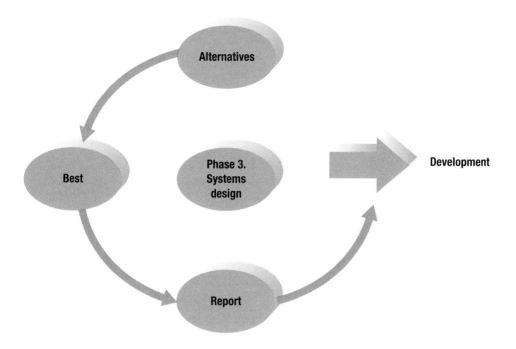

Figure 13-14 **Phase 3: Systems design**

- **Operational feasibility:** Can the system actually be made to operate in the organization, or will people—employees, managers, clients—resist it?

Selecting the Best System

When choosing the best design, managers must consider these four questions: (1) Will the system fit in with the organization's overall information system? (2) Will the system be flexible enough so it can be modified in the future? (3) Can it be made secure against unauthorized use? (4) Are the benefits worth the costs?

For example, one aspect you have to consider at Advantage Advertising is security. Should freelancers and outside vendors enter data directly into a computerized time-and-billing system, or should they keep submitting time sheets manually? In allowing these outside people to input information directly, are you also allowing them access to files they should not see? Do these files contain confidential information, perhaps information of value to rival advertising agencies?

Writing the Systems Design Report

The **systems design report** is prepared for higher management and describes the alternative designs. It presents the costs versus the benefits and outlines the effect of alternative designs on the organization. It usually concludes by recommending one of the alternatives.

 CONCEPT CHECK

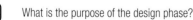

What is the purpose of the design phase?

Distinguish between economic, technical, and operational feasibility.

Identify the factors that need to be considered when choosing the best systems design.

Phase 4: Systems Development

Phase 4 is **systems development.** It has three steps: (1) acquiring software, (2) acquiring hardware, and (3) testing the new system. (See Figure 13-15.)

Acquiring Software

Application software for the new information system can be obtained in two ways. It can be purchased as off-the-shelf packaged software and possibly modified, or it can be custom designed. If any of the software is being specially created, the programming steps we will outline in Chapter 14 should be followed.

With the systems analyst's help, you have looked at time-and-billing packaged software designed for service organizations. Unfortunately, you find that none of the packaged software will do. Most of the packages seem to work well for one person (you). However, none seems to be designed for many people working together. It appears, then, that software will have to be custom designed. (We discuss the process of developing software in Chapter 14, on programming.)

Acquiring Hardware

Some new systems may not require new computer equipment, but others will. The equipment needed and the places where they are to be installed must be determined. This is a very critical area. Switching or upgrading equipment can be a tremendously expensive proposition. Will a microcomputer system be sufficient as a company grows? Are networks expandable? Will people have to undergo costly training?

The systems analyst tells you that there are several different makes and models of microcomputers currently in use at Advantage Advertising. Fortunately, all are connected by a local area network to a file server that can hold the time-and-billing data. To maintain security, the systems analyst suggests that

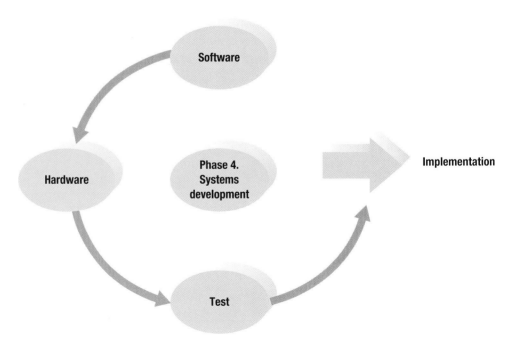

Figure 13-15 Phase 4: Systems development

an electronic mailbox be installed for freelancers and others outside the company. They can use this electronic mailbox to post their time charges. Thus, it appears that existing hardware will work just fine.

Testing the New System

After the software and equipment have been installed, the system should be tested. Sample data is fed into the system. The processed information is then evaluated to see whether results are correct. Testing may take several months if the new system is complex.

For this step, you ask some people in Creative Services to test the system. (See Figure 13-16.) You observe that some of the people have problems knowing where to enter their times. To solve the problem, the software is modified to display an improved user entry screen. After the system has been thoroughly tested and revised as necessary, you are ready to put it into use.

CONCEPT CHECK

 What is the purpose of the development phase?

 What are the ways by which application software can be obtained?

Figure 13-16 **To test a system, sample data is entered and problems are resolved**

Phase 5: Systems Implementation

Another name for Phase 5, **systems implementation,** is **conversion.** It is the process of changing—converting—from the old system to the new one and training people to use the new system. (See Figure 13-17.)

Types of Conversion

There are four approaches to conversion: *direct, parallel, pilot,* and *phased.*

- In the **direct approach,** the conversion is done simply by abandoning the old and starting up the new. This can be risky. If anything is still wrong with the new system, the old system is no longer available to fall back on.

  The direct approach is not recommended precisely because it is so risky. Problems, big or small, invariably crop up in a new system. In a large system, a problem might just mean catastrophe.

- In the **parallel approach,** old and new systems are operated side by side until the new one proves to be reliable.

  This approach is low-risk. If the new system fails, the organization can just switch to the old system to keep going. However, keeping enough equipment and people active to manage two systems at the same time can be very expensive. Thus, the parallel approach is used only in cases in which the cost of failure or of interrupted operation is great.

- In the **pilot approach,** the new system is tried out in only one part of the organization. Once the system is working smoothly in that part, it is implemented throughout the rest of the organization.

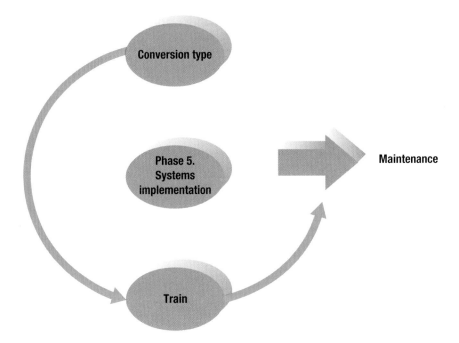

Figure 13-17 **Phase 5: Systems implementation**

The pilot approach is certainly less expensive than the parallel approach. It also is somewhat riskier. However, the risks can be controlled because problems will be confined only to certain areas of the organization. Difficulties will not affect the entire organization.

- In the **phased approach,** the new system is implemented gradually over a period of time.

The entire implementation process is broken down into parts or phases. Implementation begins with the first phase, and once it is successfully implemented, the second phase begins. This process continues until all phases are operating smoothly. This is an expensive proposition because the implementation is done slowly. However, it is certainly one of the least risky approaches.

In general, the pilot and phased approaches are the favored methods. Pilot is preferred when there are many people in an organization performing similar operations—for instance, all sales clerks in a department store. Phased is more appropriate for organizations in which people are performing different operations. For a summary of the different types of conversions, see Figure 13-18.

You and the systems analyst, with top management support, have decided on a pilot implementation. This approach was selected in part based on cost and the availability of a representative group of users. The Creative Services department previously tested the system and has expressed enthusiastic support for it. A group from this department will pilot the implementation of the time-and-billing system.

Training

Training people is important, of course. Unfortunately, it is one of the most commonly overlooked activities. Some people may begin training early, even before the equipment is delivered, so that they can adjust more easily. In some

Type	Description	Discussion
Direct	Abandon the old	Very risky; not recommended
Parallel	Run old and new side by side	Very low risk; however, very expensive; not generally recommended
Pilot	Convert part of organization first	Less expensive but riskier than parallel conversion; recommended for situations with many people performing similar operations
Phased	Implement gradually	Less risky but more expensive than parallel conversion; recommended for situations with many people performing different operations

Figure 13-18 **Types of conversion**

cases, a professional software trainer may be brought in to show people how to operate the system. However, at Advantage Advertising, the time-and-billing software is simple enough that the systems analyst can act as the trainer.

 CONCEPT CHECK

 What is the goal of the implementation phase?

 Briefly describe the four approaches to conversion.

 Which two conversion approaches are favored methods?

Phase 6: Systems Maintenance

After implementation comes **systems maintenance,** the last step in the systems life cycle. This phase is a very important, ongoing activity. Most organizations spend more time and money on this phase than on any of the others. Maintenance has two parts: a *systems audit* and a *periodic evaluation.* (See Figure 13-19.)

In the **systems audit,** the system's performance is compared to the original design specifications. This is to determine whether the new procedures are actually furthering productivity. If they are not, some redesign may be necessary.

After the systems audit, the new information system is further modified, if necessary. All systems should be evaluated from time to time to determine whether they are meeting the goals and providing the service they are supposed to.

The six-step systems life cycle is summarized in Figure 13-20.

 CONCEPT CHECK

 What is the purpose of the maintenance phase?

 Name the two parts of the maintenance phase.

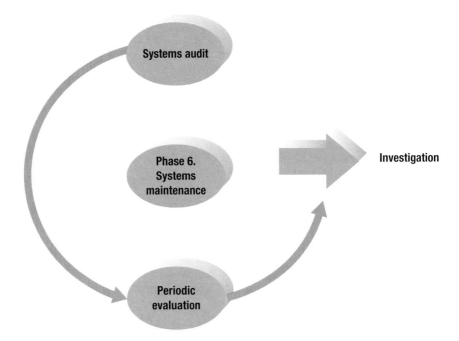

Figure 13-19 **Phase 6: Systems maintenance**

Phase	Activity
1. Preliminary investigation	Define problem, suggest alternatives, prepare short report
2. Systems analysis	Gather data, analyze data, document
3. Systems design	Design alternatives, select best alternative, write report
4. Systems development	Develop software, acquire hardware, test system
5. Systems implementation	Convert, train
6. Systems maintenance	Perform systems audit, evaluate periodically

Figure 13-20 **Summary of systems life cycle**

Prototyping and Rapid Applications Development

Is it necessary to follow every phase of the systems life cycle? It may be desirable, but often there is no time to do so. For instance, hardware may change so fast that there is no opportunity for evaluation, design, and testing as just described. Two alternative approaches that require much less time are *prototyping* and *rapid applications development*.

Prototyping

Prototyping means to build a *model* or *prototype* that can be modified before the actual system is installed. For instance, the systems analyst for Advantage Advertising might develop a proposed or prototype menu as a possible screen display for the time-and-billing system. Users would try it out and provide feedback to the systems analyst. The systems analyst would revise the prototype until the users felt it was ready to put into place. Typically, the development time for prototyping is shorter; however, it is sometimes more difficult to manage the project and to control costs. (See Figure 13-21.)

Rapid Applications Development

Rapid applications development (RAD) involves the use of powerful development software, small specialized teams, and highly trained personnel. For example, the systems analyst for Advantage Advertising would use specialized development software like CASE, form small teams consisting of select users and managers, and obtain assistance from other highly qualified analysts. Although the resulting time-and-billing system would likely cost more, the development time would be shorter and the quality of the completed system would be better.

Figure 13-21 Serena offers prototyping software.

CONCEPT CHECK

  What is prototyping?

  What is RAD?

  What is the advantage of these two approaches over the systems life cycle approach?

Careers in IT

A **systems analyst** follows the steps described in the systems life cycle. (See Figure 13-22.) Analysts plan and design new systems or reorganize a company's computer resources to best utilize them. Analysts follow the systems life cycle through all its steps: preliminary investigation, analysis, design, development, implementation, and maintenance.

Systems analyst positions normally require a bachelor's degree in computer science or information systems and technical experience. Internships and prior experience with the latest technology are a considerable advantage for those seeking jobs in this industry. Systems analysts can expect to earn an annual salary of $54,500 to $87,500. Opportunities for advancement include positions as a chief technology officer or other managerial opportunities.

To learn about other careers in information technology, visit us at www.computing2011.com and enter the keyword **careers.**

Figure 13-22 Systems analyst

A LOOK TO THE FUTURE

The Challenge of Keeping Pace

Most observers firmly believe that the pace of business is now faster than ever before. The time to develop a product and bring it to market in many cases is now months rather than years. Internet technologies, in particular, have provided tools to support the rapid introduction of new products and services.

To stay competitive, corporations must integrate these new technologies into their existing way of doing business. In many cases, the traditional systems life cycle approach takes too long—sometimes years—to develop a system. Many organizations are responding by aggressively

implementing prototyping and RAD. Others are enlisting the services of outside consulting groups that specialize in systems development.

One such company is Drapkin Technology. Drapkin provides technical expertise and managerial experience to the systems analysis and design process. Working with corporations such as Gateway and Sony, the company provides project assessment, analysis, design, development, implementation, and administration. Drapkin also can step in and quickly reorganize projects when the systems life cycle fails—a crucial service in and of itself.

Using IT at DVD Direct—a case study

SYSTEMS ANALYSIS AND DESIGN AT DVD DIRECT

DVD Direct, a fictitious organization, is an entirely Web-oriented movie rental business. Its customers order movies from DVD Direct's Web site and the movies are delivered on DVD disks by mail. While business has been good, some recent indications have pointed to possible trouble ahead. Specifically, an internal study discovered that many current and potential customers with high-bandwidth Internet connections prefer to have movies delivered over the Internet rather than by mail. Further, the study reported that current customers who recently switched to high-bandwidth connections were very likely to drop their DVD Direct membership.

In response, top management has committed to expanding DVD Direct's business model to include online delivery of movies using streaming video technology. Once an order is placed, the Internet-delivered movies would be immediately downloaded onto the member's hard disk. The movie would remain there for a week, or until the movie was played, whichever occurs first.

Alice, a recently hired marketing analyst, has proposed the creation of a Frequent Renters Club that gives members points for each streaming movie they order. As a member's points accumulate, the points can be redeemed for gifts and free rentals. To follow Alice as she meets with Bob, the vice president of marketing, to discuss the proposed Frequent Renters Club, visit us on the Web at www.computing2011.com and enter the keyword design.

"The key is to develop an information system that accurately and consistently records reward points."

SYSTEMS ANALYSIS AND DESIGN

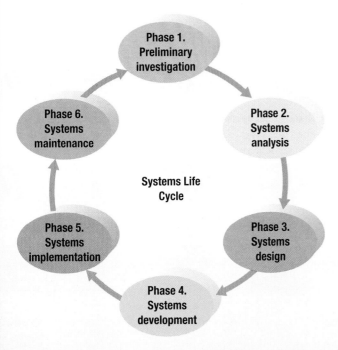

A **system** is a collection of activities and elements organized to accomplish a goal. **Systems analysis and design** is a six-phase problem-solving procedure that makes up the **systems life cycle.** The phases are

- *Preliminary investigation*—identifying problems or needs.
- *Systems analysis*—studying present system and specifying new requirements.
- *Systems design*—designing new or alternative system to meet new requirements.
- *Systems development*—acquiring, developing, and testing needed hardware and software.
- *Systems implementation*—installing new system and training people.
- *Systems maintenance*—periodically evaluating and updating system as needed.

Systems analysts are computer professionals who typically conduct systems analysis and design.

PHASE 1: PRELIMINARY INVESTIGATION

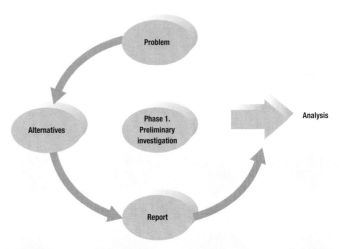

The **preliminary investigation** determines the need for a new information system. It is typically requested by an end user or a manager. Three tasks of this phase are defining the problem, suggesting alternative systems, and preparing a report.

Defining the Problem

The current information system is examined to determine who needs what information, when the information is needed, and why.

If the existing information system is large, then a **systems analyst** conducts the survey. Otherwise, the end user conducts the survey.

Suggesting Alternative Systems

Some possible alternative systems are suggested. Based on interviews and observations made in defining the problem, alternative information systems are identified.

Preparing a Short Report

To document and communicate the findings of Phase 1, preliminary investigation, a short report is prepared and presented to management.

To be a competent end user, you need to understand the importance of systems analysis and design. You need to know the six phases of the systems development life cycle: preliminary investigation, analysis, design, development, implementation, and maintenance. Additionally, you need to understand prototyping and RAD.

PHASE 2: SYSTEMS ANALYSIS

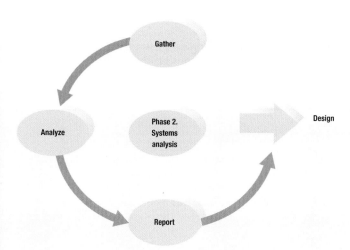

In **systems analysis,** data is collected about the present system. The focus is on determining the requirements for a new system. Three tasks of this phase are gathering data, analyzing the data, and documenting the analysis.

Gathering Data
Data is gathered by observation, interviews, questionnaires, and looking at documents. One helpful document is the **organization chart,** which shows a company's functions and levels of management.

Analyzing the Data
There are several tools for the analysis of data, including **checklists, top-down analysis, grid charts, decision tables,** and **system flowcharts.**

Documenting Systems Analysis
To document and communicate the findings of Phase 2, a **systems analysis report** is prepared for higher management.

Forms (input)	Reports (output)		
	Client billing	Personnel expense	Support cost
Time sheet	✓	✓	
Telephone log	✓		✓
Travel log	✓		✓

PHASE 3: SYSTEMS DESIGN

In the **systems design** phase, a new or alternative information system is designed. This phase consists of three tasks:

Designing Alternative Systems
Alternative information systems are designed. Each alternative is evaluated for

- **Economic feasibility**—cost versus benefits; time for the system to pay for itself.
- **Technical feasibility**—hardware and software reliability; available training.
- **Operational feasibility**—will the system work within the organization?

Selecting the Best System
Four questions should be considered when selecting the best system:

- Will the system fit into an overall information system?
- Will the system be flexible enough to be modified as needed in the future?
- Will it be secure against unauthorized use?
- Will the system's benefits exceed its costs?

Writing the Systems Design Report
To document and communicate the findings of Phase 3, a **systems design report** is prepared for higher management.

PHASE 4: SYSTEMS DEVELOPMENT

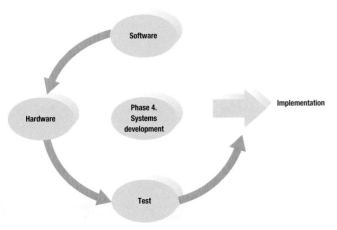

In the **systems development** phase, software and hardware are acquired and tested.

Acquiring Software

Two ways to acquire software are purchasing off-the-shelf packaged software and designing custom programs.

Acquiring Hardware

Acquiring hardware involves consideration for future company growth, existing networks, communication capabilities, and training.

Testing the New System

Using sample data, the new system is tested. This step can take several months for a complex system.

PHASE 5: SYSTEMS IMPLEMENTATION

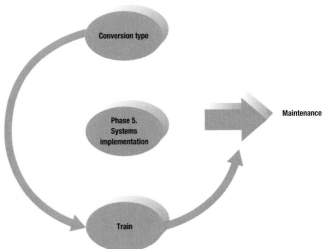

Systems implementation (conversion) is the process of changing to the new system and training people.

Types of Conversion

Four ways to convert are

- **Direct approach**—abandoning the old system and starting up the new system; can be very risky and not recommended.
- **Parallel approach**—running the old and new side by side until the new system proves its worth; very low risk; however, very expensive; not generally recommended.
- **Pilot approach**—converting only one part of the organization to the new system until new system proves its worth; less expensive but riskier than parallel conversion; recommended for situations with many people performing similar operations.
- **Phased approach**—gradually implementing the new system to the entire organization; less risky but more expensive than parallel conversion; recommended for situation with many people performing different operations.

Training

Training is important, however, often overlooked. Some people may train early as the equipment is being delivered, so they can adjust more easily. Sometimes a professional trainer is used; other times the systems analyst acts as the trainer.

PHASE 6: SYSTEMS MAINTENANCE

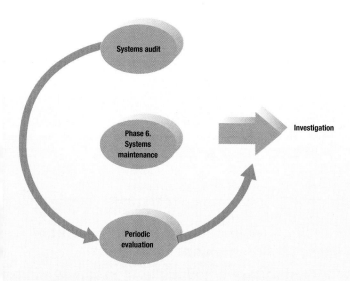

Systems maintenance consists of a systems audit followed by periodic evaluation.

Systems Audit

Once the system is operational, the systems analyst performs a **systems audit** by comparing the new system to its original design specifications.

Periodic Evaluation

The new system is periodically evaluated to ensure that it is operating efficiently.

Phase	Activity
1. Preliminary investigation	Define problem, suggest alternatives, prepare short report
2. Systems analysis	Gather data, analyze data, document
3. Systems design	Design alternatives, select best alternative, write report
4. Systems development	Develop software, acquire hardware, test system
5. Systems implementation	Convert, train
6. Systems maintenance	Perform systems audit, evaluate periodically

PROTOTYPING AND RAD

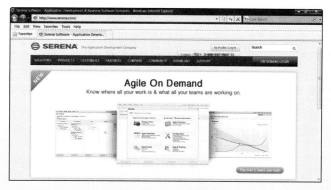

Due to time pressures, it is not always feasible to follow every phase of the systems life cycle. Two alternatives that require less time are *prototyping* and *RAD*.

Prototyping

Prototyping means to build a model or prototype that can be modified before the actual system is installed. Typically, the development time for prototyping is shorter; however, it can be more difficult to manage the project and to control costs.

Rapid Applications Development

Rapid applications development (RAD) uses powerful development software, small specialized teams, and highly trained personnel. Typically, the development costs more. However, the time is much less and the quality is often better.

CAREERS IN IT

Systems analysts plan and design new systems or reorganize a company's computer resources to better utilize them. They follow the systems life cycle through all its steps. Bachelor's degree in computer science or information systems and technical experience required. Salary range $54,500 to $87,500.

KEY TERMS

automated design tools   (377)
checklist   (375)
computer-aided software engineering
   (CASE) tools   (377)
conversion   (381)
data flow diagram   (377)
decision table   (376)
direct approach   (381)
economic feasibility   (378)
grid chart   (376)
operational feasibility   (379)
organization chart   (375)
parallel approach   (381)
phased approach   (382)
pilot approach   (381)
preliminary investigation   (371)
prototyping   (384)

rapid applications development
   (RAD)   (385)
system   (370)
system flowchart   (377)
systems analysis   (374)
systems analysis and design   (370)
systems analysis report   (377)
systems analyst (371, 385)
systems audit   (383)
systems design   (378)
systems design report   (379)
systems development   (380)
systems implementation   (381)
systems life cycle   (370)
systems maintenance   (383)
technical feasibility   (378)
top-down analysis method   (376)

To test your knowledge of these key terms with animated flash cards, visit our Web
site at www.computing2011.com and enter the keyword terms13.

MULTIPLE CHOICE

Circle the letter or fill in the correct answer.

1. In which phase of the systems life cycle are information needs identified?
   a. preliminary investigation
   b. systems analysis
   c. systems design
   d. systems development

2. This phase of the systems life cycle is known as the "ongoing phase," where the system is periodically evaluated and updated as needed.
   a. preliminary investigation
   b. systems design
   c. systems implementation
   d. systems maintenance

3. Which of the following shows levels of management and formal lines of authority?
   a. organization chart
   b. decision table
   c. pyramid diagram
   d. grid chart

4. Which of the following is *not* found on a data flow diagram?
   a. entities
   b. process
   c. locations
   d. file

5. Which of the following tasks is not part of the systems design phase?
   a. designing alternative systems
   b. selecting the best system
   c. writing a systems design report
   d. suggesting alternative solutions

6. Determining if employees, managers, and clients will resist a proposed new system is part of this feasibility study.
   a. technical feasibility
   b. economic feasibility
   c. organizational feasibility
   d. operational feasibility

7. The _____ approach conversion type simply involves abandoning the old system and using the new.
   a. direct
   b. pilot
   c. phased
   d. parallel

8. In the _____ implementation approach, the new system is broken down into smaller parts that are implemented over time.
   a. pilot
   b. direct
   c. parallel
   d. phased

9. The ongoing testing and analysis of an existing system is called systems _____.
   a. maintenance
   b. implementation
   c. design
   d. analysis

10. Which of the following is a disadvantage to prototyping?
    a. quick user feedback
    b. lengthy development times
    c. difficult to manage
    d. lack of user feedback

For an interactive multiple-choice practice test, visit our Web site at www.computing
2011.com and enter the keyword multiple13.

MATCHING

Match each numbered item with the most closely related lettered item. Write your answers in the spaces provided.

a. data flow diagram
b. economic feasibility
c. grid chart
d. organization chart
e. phased approach
f. preliminary investigation
g. systems analysis and design
h. systems analyst
i. systems design report
j. systems development

1. Six-phase procedure for examining and improving information systems. _____
2. Computer professional who studies an organization's systems. _____
3. The first phase of the systems life cycle. _____
4. Chart showing management levels and formal lines of authority. _____
5. Shows the relationship between input and output documents. _____
6. Shows the data or information flow within an information system. _____
7. Condition where cost of designing a system is justified by the benefits. _____
8. Report for higher management describing the alternative designs suggested in the design phase. _____
9. Phase consisting of developing software, acquiring hardware, and testing the new system. _____
10. Implementation gradually over a period of time. _____

For an interactive matching practice test, visit our Web site at www.computing2011 .com and enter the keyword matching13.

OPEN-ENDED

On a separate sheet of paper, respond to each question or statement.

1. What is a system? What are the six phases of the systems life cycle? Why do corporations undergo this process?
2. What are the tools used in the analysis phase? What is top-down analysis? How is it used?
3. Describe each type of system conversion. Which is the most commonly used?
4. What is systems maintenance? When does it occur?
5. Explain prototyping and RAD. When might they be used by corporations?

APPLYING TECHNOLOGY

The following questions are designed to demonstrate ways that you can effectively use technology today.

① SYSTEMS DESIGN SOFTWARE

To learn more about systems design software, visit our Web site at www.computing2011 .com and enter the keyword system. Once connected, select one of these tools and read about it. Then answer the following questions: (a) What is the product, and what does it do? (b) What types of projects could you use it for? (c) What types of professionals could use this product? Provide specific examples.

② SYSTEMS ANALYSIS SOFTWARE

There are several companies that specialize in systems analysis support software. Connect to our Web site at www.computing2011.com and enter the keyword analysis to link to one of these organizations. Explore the products the company offers. Then answer the following: (a) Describe the products designed to enhance systems analysis. (b) For each product you described, list the phase or phases of the systems life cycle it applies to. (c) Visit our Web site at www.computing2011.com and enter the keyword design to review the DVD Direct case study. Pick a product that could assist Alice and Mia, and describe how. Be specific.

③ PRELIMINARY INVESTIGATION

The first phase of the systems analysis and design process is a preliminary investigation. Perform this phase for either a new computer system you'd like to purchase or an upgrade to your current system. (Hint: See the Buyer's Guide and Upgrader's Guide at the end of this book.) Document each step of the preliminary investigation in a one-page paper: (a) Define the problem. (b) Suggest at least three alternatives. (c) Write a preliminary investigation summary.

EXPANDING YOUR KNOWLEDGE

The following questions are designed to add depth and detail to your understanding of specific topics presented within this chapter. The questions direct you to sources other than the textbook to obtain this knowledge.

1 DVD DIRECT SYSTEMS ANALYSIS AND DESIGN

DVD Direct is planning to implement a Frequent Renters Club. The key to successful implementation is the development of an information system that accurately and consistently records reward points. To learn more about DVD Direct's plans, visit us on the Web at www.computing2011.com and enter the keyword design. (a) Describe the six sequential phases of systems analysis and design as they relate to the Frequent Renters Club information system. (b) If you were developing this information system, would you use prototyping or a full systems analysis and design approach? Why? (c) If you were developing this information system, would you use rapid applications development or a full systems analysis and design approach? Why?

2 CONVERSION

To learn more about how DVD Direct plans to convert to its new information system, visit us on the Web at www.computing2011.com and enter the keyword design. Then answer the following: (a) Define the term *conversion* and briefly describe each conversion type. (b) What type of conversion do Alice and Mia use for implementing the new DVD Direct system? (c) Do you agree that this was the best choice for DVD Direct? Why or why not?

3 UML

Uniform Modeling Language, or UML, is being used more extensively in industry to assist in systems analysis. Research UML on the Internet, and then answer the following questions: (a) What is UML? (b) What details of a project does UML focus on? (c) How is defining a project with UML different than in plain English? What are the advantages and disadvantages to each?

WRITING ABOUT TECHNOLOGY

The ability to think critically and to write effectively is essential to nearly every profession. The following questions are designed to help you develop these skills by posing thought-provoking questions about computer privacy, security, and/or ethics.

LEGACY SYSTEMS

The term *legacy systems* refers to systems in which an organization has already invested significant time and money. Often, when a systems audit reveals that a system change is necessary, it is cheaper to patch the existing system rather than create a new one. Over time, this can lead to systems that are expensive to maintain and difficult to modify. Research issues related to legacy systems and write a one-page paper that addresses the following: (a) Define the term *legacy system.* (b) What problems can legacy systems present? (c) What problems can system upgrades present? (d) How can an analyst determine whether it is more cost-effective to maintain or upgrade a legacy system? (e) Identify any security and privacy concerns that might be associated with legacy systems.

MANAGING CHOICES

Consider the following scenario and then answer the questions that follow in a one-page paper: You're a manager who comes up with a new system that will make your company more efficient. However, implementing this system would make several tasks obsolete and cost many of your co-workers their jobs. (a) What is your ethical obligation to your company in this situation? (b) What is your ethical obligation to your co-workers? (c) What would you do in this situation? Defend your answer.

Programming and Languages

Competencies

After you have read this chapter, you should be able to:

1. Define programming and describe the six steps of programming.

2. Discuss design tools including top-down design, pseudocode, flowcharts, and logic structures.

3. Describe program testing and the tools for finding and removing errors.

4. Describe CASE tools and object-oriented software development.

5. Explain the five generations of programming languages.

One of the earliest versions of the Windows operating system was built on a few million lines of code. Just a few generations later, that same operating system used nearly 20 times that number. This growth could be concerning, as we imagine a future where programs are so large and take so long to program that they are unaffordable. Today's software is generally broken into smaller pieces called objects and reused. This helps streamline the development time and cost of new software.

Some experts predict that the future of programming features objects, human language, and artificial intelligence. Imagine a world where you could create a program in collaboration with your computer. You might begin by writing a paragraph describing the program you want. The computer would take those instructions and compose your software using existing code and new lines it creates.

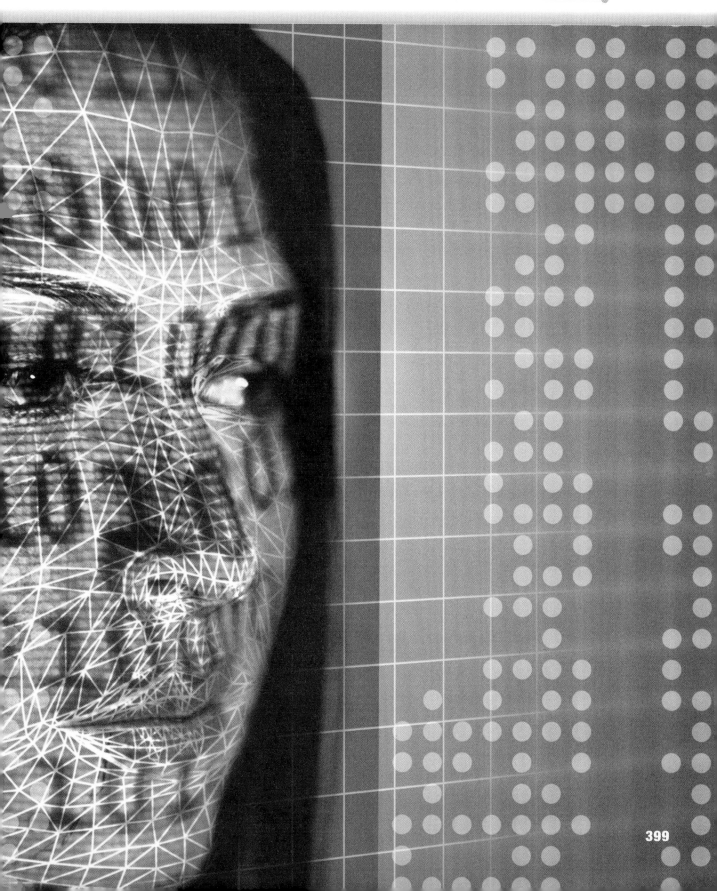

chapter **14**

399

Introduction

How do you go about getting a job? You might look through newspaper classified ads, check with employment services, write to prospective employers, and so on. In other words, you do some general problem solving to come up with a broad plan. This is similar to what you do in systems analysis and design. Once you have determined a particular job, then you do some specific problem solving. That is what you do in programming. In this chapter, we describe programming in two parts: (1) the steps in the programming process and (2) some of the programming languages available.

Why should you need to know anything about programming? The answer is simple. You might need to deal with programmers in the course of your work. You also may be required to do some programming yourself in the future. A growing trend is toward end user software development. This means that end users, like you, are developing their own application programs.

In Chapter 13, we described the six phases of the systems life cycle. Programming is part of Phase 4, systems development. Competent end users need to understand the relationship between systems development and programming. Additionally, they need to know the six steps of programming, including program specification, program design, program code, program test, program documentation, and program maintenance.

Programs and Programming

What exactly is programming? Many people think of it as simply typing words into a computer. That may be part of it, but that is certainly not all of it. Programming, as we've hinted before, is actually a *problem-solving procedure.*

What Is a Program?

To see how programming works, think about what a program is. A **program** is a list of instructions for the computer to follow to accomplish the task of processing data into information. The instructions are made up of statements used in a programming language, such as BASIC, C, or Java.

You are already familiar with some types of programs. As we discussed in Chapters 1 and 3, application programs are widely used to accomplish a variety of different types of tasks. For example, we use word processors to create documents and spreadsheets to analyze data. System programs, on the other hand, focus on tasks necessary to keep the computer running smoothly. These can be purchased and are referred to as prewritten or packaged programs. Programs also can be created or custom-made. In Chapter 13, we saw that the systems analyst looked into the availability of time-and-billing software for Advantage Advertising. Will off-the-shelf software do the job, or should it be custom written? This is one of the first things that needs to be decided in programming.

What Is Programming?

A program is a list of instructions for the computer to follow to process data. **Programming,** also known as **software development,** is a six-step procedure for creating that list of instructions. Only one of those steps consists of typing (keying) statements into a computer. (See Figure 14-1.)

The six steps are as follows:

1. *Program specification:* The program's objectives, outputs, inputs, and processing requirements are determined.
2. *Program design:* A solution is created using programming techniques such as top-down program design, pseudocode, flowcharts, and logic structures.
3. *Program code:* The program is written or coded using a programming language.
4. *Program test:* The program is tested or debugged by looking for syntax and logic errors.
5. *Program documentation:* Documentation is an ongoing process throughout the programming process. This phase focuses on formalizing the written description and processes used in the program.
6. *Program maintenance:* Completed programs are periodically reviewed to evaluate their accuracy, efficiency, standardization, and ease of use. Changes are made to the program's code as needed.

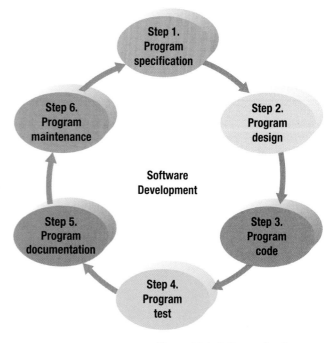

Figure 14-1 Software development

In organizations, computer professionals known as **software engineers** or **programmers** use this six-step procedure. Working closely with systems analysts in systems development, Phase 4 of the systems life cycle, programmers create software required for information systems. In a recent survey by *Money* magazine, software engineers were ranked near the top of over 100 widely held jobs based on salary, prestige, and security.

You may well find yourself working directly with a programmer or indirectly through a systems analyst. Or you may actually do the programming for a system that you develop. Whatever the case, it's important that you understand the six-step programming procedure.

 CONCEPT CHECK

 What is a program?

 What are the six programming steps?

Step 1: Program Specification

Program specification is also called **program definition** or **program analysis.** It requires that the programmer—or you, the end user, if you are following this procedure—specify five items: (1) the program's objectives, (2) the desired output, (3) the input data required, (4) the processing requirements, and (5) the documentation. (See Figure 14-2.)

Program Objectives

You solve all kinds of problems every day. A problem might be deciding how to commute to school or work or which homework or report to do first. Thus, every day you determine your **objectives**—the problems you are trying to

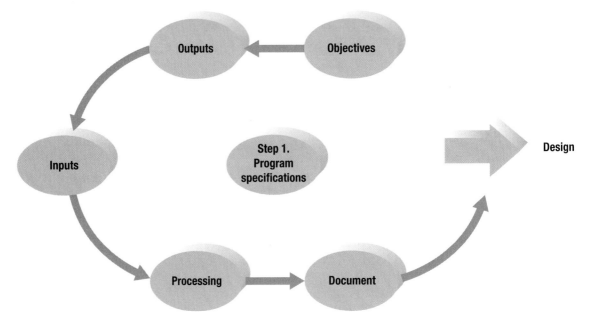

Figure 14-2 **Step 1: Program specification**

solve. Programming is the same. You need to make a clear statement of the problem you are trying to solve. (See Figure 14-3.) An example would be "I want a time-and-billing system to record the time I spend on different jobs for different clients of Advantage Advertising."

Desired Output

It is best always to specify outputs before inputs. That is, you need to list what you want to *get out* of the computer system. Then you should determine what will *go into it*. The best way to do this is to draw a picture. You—the end user, not the programmer—should sketch or write how you want the output to look when it's done. It might be printed out or displayed on the monitor.

For example, if you want a time-and-billing report, you might write or draw something like Figure 14-4. Another form of output from the program might be bills to clients.

Input Data

Once you know the output you want, you can determine the input data and the source of this data. For example, for a time-and-billing report, you can specify that one source of data to be processed should be time cards. These are usually logs or statements of hours worked submitted on paper forms. The log shown in Figure 14-5 is an example of the kind of input data used in Advantage Advertising's manual system. Note that military time is used. For example, instead of writing "5:45 P.M.," people would write "1745."

Processing Requirements

Here you define the processing tasks that must happen for input data to be processed into output. For Advantage, one of the tasks for the program will be to add the hours worked for different jobs for different clients.

Figure 14-3 **Problem definition: Make a clear statement of the problem**

Figure 14-4 **End user's sketch of desired output**

Client name: Allen Realty			Month and year: Jan '10	
Date	Worker	Regular Hours & Rate	Overtime Hours & Rate	Bill
1/2	M. Jones	5 @ $10	1 @ $15	$65.00
	K. Williams	4 @ $30	2 @ $45	$210.00

Daily Log

Worker:
Date:

Client	Job	Time in	Time out
A	TV commercial	800	915
B	Billboard ad	935	1200
C	Brochure	1315	1545
D	Magazine ad	1600	1745

Figure 14-5 **Example of input data for hours worked expressed in military time**

Program Specifications Document

As in the systems life cycle, ongoing documentation is essential. You should record program objectives, desired outputs, needed inputs, and required processing. This leads to the next step, program design.

  CONCEPT CHECK

What is program specification?

What are the five tasks of the program specification phase?

Step 2: Program Design

After program specification, you begin **program design.** (See Figure 14-6.) Here you plan a solution, preferably using **structured programming techniques.** These techniques consist of the following: (1) top-down program design, (2) pseudocode, (3) flowcharts, and (4) logic structures.

Top-Down Program Design

First determine the outputs and inputs for the program. Then use **top-down program design** to identify the program's processing steps. Such steps are

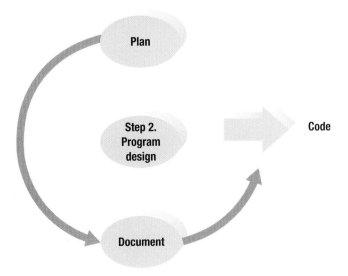

Figure 14-6 Step 2: Program design

called **program modules** (or just **modules**). Each module is made up of logically related program statements.

An example of a top-down program design for a time-and-billing report is shown in Figure 14-7. Each of the boxes shown is a module. Under the rules of top-down design, each module should have a single function. The program must pass in sequence from one module to the next until all modules have been processed by the computer. Three of the boxes—"Obtain input," "Compute hours for billing," and "Produce output"—correspond to the three principal computer system operations: *input, process,* and *output.*

Pseudocode

Pseudocode (pronounced "soo-doh-code") is an outline of the logic of the program you will write. It is like doing a summary of the program before it is written. Figure 14-8 shows the pseudocode you might write for one module in the time-and-billing program. This shows the reasoning behind determining hours—including overtime hours—worked for different jobs for one client, Client A. Again, note this expresses the *logic* of what you want the program to do.

Flowcharts

We mentioned system flowcharts in the previous chapter. Here we are concerned with **program flowcharts.** These graphically present the detailed sequence of steps needed to solve a programming problem. Figure 14-9 presents several of the standard flowcharting symbols. An example of a program flowchart is presented in Figure 14-10. This flowchart expresses all the logic for just one module—"Compute time on Client A jobs"—in the top-down program design.

Perhaps you can see from this flowchart why a computer is a computer, and not just a fancy adding machine. A computer does more than arithmetic. It also *makes comparisons*—whether something is greater than or less than, equal to or not equal to.

But have we skipped something? How do we know which kind of twists and turns to put in a flowchart so that it will work logically?

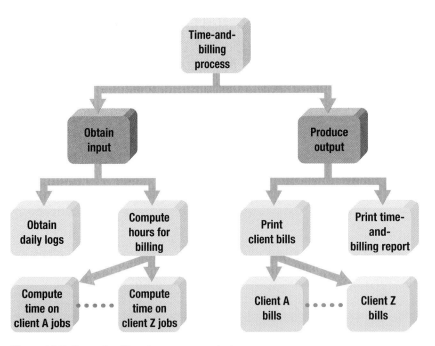

Figure 14-7 Example of top-down program design

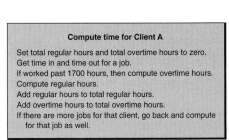

Compute time for Client A

Set total regular hours and total overtime hours to zero.
Get time in and time out for a job.
If worked past 1700 hours, then compute overtime hours.
Compute regular hours.
Add regular hours to total regular hours.
Add overtime hours to total overtime hours.
If there are more jobs for that client, go back and compute for that job as well.

Figure 14-8 Example of pseudocode

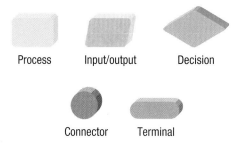

Process   Input/output   Decision

Connector   Terminal

Figure 14-9 Flowchart symbols

The answer is based on the use of logic structures, as we will explain.

Logic Structures

How do you link the various parts of the flowchart? The best way is a combination of three **logic structures** called *concatenation, selection,* and *repetition*. Using these arrangements enables you to write so-called structured programs, which take much of the guesswork out of programming. Let us look at the logic structures.

- In the **concatenation structure,** one program statement follows another. (See Figure 14-11.) Consider, for example, the "compute time" flowchart. (Refer back to Figure 14-10.) The two "add" boxes are "Add regular hours to total regular hours" and "Add overtime hours to total overtime hours." They logically follow each other. There is no question of "yes" or "no," of a decision suggesting other consequences.

- The **selection structure** occurs when a decision must be made. The outcome of the decision determines which of two paths to follow. (See Figure 14-12.) This structure is also known as an **IF-THEN-ELSE structure** because that is how you can formulate the decision. Consider, for example, the selection structure in the "compute time" flowchart, which is concerned about computing overtime hours. (Refer to Figure 14-10.) It might be expressed in detail as follows:

> **IF hour finished for this job is later than 1700 hours (5:00 P.M.),**
> **THEN overtime hours equal the number of hours past 1700 hours,**
> **ELSE overtime hours equal zero.**

- The **repetition** or **loop structure** describes a process that may be repeated as long as a certain condition remains true. The structure is called a "loop" or "iteration" because the program loops around (iterates or repeats) again and again. The repetition structure has

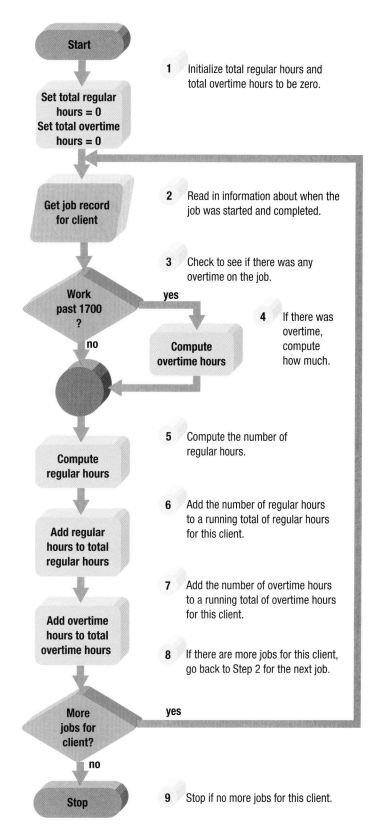

1   Initialize total regular hours and total overtime hours to be zero.

2   Read in information about when the job was started and completed.

3   Check to see if there was any overtime on the job.

4   If there was overtime, compute how much.

5   Compute the number of regular hours.

6   Add the number of regular hours to a running total of regular hours for this client.

7   Add the number of overtime hours to a running total of overtime hours for this client.

8   If there are more jobs for this client, go back to Step 2 for the next job.

9   Stop if no more jobs for this client.

Figure 14-10 Flowchart for "Compute time on Client A jobs"

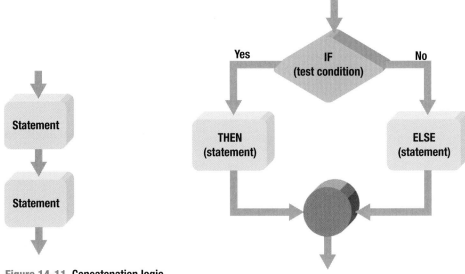

Figure 14-11 **Concatenation logic structure**

Figure 14-12 **Selection (IF-THEN-ELSE) logic structure**

two variations: *DO UNTIL* and *DO WHILE.* (See Figure 14-13.) An example of the **DO UNTIL structure** follows.

> **DO read in job information UNTIL there are no more jobs.**

An example of the **DO WHILE structure** is:

> **DO read in job information WHILE (that is, as long as) there are more jobs.**

There is a difference between the two repetition structures. You may have several statements that need to be repeated. If so, the decision when to *stop* repeating them can appear at the *beginning* of the loop (DO WHILE) or at the *end* of the loop (DO UNTIL). The DO UNTIL loop means that the loop statements will be executed at least once. This is because the statements are executed before you are asked whether to stop.

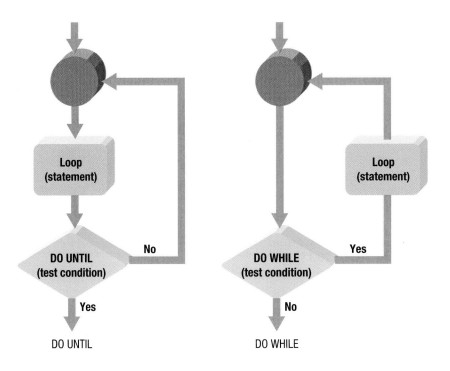

Figure 14-13 **Repetition logic structures: DO UNTIL and DO WHILE**

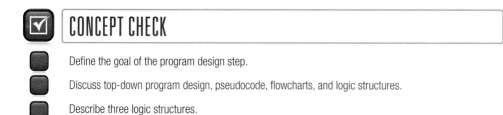

Technique	Description
Top-down design	Major processing steps, called program modules, are identified
Pseudocode	A narrative expression of the logic of the program is written
Program flowcharts	Graphic representation of the steps needed to solve the programming problem is drawn
Logic structures	Three arrangements are used in program flowcharts to write structured programs

Figure 14-14 **Summary of structured programming techniques**

A summary of components used in structured programming is presented in Figure 14-14.

The last thing to do before leaving the program design step is to document the logic of the design. This report typically includes pseudocode, flowcharts, and logic structures. Now you are ready for the next step, program code.

CONCEPT CHECK

- Define the goal of the program design step.
- Discuss top-down program design, pseudocode, flowcharts, and logic structures.
- Describe three logic structures.

Step 3: Program Code

Writing the program is called **coding.** Here you use the logic you developed in the program design step to actually write the program. (See Figure 14-15.) That is, you write out—using pencil and paper or typing on a computer keyboard—the letters, numbers, and symbols that make up the program. This is the "program code" that instructs the computer what to do. Coding is what many people think of when they think of programming. As we've pointed out, however, it is only one of the six steps in the programming process.

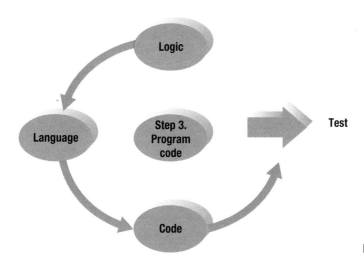

Figure 14-15 **Step 3: Program code**

The Good Program

What are the qualities of a good program? Above all, it should be reliable—that is, it should work under most conditions and produce correct output. It should catch obvious and common input errors. It also should be well documented and understandable by programmers other than the person who wrote it. After all, someone may need to make changes in the program in the future. One of the best ways to code effective programs is to write so-called **structured programs,** using the logic structures described in Step 2.

Coding

After the program logic has been formulated, the next step is to **code** or write the program using the appropriate computer language. There are numerous content-markup and programming languages. A **content-markup language** uses symbols, words, and phrases that instruct a computer how to structure information for display or processing. For example, HTML is a widely used content-markup language to create Web pages. See Figure 14-16 for a partial

```
<html>

<head>
<meta http-equiv="Content-Type" content="text/html; charset=windows-1252">
<meta http-equiv="Content-Language" content="en-us">

<title>Explore the Nile</title>
<meta name="GENERATOR" content="Microsoft FrontPage 4.0">
<meta name="ProgId" content="FrontPage.Editor.Document">

<!--mstheme--><linkrel="stylesheet" type="text/css"
href="_themes/artsy/arts1111.css"><meta name="Microsoft Theme" content="artsy 1111,
default">
<meta name="Microsoft Border" content="tb">
</head>
<body><!--msnavigation--><table border="0" cellpadding="0" cellspacing="0"
width="100%"><tr><td>

<p>
        </p>
<p>
<img border="0" src="images/logo_newletter.jpg" width="271" height="188"
align="left"></p>

<p>
 </p>

<p>
<img src="_derived/africa03.htm_cmp_artsy110_bnr.gif" width="600" height="60"
border="0" alt="Explore the Nile"></p>
```

Figure 14-16 Portion of HTML code to display Explore the Nile Web page

Language	Description
HTML	Stands for HyperText Markup Language; used to create Web pages
XML	Stands for eXtensible Markup Language; assists sharing of data across networks and different systems
XHTML	Stands for eXtended HTML; combines HTML and XML to add structure and flexibility to HTML
SVG	Stands for Scalable Vector Graphics; provides a standard for describing two-dimensional graphics

Figure 14-17 **Widely used content-markup languages**

listing of the HTML code used to display The Adventure Traveler's Explore the Nile Web page. Some of the most popular content-markup languages are presented in Figure 14-17.

A **programming language** uses a collection of symbols, words, and phrases that instruct a computer to perform specific operations. While content-markup languages focus on assigning meaning to different pieces of content, programming languages focus on processing data and information for a wide variety of different types of applications. Figure 14-18 presents the programming code using C++, a widely used programming language, to calculate the compute time module. For a description of C++ and some other widely used programming languages, see Figure 14-19.

Once the program has been coded, the next step is testing, or debugging, the program.

```cpp
#include <fstream.h>

void main (void)
{
    ifstream input_file;

    float total_regular, total_overtime, regular, overtime;
    int hour_in, minute_in, hour_out, minute_out;
    input_file.open("time.txt",ios::in);

    total_regular = 0;
    total_overtime = 0;

    while (input_file != NULL)
    {
        input_file >> hour_in >> minute_in >> hour_out >> minute_out;

        if (hour_out > 17)
            overtime = (hour_out-17) +(minute_out/(float)60);
        else
            overtime = 0;
            regular = ((hour_out - hour_in) +(minute_out
                        - minute_in)/(float)60)    - overtime;
        total_regular += regular;
        total_overtime += overtime;
    }

    cout <<"Regular: " << total_regular <<endl;
    cout <<"Overtime " << total_overtime <<endl;
}
```

Figure 14-18 **C++ code for computing regular and overtime hours**

Language	Description
C	Widely used programming language, often associated with the UNIX operating system
C++	Extends C to use objects or program modules that can be reused and interchanged between programs
C#	Extends C++ to include XML functionality and support for a new Microsoft initiative called .NET
Java	Primarily used for Internet applications; similar to C++; runs with a variety of operating systems
JavaScript	Embedded into Web pages to provide dynamic and interactive content
Visual Basic	Uses a very graphical interface, making it easy to learn and to rapidly develop Windows and other applications

Figure 14-19 Widely used programming languages

☑ CONCEPT CHECK

What is coding?

What makes a good program?

What is the difference between a content-markup and a programming language?

Step 4: Program Test

Debugging refers to the process of testing and then eliminating errors ("getting the bugs out"). (See Figure 14-20.) It means running the program on a computer and then fixing the parts that do not work. Programming errors are of two types: *syntax errors* and *logic errors*.

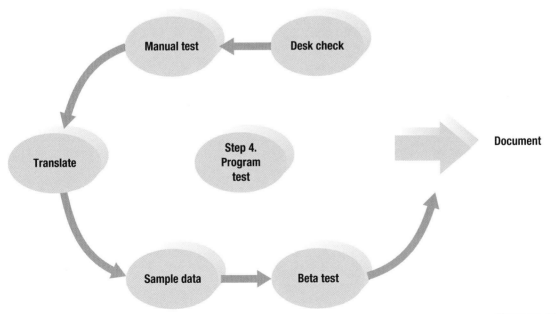

Figure 14-20 Step 4: Program test

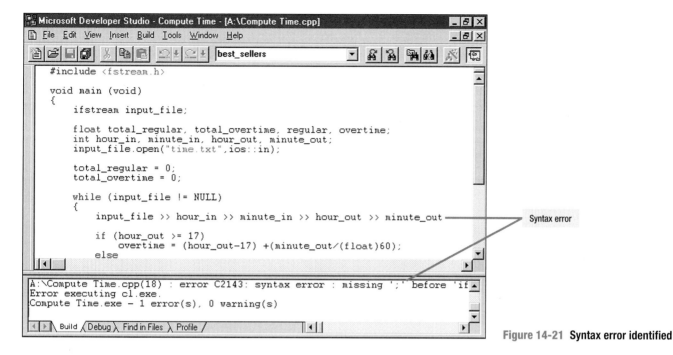

```
#include <fstream.h>

void main (void)
{
    ifstream input_file;

    float total_regular, total_overtime, regular, overtime;
    int hour_in, minute_in, hour_out, minute_out;
    input_file.open("time.txt",ios::in);

    total_regular = 0;
    total_overtime = 0;

    while (input_file != NULL)
    {
        input_file >> hour_in >> minute_in >> hour_out >> minute_out

        if (hour_out >= 17)
            overtime = (hour_out-17) +(minute_out/(float)60);
        else
```

Syntax error

```
A:\Compute Time.cpp(18) : error C2143: syntax error : missing ';' before 'if
Error executing cl.exe.
Compute Time.exe - 1 error(s), 0 warning(s)
```

Build / Debug / Find in Files / Profile

Figure 14-21 Syntax error identified

Syntax Errors

A **syntax error** is a violation of the rules of the programming language. For example, in C++, each statement must end with a semicolon (;). If the semi-colon is omitted, the program will not run due to a syntax error. For example, Figure 14-21 shows testing of the compute time module in which a syntax error was identified.

Logic Errors

A **logic error** occurs when the programmer uses an incorrect calculation or leaves out a programming procedure. For example, a payroll program that did not compute overtime hours would have a logic error.

Testing Process

Several methods have been devised for finding and removing both types of errors:

- **Desk checking:** In **desk checking** or **code review,** a programmer sitting at a desk checks (proofreads) a printout of the program. The programmer goes through the listing line by line looking for syntax and logic errors.

- **Manually testing with sample data:** Using a calculator and sample data, a programmer follows each program statement and performs every calculation. Looking for programming logic errors, the programmer compares the manually calculated values to those calculated by the programs.

- **Attempt at translation:** The program is run through a computer, using a translator program. The translator attempts to translate the written program from the programming language (such as C++) into the machine language. Before the program will run, it must be free of syntax errors. Such errors will be identified by the translating program. (See Figure 14-21.)

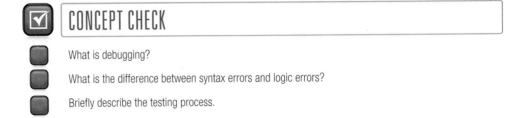

Task	Description
1	Desk check for syntax and logic errors
2	Manually test with sample data
3	Translate program to identify syntax errors
4	Run program with sample data
5	Beta test with potential users

Figure 14-22 **Step 4: Program testing process**

- **Testing sample data on the computer:** After all syntax errors have been corrected, the program is tested for logic errors. Sample data is used to test the correct execution of each program statement.
- **Testing by a select group of potential users:** This is sometimes called **beta testing.** It is usually the final step in testing a program. Potential users try out the program and provide feedback.

For a summary of Step 4: Program test, see Figure 14-22.

☑ CONCEPT CHECK

- What is debugging?
- What is the difference between syntax errors and logic errors?
- Briefly describe the testing process.

Step 5: Program Documentation

Documentation consists of written descriptions and procedures about a program and how to use it. (See Figure 14-23.) It is not something done just at the end of the programming process. **Program documentation** is carried on throughout all the programming steps. This documentation is typically within the program itself and in printed documents. In this step, all the prior documentation is reviewed, finalized, and distributed. Documentation is important for people who may be involved with the program in the future. (See Figure 14-24.) These people may include the following:

- **Users:** Users need to know how to use the software. Some organizations may offer training courses to guide users through the program. However,

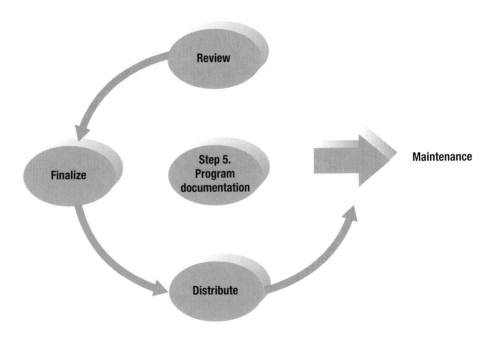

Figure 14-23 **Step 5: Program documentation**

other organizations may expect users to be able to learn a package just from the written documentation. Two examples of this sort of documentation are printed manuals and the help option within most applications.

- **Operators:** Documentation must be provided for computer operators. If the program sends them error messages, for instance, they need to know what to do about them.

- **Programmers:** As time passes, even the creator of the original program may not remember much about it. Other programmers wishing to update and modify it—that is, perform program maintenance—may find themselves frustrated without adequate documentation. This kind of documentation should include text and program flowcharts, program listings, and sample output. It also might include system flowcharts to show how the particular program relates to other programs within an information system.

Figure 14-24 **Program documentation: An ongoing process**

 CONCEPT CHECK

 What is documentation?

 When does program documentation occur?

 Who is affected by documentation?

Step 6: Program Maintenance

The final step is **program maintenance.** (See Figure 14-25.) As much as 75 percent of the total lifetime cost for an application program is for maintenance. This activity is so commonplace that a special job title, **maintenance programmer,** exists. (See Figure 14-26.)

The purpose of program maintenance is to ensure that current programs are operating error free, efficiently, and effectively. Activities in this area fall into two categories: operations and changing needs.

Operations

Operations activities concern locating and correcting operational errors, making programs easier to use, and standardizing software using structured programming techniques. For properly designed programs, these activities should be minimal.

Changing Needs

The category of changing needs is unavoidable. All organizations change over time, and their programs must change with them. Programs need to be adjusted for a variety of reasons, including new tax laws, new information

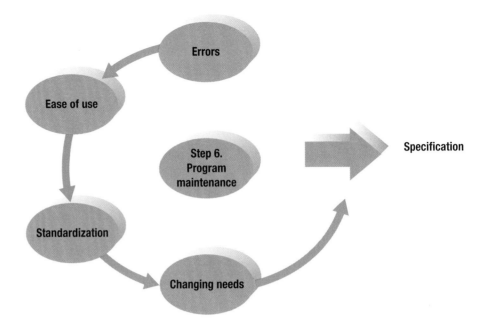

Figure 14-25 Step 6: Program maintenance

needs, and new company policies. Significant revisions may require that the entire programming process begin again with program specification.

Ideally, a software project sequentially follows the six steps of software development. However, some projects start before all requirements are known. In these cases, the SDLC becomes a more cyclical process, repeated several times throughout the development of the software. For example, **agile development,** a popular development methodology, starts by getting core functionality of a program working, then expands on it until the customer is satisfied with the results. All six steps are repeated over and over as quickly as possible to create incrementally more functional versions of the application.

Figure 14-27 summarizes the six steps of the programming process.

Figure 14-26 Program maintenance: Ensure program is operating correctly

Step	Primary Activity
1. Program specification	Determine program objectives, desired output, required input, and processing requirements
2. Program design	Use structured programming techniques
3. Program code	Select programming language; write the program
4. Program test	Perform desk check (code review) and manual checks; attempt translation; test using sample data; beta test with potential users
5. Program documentation	Write procedure for users, operators, and programmers
6. Program maintenance	Adjust for errors, inefficient or ineffective operations, nonstandard code, and changes over time

Figure 14-27 Summary of six steps in programming

CONCEPT CHECK

 What is the purpose of program maintenance?

 Discuss operational activities.

 What are changing needs and how do they affect programs?

CASE and OOP

You hear about efficiency and productivity everywhere. They are particularly important for software development. Two resources that promise to help are *CASE tools* and *object-oriented software development.*

CASE Tools

Professional programmers are constantly looking for ways to make their work easier, faster, and more reliable. One tool we mentioned in Chapter 13, CASE, is meeting this need. **Computer-aided software engineering (CASE) tools** provide some automation and assistance in program design, coding, and testing. (See Figure 14-28.)

Object-Oriented Software Development

Traditional systems development is a careful, step-by-step approach focusing on the procedures needed to complete a certain objective. **Object-oriented software development** focuses less on the procedures and more on defining the relationships between previously defined procedures or "objects." **Object-oriented programming (OOP)** is a process by which a program is organized into objects. Each **object** contains both the data and processing operations necessary to perform a task. Let's explain what this means.

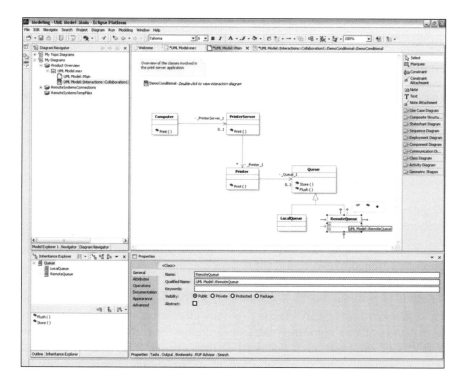

Figure 14-28 CASE tool: Providing code-generation assistance

In the past, programs were developed as giant entities, from the first line of code to the last. This has been compared to building a car from scratch. Object-oriented programming is like building a car from prefabricated parts—carburetor, alternator, fenders, and so on. Object-oriented programs use objects that are reusable, self-contained components. Programs built with these objects assume that certain functions are the same. For example, many programs, from spreadsheets to database managers, have an instruction that will sort lists of names in alphabetical order. A programmer might use this object for alphabetizing in many other programs. There is no need to invent this activity anew every time. C++ is one of the most widely used object-oriented programming languages.

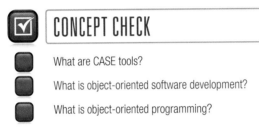

CONCEPT CHECK

What are CASE tools?

What is object-oriented software development?

What is object-oriented programming?

Generations of Programming Languages

Computer professionals talk about **levels** or **generations** of programming languages, ranging from "low" to "high." Programming languages are called **lower level** when they are closer to the language the computer itself uses. The computer understands the 0s and 1s that make up bits and bytes. Programming languages are called **higher level** when they are closer to the language humans use—that is, for English speakers, more like English.

There are five generations of programming languages: (1) machine languages, (2) assembly languages, (3) procedural languages, (4) task-oriented languages, and (5) problem and constraint languages.

Machine Languages: The First Generation

We mentioned in Chapter 6 that a byte is made up of bits, consisting of 1s and 0s. These 1s and 0s may correspond to electricity's being on or off in the computer. They also may correspond to a magnetic charge being present or absent on storage media such as disk or tape. From this two-state system, coding schemes have been developed that allow us to construct letters, numbers, punctuation marks, and other special characters. Examples of these coding schemes, as we saw, are ASCII, EBCDIC, and Unicode.

Data represented in 1s and 0s is said to be written in **machine language.** To see how hard this is to understand, imagine if you had to code this:

1111001001110011110100100001000001110000000101011

Machine languages also vary according to make of computer—another characteristic that makes them hard to work with.

Assembly Languages: The Second Generation

Before a computer can process or run any program, the program must be converted or translated into machine language. **Assembly languages** use abbreviations or mnemonics such as ADD that are automatically converted to the appropriate sequence of 1s and 0s. Compared to machine languages, assembly languages are much easier for humans to understand and to use. The machine language code we gave above could be expressed in assembly language as

> **ADD 210(8,13),02B(4,7)**

This is still pretty obscure, of course, and so assembly language is also considered low level.

Assembly languages also vary from computer to computer. With the third generation, we advance to high-level languages, many of which are considered **portable languages.** That is, they can be run on more than one kind of computer—they are "portable" from one machine to another.

High-Level Procedural Languages: The Third Generation

People are able to understand languages that are more like their own (e.g., English) than machine languages or assembly languages. These more English-like programming languages are called "high-level" languages. However, most people still require some training to use higher-level languages. This is particularly true of procedural languages.

Procedural languages, also known as **3GLs (third-generation languages),** are designed to express the logic—the procedures—that can solve general problems. Procedural languages, then, are intended to solve general problems. C++ is a procedural language widely used by today's programmers. For example, C++ was used in Advantage's time-and-billing report. (See again Figure 14-18 for the compute time module of this program.)

Consider the following C++ statement from a program that assigns letter grades based on the score of an exam.

> **if (score > = 90) grade = 'A';**

This statement tests whether the score is greater than or equal to 90. If it is, then the letter grade of A is assigned.

Like assembly languages, procedural languages must be translated into machine language so that the computer processes them. Depending on the language, this translation is performed by either a *compiler* or an *interpreter*.

- A **compiler** converts the programmer's procedural language program, called the **source code,** into a machine language code, called the **object code.** This object code can then be saved and run later. Examples of procedural languages using compilers are the standard versions of Pascal, COBOL, and FORTRAN.

- An **interpreter** converts the procedural language one statement at a time into machine code just before it is to be executed. No object code is saved. An example of a procedural language using an interpreter is the standard version of BASIC.

What is the difference between using a compiler and using an interpreter? When a program is run, the compiler requires two steps. The first step is to convert the entire program's source code to object code. The second step is to run the object code. The interpreter, in contrast, converts and runs the program one line at a time. The advantage of a compiler language is that once the object code has been obtained, the program executes faster. The advantage of an interpreter language is that programs are easier to develop.

Task-Oriented Languages: The Fourth Generation

Third-generation languages are valuable, but they require training in programming. Task-oriented languages, also known as **4GLs (fourth-generation** languages) and **very high-level languages,** require little special training on the part of the user.

Unlike general-purpose languages, **task-oriented languages** are designed to solve specific problems. While 3GLs focus on procedures and how logic can be combined to solve a variety of problems, 4GLs are nonprocedural and focus on specifying the specific tasks the program is to accomplish. 4GLs are more Englishlike, easier to program, and widely used by nonprogrammers. Some of these fourth-generation languages are used for very specific applications. For example, **IFPS (interactive financial planning system)** is used to develop financial models. Many 4GLs are part of a database management system. 4GLs include query languages and application generators:

- **Query languages: Query languages** enable nonprogrammers to use certain easily understood commands to search and generate reports from a database. One of the most widely used query languages is SQL (structured query language). For example, let's say that Advantage Advertising has a database containing all customer calls for service and that their management would like a listing of all clients who incurred overtime charges. The SQL command to create this list is

> **SELECT client FROM dailyLog WHERE serviceEnd > 17**

This SQL statement selects or identifies all clients (a field name from the dailyLog table) that required service after 17 (military time for 5:00 P.M.). Microsoft Access can generate SQL commands like this one by using its Query wizard.

- **Application generators:** An **application generator** or a **program coder** is a program that provides modules of prewritten code. When using an application generator, a programmer can quickly create a program by referencing the module(s) that performs certain tasks. This greatly reduces the time to create an application. For example, Access has a report generation application and a Report wizard for creating a variety of different types of reports using database information.

Problem and Constraint Languages: The Fifth Generation

As they have evolved through the generations, computer languages have become more humanlike. Clearly, the fourth-generation query languages using commands that include words like SELECT, FROM, and WHERE are much more humanlike than the 0s and 1s of machine language. However, 4GLs are still a long way from the natural languages such as English and Spanish that people use.

The standard definition of a **fifth-generation language (5GL)** is a computer language that incorporates the concepts of artificial intelligence to allow a person to provide a system with a problem and some constraints, and then request a solution. Additionally, these languages would enable a computer to *learn* and to *apply* new information as people do. Rather than coding by keying in specific commands, we would communicate more directly to a computer using **natural languages.**

Consider the following natural language statement that might appear in a 5GL program for recommending medical treatment.

> **Get patientDiagnosis from patientSymptoms "sneezing", "coughing", "aching"**

Generation	Sample Statement
First: Machine	1111001001110011110100100001000001110000000101011
Second: Assembly	ADD 210(8, 13),02B(4, 7)
Third: Procedural	if (score > = 90) grade = 'A';
Fourth: Task	SELECT client FROM dailyLog WHERE serviceEnd > 17
Fifth: Problems and Constraints	Get patientDiagnosis from patientSymptoms "sneezing", "coughing", "aching"

Figure 14-29 Summary of five programming generations

See Figure 14-29 for a summary of the generations of programming languages.

CONCEPT CHECK

What distinguishes a lower-level language from a higher-level language?

Outline the five generations of programming languages.

Careers in IT

Computer **programmers** create, test, and troubleshoot programs used by computers (see Figure 14-30). Programmers also may update and repair existing programs. Most computer programmers are employed by companies that create and sell software, but programmers also may be employed in various other businesses. Many computer programmers work on a project basis as consultants, meaning they are hired by a company only to complete a specific program. As technology has developed, the need for programmers to work on the most basic computer functions has decreased. However, demand for computer programmers with specializations in advanced programs continues.

Jobs in programming typically require a bachelor's degree in computer science or information systems. However, there are positions available in the field for those with a two-year degree. Employers looking for programmers typically put an emphasis on previous experience. Programmers who have patience, think logically, and pay attention to detail are continually in demand. Additionally, programmers who can communicate technical information to nontechnical people are preferred.

Computer programmers can expect to earn an annual salary in the range of $51,500 to $88,000. Advancement opportunities for talented programmers include a lead programmer position or supervisory positions. Programmers with specializations and experience also may have an opportunity to consult. To learn about careers in information technology, visit us at www.computing2011.com and enter the keyword **careers**.

Figure 14-30 Programmer

A LOOK TO THE FUTURE

Using a Wish List to Create a Program

What if you could instruct a computer to code a program with a simple wish list written in English? What if syntax errors didn't happen? What if the computer asked you to clarify your meaning rather than just report an error? What if you could create a program that would run on a Windows PC, an Apple Mac, or even a Linux computer? At Synapse Solutions they believe they have created a system that meets these needs.

Traditional programming relies on a compiler and a translator to communicate the desires of the programmer to the computer. There are also precise rules that must be followed to correctly communicate with the computer. Natural language programming (using a human language to talk to the computer) has been the dream of programmers for a long time.

Human languages can be confusing to a machine because it is possible to have double meanings and uncertainty.

Synapse Solutions has created a system called MI-tech that has an understanding of word order and meaning in English. To program using the system, you enter a "wish list" and the computer translates these sentences into machine language. If the system does not understand a "wish," it makes a request for clarification. It also uses a dictionary to look up words it doesn't recognize.

Would you like to create your own applications? What if you could create a Web page using a list of what you would like to appear on the page? Synapse Solutions believes it will soon be possible to use its system to do just that. What other programs do you think could utilize this system? Do you think someday all computer users will be programmers?

Using IT at DVD Direct—a case study

PROGRAMMING AT DVD DIRECT

DVD Direct, a fictitious organization, is an entirely Web-oriented movie rental business in which customers select movies to rent from the company's Web site and choose the delivery method. One way is to receive selected movies on DVD disks by mail. This is how the business originally started out. The other way is to immediately download the movies onto the member's hard disk. Online delivery is a recent innovation. To encourage the choice of online delivery (which is more cost-effective for DVD Direct), a Frequent Renters Club has been established. Whenever members select online delivery, they receive reward points that can be redeemed for a variety of items.

To support the record keeping of the Frequent Renters Club, an information system was developed by Alice, a marketing analyst, and Mia, a systems analyst. The hardware needed to support the system was leased, and most of the software was purchased from an outside vendor. Mia created one program that integrated a login screen to the Frequent Renters Club Web site. After some initial modifications, the Frequent Renters Club has been successfully operating for the past two months.

One morning, Mia receives a telephone call from Bob, the vice president of marketing, asking her to come to the meeting room to discuss the login program she wrote for the Frequent Renters Club Web site and to bring all her documentation from the project. This is a bit of a surprise, and Mia wonders what it could be about. The system has been up and running for two months without problems. The login program is quite simple. Could that in itself somehow be the problem? Why aren't they meeting in Bob's office? To follow Alice into the meeting, visit us on the Web at www.computing2011.com and enter the keyword programming.

"Hi, Mia. Good morning! I'd like you to meet Nicole, Oscar, and Laurence."

PROGRAMS AND PROGRAMMING

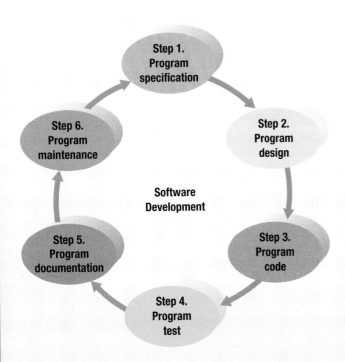

A **program** is a list of instructions for a computer to follow. **Programming (software development)** is a six-step procedure for creating programs.

The steps are

- Program specification—defining objectives, inputs, outputs, and processing requirements.
- Program design—creating a solution using structured programming tools and techniques such as **top-down program design, pseudocode, program flowcharts,** and **logic structures.**
- Program code—writing or coding the program using a **programming language.**
- Program test—testing or debugging the program by looking for **syntax** and **logic errors.**
- Program documentation—ongoing process throughout the programming process.
- Program maintenance—periodically evaluating programs for accuracy, efficiency, standardization, and ease of use and modifying program code as needed.

STEP 1: PROGRAM SPECIFICATION

Program specification, also called **program definition** or **program analysis,** consists of specifying five tasks related to objectives, outputs, inputs, requirements, and documentation.

Program Objectives
The first task is to clearly define the problem to solve in the form of program **objectives.**

Desired Output
Next, focus on the desired output before considering the required inputs.

Input Data
Once outputs are defined, determine the necessary input data and the source of the data.

Processing Requirements
Next, determine the steps necessary (processing requirements) to use input to produce output.

Program Specifications Document
The final task is to create a specifications document to record this step's program objectives, outputs, inputs, and processing requirements.

To be a competent end user, you need to understand the six steps of programming: program specification, program design, program coding, program test, program documentation, and program maintenance. Additionally, you need to be aware of CASE, OOP, and the generations of programming languages.

STEP 2: PROGRAM DESIGN

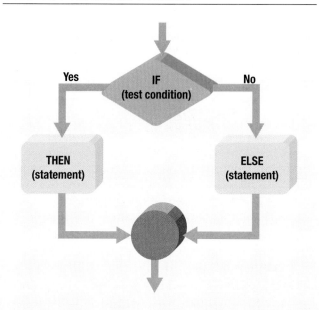

In **program design,** a solution is designed using, preferably, **structured programming techniques,** including the following.

Top-Down Program Design

In **top-down program design,** major processing steps, called **program modules** (or **modules**), are identified.

Pseudocode

Pseudocode is an outline of the logic of the program you will write.

Flowcharts

Program flowcharts are graphic representations of the steps necessary to solve a programming problem.

Logic Structures

Logic structures are arrangements of programming statements. Three types are

- **Concatenation**—one program statement followed by another.
- **Selection (IF-THEN-ELSE)**—when a decision must be made.
- **Repetition (loop) (DO UNTIL** and **DO WHILE)**—when process is repeated until condition is true.

STEP 3: PROGRAM CODE

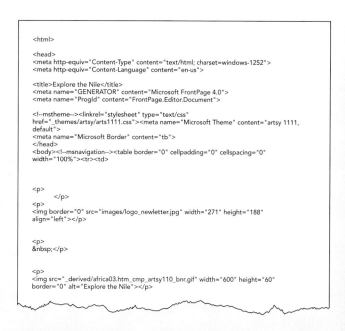

Coding is writing a program. There are several important aspects of writing a program. Two are writing good programs and actually writing or coding.

Good Programs

Good programs are reliable, detect obvious and common errors, and are well documented. The best way to create good programs is to write **structured programs** using the three basic logic structures presented in Step 2.

Coding

There are hundreds of different programming languages. Two types are

- **Content-markup languages** that instruct a computer how to process different types of information. A widely used content-markup language is HTML, used to create Web pages.
- **Programming languages** that instruct a computer to perform specific operations. C++ is a widely used programming language.

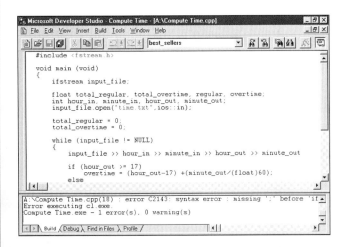

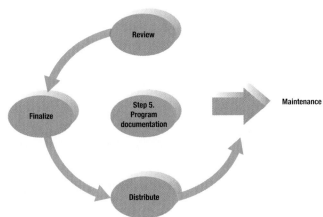

Debugging is a process of testing and eliminating errors in a program. Syntax and logic are two types of programming errors.

Syntax Errors

Syntax errors are violations of the rules of a programming language. For example, omitting a semicolon at the end of a C++ statement is a syntax error.

Logic Errors

Logic errors are incorrect calculations or procedures. For example, failure to include calculation of overtime hours in a payroll program is a logic error.

Testing Process

Five methods for testing for syntax and logic errors are

- **Desk checking (code review)**—careful reading of a printout of the program.
- **Manual testing**—using a calculator and sample data to test for correct programming logic.
- **Attempt at translation**—running the program using a translator program to identify syntax errors.
- **Testing sample data**—running the program and testing the program for logic errors using sample data.
- **Testing by users (beta testing)**—final step in which potential users try the program and provide feedback.

Program documentation consists of a written description of the program and the procedures for running it. People who use documentation include

- **Users,** who need to know how to use the program. Some organizations offer training courses; others expect users to learn from written documentation.
- **Operators,** who need to know how to execute the program and how to recognize and correct errors.
- **Programmers,** who may need to update and maintain the program in the future. Documentation could include text and program flowcharts, program listings, and sample outputs.

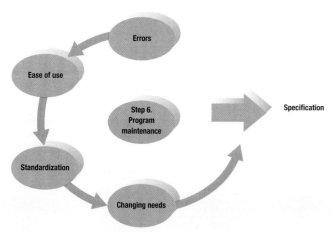

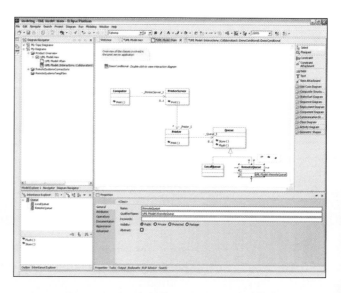

Program maintenance is designed to ensure that the program operates correctly, efficiently, and effectively. Two categories of maintenance activities are the following.

Operations

Operations activities include locating and correcting errors, improving usability, and standardizing software.

Changing Needs

Organizations change over time and their programs must change with them. **Agile development** starts with core program functionality, then expands until the customer is satisfied with the results.

CASE

Computer-aided software engineering (CASE) tools provide automation and assistance in program design, coding, and testing.

OOP

Traditional systems development focuses on procedure to complete a specific objective.

Object-oriented software development focuses less on procedures and more on defining relationships between previously defined procedures or objects. **Object-oriented programming (OOP)** is a process by which a program is divided into modules called **objects**. Each object contains both the data and processing operations necessary to perform a task.

PROGRAMMING LANGUAGE GENERATIONS

Programming languages have **levels** or **generations** ranging from low to high. **Lower-level** languages are closer to the 0s and 1s language of computers. **Higher-level** languages are closer to the languages of humans.

CAREERS IN IT

Programmers create, test, and troubleshoot programs. They also update and repair existing programs. Bachelor's or specialized two-year degree in computer science or information systems. Salary range $51,500 to $88,000.

KEY TERMS

agile development   (414)
application generator   (418)
assembly language   (416)
beta testing   (412)
code   (408)
code review   (411)
coding   (407)
compiler   (417)
computer-aided software engineering
   (CASE) tools   (415)
concatenation structure   (405)
content-markup language   (408)
debugging   (410)
desk checking   (411)
DO UNTIL structure   (406)
DO WHILE structure   (406)
documentation   (412)
fifth-generation language (5GL)   (418)
fourth-generation language
   (4GL)   (417)
generations   (416)
higher level   (416)
IF-THEN-ELSE structure   (405)
IFPS (interactive financial planning
   system)   (418)
interpreter   (417)
levels   (416)
logic error   (411)
logic structure   (405)
loop structure   (405)
lower level   (416)
machine language   (416)
maintenance programmer   (413)
module   (404)
natural language   (418)
object   (415)
object code   (417)

object-oriented programming
   (OOP)   (415)
object-oriented software
   development   (415)
objectives   (401)
operators   (413)
portable language   (417)
procedural language   (417)
program   (400)
program analysis   (401)
program coder   (418)
program definition   (401)
program design   (403)
program documentation   (412)
program flowchart   (404)
program maintenance   (413)
program modules   (404)
program specification   (401)
programmer (401, 413, 419)
programming   (400)
programming language   (409)
pseudocode   (404)
query language   (418)
repetition structure   (405)
selection structure   (405)
software development   (400)
software engineer   (401)
source code   (417)
structured program   (408)
structured programming
   techniques   (403)
syntax error   (411)
task-oriented language   (418)
third-generation language (3GL)   (417)
top-down program design   (403)
user   (412)
very high-level language   (418)

To test your knowledge of these key terms with animated flash cards, visit our Web site at www.computing2011.com and enter the keyword terms14.

MULTIPLE CHOICE

Circle the letter or fill in the correct answer.

1. A(n) _____ is a list of instructions detailing the steps needed to perform a task.
    - **a.** program
    - **b.** punch card
    - **c.** agenda
    - **d.** plan

2. In the course of creating program specifications, the end user should sketch out the desired
    - **a.** input
    - **b.** output
    - **c.** splash logo
    - **d.** icon

3. In a _____ structure, one statement follows the other with no conditions having to be met.
    - **a.** selection
    - **b.** loop
    - **c.** concatenation
    - **d.** conditional

4. A _____ language uses symbols, words, and phrases that instruct a computer how to structure information for display or processing.
    - **a.** Java
    - **b.** 5GL
    - **c.** content-markup
    - **d.** natural

5. A program error that violates the rules of the programming language is a _____ error.
    - **a.** modular
    - **b.** logic
    - **c.** syntax
    - **d.** language

6. This tool provides automation and assistance in program design, coding, and testing.
    - **a.** CAUSE (computer-assisted Unix software environment) tool
    - **b.** CASE (computer-aided software engineering) tool
    - **c.** CLOC (computer-licensed operations code) tool
    - **d.** CULP (combined-users licensed protocols) tool

7. Which of the following lines of code comes from a first-generation computer language?
    - **a.** ADD 255(3,10), 02B(4,5)
    - **b.** 00010 1010 1101 0001 1010
    - **c.** this Total = TotalA + TotalC
    - **d.** set total to sum of totals

8. C++ is considered a(n)
    - **a.** machine language
    - **b.** assembly language
    - **c.** procedural language
    - **d.** natural language

9. Task-oriented languages are the _____ generation of programming languages.
    - **a.** first
    - **b.** second
    - **c.** third
    - **d.** fourth

10. Fourth-generation languages use
    - **a.** procedural statements
    - **b.** nonprocedural statements
    - **c.** assemblers
    - **d.** symbols

For an interactive multiple-choice practice test, visit our Web site at www.computing 2011.com and enter the keyword multiple14.

MATCHING

Match each numbered item with the most closely related lettered item. Write your answers in the spaces provided.

a. assembly
b. coding
c. logic error
d. maintenance programmer
e. OOP
f. program specification
g. programmer
h. program
i. pseudocode
j. repetition structure

1. A list of instructions for the computer to follow to process data. _____
2. Computer professional who creates new software or revises existing software. _____
3. Programming step in which objectives, outputs, inputs, and processing requirements are determined. _____
4. An outline of the logic of the program to be written. _____
5. Logic structure in which a process may be repeated as long as a certain condition remains true. _____
6. Actual writing of a program. _____
7. Error that occurs when an incorrect calculation or incorrect procedure is used in a program. _____
8. Computer specialist whose job is to ensure current programs run error free, efficiently, and effectively. _____
9. Process by which a program is organized into objects. _____
10. Languages that use abbreviations or mnemonics. _____

For an interactive matching practice test, visit our Web site at www.computing2011.com and enter the keyword matching14.

OPEN-ENDED

On a separate sheet of paper, respond to each question or statement.

1. Identify and discuss each of the six steps of programming.
2. Describe CASE tools and OOP. How does CASE assist programmers?
3. What is meant by "generation" in reference to programming languages? What is the difference between low-level and high-level languages?
4. What is the difference between a compiler and an interpreter?
5. What are logic structures? Describe the differences between the three types.

APPLYING TECHNOLOGY

The following questions are designed to demonstrate ways that you can effectively use technology today.

 ## VERSION CONTROL SYSTEMS

A version control system is an invaluable tool for large programming projects. Learn more about version control systems by visiting our Web site at www.computing2011.com and entering the keyword version to link to a version control software Web site. Once connected, read about version control and then answer the following: (a) What is version control? Who uses it? (b) Describe what version control does. Be specific. (c) When is version control not a useful choice? Why?

 ## .NET FRAMEWORK

Microsoft's .NET Framework is a platform for developing applications that run on computers, small devices like mobile phones and PDAs, and even across the Internet. Visit our Web site at www.computing2011.com and enter the keyword net to link to the .NET site. Read about the .NET Framework and then answer the following questions: (a) What are the basic components of the .NET Framework? (b) What programming languages does the .NET Framework include? (c) What are the benefits of using the .NET Framework for software developers?

③ INTEGRATED DEVELOPMENT ENVIRONMENTS

As discussed in the chapter, source code is written in a programming language and then compiled or interpreted. Most programmers use an integrated development environment (IDE). Research IDEs on the Web and then answer the following: (a) What is an IDE? What purpose does it serve? (b) What features are common to most IDEs? (c) In the DVD Direct case study, Mia programmed the login application herself. Locate and describe an IDE that would be appropriate for her chosen programming language.

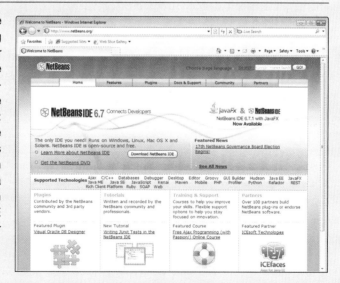

EXPANDING YOUR KNOWLEDGE

The following questions are designed to add depth and detail to your understanding of specific topics presented within this chapter. The questions direct you to sources other than the textbook to obtain this knowledge.

① DVD DIRECT PROGRAM DEVELOPMENT

To encourage online delivery of DVD disks, DVD Direct has established a Frequent Renters Club. Whenever a member orders an online movie, he or she receives reward points that can be redeemed for a variety of items. Alice and Mia have been actively developing an information system to support the record-keeping activity of the Frequent Renters Club. Mia has created a program that integrates a login screen to the Frequent Renters Club Web site. To learn more about this program, visit us on the Web at www.computing2011.com and enter the keyword programming. Describe the steps Mia followed to develop this program.

② SOURCE CODE GENERATORS

Generally, the human resources that are devoted to a successful software project are its greatest single expense. Programming and testing applications are time-consuming tasks. Recently, source code generators have become popular for handling some of the more routine programming tasks. Research source code generators on the Web and answer the following questions: (a) What are source code generators? (b) How do source code generators work? (c) What programming tasks are source code generators best for? Why? (d) What programming tasks are beyond what source code generators can accomplish? Why?

③ CAPABILITY MATURITY MODEL

Continuous improvement of the software development process is critical for an organization. The Capability Maturity Model, or CMM, is a way to address this need. Visit our Web site at www.computing2011.com and enter the keyword CMM to link to the CMM site. Read about CMM and then answer the following: (a) What is CMM? Who created it? (b) List the five CMM levels and describe the characteristics of each. (c) What CMM level was DVD Direct working at? Justify your answer. (d) Based on the CMM, what steps can DVD Direct take to use Mia's experience to improve their next software project? Be specific.

WRITING ABOUT TECHNOLOGY

The ability to think critically and to write effectively is essential to nearly every profession. The following questions are designed to help you develop these skills by posing thought-provoking questions about computer privacy, security, and/or ethics.

 ## BUGS

Several years ago, two people died and a third was maimed after receiving excessive radiation from a medical machine. It was only after the second incident that the problem was located—a bug in the software that controlled the machine. Consider the possible consequences of software failure in situations where life is at stake and then answer the following questions in a one-page paper: (a) Are there situations when software bugs are unethical? Explain your answer. (b) No program of any significant complexity can reasonably be fully tested. When is it ethical to say that software is "tested enough"? (c) What responsibility does a programmer have in situations when a program fails in the field? What about the software company he or she works for? Does the consumer share any responsibility? Justify your answers.

 ## SECURITY AND PRIVACY

Security and privacy are important concerns in the development of any information system. Answer the following questions in a one-page paper: (a) In the development process, who would you expect to have the responsibility of identifying security and privacy concerns? (b) In what phase of the systems life cycle would security and privacy concerns be identified? (c) To learn about security and privacy concerns for DVD Direct, visit us on the Web at www.computing2011.com and enter the keyword programming. Then identify DVD Direct's most important security and privacy concerns. Be as specific as possible.

Your Future and Information Technology

Competencies

After you have read this chapter, you should be able to:

1. Explain why it's important to have an individual strategy to be a "winner" in the information age.

2. Describe how technology is changing the nature of competition.

3. Discuss four ways people may react to new technology.

4. Describe how you can stay current with your career.

5. Describe different careers in information technology.

In the past, to maximize your business contacts it may have been necessary to carry business cards with your contact information and frequently attend conferences in your field. Today social networking sites are available for business contacts, allowing users to meet potential business partners around the world or across the street without leaving the office.

Some experts predict that social networking in the business world will soon feature the use of moblie devices. Presence technology and social networking data may combine to make it possible to turn your daily commute into a potential business meeting. Imagine viewing the portfolios of people waiting on the subway next to you or striking up a conversation with a potential business partner based on a mutual friend. It may even be possible to interview for a job on the fly after someone views your resume on their mobile device.

chapter **15**

Introduction

Throughout this book, we have emphasized practical subjects that are useful to you now or will be very soon. Accordingly, this final chapter is not about the far future, say, 10 years from now. Rather, it is about today and the near future—about developments whose outlines we can already see. It is about how organizations adapt to technological change. It is also about what you as an individual can do to keep your computer competency up to date.

Are the times changing any faster now than they ever have? It's hard to say. People who were alive when radios, cars, and airplanes were being introduced certainly lived through some dramatic changes. Has technology made our own times even more dynamic? Whatever the answer, it is clear we live in a fast-paced age. The challenge for you as an individual is to devise ways to stay current and to use technology to your advantage. For example, you can use the Web to locate job opportunities.

To stay competent, end users need to recognize the impact of technological change on organizations and people. They need to know how to use change to their advantage and how to be winners. Although end users do not need to be specialists in information technology, they should be aware of career opportunities in the area.

Changing Times

Figure 15-1 Automated teller machines are examples of technology used in business strategy

Almost all businesses have become aware that they must adapt to changing technology or be left behind. Most organizations are now making formal plans to keep track of technology and implement it in their competitive strategies. For example, banks have found that automated teller machines (ATMs) are vital to retail banking. (See Figure 15-1.) Not only do they require fewer human tellers, but also they are available 24 hours a day. More and more banks also are trying to go electronic, doing away with paper transactions wherever possible. ATM cards are used to buy almost anything from gas to groceries.

What's next for the banking industry? Almost all banks also are trying to popularize home banking so that customers can use microcomputers for certain financial tasks. Some banks, known as Internet banks, have even done away with physical bank buildings and conduct all business over the Web. (See Figure 15-2.) In addition, banks are exploring the use of some very sophisticated application programs. These programs will accept cursive writing (the handwriting on checks) directly as input, verify check signatures, and process the check without human intervention.

Clearly, such changes do away with some jobs—those of many bank tellers and cashiers, for example. However, they create opportunities for other people. New technology requires people who are truly capable of working with it. These are not the people who think every piece of equipment is so simple they can just turn it on and use it. Nor are they those who think each new machine is a potential disaster. In other words, new technology needs people who are not afraid to learn about it and are able to manage it. The real issue, then, is not how to make technology better. Rather, it is how to integrate the technology with people.

You are in a very favorable position compared with many other people in industry today. After reading the previous chapters, you have learned more than just the basics of hardware, software, connectivity, and the Internet. You have learned about the most current technology. You are therefore able to use these tools to your advantage—to be a winner.

How do you become and stay a winner? In brief, the answer is: You must form your own individual strategy for dealing with change. First let us look at how businesses are handling technological change. Then let's look at how people are reacting to these changes. Finally, we will offer a few suggestions that will enable you to keep up with and profit from the information revolution.

Figure 15-2 Internet banks conduct business over the Web

 CONCEPT CHECK

 Cite examples of ways computers are changing the business world.

 What are the human requirements of new technology?

Technology and Organizations

Technology can introduce new ways for businesses to compete with each other. Some of the principal changes are as follows.

New Products

Technology creates products that operate faster, are priced cheaper, are often of better quality, or are wholly new. Indeed, new products can be individually tailored to a particular customer's needs. For example, financial services companies such as Merrill Lynch have taken advantage of technology to launch cash management accounts. (See Figure 15-3.) These accounts combine information on a person's checking, savings, credit card, and securities accounts into a single monthly statement. It automatically sets aside "idle" funds into interest-bearing money market funds. Customers can access their accounts on the Web and get a complete picture of their financial condition at any time. However, even if they don't pay much attention to their statements, their surplus funds are invested automatically.

New Enterprises

Information technology can build entirely new businesses. Two examples are Internet service providers and Web site development companies.

- Just a few years ago, the only computer connectivity options available to individuals were through online service providers like America Online and

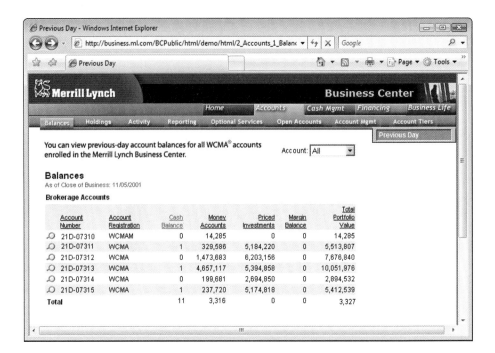

Figure 15-3 Merrill Lynch's cash management account

through colleges and universities. Now, hundreds of national service providers and thousands of local service providers are available.

• Thousands of small companies specializing in Web site development have sprung up in the past few years. These companies help small- to medium-sized organizations by providing assistance in evaluating, creating, and maintaining Web sites.

New Customer and Supplier Relationships

Businesses that make their information systems easily available may make their customers less likely to take their business elsewhere. For instance, Federal Express, the overnight package delivery service, does everything possible to make its customers dependent on it. Upon request, customers receive airbills with their name, address, and account number preprinted on them, making shipping and billing easier. Package numbers are scanned into the company's information system so that they can be tracked from pickup point to destination. (See Figure 15-4.) Thus, apprehensive customers can be informed very quickly of the exact location of their package as it travels toward its destination.

Figure 15-4 New technology helps FedEx maintain customer loyalty

CONCEPT CHECK

What is the role of technology in creating new products?

Describe two new enterprises built by information technology.

Discuss how technology can create new customers and affect supplier relationships.

Technology and People

Clearly, recent technological changes, and those sure to come in the near future, will produce significant changes and opportunities in the years ahead. How should we be prepared for them?

People have different coping styles when it comes to technology. It has been suggested, for instance, that people react to changing technology in one of four ways: cynicism, naivete, frustration, and proactivity.

Cynicism

The **cynic** feels that, for a manager at least, the idea of using a microcomputer is overrated. (See Figure 15-5.) Learning and using it take too much time, time that could be delegated to someone else. Doing spreadsheets and word processing, according to the cynic, are tasks that managers should understand. However, the cynic feels that such tasks take time away from a manager's real job of developing plans and setting goals for the people being supervised.

Cynics may express their doubts openly, especially if they are top managers. Or they may only pretend to be interested in microcomputers, when actually they are not interested at all.

Naivete

Many **naive** people are unfamiliar with computers. They may think computers are magic boxes capable of solving all kinds of problems that computers really can't handle. On the other hand, some naive persons are actually quite familiar with computers but underestimate the difficulty of changing computer systems or of generating certain information.

Frustration

The **frustrated** person may already be quite busy and may hate having to take time to learn about microcomputers. Such a person feels it is an imposition to have to learn something new or is too impatient to try to understand the manuals explaining what hardware and software are supposed to do. The result is continual frustration. (See Figure 15-6.) Some people are frustrated because they try to do too much. Or they're frustrated because they find manuals difficult to understand. In some cases poorly written manuals are at fault.

Proactivity

Webster's Collegiate Dictionary defines **proactive,** in part, as "acting in anticipation of future problems, needs, or changes." A proactive person looks at technology in a positive realistic way. (See Figure 15-7.) They are not cynics, underestimating the likely impact of technology on their

Figure 15-5 The cynic: "These gadgets are overrated."

Figure 15-6 The frustrated person: "This stuff doesn't make sense half the time."

Figure 15-7 The proactive person: "How can I use this new tool?"

lives. They are not naive, overestimating the ability of technology to solve the world's or their problems. They do not become frustrated easily and give up using technology. Proactive people are positive in their outlook and look at new technology as providing new tools that, when correctly applied, can positively impact their lives.

Most of us fall into one of the four categories. Cynicism, naivete, frustration, and proactivity are common human responses to change. Do you see yourself or others around you responding to technology in any of these ways? For those who respond negatively, just being aware of their reaction can help them become more positive and proactive to tomorrow's exciting new changes in technology.

☑ CONCEPT CHECK

 Describe three negative ways people cope with technological changes in the workplace.

 Describe one positive way people cope with technological change in the workplace.

 Define proactive.

How You Can Be a Winner

So far we have described how progressive organizations are using technology in the information age. Now let's concentrate on you as an individual. (See Making IT Work for You: Locating Job Opportunities Online on pages 440 and 441.) How can you stay ahead? Here are some ideas.

Stay Current

Whatever their particular line of work, successful professionals keep up both with their own fields and with the times. We don't mean you should try to become a computer expert and read a lot of technical magazines. Rather, you should concentrate on your profession and learn how computer technology is being used within it.

Every field has trade journals, whether the field is interior design, personnel management, or advertising. Most such journals regularly present articles about the uses of computers. It's important that you also belong to a trade or industry association and go to its meetings. Many associations sponsor seminars and conferences that describe the latest information and techniques.

Another way to stay current is by participating electronically with special-interest newsgroups on the Internet.

Maintain Your Computer Competency

Actually, you should try to stay ahead of the technology. Books, journals, and trade associations are the best sources of information about new technology that applies to your field. The general business press—*BusinessWeek, Fortune, Inc., The Wall Street Journal,* and the business section of your local newspaper—also carries computer-related articles.

However, if you wish, you can subscribe to a magazine that covers micro-

Figure 15-8 Professional organizations and contacts help you keep up in your field

computers and information more specifically. Examples are *InfoWorld, PC World,* and *MacWorld.* You also may find it useful to look at newspapers and magazines that cover the computer industry as a whole. An example of such a periodical is *ComputerWorld.* Most of these magazines also have online versions available on the Web.

Develop Professional Contacts

Besides being members of professional associations, successful people make it a point to maintain contact with others in their field. They stay in touch by telephone, e-mail, and newsgroups and go to lunch with others in their line of work. Doing this lets them learn what other people are doing in their jobs. It tells them what other firms are doing and what tasks are being automated. Developing professional contacts can keep you abreast not only of new information but also of new job possibilities. (See Figure 15-8.) It also offers social benefits. An example of a professional organization found in many areas is the local association of Realtors.

Develop Specialties

Develop specific as well as general skills. You want to be well-rounded *within* your field, but certainly not a "jack of all trades, master of none." Master a trade or two within your profession. At the same time, don't become identified with a specific technological skill that might very well become obsolete.

The best advice is to specialize to some extent. However, don't make your specialty so tied to technology that you'll be in trouble if the technology shifts. For example, if your career is in marketing or graphics design, it makes sense to learn about desktop publishing and Web page design. (See Figure 15-9.) In this way, you can learn to make high-quality, inexpensive graphics layouts. It would not make as much sense for you to become an expert on, say, the various types of monitors used to display the graphics layouts because such monitors are continually changing.

Expect to take classes during your working life to keep up with developments in your field. Some professions require more keeping up than others—a

Figure 15-9 Desktop publishing: A good specialty to develop for certain careers

Making IT work for you

LOCATING JOB OPPORTUNITIES ONLINE

Did you know that you can use the Internet to find a job? You can locate and browse through job listings. You can even electronically post your resume for prospective employers to review.

Browsing Job Listings   Three well-known job search sites on the Web are Yahoo! HotJobs (hotjobs.yahoo.com), Monster (monster.com), and CareerBuilder (careerbuilder.com). You can connect to these sites and browse through job opportunities. For example, after connecting to careerbuilder.com, you can search for a job by following steps similar to those shown below.

1 ● Visit **www.careerbuilder.com.**

   ● Click *Find Jobs.*

   ● Enter location to search.

   ● Select job categories to search.

   ● Enter optional keywords to refine your search.

   ● Click the *Find Jobs* button.

2 ● Select a job title from the table of results to learn more about that job posting.

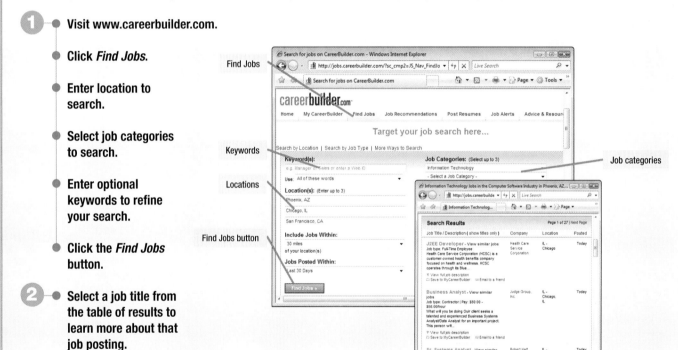

Posting Your Resume   To make your qualifications known to prospective employers, you can post your resume at the job search site.

1 ● **Click** *Post Resumes.*

   ● **If you do not have a resume to upload, select** *Resume Builder* **to create one.**

2 ● **Follow the step-by-step instructions on the screen and fill in blanks to create a professional resume.**

Your resume is posted and searchable by potential employers.

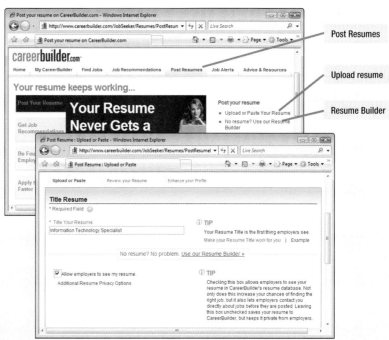

Post Resumes

Upload resume

Resume Builder

Automated Alerts   To help you find a job faster, you can set up automatic searches. When new jobs are posted that match your search, you can be alerted instantly by e-mail or mobile phone.

1 ● **Click** *Job Alerts.*

   ● **Fill in the search form similar to the** *Browse Job Listings* **section on the previous page.**

   ● **Provide your e-mail address and/or mobile phone number to receive alerts as new matching jobs are posted.**

Job Alerts

Your agent will search new job listings and alert you to new opportunities by e-mail.

The Web is continually changing, and some of the specifics presented in this Making IT Work for You may have changed.

To learn about other ways to make information technology work for you, visit our Web site at www.computing2011.com and enter the keyword miw.

computer specialist, for example, compared to a human resources manager. Whatever the training required, always look for ways to adapt and improve your skills to become more productive and marketable. There may be times when you are tempted to start all over again and learn completely new skills. However, a better course of action may be to use emerging technology to improve your present base of skills. This way you can build on your current strong points and then branch out to other fields from a position of strength.

Be Alert for Organizational Change

Every organization has formal lines of communication—for example, supervisor to middle manager to top manager. However, there is also the *grapevine*— informal lines of communication. (See Figure 15-10.) Some service departments will serve many layers of management and be abreast of the news on all levels. For instance, the art director for advertising may be aware of several aspects of a companywide marketing campaign. Secretaries and administrative assistants know what is going on in more than one area.

Being part of the office grapevine can alert you to important changes—for instance, new job openings—that can benefit you. However, you always have to assess the validity of what you hear on the grapevine. Moreover, it's not advisable to be a contributor to office gossip. Behind-the-back criticisms of other people have a way of getting back to the person criticized.

Be especially alert for new trends within the organization—future hiring, layoffs, automation, mergers with other companies, and the like. Notice which areas are receiving the greatest attention from top management. One tip-off is to see what kind of outside consultants are being brought in. Independent consultants are usually invited in because a company believes it needs advice in an area with which it has insufficient experience.

Look for Innovative Opportunities

You may understand your job better than anyone—even if you've only been there a few months. Look for ways to make it more efficient. How can present procedures be automated? How can new technology make your tasks easier? Discuss your ideas with your supervisor, the training director, or the head of the information systems department. Or discuss them with someone else who

Figure 15-10 Informal communication can alert you to important organizational changes

can see that you get the recognition you deserve. (Co-workers may or may not be receptive and may or may not try to take credit themselves.)

A good approach is to present your ideas in terms of saving money rather than "improving information." Managers are generally more impressed with ideas that can save dollars than with ideas that seem like potential breakthroughs in the quality of decisions.

In general, it's best to concentrate on the business and organizational problems that need solving. Then look for a technological way of solving them. That is, avoid becoming too enthusiastic about a particular technology and then trying to make it fit the work situation.

 ## CONCEPT CHECK

 Outline the strategies you can use to stay ahead and be successful in your career.

 Discuss the advantages and disadvantages of specialization.

 Describe how you would stay alert for organizational changes.

Careers in IT

Being a winner does not necessarily mean having a career in information systems. There are, however, several jobs within information technology that you might like to consider. We have discussed many of these careers in the preceding chapters. (See Figure 15-11.)

To learn more about these careers, visit our Web site at www.computing 2011.com and enter the keyword **careers.**

Career	Responsibilities
Computer support specialist	Provides technical support to customers and other users
Computer technician	Repairs and installs computer components and systems
Computer trainer	Instructs users on the latest software or hardware
Cryptographer	Designs, tests, and researches encryption procedures
Data entry worker	Inputs customer information, lists, and other types of data
Database administrator	Uses database management software to determine the most efficient ways to organize and access data
Desktop publisher	Creates and formats publication-ready material
Information systems manager	Oversees the work of programmers, computer specialists, systems analysts, and other computer professionals
Network administrator	Creates and maintains networks
Programmer	Creates, tests, and troubleshoots computer programs
Software engineer	Analyzes users' needs and creates application software
Systems analyst	Plans and designs information systems
Technical writer	Prepares instruction manuals, technical reports, and other scientific or technical documents
Webmaster	Develops and maintains Web sites and Web resources

Figure 15-11 Careers in information systems

A LOOK TO THE FUTURE

Maintaining Computer Competency and Becoming Proactive

This is not the end; it is the beginning. Being a skilled computer end user and having computer competency are not a matter of thinking, "Someday I'll have to learn all about that." They are a matter of living in the present and keeping an eye on the future. Computer competency also demands the discipline to keep up with emerging technology. Yet it is important not to focus on the "what ifs" of technology. Computer competency demands concentration on your goals and dedication to learning how the computer can aid you in obtaining these goals. Being an end user, in short, is not about trying to avoid failure. Rather, it is about always moving toward success—about taking control of the exciting new tools available to you.

CHANGING TIMES

Individuals, businesses, and organizations must adapt to changing technology or be left behind.

Banking Industry
The banking industry uses automated teller machines (ATMs) to provide 24-hour service without incurring additional employee costs. Internet banks conduct all business over the Web.

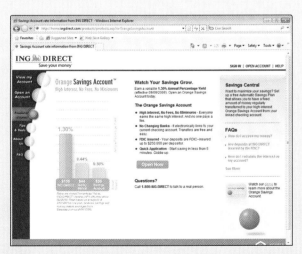

Many changes do away with jobs. Technology, however, creates opportunities. New technology requires people who are truly capable of working with it. To become and stay a winner, you must form your own individual strategy for dealing with changes.

TECHNOLOGY AND ORGANIZATIONS

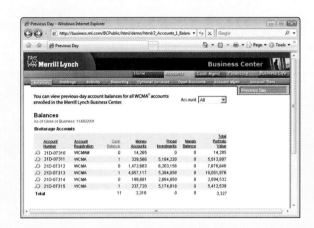

Technology can introduce new ways for businesses to compete with each other. They can compete by *creating new products, establishing new enterprises,* and *developing new customer and supplier relationships.*

New Products
Technology creates products that operate faster, are priced more cheaply, are often better quality, or are wholly new. New products can be individually tailored to a particular customer's needs.

New Enterprises
Technology can build entirely new businesses. Two examples:

- Internet service providers—just a few years ago, only a few Internet service providers were available. Now, thousands of national and local providers are available.
- Web site development companies—thousands of small companies specializing in developing Web sites have sprung up in just the past few years.

New Customer and Supplier Relationships
Businesses that make their information systems easily available may make their customers less likely to take their business elsewhere (e.g., overnight delivery services closely track packages and bills).

To stay competent, you need to recognize the impact of technological change on organizations and people. You need to know how to use change to your advantage and how to become a winner. Although you do not need to be a specialist in information technology, you should be aware of career opportunities in the area.

TECHNOLOGY AND PEOPLE

People have different coping styles when it comes to technology. Four common reactions to new technology are cynicism, naivete, frustration, and proactivity.

Cynicism

The **cynics** feel that new technology is over-rated and too troublesome to learn. Some cynics openly express their doubts. Others pretend to be interested.

Naivete

Naive people may be unfamiliar or quite familiar with computers. People who are unfamiliar tend to think of computers as magic boxes. Even those familiar with technology often underestimate the time and difficulty of using technology to generate information.

Frustration

Frustrated users are impatient and irritated about taking time to learn new technology. Often these people have too much to do, find manuals difficult to understand, and/or feel stupid.

Proactivity

A **proactive** person looks at technology in a positive and realistic way. He or she is not cynical, naive, or frustrated regarding new technology. Proactive people are positive and look at new technology as providing new tools that can positively impact their lives.

HOW YOU CAN BE A WINNER

There are six ongoing activities that can help you be successful.

Stay Current

Read trade journals and the general business press, join professional associations, and participate in interest groups on the Internet.

Maintain Your Computer Competency

Stay current by reading computer-related articles in the general press and trade journals.

Develop Professional Contacts

Stay active in your profession and meet people in your field. This provides information about other people, firms, job opportunities, and social contacts.

Develop Specialties

Develop specific as well as general skills. Expect to take classes periodically to stay current with your field and technology.

Be Alert for Organizational Change

Use formal and informal lines of communication. Be alert for new trends within the organization.

Look for Innovative Opportunities

Look for ways to increase efficiency. Present ideas in terms of saving money rather than "improving information."

Computer Support Specialist

Computer support specialists provide technical support to customers and other users.

Computer Technician

Computer technicians repair and install computer components and systems.

Computer Trainer

Computer trainers instruct users on the latest software or hardware.

Cryptographer

Cryptographers design, test, and research encryption procedures.

Data Entry Worker

Data entry workers input customer information, lists, and other types of data.

Database Administrator

Database administrators use database management software to determine the most efficient ways to organize and access data.

Desktop Publisher

Desktop publishers create and format publication-ready material.

Information Systems Manager

Information systems managers oversee the work of programmers, computer specialists, systems analysts, and other computer professionals.

Network Administrator

Network administrators create and maintain networks.

Programmer

Programmers create, test, and troubleshoot computer programs.

Software Engineer

Software engineers analyze users' needs and create application software.

Systems Analyst

Systems analysts plan and design information systems.

Technical Writer

Technical writers prepare instruction manuals, technical reports, and other scientific or technical documents.

Webmaster

Webmasters develop and maintain Web sites and Web resources.

KEY TERMS

computer support specialist   (443)
computer technician   (443)
computer trainer   (443)
cryptographer   (443)
cynic   (437)
data entry worker   (443)
database administrator (DBA)   (443)
desktop publisher   (443)
frustrated   (437)

information systems manager   (443)
naive   (437)
network administrator   (443)
proactive   (437)
programmer   (443)
software engineer   (443)
systems analyst   (443)
technical writer   (443)
Webmaster   (443)

To test your knowledge of these key terms with animated flash cards, visit our Web site at www.computing2011.com and enter the keyword terms15.

MULTIPLE CHOICE

Circle the letter or fill in the correct answer.

1. Changes in technology require people who
   a. are not afraid to learn and manage new technology
   b. know just the basics about the technology
   c. think each new machine is a potential disaster
   d. think every piece of equipment is so simple they can just turn it on and use it

2. One of the advantages of the changes in information technology is
   a. data can be lost and/or stolen
   b. new businesses are created
   c. new skills are constantly in demand
   d. people are put out of work

3. The _____ user believes that learning and using computers take time away from his or her real job.
   a. cynical
   b. frustrated
   c. naive
   d. proactive

4. Generally, a proactive person
   a. feels that the idea of using a microcomputer is overrated
   b. is unfamiliar with computers
   c. hates to take time to learn about microcomputers
   d. looks at technology in a positive, realistic way

5. To maintain your computer competence, you should try to stay ahead of technology by
   a. learning a new trade
   b. quitting your current job and going back to school
   c. reading books, journals, newspapers, and magazines
   d. reviewing the systems life cycle

6. Successful people make it a point to
   a. avoid contact with others
   b. develop nonspecific skills
   c. get their education and relax
   d. maintain contact with others in their field

7. These individuals design, test, and research encryption procedures.
   a. database administrators
   b. computer trainers
   c. cryptographers
   d. technical writers

8. _____ oversee the work of programmers, computer specialists, and other computer professionals.
   a. Database administrators
   b. Information systems managers
   c. Network managers
   d. Systems analysts

9. These individuals are responsible for creating, testing, and troubleshooting computer programs.
   a. database administrators
   b. network managers
   c. programmers
   d. systems analysts

10. _____ develop and maintain Web sites and Web resources.
    a. Network managers
    b. Programmers
    c. Systems analysts
    d. Webmasters

For an interactive multiple-choice practice test, visit our Web site at www.computing 2011.com and enter the keyword multiple15.

MATCHING

Match each numbered item with the most closely related lettered item. Write your answers in the spaces provided.

a. computer technician
b. computer trainer
c. cynic
d. database administrator
e. network administrator
f. programmer
g. software engineer
h. systems analyst
i. technical writer
j. Webmaster

1. Computer user who feels the idea of using micro-computers is overrated. _____
2. A computer specialist employed to evaluate, create, and maintain Web sites. _____
3. Computer professional who creates, tests, and troubleshoots computer programs. _____
4. Computer specialist who uses database management software to determine the most efficient ways to organize and access data. _____
5. Computer professional who analyzes users' needs and creates application software. _____
6. Computer professional who plans and designs information systems. _____
7. Computer professional who repairs and installs computer components and systems. _____
8. Computer professional who creates and maintains networks. _____
9. Computer professional who instructs users on the latest software or hardware. _____
10. Computer professional who prepares instruction manuals, technical reports, and other scientific or technical documents. _____

For an interactive matching practice test, visit our Web site at www.computing 2011.com and enter the keyword matching15.

OPEN-ENDED

On a separate sheet of paper, respond to each question or statement.

1. Why is strategy important to individual success in the information age? What is your strategy?
2. Describe how technology changes the nature of competition.
3. How can your computer competencies and knowledge help you get ahead in today's market?
4. What does proactive mean? What is a proactive computer user? What advantages does this type of user have over the other types?
5. Discuss several different careers in information technology. Which are of interest to you?

APPLYING TECHNOLOGY

The following questions are designed to demonstrate ways that you can effectively use technology today. The first question relates directly to this chapter's Making IT Work for You feature.

1 JOBS ONLINE

Did you know that you can use the Internet to find a job? You can browse through job listings, post resumes for prospective employers, and even use special agents to continually search for that job that's just right for you. To learn more about online job searches, review Making IT Work for You: Locating Job Opportunities Online on pages 440 and 441. Then visit our Web site at www.computing 2011.com and enter the keyword jobs. Once at that site, play the video and answer the following: (a) What locations and categories were selected for the job search? (b) Describe the process for posting a resume. (c) What search criteria were used to set up the job search agent?

2 MAINTAIN COMPUTER COMPETENCE

There are several sources of information to help keep you up to date on current computing trends. Visit our Web site at www.computing 2011.com and enter the keyword competence to link to a few computing sites. Explore the sites and then answer the following: (a) List the sites you visited and describe the focus of each. (b) Which of these sites was most useful? Why? (c) Which of these sites was least useful? Why? (d) What are other ways you can stay in step with current computing issues?

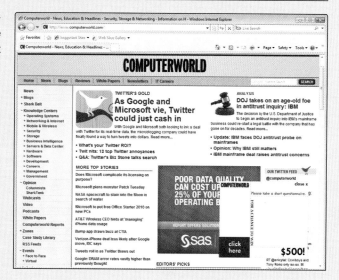

EXPANDING YOUR KNOWLEDGE

The following questions are designed to add depth and detail to your understanding of specific topics presented within this chapter. The questions direct you to sources other than the textbook to obtain this knowledge.

1 YOUR CAREER

Have you thought about what your career might be? Perhaps it is in marketing, education, or information technology. If you have a career in mind, conduct a Web search to learn more about your chosen career. If you don't have a career in mind, select one of the information systems careers presented in this chapter and conduct a Web search to learn more about that career. After reviewing at least five sites, answer the following: (a) Describe your career of choice. (b) Why did you choose that career? (c) How is information technology used in this career? (d) How will changing technology impact your chosen career?

2 RESUME ADVICE

There are several excellent resources available online to help you write a winning resume. Conduct a Web search using the keywords "resume help" to learn more. Review at least five sites and then compose a sample resume for yourself, applying the information from the sites.

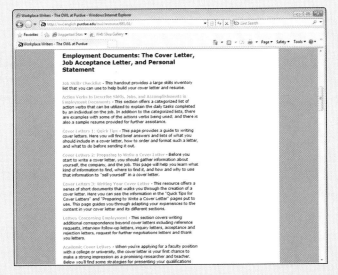

WRITING ABOUT TECHNOLOGY

The ability to think critically and to write effectively is essential to nearly every profession. The following questions are designed to help you develop these skills by posing thought-provoking questions about computer privacy, security, and/or ethics.

① WRITING ABOUT PRIVACY AND ETHICS

Regardless of your career path, critical thinking, analysis, and writing are essential skills. In each of the preceding chapters, the Writing About Technology feature presented questions about privacy and ethics. These questions are designed to help you develop critical thinking, analysis, and writing skills. Select the five questions you feel are most important to privacy or ethics from the Writing About Technology questions in the preceding chapters. Write a two-page paper that addresses the questions you chose and describe why they are of interest to you.

② WRITING ABOUT SECURITY

The importance of computer security is often overshadowed by the functions and features of new technology. The Writing About Technology feature presented many questions about security in the preceding chapters. These questions are designed to increase your awareness of important computer security topics and further develop your writing skills. Select the five questions you feel are most important to security from the Writing About Technology questions in the preceding chapters. Write a two-page paper that addresses the questions you chose and describe why they are of interest to you.

The Evolution of the Computer Age

Many of you probably can't remember a world without computers, but for some of us, computers were virtually unknown when we were born and have rapidly come of age during our lifetime.

Although there are many predecessors to what we think of as the modern computer—reaching as far back as the 18th century, when Joseph Marie Jacquard created a loom programmed to weave cloth and Charles Babbage created the first fully modern computer design (which he could never get to work)—the computer age did not really begin until the first computer was made available to the public in 1951.

The modern age of computers thus spans slightly more than 50 years (so far), which is typically broken down into five generations. Each generation has been marked by a significant advance in technology.

- **First Generation (1951–57):** During the first generation, computers were built with vacuum tubes— electronic tubes that were made of glass and were about the size of light bulbs.

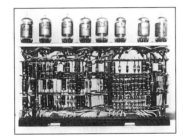

- **Second Generation (1958–63):** This generation began with the first computers built with transistors—small devices that transfer electronic signals across a resistor. Because transistors are much smaller, use less power, and create less heat than vacuum tubes, the new computers were faster, smaller, and more reliable than the first-generation machines.

- **Third Generation (1964–69):** In 1964, computer manufacturers began replacing transistors with integrated circuits. An integrated circuit (IC) is a complete electronic circuit on a small chip made of silicon (one of the most abundant elements in the earth's crust). These computers were more reliable and compact than computers made with transistors, and they cost less to manufacture.

- **Fourth Generation (1970–90):** Many key advances were made during this generation, the most significant being the microprocessor—a specialized chip developed for computer memory and logic. Use of a single chip to create a smaller "personal" computer (as well as digital watches,

pocket calculators, copy machines, and so on) revolutionized the computer industry.

- **Fifth Generation (1991–2011 and beyond):** Our current generation has been referred to as the "Connected Generation" because of the industry's massive effort to increase the connectivity of computers. The rapidly expanding Internet, World Wide Web, and intranets have cre-

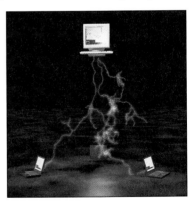

ated an information superhighway that has enabled both computer professionals and home computer users to communicate with others across the globe.

This appendix provides you with a timeline that describes in more detail some of the most significant events in each generation of the computer age.

First Generation: The Vacuum Tube Age

1951 Dr. John W. Mauchly and J. Presper Eckert Jr. introduce the first commercially available electronic digital computer—the UNIVAC—built with vacuum tubes. This computer was based on their earlier ENIAC (Electronic Numerical Integrator and Computer) design completed in 1946.

1951–53 IBM adds computers to its business equipment products and sells over 1,000 IBM 650 systems.

1951	1952	1953	1954	1955	1956	1957

1957 Introduction of first high-level programming language—FORTRAN (FORmula TRANslator).

1952 Development team led by Dr. Grace Hopper, former U.S. Navy programmer, introduces the A6 Compiler—the first example of software that converts high-level language symbols into instructions that a computer can execute.

Second Generation: The Transistor Age

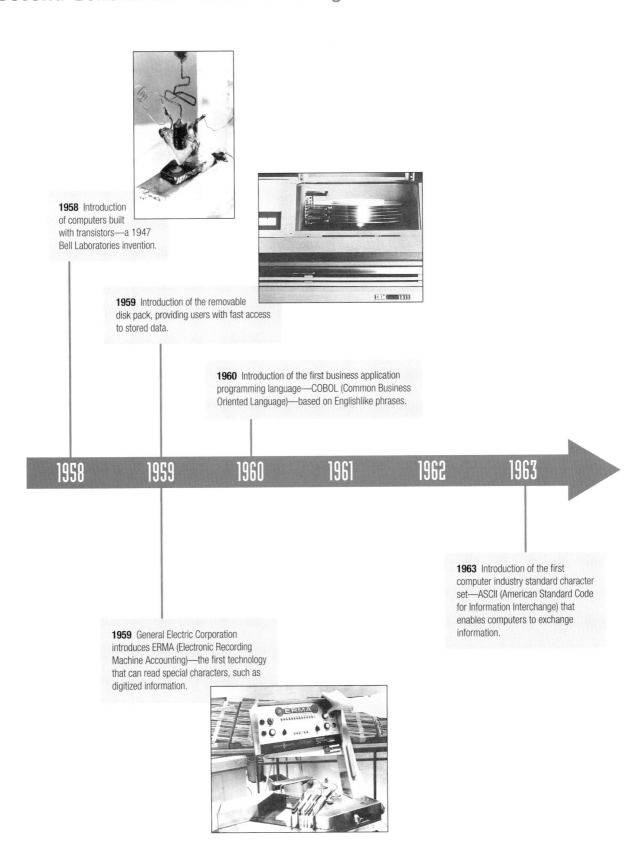

1958 Introduction of computers built with transistors—a 1947 Bell Laboratories invention.

1959 Introduction of the removable disk pack, providing users with fast access to stored data.

1960 Introduction of the first business application programming language—COBOL (Common Business Oriented Language)—based on Englishlike phrases.

| 1958 | 1959 | 1960 | 1961 | 1962 | 1963 |

1963 Introduction of the first computer industry standard character set—ASCII (American Standard Code for Information Interchange) that enables computers to exchange information.

1959 General Electric Corporation introduces ERMA (Electronic Recording Machine Accounting)—the first technology that can read special characters, such as digitized information.

Third Generation: The Integrated Circuit Age

1964 Introduction of computers built with an integrated circuit (IC), which incorporates multiple transistors and electronic circuits on a single silicon chip.

1965 Digital Equipment Corporation (DEC) introduces the first minicomputer.

1969 Introduction of ARPANET and the beginning of the Internet.

| 1964 | 1965 | 1966 | 1967 | 1968 | 1969 |

1965 Introduction of the BASIC programming language.

1969 IBM announces its decision to offer unbundled software, priced and sold separately from the hardware.

1964 IBM introduces its System/360 line of compatible computers, which can all use the same programs and peripherals.

Fourth Generation: The Microprocessor Age

1970 Introduction of computers built with chips that used LSI (large-scale integration).

1975 First local area network (LAN)—Ethernet—developed at Xerox PARC (Palo Alto Research Center).

1977 Apple Computer, Inc., founded by Steve Wozniak and Steve Jobs, and Apple I introduced as an easy-to-use "hobbyist" computer.

| 1970 | 1971 | 1972 | 1973 | 1974 | 1975 | 1976 | 1977 | 1978 | 1979 |

1971 Dr. Ted Hoff of Intel Corporation develops a microprogrammable computer chip—the Intel 4004 microprocessor.

1975 The MITS, Inc., Altair becomes the first commercially successful microcomputer, selling for less than $400 a kit.

1979 Introduction of the first public information services—Compuserve and the Source.

1980 IBM asks Microsoft founder, Bill Gates, to develop an operating system—MS-DOS— for the soon-to-be-released IBM personal computer.

1981 Introduction of the IBM PC, which contains an Intel microprocessor chip and Microsoft's MS-DOS operating system.

1989 Introduction of Intel 486—the first 1,000,000-transistor microprocessor.

| 1980 | 1981 | 1982 | 1983 | 1984 | 1985 | 1986 | 1987 | 1988 | 1989 | 1990 |

1984 Apple introduces the Macintosh Computer, with a unique, easy-to-use graphical user interface.

1985 Microsoft introduces its Windows graphical user interface.

1990 Microsoft releases Windows 3.0, with an enhanced graphical user interface and the ability to run multiple applications.

The Evolution of the Computer Age **459**

Fifth Generation: The Age of Connectivity

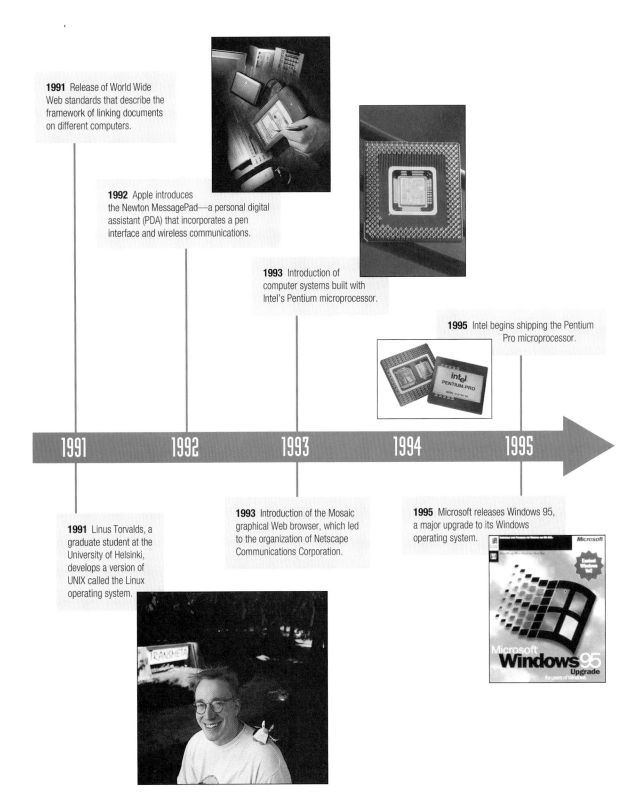

1991 Release of World Wide Web standards that describe the framework of linking documents on different computers.

1992 Apple introduces the Newton MessagePad—a personal digital assistant (PDA) that incorporates a pen interface and wireless communications.

1993 Introduction of computer systems built with Intel's Pentium microprocessor.

1995 Intel begins shipping the Pentium Pro microprocessor.

1991 **1992** **1993** **1994** **1995**

1991 Linus Torvalds, a graduate student at the University of Helsinki, develops a version of UNIX called the Linux operating system.

1993 Introduction of the Mosaic graphical Web browser, which led to the organization of Netscape Communications Corporation.

1995 Microsoft releases Windows 95, a major upgrade to its Windows operating system.

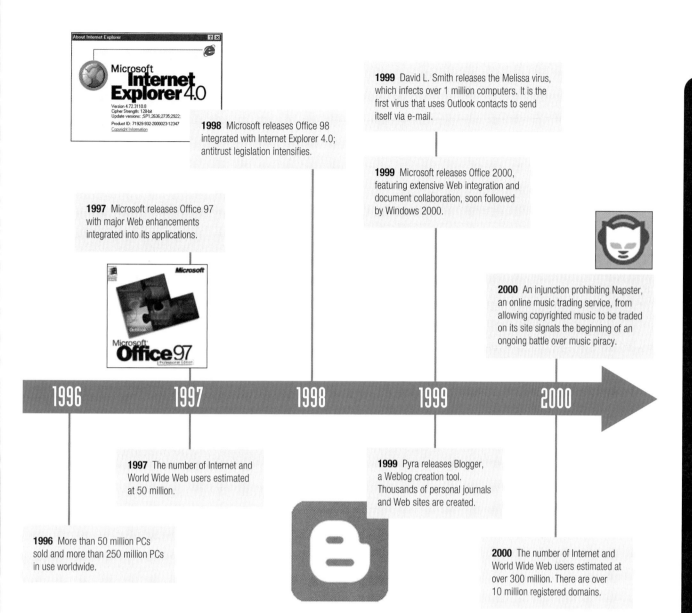

1999 David L. Smith releases the Melissa virus, which infects over 1 million computers. It is the first virus that uses Outlook contacts to send itself via e-mail.

1998 Microsoft releases Office 98 integrated with Internet Explorer 4.0; antitrust legislation intensifies.

1999 Microsoft releases Office 2000, featuring extensive Web integration and document collaboration, soon followed by Windows 2000.

1997 Microsoft releases Office 97 with major Web enhancements integrated into its applications.

2000 An injunction prohibiting Napster, an online music trading service, from allowing copyrighted music to be traded on its site signals the beginning of an ongoing battle over music piracy.

1996 1997 1998 1999 2000

1997 The number of Internet and World Wide Web users estimated at 50 million.

1999 Pyra releases Blogger, a Weblog creation tool. Thousands of personal journals and Web sites are created.

1996 More than 50 million PCs sold and more than 250 million PCs in use worldwide.

2000 The number of Internet and World Wide Web users estimated at over 300 million. There are over 10 million registered domains.

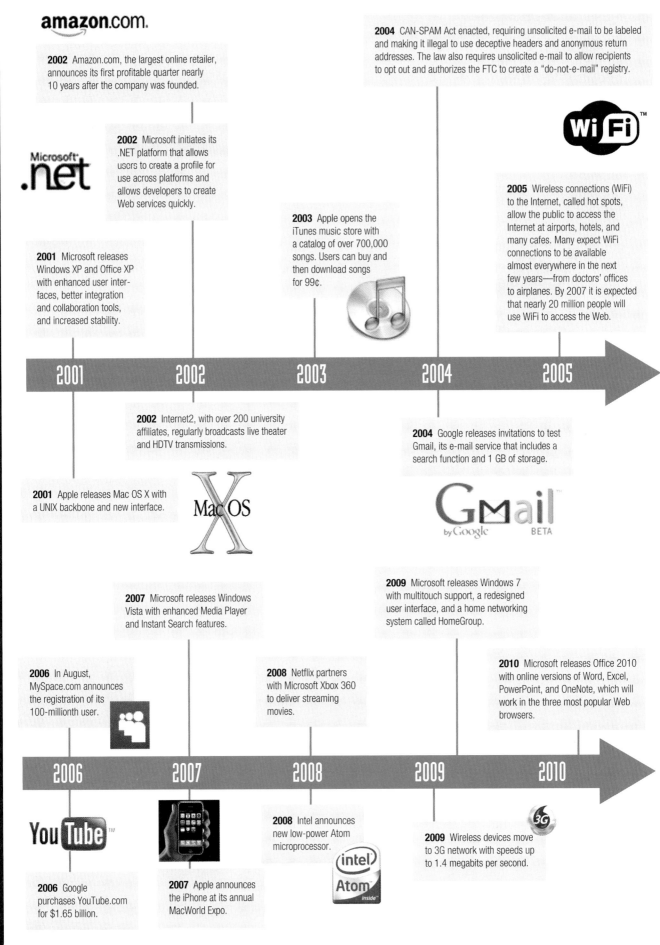

amazon.com.

2002 Amazon.com, the largest online retailer, announces its first profitable quarter nearly 10 years after the company was founded.

2004 CAN-SPAM Act enacted, requiring unsolicited e-mail to be labeled and making it illegal to use deceptive headers and anonymous return addresses. The law also requires unsolicited e-mail to allow recipients to opt out and authorizes the FTC to create a "do-not-e-mail" registry.

Microsoft®
.net

2002 Microsoft initiates its .NET platform that allows users to create a profile for use across platforms and allows developers to create Web services quickly.

2003 Apple opens the iTunes music store with a catalog of over 700,000 songs. Users can buy and then download songs for 99¢.

2005 Wireless connections (WiFi) to the Internet, called hot spots, allow the public to access the Internet at airports, hotels, and many cafes. Many expect WiFi connections to be available almost everywhere in the next few years—from doctors' offices to airplanes. By 2007 it is expected that nearly 20 million people will use WiFi to access the Web.

2001 Microsoft releases Windows XP and Office XP with enhanced user interfaces, better integration and collaboration tools, and increased stability.

2001 | **2002** | **2003** | **2004** | **2005**

2002 Internet2, with over 200 university affiliates, regularly broadcasts live theater and HDTV transmissions.

2004 Google releases invitations to test Gmail, its e-mail service that includes a search function and 1 GB of storage.

2001 Apple releases Mac OS X with a UNIX backbone and new interface.

Mac OS X

Gmail by Google BETA

2007 Microsoft releases Windows Vista with enhanced Media Player and Instant Search features.

2009 Microsoft releases Windows 7 with multitouch support, a redesigned user interface, and a home networking system called HomeGroup.

2006 In August, MySpace.com announces the registration of its 100-millionth user.

2008 Netflix partners with Microsoft Xbox 360 to deliver streaming movies.

2010 Microsoft releases Office 2010 with online versions of Word, Excel, PowerPoint, and OneNote, which will work in the three most popular Web browsers.

2006 | **2007** | **2008** | **2009** | **2010**

You Tube™

2008 Intel announces new low-power Atom microprocessor.

2009 Wireless devices move to 3G network with speeds up to 1.4 megabits per second.

2006 Google purchases YouTube.com for $1.65 billion.

2007 Apple announces the iPhone at its annual MacWorld Expo.

intel Atom inside™

462   The Evolution of the Computer Age

The Buyer's Guide How to Buy Your Own Microcomputer System

FOUR STEPS IN BUYING A MICROCOMPUTER SYSTEM

The following is not intended to make buying a microcomputer an exhausting experience. Rather, it is to help you clarify your thinking about what you need and can afford.

The four steps in buying a microcomputer system are presented on the following pages. We divide each step into two parts based on the assumptions that both your needs and the money you have to spend on a microcomputer may change.

STEP 1

What Needs Do I Want a Computer to Serve?

The trick is to distinguish between your needs and your wants. Sure, you *want* a cutting-edge system powerful enough to run every conceivable program you'll ever need. And you want a system fast enough to process them all at the speed of light. But do you *need* this? Your main concern is to address the following two questions:

- What do I need a computer system to do for me today?

- What will I need it to do for me in another year or two?

The questionnaire at the end of this guide will help you determine the answers to both questions.

Suggestions

Consider the type of computer most available on campus. Some schools favor Apple computers; others favor Windows-based computers. If you own a system that's incompatible with most computers on campus, you may be stuck if your computer breaks down.

Look ahead and determine whether your major requires a computer. Business and engineering students may find one a necessity; physical education and drama majors may not. Your major also may determine the kind of computer that's best. A journalism major may want a Windows-based notebook. An architecture major may want a powerful desktop Macintosh with a laser printer that can produce elaborate drawings. Ask your academic advisor for some recommendations.

Example

Suppose you are a college student beginning your sophomore year, with no major declared. Looking at the courses you will likely take this year, you decide you will probably need a computer mainly for word processing. That is, you need a system that will help you write short (10- to 20-page) papers for a variety of courses.

By this time next year, however, you may be an accounting major. Having talked to some juniors and seniors, you find that courses in this major, such as financial accounting, will require you to use elaborate spreadsheets. Or maybe you will be a fine arts or architecture major. Then you may be required to submit projects for which drawing and painting desktop publishing software would be helpful.

STEP 2

How Much Money Do I Have to Spend on a Computer System?

When you buy your first computer, you are not necessarily buying your last. Thus, you can think about spending just the bare-bones amount for a system that meets your needs while in college. Then you might plan to get another system later on.

You know the amount of money you have to spend. Your main concern is to answer the following two questions:

- How much am I prepared to spend on a computer system today?

- How much am I prepared to spend in another year or two?

The questionnaire at the end of this guide asks you this.

Suggestions

You can probably buy a good used computer of some sort for under $300 and a printer for under $50. On the other hand, you might spend $1,000 to $2,500 on a new state-of-the-art system. When upgraded, this computer could meet your needs for the next five years.

There is nothing wrong with getting a used system if you have a way of checking it out. For a reasonable fee, a computer-repair shop can examine it prior to your purchase. Look at newspaper ads and notices on campus bulletin boards for good buys on used equipment. Also try the Internet. If you stay with recognized brands, such as Apple, IBM, Compaq, or Dell, you probably won't have any difficulties.

If you're buying new equipment, be sure to look for student discounts. Most college bookstores, for instance, offer special prices to students. Also check the Web. There are numerous sites specializing in discounted computer systems.

Example

Perhaps you have access to a microcomputer at the campus student computing center, the library, or the dormitory. Or you can borrow a friend's. However, this computer isn't always available when it's convenient for you. Moreover, you're not only going to college, but you're also working, so both time and money are tight. Having your own computer would enable you to write papers when it's convenient for you. Spending more than $350 might cause real hardship, so a new microcomputer system may be out of the question. You'll need to shop the newspaper classified ads or the campus bulletin boards to find a used but workable computer system.

Or maybe you can afford to spend more now—say, between $1,000 and $2,000—but probably only $500 next year. By this time next year, however, you'll know your major and how your computer needs have changed.

STEP 3

What Kind of Software Will Best Serve My Needs?

Most computer experts urge that you determine what software you need before you buy the hardware. The reasoning here is that some hardware simply won't run the software that is important to you. This is certainly true once you get into *sophisticated* software. Examples include specialized programs available for certain professions (such as certain agricultural or retail-management programs). However, if all you are interested in today are the basic software tools—word processing, spreadsheet, and communications programs—these are available for nearly all microcomputers. The main caution is that some more recent versions of application software won't run on older hardware. Still, if someone offers you a free computer, don't say no because you feel you have to decide what software you need first. You will no doubt find it sufficient for many general purposes, especially during your early years in college.

That said, you are better served if you follow step 3 after step 2—namely, finding the answers to the following two questions:

- **What kind of software will best serve my needs today?**
- **What kind will best serve my needs in another year or two?**

The questionnaire at the end of this guide will help you determine your answers.

Suggestions

No doubt some kinds of application software are more available on your campus—and in certain departments on your campus—than others. Are freshman and sophomore students mainly writing their term papers in Word, WordPerfect, or Apple Pages? Which spreadsheet is most often used by business students: Excel, Apple iWork's Numbers, or Quattro Pro? Which desktop publishing program is most favored by graphic arts majors: PageMaker, Quark Express, or MS Publisher? Do engineering and architecture majors use their own machines for CAD/CAM applications? Start by asking other students and your academic advisor.

If you're looking to buy state-of-the-art software, you'll find plenty of advice in various computer magazines. Several of them rate the quality of newly issued programs. Such periodicals include *PC World* and *MacWorld*.

Example

Suppose you determine that all you need is software to help you write short papers. In that case, nearly any kind of word processing program would do. But will this software be sufficient a year or two from now? Looking ahead, you guess that you'll major in theater arts and minor in screenwriting, which you may pursue as a career. At that point, a simple word processing program might not do. You learn from juniors and seniors in that department that screenplays are written using special screenwriting programs. This is software that's not available for some computers. Or, as an advertising and marketing major, you're expected to turn word-processed promotional pieces into brochures. For this, you need desktop publishing software. Or, as a physics major, you discover you will need to write reports on a word processor that can handle equations. In short, you need to look at your software needs not just for today but also for the near future. You especially want to consider what programs will be useful to you in building your career.

STEP 4

What Kind of Hardware Will Best Serve My Needs?

A bare-bones hardware system might include a three-year-old desktop or notebook computer with a CD-ROM disc drive and a hard-disk drive. It also should include a monitor and a printer. On the one hand, as a student—unless you're involved in some very specialized activities—it's doubtful you'll really need such things as voice-input devices, touch screens, scanners, and the like. On the other hand, you will probably need speakers and a DVD-ROM drive. The choices of equipment are vast.

As with the other steps, the main task is to find the answers to the following two questions:

- **What kind of hardware will best serve my needs today?**

- **What kind will best serve my needs in another year or two?**

There are several questions on the questionnaire at the end of this guide to help you determine answers to these concerns.

Suggestions

Clearly, you should let the software be your guide in determining your choice of hardware. Perhaps you've found that the most popular software in your department runs on an Apple computer rather than a Windows-based computer. If so, that would seem to determine your general brand of hardware.

Whether you buy IBM or Macintosh, a desktop or a notebook, we suggest you get a hard-disk drive with at least 40 gigabytes of storage, a DVD drive, at least 512 megabytes of memory, and an ink-jet printer.

As with software, several computer magazines not only describe new hardware but also issue ratings. See *PC World* and *MacWorld,* for example.

Example

Right now, let's say, you're mainly interested in using a computer to write papers, so almost anything would do. But you need to look ahead.

Suppose you find that Word seems to be the software of choice around your campus. You find that Word 2007 will run well on a Pentium machine with 256 megabytes of memory and a 1.5-gigabyte hard disk. Although this equipment is now outdated, you find from looking at classified ads that there are many such used machines around. Plus, they cost very little—well under $500 for a complete system.

Your choice then becomes: Should I buy an inexpensive system now that can't be upgraded, then sell it later and buy a better one? Or should I buy at least some of the components of a good system now and upgrade it over the next year or so?

As an advertising major, you see the value of learning desktop publishing. This will be a useful if not essential skill once you embark on a career. In exploring the software, you learn that Word includes some desktop publishing capabilities. However, the hardware you previously considered simply isn't sufficient. Moreover, you learn from reading about software and talking to people in your major that there are better desktop publishing programs. Specialized desktop publishing programs like Ventura Publisher are considered more versatile than Word. Probably the best software arrangement, in fact, is to have Word as a word processing program and Ventura Publisher for a desktop publishing program.

To be sure, the campus has computers that will run this software available to students. If you can afford it, however, you're better off having your own. Now, however, we're talking about a major expense. A computer running a multicore microprocessor, with 6 gigabytes of memory, a rewriteable DVD disc drive, and a 400-gigabyte hard disk, plus a modem, color monitor, and laser printer, could cost in excess of $1,500.

DEVELOPING A PHILOSOPHY ABOUT COMPUTER PURCHASING

It's important not to develop a case of "computer envy." Even if you buy the latest, most expensive microcomputer system, in a matter of months something better will come along. Computer technology is still in a very dynamic state, with more powerful, versatile, and compact systems constantly hitting the marketplace. So what if your friends have the hottest new piece of software or hardware? The main question is: Do you need it to solve the tasks required of you or to keep up in your field? Or can you get along with something simpler but equally serviceable?

Visual Summary The Buyer's Guide:
How to Buy Your Own Microcomputer System

NEEDS

What do I need a computer system to do for me today? In another year or two?

I WISH TO USE THE COMPUTER FOR:

	Today	1–2 years
Word processing—writing papers, letters, memos, or reports	❏	❏
Business or financial applications—balance sheets, sales projections, expense budgets, or accounting problems	❏	❏
Record keeping and sorting—research bibliographies, scientific data, or address files	❏	❏
Graphic presentations of business, scientific, or social science data	❏	❏
Online information retrieval to campus networks, service providers, or the Internet	❏	❏
Publications, design, or drawing for printed newsletters, architectural drawing, or graphic arts	❏	❏
Multimedia for video games, viewing, creating, presenting, or research	❏	❏
Other (specify): _____	❏	❏

BUDGET

How much am I prepared to spend on a system today? In another year or two?

I CAN SPEND:

	Today	1–2 years
Under $500	❏	❏
Up to $1,000	❏	❏
Up to $1,500	❏	❏
Up to $2,000	❏	❏
Up to $2,500	❏	❏
Over $3,000	❏	❏
(specify): _____		

Buying a Microcomputer System	
Step	Questions
1	*My needs:* What do I need a computer system to do for me today? In another year or two?
2	*My budget:* How much am I prepared to spend on a system today? In another year or two?
3	*My software:* What kind of software will best serve my needs today? In another year or two?
4	*My hardware:* What kind of hardware will best serve my needs today? In another year or two?

To help clarify your thinking about buying a microcomputer system, complete the questionnaire by checking the appropriate boxes.

SOFTWARE

What kinds of software will best serve my needs today? In another year or two?

The Application Software I Need Includes:

	Today	1–2 years
Word processing—Word, WordPerfect, or other (specify): _____	❏	❏
Spreadsheet—Excel, iWork's Numbers, or other (specify): _____	❏	❏
Database—Access, Paradox, or other (specify): _____	❏	❏
Presentation graphics—PowerPoint, Freelance, CorelPresentations, or other (specify): _____	❏	❏
Browsers—Mozilla Firefox, Apple Safari, Microsoft Internet Explorer, or other (specify): _____	❏	❏
Other—integrated packages, software suites, graphics, multimedia, Web authoring, CAD/CAM, other (specify): _____	❏	❏

The System Software I Need:

	Today	1–2 years
Windows 7	❏	❏
Windows Vista	❏	❏
Mac OS	❏	❏
UNIX	❏	❏
Other (specify): _____	❏	❏

HARDWARE

What kinds of hardware will best serve my needs today? In another year or two?

The Hardware I Need Includes:

	Today	1–2 years
Microprocessor—Celeron, Apple G4, other (specify): _____	❏	❏
Memory—(specify amount): _____	❏	❏
Monitor—size (specify): _____	❏	❏
Optical disc drive—CD-ROM, DVD-ROM (specify type, speed, and capacity): _____	❏	❏
Hard-disk drive—(specify capacity): _____	❏	❏
Portable computer—laptop, notebook, netbook, personal digital assistant (specify): _____	❏	❏
Printer—ink-jet, laser, color (specify): _____	❏	❏
Other—modem, network card, speakers, fax, surge protector (specify): _____	❏	❏

The Upgrader's Guide How to Upgrade Your Microcomputer System

If you own a microcomputer, chances are that your machine is not the latest and greatest. Microcomputers are always getting better—more powerful and faster. While that is a good thing, it can be frustrating trying to keep up.

What can you do? If you have lots of money, you can simply buy a new one. Another alternative is to upgrade or add new components to increase the power and speed of your current microcomputer. You probably can increase your system's performance at a fraction of the cost of a new one.

THREE STEPS IN UPGRADING A MICROCOMPUTER SYSTEM

The following is not intended to detail specific hardware upgrades. Rather, it is intended to help you clarify your thinking about what you need and can afford.

The three steps in upgrading a microcomputer system are presented on the following pages. Each step begins by asking a key question and then provides some suggestions or factors to consider when responding to the question.

STEP 1

Is It Time to Upgrade?

Almost any upgrade you make will provide some benefit; the trick is determining if it is worth the monetary investment. It is rarely practical to rebuild an older computer system into a newer model piece by piece. The cost of a complete upgrade typically far exceeds the purchase price of a new system. But if your system is just a piece or two away from meeting your needs, an upgrade may be in order.

Clearly defining what you hope to gain with an upgrade of some of your system's hardware will enable you to make the most relevant and cost-effective selections. Before deciding what to buy, decide what goal you hope to accomplish. Do you want to speed up your computer's performance? Do you need more

space to save your files? Do you want to add a new component such as a DVD-RW drive?

Suggestions

A good place to start is to look at the documentation on the packaging of any software you use or plan to use. Software manufacturers clearly label the minimum requirements to use their products. These requirements are usually broken down into categories that relate to specific pieces of hardware. For instance, how much RAM (random access memory) does a new program require? How much hard disk space is needed? Keep in mind these ratings are typically the bare minimum. If your system comes very close to the baseline in any particular category, you should still consider an upgrade.

Another thing to investigate is whether there is a software solution that will better serve your needs. For instance, if you are looking to enhance performance or make more room on your hard disk, there are diagnostic and disk optimization utility programs that may solve your problem. In Chapter 5, we discuss a variety of utility programs, such as Norton SystemWorks, that monitor, evaluate, and enhance system performance and storage capacity.

Typical objectives of an upgrade are to improve system performance, increase storage capacity, or add new technology.

STEP 2

What Should I Upgrade?

Once you have clearly defined your objectives, the focus shifts to identifying specific components to meet those objectives.

Suggestions

If your objective is to improve performance, three components to consider are RAM, the microprocessor, and expansion cards. If your objective is to increase storage capacity, two components to consider are hard-disk drive and optical disc drive. If you are adding new technology, consider the capability of your current system to support new devices.

Performance

If you want to increase the speed of your computer, consider increasing the amount of RAM. In most cases, this upgrade is relatively inexpensive and will yield the highest performance result per dollar invested. How much your system's performance will increase depends on how much RAM you start with, the size of programs you run, and how often you run large programs.

Another way to increase speed is to replace your system's microprocessor. Processor speed is measured in gigahertz (GHz). This rating is not a direct measurement of how fast the processor works, but rather it gives you a general idea of how it compares to other processors. (Computing magazines such as *PC World* often publish articles comparing the relative effectiveness of different processors.) The concept behind a microprocessor upgrade is simple: A faster processor will process faster. This is often an expensive upgrade and not as cost-effective as increasing RAM.

If you are looking at upgrading for a specific type of application, perhaps an expansion card is your answer. Expansion cards connect to slots on the system board, provide specialized support, and often free up resources and increase overall system performance. For example, if you run graphics-intensive programs, such as a drafting program or a video game, a video-card upgrade may be a good buy. An upgraded video card can be used to support higher resolution displays, handle all video data, and speed up overall system performance.

Storage Capacity

It's not hard to know when it's time to upgrade your storage capacity. If you frequently have to delete old files to make way for new ones, then it is probably time for more space. A larger or an additional hard drive is usually the solution. Two things to consider when comparing new hard drives are (1) size, which is usually rated in gigabytes (GB) of data the drive can hold, and (2) seek time, which is a rating of the average time it takes the drive to access any particular piece of data.

If you are storing a lot of data that you no longer use, such as old term papers, you might consider adding a high-capacity floppy disk drive. This is usually cheaper and is a good way to archive and transport data. Access time is slower than from a hard drive, so this is an option best suited for infrequently used data or for backing up data.

New Technology

Perhaps you are not looking to modify existing hardware but would like to add a new device. Examples include large high-resolution monitors, DVD-RW drives, and high-speed printers.

The key consideration is whether the new device will work with your existing hardware. The requirements for these devices are typically printed on the outside packaging or available at the product's Web site. If not, then refer to the product's operating manuals. Obviously, if your current system cannot support the new technology, you need to evaluate the cost of the new device plus the necessary additional hardware upgrades.

STEP 3

Who Should Do the Upgrade?

Once you've decided that the cost of the upgrade is justified and you know what you want to upgrade, the final decision is who is going to do it. Basically, there are two choices. You can either do it yourself or pay for professional installation.

Suggestions

The easiest way, and many times the best way, is to have a professional perform the upgrade. If you select this option, be sure to include the cost of installation in your analysis. If you have had some prior hardware experience or are a bit adventurous, you may want to save some money and do it yourself.

Visit a few computer stores that carry the upgrades you have selected. Most stores that provide the parts will install them as well. Talk with their technical people, describe your system (better yet, bring your system unit to the store), and determine the cost of professional installation. If you are thinking of doing it yourself, ask for their advice. Ask if they will provide assistance if you need it.

If you decide to have the components professionally installed, get the total price in writing and inquire about any guarantees that might exist. Before leaving your system, be sure that it is carefully tagged with your name and address. After the service has been completed, pay by credit card and thoroughly test the upgrade. If it does not perform satisfactorily, contact the store and ask for assistance. If the store's service is not satisfactory, you may be able to have your credit card company help to mediate any disputes.

Visual Summary The Upgrader's Guide: How to Upgrade Your Microcomputer System

Upgrading a Microcomputer System	
Step	**Questions**
1	*Needs:* Is it time to upgrade? What do I need that my current system is unable to deliver?
2	*Analysis:* What should I upgrade? Will the upgrade meet my needs and will it be cost-effective?
3	*Action:* Who should do the upgrade? Should I pay a professional or do it myself?

NEEDS

Is it time to upgrade? What do I need that my current system is unable to deliver?

I Am Considering an Upgrade to:

❏ **Improve performance because**
  ❏ My programs run too slowly
  ❏ I cannot run some programs I need

❏ **Increase storage capacity because**
  ❏ I don't have enough space to store all my files
  ❏ I don't have enough space to install new programs
  ❏ I need a secure place to back up important files
  ❏ I'd like to download large files from the Internet

❏ **Add new technology**
  ❏ DVD-RW
  ❏ High-performance monitor
  ❏ Printer
  ❏ TV tuner card
  ❏ Enhanced video card
  ❏ Enhanced sound card
  ❏ Other _____

ANALYSIS

What should I upgrade? Will the upgrade meet my needs and will it be cost-effective?

I Will Improve:

❏ **Performance by**
  ❏ Adding random-access memory (RAM)
    Current RAM (MB) _____
    Upgrade to _____
    Cost $ _____
    Expected improvement _____
    Other factors _____
  ❏ Replacing the current microprocessor
    Current processor _____
    Upgrade processor _____
    Cost $ _____
    Expected improvement _____
    Other factors _____
  ❏ Adding an expansion card
    Type _____
    Purpose _____
    Cost $ _____
    Expected improvement _____
    Other factors _____

❏ **Storage capacity by**
  ❏ Adding a hard-disk drive
    Current size (GB) _____
    Upgrade size (GB) _____
    Cost $ _____
    Expected improvement _____
    Other factors _____

❏ Adding a Zip disk drive

    Upgrade size (GB) _____

    Cost $ _____

    Type _____

    Expected improvement _____

    Other factors _____

❏ **Functionality by adding**

    New technology _____

    System requirements _____

    Cost $ _____

    Expected improvement _____

    Other factors _____

To help clarify your thinking about upgrading a microcomputer system, complete the questionnaire by checking the appropriate boxes.

ACTION

Who should do the upgrade? Should I do it myself or should I pay a professional?

The Two Choices are:

❏ **Professional installation**

The easiest way, and many times the best way, is to have a professional perform the upgrade. If you select this option, be sure to include the cost of installation in your analysis. Pay with a credit card, and make sure your system is tagged with your name and address before you part with it.

❏ **Do-it-yourself installation**

If you have had some prior hardware experience or are a bit adventurous, you may want to save some money and do it yourself. Avoid touching sensitive electronic parts and be sure to ground yourself by touching an unpainted metal surface in your computer.

Glossary

3G Cellular Network: A network that allows devices such as cell phones and properly equipped laptop computers to download data from the Internet.

3GLs (third-generation languages): High-level procedural language. *See* Procedural language.

4GLs (fourth-generation languages): Very high-level or problem-oriented languages. *See* Task-oriented language.

5GLs (fifth-generation languages): *See* Fifth-generation language.

802.11: *See* Wi-Fi (wireless fidelity).

A

AC adapter: Notebook computers use AC adapters that are typically outside the system unit. They plug into a standard wall outlet, convert AC to DC, provide power to drive the system components, and can recharge batteries.

Access: Refers to the responsibility of those who have data to control who is able to use that data.

Access speed: Measures the amount of time required by the storage device to retrieve data and programs.

Accounting: The organizational department that records all financial activity from billing customers to paying employees.

Accounts payable: The activity that shows the money a company owes to its suppliers for the materials and services it has received.

Accounts receivable: The activity that shows what money has been received or is owed by customers.

Accuracy: Relates to the responsibility of those who collect data to ensure that the data is correct.

Active-matrix monitor: Type of flat-panel monitor in which each pixel is independently activated. Displays more colors with better clarity; also known as thin film transistor (TFT) monitor.

Ad network cookies: Cookies that monitor your activities across all sites you visit and are continually active in collecting information on your Web activities.

Add a Device Wizard: A Windows wizard that provides step-by-step guidance for selecting and installing an appropriate printer driver for a new printer.

Address: Located in the header of an e-mail message; the e-mail address of the persons sending, receiving, and, optionally, anyone else who is to receive copies.

Advanced graphics card: Provides high-quality 3D graphics and animation for games and simulations.

Advanced Research Project Agency Network (ARPA-NET): A national computer network from which the Internet developed.

Adware cookie: *See* Ad network cookies.

Agile development: A development methodology that starts by getting core functionality of a program working, then expands on it until the customer is satisfied with the results.

AJAX: An advanced use of JavaScript found on many interactive sites. This technology is used to create interactive Web sites that respond quickly like traditional desktop application software.

Analog: Continuous signals that vary to represent different tones, pitches, and volume.

Analog signal: Signals that represent a range of frequencies, such as the human voice. They are a continuous electronic wave signal as opposed to a digital signal that is either on or off. To convert the digital signals of your computer to analog and vice versa, you need a modem. Another cable connects the modem to the telephone wall jack.

Analytical graphs or charts: Form of graphics used to put numeric data into objects that are easier to analyze, such as bar charts, line graphs, and pie charts.

Animation: Feature involving special visual and sound effects like moving pictures, audio, and video clips that play automatically when selected.

Antispyware: *See* spy removal programs.

Antivirus program: A utility program that guards a computer system from viruses or other damaging programs.

Applets: Web pages contain links to programs called applets, which are written in a programming language called Java. These programs are used to add interest to a Web site by presenting animation, displaying graphics, providing interactive games, and so forth.

Application generation subsystem: Provides tools to create data entry forms and specialized programming languages that interface or work with common languages, such as C or Visual Basic.

Application generator: Also called program coder; provides modules of prewritten code to accomplish various tasks, such as calculation of overtime pay.

Application service provider (asp): A business that provides computer-based services over the Internet, usually for a fee.

Application software: Software that can perform useful work, such as word processing, cost estimating, or accounting tasks. The user primarily interacts with application software.

Arithmetic-logic unit (ALU): The part of the CPU that performs arithmetic and logical operations.

Arithmetic operation: Fundamental math operations: addition, subtraction, multiplication, and division.

Artificial intelligence (AI): A field of computer science that attempts to develop computer systems that can mimic or simulate human thought processes and actions.

Artificial reality: *See* Virtual reality.

ASCII (American Standard Code for Information Interchange): Binary coding scheme widely used on all computers, including microcomputers. Eight bits form each byte, and each byte represents one character.

Assembly language: A step up from machine language, using names instead of numbers. These languages use abbreviations or mnemonics, such as ADD, that are automatically converted to the appropriate sequence of 1s and 0s.

Aspect ratio: The width of a monitor divided by its height. Common aspect ratios for monitors are 4:3 (standard) and 16:10 (wide screen).

Asymmetric digital subscriber line (ADSL): One of the most widely used types of telephone high-speed connections (DSL).

Attachment: A file, such as a document or worksheet, that is attached to an e-mail message.

Attribute: A data field represents an attribute (description or characteristic) of some entity (person, place, thing, or object). For example, an employee is an entity with many attributes, including his or her last name, address, phone, etc.

Auction house sites: Web sites that operate like a traditional auction to sell merchandise to bidders.

Audio editing software: Allows you to create and edit audio clips like filtering out pops and scratches in an old recording.

Automated design tool: Software package that evaluates hardware and software alternatives according to requirements given by the systems analyst. Also called computer-aided software engineering (CASE) tools.

B

Backbone: *See* Bus.

Backup: A Windows utility program. *See* Backup program.

Backup and restore: A utility program included with the many versions of Windows that makes a copy of all files or selected files that have been saved onto a disk.

Backup program: A utility program that helps protect you from the effects of a disk failure by making a copy of selected or all files that have been saved onto a disk.

Balance sheet: Lists the overall financial condition of an organization.

Bandwidth: Bandwidth determines how much information can be transmitted at one time. It is a measurement of the communication channel's capacity. There are three bandwidths: voice and, medium band, and broadband.

Bar code: Code consisting of vertical zebra-striped marks printed on product containers, read with a bar code reader.

Bar code reader: Photoelectric scanner that reads bar codes for processing.

Bar code scanner: *See* Bar code reader.

Base station: *See* Wireless access point.

Baseband: Bandwidth used to connect individual computers that are located close to one another. Though it supports high-speed transmission, it can only carry a single signal at a time.

Basic application: Applications used for doing common tasks, such as browsers and word processors, spreadsheets, databases, management systems, and presentation graphics. Also known as productivity applications.

Batch processing: Processing performed all at once on data that has been collected over time.

BD (Blu-ray Discs): A type of high-definition disc with a capacity of 25 to 50 gigabytes.

Beta testing: Testing by a select group of potential users in the final stage of testing a program.

Binary system: Numbering system in which all numbers consist of only two digits: 0 and 1.

Biometric scanning: Devices that check fingerprints or retinal scans.

Bit (binary digit): Each 1 or 0 is a bit; short for binary digit.

Bitmap image: Graphic file in which an image is made up of thousands of dots (pixels).

BitTorrent: A peer-to-peer file-sharing protocol used for distributing large amounts of data over the Internet.

Blog: *See* Web log.

Bluetooth: A recent wireless technology that allows nearby devices to communicate without the connection of cables or telephone systems.

Boot camp: Feature of Leopard, the new version of Mac OS, that allows appropriately equipped Apple computers to run both Mac OS and Windows XP.

Booting: Starting or restarting your computer.

Botnet: A collection of zombie computers.

Broadband: Bandwidth that includes microwave, satellite, coaxial cable, and fiber-optic channels. It is used for very high-speed computers.

Browser: Special Internet software connecting you to remote computers; opens and transfers files, displays text and images, and provides an uncomplicated interface to the Internet and Web documents. Examples of browsers are Internet Explorer and Netscape Navigator.

Bulleted list: The sequence of topics arranged on a page and organized by bullets.

Bus: All communication travels along a common connecting cable called a bus or a backbone. As information passes along the bus, it is examined by each device on the system board to see if the information is intended for that device. *See* Bus line and Ethernet.

Bus line: Electronic data roadway, along which bits travel, connects the parts of the CPU to each other and links the CPU with other important hardware. The common connecting cable in a bus network.

Bus network: Also known as Ethernet. Network in which all communications travel along a common connecting cable called a bus. Each device in the network handles its own communications control. There is no host computer or file server.

Bus width: The number of bits traveling simultaneously down a bus is the bus width.

Business suite: *See* Productivity suites.

Business-to-business (B2B):   A type of electronic commerce that involves the sale of a product or service from one business to another. This is typically a manufacturer–supplier relationship.

Business-to-consumer (B2C):   A type of electronic commerce that involves the sale of a product or service to the general public or end users.

Button: A special area you can click to make links that "navigate" through a presentation.

Byte: Unit consisting of eight bits. There are 256 possible bit combinations in a byte and each byte represents one character.

C

Cable: Cords used to connect input and output devices to the system unit.

Cable modem: Allows all digital communication, which is a speed of 27 million bps.

Cable service: Service provided by cable television companies using existing television cables.

Cache memory: Area of random-access memory (RAM) set aside to store the most frequently accessed information. Cache memory improves processing by acting as a temporary high-speed holding area between memory and the CPU, allowing the computer to detect which information in RAM is most frequently used.

Capacity: Capacity is how much data a particular storage medium can hold and another characteristic of secondary storage.

Carder: Criminal who steals credit cards over the Internet.

Carrier package: The material that chips are mounted on which then plugs into sockets on the system board.

Cathode-ray tube (CRT) monitor: Desktop-type monitor built in the same way as a television set. The most common type of monitor for office and home use. These monitors are typically placed directly on the system unit or on top of a desk.

CD: *See* Compact disc.

CD-R: Stands for CD-recordable. This optical disc can be written to only once. After that it can be read many times without deterioration but cannot be written on or erased. Used to create custom music CDs and to archive data.

CD-ROM (compact disc–read only memory):   Optical disc that allows data to be read but not recorded. Used to distribute large databases, references, and software application packages.

CD-RW (compact disc rewriteable):   A reusable, optical disc that is not permanently altered when data is recorded. Used to create and edit large multimedia presentations.

Cell: The space created by the intersection of a vertical column and a horizontal row within a worksheet in a program like Microsoft Excel. A cell can contain text or numeric entries.

Cellular service: Links car phones and portable phones.

Center for European Nuclear Research (CERN):   In Switzerland, where the Web was introduced in 1992.

Central processing unit (CPU):   The part of the computer that holds data and program instructions for processing the data. The CPU consists of the control unit and the arithmetic-logic unit. In a microcomputer, the CPU is on a single electronic component called a microprocessor chip.

Character: A single letter, number, or special character, such as a punctuation mark or $.

Character effect: Changes the appearance of font characters by using bold, italic, shadow, and colors.

Character encoding standards: Assign unique sequence of bits to each character.

Chart: Displaying numerical data in a worksheet as a pie chart or a bar chart, making it easier to understand.

Checklist: In analyzing data, a list of questions helps guide the systems analyst and end user through key issues for the present system.

Child node: A node one level below the node being considered in a hierarchical database or network. *See* Parent node.

Chip: A tiny circuit board etched on a small square of sandlike material called silicon. A chip is also called a silicon chip, semiconductor, or integrated circuit.

Citation: The source of information used in developing a report.

Clarity: Indicated by the resolution, or number of pixels, on a monitor. The greater the resolution, the better the clarity.

Class: In an object-oriented database, classes are similar objects grouped together.

Client: A node that requests and uses resources available from other nodes. Typically, a client is a user's microcomputer.

Client/server network: Network in which one powerful computer coordinates and supplies services to all other nodes on the network. Server nodes coordinate and supply specialized services, and client nodes request the services.

Clip art: Graphic illustrations representing a wide variety of topics.

Clock speed: Also called clock rate. It is measured in gigahertz, or billions of beats per second. The faster the clock speed, the faster the computer can process information and execute instructions.

Coaxial cable: High-frequency transmission cable that replaces the multiple wires of telephone lines with a single solid-copper core. It is used to deliver television signals as well as to connect computers in a network.

Code: Writing a program using the appropriate computer language.

Code review: *See* Desk checking.

Coding: Actual writing of a computer program, using a programming language.

Cold boot: Starting the computer after it has been turned off.

Column: Using Microsoft Excel, for example, a vertical block of cells one cell wide all the way down the worksheet.

Combination key: Keys such as the Ctrl key that perform an action when held down in combination with another key.

Commercial database: Enormous database an organization develops to cover certain particular objects. Access to this type of database is usually offered for a fee or subscription. Also known as data bank and informational utility.

Common data item: In a relational database, all related tables must have a common data item or key field.

Common interest site: A site that brings together individuals that share common interests or hobbies.

Communication channel: The actual connecting medium that carries the message between sending and receiving devices. This medium can be a physical wire, cable, or wireless connection.

Communication device: Computer systems that communicate with other computer systems using modems. For example, it modifies computer output into a form that can be transmitted across standard telephone lines.

Communication system: Electronic system that transmits data over communication lines from one location to another.

Compact disc (CD): Widely used optical disc format. It holds 650 MB (megabytes) to 1 GB (gigabyte) of data on one side of the CD.

Compact disc–read only memory: *See* CD-ROM.

Compact disc rewriteable: *See* CD-RW.

Company database: Also called shared database. Stored on a mainframe, users throughout the company have access to the database through their microcomputers linked by a network.

Compiler: Software that converts the programmer's procedural-language program (source code) into machine language (object code). This object code can then be saved and run later.

Computer-aided design/computer-aided manufacturing (CAD/CAM) system: Knowledge work systems that run programs to integrate the design and manufacturing activities. CAD/CAM is widely used in manufacturing automobiles.

Computer-aided software engineering (CASE) tool: A type of software development tool that helps provide some automation and assistance in program design, coding, and testing. *See* Automated design tool.

Computer competency: Becoming proficient in computer-related skills.

Computer crime: Illegal action in which a perpetrator uses special knowledge of computer technology. Criminals may be employees, outside users, hackers and crackers, and organized crime members.

Computer ethics: Guidelines for the morally acceptable use of computers in our society.

Computer Fraud and Abuse Act: Law allowing prosecution of unauthorized access to computers and databases.

Computer monitoring software: The most invasive and dangerous type of spyware. These programs record every activity made on your computer, including credit card numbers, bank account numbers, and e-mail messages.

Computer network: Communications system connecting two or more computers and their peripheral devices to exchange information and share resources.

Computer support specialist: Specialists include technical writers, computer trainers, computer technicians, and help-desk specialists who provide technical support to customers and other users.

Computer technician: Specialist who installs hardware and software and troubleshoots problems for users.

Computer trainer: Computer professional who provides classes to instruct users.

Computer virus: Destructive programs that can come in e-mail attachments and spam.

Concatenation structure: Logic structure in which one program statement follows another.

Connectivity: Capability of the microcomputer to use information from the world beyond one's desk. Data and information can be sent over telephone or cable lines and through the air so that computers can talk to each other and share information.

Consumer-to-consumer (C2C): A type of electronic commerce that involves individuals selling to individuals.

Content-markup language: Also known as markup language. Uses symbols, words, and phrases that instruct a computer on how to display information to the user. For example, HTML is a content-markup language used to display Web pages.

Content template: Includes suggested content for each slide in a PowerPoint presentation.

Contextual tab: A type of tab found in Microsoft Word that only appears when needed and anticipates the next operations to be performed by the user.

Control unit: Section of the CPU that tells the rest of the computer how to carry out program instructions.

Conversion: Also known as systems implementation; four approaches to conversion: direct, parallel, pilot, and phased. *See* Systems implementation.

Cookies: Programs that record information on Web site visitors.

Coprocessor: Specialized processing chip designed to improve specific computer operations, such as the graphics coprocessor.

Copyright: A legal concept that gives content creators the right to control use and distribution of their work.

Cordless mouse: A battery-powered mouse that typically uses radio waves or infrared light waves to communicate with the system unit. Also known as wireless mouse.

Cracker: One who gains unauthorized access to a computer system for malicious purposes.

Cryptographer: Designs, tests, and researches encryption procedures.

Cryptography: The science of disguising and revealing encrypted information.

Cybercash: *See* Digital cash.

Cylinder: Hard disks store and organize files using tracks, sectors, and cylinders. A cylinder runs through each track of a stack of platters. Cylinders differentiate files stored on the same track and sector of different platters.

Cynic: Individual who feels that the idea of using a microcomputer is overrated and too troublesome to learn.

D

Dashboard Widgets: A collection of specialized programs on the Mac OS X operating system that constantly updates and displays information such as stock prices and weather information.

Data: Raw, unprocessed facts that are input to a computer system that will give compiled information when the computer processes those facts. Data is also defined as facts or observations about people, places, things, and events.

Data administration subsystem: Helps manage the overall database, including maintaining security, providing disaster recovery support, and monitoring the overall performance of database operations.

Data bank: *See* Commercial database.

Data cube: A multidimensional data model. *Also see* Multidimensional database.

Data definition subsystem: This system defines the logical structure of the database by using a data dictionary.

Data dictionary: Dictionary containing a description of the structure of data in a database.

Data entry worker: Inputs customer information, lists, and other types of data.

Data flow diagram: Diagram showing data or information flow within an information system.

Data integrity: Database characteristics relating to the consistency and accuracy of data.

Data maintenance: Maintaining data includes adding new data, deleting old data, and editing existing data.

Data manipulation subsystem: Provides tools to maintain and analyze data.

Data mining: Technique of searching data warehouses for related information and patterns.

Data processing system (DPS): Transaction processing system that keeps track of routine operations and records these events in a database. Also called transaction processing system (TPS).

Data projector: Specialized device, similar to slide projector, that connects to microcomputers and projects computer output.

Data redundancy: A common database problem in which data is duplicated and stored in different files.

Data security: Protection of software and data from unauthorized tampering or damage.

Data warehouse: Data collected from a variety of internal and external databases and stored in a database called a data warehouse. Data mining is then used to search these databases.

Data worker: Person involved with the distribution and communication of information, such as secretaries and clerks.

Database: A collection of related information, like employee names, addresses, and phone numbers. It is organized so that a computer program can quickly select the desired pieces of information and display them for you.

Database administrator (DBA): Uses database management software to determine the most efficient way to organize and access data.

Database file: File containing highly structured and organized data created by database management programs.

Database management system (DBMS): To organize, manage, and retrieve data. DBMS programs have five subsystems: DBMS engine, data definition, data manipulation, applications generation, and data administration. An example of a database management system is Microsoft Access. *See* Database manager.

Database manager: Software package used to set up, or structure, a database such as an inventory list of supplies. It also provides tools to edit, enter, and retrieve data from the database.

Database model: Defines rules and standards for all data in a database. There are five database models: hierarchical, network, relational, multidimensional, and object-oriented. For example, Access uses the relational data model.

DBMS engine: Provides a bridge between the logical view of data and the physical view of data.

Debugging: Programmer's word for testing and then eliminating errors in a program. Programming errors are of two types: syntax and logic errors.

Decision model: The decision model gives the decision support system its analytical capabilities. There are three types of models included in the decision model: tactical, operational, and strategic models.

Decision support system (DSS): Flexible analysis tool that helps managers make decisions about unstructured problems, such as effects of events and trends outside the organization.

Decision table: Table showing decision rules that apply when certain conditions occur and what action should take place as a result.

Demand report: A demand report is produced on request. An example is a report on the numbers and types of jobs held by women and minorities done at the request of the government.

Demodulation: Process performed by a modem in converting analog signals to digital signals.

Denial of service (DoS) attack: A variant virus in which Web sites are overwhelmed with data and users are unable to access the Web site. Unlike a worm that self-replicates, a DoS attack floods a computer or network with requests for information and data.

Density: Refers to how tightly the bits (electromagnetic charges) can be packed next to one another on a floppy disk.

Design template: Provides professionally selected combinations of color schemes, slide layouts, and special effects for presentation graphics.

Desk checking: Process of checking out a computer program by studying a printout of the program line by line, looking for syntax and logic errors.

Desktop: The screen that is displayed on the monitor when the computer starts up. All items and icons on the screen are considered to be on your desktop and are used to interact with the computer.

Desktop computer: Computer small enough to fit on top of or along the side of a desk and yet too big to carry around.

Desktop operating systems: *See* Stand-alone operating system.

Desktop publisher: One who creates and formats publication-ready material.

Desktop publishing program: Program that allows you to mix text and graphics to create publications of professional quality.

Desktop system unit: A system unit that typically contains the system's electronic components and selected secondary storage devices. Input and output devices, such as the mouse, keyboard, and monitor, are located outside the system unit.

Device driver: Every device that is connected to the computer has a special program associated with it called a device driver that allows communication between the operating system and the device.

Diagnostic program: *See* Troubleshooting program.

Dialog box: Provides additional information and requests user input.

Dial-up service: Method of accessing the Internet using a high-speed modem and standard telephone lines.

Dictionary attack: Uses software to try thousands of common words sequentially in an attempt to gain unauthorized access to a user's account.

Digital: Computers are digital machines because they can only understand 1s and 0s. It is either on or off. For example, a digital watch states the exact time on the face, whereas an analog watch has the second hand moving in constant motion as it tells the time.

Digital camera: Similar to a traditional camera except that images are recorded digitally in the camera's memory rather than on film.

Digital cash: Currency for Internet purchases. Buyers purchase digital cash from a third party (a bank that specializes in electronic currency) by transferring funds from their banks.

Digital media player: Also known as digital music player; a specialized device for storing, transferring, and playing audio files.

Digital Millennium Copyright Act: Law that makes it legal for a program owner to make only his or her own backup copies of a software program. However, it is illegal for those copies to be resold or given away.

Digital music player: Also known as digital media player; a specialized device for storing, transferring, and playing audio files.

Digital rights management (DRM): Encompasses various technologies that control access to electronic media and files.

Digital signal: Computers can only understand digital signals. Before processing can occur within the system unit, a conversion must occur from what we understand (analog) to what the system unit can electronically process (digital). *See* Analog signal.

Digital subscriber line (DSL): Provides high-speed connection using existing telephone lines.

Digital subscriber line (DSL) service: Service provided by telephone companies using existing telephone lines to provide high-speed connections.

Digital versatile disc (DVD): A type of optical disc similar to CD-ROMs except that more data can be packed into the same amount of space. *Also see* DVD (digital versatile disc).

Digital video camera: Input device that records motion digitally.

Digital video disc: *See* DVD (digital versatile disc).

DIMM (dual in-line memory module): An expansion module used to add memory to the system board.

Direct access: A fast approach to external storage, provided by disks, where information is not in a set sequence.

Direct approach: Approach for systems implementation whereby the old system is simply abandoned for the new system.

Directory search: A search engine option that provides a directory or list of categories or topics to choose from, such as Arts & Humanities, Business & Economics, or Computers & Internet, that help you narrow your search until a list of Web sites appears.

Directory server: A specialized server that manages resources such as user accounts for an entire network.

Disaster recovery plan: Plan used by large organizations describing ways to continue operations following a disaster until normal computer operations can be restored.

Disk: *See* Floppy disk.

Disk caching: Method of improving hard-disk performance by anticipating data needs. Frequently used data is read from the hard disk into memory (cache). When needed, data is then accessed directly from memory, which has a much faster transfer rate than from the hard disk. Increases performance by as much as 30 percent.

Disk Cleanup: A Windows troubleshooting utility that eliminates nonessential files.

Disk Defragmenter: A Windows utility that optimizes disk performance by eliminating unnecessary fragments and rearranging files.

Display screen: *See* Monitor.

Distributed database: Database that can be made accessible through a variety of communications networks, which allow portions of the database to be located in different places.

Distributed processing network: System in which computing power is located and shared at different locations.

DO UNTIL structure: Loop structure in programming that appears at the end of a loop. The DO UNTIL loop means that the loop statements will be executed at least once. In other words, this program tells you to DO option one UNTIL it is no longer true.

DO WHILE structure: Loop structure in programming that appears at the beginning of a loop. The DO WHILE loop will keep executing as long as there is information to be processed. For example, DO option one WHILE (or as long as) option one remains true.

Document: Any kind of text material.

Document file: File created by a word processor to save documents such as letters, research papers, and memos.

Document scanner: Similar to a flatbed scanner except that it can quickly scan multipage documents. It automatically feeds one page of a document at a time through a scanning surface.

Document theme: Built-in sets of colors, fonts, and effects that can be quickly applied to an entire presentation.

Documentation: Written descriptions and procedures about a program and how to use it. *See* Program documentation.

Domain name: The second part of the URL; it is the name of the server where the resource is located. For example, www.mtv.com.

Domain name server (DNS): Internet addressing method that assigns names and numbers to people and computers. Because the numeric IP addresses are difficult to remember, the DNS server was developed to automatically convert text-based addresses to numeric IP addresses.

Dot-matrix printer: A type of printer that forms characters and images using a series of small pins on a print head. Used where high-quality output is not required.

Dot pitch: Distance between each pixel. The lower the dot pitch, the shorter the distance between pixels, and the higher the clarity of images produced.

Dots-per-inch (dpi): Printer resolution is measured in dpi. The higher the dpi, the better the quality of images produced.

Downloadable office suite: Office suite that is offered for free as downloadable software and then is stored on your desktop computer just like a traditional office suite.

Downloading: Process of transferring information from a remote computer to the computer one is using.

Drawing program: Program used to help create artwork for publications. *See* Illustration program.

Driver: *See* Device driver.

DS3: Provides support for very high-speed, all-digital transmission for large corporations.

DSL: *See* Digital subscriber line.

Dual-scan monitor: *See* Passive-matrix monitor.

DVD (digital versatile disc or digital video disc): Similar to CD-ROMs except that more data can be packed into the same amount of space. DVD drives can store 4.7 GB to 17 GB on a single DVD disc or 17 times the capacity of CDs.

DVD player: Also known as DVD-ROM drives. *See* DVD.

DVD–R (DVD recordable): A DVD with a write-once format that differs slightly from the format of DVD+R. Typically used to create permanent archives for large amounts of data and to record videos.

DVD+R (DVD recordable): A DVD with a write-once format that differs slightly from the format of DVD−R. Typically used to create permanent archives for large amounts of data and to record videos.

DVD-RAM (DVD random-access memory): A high-capacity, maximum-performance disc that allows the user to read the information, write over it, and erase the data if necessary. Used like a floppy disk to copy, delete files, and run programs. It has up to 8 times the storage capacity of a CD and also can be used to read CD and DVD formats.

DVD-ROM (DVD–read-only memory): Used to distribute full-length feature films with theater-quality video and sound. Also known as DVD players. Are read-only.

DVD–RW (DVD rewriteable): A type of reusable DVD disc that is more flexible than the DVD-RAM. DVD–RW is able to create and read CD discs along with creating and editing large-scale multimedia presentations.

DVD+RW (DVD rewriteable): Another DVD format to record and erase repeatedly. Able to create and read CD discs along with creating and editing large-scale multimedia presentations.

DVI (Digital Video Interface) port: A type of port that provides a connection to a digital monitor.

E

EBCDIC (Extended Binary Coded Decimal Interchange Code): Binary coding scheme that is a standard for minicomputers and mainframe computers.

E-book reader: Handheld, book-sized devices that display text and graphics. Using content downloaded from the Web or special cartridges, these devices are used to read newspapers, magazines, and books.

E-commerce: Buying and selling goods over the Internet.

E-learning: A Web application that allows one to take educational courses online.

E-mail: Communicate with anyone in the world who has an Internet address or e-mail account with a system connected to the Internet. You can include a text message, graphics, photos, and file attachments.

E-paper: Requires power only when changing pages, and not the entire time a page is displayed on the screen.

Economic feasibility: Comparing the costs of a new system to the benefits it promises.

Editing: Features that modify a document such as using a thesaurus, find and replace, or spell check.

Electronic commerce (e-commerce): Buying and selling goods over the Internet.

Electronic mail: Transmission of electronic messages over the Internet. Also known as e-mail.

Electronic paper: *See* e-paper.

Electronic profile: Using publicly and privately available databases, information resellers create electronic profiles, which are highly detailed and personalized descriptions of individuals.

Embedded operating system: An operating system that is completely stored within the ROM (read-only memory) of the device that it is in; used for handheld computers and smaller devices like PDAs.

Encryption: Coding information so that only the user can read or otherwise use it.

Encryption key: A binary number used to gain access to encrypted information.

End user: Person who uses microcomputers or has access to larger computers.

Enterprise storage system: Using mass storage devices, a strategy is designed for organizations to promote efficient and safe use of data across the networks within their organizations.

Entity: In an object-oriented database, a person, place, thing, or event that is to be described.

Erasable optical disc: Optical disc on which the disk drive can write information and also erase and rewrite information. Also known as CD-RW or compact disc rewriteable.

Ergonomic keyboard: Keyboard arrangement that is not rectangular and has a palm rest, which is designed to alleviate wrist strain.

Ethernet: Otherwise known as Ethernet bus or Ethernet LAN. The Ethernet bus is the pathway or arterial to which all nodes (PCs, file servers, print servers, Web servers, etc.) are connected. All of this is connected to a local area network (LAN) or a wide area network (WAN). *See* Bus network.

Ethernet cable: Twisted-pair cable commonly used in networks and to connect a variety of components to the system unit.

Ethernet port: A high-speed networking port that allows multiple computers to be connected for sharing files or for high-speed Internet access.

Ethics: Standards of moral conduct.

Exception report: Report that calls attention to unusual events.

Executive information system (EIS): Sophisticated software that can draw together data from an organization's databases in meaningful patterns and highly summarized forms.

Executive support system (ESS): *See* Executive information system.

Expansion bus: Connects the CPU to slots on the system board. There are different types of expansion buses such as industry standard architecture (ISA), peripheral component interconnect (PCI), accelerated graphics port (AGP), universal serial bus (USB), and FireWire buses. *See* System bus.

Expansion card: Optional device that plugs into a slot inside the system unit to expand the computers' abilities. Ports on the system board allow cables to be connected from the expansion board to devices outside the system unit.

Expansion slots: Openings on a system board. Users can insert optional devices, known as expansion cards, into these slots, allowing users to expand their systems. *See* Expansion card.

Expert system: Computer program that provides advice to decision makers who would otherwise rely on human experts. It's a type of artificial intelligence that uses a database to provide assistance to users.

ExpressCard: Technology replacing the PC Card to provide a direct connection to the system bus. *Also see* PC Card.

External data: Data gathered from outside an organization. Examples are data provided by market research firms.

External hard drive: Uses the same technology as an internal hard disk but is used primarily to complement an internal hard disk by providing additional storage. They are typically connected to a USB or FireWire port on the system unit and are easily removed.

Extranet: Private network that connects more than one organization.

F

Family Educational Rights Privacy Act (FERPA): A federal law that restricts disclosure of educational records.

Fax machine: A device for sending and receiving images over telephone lines.

Fiber-optic cable: Special transmission cable made of glass tubes that are immune to electronic interference. Data is transmitted through fiber-optic cables in the form of pulses of light.

Field: Each column of information within a record is called a field. A field contains related information on a specific item like employee names within a company department.

Fifth-generation language (5GL): Computer language that incorporates the concept of artificial intelligence to allow direct human communication.

File: A collection of related records that can store data and programs. For example, the payroll file would include payroll information (records) for all of the employees (entities).

File compression: Process of reducing the storage requirements for a file.

File compression program: Utility programs that reduce the size of files so they require less storage on the computer and can be sent more efficiently over the Internet. Examples of such programs are WinZip and Wizard.

File decompression: Process of expanding a compressed file.

File server: Dedicated computer with large storage capacity providing users access to shared folders or fast storage and retrieval of information used in that business.

File transfer protocol (FTP): Internet service for uploading and downloading files.

Filter: (1) A filter blocks access to selected Web sites. (2) A filter will locate or display records from a table that fit a set of conditions or criteria when using programs like Excel.

Find and replace: An editing tool that finds a selected word or phrase and replaces it with another. Click *edit, find*.

Firewall: Security hardware and software. All communications into and out of an organization pass through a special security computer, called a proxy server, to protect all systems against external threats.

FireWire bus: Operates much like USB buses on the system board but at higher speeds.

FireWire port: Used to connect high-speed printers, and even video cameras, to system unit.

Flash: An interactive animation program from Adobe that is usually full screen and highly dynamic, displaying moving text or complicated interactive features.

Flash drive: *See* USB drive.

Flash memory: RAM chips that retain data even when power is disrupted. Flash memory is an example of solid-state storage and is typically used to store digitized images and record MP3 files.

Flash memory card: A solid-state storage device widely used in notebook computers. Flash memory also is used in a variety of specialized input devices to capture and transfer data to desktop computers.

Flat-panel monitor: Or liquid crystal display (LCD) monitor. These monitors are much thinner than CRTs and can be used for desktop systems as well.

Flatbed scanner: An input device similar to a copying machine.

Floppy disk: Flat, circular piece of magnetically treated mylar plastic that rotates within a jacket. A floppy disk is 3½ inches and holds 1.44 MB of information. It is a portable or removable secondary storage device.

Floppy disk drive (FDD): A drive that stores data and programs by altering the electromagnetic charges on the disk's surface.

Folder: A named area on a disk that is used to store related subfolders and files.

Font: Also known as typeface, is a set of characters with a specific design.

Font size: The height of a character measured in points, with each point being $1/72$ inch.

Form: Electronic forms reflecting the contents of one record or table. Primarily used to enter new records or make changes to existing records.

Format: Features that change the appearance of a document like font, font sizes, character effects, alignment, and bulleted and numbered lists.

Formula: Instructions for calculations in a spreadsheet. It is an equation that performs calculations on the data contained within the cells in a worksheet or spreadsheet.

Fourth-generation language (4GL): Task-oriented languages are designed to solve a specific problem and require little special training on the part of the end user.

Fragmented: Storage technique that breaks up large files and stores the parts wherever space is available in adjacent sectors and clusters.

Freedom of Information Act of 1970: Law giving citizens the right to examine data about them in federal government files, except for information restricted for national security reasons.

Friend: An individual on a list of contacts for an instant messaging server.

Friend-of-a-friend site: A site designed to bring together two people who do not know one another but share a common friend.

Frustrated: Person who feels it is an imposition to have to learn something new like computer technology.

Function: A built-in formula in a spreadsheet that performs calculations automatically.

Fuzzy logic: Used by expert systems to allow users to respond by using qualitative terms, such as *great* and *OK*.

G

Galleries: Feature of Microsoft Office 2007 that simplifies the process of making selections from a list of alternatives by replacing dialog boxes with visual presentations of results.

Game port: Were used to connect video game controllers and joysticks.

General ledger: Activity that produces income statements and balance sheets based on all transactions of a company.

Generations (of programming languages): The five generations are machine languages, assembly languages, procedural languages, problem-oriented languages, and natural languages. *See* Levels.

Global positioning system (GPS): Devices use location information to determine the geographic location of your car, for example.

GPU (graphics processing unit): *See* Graphics coprocessor.

Gramm-Leach-Bliley Act: A law that protects personal financial information.

Grammar checker: In word processing, a tool that identifies poorly worded sentences and incorrect grammar.

Graphical map: Diagram of a Web site's overall design.

Graphical user interface (GUI): Special screen that allows software commands to be issued through the use of graphic symbols (icons) or pull-down menus.

Graphics coprocessor: Designed to handle requirements related to displaying and manipulating 2-D and 3-D graphic images.

Graphics suite: Group of graphics programs offered at a lower cost than if purchased separately, like CorelDraw.

Grid chart: Chart that shows the relationship between input and output documents.

Groups: In Microsoft Word, each tab is organized into groups that contain related items.

Group decision support system (GDSS): System used to support the collective work of a team addressing large problems.

Guest operating system: Operating system that operates on virtual machines.

H

Hacker: Person who gains unauthorized access to a computer system for the fun and challenge of it.

Handheld computer: *See* Personal digital assistant (PDA) and Palm computers.

Handheld computer system unit: Smallest type of system unit, designed to fit into the palm of one hand.

Handwriting recognition software: Translates handwritten notes into a form that the system unit can process.

Hard disk: Enclosed disk drive containing one or more metallic disks. Hard disks use magnetic charges to record data and have large storage capacities and fast retrieval times.

Hardware: Equipment that includes a keyboard, monitor, printer, the computer itself, and other devices that are controlled by software programming.

HD DVD (high-definition DVD): A high-definition disc with a format similar to DVD with a much higher storage capacity. *Also see* DVD.

Head crash: When a read-write head makes contact with the hard disk's surface or particles on its surface, the disk surface becomes scratched and some or all data is destroyed.

Header: A typical e-mail has three elements: header, message, and signature. The header appears first and includes addresses, subject, and attachments.

Headphones: Audio-output devices connected to a sound card in the system unit. The sound card is used to capture as well as play back recorded sound.

Help: A feature in most application software providing options that typically include an index, a glossary, and a search feature to locate reference information about specific commands.

Health Insurance Portability and Accountability Act (HIPAA): A federal law that protects medical records.

Hexadecimal system (hex): Uses 16 digits to represent binary numbers.

Hi def (high definition) disc: The next generation of optical disc, which offers increased storage capacities.

Hierarchical database: Database in which fields or records are structured in nodes. Organized in the shape of a pyramid, and each node is linked directly to the nodes beneath it. Also called one-to-many relationship.

Hierarchical network: *See* Tree network.

High-capacity floppy disk: Also a 3½-inch floppy-disk cartridge. It is thicker than a floppy disk and requires a special drive. For example, Zip disks.

High Definition Multimedia Interface (HDMI): Port that provides high-definition video and audio, making it possible to use a computer as a video jukebox or an HD video recorder.

High-definition television (HDTV): All-digital television that delivers a much clearer and more detailed widescreen picture.

Higher level: Programming languages that are closer to the language humans use.

History file: Created by browser to store information on Web sites visited by your computer system.

Hits: The sites that a search engine returns after running a keyword search, ordered from most likely to least likely to contain the information requested.

Home network: LAN network for homes allowing different computers to share resources, including a common Internet connection.

Home software: *See* Integrated package.

Host: Also called a server or provider, is a large centralized computer.

Host operating system: Operating system that runs on the physical machine.

Household robot: Robot designed to vacuum or scrub floors, mow lawns, patrol the house, or simply provide entertainment.

HTML: *See* Hypertext Markup Language.

HTML editor: *See* Web authoring program.

Hub: The center or central node for other nodes. This device can be a server or a connection point for cables from other nodes.

Human resources: The organizational department that focuses on the hiring, training, and promoting of people, as well as any number of human-centered activities within the organization.

Hybrid network: A combination of different topologies.

Hyperlink: Connection or link to other documents or Web pages that contain related information.

Hypertext Markup Language (HTML): Programming language that creates document files used to display Web pages.

Icons: Graphic objects on the desktop used to represent programs and other files.

Identity theft: The illegal assumption of someone's identity for the purpose of economic gain.

IF-THEN-ELSE structure: Logical selection structure whereby one of two paths is followed according to IF, THEN, and ELSE statements in a program. *See* Selection structure.

IFPS (interactive financial planning system): A 4GL language used for developing financial models.

Illusion of anonymity: The misconception that being selective about disclosing personal information on the Internet can prevent an invasion of personal privacy.

Illustration program: Also known as drawing programs; used to create digital illustrations and modify vector images and thus create line art, 3-D models, and virtual reality.

Image editor: An application for modifying bitmap images.

Image gallery: Libraries of electronic images.

Immersive experience: Allows the user to walk into a virtual reality room or view simulations on a virtual reality wall.

Income statement: A statement that shows a company's financial performance, income, expenses, and the difference between them for a specific time period.

Individual database: Collection of integrated records used mainly by just one person. Also called microcomputer database.

Industrial robot: Robot used in factories to perform a variety of tasks. For example, machines used in automobile plants to do painting and polishing.

Information: Data that has been processed by a computer system.

Information broker: *See* Information reseller.

Information reseller: Also known as information broker. It gathers personal data on people and sells it to direct marketers, fund-raisers, and others, usually for a fee.

Information system: Collection of hardware, software, people, data, and procedures that work together to provide information essential to running an organization.

Information systems manager: Oversees the work of programmers, computer specialists, systems analysts, and other computer professionals.

Information technology (IT): Computer and communication technologies, such as communication links to the Internet, that provide help and understanding to the end user.

Information utility: *See* Commercial database.

Information worker: Employee who creates, distributes, and communicates information.

Infrared: Uses infrared light waves to communicate over short distances. Sometimes referred to as line-of-sight communication because light waves can only travel in a straight line.

Infrared Data Association (IrDA) port: A wireless mechanism for transferring data between devices using infrared light waves.

Ink-jet printer: Printer that sprays small droplets of ink at high speed onto the surface of the paper, producing letter-quality images, and can print in color.

Input device: Piece of equipment that translates data into a form a computer can process. The most common input devices are the keyboard and the mouse.

Instant messaging (IM): A program allowing communication and collaboration for direct, "live," connections over the Internet between two or more people.

Integrated circuit: *See* Silicon chip.

Integrated package: A single program providing functionality of a collection of programs but not as extensive as a specialized program like Microsoft Word. Popular with home users who are willing to sacrifice some advanced features for lower cost and simplicity.

Interactivity: User participation in a multimedia presentation.

Internal data: Data from within an organization consisting principally of transactions from the transaction processing system.

Internal hard disk: Storage device consisting of one or more metallic platters sealed inside a container. Internal hard disks are installed inside the system cabinet of a microcomputer. It stores the operating system and major applications like Word.

Internet: A huge computer network available to everyone with a microcomputer and a means to connect to it. It is the actual physical network made up of wires, cables, and satellites as opposed to the Web, which is the multimedia interface to resources available on the Internet.

Internet scam: Using the Internet, a fraudulent act or operation designed to trick individuals into spending their time and money for little or no return.

Internet security suite: Collection of utility programs designed to make using the Internet easier and safer.

Internet service provider (ISP): Provides access to the Internet.

Internet telephone: Low-cost alternative to long-distance telephone calls using electronic voice delivery.

Internet telephony: *See* Telephony.

Interpreter: Software that converts a procedural language one statement at a time into machine language just before the statement is executed. No object code is saved.

Intranet: Like the Internet, it typically provides e-mail, mailing lists, newsgroups, and FTP services, but it is accessible only to those within the organization. Organizations use intranets to provide information to their employees.

Intrusion detection system (NIDS): Using sophisticated statistical techniques to analyze all incoming and outgoing network traffic, this system works with firewalls to protect an organization's network.

Inventory: Material or products that a company has in stock.

Inventory control system: A system that keeps records of the number of each kind of part or finished good in the warehouse.

IP address (Internet Protocol address): The unique numeric address of a computer on the Internet that facilitates the delivery of e-mail.

IP telephony: *See* Telephony.

J

Java: Programming language for creating special programs like applets. *See* Applets.

JavaScript: A scripting language that adds basic interactivity to Web pages.

Joystick: Popular input device for computer games. You control game actions by varying the pressure, speed, and direction of the joystick.

K

Key: Another term for encryption key.

Key field: The common field by which tables in a database are related to each other. This field uniquely identifies the record. For example, in university databases, a key field is the Social Security number. Also known as primary key.

Keyboard: Input device that looks like a typewriter keyboard but has additional keys.

Keyboard port: Were used to connect keyboards to the system unit.

Keystroke logger: Also known as computer monitoring software and sniffer programs. They can be loaded onto your computer without your knowledge.

Keyword search: A type of search option that causes the search engine to compare your entry against its database and return with a list of sites, or hits, that contain the keyword you entered.

Kilobits per second (Kbps): Speed at which data is transferred.

Knowledge base: A system that uses a database containing specific facts, rules to relate these facts, and user input to formulate recommendations and decisions.

Knowledge-based systems: Programs duplicating human knowledge. It's like capturing the knowledge of a human expert and making it accessible through a computer program.

Knowledge work system (KWS): Specialized information system used to create information in a specific area of expertise.

Knowledge worker: Person involved in the creation of information, such as an engineer and a scientist.

L

Label: Provides structure to a worksheet by describing the contents of the rows and columns. *See* Text entry.

Land: *See* Lands and pits.

Lands and pits: Flat and bumpy areas, respectively, that represent 1s and 0s on the optical disc surface to be read by a laser.

Language translator: Converts programming instructions into a machine language that can be processed by a computer.

Laptop computer: *See* Notebook computer and Notebook system unit.

Laser printer: Printer that creates dotlike images on a drum, using a laser beam light source.

Legacy port: Was common on microcomputer systems to connect specific types of devices. They have largely been replaced by faster, more flexible ports such as the universal serial bus (USB).

Levels: Generations or levels of programming languages ranging from "low" to "high." *See* Generations (of programming languages).

Link: A connection to related information.

Linux: Type of UNIX operating system initially developed by Linus Torvalds, it is one of the most popular and powerful alternatives to the Windows operating system.

Liquid crystal display (LCD): A technology used for flat-panel monitors.

Local area network (LAN): Network consisting of computers and other devices that are physically near each other, such as within the same building.

Location: For browsers to connect to resources, locations or addresses must be specified. Also known as uniform resource locators or URLs.

Logic error: Error that occurs when a programmer has used an incorrect calculation or left out a programming procedure.

Logic structure: Programming statements or structures called sequence, selection, or loop that control the logical sequence in which computer program instructions are executed.

Logical operation: Comparing two pieces of data to see whether one is equal to ($=$), less than ($<$), or greater than ($>$) the other.

Logical view: Focuses on the meaning and content of the data. End users and computer professionals are concerned with this view as opposed to the physical view, with which only specialized computer professionals are concerned.

Loop structure: Logic structure in which a process may be repeated as long as a certain condition remains true. This structure is called a "loop" because the program loops around or repeats again and again. There are two variations: DO UNTIL and DO WHILE.

Low bandwidth: *See* Voiceband.

Lower level: Programming language closer to the language the computer itself uses. The computer understands the 0s and 1s that make up bits and bytes.

M

Mac OS: Operating system designed for Macintosh computers.

Mac OS X: Macintosh operating system featuring a user interface called Aqua.

Machine language: Language in which data is represented in 1s and 0s. Most languages have to be translated into machine language for the computer to process the data. Either a compiler or an interpreter performs this translation.

Magnetic card reader: A card reader that reads encoded information from a magnetic strip on the back of a card.

Magnetic-ink character recognition (MICR): Direct-entry scanning devices used in banks. This technology is used to automatically read the numbers on the bottom of checks.

Magnetic tape: To find specific information, you will have to go through the tape sequentially until that data comes up. On the other hand, using an audio compact disc, select the song and the disc moves directly to that song. Tape may be slow, but it is effective and a commonly used tool for backing up data.

Magnetic tape reel: Typically ½-inch wide and ½-mile long, this type of magnetic tape is used by mainframe computers due to its massive storage capacity.

Magnetic tape streamer: Device that allows duplication (backup) of the data stored on a microcomputer hard disk.

Mainframe computer: This computer can process several million program instructions per second. Sizeable organizations rely on these room-size systems to handle large programs and a great deal of data.

Maintenance programmer: Programmers who maintain software by updating programs to protect them from errors, improve usability, standardize, and adjust to organizational changes.

Malware: Short for malicious software.

MAN: *See* Metropolitan area network.

Management information system (MIS): Computer-based information system that produces standardized reports in a summarized and structured form. Generally used to support middle managers.

Many-to-many relationship: In a network database, each child node may have more than one parent node and vice versa.

Marketing: The organizational department that plans, prices, promotes, sells, and distributes an organization's goods and services.

Markup language: *See* Content-markup language.

Mass storage: Refers to the tremendous amount of secondary storage required by large organizations.

Mass storage devices: Devices such as file servers, RAID systems, tape libraries, optical jukeboxes, and more.

Mechanical mouse: Traditional and most widely used type of mouse. It has a ball on the bottom and is attached with a cord to the system unit.

Media: Media are the actual physical material that holds the data, such as a floppy disk, which is one of the important characteristics of secondary storage. Singular of media is medium.

Media center system unit: Use powerful desktop system hardware with specialized graphics cards for interfacing with televisions and other home entertainment devices.

Medium: *See* Media.

Medium band: Bandwidth of special leased lines, used mainly with minicomputers and mainframe computers.

Memory: Memory is contained on chips connected to the system board and is a holding area for data instructions and information (processed data waiting to be output to secondary storage). RAM, ROM, and CMOS are three types of memory chips.

Menu: List of commands.

Menu bar: Menus are displayed in a menu bar at the top of the screen.

Mesh network: A topology requiring each node to have more than one connection to the other nodes so that if a path between two nodes is disrupted, data can be automatically rerouted around the failure using another path.

Message: The content portion of e-mail correspondence.

Metasearch engine: Program that automatically submits your search request to several indices and search engines and then creates an index from received information. One of the best known is Dogpile.

Method: In an object-oriented database, description of how the data is to be manipulated.

Metropolitan area network (MAN): These networks are used as links between office buildings in a city.

Microblog: Publishes short sentences that only take a few seconds to write, rather than long stories or posts like a traditional blog.

Microcomputer: Small, low-cost computer designed for individual users. These include desktop, notebook, and personal digital assistant computers.

Microcomputer database: *See* Individual database.

Microprocessor: The central processing unit (CPU) of a microcomputer controls and manipulates data to produce information. The microprocessor is contained on a single integrated circuit chip and is the brains of the system.

Microwave: Communication using high-frequency radio waves that travel in straight lines through the air.

Middle management: Middle-level managers deal with control and planning. They implement the long-term goals of the organization.

MIDI: *See* Musical instrument digital interface.

Midrange computer: Also known as a minicomputer.

Minicomputer: Refrigerator-sized machines falling in between microcomputers and mainframes in processing speed and data-storing capacity. Medium-sized companies or departments of large companies use minicomputers.

Mistaken identity: When the electronic profile of one person is switched with another.

Mobile browser: Special browsers designed to run on portable devices.

Mobile robots: Robots that act as transports and are used for a variety of different tasks.

Modem: Short for modulator-demodulator. It is a communication device that translates the electronic signals from a computer into electronic signals that can travel over telephone lines.

Modem card: Also known as an internal modem, a card that allows distant computers to communicate with one another by converting electronic signals from within the system unit into electronic signals that can travel over telephone lines and other types of connections.

Modulation: Process of converting digital signals to analog signals.

Module: *See* Program module.

Monitor: Output device like a television screen that displays data processed by the computer.

Motherboard: Also called a system board; the communications medium for the entire system.

Mouse: Device that typically rolls on the desktop and directs the cursor on the display screen.

Mouse pointer: Typically in the shape of an arrow.

Mouse port: Was used to connect a mouse to the system unit.

Multicore chip: A new type of chip that provides two independent CPUs, allowing two programs to run simultaneously. *Also see* Central processing unit.

Multidimensional database: Data can be viewed as a cube having three or more sides consisting of cells. Each side of the cube is considered a dimension of the data; thus, complex relationships between data can be represented and efficiently analyzed. Sometimes called a data cube and designed for analyzing large groups of records.

Multifunctional devices (MFD): Devices that typically combine the capabilities of a scanner, printer, fax, and copying machine.

Multimedia: Technology that can link all sorts of media into one form of presentation, such as video, music, voice, graphics, and text.

Multimedia authoring programs: Programs used to create multimedia presentations bringing together video, audio, graphics, and text elements into an interactive framework. Macromedia Director, Authorware, and Toolbook are examples of multimedia authoring programs.

Multitasking: Operating system that allows a single user to run several application programs at the same time.

Multi-touch screen: Can be touched with more than one finger, which allows for interactions such as rotating graphical objects on the screen with your hand or zooming in and out by pinching and stretching your fingers.

Musical instrument digital interface (MIDI): A standard that allows musical instruments to connect to the system using MIDI ports.

N

Naive: People who underestimate the difficulty of changing computer systems or generating information.

National service provider: Internet service providers, such as America Online (AOL), that provide access through standard telephone or cable connections and allow users to access the Internet from almost anywhere within the country for a standard fee.

Natural language: Language designed to give people a more human connection with computers.

Netbook: A type of microcomputer that is smaller, lighter, and less expensive than a notebook computer.

Netbook system unit: Similar to notebook system units but smaller, less powerful, and less expensive.

Network: The arrangement in which various communications channels are connected through two or more computers. The largest network in the world is the Internet.

Network adapter card: Connects the system unit to a cable that connects to other devices on the network.

Network administrator: Also known as network manager. Computer professional who ensures that existing information and communication systems are operating effectively and that new ones are implemented as needed. Also responsible for meeting security and privacy requirements.

Network architecture: Describes how networks are configured and how the resources are shared.

Network attached storage (NAS): Similar to a file server except simpler and less expensive. Widely used for home and small business storage needs.

Network database: Database with a hierarchical arrangement of nodes, except that each child node may have more than one parent node. Also called many-to-many relationship.

Network gateway: Connection by which a local area network may be linked to other local area networks or to larger networks.

Network interface card (NIC): Also known as a network adapter card. They are used to connect a computer to one or more computers forming a communication network whereby users can share data, programs, and hardware.

Network operating system (NOS): Interactive software between applications and computers coordinating and directing activities between computers on a network. This operating system is located on one of the connected computers' hard disks, making that system the network server.

Network server: *See* Network operating system. This computer coordinates all communication between the other computers. Popular network operating systems include NetWare and Windows NT Server.

Node: Any device connected to a network. For example, a node is a computer, printer, or data storage device and each device has its own address on the network. Also, within hierarchical databases, fields or records are structured in nodes.

Notebook computer: Portable computer, also known as a laptop computer, weighing between 4 and 10 pounds.

Notebook system unit: A small, portable system unit that contains electronic components, selected secondary storage devices, and input devices.

Numbered list: Sequence of steps or topics on a page organized by numbers.

Numeric entry: In a worksheet or spreadsheet, typically used to identify numbers or formulas.

Numeric keypad: Enters numbers and arithmetic symbols and is included on all computer keyboards.

O

Object: An element, such as a text box, that can be added to a workbook, which can be selected, sized, and moved. For example, if a chart (object) in an Excel workbook file (source file) is linked to a word document (destination file), the chart appears in the word document. In this manner, the object contains both data and instructions to manipulate the data.

Object code: Machine language code converted by a compiler from source code. Object code can be saved and run later.

Object-oriented database: A more flexible type of database that stores data as well as instructions to manipulate data and is able to handle unstructured data such as photographs, audio, and video. Object-oriented databases organize data using objects, classes, entities, attributes, and methods.

Object-oriented programming (OOP): Methodology in which a program is organized into self-contained, reusable modules called objects. Each object contains both the data and processing operations necessary to perform a task.

Object-oriented software development: Software development approach that focuses less on the tasks and more on defining the relationships between previously defined procedures or objects.

Objectives: In programming, it is necessary to make clear the problems you are trying to solve to create a functional program.

Office automation system (OAS): System designed primarily to support data workers. It focuses on managing documents, communicating, and scheduling.

Office software suites: *See* Productivity suites.

Office suites: *See* Productivity suites.

One-to-many relationship: In a hierarchical database, each entry has one parent node, and a parent may have several child nodes.

Online: Being connected to the Internet is described as being online.

Online banking: A feature provided by banking institutions that allows customers to perform banking operations using a Web browser.

Online identity: The information that people voluntarily post about themselves online.

Online office suite: Office suite stored online and available anywhere the Internet can be accessed.

Online processing: *See* Real-time processing.

Online shopping: The buying and selling of a wide range of consumer goods over the Internet.

Online stock trading: Allows investors to research, buy, and sell stocks and bonds over the Internet.

Online storage service: Provide users with storage space that can be accessed from a Web site.

Operating system: Software that interacts between application software and the computer, handling such details as running programs, storing and processing data, and coordinating all computer resources, including attached peripheral devices. It is the most important program on the computer. Windows 7, Windows Vista, and Mac OS X are examples of operating systems.

Operational feasibility: Making sure the design of a new system will be able to function within the existing framework of an organization.

Operational model: A decision model that helps lower-level managers accomplish the organization's day-to-day activities, such as evaluating and maintaining quality control.

Operators: Operators handle correcting operational errors in any programs. To do that, they need documentation, which gives them the understanding of the program, thus enabling them to fix any errors.

Optical audio connection: Port used to integrate computers into high-end audio and home theatre systems.

Optical carrier (OC): Provide support for very high-speed, all-digital transmission for large corporations.

Optical-character recognition (OCR): Scanning device that uses special preprinted characters, such as those printed on utility bills, that can be read by a light source and changed into machine-readable code.

Optical disc: Storage device that can hold over 17 gigabytes of data, which is an equivalent of several million typewritten pages. Lasers are used to record and read data on the disc. The two basic types of optical discs are compact discs (CDs) and digital versatile or video discs (DVDs).

Optical disc drive: A disc is read by an optical disc drive using a laser that projects a tiny beam of light. The amount of reflected light determines whether the area represents a 1 or a 0.

Optical-mark recognition (OMR): Device that senses the presence or absence of a mark, such as a pencil mark. As an example, an OMR device is used to score multiple choice tests.

Optical mouse: A type of mouse that emits and senses light to detect mouse movement.

Optical scanner: Device that identifies images or text on a page and automatically converts them to electronic signals that can be stored in a computer to copy or reproduce.

Organic light-emitting diode (OLED): Has the benefits of lower power consumption and longer battery life, as well as possibilities for much thinner displays.

Organization chart: Chart showing the levels of management and formal lines of authority in an organization.

Organizational online storage: High-speed Internet connection to a dedicated remote organizational Internet drive site.

Output device: Equipment that translates processed information from the central processing unit into a form that can be understood by humans. The most common output devices are monitors and printers.

P

Packet: Before a message is sent on the Internet, it is broken down into small parts called packets. Each packet is then sent separately over the Internet. At the receiving end, the packets are reassembled into the correct order.

Pages: In Microsoft PowerPoint, another name for slides.

Page layout program: *See* Desktop publishing program.

Palm computer: Also known as a handheld computer. These systems combine pen input, writing recognition, personal organizational tools, and communications capabilities. They contain an entire computer system, including the electronic components, secondary storage, and input and output devices.

Parallel approach: Systems implementation in which old and new systems are operated side by side until the new one has shown it is reliable.

Parallel port: Used to connect external devices that send or receive data over a short distance. Mostly used to connect printers to the system unit.

Parallel processing: Used by supercomputers to run large and complex programs.

Parent node: Node one level above the node being considered in a hierarchical database or network. Each entry has one parent node, although a parent may have several child nodes. Also called one-to-many relationship.

Passive-matrix monitor: Monitor that creates images by scanning the entire screen. This type requires little energy but clarity of images is not sharp. Also known as dual-scan monitor.

Password: Special sequence of numbers or letters that limits access to information, such as electronic mail.

Payroll: Activity concerned with calculating employee paychecks.

PC Card: Also known as Personal Computer Memory Card International Association (PCMCIA) card. Credit card–sized expansion cards developed for portable computers.

PCI Express (PCIe): New type of bus that is 30 times faster than PCI bus.

PDA keyboard: Miniature keyboard for PDAs used to send e-mail, create documents, and more.

Peer-to-peer (P2P) network: Network in which nodes can act as both servers and clients. For example, one microcomputer can obtain files located on another microcomputer and also can provide files to other microcomputers.

People: End users who use computers to make themselves more productive.

Perception system robot: Robot that imitates some of the human senses.

Periodic report: Reports for a specific time period as to the health of the company or a particular department of the company.

Peripheral component interconnect (PCI): Bus architecture that combines the capabilities of MCA and EISA with the ability to send video instructions at speeds to match the microprocessor. PCI is a 32-bit or 64-bit speed bus that is over 20 times faster than an ISA bus.

Person-to-person auction site: A type of Web auction site where the owner provides a forum for numerous buyers and sellers to gather.

Personal area network (PAN): A type of wireless network that works within a very small area—your immediate surroundings.

Personal digital assistant (PDA): A device that typically combines pen input, writing recognition, personal organizational tools, and communication capabilities in a very small package. Also called handheld PC and palm computer.

Personal laser printer: Inexpensive laser printer widely used by single users to produce black-and-white documents.

Personal software: *See* Integrated package.

Phased approach: Systems implementation whereby a new system is implemented gradually over a period of time.

Phishing: An attempt to trick Internet users into thinking a fake but official-looking Web site or e-mail is legitimate.

Photo editor: *See* Image editor.

Photo printer: A special-purpose ink-jet printer designed to print photo-quality images from digital cameras.

Physical security: Activity concerned with protecting hardware from possible human and natural disasters.

Physical view: This focuses on the actual format and location of the data. *See* Logical view.

Picture elements: *See* Pixel.

Pilot approach: Systems implementation in which a new system is tried out in only one part of the organization. Later it is implemented throughout the rest of the organization.

Pit: *See* Lands and pits.

Pixel (picture elements): Smallest unit on the screen that can be turned on and off or made different shades. Pixels are individual dots that form images on a monitor. The greater the resolution, the more pixels and the better the clarity.

Pixel pitch: The distance between each pixel on a monitor.

Plagiarism: Representing some other person's work and ideas as your own without giving credit to the original source.

Plagiarist: Someone who engages in plagiarism.

Platform: The operating system. Application programs are designed to run with a specific platform. *See* Operating system.

Platform scanner: Handheld direct-entry device used to read special characters on price tags. Also known as wand reader.

Platter: Rigid metallic disk; multiple platters are stacked one on top of another within a hard disk drive.

Plotter: Special-purpose output device for producing bar charts, maps, architectural drawings, and three-dimensional illustrations.

Plug and Play: Set of hardware and software standards developed to create operating systems, processing units, expansion cards, and other devices that are able to configure themselves. When the computer starts up, it will search for the Plug and Play device and automatically configure it to the system.

Plug-in: Program that is automatically loaded and operates as part of a browser.

Pointer: For a monitor, a pointer is typically displayed as an arrow and controlled by a mouse. For a database, a pointer is a connection between a parent node and a child node in a hierarchical database.

Pointing stick: Device used to control the pointer by directing the stick with your finger.

Pointers: Within a network database, pointers are additional connections between parent nodes and child nodes. Thus, a node may be reached through more than one path and can be traced down through different branches.

Port: Connecting socket on the outside of the system unit. Used to connect input and output devices to the system unit.

Portable language: Language that can be run on more than one type of computer.

Portable printer: Small and lightweight printers designed to work with notebook computers.

Portable scanner: A handheld device that slides across an image to be scanned, making direct contact.

Power supply unit: Desktop computers have a power supply unit located within the system unit that plugs into a standard wall outlet, converting AC to DC, which becomes the power to drive all of the system unit components.

Preliminary investigation: First phase of the systems life cycle. It involves defining the problem, suggesting alternative systems, and preparing a short report.

Presentation file: A file created by presentation graphics programs to save presentation materials. For example, a file might contain audience handouts, speaker notes, and electronic slides.

Presentation graphics: Graphics used to combine a variety of visual objects to create attractive and interesting presentations.

Primary key: *See* Key field.

Primary storage: Holds data and program instructions for processing data. It also holds processed information before it is output. *See* Memory.

Printer: Device that produces printed paper output.

Privacy: Computer ethics issue concerning the collection and use of data about individuals.

Proactive: Person who looks at technology in a positive, realistic way.

Procedural language: Programming language designed to focus on procedures and how a program will accomplish

a specific task. Also known as 3GLs or third-generation languages.

Procedures: Rules or guidelines to follow when using hardware, software, and data.

Processing rights: Refers to which people have access to what kind of data.

Processor: *See* Central processing unit.

Production: The organizational department that actually creates finished goods and services using raw materials and personnel.

Productivity suites: Also known as office suites; contain professional-grade application programs, including word processing, spreadsheets, and more. A good example is Microsoft Office.

Program: Instructions for the computer to follow to process data. *See* Software.

Program analysis: *See* Program specification.

Program coder: *See* Application generator.

Program definition: *See* Program specification.

Program design: Creating a solution using programming techniques, such as top-down program design, pseudocode, flowcharts, logic structures, object-oriented programming, and CASE tools.

Program documentation: Written description of the purpose and process of a program. Documentation is written within the program itself and in printed documents. Programmers will find themselves frustrated without adequate documentation, especially when it comes time to update or modify the program.

Program flowchart: Flowchart graphically presents a detailed sequence of steps needed to solve a programming problem.

Program maintenance: Activity of updating software to correct errors, improve usability, standardize, and adjust to organizational changes.

Program module: Each module is made up of logically related program statements. The program must pass in sequence from one module to the next until the computer has processed all modules.

Program specification: Programming step in which objectives, output, input, and processing requirements are determined.

Programmer: Computer professional who creates new software or revises existing software.

Programming: A program is a list of instructions a computer will follow to process data. Programming, also known as software development, is a six-step procedure for creating that list of instructions. The six steps are program specification, program design, program code (or coding), program test, program documentation, and program maintenance.

Programming language: A collection of symbols, words, and phrases that instruct a computer to perform a specific task.

Project manager: Software that enables users to plan, schedule, and control the people, resources, and costs needed to complete a project on time.

Property: Computer ethics issue relating to who owns data and rights to software.

Protocol: Rules for exchanging data between computers. The protocol http:// is the most common.

Prototyping: Building a model or prototype that can be modified before the actual system is installed.

Proxy server: Computer that acts as a gateway or checkpoint in an organization's firewall. *See* Firewall.

Pseudocode: An outline of the logic of the program to be written. It is the steps or the summary of the program before you actually write the program for the computer. Consequently, you can see beforehand what the program is to accomplish.

Purchase order: A form that shows the name of the company supplying the material or service and what is being purchased.

Purchasing: Buying of raw materials and services.

Q

Query: A question or request for specific data contained in a database. Used to analyze data.

Query-by-example: A specific tool in database management that shows a blank record and lets you specify the information needed, like the fields and values of the topic you are looking to obtain.

Query language: Easy-to-use language and understandable to most users. It is used to search and generate reports from a database. An example is the language used on an airline reservation system.

R

Radio Frequency (RF): Uses radio signals to communicate between wireless devices.

Radio frequency card reader: A device that reads cards having embedded radio frequency identification (RFID) information.

Radio frequency identification (RFID): A system that uses radio waves to read encoded information from a microchip.

RAID system: Several inexpensive hard-disk drives connected to improve performance and provide reliable storage.

RAM: *See* Random access memory.

Random access memory (RAM): Volatile, temporary storage that holds the program and data the CPU is presently processing. It is called temporary storage because its contents will be lost if electrical power to the computer is disrupted or the computer is turned off.

Range: A series of continuous cells in a worksheet.

Rapid applications development (RAD): Involves the use of powerful development software and specialized teams as an alternative to the systems development life cycle approach. Time for development is shorter and quality of the completed systems development time is better, although cost is greater.

Raster image: *See* Bitmap image.

Read-only memory (ROM): Refers to chips that have programs built into them at the factory. The user cannot

change the contents of such chips. The CPU can read or retrieve the programs on the chips but cannot write or change information. ROM stores programs that boot the computer, for example. Also called firmware.

Real-time processing: Or online processing. Occurs when data is processed at the same time a transaction occurs.

Recalculation: If you change one or more numbers in your spreadsheet, all related formulas will automatically recalculate and charts will be recreated.

Record: Each row of information in a database is a record. Each record contains fields of data about some specific item, like employee name, address, phone, and so forth. A record represents a collection of attributes describing an entity.

Redundant arrays of inexpensive disks (RAIDs): Groups of inexpensive hard-disk drives related or grouped together using networks and special software. They improve performance by expanding external storage.

Refresh rate: How often a displayed image is updated or redrawn on the monitor.

Relation: A table in a relational database in which data elements are stored in rows and columns.

Relational database: A widely used database structure in which data is organized into related tables. Each table is made up of rows called records and columns called fields. Each record contains fields of data about a specific item.

Repetition structure: *See* Loop structure.

Reports: Can be lists of fields in a table or selected fields based on a query. Typical database reports include sales summaries, phone lists, and mailing labels.

Research: The organizational department that identifies, investigates, and develops new products and services.

Resolution: A measurement in pixels of a monitor's clarity. For a given monitor, the greater the resolution, the more pixels and the clearer the image.

Reuniting site: A site that connects people who have known one another but have lost touch.

Reverse directory: A special telephone directory listing telephone numbers sequentially, followed by subscriber names.

RFID tag: Information chips that are embedded in merchandise to track their location.

Ribbons: Feature of Microsoft Office 2007 that replaces menus and toolbars by organizing commonly used commands into a set of tabs.

Ring network: Network in which each device is connected to two other devices, forming a ring. There is no host computer, and messages are passed around the ring until they reach the correct destination.

Robot: Robots are computer-controlled machines that mimic the motor activities of living things, and some robots can solve unstructured problems using artificial intelligence.

Robot network: *See* Botnet.

Robotics: Field of study concerned with developing and using robots.

Roller ball: *See* Trackball.

ROM: *See* Read-only memory.

Row: A horizontal block of cells one cell high all the way across the worksheet.

S

Sales order processing: Activity that records the demands of customers for a company's products or services.

Satellite: This type of communication uses satellites orbiting about 22,000 miles above the earth as microwave relay stations.

Satellite/air connection services: Connection services that use satellites and the air to download or send data to users at a rate seven times faster than dial-up connections.

Scam: A fraudulent or deceptive act or operation designed to trick individuals into spending their time and money for little or no return.

Schema: *See* Data dictionary.

Search engine: Specialized programs assisting in locating information on the Web and the Internet.

Search services: Organizations that maintain databases relating to information provided on the Internet and also provide search engines to locate information.

Secondary storage: Permanent storage used to preserve programs and data that can be retained after the computer is turned off. These devices include floppy disks, hard disks, magnetic tape, CDs, DVDs, and more.

Secondary storage device: These devices are used to save, backup, and transport files from one location or computer to another. *See* Secondary storage.

Sector: Section shaped like a pie wedge that divides the tracks on a disk.

Secure file transfer protocol (SFTP): *See* File transfer protocol.

Security: The protection of information, hardware, and software.

Selection structure: Logic structure that determines which of two paths will be followed when a program must make a decision. Also called IF-THEN-ELSE structures. If something is true, then do option one, or else do option two.

Semiconductor: Silicon chip through which electricity flows with some resistance.

Sequential access: An approach to external storage, provided by magnetic tape, where information is stored in sequence. *See* Magnetic tape.

Serial Advanced Technology Attachment (SATA): New type of bus used to connect magnetic and optical disc drives to the system board with far greater speed than other types of buses.

Serial port: Used to connect external devices that send or receive data one bit at a time over a long distance. Used for mouse, keyboard, modem, and many other devices.

Server: A host computer with a connection to the Internet that stores document files used to display Web pages.

Depending on the resources shared, it may be called a file server, printer server, communication server, Web server, or database server.

Shared laser printer: More expensive laser printer used by a group of users to produce black-and-white documents. These printers can produce over 30 pages a minute.

Sheet: A rectangular grid of rows and columns. *See* Spreadsheet or Worksheet.

Signature: Provides additional information about a sender of an e-mail message, such as name, address, and telephone number.

Silicon chip: Tiny circuit board etched on a small square of sandlike material called silicon. Chips are mounted on carrier packages, which then plug into sockets on the system board.

Slide: A PowerPoint presentation is made up of many slides shown in different views and presentation styles.

Slot: Area on a system board that accepts expansion cards to expand a computer system's capabilities.

Smart card: Card about the size of a credit card containing a tiny built-in microprocessor. It can be used to hold such information as personal identification, medical and financial knowledge, and credit card numbers. Information on this card is protected by a password, which offers security and privacy.

Smart phone: A type of cell phone that offers a variety of advanced functionality, including Internet and e-mail.

Snoopware: Programs that record virtually every activity on a computer system.

Social networking: Using the Internet to connect individuals.

Socket: Sockets provide connection points on the system board for holding electronic parts.

Software: Computer program consisting of step-by-step instructions, directing the computer on each task it will perform.

Software development: *See* Programming.

Software engineer: Programming professional or programmer who analyzes users' needs and creates application software.

Software environment: Operating system, also known as software platform, consisting of a collection of programs to handle technical details depending on the type of operating system. For example, software designed to run on an Apple computer is compatible with the Mac OS environment.

Software piracy: Unauthorized copying of programs for personal gain.

Software platform: *See* Software environment.

Software suite: Individual application programs that are sold together as a group.

Solid-state drive (SSD): Designed to be connected inside a microcomputer system the same way an internal hard disk would be, but contains solid-state memory instead of magnetic disks to store data.

Solid-state storage: A secondary storage device that has no moving parts. Data is stored and retrieved electronically directly from these devices, much as they would be from conventional computer memory.

Sony/Philips Digital Interconnect Format (S/PDIF): *See* Optical audio connection.

Sort: Tool that rearranges a table's records numerically or alphabetically according to a selected field.

Sound card: Device that accepts audio input from a microphone and converts it into a form that can be processed by the computer. Also converts internal electronic signals to audio signals so they can be heard from external speakers.

Source code: When a programmer originally writes the code for a program in a particular language. This is called source code until it is translated by a compiler for the computer to execute the program. It then becomes object code.

Spam: Unwelcome and unsolicited e-mail that can carry attached viruses.

Spam blocker: Software that uses a variety of different approaches to identify and eliminate spam or junk mail.

Speakers: Audio-output devices connected to a sound card in the system unit. The sound card is used to capture as well as play back recorded sound.

Specialized application: Programs that are narrowly focused on specific disciplines and occupations. Some of the best known are multimedia, Web authoring, graphics, virtual reality, and artificial intelligence.

Specialized search engine: Search engine that focuses on subject-specific Web sites.

Specialized suite: Programs that focus on specialized applications such as graphics suites or financial planning suites.

Speech recognition: The ability to accept voice input to select menu options, and to dictate text.

Spelling checker: Program used with a word processor to check the spelling of typed text against an electronic dictionary.

Spider: Special programs that continually look for new information and update the search servers' databases.

Spike: *See* Voltage surge.

Spotlight: An advanced search tool on the Mac OS X operating system for locating files, e-mail messages, and more.

Spreadsheet: Computer-produced spreadsheet based on the traditional accounting worksheet that has rows and columns used to present and analyze data.

Spy removal programs: Programs such as Spybot and Spysweeper, designed to detect Web bugs and monitor software.

Spyware: Wide range of programs designed to secretly record and report an individual's activities on the Internet.

Stand-alone operating system: Also called desktop operating systems; a type of operating system that controls a single desktop or notebook computer.

Star network: Network of computers or peripheral devices linked to a central computer through which all communications pass. Control is maintained by polling. The configuration of the computers looks like a star surrounding and connected to the central computer in the middle.

Stock photograph: Photographs on a variety of subject material from professional models to natural landscapes.

Storage area network (SAN): An architecture that links remote computer storage devices such as enterprise storage systems to computers so that the devices are available as locally attached drives.

Storage device: Hardware that reads data and programs from storage media. Most also write to storage media.

Strategic model: A decision model that assists top managers in long-range planning, such as stating company objectives or planning plant locations.

Strategy: A way of coordinating the sharing of information and resources. The most common network strategies are terminal, peer-to-peer, and client/server networks.

Structured program: Program that uses logic structures according to the program design and the language in which you have chosen to write the program. Each language follows techniques like pseudocode, flowcharts, and logic structures.

Structured programming techniques: Techniques consisting of top-down program design, pseudocode, flowcharts, and logic structures.

Structured query language (SQL): A program control language used to create sophisticated database applications for requesting information from a database.

Styles: A feature found in most word processors that quickly applies predefined formats.

Stylus: Penlike device used with tablet PCs and PDAs that uses pressure to draw images on a screen. A stylus interacts with the computer through handwriting recognition software.

Subject: Located in the header of an e-mail message; a one-line description used to present the topic of the message.

Supercomputer: Fastest calculating device ever invented, processing billions of program instructions per second. Used by very large organizations like NASA.

Supervisor: Manager responsible for managing and monitoring workers. Supervisors have responsibility for operational matters.

Surf: Move from one Web site to another.

Surge protector: Device separating the computer from the power source of the wall outlet. When a voltage surge occurs, a circuit breaker is activated, protecting the computer system.

Switch: The center or central node for other nodes. This device coordinates the flow of data by sending messages directly between sender and receiver nodes.

Syntax error: Violation of the rules of a language in which the computer program is written. For example, leaving out a semicolon would stop the entire program from working because it is not the exact form the computer expects for that language.

System: Collection of activities and elements designed to accomplish a goal.

System board: Flat board that usually contains the CPU and memory chips connecting all system components to one another.

System bus: There are two categories of buses. One is the system bus that connects the CPU to the system board. The other is the expansion bus that connects the CPU to slots on the system board.

System chassis: *See* System unit.

System flowchart: A flowchart that shows the flow of input data to processing and finally to output, or distribution of information.

System software: "Background" software that enables the application software to interact with the computer. System software consists of the operating system, utilities, device drivers, and language translators. It works with application software to handle the majority of technical details.

System unit: Part of a microcomputer that contains the CPU. Also known as the system cabinet or chassis, it is the container that houses most of the electronic components that make up the computer system.

Systems analysis: This second phase of the systems life cycle determines the requirements for a new system. Data is collected about the present system and analyzed, and new requirements are determined.

Systems analysis and design: Six phases of problem solving procedures for examining information systems and improving them.

Systems analysis report: Report prepared for higher management describing the current information system, the requirements for a new system, and a possible development schedule.

Systems analyst: Plans and designs information systems.

Systems audit: A systems audit compares the performance of a new system to the original design specifications to determine if the new procedures are actually improving productivity.

Systems design: Phase three of the systems life cycle, consisting of designing alternative systems, selecting the best system, and writing a systems design report.

Systems design report: Report prepared for higher management describing alternative designs, presenting cost versus benefits, and outlining the effects of alternative designs on the organization.

Systems development: Phase four of the systems life cycle, consisting of developing software, acquiring hardware, and testing the new system.

Systems implementation: Phase five of the systems life cycle is converting the old system to the new one and training people to use the new system. Also known as conversion.

Systems life cycle: The six phases of systems analysis and design are called the systems life cycle. The phases are preliminary investigation, systems analysis, systems design, systems development, systems implementation, and systems maintenance.

Systems maintenance: Phase six of the systems life cycle consisting of a systems audit and periodic evaluation.

T

T1: High-speed lines that support all digital communications, provide very high capacity, and are very expensive.

T3: Copper lines combined to form higher-capacity options.

Tab: Used to divide the ribbon into major activity areas, with each tab being organized into groups that contain related items.

Table (in database): The list of records in a database. Tables make up the basic structure of a database. Their columns display field data and their rows display records. *See* Field and Record.

Tablet PC: A type of notebook computer that accepts handwritten data, using a stylus or pen, that is converted to standard text and can be processed by a word processor program.

Tablet PC system unit: Similar to notebook system units. Two basic categories are convertible and slate. A stylus or pen is used to input data.

Tactical model: A decision model that assists middle-level managers to control the work of the organization, such as financial planning and sales promotion planning.

Tape cartridges: *See* Magnetic tape streamer.

Tape library: Device that provides automatic access to data archived on a large collection or library of tapes.

Task-oriented language: Programming language that is nonprocedural and focuses on specifying what the program is to accomplish. Also known as 4GLs or very high-level languages.

Technical feasibility: Making sure hardware, software, and training will be available to facilitate the design of a new system.

Technical writer: Prepares instruction manuals, technical reports, and other scientific or technical documents.

Telephone line: A transmission medium for both voice and data.

Telephone modem: Used to connect a computer directly to a telephone line.

Telephony: Communication that uses the Internet rather than traditional communication lines to connect two or more people via telephone.

Terminal server network: Network system in which processing power is centralized in one large computer, usually a mainframe. The nodes connected to this host computer are terminals, with little or no processing capabilities, or they are microcomputers running special software allowing them to act as terminals.

Text entry: In a worksheet or spreadsheet, a text entry is typically used to identify or label information entered into a cell as opposed to numbers and formulas. Also known as labels.

Thermal printer: Printer that uses heat elements to produce images on heat-sensitive paper.

Thesaurus: A word processor feature that provides synonyms, antonyms, and related words for a selected word or phrase.

Thin film transistor (TFT) monitor: Type of flat-panel monitor activating each pixel independently.

Third-generation language (3GL): *See* Procedural language.

Toggle key: These keys turn a feature on or off like the CAPS LOCK key.

Toolbar: Bar located typically below the menu bar containing icons or graphical representations for commonly used commands.

Top-down analysis method: Method used to identify top-level components of a system, then break these components down into smaller parts for analysis.

Top-down program design: Used to identify the program's processing steps, called program modules. The program must pass in sequence from one module to the next until the computer has processed all modules.

Top-level domain (TLD): Last part of an Internet address; identifies the geographical description or organizational identification. For example, using www.aol.com, the .com is the top-level domain code and indicates it is a commercial site. *Also see* Domain name.

Top management: Top-level managers are concerned with long-range (strategic) planning. They supervise middle management.

Topology: The configuration of a network. The four principal network topologies are *star, bus, ring,* and *hierarchical.*

Touch pad: Used to control the pointer by moving and tapping your finger on the surface of a pad.

Touch screen: Monitor screen allowing actions or commands to be entered by the touch of a finger.

Track: Closed, concentric ring on a disk on which data is recorded. Each track is divided into sections called sectors.

Trackball: Device used to control the pointer by rotating a ball with your thumb. Also called a roller ball.

Traditional cookies: Intended to provide customized service. A program recording information on Web site visitors within a specific site. When you leave the site, the cookie becomes dormant and is reactivated when you revisit the site.

Traditional floppy disk: A two-sided, high-density, 3½-inch disk with a capacity of 1.44 megabytes. *Also see* Floppy disk.

Traditional keyboard: Full-sized, rigid, rectangular keyboard that includes function, navigational, and numeric keys.

Transaction processing system (TPS): System that records day-to-day transactions, such as customer orders, bills, inventory levels, and production output. The TPS tracks operations and creates databases.

Transfer rate: Or transfer speed, is the speed at which modems transmit data, typically measured in bits per second (bps).

Transition: Used to animate how a presentation moves from one slide to the next.

Transmission control protocol/Internet protocol (TCP/IP): TCP/IP is the standard protocol for the Internet. The essential features of this protocol involve (1) identifying sending and receiving devices and (2) reformatting information for transmission across the Internet.

Tree network: Also known as a hierarchical network. A topology in which each device is connected to a central node, either directly or through one or more other devices. The central node is then connected to two or more subordinate nodes that in turn are connected to other subordinate nodes, and so forth, forming a treelike structure.

Trojan horse: Program that is not a virus but is a carrier of virus(es). The most common Trojan horses appear as free computer games, screen savers, or antivirus programs. Once downloaded they locate and disable existing virus protection and then deposit the virus.

Troubleshooting program: A utility program that recognizes and corrects computer-related problems before they become serious. Also called diagnostic programs.

Twisted pair: Cable consisting of pairs of copper wire that are twisted together.

Twitter: The most popular microblogging site that enables you to add new content from your browser, instant messaging application, or even a mobile phone.

TV tuner card: Contains TV tuner card and video converter changing the TV signal into one that can be displayed on your monitor. Also known as video recorder cards and video capture cards.

Unicode: A 16-bit code designed to support international languages, like Chinese and Japanese.

Uniform resource locator (URL): For browsers to connect you to resources on the Web, the location or address of the resources must be specified. These addresses are called URLs.

Uninstall program: A utility program that safely and completely removes unwanted programs and related files.

Universal instant messenger: An instant messaging service that communicates with any other messaging service programs.

Universal Product Code (UPC): A barcode system that identifies the product to the computer, which has a description and the latest price for the product.

Universal serial bus (USB): Combines with a PCI bus on the system board to support several external devices without inserting cards for each device. USB buses are used to support high-speed scanners, printers, and video-capturing devices.

Universal serial bus (USB) port: Expected to replace serial and parallel ports. They are faster, and one USB port can be used to connect several devices to the system unit.

UNIX: An operating system originally developed for minicomputers. It is now important because it can run on many of the more powerful microcomputers.

Uploading: Process of transferring information from the computer the user is operating to a remote computer.

USB drive: The size of a key chain, these hard drives connect to a computer's USB port enabling a transfer of files; has a capacity of up to 64GB.

User: Any individual who uses a computer. *See* End user.

User interface: Means by which users interact with application programs and hardware. A window is displayed with information for the user to enter or choose, and that is how users communicate with the program.

Utility: Performs specific tasks related to managing computer resources or files. Norton Utility for virus control and system maintenance is a good example of a utility. Also known as service programs.

Utility suite: A program that combines several utilities in one package to improve system performance. McAfee Office and Norton SystemWorks are examples.

V

Vector: Another common type of graphic file. A vector file contains all the shapes and colors, along with starting and ending points, necessary to recreate the image.

Vector illustration: *See* Vector image.

Vector image: Graphics file made up of a collection of objects such as lines, rectangles, and ovals. Vector images are more flexible than bitmaps because they are defined by mathematical equations so they can be stretched and resized. Illustration programs create and manipulate vector graphics. Also known as vector illustrations.

Very high-level languages: Task-oriented languages that require little special training on the part of the user.

VGA (Video Graphic Adapter) port: A type of port that provides a connection to an analog monitor.

Video editing software: Allows you to reorganize, add effects, and more to your video footage.

Videoconferencing system: Computer system that allows people located at various geographic locations to have in-person meetings.

Virtual environment: *See* Virtual reality.

Virtualization: A process that allows a single physical computer to support multiple operating systems that operate independently.

Virtualization software: Software that creates virtual machines.

Virtual keyboard: Display an image of a keyboard on a touch screen device. The screen functions as the actual input device, which is why the keyboard is considered virtual.

Virtual machine: A software implementation of a computer that executes programs like a physical computer.

Virtual memory: Feature of an operating system that increases the amount of memory available to run programs. With large programs, parts are stored on a secondary device like your hard disk. Then each part is read in RAM only when needed.

Virtual private network (VPN): Creates a secure private connection between a remote user and an organization's internal network. Special VPN protocols create the equivalent of a dedicated line between a user's home or laptop computer and a company server.

Virtual reality: Interactive sensory equipment (headgear and gloves) allowing users to experience alternative realities generated in 3-D by a computer, thus imitating the physical world.

Virtual reality wall: An immersive experience whereby you are viewing simulations on a virtual reality wall in stereoscopic vision.

Virus: Hidden instructions that migrate through networks and operating systems and become embedded in different programs. They may be designed to destroy data or simply to display messages.

Voice over IP (VoIP): Transmission of telephone calls over networks. *See also* Telephony.

Voice recognition system: Using a microphone, sound card, and specialty software, the user can operate a computer and create documents using voice commands.

Voiceband: Bandwidth of a standard telephone line. Also known as low bandwidth.

Voltage surge (spike): Excess of electricity that may destroy chips or other electronic computer components.

VR: *See* Virtual reality.

W

WAN: *See* Wide area network.

Wand reader: Special-purpose handheld device used to read OCR characters.

Warm boot: Restarting your computer while the computer is already on and the power is not turned off.

Web: Introduced in 1992 and prior to the Web, the Internet was all text. The Web made it possible to provide a multimedia interface that includes graphics, animations, sound, and video.

Web auction: Similar to traditional auctions except that all transactions occur over the Web; buyers and sellers seldom meet face-to-face.

Web authoring: Creating a Web site.

Web authoring program: Word processing program for generating Web pages. Also called HTML editor or Web page editor. Widely used Web authoring programs include Macromedia Dreamweaver and Microsoft FrontPage.

Web-based applications: By using the Web to connect with an application service provider (asp), you can copy an application program to your computer system's memory and then run the application.

Web-based file transfer services: A type of file transfer service that uses a Web browser to upload and download files, allowing you to copy files to and from your computer across the Internet.

Web-based service: Web site that provides free access to programs that run within a browser window; for example, Google Apps.

Web bug: Program hidden in the HTML code for a Web page or e-mail message as a graphical image. Web bugs can migrate whenever a user visits a Web site containing a Web bug or opens infected e-mail. They collect information on the users and report back to a predefined server.

Web log: A type of personal Web site where articles are regularly posted.

Web page: Browsers interpret HTML documents to display Web pages.

Web page editor: *See* Web authoring program.

Web utilities: Specialized utility programs making the Internet and the Web easier and safer. Some examples are plug-ins that operate as part of a browser and filters that block access and monitor use of selected Web sites.

WebCam: Specialized digital video camera for capturing images and broadcasting to the Internet.

Webmaster: Develops and maintains Web sites and Web resources.

What-if analysis: Spreadsheet feature in which changing one or more numbers results in the automatic recalculation of all related formulas.

Wheel button: Some mice have a wheel button that can be rotated to scroll through information displayed on the monitor.

Wide area network (WAN): Countrywide and worldwide networks that use microwave relays and satellites to reach users over long distances.

Wi-Fi (wireless fidelity): Wireless standard also known as 802.11, used to connect computers to each other and to the Internet.

Wiki: A Web site that allows people to fill in missing information or correct inaccuracies on it by directly editing the pages.

Window: A rectangular area containing a document or message.

Windows: An operating environment extending the capability of DOS.

Windows 7: The newest version of the Windows operating system, released in 2009.

Windows Update: A utility provided in the Windows platform that allows you to update the device drivers on your computer.

Windows Vista: An upgrade to Windows XP with improved security, three-dimensional workspace, and filtering capabilities.

Wireless access point: Or base station. The receiver interprets incoming radio frequencies from a wireless LAN and routes communications to the appropriate devices, which could be separate computers, a shared printer, or a modem.

Wireless keyboard: Transmits input to the system through the air, providing greater flexibility and convenience.

Wireless LAN (WLAN): Uses radio frequencies to connect computers and other devices. All communications pass through the network's centrally located wireless receiver or base station and are routed to the appropriate devices.

Wireless modem: Modem that connects to the serial port but does not connect to telephone lines. It receives through the air.

Wireless mouse: *See* Cordless mouse.

Wireless revolution: A revolution that is expected to dramatically affect the way we communicate and use computer technology.

Wireless service provider: Provides Internet connections for computers with wireless modems and a wide array of wireless devices. They do not use telephone lines.

Wireless wide area network (WWAN) modem: *See* Wireless modem.

Word: The number of bits (such as 16, 32, or 64) that can be accessed at one time by the CPU.

Word processor: The computer and the program allow you to create, edit, save, and print documents composed of text.

Word wrap: Feature of word processing that automatically moves the cursor from the end of one line to the beginning of the next.

Workbook file: Contains one or more related worksheets or spreadsheets. *See* Spreadsheet.

Worksheet: Also known as a spreadsheet, or sheet; a rectangular grid of rows and columns used in programs like Excel.

Worksheet file: Created by electronic spreadsheets to analyze things like budgets and to predict sales.

Worm: Virus that doesn't attach itself to programs and databases but fills a computer system with self-replicating information, clogging the system so that its operations are slowed or stopped.

WYSIWYG (what you see is what you get) editors: Web authoring programs that build a page without requiring direct interaction with the HTML code and then preview the page described by the HTML code.

Z

Zombie: A computer infected by a virus, worm, or Trojan horse that allows it to be remotely controlled for malicious purposes.

Credits

Photo

p. 3	© Enamul Hoque/Rod Steele/Getty Images
p. 4 top left	© Sydney Shaffer/zefa/Corbis
p. 4 bottom	Microsoft product box shot(s) reprinted with permission from Microsoft Corporation.
p. 4 top right	Microsoft product box shot(s) reprinted with permission from Microsoft Corporation.
p. 5 left	© Willis Technology
p. 5 right	© Guy Crittenden/Getty Images
p. 7 top left	© ColorBlind Images/Getty Images
p. 7 bottom left	© AAGAMIA/Getty Images
p. 7 center	© Goodshoot/Punchstock
p. 7 right	© Ron Levine/Getty Images
p. 9 left	Microsoft screen shot reprinted with permission from Microsoft Corporation.
p. 11 top	Courtesy of IBM.
p. 11 center left	Courtesy of Apple.
p. 11 center middle	Courtesy of Apple.
p. 11 bottom left	© FURGOLLE/Image Point FR/Corbis
p. 11 bottom middle	Courtesy of Nokia.
p. 11 center right	Courtesy of Hewlett-Packard Company.
p. 11 bottom right	© PRNewsFoto/RadioShack Corporation
p. 12	© Willis Technology
p. 13 top	© Willis Technology
p. 13 bottom left	Courtesy of Samsung.
p. 13 bottom right	© Willis Technology
p. 15 top left	Courtesy of Apple.
p. 15 top center	Courtesy of Nokia.
p. 15 top right	Courtesy of LG Electronics.
p. 15 bottom left	© PRNewsFoto/Verizon Wireless
p. 15 bottom right	© PRNewsFoto/Verizon Wireless
p. 16	© Westend61/Getty Images
p. 17	© Colin Anderson/Getty Image
p. 18 left	© Sydney Shaffer/zefa/Corbis
p. 18 right	© AAGAMIA/Getty Images
p. 19 left	Microsoft product box shot(s) reprinted with permission from Microsoft Corporation.
p. 19 left	Microsoft product box shot(s) reprinted with permission from Microsoft Corporation.
p. 19 right	© Willis Technology
p. 24	Courtesy of Nokia.
p. 25	© Image Source/Getty Images
p. 26	© Huntstock/Getty Images
p. 29	© Colin Anderson/Getty Image
p. 51	© Peter Cade/Getty Images
p. 52	© Tom Ackerman/Getty Images
p. 53	© George Gutenberg/Beateworks/Corbis
p. 65	© Kheng Guan Toh/Veer
p. 84	Microsoft product box shot(s) reprinted with permission from Microsoft Corporation.
p. 85	Microsoft product box shot(s) reprinted with permission from Microsoft Corporation.
p. 88	© Stockbyte/Getty Images
p. 89	© Colin Anderson/Getty Image
p. 92	© Stockbyte/Getty Images
p. 101	© Design Pics/SuperStock
p. 102 top left	Courtesy of Adobe Systems Incorporated.
p. 102 bottom left	Courtesy of Adobe Systems Incorporated.
p. 102 center	Courtesy of Apple.
p. 102 right	Microsoft product box shot(s) reprinted with permission from Microsoft Corporation.
p. 105	Courtesy of Corel Corporation.
p. 112	© Chris Salvo/Getty Images
p. 113 top	© AP Photo/Steve Pope
p. 113 bottom	© Getty Images
p. 114 top	© Romilly Lockyer/Getty Images
p. 114 bottom	© Ciaran Griffin/Getty Images
p. 115	© John Lund/Getty Images
p. 118 top left	© Chris Salvo/Getty Images
p. 118 bottom	© AP Photo/Steve Pope
p. 118 top right	© Getty Images
p. 127	© Howard Grey/Getty Images
p. 129 left	© Sydney Shaffer/zefa/Corbis
p. 129 center	Microsoft product box shot(s) reprinted with permission from Microsoft Corporation.
p. 129 center	Microsoft product box shot(s) reprinted with permission from Microsoft Corporation.
p. 131 top	Courtesy of Research In Motion Limited.

p. 131 bottom	© Willis Technology
p. 143	© Thomas Barwick/Getty Images
p. 144	© Lucas Racasse/Getty Images
p. 145 left	Microsoft product box shot(s) reprinted with permission from Microsoft Corporation.
p. 155	© Photodisc/Getty Images
p. 157 top left	Courtesy of Apple.
p. 157 top right	Courtesy of Nokia.
p. 157 center left	Courtesy of Apple.
p. 157 center right	© FURGOLLE/Image Point FR/ Corbis
p. 157 bottom left	Courtesy of Hewlett-Packard Company.
p. 157 bottom right	© PRNewsFoto/RadioShack Corporation
p. 158 left	Courtesy of Hewlett-Packard Company.
p. 160	© Willis Technology
p. 161 top left	© Willis Technology
p. 161 top right	© Willis Technology
p. 161 bottom	© Willis Technology
p. 163	© Willis Technology
p. 165 left	© Willis Technology
p. 165 right	© Willis Technology
p. 166 left	© Willis Technology
p. 166 right	© Willis Technology
p. 167	© Willis Technology
p. 170	© Willis Technology
p. 172 top	© Willis Technology
p. 172 bottom left	© Willis Technology
p. 172 bottom right	© Willis Technology
p. 173	© Shalom Ormsby/Getty Images
p. 174	© Colin Anderson/Getty Image
p. 175 top left	Courtesy of Apple.
p. 175 top right	© Willis Technology
p. 175 bottom right	© Willis Technology
p. 176	© Willis Technology
p. 177	© Willis Technology
p. 185	© Blend Images/Getty Images
p. 187 top left	© John Lund/Paula Zacharias/ Getty Images
p. 187 top right	© AP Photo/Mark Lennihan
p. 187 bottom	© Willis Technology
p. 188 bottom	© Willis Technology
p. 189 top left	Courtesy of Microsoft Corporation.
p. 189 top right	Courtesy of Kensington Computer Products Group.
p. 189 bottom	© Jonnie Miles/Getty Images
p. 190 top left	© Photodisc/Getty Images
p. 190 top right	© Thinkstock Images/Getty Images
p. 190 bottom	© Dimitri Vervitsiotis/Getty Images
p. 191 left	© ColorBlind Images/Getty Images
p. 191 right	© Yamada Taro/Getty Images
p. 192 top left	© Ryan McVay/Getty Images
p. 192 right	Courtesy of Hewlett-Packard Company.
p. 192 bottom left	Courtesy of Logitech.
p. 193 left	© Getty Images
p. 193 right	© Phil Degginger/Getty Images
p. 194 top	© Junior Gonzalez/Getty Images
p. 194 bottom	© Royalty-Free/Corbis
p. 195 top left	© Beth Dixson/Getty Images
p. 195 top right	© Sullivan/Corbis
p. 198 top	Courtesy of Sony Electronics Inc.
p. 198 bottom	© Jose Luis Pelaez, Inc./CORBIS
p. 199 left	Courtesy of Sony Electronics Inc.
p. 199 right	Courtesy of Sony Electronics Inc.
p. 200	
p. 201	Courtesy of Amazon.com, Inc. Used with permission.
p. 203 top	Courtesy of Hewlett-Packard Company.
p. 203 bottom	Courtesy of Dell Inc.
p. 204	Courtesy of Hewlett-Packard Company.
p. 205	Courtesy of Apple.
p. 206	Courtesy of Linksys.
p. 207	© Justin Guariglia/Getty Images
p. 208	© Jason Reed/Ryan McVay/Getty Images
p. 209 left	© John Lund/Paula Zacharias/ Getty Images
p. 209 right	© Junior Gonzalez/Getty Images
p. 210	© Royalty-Free/Corbis
p. 210 right	Courtesy of Sony Electronics Inc.
p. 211 left	Courtesy of Hewlett-Packard Company.
p. 211 right	Courtesy of Linksys.
p. 219	© Digital Vision/Getty Images
p. 221	© Getty Images
p. 222	Courtesy of Iomega.
p. 223	Courtesy of Iomega.
p. 224 top left	© Willis Technology
p. 224 bottom left	© Willis Technology
p. 224 right	© Willis Technology
p. 225 left	© Willis Technology
p. 225 right	© Willis Technology
p. 227	Courtesy of Iomega.
p. 231	© Willis Technology
p. 232	Courtesy of Quantum Corporation.
p. 234	© ColorBlind Images/Getty Images
p. 235	© Colin Anderson/Getty Image
p. 236 left	© Getty Images
p. 236 right	Courtesy of Iomega.

p. 446 left	© Jupiterimages/Getty Images	p. 34	Microsoft product screen shot(s) reprinted with permission from Microsoft Corporation.
p. 446 right	© Getty Images		
p. 447 left	© Thomas Northcut/Getty Images	p. 67	Microsoft product screen shot(s) reprinted with permission from Microsoft Corporation.
p. 447 right	© Thomas Northcut/Getty Images		
p. 454 top left	IBM Corporate Archives.	p. 68	Microsoft product screen shot(s) reprinted with permission from Microsoft Corporation.
p. 454 bottom left	Courtesy of the Computer History Museum.		
p. 454 top right	IBM Corporate Archives.	p. 68–69	Microsoft product screen shot(s) reprinted with permission from Microsoft Corporation.
p. 454 bottom right	© Masahiro Sano/Corbis		
p. 455 top left	IBM Corporate Archives.		
p. 455 top right	© Bettman/Corbis	p. 84	Microsoft product screen shot(s) reprinted with permission from Microsoft Corporation.
p. 455 bottom	Courtesy of the Computer History Museum.		
p. 455 center	IBM Corporate Archives.	p. 85	Microsoft product screen shot(s) reprinted with permission from Microsoft Corporation.
p. 456 top left	Courtesy of the Computer History Museum.		
p. 456 top right	IBM Corporate Archives.	p. 98	© OSNews.com, 2010
p. 456 bottom	Courtesy of the Computer History Museum.	p. 106	Microsoft product screen shot(s) reprinted with permission from Microsoft Corporation.
p. 457 top left	IBM Corporate Archives.		
p. 457 top right	Courtesy of the Computer History Museum.	p. 107	Microsoft product screen shot(s) reprinted with permission from Microsoft Corporation.
p. 457 bottom	IBM Corporate Archives.	p. 133	Microsoft product screen shot(s) reprinted with permission from Microsoft Corporation.
p. 458 top left	Courtesy of the Computer History Museum.		
p. 458 top right	Courtesy of Apple.	p. 136–137	Microsoft product screen shot(s) reprinted with permission from Microsoft Corporation.
p. 458 bottom	Courtesy of the Computer History Museum.		
p. 459 top	Courtesy of Microsoft Corporation.	p. 142	Microsoft product screen shot(s) reprinted with permission from Microsoft Corporation.
p. 459 center left	Courtesy of the Computer History Museum.		
p. 459 center right	Courtesy of the Computer History Museum.	p. 167–169	Microsoft product screen shot(s) reprinted with permission from Microsoft Corporation.
p. 459 bottom	Courtesy of Apple.	p. 196–197	Microsoft product screen shot(s) reprinted with permission from Microsoft Corporation.
p. 460 top left	Courtesy of Apple.		
p. 460 top right	Courtesy Intel.		
p. 460 center	Courtesy Intel.	p. 262	Microsoft product screen shot(s) reprinted with permission from Microsoft Corporation.
p. 460 bottom left	© AP Photo/Paul Sakuma		
p. 460 bottom right	Microsoft product box shot(s) reprinted with permission from Microsoft Corporation.	p. 278	Copyright, 2010 Internet.com All rights reserved. Reprinted with permission from http://www.internet.com.
p. 461	Microsoft product box shot(s) reprinted with permission from Microsoft Corporation.	p.352	Copyright 2010 LexisNexis, a division of Reed Elsevier Inc. All Rights Reserved. LexisNexis and the Knowledge Burst logo are registered trademarks of Reed Elsevier Properties Inc. and are used with the permission of LexisNexis.

Screen shot

p. 4, 19	Microsoft product screen shot(s) reprinted with permission from Microsoft Corporation.		
		p. 429	Sunsoft
p. 9	Microsoft product screen shot(s) reprinted with permission from Microsoft Corporation.	p. 435, 445	© ING Direct USA, 2008.

Subject Index

A

AC adapters, 172
Access, 79, 283
Access by unauthorized persons, 296
Access data dictionary form, 345
Access data entry form, 346
Access point, 259, 262
Access speed, 221
Access to Internet, 31
Accounting, 315, 316, 320
Accounts payable, 321
Accounts receivable, 320
Accuracy, 46, 283
ACI, 143–144
Acrobat Reader, 50
Active-matrix monitor, 199
Ad-Aware, 289
Ad network, 287
Add a Device Wizard, 139
Addresses, 32, 34
Adobe, 79
Adobe Creative Suite, 105
Adobe Dreamweaver, 111
Adobe Illustrator, 104
Adobe Photoshop, 103
ADSL, 254
Advance fee loans, 295
Advanced graphics cards, 165
Advanced Research Project Agency Network (ARPANET), 30
Adware cookies, 287
Age of connectivity (1911–2011 and beyond), 454, 460–462
Agents (intelligent programs), 89
Agile development, 414
AI, 112–114
Airline reservation systems, 265
AJAX, 33
Alternative office suites, 85
Alternative systems design, 378–379
ALU, 162
Amazon Kindle, 201
American Standard Code for Information Interchange (ASCII), 159
Amerivault, 231
Analog signals, 158, 252
Analytical graphs, 74
Animations, 82, 83, 110
Anticipating, 299
Antispyware, 289
Antivirus programs, 135, 294
AOL Search, 44
Apple, 231
Apple GarageBand, 108
Apple iMovie, 105
Apple iTunes, 226, 341
Applets, 33
AppleWorks, 84

Application generation subsystem, 346
Application generator, 418
Application service provider (asp), 49
Application software, 9–10
  careers, 88
  database management systems, 78–81
  defined, 66
  Google Docs, 86–87
  integrated packages, 84
  intelligent programs, 89
  presentation graphics, 82–83
  specialized. *See* Specialized applications
  speech recognition, 68–69
  spreadsheets, 73–78
  suites, 85–88
  word processors, 70–73
Arithmetic-logic unit (ALU), 162
Arithmetic operations, 162
ARPANET, 30
Artificial intelligence (AI), 112–114
Artificial reality, 112
ASCII, 159
ASCII code, 159
Asimo robot, 113
Ask, 44
ASP, 49
Aspect ratio, 199
Assembly languages, 416–417, 419
Asymmetric digital subscriber line (ADSL), 254
Athlon 64 X2 processor, 163
ATM, 342–343, 434
Atom processor, 163
Attached WebCam, 195
Attachments, 35
Attempt at translation, 411
Attribute, 342, 350
Auction fraud, 295
Auction house sites, 48
Audio editing software, 108
Audio-input devices, 195
Audio-output devices, 205
Authority, 45
AutoCorrect, 72
Automated design tools, 377, 378
Automated teller machine (ATM), 342–343, 434
Autonomic Computing Initiative (ACI), 143–144

B

B2B e-commerce, 47
B2C e-commerce, 47
Backup and Restore, 135–136
Backup programs, 135
Backups, 298
Balance sheets, 321

Tips Index